COUNSELING
Children & <small>THIRD EDITION</small>
Adolescents

Ann Vernon
University of Northern Iowa

LOVE PUBLISHING COMPANY®
Denver • London • Sydney

To my son,
Eric J. Vernon,
with pride and appreciation
for the person he is.

 Published by Love Publishing Company
P.O. Box 22353
Denver, Colorado 80222
www.lovepublishing.com

Third Edition

Library of Congress Catalog Card Number 2003107621

Contents

Preface

Not so many years ago children entertained themselves by engaging in simple pleasures such as capturing fireflies in a jar, soaring high on a tire swing, or playing board games, hide and go seek, and tag. These forms of diversion were inexpensive, creative, and healthy—in sharp contrast to what many of today's youth do for fun. Without DVD's, game cubes, or video games they are lost—and even more so if families can't afford these entertainment options.

In so many ways the world is more complex than it was even a decade ago when the first edition of this book was published. At that time I wrote about how children and adolescents were faced with many challenges; that in addition to normal growing up problems, young people had to deal with the complexities of our contemporary society. The same holds true today, but to a much greater degree. Children are growing up too fast, too soon. While they may be young chronologically, they are exposed to adult issues through the media and the internet, as well as from their day-to-day experiences, they are not developmentally equipped to deal with sexuality, drugs, and violence, for example. The ramifications are significant, and school and mental health counselors play an important role in helping young people deal with the challenges of growing up. By listening to their stories, employing effective interventions, advocating for them, and educating parents and other professionals about child and adolescent development and other important issues, we can make their journey through life less difficult.

This third edition builds on the second edition revisions in several ways. There are more case studies that illustrate application of principles, and there is a new section on helping children and adolescents deal with sudden crisis such as the events of 9/11. There is also more emphasis on applications with clients from diverse cultures. A graphic in the first chapter illustrates how developmental levels impact the way children and adolescents deal with both situational and developmental issues and how important it is to intervene early in order to prevent more serious self-defeating behaviors.

Contributing authors have made revisions in all chapters. The chapter on working with young multicultural clients has been written from a new perspective, and the information contained in this chapter should equip the reader to intervene more effectively with diverse populations. In addition, readers working in school settings should find the revised chapter on a developmental counseling curriculum to be particularly helpful in program implementation. And as a foundation for the work we do with children, readers are directed to important additions to the chapter on employing creative interventions. The final chapters on working with parents and families emphasize the necessity of working with the system even when the identified client may be the child or adolescent.

The authors of this book are all well-respected authorities in their field and have provided pertinent, up-to-date information that will increase the reader's knowledge about effective counseling strategies for children and adolescents. Each chapter contains practical as well as theoretical information, along with case studies or sample group/classroom activities to illustrate application of concepts. The numerous examples interspersed throughout the text provide for interesting reading as well. It is my hope that this third edition will be a valuable resource that students and practitioners will use to help make a difference for today's children and families.

Ann Vernon

Meet the Editor

Ann Vernon, Ph.D., LMHC, is professor and coordinator of the counselor education program at the University of Northern Iowa in Cedar Falls. In addition, Dr. Vernon maintains a part-time private practice where she specializes in working with children, adolescents, and their parents. Dr. Vernon is a frequent speaker at professional conferences and conducts workshops throughout the United States and Canada on a variety of topics pertaining to children and adolescents. She is the Vice President of the Albert Ellis Board of Trustees and the author of numerous books and articles, including *What Works with Children and Adolescents, The Passport Program,* and *Thinking, Feeling, Being.*

Meet the Contributors

James J. Bergin, Ed.D., is a professor at Georgia Southern University of Statesboro and coordinator of counselor education programs. Dr. Bergin has held leadership positions and editorial responsibilities for both state and national counseling associations, including supervisor and postsecondary Vice President of the American School Counselor Association. He has authored numerous articles and book chapters and is a recipient of the Carl Perkins Award.

Loretta J. Bradley, Ph.D., is professor of counselor education and chair of the Division of Educational Psychology and Leadership at Texas Tech University. Dr. Bradley has held major leadership roles including past president of the Association for Counselor Education and Supervision (ACES) and president of the American Counseling Association (ACA). She is a licensed professional counselor and a licensed marriage and family therapist. Dr. Bradley is the co-recipient of the ACA Research Award and the ACES Research Award.

Dr. Roberto Clemente, Ph.D., holds a Masters Degree in school counseling from the University of Puerto Rico and a doctoral degree in Counselor Education from Oregon State University. He has written several professional articles in national and state journals on multicultural counseling. Dr. Clemente conducts workshops on diversity, multiculturalism, and artistic interventions throughout the U.S. He is currently an associate professor at the University of Northern Iowa.

Larry Golden, Ph.D., chairs the Department of Counseling, Educational Psychology, and Adult and Higher Education at the University of Texas at San Antonio. He is a licensed psychologist with specialization in counseling children and families. Dr. Golden has published several books including *Psychotherapeutic Techniques in School Psychology, Helping Families Help Children, Preventing Adolescent Suicide,* and several books on case studies.

L. J. Gould, Ed.D., is at Texas Tech University. Dr. Gould teaches in the counselor education program and has been engaged in writing and consulting. Previous publications have focused on gender stereotyping, career development, counselor career satisfaction and integrative theory.

C. Bret Hendricks, Ed.D., LPC, is assistant professor in the counselor education program at Texas Tech University. His research interests are career development, the use of music therapy techniques, and substance abuse studies.

Marcy C. Hunt-Morse, Ph.D., received her doctoral degree in Counseling Psychology from the University of Oregon. She currently works as an Academic Advisor at the University of Oregon and works in the community providing clinical services with an Employee Assistance Program. Dr. Morse has special interests in adolescent pregnancy, parenting, and developmental and life transitions.

Terry Kottman, Ph.D., NCC, RPT-S, LMHC, recently founded The Encouragement Zone, a center where she provides play therapy training, counseling, coaching, and "playshops" for women. Dr. Kottman is a Registered Play Therapist-Supervisor and maintains a small private practice, providing personal and professional coaching, consultation, and supervision. She regularly presents workshops on play therapy, activity-based counseling, counseling children, and school counseling. Dr. Kottman spent eight years as a professor of counselor education at the University of Northern Iowa and five years as a professor of counselor education at the University of North Texas.

John M. Littrell, Ed.D., is a professor in the Department of Educational Leadership and Policy Studies at Iowa State University. He serves as the program coordinator for the Counselor Education program and is author of 30 articles and five book chapters. He has authored *Brief Counseling in Action* and produced five brief counseling videotapes. Dr. Littrell has presented 25 national and international brief counseling workshops for the American Counseling Association.

William P. McFarland, Ed.D., is the coordinator of school counseling at Western Illinois University where he teaches courses in counseling children and adolescents. Dr. McFarland is a former school counselor and has published several articles on counseling children and adolescents, including a recent article on working with gay and lesbian youth. Dr. McFarland has presented at state and national conferences on issues related to child and adolescent development.

Ellen Hawley McWhirter, Ph.D., is an associate professor in the counseling psychology program at the University of Oregon. Dr. McWhirter is the author of *Counseling for Empowerment* and co-author of *At-risk Youth: A Comprehensive Response*. In addition, she has numerous other publications in the areas of adolescent career development, at-risk youth, and applying her empowerment model to aspects of counseling and counselor training.

Robert J. Nejedlo, Ph.D., is the author of 52 professional publications and a former school counselor at Niles North Township High School in Skokie, Illinois. He was a professor at Northern Illinois University for 30 years, 10 of which he directed the Counseling and Student Development Center. He served as President of the American Counseling Association 1988-1989.

Jean Sunde Peterson, Ph.D., teaches in the Department of Educational Studies and coordinates the school counselor preparation program at Purdue University. She is a former classroom teacher, state teacher of the year, and school and mental health counselor. Dr. Peterson is the author of two *Talk with Teens* books, as well as many other publications related to teaching, school counseling, at-risk youth, and affective concerns of high-ability students.

Michael E. Spagna, Ph.D., received his Ph.D. in special education from the University of California at Berkeley. He is an associate professor in the Department of Special Education at California State University, Northridge, where his professional interests include collaboration with helping professionals in meeting the needs of exceptional students.

Rachel E. Shepard, Ph.D., received her doctoral degree in Counseling Psychology from the University of Oregon. She is completing her psychologist residency in private practice, providing individual and couples therapy to adults and adolescents for eating disorders, anxiety disorders, affective disorders, adjustment disorders, and trauma spectrum disorders. She is engaged in research and writing with special interest on eating disorders.

Shari Tarver-Behring, Ph.D., is an associate professor and school counseling coordinator at California State University, Northridge. Dr. Tarver-Behring is a credentialed school psychologist and counselor as well as a licensed psychologist in California. In addition to her extensive clinical and teaching experience in the area of child and adolescent psychology, Dr. Tarver-Behring has published and presented in the areas of school consultation with diverse youth, the school counselor's role in full inclusion, and school interventions for at-risk youth.

Toni R. Tollerud, Ph.D., has been an educator for over 33 years, participating as senior high teacher, counselor, pre-school teacher, community college counselor and counselor educator at Northern Illinois University. In 1999 she became the Executive Director of the Illinois School Counselors' academy, a program that provides professional development to school counselors. She has numerous publications in the area of school counseling. In

2001, she was named the Counselor Advocate of the Year by the American School Counseling Association.

Kirk Zinck, Ph.D., is a licensed marriage and family therapist who provides clinical services to coastal villages in Alaska. His background includes school counseling, clinical counseling and supervision, graduate instruction, and professional research. Dr. Zinck is a clinical member of the American Association for Marriage and Family Therapy, a National Certified Counselor, and a National Certified School Counselor. He and Dr. John Littrell have collaborated on research articles, book chapters, and an instructional videotape explaining the brief counseling process.

Working With Children, Adolescents, and Their Parents: Practical Application of Developmental Theory

Ann Vernon

A single-parent father and his 15-year-old son arrived for an appointment with a mental health counselor. The father told the counselor that he and his son Kevin had recently begun to have some major arguments about curfew and chores. They both wanted to address these problems before they escalated. The counselor, who previously had seen Kevin for school performance and sibling relationship issues, thought him to be a "good kid" who was concerned about his grades but had to work hard to keep them up. The counselor recalled that although Kevin had trouble controlling his temper when his younger brother did things that annoyed him, Kevin had learned new ways to handle his anger and frustration and the relationship between father and son had improved considerably.

As the father and son described their recent conflict, the counselor became aware that the father was seeing his son's refusal to do assigned chores as defiance and was assuming that this defiant behavior would begin to surface in other areas. When the counselor asked Kevin to talk from his perspective, she began to sense that, although this adolescent did not necessarily like doing chores, the real issue was the arbitrary way in which his dad was instructing him to do them. Kevin also told the counselor that he resented his curfew being earlier than most of his friends' curfews, but he admitted that he had not talked to his dad about this because Kevin assumed it wouldn't do any good. Instead, he sometimes stayed out later than his curfew and then argued with Dad when Kevin was grounded for being late.

Based on what these two clients had shared, the counselor believed that many of the problems they were experiencing were a result of the difficulties inherent in the transition from childhood to adolescence. She explained to them that significant changes occur in parent–child relationships during this period, one of which is that adolescents are naturally struggling to achieve independence and need the opportunity to make some of their own decisions. Therefore, when parents tell their children what, when, and how to do things, adolescents hear their parents' words as a command and feel like they are being treated as children who are not responsible enough to make any decisions.

The counselor assured the father that she did not mean that his son should have no responsibility, but she believed that he probably would be less defiant if Dad were to phrase his requests in a way that would allow Kevin to take more control of the tasks. She also explained that, at Kevin's age, many adolescents assume things without checking them out and do not have the cognitive ability to carefully analyze situations and anticipate consequences. Therefore, it was normal for Kevin to assume that his dad would not negotiate on curfew and to take matters into his own hands by ignoring his curfew.

Assimilating this information about adolescent development, Kevin's father was able to reframe the issue of defiance and recognize that his son was attempting to assert his independence, which is normal for people his age. At this point, Kevin and his father were able to work out a contract for chores and curfew that had reasonable timelines and consequences if Kevin were to fail to do what they had agreed upon.

As this vignette illustrates, knowledge about developmental characteristics is essential in assessment and intervention with children, adolescents, and their parents. Without this perspective, problems can be easily misconstrued. Parents in particular may assume that the symptom they see is indicative of something more pervasive if they fail to take into account what is normal at each stage of development.

Model of Developmental Levels

It is also important to understand how children's level of development influences how they respond to their attainment of basic needs, as well as to normal developmental issues and more significant situational problems. The model in Figure 1.1 illustrates this more specifically. In the center of the triangle are basic needs that, according to Maslow (1968), all human beings have: the needs for safety, belongingness, love, and respect. When these basic needs are not met, children respond to the deficits depending on their developmental level in one or more of the areas listed in the next level: self, emotional, cognitive, physical, and social.

For example, young children in the preoperational stage of development will respond very differently to a basic need for safety than will adolescents who have begun to develop abstract thinking skills. Young children do not have the ability to

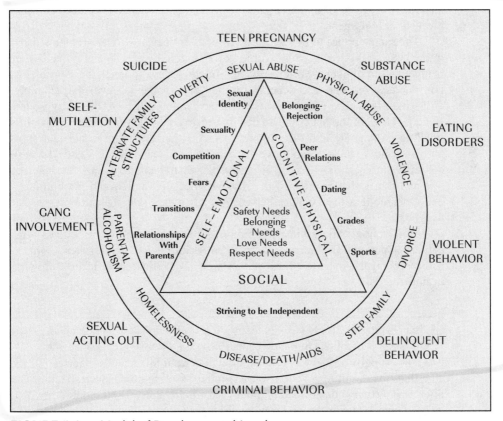

FIGURE 1.1   *Model of Developmental Levels*

clearly identify or express their feelings, do not understand all of the ramifications of the situation, and have difficulty generating effective coping skills. The implication, therefore, is that the experience itself is mediated by the level of development and impacts children differently depending on that level.

In this model the level of development also influences how children respond to the normal developmental problems that most children and adolescents experience to some extent and are listed in the first circle of the model: puberty, friendship, grades, mastery and competition, and so forth. Once again, how they respond to these typical problems depends upon their level of development. For instance, self-conscious pre-teens whose abstract thinking skills are limited can easily overgeneralize about how terrible it is to give a speech in front of peers. Instead of realizing that others probably feel very much the same way and that not everyone will be staring at them or noticing their pimples, they assume that their only option is to skip class to avoid the situation. Had they been more advanced in their level of cognitive development, they would have been able to identify alternative ways to deal with this typical problem associated with puberty and physical development.

The same applies to how children respond to the situational problems listed in the next circle: living with divorced or alcoholic parents, being homeless, or being a victim of abuse. Fortunately, not all children experience these problems, but how they respond also depends on their developmental level. For example, an 8-year-old whose mother abandoned the family will have difficulty understanding how her mother could do this if she loves her daughter. The 8-year-old's thinking is concrete and dichotomous: Her mother either loves her and stays with the family or she doesn't love her daughter and leaves. A 17-year-old whose cognitive skills are more advanced would be able to recognize other relevant factors and issues that influenced her mother's decision and would not automatically assume that just because her mother left meant that she did not love her daughter.

Finally, how children interpret and respond to basic needs, as well as typical and situational problems, can result in various self-defeating behaviors, as listed around the outside edges of the circles and illustrated in the following example.

After 9-year-old Rosa's parents lost their jobs, the family was homeless for several months. On many nights Rosa could not sleep because she was cold, hungry, or frightened. Even though her parents usually made sure that Rosa went to school, she was embarrassed to go because she often was dirty and disheveled and didn't like being teased and taunted by her peers, which happened repeatedly. Rosa kept her feelings to herself, but as the humiliation increased, her self-worth plummeted; she believed she was as ugly and worthless as what her classmates claimed.

Eventually Rosa's parents both secured new jobs, and they once again were able to live in an apartment, but Rosa's situation at school did not improve. She lacked both the confidence and the social skills that she needed to be accepted by her peers. In junior high she began to develop physically, and suddenly she became the center of attention because boys were attracted to her. For the first time, she felt like she belonged. Before long she became sexually active, which was her way to feel loved and respected. Unfortunately, her physical maturity was not accompanied by maturity in other areas of development; she didn't think about the consequences of her sexual activity, lacked the social skills to assertively deal with the pressure to have sex, and illogically attributed her popularity with boys as the way to feel worthwhile. By age 15 she was pregnant and dropped out of school.

As this vignette illustrates, the way youngsters process the experiences depicted in this model is influenced by their developmental maturity. Helping professionals need to recognize this reality and take an active role in helping their counselees develop the social, emotional, cognitive, and self-development skills they need to handle the normal and situational challenges of growing up. To some extent, the importance of incorporating a developmental perspective into the counseling process with clients of all ages has been acknowledged, but developmental theory has been applied primarily through comprehensive counseling programs that focus on prevention through classroom and small-group work and not on assessment and intervention in individual counseling (Vernon, 1993).

Although the preventive focus is extremely important, it also is critical to consider developmental factors in problem conceptualization, in designing or selecting age-appropriate assessment instruments, and in developing interventions that take into account the child's developmental capabilities. In addition, because adult models of assessment and treatment cannot be extrapolated to young clients, knowledge of development is essential in selecting appropriate interventions that will engage children in the counseling process (Vernon, 2002).

As seen in the vignette at the beginning of this chapter, it is also important for counselors to convey information about developmental norms and competencies in consultations with parents. If parents have a better understanding about what to expect with their children at various stages of development, they have a better perspective from which to assess symptoms they may see as problematic.

This chapter covers characteristics and applications in counseling and consulting for early childhood, middle childhood, early adolescence, and mid-adolescence. Typical characteristics and developmental problems are described for these children, ages 4–18, in five areas of development: physical, cognitive, self, social, and emotional.

Developmental Characteristics of Early Childhood

Physical Development

Young children seem to be in perpetual motion as they explore their world and focus their energy on a variety of things. Although physical growth is slower during the preschool years than in earlier years, gross motor skills such as running, jumping, throwing, and climbing improve dramatically during this period (Berger & Thompson, 1991; Trawick–Smith, 2000). Fine motor skills develop more slowly, but 4-year-olds can copy designs and 5-year-olds can reproduce letters and copy short words (Owens, 2002). Although their muscles have increased in size and strength, they are still immature in function compared to children in middle childhood. Gradually, 4- and 5-year-olds lose their baby fat, and by age 6 their body proportions are similar to those of an adult (Owens, 2002). Because their growth is slower than it was earlier, preschoolers tend to have smaller appetites.

Cognitive Development

To the 4- and 5-year-old preschooler, the world is a fascinating place. With the help of their imaginations, anything is possible. Ordinary playrooms become transformed into museums, and imaginary friends are frequent dinner-table guests. Typical preschoolers are curious, energetic, and eager.

Preoperational thinking characterizes preschoolers' cognitive development (Berk, 2001; McDevitt & Ormrod, 2002; Santrock & Yussen, 1992). Although they are beginning to reason more logically if they are asked to think about familiar things in a familiar context, they still rely heavily on solving a problem based on what they hear or see rather than by logical reasoning. McDevitt and Ormrod noted, however, that preschoolers can think more logically than Piaget suggested and that they can draw logically valid conclusions such as making appropriate inferences when they listen to a story. They do have difficulty with abstract concepts such as divorce and death (Berk, 2001).

Also characteristic of their cognitive style is *unidimensional thought* (Trawick–Smith, 2000), the tendency to center on their perceptions, or on one aspect of the situation, rather than on a broader view. This style of thinking interferes with their ability to understand cause and effect and makes it difficult for them to see that the same object or situation can have two identities. For example, many preschoolers cannot grasp the concept that their teacher could also be a parent.

Two other characteristics of preschoolers' thinking are animism and artificialism (Vernon & Al–Mabuk, 1995). *Animism* refers to the attribution of lifelike qualities to inanimate objects, such as comforting a doll when it falls. *Artificialism* is the belief that people cause natural phenomena, such as thinking that rain occurs because fire fighters are spraying water from the sky. Both of these characteristics contribute to the preschoolers' ability to engage in make-believe play.

Another important facet of cognitive development during this period is language. By age 5, children can understand almost anything explained to them in context if the examples are specific (Bjorklund, 2000). They are able to introduce new topics into a conversation but have difficulty maintaining a sustained dialogue about one idea (Owens, 1996). They also struggle with abstract nouns and concepts such as time and space, as characterized by the frequent question, "Are we there yet?"

Self-Development

Preschoolers are egocentric—assuming that everyone thinks and feels as they do. They have difficulty seeing things from another's perspective. This egocentrism is reflected in their excessive use of "my" and "mine." Their self-esteem is quite high (McDevitt & Ormrod, 2002), and they tend to overestimate their own abilities, thinking that they are competent in everything (Seifert & Hoffnung, 1997). This belief is advantageous during this period, when they have so many new tasks to master. With each mastery, their sense of initiative and competence increases.

Another self-development issue relates to preschoolers' self-control, which increases during this period. Preschoolers are better at modifying and controlling their own impulses and are not as frustrated and intolerant if their needs are not met immediately (Berk, 2001; Turner & Helms, 1995).

Preschoolers also show an increase in initiative during this period. As children enter preschool, they face more challenges and assume more responsibilities. In turn, their self-initiated behaviors increase.

Social Development

Play serves an extremely important function for children at this age. Most of the play for 4-year-olds is *associative;* they interact and share, and although they are engaging in a common activity, they do not assign roles and are not very clear about their goals (Owens, 2002). By age 5, they begin to engage in more cooperative play: taking turns, creating games, and forming groups to do something. In this type of play, one or more children organize the activity and others assume different roles (Berk, 1999; Seifert & Hoffnung, 1997; Vandenberg, 1998).

Children at this age do not understand give-and-take, and are most likely to be egocentric and unable to see another child's point of view (Kaplan, 2000). They also have difficulty understanding intentionality, so they may misinterpret others' behavior and respond inappropriately.

Gender differences are quite apparent at this age. Boys more readily engage in rough, noisy, aggressive play, and girls are more nurturing and cooperative (LeFrancois, 1992). By age 5 they associate toughness with males and gentleness with females (Owens, 2002).

Emotional Development

Although their vocabularies are expanding and they are beginning to understand which emotions are appropriate to specific situations (Izard & Ackerman, 2000), preschoolers still have a rather limited vocabulary for expressing how they feel. As a result, they often express their feelings behaviorally. According to Berk (1999), children at this age have difficulty understanding that they can experience different emotions about a situation simultaneously, although they can understand the concept of experiencing different emotions at different times.

Toward the end of the preschool period, children have a better understanding of why others are upset, and they begin to respond verbally or physically to others' emotions. Their understanding of other peoples' emotions is limited, however, by their perception, and they tend to focus on the most obvious aspects of an emotional situation, such as being angry, happy, or sad (Vernon & Al–Mabuk, 1995).

Counseling Applications for Early Childhood

Helping professionals who work with 4- and 5-year-olds need to remain cognizant of the physical, intellectual, social, emotional, and self-development characteristics of these young clients during both the assessment and intervention process. Because the attention span of preschoolers is limited, practitioners should use a variety of techniques to engage their young clients. These children require very concrete approaches. Their ability to remember concepts is enhanced if they can manipulate objects, have a visual representation of the concept, or engage in some form of play to help them resolve issues. Traditional forms of counseling that rely primarily on talking and listening do not work well for young clients (DiGiuseppe, 1999; Vernon, 2002). Chapters 3 and 4 of this book describe in detail appropriate interventions to use with young children.

Typical Problems Experienced During Early Childhood

The social and emotional development of preschoolers may be manifested in their difficulty engaging in cooperative play. They sometimes have difficulty getting along because of their limited ability to understand give-and-take or to see situations from perspectives other than their own egocentric view. In addition, the tendency of young children to take things quite literally can result in fear. For example, parents who tell their preschooler that Grandma just "went to sleep" when in reality she died should not be surprised when their child is afraid to go to sleep at night.

Elkind (1991) related the example of a young child who refused to go home from preschool because he was going to meet his new "half brother." As he discussed his fear, it became apparent that he actually thought he would be seeing half of a brother! This type of thinking is characteristic of preschoolers, and it is similar to many of the other fears and uncertainties that 4- and 5-year-olds experience because of their preoperational thinking: fear of dark rooms, fear of noises at night, fear of monsters, fear of bad people (Bee, 2000). In addition, they may be hesitant to leave the house to play in the yard, visit a friend, or be left at preschool because they are afraid of being separated from a parent.

In addition to these typical problems, many other situational problems, such as divorce, abuse, and parental alcoholism, affect the lives of children. Practitioners must keep in mind that the way they process typical developmental problems and more serious situational issues alike is directly related to the developmental capabilities of these young children.

Case Studies of Young Children

Joshua

Five-year-old Joshua had started refusing to go outdoors to play in the yard. This behavior was confusing to his parents because until the past month, he had showed no hesitation about playing in the neighborhood with his friends. The parents were not aware of any traumatic incident that had occurred when Joshua had been playing outside, nor did they see any other problematic symptoms. They referred him to a counselor for help.

The counselor first reassured the parents that this problem is common in children of this age because they have a vivid imagination, take things literally, and have limited ability to process concepts. She explained to them that she first would attempt to determine specifically what Joshua was afraid of and then develop some interventions to help him deal with the problem.

In working with Joshua, the counselor had him draw a picture of himself playing in the yard. He readily drew himself with several friends playing in the sand pile. The counselor told him that she knew he did not want to play outside much anymore, and she asked if he was afraid of something in the yard. At first Joshua denied having any fear, saying that he didn't want to go outside because it was too cold or because his friends couldn't play. The counselor then read him a book, *Dark Closets and Voices in the Night* (Coleman, 1991), to help normalize his fears.

After hearing the story, Joshua did admit that he was a little scared to go outside but couldn't verbalize why, so the counselor asked Joshua to draw a picture to show what he thought might happen. Based on the picture, it appeared that he thought there were "bogeymen" hiding in the trees and that they would come out and hurt him.

To empower Joshua to handle this fear, as well as other fears he might have, the counselor used a combination of empowerment strategies, self-talk, and puppet play, specifically addressing the imaginative fear that seemed very real to this 5-year-old.

First, she asked Joshua if he could think of anything that he could put in the yard or on the fence that might scare the bogeymen away. After some brainstorming, he and the counselor decided that Joshua could make scary masks to hang around the yard. The counselor also knew that Joshua had a dog, so the counselor suggested that Joshua put up a sign reading, "This is a bogeyman guard dog." Next, the counselor helped Joshua generate some statements he could say to himself when he was going outside: "My dog will scare them away," "The masks will scare them away," and "Even if they aren't scared away, my friends are there with me and we can protect each other." She also suggested that Joshua buy a whistle that he could blow to alert his parents if he felt threatened. Finally, the counselor had Joshua use puppets to act out different ways he could react if he thought he saw a bogeyman in the yard.

In conferring with Joshua's parents, the counselor again stressed that his behavior seemed normal for a child his age and that they might see some of this fear transferred to monsters in his room at night. She emphasized that these fears do seem very real and probable to a young child and cautioned them to take the fear seriously and not let his siblings tease him about it. The counselor asked the parents to help Joshua rehearse his self-talk and make his masks. She concluded by saying that if these interventions were unsuccessful, other approaches could be tried.

As this case illustrates, the counselor conceptualized the problem by taking into account how children this age experience the world and process experiences. The interventions she suggested and implemented were concrete and addressed the problem in a variety of ways.

Tanya

Just after kindergarten started in the fall, 5-year-old Tanya cried and screamed when the class went to the pool for swimming class. When the teacher discussed Tanya's behavior with her parents, they said they were not too surprised because they lived on a farm and rarely had opportunities to take their children swimming. They noted that Tanya had problems adjusting to other new experiences as well. They requested that the school counselor work with their daughter to see what could be done to help her get over this fear.

When first meeting with Tanya, the counselor read her a book about going swimming, entitled *Wiggle-Butts and Up Faces* (Kolbisen, 1989). They discussed how the character in the story felt about going swimming, and how he learned to deal with his fears by teaching his stuffed animals how to breathe, float, and kick while in the water and by practicing in the bathtub. The counselor suggested that Tanya might want to try some of these things at home.

Next, the counselor brought out several paper plates and markers. On different plates she drew a sad face, a worried/scared face, an angry face, and a happy face, discussing the feelings as she drew. Then she asked Tanya to pick out the paper-plate faces that described how she felt about going swimming. After Tanya selected the worried/scared face, the counselor asked her to talk about what scared her about going swimming. Tanya said she was afraid she would drown, that no one would see her if she needed help, and that she was afraid other kids would splash her or push her. After talking more about these feelings, the counselor offered to go with her the next time Tanya had swimming class. The counselor said that they both would just sit by the water and watch what was going on. Tanya agreed to do that.

During that next swimming class, the counselor and Tanya sat by the pool. Periodically, the counselor asked Tanya if she had seen any of her classmates drown, if she noticed that they seemed unhappy when the water splashed on them, and whether lots of adults were around watching the children carefully. Then, at the end of the class period, she asked Tanya if her feelings about going swimming had changed any. Tanya said no. The counselor suggested that they repeat this procedure at the next swimming class, and Tanya agreed.

At the second class they sat closer to the pool, and after the class they talked with two of Tanya's friends. The counselor asked them what they liked best about swimming and if they had been afraid at first to get in the water. One of the boys said he had been afraid, but ever since he knew he could stay in the shallow end, he wasn't afraid anymore. He showed Tanya that when he stood up in the water, it came only to his stomach.

During the next swimming class the counselor suggested that she and Tanya put their feet in the water. She explained that at first the water might feel cold, but that it gradually would feel warmer. She periodically asked Tanya questions related to her fears, and by the end of the session, Tanya agreed to try to get in the water for a few minutes during the next class. Prior to that class, the counselor met with her and taught her the following rational self-statements to help her deal with her fears:

"There are lots of adults around to help me if I'm scared."

"No one in my class has drowned, so I probably won't either."

"Everyone looks like they are having fun, so maybe I will, too."

"Even though the water will be cold at first, I know it will get warmer once I'm in the pool."

Tanya's first attempt at spending a few minutes in the water was successful, and she increased her time in the pool the following week. At their next counseling session the counselor had her draw a picture of how she felt about swimming now, and she portrayed herself as laughing as she splashed in the water. From then on, Tanya no longer cried on swimming day.

Developmental Characteristics of Middle Childhood

Physical Development

During middle childhood, ages 6–11, physical growth is relatively stable (Bee, 2000; McDevitt & Ormrod, 2002). Children do grow taller, their body proportions change, and their muscles grow stronger (Schickendanz, Schickendanz,

Forsyth, & Forsyth, 1998), but because of the slow rate of growth, they experience a high degree of self-control over their bodies. Movement becomes more controlled and complex (Owens, 2002). Children at this level are able to master most motor skills and become much more agile and adept at running, skipping, jumping, and riding a bike. By the end of this period, there is a major improvement in their fine motor skills as well.

Because children's bodies mature at different rates, some 10- and 11-year-olds are entering puberty. Height and weight growth spurts, which begin at different times for different children, contribute to self-consciousness and embarrassment (Vernon & Al–Mabuk, 1995).

Cognitive Development

According to Piaget (1967), a transitional period between preoperational and concrete operational thought occurs between the ages of 5 and 7. By age 8, children have become concrete operational thinkers. As a result, they are able to understand reversibility, reciprocity, identity, and classification. They also develop the skill of *conservation,* the ability to understand that the quantity remains the same even if the appearance changes (Owens, 2002). They begin to apply these principles in a variety of contexts such as friendships, rules in games, and team play, as well as in academic contexts (Vernon, 1993).

During this period of development, children's thinking becomes more logical and their problem-solving abilities are enhanced. Because they are concrete thinkers, however, they still cannot reason abstractly or consider possibilities, which influences the way they approach situations. For example, if their best friend does not sit by them, they assume that they did something that made the friend angry, rather than consider a variety of other possibilities.

During middle childhood, children learn best by questioning, exploring, and engaging in guided participation through social interaction (Gauvain, 2001). Their language development continues; they are beginning to understand more abstract concepts and use vocabulary in more sophisticated ways (Berk, 1999). By the end of middle childhood, children's vocabulary will expand to more than 40,000 words (Owens, 2002). Even in middle childhood, children rely on intonation more than context to help them understand another person's intent (Shwe, 1999).

Self-Development

Children's self-understanding expands during this period, and instead of describing themselves superficially, they have a multidimensional view of themselves (Owens, 2002). Consequently, they are able to describe themselves in terms of several competencies at once: "I am short, a good reader, and a fast runner." Furthermore, they can provide justification for their attributes: "I'm smart because I got an A on a test." During middle childhood they begin to see themselves as having more complex personalities (Harter, Waters, & Whitesell, 1998), and they are beginning to develop more of an internal locus of control (Vernon & Al–Mabuk, 1995).

As they enter school and begin to compare themselves to others, they become self-critical, feel inferior, and may develop lower self-esteem (Cole & Cole, 1996). They may be more inhibited about trying new things, and they are sensitive to feedback from peers. As they become aware of their specific areas of competence and more aware of their personal strengths and weaknesses, they may experience either self-confidence or self-doubt (Bee, 2000).

According to Harter (1996), children develop a concept of their overall worth at around age 8. At this time their self-esteem begins to solidify and they behave according to their preconceived ideas of themselves (Harter, Waters, & Whitesell, 1998).

Social Development

During the primary school years, socialization with peers is a major issue. Acceptance in a group and having a "best friend" contribute to children's sense of competence. As they learn to deal with peer pressure, rejection, approval, and conformity, they begin to formulate values, behaviors, and beliefs that facilitate their social development (Pruitt, 1998).

Friendships serve other important functions. Through association with peers, children learn to develop a broader view of the world, experiment with ideas and roles, and learn important interaction skills. As they participate in activities, they learn to cooperate and compromise, to make and break rules, to assume roles as leaders and followers, and to understand others' points of view (Vernon & Al-Mabuk, 1995).

By age 7, children begin to outgrow their egocentrism and adopt more pro-social behaviors. According to Selman (1980) and Selman and Schultz (1990), children in this stage of development realize that other people have thoughts and feelings different from their own, although they still have overly simplistic perceptions of others' perspectives. In the upper elementary grades, they begin to realize that others may have mixed or contradictory feelings about a situation, and they understand that how people act may not reflect accurately what they feel (McDevitt & Ormrod, 2002). As children continue to mature and develop the ability to see things from another's perspective, they become more adept at interpreting social cues and evaluating input (Cole & Cole, 1996; Pruitt, 1998). As a result, they become better able to resolve conflicts and solve social problems.

Emotional Development

During this period, children begin to experience more complex emotions such as guilt, shame, and pride. They also are increasingly aware that people are capable of having more than one emotion at once. These children are more adept at hiding their emotions when they don't want to hurt someone's feelings (Berk, 1999; Borich & Tombari, 1995).

Generally, children at this age are more sensitive, empathic, and better able to recognize and communicate their feelings to others. They realize that feelings can change and that they are not the cause of another person's discomfort (Kaplan, 2000; Turner & Helms, 1995). Because they are experiencing many new situations that require mastery, their anxiety about school performance or peer inclusion is common (Vernon, 1993).

Counseling Applications for Middle Childhood

Middle childhood spans a number of years and many "firsts," particularly those associated with school and friends. School and mental health professionals need to keep in mind that children in the concrete stage of development have a limited ability to think logically and see possibilities. Despite the gradual improvement in their problem-solving abilities, these children continue to need adult guidance to consistently apply their skills to common problems.

Professionals working with this age group should continue to employ concrete interventions to help the children resolve problems. As described in Chapter 3, bibliotherapy, art activities, puppets, role play, and games are appropriate interventions for this age group.

Typical Problems Experienced During Middle Childhood

The most common stressors for children at this age are school related: failing a test, getting a bad report card, or not receiving the teacher's approval (Owens, 2002). Owens also noted other stressors related to family: arguing, sibling issues, and parental separation. Appearance and health issues, too, were cited as stressors. Porter (1999) identified other typical concerns of children at this age. In particular, this author noted issues surrounding peer relationships: being different from other children, losing friends, being accepted by peers, being picked on, or being lonely. They also worry about needing to be perfect, struggle with self-confidence, and experience frustration in becoming more independent (Porter, 1999).

Far too many young children also must deal with more serious situational problems, such as growing up in abusive or alcoholic homes, living in poverty, or dealing with difficult adjustments to parental divorce and remarriage. Regardless of the type of problem, whether it is a normal challenge of growing up or a more serious situational problem, practitioners should design interventions that are concrete in nature to engage the child in problem solving, regardless of the type of problem. With those in middle childhood, simply talking about the problem is usually not effective (Vernon, 2002).

Case Studies from Middle Childhood

Jennifer

Jennifer, age 9, was referred to a counselor because she was afraid to take tests. Although she was a good student, she became so anxious prior to and during a test that she sometimes missed school on the day of the test or felt sick to her stomach at school as the test time approached. Jennifer tended to be very self-critical and was very hard on herself if she didn't get a perfect score.

To get a more accurate assessment of the problem, the counselor asked Jennifer to describe the following:

- What she is thinking prior to taking a test
- What she is feeling physically prior to taking a test
- What she imagines will happen as she takes the test
- How she feels emotionally before and during the test

The counselor also asked Jennifer what she had tried to do to solve the problem.

Based on what this young client said, the counselor confirmed her hypothesis that Jennifer was perfectionistic and looked at the test-taking situation as an "all or nothing, pass/fail" event. In addition, Jennifer always imagined the worst, even though she seldom received less than a perfect score. This sort of absolutist thinking is common in children of Jennifer's age, but counselors should help them see that there is a range of possibilities. To help Jennifer with this, the counselor placed a strip of masking tape on the floor and positioned note cards stating the following along the line in the order shown here:

1. Fail by getting everything wrong.
2. Get a bad grade and miss a lot.
3. Get an average grade and miss quite a few.
4. Get a very high grade but still miss a few.
5. Get the top grade and not miss any.

Next, she asked Jennifer to stand at the position on the line that represented where her test scores were most of the time. Then the counselor asked Jennifer to stand on the spot that represented where she was if she didn't get a perfect score. As the counselor suspected, Jennifer stood first at the far end of the line (top grade, not miss any), then at the next level down.

The counselor then gave Jennifer two pairs of old eyeglasses. She described one pair as the "doom and gloom" glasses and said that when Jennifer put them on, she would imagine only terrible things happening when she took a test. She asked Jennifer to put on the glasses and verbalize those thoughts while the counselor recorded them. Then, she asked Jennifer to put on the other pair, which the counselor described as "rose-colored" glasses. When Jennifer had these glasses on, things would look very good. The counselor asked Jennifer to verbalize her thoughts when she wore the rose-colored glasses.

The counselor explained to Jennifer that because she had never failed a test before, or had ever received an average or below-average grade, Jennifer probably didn't need to wear the "doom and gloom" glasses. The counselor pointed out that if Jennifer pretended to put on the rose-colored glasses before each test, she could say positive things to herself, such as, "I usually do very well, so why should I even think I won't do well this time?" "Even if I get a few wrong, does this mean I'm a stupid kid?" "If I get too nervous, I'll worry too much and make myself sick, but if I just work hard, I'll probably do okay." After the counselor modeled these rational self-statements to Jennifer, the two of them generated a few more together and put them on note cards that Jennifer could look at prior to taking a test.

As a final intervention, the counselor taught Jennifer some relaxation exercises from *The Second Centering Book* (Hendricks & Roberts, 1977). The counselor also had Jennifer interview her sister, her father, and her grandmother about times they had made a mistake, whether they had ever scored less than perfect on an exam, and their individual strengths and weaknesses. This activity helped Jennifer see that other people had strong and weak areas, that they made mistakes, and that they had scored less than perfect on tests and it hadn't been a catastrophe.

The counselor explained to Jennifer's parents that it was normal for Jennifer to feel more pressure at school at age 9 than she had previously because she was more aware of her performance in relation to others. The counselor emphasized the importance of the parents' sharing some of their "less than perfect" experiences with Jennifer, reinforcing the importance of effort versus the final grade, and helping her avoid thinking the worst by looking at her "track record" of performance. The counselor also recommended that they read together the story "The Less Than Perfect Prince" from *Color Us Rational* (Waters, 1979), a story about a prince who learns that he and the world can't be perfect. Finally, the counselor explained the relaxation exercises she had taught Jennifer so the parents could help their daughter use them at home.

Ian

Ian, a second-grader, visited the school counselor because he said everyone was picking on him. To get a more accurate picture of the problem, the counselor asked Ian to act out with 15 small action figures what happened when others picked on him. When Ian acted out the situation, the counselor noted that of the 15 action figures involved in the game, only a few seemed to be actively involved in picking on Ian—calling him names and trying to prevent him from participating in the game. When questioned about this, Ian agreed that not everyone picked on him but said that he hated going out for recess because the kids were so mean to him.

The counselor then asked Ian to tell him more specifically how these kids picked on him. Ian discussed in detail some of the things they did to him. He said that what bothered him the most was when they called him a pig and said he was fat and ugly and couldn't run fast. The counselor listened carefully to this young client, then took out a mirror and handed it to him. "Ian," he said, "look into this mirror and tell me what you see." Ian looked in the mirror and said that he saw himself. "Do you see a fat, ugly kid?" "No," Ian responded. The counselor then asked, "Do you see something with pink ears and a snout in the mirror?" "Of course not," Ian replied. "Then, Ian, if you aren't what they say you are, what is there to be upset about?"

Ian replied that the kids shouldn't call him names, and the counselor agreed that it wasn't nice to call others names but stressed that usually we can't control what others do. He explained to Ian that together they might be able to come up with some ideas that Ian could use so he didn't upset himself so much when others behaved badly toward him.

Together, Ian and the counselor brainstormed some things that might help Ian, including making up a silly song or a limerick that he could say to himself to make him laugh instead of feeling upset when others called him names that he knew weren't true. Ian liked the idea of the limerick and, with a little help from the counselor, he wrote the following:

> *You shouldn't call me a pig,*
> *But if you do, it's nothing big.*
> *I'm not what you say,*
> *So have it your way,*
> *But I'm not a pig in a hole that I dig.*

After developing the limerick, the counselor asked Ian to repeat it aloud several times until he had memorized it. They agreed that Ian would say this to himself the next time his classmates teased him so he could laugh instead of getting so upset. Before sending him back to the classroom, the counselor asked Ian what he had learned during their session. Ian immediately stated that he knew he didn't have to be upset if others teased him about things that weren't true and that he felt better because he had a plan to try.

Developmental Characteristics of Early Adolescence

Physical Development

During early adolescence (ages 10 to 14) physical changes occur more rapidly than at any other time in the lifespan with the exception of infancy (Dusek, 1996; Steinberg, 1996). The increased production of sex hormones and the changes associated with puberty begin at about age 10½ for females and 12½ for males, although there is considerable variation. Following the onset of puberty, maturation of the reproductive system (the ovaries in females and the testes in males) and the appearance of secondary sex characteristics (growth of pubic hair, development of facial hair and voice change in males, breast development and widening of the hips in females) begin. Also, this age is characterized by a growth spurt that lasts approximately 3 years and begins about 2 years earlier in girls than in boys (Cobb, 2001).

Because young adolescents' rate of maturity varies tremendously, self-consciousness and anxiety are common. Males and females alike may become clumsy and uncoordinated for a time because the size of their hands and feet may be disproportionate to other body parts. In addition, their rate of physical change affects how they see themselves (McDevitt & Ormrod, 2002). Early adolescents want to be like everyone else and are painfully aware of appearing awkward or different (Owens, 2002). Because they don't want others to see their bodies, "locker room phobia" is common during this period of development (Jaffe, 1998).

The physical and hormonal changes characteristic of early adolescence can cause early adolescents to become confused. Sexual thoughts and feelings abound, often accompanied by feelings of shame and guilt. Young adolescents are curious about sex and wonder if others feel the same way they do. Straightforward information about sex is extremely important prior to and during early adolescence.

Cognitive Development

During early adolescence the shift from concrete to formal operational thinking begins. Although this change actually begins at about age 11, it is not attained until age 15 to 20 (Kaplan, 2000). As they move into more formal operational thinking, adolescents begin to think more abstractly, develop the ability to hypothesize, and consider alternatives (Dusek, 1996; Kaplan, 2000). Although they also can reason more logically and can predict consequences of events and behaviors, they do not always apply these skills to themselves. Thus, they may apply their skill in logic to their work in mathematics but not logically assume that if they stay out past their curfew, there might be a consequence (Vernon, 1993). Young adolescents are unable to link events, feelings, and situations, which Schave and Schave (1989) labeled as the "time warp" concept. As a result, young adolescents may fail to connect flunking a test with not studying for it, or not associate being grounded with coming in late. If they were to associate these events, they might be overwhelmed by guilt, shame, or anger, so the time warp allows them to avoid responsibility.

According to Schave and Schave (1989), the shift from concrete to formal operational thinking is "the most drastic and dramatic change in cognition that occurs in anyone's life" (p. 7). With these new abilities, young adolescents are able to detect inconsistencies, think about future changes, see possibilities, think of logical rebuttals, and hypothesize about the logical sequence of events (Bee, 2000). It is important to remember that there is considerable variability in the extent to which formal operational thinking is attained and applied consistently during early adolescence (Cobb, 2001). Because it is easy to assume that these adolscents are capable of more mature cognitive thought than they actually are, working with them can be confusing.

Self-Development

The task of self-definition and integration begins during early adolescence (Dusek, 1996; Jaffe, 1998). As early adolescents engage in their self-development search, they push for autonomy (Cobb, 2001). At the same time, they are still immature and lack life experience (Weisfeld, 1999). These contrasts, coupled with their cognitive, physical, and pubertal changes, leave them vulnerable. As a result, they show increased dependency, which can be confusing to them and to the adults in their lives.

In some ways young adolescents contradict themselves. They want to be unique, yet they want to look like everyone else. In addition, they are both self-conscious and egocentric, assuming that everyone is looking at them or thinking about them (Dusek, 1996). Elkind (1988) termed this belief that others are as concerned with us as we are the "imaginary audience." As a result of this type of thinking, early adolescents fantasize about how others will react to them and become overly sensitive about their performance and appearance. Because they feel awkward and ugly, self-esteem usually decreases during this period of development (Vernon, 1993).

At the same time, early adolescents can be highly egocentric, seeing themselves as more important than they really are or assuming that no one else experiences things the way they do (Bjorklund, 2000; Owens, 2002). They also assume that because they are unique, they are also invulnerable. Elkind (1984) labeled this the "personal fable"—because adolescents believe they are special, they think bad things can happen to others but not to them. The personal fable accounts for self-deprecating as well as self-aggrandizing behavior, in which the adolescent assumes that he or she will be heroic and world-famous.

Social Development

Because young adolescents look to peers as a source of support (McDevitt & Ormrod, 2002), they are sensitive and vulnerable to humiliation by peers (Vernon & Al-Mabuk, 1995). Peers play an increasingly significant role in their lives and are an important part of their socialization. Thus, while peer relationships can be a source of pleasure, they also can be negative, and dealing with rejection is a major stressor at this age. Because they have a strong need to belong (Cobb, 2001), young adolescents have to learn to contend with peer pressure and decisions about which group to associate with. This is the period when cliques and distinct groups emerge, with specific "rules" about how to dress and behave.

As adolescents mature, their relationships become more complex (Weisfeld, 1999). Because some adolescents still have difficulty stepping outside themselves and looking at their own behavior objectively, they may behave in obnoxious ways. This, in turn, influences how others respond to them. They also continue to have trouble taking others' viewpoints into account because they still are preoccupied with their own needs (Jaffe, 1998; Seifert & Hoffnung, 1997).

Young adolescents also struggle with popularity. Cobb (2001) noted that being good in sports contributes to popularity for boys, and being a social leader is important for girls. Fitting into a group seems to be based on figuring out what the group is doing; the better able the adolescent is to do this, the more popular he or she will be.

Emotional Development

Many early adolescents ride an emotional roller coaster. They are more emotionally volatile (McDevitt & Ormrod, 2002); moodiness, accompanied by emotional outbursts, is common. Troublesome emotions such as anxiety, shame, depression, guilt, and anger also occur more frequently (Vernon, 1993). Because these negative emotions can be overwhelming and cause adolescents to feel vulnerable, they often mask their feelings of fear and vulnerability with anger, which typically distances people and often results in increased conflict with adults, who all too often react to the anger and fail to recognize the true feelings.

The increased intensity of emotions permeates all facets of life. Early adolescents feel anxious about the emotions they are experiencing, but because they are unable to think abstractly, for the most part, they tend to view situations from an "either–or" perspective and they do not make good choices about how to deal with the anxiety because they are unable to generate alternatives. This, in turn, may result in more anxiety or guilt and shame.

Adults who interact with young adolescents must recognize their emotional vulnerabilty and not exacerbate the problem by reacting insensitively. Educating young adolescents about what they are experiencing also is essential because it is far too easy for them to feel overwhelmed by their negative emotions and deal with them in nonconstructive ways.

Counseling Applications for Early Adolescence

Working with young adolescents can be challenging because it often is difficult to get at the underlying feelings they mask with their anger, apathy, or acting out. Helping professionals need to remember that the attainment of formal operational thinking occurs gradually, and that many of the problem behaviors they see are a result of incompetencies in thinking and reasoning. The rapid achievement of physical maturity often leads adults to assume that adolescents are more mature than they actually are.

Despite all the worries and concerns that result from the many significant changes during early adolescence, many researchers contend that what the adolescent experiences is part of a normal, healthy, developmental process (Jaffe, 1998; Kaplan, 2000; Seifert & Hoffnung, 1997). Furthermore, research has shown that the majority of adolescents do not resort to drug dependence, delinquent acting-out, school failure, sexual promiscuity, or other self-destructive behaviors (Jaffe, 1998; Owens, 2002; Schickendanz et al., 1998). Nevertheless, adult guidance is useful for helping adolescents deal with their worries and problems, whether typical or more severe.

Typical Problems Experienced During Early Adolescence

Young adolescents are easily overwhelmed by their feelings, and many of their problems result from their inability to deal effectively with these feelings. Anger, depression, and mood swings are common (Vernon, 2002). Because they tend to be overly sensitive, early adolescents may overreact to relationship issues with friends and parents. They worry excessively about how they look, how they act, and whether they belong. They also have concerns about dealing with their own sexuality.

Relationships with others can be difficult during this period. As adolescents struggle for independence, they may be loving and affectionate with parents one minute and hostile and rejecting the next (Vernon & Al-Mabuk, 1995). Changing friends is common as they attempt to piece together their identity and see where they fit in socially. They typically resist authority, signifying their need to assert their independence.

Adults often overreact to adolescent behavior and assume that their illogical actions are intentional. The adults' overreaction creates additional problems for adolescents, and they may respond with defiance or withdrawal. Mental health professionals working with adolescents must remember that adolescents are confused and that concrete strategies may still be necessary to help them look at cause and effect, alternative behaviors, and long-range implications.

Case Studies of Young Adolescents

Cory

Cory's mother referred her eighth grade son to a counselor at a local mental health center because the school had called to inform her that he had skipped school the last 5 days. For several years she'd had to leave for work before it was time for Cory to go to school, but his school attendance had never been a problem. She indicated that he seemed happy at home and had several close friends. He had struggled some with grades in seventh grade but generally got average grades. There had been no major changes in his life other than the transition to junior high last year.

When the counselor saw Cory for the first time, the counselor immediately noticed that although he was very tall, Cory's feet and hands were still too big for his body, making him appear clumsy and awkward. He had noticeable acne and seemed somewhat immature compared to other eighth-graders the counselor had worked with. Cory didn't deny skipping school, but he wasn't willing to talk about why he did it. To try to elicit more information from him, the counselor asked Cory to complete the following unfinished sentences:

1. When I go to school, I feel _____
2. The part of the school day I like best is _____
3. The part of the school day I like least is _____
4. The subject I like best is _____
5. The subject that is easiest for me is _____
6. The subject I like least is _____
7. The subject that is hardest for me is_____
8. If I could change something about school, I would change _____ ____
9. Other kids in this school _____
10. Teachers in this school _____

Cory's responses to these questions indicated two problem areas: speech class and physical education. The counselor hypothesized that Cory was overly sensitive about his body and didn't want to undress in the locker room before and after physical education. Likewise, the counselor assumed that Cory wanted to skip speech class because he was self-conscious about getting up in front of the other 25 students to give a speech.

After some discussion, Cory admitted that he felt self-conscious in these classes. The counselor explained the concept of the "imaginary audience" to him and assured Cory that his classmates probably had the same concerns. He asked Cory to assess how helpful skipping school had been in dealing with these problems and obtained a commitment from Cory to work on more productive ways to handle the situation.

The counselor then had Cory work on an adaptation of an activity called "Magnify" (Pincus, 1990). The counselor listed several events and instructed Cory to magnify their importance by turning them into catastrophes. For example:

1. You walk to the front of the room to give a speech.
   Catastrophic thoughts: _____
2. You go into the locker room to change for physical education.
   Catastrophic thoughts: _____

After Cory identified the worst-case scenarios, the counselor taught him to look at the probable situation by having him work on an adaptation of an activity called "Getting Straight Our Magnifications" (Pincus, 1990). In this activity, best-case, worst-case, and probable scenarios were identified. For example:
You walk to the front of the room to give a speech.

Best-case scenario: _____

Worst-case scenario: _____

Probable scenario: _____

As he identified the best, worst, and probable outcomes and identified his catastrophic thoughts for several different situations, Cory began to dispute some of his anxieties about speech and physical education. Next, the counselor helped Cory develop self-statements to deal with the anxiety. Among them were the following:

- Even though it seems like everyone is looking at me when I give a speech, probably only a few people are, and that's not the end of the world.
- If I mess up when I'm giving a speech, I'm not a total jerk.
- If I'm embarrassed to undress in physical education, probably other kids are too, so it's not worth skipping school over.

Following these activities, Cory and the counselor looked at the consequences of skipping school and brainstormed better ways for Cory to handle his anxiety. The counselor recommended that he read *Life Happens* (McCoy & Wibbelsman, 1996) to help him see that his thoughts and feelings were normal. Together they drew up a contract for school attendance.

Consulting with Cory's mother, the counselor explained the concept of the imaginary audience and assured her that her son's solution to the problem no doubt seemed logical to him because of the cognitive incompetencies characteristic of youth at this stage of development. The counselor suggested that she visit with the speech teacher to discuss the possibility of utilizing small groups for some of the speech activities because students in the small group wouldn't feel as anxious about performing. Finally, he praised the mother for being firm about Cory's school attendance, yet understanding about why Cory had chosen to behave as he had.

Maria

Maria, a sixth-grader, referred herself to the school counselor because she was having problems with friends. First of all, her best friend had been ignoring her and wasn't spending much time with her. Although this bothered her a lot, she was more upset that some girls had started an *I Hate Maria* club and that to get into the club, her classmates had to say bad things about her.

Although Maria was highly verbal, she rambled a lot. To help her focus on some of her thoughts and feelings about these issues, the counselor had her fill in the blanks in the following series of open-ended sentences:

1. If my best friend does not do things with me, it means that _____ _____

2. If some kids in my class join the *I Hate Maria* club, I feel _____ _____ and I think that_____

3. If other kids say mean things about me, I feel_____and I think_____

4. What I wish would happen is_____

5. What I think I can control about this situation is_____ _____

Based on her responses, Maria seemed to feel helpless, sad, and inadequate, which are normal responses for early adolescents, who place great importance on peer relationships.

Because Maria felt sad and inadequate rather than angry at her peers, the counselor chose to focus on her self-concept and what she thought being rejected by some friends said about her. He adapted an activity called *Glad To Be Me* (Vernon, 1989) to help this 12-year-old see that rejection from others does not mean she is not a worthwhile person. He also challenged Maria to take a good look at herself and ask herself whether she was what the club members said she was.

He asked her for some examples of what she thought others were saying about her and then asked her to prove to him that she was stupid, that she was a stuck-up snob, and that she couldn't roller blade well. Maria admitted that none of these things said about her was true and that even if others thought they were, that didn't have to change who she was.

The counselor then talked to Maria about what she could and could not control in this situation, and helped her see that she could control her own thoughts by reminding herself that she wasn't what some of her classmates said she was, but that she couldn't control her classmates.

Next, the counselor helped Maria put the problem in perspective by asking her to make a list of all the boys and girls in her class. He then asked her to cross out the names of the kids who were in the club, put an asterisk beside the names of the kids who were still nice to her, and put a star next to the names of the kids she could still consider good friends. By doing this, Maria realized that only a small percentage of her classmates were actually in the club, that most of them were still nice to her, and that she still had several good friends. This activity helped her to see that she had been overgeneralizing about the club. She'd been thinking that *everyone* was in it and that they all were against her.

As a final activity, the counselor discussed the concept of coping self-statements, things Marie could say to herself to help her cope more effectively with problems. After giving an example, he asked Maria to write several positive self-statements on index cards so she could refer to them in the future. He also suggested that Maria read *The Friendship Hotline* (Krulik, 1999), to help her realize that friendships change, and encouraged her to keep a journal about her feelings related to these friendship issues.

Developmental Characteristics of Mid-Adolescence

Physical Development

Typically at about age 15 for females and 17 for males, the growth spurt ends (McDevitt & Ormrod, 2002). Depending on when he or she entered puberty, however, the 15- to 18-year-old's physical development might continue rather rapidly or slow down gradually. Because males typically lag behind females in the rate of physical development in early adolescence, females tend to tower over males until this trend is reversed in mid-adolescence (Jaffe, 1998).

By mid-adolescence, females usually have achieved full breast growth, have started to menstruate, and have pubic hair (Dusek, 1996). Males experience a lowering of their voice by age 15 (McDevitt & Ormrod, 2002), and facial hair appears approximately a year later (Kaplan, 2000).

Sexual urges are strong during mid-adolescence, which can evoke anxiety in adolescents and their parents. Becoming sexually active is often unplanned, and most adolescents have knowledge about the risks of sexually transmitted diseases and pregnancy (Owens, 2002). Still, unprotected sex is common because they see themselves as immune from the consequences (Vernon & Al-Mabuk, 1995). Although most teenagers aren't obsessed by sex or having intercourse on a regular basis, good sex education is imperative (Kaplan, 2000).

Cognitive Development

Formal operational thinking continues to develop during mid-adolescence, and their new cognitive capabilities allow 15- to 18-year-olds to think and behave in significantly different ways than before. For example, as they develop the ability to think more abstractly, they can hypothesize, can think about the future, and are less likely to conceptualize everything in either–or terms because their thought processes are more flexible. Formal operational thinking moves adolescents into the realm of possibility, at which their thinking is more multidimensional and relativistic (Owens, 2002). During mid-adolescence, they are capable of pondering and philosophizing about moral, social, and political issues and are better able to distinguish the real and concrete from the abstract and possible (Frankel, 1998; Jaffe, 1998).

Although their cognitive abilities have improved considerably since early adolescence, adolescents at ages 15 to 18 are still likely to be inconsistent in their thinking and behaving (Cobb, 2001). They might be able to see alternatives but still lack the experience or self-understanding to make appropriate choices.

Self-Development

Adolescents at this stage are preoccupied with achieving independence and finding their identities—discovering who they are and are not (Cobb, 2001). Finding themselves involves establishing a vocational, political, social, sexual, moral, and religious identity (Erikson, 1968). They do this by trying on various roles and responsibilities; engaging in discussions; observing adults and peers; speculating about possiblities; dreaming about the future; and doing a lot of self-questioning, experimenting, and exploring. During this period of development, they may spend more alone time, contemplating ideas and trying to clarify their values, beliefs, and direction in life.

Mid-adolescents generally are more self-confident than they were earlier and do not feel the need to look like carbon copies of their peers. Actually, they may strive to do the opposite, dying their hair green if someone else's is red or wearing quirky clothes from secondhand stores to "make a statement." This self-assertion extends to other areas as well. Mid-adolescents are more capable of resisting peer pressure because of their increased self-confidence and their ability to look beyond the immediate present and speculate about long-term consequences (Vernon, 1993).

There has been considerable discussion about whether there are gender differences in the process of identity formation. Cobb (2001) summarized the research, noting that the process is comparable for both sexes, but the particular content that adolescents address in achieving their identify can differ for either gender. Cultural values also contribute to identity development, as our sense of self reflects an awareness of how others see us (Cobb, 2001).

Social Development

Peer relationships continue to be important during this stage of development. Mid-adolescents spend more time with peers, and this serves several important functions: to try out various roles, to learn to tolerate individual differences, and to prepare themselves for adult interactions as they form more intimate relationships (Dusek, 1996).

If they have attained formal operational thinking, adolescents approach relationships with more wisdom and maturity. With their higher level of self-confidence, they are not as dependent on friends for emotional support, and by the end of this period, they begin to select friendships based on compatibility, common interests, shared experiences, and what they can contribute to the relationship (Dusek, 1996; Jaffe, 1998).

During mid-adolescence, intimate friendships increase, which helps them become more socially sensitive. Females seek intimate friendships sooner than males do, these relationships are more intense, and their development of intimacy is more advanced than it is for males (Dusek, 1996). As they become less egocentric, they are better able to recognize and deal with the shortcomings in relationships. As a result, friendship patterns become more stable and less exclusive (Steinberg,1996). Dating and sexual experimentation generally increase during this period, but, according to Cobb (2001), although teenagers are more likely to be sexually active now than before, Jensen, de Gaston, and Weed (1994) reported that many adolescents engage in intercourse infrequently.

Emotional Development

As they attain formal operational thinking, mid-adolescents have fewer rapid mood fluctuations and therefore are not as overwhelmed by their emotions. They tend to be less defensive and are more capable of expressing their feelings rather than acting them out behaviorally (Vernon & Al-Mabuk, 1995). Some adolescents, however, perceive their lives as quite stressful and think their problems exceed their ability to cope effectively. This contributes to the higher rate of suicide at this stage of development (Masten, Neemann, & Andenas, 1994).

Toward the end of this developmental stage, many adolescents are lonely and ambivalent. As their needs and interests change, they may be gradually growing away from their friends. As high school graduation approaches, they might be apprehensive about the future. Some experience self-doubt and insecurity if they compare themselves to peers or when they explore the skills and abilities they need to qualify for a certain job or for postsecondary education.

Once they have developed formal operational thinking skills, adolescents are better able to deal with emotionally charged issues. They are not as impulsive or as likely to behave irrationally or erratically in response to emotional upset. How adolescents at this stage of development manage their emotions varies widely and is dependent on their level of cognitive maturation.

Counseling Applications for Mid-Adolescence

Counseling the mid-adolescent is easier than working with the 11- to 14-year-old, but a lot depends on the extent to which the adolescent has obtained formal operational thinking. In general, the older adolescent does not feel as vulnerable, is better able to express feelings rather than masking them through acting out, and is more willing to be in counseling. That is not to say that all older adolescents are this way; a lot depends on the nature of the problem and the personality of the adolescent.

For the most part, though, they are better able to express themselves verbally, and it is easy to assume that concepts don't have to be reinforced in concrete ways. Because adolescents vary in their level of maturity, and because some are visual rather than auditory learners, it is still appropriate to use activities to help illustrate points. Short homework assignments such as bibliotherapy or journaling is helpful for this age group.

Typical Problems Experienced During Mid-Adolescence

Although the emotional turbulence lessens significantly during mid-adolescence, a new set of circumstances arise that can create problems for 15- to 18-year-olds. Specifically, adolescents in this age-group are dealing with more complex relationships that may involve sexual intimacy (Owens, 2002) and with decisions about their future. Teenagers are concerned with getting enough out of high school to prepare them for life (Kaplan, 2000). They also express confusion about career choice, and they worry about money. The transition from high school to postsecondary plans results in mixed feelings of elation, ambivalence, and loss (Vernon & Al-Mabuk, 1995). Relationships with their families may be strained as they push for more autonomy, yet are anxious about being too independent.

Mid-adolescence serves as a stepping stone to the young adult world with its even greater challenges and new opportunities. This can be an exciting time but also can create anxiety. Mental health professionals working with adolescents need to be aware of the ambivalence that mid-adolescents likely feel. Counselors must be sensitive to both the anxiety and the excitement that many adolescents feel about making a significant transition that will involve a change in roles, relationships, routine, and assessment of self.

Case Studies of Mid-Adolescents

Stacie

Stacie, age 17, initiated contact with the school counselor to discuss her relationship with her boyfriend. She said the relationship had been very good for the first few months, but lately they had been arguing so much that she was afraid Matt would break up with her. Whenever they went out, she constantly wanted reassurance that he cared about her, which irritated him. When she persisted, he ignored her. If he didn't call when he said he would, she got anxious, and she would get upset if he didn't return her phone calls right away. She was certain that he was seeing other girls and assumed that something was wrong with her. Her response to this situation was to sit at home and wait for his phone calls, to call his friends to see where he was, and to stay awake at night thinking about the situation. She felt depressed and anxious.

In talking further with Stacie, most of their arguments seemed to arise because Stacie wanted to spend all her time with Matt and he was insisting on having some space. When Stacie expressed concern about what he would do if he wasn't with her as much, the counselor had her make a list of all the possible things that could happen. She then asked Stacie to put a checkmark next to the things she could prove had happened. When Stacie completed this task, the counselor explained that there is a difference between probability and possibility, and that one way of distinguishing between them is to look at past evidence.

For example, although Matt possibly could take out another girl, to her knowledge had he ever done this? It was possible that he could get killed in a car accident, but had he ever driven recklessly or while drunk when she had been with him? The counselor instructed Stacie to use this type of questioning to help her deal with her anxiety about things that could happen when Matt wasn't with her. Many of them, she would find, were unlikely based on past history and her information about Matt.

Next, the counselor discussed issues of control in the relationship. She tied some strings to her arms and legs and asked Stacie to pull on them. The harder Stacie pulled, the more the counselor resisted. They discussed the idea that Stacie's attempts to control Matt would probably drive him away, which Stacie acknowledged had happened once already. To help her deal with this, the counselor helped Stacie make a list of things she could say to herself when she felt like she wanted to control her boyfriend, such as: "Will it do more harm than good to control?" "What's the worst thing that could happen if I don't control him?" "Can I really control another person?"

As Stacie talked about her relationship with Matt, she brought up times when she wasn't being controlling but Matt still was not treating her with respect. The counselor gave Stacie some handouts on personal rights and assertion and explained the concepts. They then role-played assertive and nonassertive responses to some issues Stacie generated.

When Stacie left the session, she admitted feeling less anxious. She indicated that she could work on several things to help her deal with these relationship issues.

Michael

Michael's mother referred him to a mental health counselor because he was a senior in high school and had no idea what he wanted to do after graduation. His mother explained to the counselor that she was a single parent who had a hard time making ends meet, so Michael's options were somewhat limited. She thought Michael was angry about this, but he refused to talk to her about it and seemed to be increasingly anxious whenever anyone asked about his future plans.

Michael was reluctant to talk and resented being in counseling, so the counselor asked him to complete two short activities. For the first activity, he gave Michael a paper bag and asked him to write words that he thought described the Michael that most people knew—his public persona. Then the counselor gave him several slips of paper and asked him to jot down words describing his private self—the self that others didn't see. To show what he meant, the counselor explained that others might, for example, see Michael as self-assured, whereas on the inside he might be afraid about making a good impression on others.

The counselor stressed to Michael that he did not have to say what was on the inside of the bag unless he chose to do so. This paper-and-pencil activity seemed to help Michael relax, and he was fairly open about the outside of his bag, through which he revealed that most people saw him as a competent athlete and as a self-confident individual. He chose not to write anything from the inside of the bag but, based on what his mother had said, the counselor hypothesized that Michael was not as confident at this point in life as he liked others to think he was.

The second activity dealt more specifically with feelings about his impending graduation. The counselor first asked Michael to list ways that he thought his relationships with others would change after graduation. Next he asked Michael to identify how his role would change once he was no longer in high school. Finally he asked Michael to list several "feeling words" that described how he felt about graduating.

Based on Michael's responses, he seemed to have a lot of ambivalence about graduating, coupled with feelings of loss. The counselor explained that, because high school graduation is such a major transition, having mixed feelings about it is normal and Michael, like all high school graduates, would be experiencing losses: the loss of a familiar routine, loss of friendships as people branch off in new directions, and loss of status, as he probably would no longer be participating competitively in the sports in which he excelled.

This activity helped Michael identify some of his feelings, and he was willing to discuss some of them with the counselor. As a follow-up activity, the counselor asked Michael if he would be willing to complete a "loss graph" to help him deal more effectively with his feelings. Michael agreed to do this during the next session.

At the second session the counselor reviewed some of the things they had discussed during the initial session and then asked Michael to draw a line across a sheet of paper. At one end of the line he was to put a date signifying the beginning of middle school, as Michael had said in the previous session that he had been with his current friends since that time. The counselor then asked Michael to put his graduation date at the other end of the line. After he had done this, he was to divide the line into specific grade levels and make separate markers for significant events, both positive and negative.

The counselor asked Michael to write on the graph several words about each event, placing the positive ones above the line and the negative ones below. He explained to Michael that the purpose of this activity was to help him get more in touch with his memories about middle school and high school. Once he had done so, they could begin looking ahead to the future. The counselor encouraged Michael to look back through scrapbooks as a way to help him remember these years.

Michael spent a considerable amount of time on this activity and was willing to share some of his memories with the counselor. Together they discussed how things wouldn't be the same again and identified some ways by which Michael could reach closure with friends who were leaving the state—for example, by writing a letter to them, telling them what their relationship had meant to him and planning a special outing with them.

During the next session Michael and the counselor talked about the future. Michael was able to express some anger at the fact that, because his parents were divorced, he didn't have as many options as some of his friends. But he also acknowledged that he hadn't been applying for scholarships or investigating other options. The counselor hypothesized that perhaps Michael hadn't been ready to move on because he was happy with things the way they were, and Michael agreed. He now realized, however, that he had to put the past behind him, and he admitted that the loss graph had helped him to put that in perspective. Now he felt like he needed to take some action.

The counselor suggested that Michael visit with the school counselor to review the interest inventories he had completed during his junior year and to get some scholarship applications. Because he sensed that Michael was becoming somewhat overwhelmed with everything involved in the transition to life after high school, the counselor suggested that Michael get three envelopes and label them as follows: this week, this month, and in the future. He explained that when Michael felt overwhelmed or worried about any aspect of graduation and future planning, he write down the worry and then put it in the appropriate envelope. In this way, Michael could stop himself from thinking about everything at once and would be able to manage things more effectively.

At this point, the counselor suggested that Michael come back for a check-up visit in a month. At that time they would evaluate to see what progress he was making in dealing with the practical and the emotional challenges associated with this major transition.

Summary

Children at various developmental levels have some physical, cognitive, self, social, and emotional characteristics in common. These levels are delineated here as early childhood, mid-childhood, early adolescence, and mid-adolescence. Armed with this developmental information, practitioners can make more accurate assessments and design more helpful interventions. In assessment, age-specific developmental characteristics can serve as a barometer to indicate how a child is progressing relative to normal developmental guidelines. Without such a barometer, parents and professionals can easily misconstrue or misdiagnose problems; with it, they have a general sense of what's "normal."

Developmental knowledge is also critical in designing effective interventions. Children and adolescents don't respond well to many of the counseling approaches that work with adults. Because children's attention spans are more limited—at least until adolescence—than adults', helping professionals who work with children must be more creative and use visual and kinesthetic methods as well as auditory methods. Games, art activities, play, simulation activities, music, and drama—all are examples of interventions that take into consideration the developmental capabilities of children and adolescents. These interventions are described in greater detail in subsequent chapters of this book.

Too often, parents and teachers think children (adolescents in particular) are being obnoxious when they actually are acting the way they are because that is the best way they know to process information in the given situation. Growing up is challenging. All children, to some extent, experience the normal developmental issues identified in this chapter. Sadly, many children today also have significant situational concerns such as growing up in abusive or alcoholic families, adjusting to parental divorce or remarriage, being homeless, or living in poverty. How children respond to these problems, in addition to their basic needs, has a bearing on whether they will or will not engage in self-defeating behaviors. Helping professionals who are well grounded in developmental theory will be better equipped to understand how young clients process information and how to work most effectively with them to facilitate problem resolution before it reaches that point.

References

Bee, H. (2000). *The developing child* (9th ed.). Needham Heights, MA: Allyn & Bacon.

Berger, K., & Thompson, R. (1991). *The developing person through childhood and adolescence.* New York: Worth.

Berk, L. E. (1999). *Infants and children.* Boston: Allyn & Bacon.

Berk, L. E. (2001). *Awakening children's minds.* New York: Oxford University Press.

Bjorklund, D. F. (2000). *Children's thinking: Developmental function and individual differences* (3rd ed.). Belmont, CA: Wadsworth.

Borich, G. D., & Tombari, M. L. (1995). *Educational psychology: A contemporary approach.* New York: HarperCollins.

Cobb, N. J. (2001). *Adolescence: Continuity, change, and diversity* (4th ed.). Mountain View, CA: Mayfield Publishing.

Cole, M., & Cole, S. R. (1996). *The development of children* (3rd ed.). New York: W. H. Freeman.

Coleman, P. (1991). *Dark closets and noises in the night.* Mahwah, NJ: Paulist Press.

DiGiuseppe, R. (1999). Rational emotive behavior therapy. In H. T. Prout and D. T. Brown, *Counseling and psychotherapy with children and adolescents: Theory and practice for school settings* (pp. 252–293). New York: John Wiley & Sons, Inc.

Dusek, J. B. (1996). *Adolescent development and behavior* (3rd ed.). Upper Saddle River, NJ: Prentice–Hall.

Elkind, D. (1984). *All grown up and no place to go: Teenagers in crisis.* Reading, MA: Addison–Wesley.

Elkind, D. (1988). *The hurried child: Growing up too fast too soon.* Reading, MA: Addison–Wesley.

Elkind, D. (1991). Development in early childhood. *Elementary School Guidance and Counseling, 26,* 12–21.

Erikson, E. (1968). *Identity: Youth and crisis.* New York: W. W. Norton.

Frankel, R. (1998). *The adolescent psyche.* New York: Routledge.

Gauvain, M. (2001). *The social context of cognitive development.* New York: Guilford Press.

Harter, S. (1996). *The construction of the self: A developmental perspective.* New York: Guilford.

Harter, S., Waters, P., & Whitesell, N. R. (1998). Relationship self-worth: Differences in perceived worth as a person across interpersonal contexts among adolescents. *Child Development, 69,* 756–766.

Hendricks, G., & Roberts, T. B. (1977). *The second centering book: More awareness activities for children, parents, and teachers.* Englewood Cliffs, NJ: Prentice–Hall.

Izard, C. E., & Ackerman, B. P. (2000). Motivation, organization, and regulatory functions of discrete emotions. In M. Lewis & J. M. Haviland–Jones (Eds.), *Handbook of emotions* (pp. 253–264). New York: Guilford Press.

Jaffe, M. L. (1998). *Adolescence.* Danvers, MA: John Wiley & Sons.

Jensen, L. C., de Gaston, J. F., & Weed, S. E. (1994). Sexual behavior of nonurban students in grades 7 and 8: Implications for public policy and sex education. *Psychological Reports, 75,* 1504–1506.

Kaplan, P. S. (2000). *A child's odyssey.* (3rd ed.). Belmont, CA: Wadsworth.

Kolbisen, I. M. (1989). *Wiggle-butts and up-faces.* Half Moon Bay, CA: I Think I Can.

Krulik, N. (1999). *The friendship hotline.* New York: Price, Stern, & Sloan.

LeFrancois, G. R. (1992). *Of children: An introduction to child development.* Belmont, CA: Wadsworth.

Maslow, A. H. (1968). *Toward a psychology of being* (2nd ed.). Princeton, NJ: D. Van Nostrand.

Masten, A. S., Neemann, J., & Andenas, S. (1994). Life events and adjustment in adolescents: The significance of event independence, desirability, and chronicity. *Journal of Research on Adolescence, 4,* 71–97.

McCoy, K., & Wibbelsman, C. (1996). *Life happens.* New York: Perigee Press.

McDevitt, T. M., & Ormrod, J. E. (2002). *Child development and education.* Upper Saddle River, NJ: Pearson Education.

Owens, K. B. (2002). *Child and adolescent development: An integrated approach.* Belmont, CA: Wadsworth.

Owens, R. E., Jr. (1996). *Language development* (4th ed.). Boston: Allyn & Bacon.

Piaget, J. (1967). *Six psychological studies.* New York: Random House.

Pincus, D. (1990). *Feeling good about yourself.* Carthage, IL: Good Apple.

Porter, L. (1999). *Young children's behavior: Practical approaches for caregivers and teachers.* Sydney, Australia.

Pruitt, D. B. (Ed.) (1998). *Your child: What every parent needs to know about childhood development from birth to preadolescence.* New York: HarperCollins.

Santrock, J., & Yussen, S. (1992). *Child development: An introduction.* Dubuque, IA: William C. Brown.

Schave, D., & Schave, B. F. (1989). *Early adolescence and the search for self: A developmental perspective.* New York: Praeger.

Schickendanz, J. A., Schickendanz, D. J., Forsyth, P. D., & Forsyth, G. A. (1998). *Understanding children and adolescents* (3rd ed.). Needham Heights, MA: Allyn & Bacon.

Seifert, K. L., & Hoffnung, R. J. (1997). *Child and adolescent development* (4th ed.). Boston: Houghton Mifflin.

Selman, R. (1980). *The growth of interpersonal understanding: Developmental and clinical analyses.* New York: Academic Press.

Selman, R. L., & Schultz, L. J. (1990). *Making a friend in youth: Developmental theory and pair therapy.* Chicago: University of Chicago Press.

Shwe, H. I. (1999). Gricean pragmatics in preschoolers: Young children's understanding of sarcasm and irony. *Dissertation Abstracts International, 59,* Sciences and Engineering.

Steinberg, L. (1996). *Adolescence.* New York: Al Knopf.

Steinberg, L. D., & Levine, A. (1990). *You and your adolescent: A parent's guide for ages 10 to 20.* New York: Harper & Row.

Trawick–Smith, J. (2000). *Early childhood development* (2nd ed.). Upper Saddle River, NJ: Prentice–Hall.

Turner, J. S., & Helms, D. B. (1995). *Lifespan development* (5th ed.). Fort Worth, TX: Harcourt Brace.

Vandenberg, B. (1998). Real and not real: A vital developmental dichotomy. In O. N. Saracho & B. Spodek (Eds.), *Multiple perspectives on play in early childhood education* (pp. 295–305). Albany: University of New York Press.

Vernon, A. (1989). *Thinking, feeling, behaving: An emotional education curriculum for children.* Champaign, IL: Research Press.

Vernon, A. (1993). *Developmental assessment and intervention with children and adolescents.* Alexandria, VA: American Counseling Association.

Vernon, A., & Al-Mabuk, R. (1995). *What growing up is all about: A parent's guide to child and adolescent development.* Champaign, IL: Research Press.

Vernon, A. (2002). *What works when with children and adolescents: A handbook of individual counseling techniques.* Champaign, IL: Research Press.

Waters, V. (1979). *Color us rational.* New York: Institute for Rational Living.
Weisfeld, G. (1999). *Evolutionary principles of human adolescence.* New York: Basic Books.

The Individual
Counseling Process

Jean Peterson

A 4-year-old comes to counseling because her father, who is separated from her mother, has made allegations that her mother has been emotionally abusive to her.

An 8-year-old sees a counselor because a teacher is concerned about his aggressive behavior.

A 10-year-old asks to see a school counselor because of tension in her family during divorce proceedings.

A 12-year-old is referred for counseling by the courts because of his drug use and shoplifting.

A 15-year-old is sent to a counselor by her parents because of her perfectionism, anxiety, and insomnia.

A 16-year-old reveals, in an essay written for her English class, that she has experienced date rape. The teacher, who also suspects an eating disorder, refers the girl to the school counselor.

A 17-year-old who is depressed and suicidal discusses these issues with a counselor.

Clients and issues like these are part of the daily work of school and agency counselors. Some of these professionals have had training in interventions specifically geared to children and adolescents, have developed a repertoire of effective strategies, and enjoy working with the problems this age group presents. Many other counselors working with young clients, however, are uncomfortable doing so. They have had little or no training or supervision in counseling children and adolescents. They feel frustrated with their clients' lack of autonomy or do not understand child and adolescent development. They feel inept during counseling sessions, and the children or adolescents they counsel feel uncomfortable and unresponsive in return. These counselors apply strategies that are appropriate only for adults, with the result that the counselor and the young client alike feel frustrated. What works for adults probably will not be effective with children and adolescents, and significant adaptations can and should be made.

This chapter addresses what counselors need to know to counsel children and adolescents effectively. The major focus is on building a relationship with younger clientele and adapting counseling skills for these clients.

Basic Guidelines for Working With Young Clients

Various scholars have offered guidelines for counseling children and adolescents. Some basic admonitions are the following.

1. Because children often have misconceptions about counseling (Muro & Kottman, 1995; Myrick, 1997), counselors should include information about the counseling process.
2. Children are socially embedded; therefore, counselors should consult with some significant adults in their life (Clark, 1993; Kottman, 1995).
3. Counselors need to be aware of their clients' developmental stage and use interventions appropriate for their developmental level (Bradley & Gould, 1999; Muro & Kottman, 1995; O'Brien & Burnett, 2000).
4. Children and adolescents need to be accepted as they are (Axline, 1969).
5. Reluctance and resistance are common, even in young clients who self-refer (Myrick, 1997). Respecting these protective behaviors helps to build trust (Orton, 1997).

6. Active listening is more important than expert questioning (Hughes & Baker, 1990; Semrud–Clikeman, 1995; Thompson & Rudolph, 2000).

7. When working with children, patience is important; building trust with a young client can be a slow process (Golden, 1993; Herlihy, 1993).

8. A strong counselor–client relationship is important (Kottman, 1995) and is a "necessary but not sufficient condition" (Semrud–Clikeman, 1995, p. 91) for change to occur.

9. Specific intervention strategies are needed for change (De Jong & Berg, 1998; Kottman, 1995; Littrell, 1998; Vernon, 2002).

10. Emphasis on the here-and-now is more powerful and exciting for the client but also is more threatening than there-and-then statements, which diffuse the intensity of the present (Myrick, 1997).

11. Paying attention to strengths and eventually helping young clients to apply their strengths in making changes is an effective counseling strategy (Muro & Kottman, 1995).

12. Counselors who work in schools should be sensitive to teachers' time constraints and need for information about the counseling process (Muro & Kottman, 1995).

13. Session length should be adapted to the setting and the needs of the client (Myrick, 1997).

Counselors working with children and adolescents should be aware of how easily they can become enmeshed or overinvolved in young clients' lives. It is easy to want to "rescue" children and adolescents, to second-guess their parents, and to lose objectivity, particularly when the counselor connects at an emotional level with the issues at hand, including a client's vulnerability and lack of autonomy. In regard to rescuing—excessive reassurances, consoling, and even humor and teasing actually might communicate a lack of understanding or the counselor's own discomfort (Erdman & Lampe, 1996). With young clients in particular, counselors must maintain objectivity and good boundaries, not just to be of maximum assistance but also for long-term health of the counselor.

Counselors also may be tempted to give material "treats" to children. Turley (1993) stated that a counselor's gift to a child is, instead, "time, a caring person, a place where there [are] unusual freedoms, togetherness" (p. 199). To establish a habit of giving material gifts or food, even if only small and seemingly inconsequential, may obscure boundaries, create expectations, foster manipulation of either client or counselor, or distort the idea of counseling.

Resistance

Because children and adolescents are often referred involuntarily for counseling, they naturally may feel uncertain or reluctant during the counseling sessions.

Counselors should expect some resistance and consider this to be a reasonable reaction (Ritchie, 1994). Orton (1997) defined *resistance* as

> the child's attempts at self-protection through the use of defensive behavior. . . . When children are threatened, they protect themselves by withdrawing, acting out, regressing, or evidencing other problem behaviors. Rather than challenging a child's resistance to treatment, the therapist should explore the reasons for the resistance. Children may refuse to participate because they fear reprisals from parents for revealing "family secrets," they have not been adequately prepared about what to expect, their previous experiences with adults have been hurtful and disappointing, or they have a strong belief that they are (as one youngster put it) "a hopeless case." (p. 178)

Resistance is a common response to moving too quickly or interpreting prematurely. Children and adolescents may show resistance with fantasy, crises, silence, chattering, belligerence, storytelling, or other avoidant maneuverings, including missing sessions. They may resist because they do not desire to change (Herlihy, 1993) or because they feel a need for control, in response to perceptions that adults are trying to "fix" them. Adolescents in particular may see counselors as their parents' "hired guns" (Golden & Norwood, 1993). Some young clients also resist understanding counselor interpretations (Clark, 1993), such as statements linking past to present, because of their level of abstraction or as a reaction to uncomfortable or overwhelming feelings.

These defenses are not necessarily maladaptive. According to Semrud–Clikeman (1995), they may help the child or adolescent cope with daily life. Stripping these defenses away is not always necessary for health. Counselors must sort out which mechanisms are adaptive and which inhibit growth and development and must challenge the latter appropriately and constructively.

Several authors have offered suggestions for working with resistance and making it therapeutically useful. Orton (1997) encouraged counselors to respect their young clients' refusal to allow access to their private thoughts and feelings, noting that this respect helps to build trust and reduce anxiety. Writing in regard to working with families, Sampson, Sato, and Miyashita (1993) acknowledged the function of resistance and offered ways to reframe it. Resistance in counseling also presents an opportunity for the counselor to draw parallels to possible resistance in other settings (Semrud–Clikeman, 1995).

Strategies that might be employed to address resistance in young clients include play therapy, role-playing, counselor self-disclosure about the resistance, a counselor comment concerning a probable cause of the resistance, and confrontation (Thompson & Rudolph, 2000). Structured exercises also may help to move the counseling relationship forward when resistance occurs (Peterson, 1993, 1995), especially with chronologically or developmentally young children

(Thompson & Rudolph, 2000). Ritchie (1994) promoted gaining the young client's commitment to change through indirect confrontation with puppets, media, or stories; through paradox and reframing; and through modeling and role-plays. Oaklander (1997) emphasized that strengthening the child's inner support structure is essential to being able to work through deep-seated emotions.

With a resistant adolescent, another effective and empowering strategy is to acknowledge and "go with" the reluctance, leaving room for choice. This strategy is illustrated by the following statement by a veteran counselor of adolescents:

> I know you don't feel like talking today. We can just sit here together. I'm not going to go away. You can choose to talk or you can say nothing. If you choose not to talk, I might sit here with you, or I might just leave you alone and work quietly at my desk over there, if it seems that you'd prefer that. I'll decide later. You can decide about the talking. It's your time here, and you can use it as you like.

Thompson and Rudolph (2000) commented that sometimes a child simply does not have anything to discuss. They encouraged counselors to come to sessions with a tentative plan that they can turn to when there are unexpected silent periods. In general, counselors need to evaluate what is happening when sessions become blocked and whether a lack of skill or lack of planning may be contributing.

Parents, too, may demonstrate resistance. They may resist necessary treatment for a child, attempt to sit in on their child's session (Semrud–Clikeman, 1995), object to their own involvement in the counseling process, deny connections between their own issues and their child's presenting problem (Kottman, 1993), and even sabotage therapy out of envy, jealousy, competition, and narcissism (Hailparn & Hailparn, 2000). Parents' pretreatment expectancies for their child also play a role in treatment participation, attendance, and premature termination. Those expectations may be lower in situations reflecting socioeconomic disadvantage, ethnic minority status, severity of child dysfunction, child age, and parental stress and depression (Nock & Kazdin, 2001). Semrud–Clikeman (1995) recommended that counselors establish contact with parents during the initial stages of counseling, to help lessen parental anxieties.

The Counseling Process

Typically, the counseling process involves moving through the following stages:

Intake
Meeting for the first session
Establishing a relationship and developing focus
Working together toward change
Closure

Intake

The intake process may involve a telephone interview with one parent, a face-to-face interview with the young client and one or more members of the family, a meeting with just the client, or a combination of these and other possible scenarios. What and how much is discussed in regard to informed consent and confidentiality, for example, depends on who is present. Orton (1997) pointed out that the intake process may involve one or several sessions, depending on the counselor's orientation and whether other members of the child's family are to be interviewed. She emphasized the importance of nonjudgmental respect for the verbal and nonverbal expressions of all who are interviewed. According to Orton, the intake interview is

> an essential part of the counseling process because it helps the counselor establish a relationship with the child and the family that will form the basis for all future counseling and therapy. A successful intake interview offers a glimpse into the interpersonal world of the child and provides valuable insight into the family dynamics. Most practitioners, regardless of their theoretical orientation, use the interview process to gather information that will help them conceptualize the case and design an appropriate treatment plan. (p. 148)

Intake information typically includes the age and grade of the child or adolescent, the reason for referral, the child's date of birth and birth order, names and ages of siblings and parents, parents' employment, the child's birth and medical history, medications, developmental history, strengths and weaknesses, family and school relationships, activities, and other information pertinent to the reason for referral. If the child is of school age, the counselor might ask the parents to request pertinent information from school records for his or her review or might ask them to sign a release of information giving the counselor permission to make that request. If the young client is being seen in a school setting, the type of intake interview described here may not be feasible.

According to Semrud–Clikeman (1995), after gathering a variety of pertinent data, the counselor might ask the parents what they expect from the counseling experience for their child and whether they have had counseling experiences themselves. The counselor should explain that children might not experience counseling in the same way that adults do. If the child is not present, the counselor might discuss how the parents can explain to their child what to expect in counseling. At ages 3 to 5 it is appropriate to refer to "playing games," but with older children it is best to say that they will, for example, "see an adult who works with children who may have some problems in school" (p. 34). Telling children and adolescents about their counseling session the night before or the morning of the first interview gives them less time to worry.

Informing Clients and Others About "Counseling"

Counselors should talk about what counseling is, not only with children and adolescents but also with their parents if the parents have anxieties about the process (Myrick, 1997). Young clients may be confused about what they will experience. The adults may also not know what to expect from counseling or may have misconceptions about it, such as that counselors "give advice" (Thompson & Rudolph, 2000). As part of informed consent, some discussion of the counseling process is warranted, even with very young children.

With children, as with adults, the counselor's "definition" of counseling, his or her behaviors, and the goals set forth should be in accord with the client's culture and worldview (Herring, 1997; Ivey, Ivey, & Simek–Morgan, 1997; Sue, Ivey, & Pedersen, 1996). Given the commonly held premise that counseling is collaborative (Corey, Corey, & Callanan, 1998), an explanation of the process may help to demystify it for the client and consequently empower him or her. The following list, drawn from the ideas of a number of scholars, describes a variety of ways by which the counseling process can be explained to clients (Erdman & Lampe, 1996; Golden & Norwood, 1993; Hansen, Rossberg, & Cramer, 1994; Ivey, 1986; Thompson & Rudolph, 2000). The words that are used—as is true in all areas of counseling—should be developmentally appropriate.

- Counseling is for normal people who have "something to work on" in their lives.
- Counseling can help people to feel better and live more effectively.
- Counseling can help people "not to feel stuck anymore" about something.
- Counseling can help people make changes.
- Counselors can help people discover their strengths.
- Counseling can help to prevent problems in living.
- Counselors listen carefully to people to learn what they feel, what they think about, what they enjoy and dislike, and what they are confused about.
- Counselors can help people make sense of things that seem confusing or complicated.
- Counselors support and look for good things in people, instead of judging, criticizing, or looking for things that are wrong with them.
- Counselors believe that, with a little help, people can figure out how to move ahead.
- Rather than giving advice, counselors usually try to help people solve their own problems.

Developmental Considerations

Many developmental changes occur in children and adolescents during the preschool and school years, and even small age increments may translate into significant developmental differences in behavior. Therefore, the counselor must think carefully about the presumed physical, cognitive, social, and emotional development of a young client before the first meeting, and then continue to consider developmental aspects throughout the counseling process. Play media, structured and unstructured activities, vocabulary, and cognitive strategies—all should be developmentally appropriate if they are to be optimally effective. At the same time, counselors should be alert to asynchronous development (Wright, 1990), in which intellectual, social, physical, and emotional development are at varying levels, and to other anomalies as well. In addition, the potential diversity of developmental trajectories among nonheterosexual children and adolescents should be recognized, along with their differences from heterosexual youth (Savin–Williams & Diamond, 1999).

Ethical and Legal Concerns

Summarizing the major implications of the 1989 United Nations Convention on the Rights of the Child for mental health practice, Melton (1991) listed the following:

— high-quality services for children
— children as active partners in treatment
— child counseling supporting family integrity
— the provision of alternatives to residential placement
— protection from harm
— and the centrality of prevention

Taking into consideration the clients' age and maturity, counselors should strive to regard children as equal partners in the counseling relationship with the right to participate in setting goals and planning treatment, the right to expect privacy and feedback, and the right to refuse or end treatment (Orton, 1997). Orton, however, did note a number of inherent difficulties regarding equal partnership:

> First, children generally do not have sufficient understanding and ability to make informed decisions on their own about whether to accept or refuse different therapeutic interventions; second, young children are not considered legally competent because they have not reached the statutory age; and third, children rarely come to therapy voluntarily. (p. 357)

In addition to having a professional obligation to the child, the counselor has an obligation to the parents. The counselor has to be ready to deal with difficulties related to these relationships. During the intake interview and later sessions, parents may resist a child's goals (Herlihy, 1993), the counselor's treatment approach, a least-restrictive alternative to placement, or even counseling in general (Semrud–Clikeman, 1995). As expressed by Semrud–Clikeman (1995), the "therapist's primary responsibility is to protect the child's rights while maintaining his or her professional and legal obligations to the child's parents. This is not an easy task" (p. 357).

The age at which a child is considered competent to give informed consent varies from state to state, and counselors are responsible for knowing the laws and statutes of the states in which they practice (Orton, 1997). Parents' wishes can be overridden if the state decides that parents are not providing adequately for a child's physical or psychosocial needs (Swenson, 1993). As Gustafson and McNamara (1987) noted, "Most jurisdictions allow minors to consent to treatment without parental knowledge in specific situations in which obtaining parental consent may jeopardize the likelihood that the minor will receive that treatment" (p. 503). These situations include, among others, substance abuse, sexual abuse, pregnancy, sexually transmitted diseases, and contraception. Treatment for mature minors and emancipated minors, emergency treatment, and court-ordered treatment also are recognized as general exceptions to the requirement for parental consent (Gustafson & McNamara, 1987; Swenson, 1993), and no general rule requires counselors to obtain parental consent concerning a child who has the ability to make an informed decision (Thompson & Rudolph, 2000).

In regard to informed consent, counselors have to make sure that child and parents alike understand the types of services available, the fees (if applicable), and potential risks and benefits, and that written permission will be sought if there is need to release information to other professionals (Orton, 1997). All of these areas should be covered in a written professional-services agreement to be signed prior to the start of therapy (Swenson, 1993). Even though a child's signature may not be legally binding, having the child sign a consent form reinforces the counselor's responsibility to inform all who are involved about the counseling process and reinforces the rights of both child and parents.

Because adults often become involved when a child or adolescent is being counseled, it is important to clarify confidentiality issues with them prior to the start of counseling. Adults' involvement may take many forms. For example, the counselor may contact the parents to gain information about the family system and how the parents perceive their child. Or the parents may contact the counselor for information about their child—information they probably have a legal right to know (Salo & Shumate, 1993). Teachers, principals, and special-services personnel may request that the school counselor divulge information about children (Huey, 1996), and agency personnel may request information from schools. All too often, teachers and counselors assume that these clients are "just children" and that the rules of confidentiality do not apply. In a survey conducted by Wagner (1981), elementary-school counselors were the least stringent about maintaining confidentiality.

Counselors should be aware that all pertinent ethical codes emphasize the right to privacy for all clients and client choice about who shall receive information (American Association for Marriage and Family Therapy, 1991; American Counseling Association, 1995; American Psychological Association, 1995; American School Counselor Association, 1992; National Association of Social Workers, 1996), with some significant exceptions: when there is a duty to warn or protect; when the client consents to disclosure; when reimbursement or other legal rules require it; when there is an emergency; or when the client has waived confidentiality by bringing a lawsuit (Stromberg, 1993). Ferris and Linville (1988) pointed out that the consultation component in the developmental model of school counseling has the potential to compromise this ethical standard and that school counselors therefore must develop skills to help them analyze specific situations.

As previously mentioned, whatever the age of the child or adolescent, at the outset of the counseling relationship, confidentiality guidelines should be clarified with the client, with any involved parents or guardians, and, in the school setting, with faculty and administrators (Huey, 1996). Even though parents have a legal right to information (Remley, 1990; Salo & Shumate, 1993; Semrud–Clikeman, 1995), the counselor should make some or all of the following points to them (Huey, 1996; Remley, 1988, 1990; Semrud–Clikeman, 1995; Schmidt, 1996):

- Any inquiry for information by a parent will be discussed first with the client and must be agreed to by the client.
- It is not in the client's best interest for a counselor to share information, except in cases in which the counselor believes that sharing information is necessary to protect the welfare of the child or others.
- A trusting relationship is basic to effective counseling, and insisting that information be shared may undermine both the counseling relationship and the counseling process.
- School-age clients often want their parents to know what they are saying in sessions, and no assumption will be made to the contrary; however, the client will have the choice regarding what is shared.
- The counseling process promotes empowerment through choice, and the child or adolescent will explore issues and decisions with empowerment and choice in mind.
- The counselor will try to help the young client tell the parents what they need to know, even practicing the telling, if appropriate, but the parents must recognize that telling or not telling is the client's choice.
- A joint session, involving counselor, client, and parent(s), is an option if there is an issue to be discussed.
- If parents object to any of these points, they may decide, if counseling is not mandated, not to initiate or to discontinue counseling.

Most parents are sensitive to their child's right to privacy and accept that specifics from sessions will not be shared with them, as long as they are kept generally informed about progress (Semrud–Clikeman, 1995).

In another issue related to confidentiality, Salo and Shumate (1993) noted that counselors always should obtain permission from a custodial parent before revealing information to a noncustodial parent. Remley (1990) recommended that counselors keep careful written notes, bearing in mind that documentation is potentially public information. According to Thompson and Rudolph (2000), in states that have no licensure law providing for privileged communication, counselors have no recourse except to reveal information if subpoenaed. But they note that

> some courts, more tolerant than others, allow the counselor to share the privileged information with the judge in private to determine if the information is necessary to the proceeding or if public disclosure would be too hurtful to those involved, such as children who are a part of the case. (p. 505)

Regarding confidentiality, children and adolescents may be told that, even though the counselor will not divulge to parents, teachers, or administrators *what* the children say in sessions, the counselor may think it is appropriate to share their *feelings about* certain situations (Huey & Remley, 1988), especially situations in which the client seems to have been misunderstood or in which significant adults do not seem to be aware of the impact of an event.

In general, the counselor should recognize that his or her explanation of confidentiality will be processed differently at each level of cognitive development and therefore requires appropriate vocabulary. Adolescents may have an automatic distrust in regard to confidentiality. Young children actually may be frightened by something that is presented so seriously. Wording such as the following probably will not induce fear and usually is effective:

> What we talk about here—I don't tell anybody else. Everything you say is confidential. That means I don't talk about it with other people. If anyone asks me about what I talk about with kids, I check it out with the kids—whether they want me to say anything. And I go by what they say. At times I *have* to tell somebody, though, if I think you're a danger to yourself or if you're going to hurt someone else. If I believe you are being abused or hurt or someone is putting you in danger, I'd also have to tell that to someone who could do something about it. The law says I have to do that. Otherwise, what we talk about is kept confidential. So what do you think of these rules that I have to go by?

Semrud–Clikeman (1995) emphasized the ethical principle of counselor competence for counselors working with young clients, recommending that counselors seek supervision from an experienced colleague or establish a network for consultation whenever they feel unsure about their ability to be effective with children or adolescents. She also called attention to the issue of establishing who will participate in counseling: the child/adolescent, the parent, the teacher, or perhaps some combination of these. In a school, the referring teacher might, for example, be the sole participant if the child is resistant, especially if improving the teacher-student relationship is the focus. Because the cooperation and assistance of adults in a child's life usually are necessary for changes in behavior, it is important to have contact with at least one significant adult during the counseling process.

In regard to contact with parents, a parent might establish "unspoken boundaries" to maintain parent–child enmeshment and to prevent a close relationship from developing between the child and the counselor (Semrud–Clikeman, 1995). Involving parents early in the process can help to alleviate this problem.

Conceptualizing the Client as Part of a System

Everyone is part of various systems, such as family, work environment, school, social groups, and ethnic group. Everyone is "in relationship." Systemic considerations are important when counseling any client, but they are especially important when counseling children and adolescents because many of their problems exist within the context of a system (Thompson & Rudolph, 2000). Family might play an integral role in the child's developing and maintaining anxiety, for example. This is a symptom that has a potentially deleterious impact on success in school and peer relationships (Bolton, 2000).

Before meeting with young clients, the counselor should attempt to obtain information about the systems in which they are involved. Adults are the best source for this important information, since children, especially young children, often lack the ability to articulate it. School counselors can ask teachers for this information or can look at school records. All counselors can interview parents by phone or in person or make inquiries during the initial phone contact if a parent initiated the call. Semrud–Clikeman (1995) emphasized the need for counselors to determine whether it is permissible to call a parent at work, to ask if they are calling at a convenient time, and to leave messages that contain no more than their name and number. Orton (1997) advocated building a partnership with parents during this contact, validating and valuing them and simultaneously gaining insight about their parenting style and interaction with the child, in addition to forming hypotheses about the potential impact of family structure and marital and other family conflict on the child (Buchanan & Waizenhofer, 2001).

Consider the following scenario concerning 7-year-old Ben, who has been referred for counseling because he is having difficulty concentrating in school. Prior to the start of counseling, the counselor should know that Ben is his parents' only child and he lives 3 days each week with Mom and 4 days with Dad. Each parent has recently remarried, and Ben now has four step-siblings, two in each household. Step-grandma babysits for Ben and his step-siblings before and after school. Ben's stepfather is considering a job transfer to a city 2 hours distant. Ben rarely interacts in the classroom and recently became agitated and cried uncontrollably when a classmate wanted to look at a small toy Ben had brought to school. Recent written assignments have been incomplete, and he has difficulty staying on task.

Before meeting with a child, the counselor should consider some hypotheses. Might a reported problem have a function (e.g., to escape, to call attention to a situation, to provoke adults to communicate, to avoid feeling)? Given the circumstances, what might a problem protect or deflect (e.g., others' concerns, uncomfortable feelings) or express (e.g., grief, agitation)? What other factors might be contributing to a problem? Ben, for instance, might be grieving losses associated with his new living arrangements, which may include little time alone with either parent and sharing space with step-siblings. Perhaps he is concerned that if his stepfather and mother move, time with his father will be more difficult to arrange. He could be angry about all of the changes in his life, and he might not be sleeping well at night because of everything occurring in his family system. Both households may have marital tensions. Ben may fear unsettling both households if he expresses strong feelings.

Even though forming tentative hypotheses can be helpful, more comprehensive assessment is necessary before considering the direction to take in regard to what is occurring within the school system. It is difficult to isolate specific family factors in accounting for children's issues, given the circularity of influences, the complex structures of families, and the simultaneous developmental transitions within individuals and families (Minuchin, 2001). In short, counselors should resist the temptation to "label" a child or adolescent based only on the situation described by the referral source. In Ben's case, for instance, systemic factors at school also could be involved in his lack of concentration.

Among many pertinent systemic factors, counselors should consider cultural context when conceptualizing a family. This would include, for example, acculturation status, ethnic composition of the neighborhood, language preference and facility, education, religion, and cultural explanation of the presenting problem (Ponterotto, Gretchen, & Chauhan, 2001). Sociocultural environment also affects cultural groups' perceptions of ideal family functioning (Garcia & Peralbo, 2000). Papilia, Olds, and Feldman (1998) noted that preferred gender roles in families may reflect cultural values, gender behaviors in a person's household, and media stereotypes. They also observed that, in general, disciplinary methods seem to vary according to geographical location, socioeconomic circumstances, and religious affiliation.

Meeting for the First Session

The Physical Setting

Regardless of the age of a child or adolescent, the counselor should create a physically and psychologically comfortable environment for counseling (Erdman & Lampe, 1996). The meeting room should be cheerful and should contain furnishings, sturdy toys, and activities that offer choice and that are appropriate for children and adolescents of various age levels, as well as for their parents (Orton, 1997). The toys in the room should meet a variety of interests and promote exploration and creative expression (Landreth, 1991). Erdman and Lampe (1996) recommended that counselors sit at their clients' eye level, inquire about their comfort, and use office furniture that does not contribute to the "disempowering and intimidating" feeling of having feet dangling or "sinking down into large chairs or couches" (p. 375).

Building Rapport and Defining the Problem

When working with young clients, counselors often direct the first few sessions to becoming acquainted. Developing a working relationship tends to take longer with children than with adults, as children typically need more time to accept the counselor as someone who can help them (Orton, 1997). Myrick (1997) recommended that counselors follow the client's lead and offer facilitative comments and responses. For example, if the child or adolescent has self-referred, the counselor might ask, "What did you want to see me about?" If the client has been referred by someone else, the counselor should clarify the reasons for the referral, check out the child's perceptions of the referral, not attempt to speak for teachers or others, and move the focus to the child's input. Semrud–Clikeman (1995) suggested a mini-interview format for gaining an understanding of the child's or adolescent's personal experiences, worldview, and family environment. The information gained may be useful in later sessions when exploring feelings and situations in the present.

Paying attention to the counselor–client relationship is important when working with children and adolescents alike. It is particularly important to focus on the relationship, especially at the outset, when working with young children who are guarded and defensive (Erdman & Lampe, 1996) or who have little knowledge about the counseling process and why they are to be involved in it (Myrick, 1997). The child initially may see the counselor as just one more rule-making, disciplinary authority figure, especially if an adult has sent him or her to the counselor (Kottman, 1990). When a child is troubled and highly resistant, gaining his or her acceptance may be a difficult challenge (Kranz & Lund, 1993). The "joining" process may be long. Several sessions may have no immediate goal other than to forge a trusting, unconditional relationship with a child in whose world adults are perhaps highly reactive, conditional, unpredictable, critical, and abusive.

For the child to learn that a trusting relationship is possible, helpful, and satisfying may itself be a worthy goal of the counseling process—a corrective emotional experience. Helping a child learn to trust and feel valued, described by Semrud–Clikeman (1995) as "align[ing] early experiences into a different mold" (p. 11), may help the child function more effectively in the classroom and elsewhere. Vernon (1993) offered a number of suggestions for building rapport in these and other situations—for example, chatting about hobbies, activities, and pastimes; being personal but not a "buddy"; showing genuine interest and concern; and taking the client's lead concerning comfortable seating. Vernon (2002) also recommended playing games.

Active listening is basic to both building rapport and defining the problem. From the outset, counselors should listen for a problem that has not been solved, associated feelings, and expectations about what the counselor should do about the problem (Thompson & Rudolph, 2000). Giving a young client feedback in the form of clarification and paraphrasing will help the counselor to confirm his or her understanding of the problem. Counselors should be aware, however, that sometimes a child or adolescent needs time to sort out what has been said. At these times, silence can be useful and productive. Young clients may use the time to consider their responses (Orton, 1997; Thompson & Rudolph, 2000) or, motivated by anxiety, to move "to deeper levels of thinking, feeling, and self-disclosure" (Gumaer, 1984).

When working with children and adolescents, as with adults, the counselor should be aware of cultural differences in eye contact, proximity preferences, response to stress, socioeconomic and sociocultural circumstances (Semrud–Clikeman, 1995), and even how circumstances are interpreted (Garbarino & Stott, 1989). Peterson (1999) provided a useful review of uniquely valued behaviors for people of different cultures that might help counselors decide how best to affirm a nonmainstream youth's culture.

Regarding African American individuals, for example, Mosley–Howard and Burgan Evans (2000) emphasized indigenous cultural strengths—namely, connection with extended family, pride in heritage, negotiation between two cultures, and spirituality and involvement with the church. Non-Hispanic counselors' relationships with Hispanic children will likely be enhanced if counselors respect clients' preferences in interpersonal distance, develop a smooth and pleasant relationship, and do not exploit the client's deference in that relationship. The cultural value of familialism also can be important if family-related reasons can be connected to desired behavioral changes (Herring, 1997). Semrud–Clikeman (1995) suggested that counselors seek out individuals who are similar in background to a client from an unfamiliar culture and question them about various behaviors and values. Ethnically matching the helping professional and the client also may result in improved functioning (Chapman, 2000).

The counselor in the following situation applied what she knew about the culture of Native Americans, especially how starkly it contrasts dominant-culture practices surrounding death:

Ten-year-old Sidney had been referred to Sarah, a school counselor in a large elementary school, because he had been absent from school for several days, had fallen far behind his class in assignments, and seemed listless and uncommunicative. His already low level of interaction with his mostly Anglo classmates, and even with the one other Native American boy in class, had also declined. His teacher had communicated to the counselor that there had been a death in the family recently but could not understand why Sidney wasn't "snapping out of it," as it was "just his grandmother."

The counselor recognized that Sidney's lack of eye contact meant deference and respect, and she noted his flat affect as he sat before her. So that she would not be uncomfortably direct in her approach, she made a few gentle "small-talk" comments and then apologized for not being aware until an hour earlier that his grandmother had died. She invited Sidney to tell her about his grandmother, and he began to explain that she had essentially raised him and his siblings after his mother developed a disabling condition shortly after Sidney was born.

Sarah recognized Sidney's deep grief and listened attentively as he responded quietly to her open-ended questions. He explained various extended-family relationships and told her about the recent days of community mourning. Near the end of the session, she asked if Sidney thought she should talk with his aunt, who now seemed to be the family leader. With his permission, Sarah contacted the aunt and made an important connection between school and family, learning at the same time that the family had been concerned about Sidney's withdrawal.

Assessment

Some form of early and ongoing assessment is warranted for accurate client conceptualization and effective strategic planning. Vernon (1993) advocated the use of creative and practical developmental assessment, describing it as qualitative, interactive with the counseling process, based on developmental theory, and involving child, practitioner, and significant other adults. Because children and adolescents are undergoing significant developmental changes, an assessment framework that provides a comprehensive sense of a child's developmental progress and potential interventions is more useful than a battery of tests alone. "Since certain behaviors are expected at certain stages" (Semrud–Clikeman, 1995, p. 10), assessment has to look at motor, cognitive, emotional, and social development (Orton, 1997).

Informal and formal assessment procedures can both be used. Myrick (1997) considered informal assessment valuable for focusing on the areas of physical development (including manner, grooming, posture, and energy level), social development (including speech flow, attitudes, and friendships), cognitive development (including logic, sense of reality, consequences, and values), cultural development (including religious and environmental influences and sense of stigmatization), history (including relevant events), future perspective (including goals, sense of responsibility, and sense of control), and the presenting problem, noting that some school counselors develop their own norms in these areas. Other tools useful in informal assessment are art, puppets, storytelling, board games, free play, unfinished-sentence activities, role-play activities, play-therapy strategies (Gitlin–Weiner, Sandgrund, & Schaefer, 2000), lifestyle questionnaires, and writing activities (Orton, 1997; Schmidt, 1996). Narrative descriptions of family systems in response to story stems can provide valuable information related to marital conflict, parental acceptance, and behavioral control in relation to presenting issues (Shamir, DuRocher Schudlich, & Cummings, 2001). Drawing the ideal self encourages young clients to be actively involved in the therapeutic process and can enhance self-understanding (Moran, 2001). A multiple-intelligences framework can be useful to tap into varied talents during and following assessment with young children (O'Brien & Burnett, 2000).

Achenbach's (1990) multi-modal, multi-informant paradigm for diagnosis is an informal assessment procedure in which the counselor gathers data from a number of sources to see how the client compares with others of the same age in similar situations. An informal, holistic approach that can be helpful in designing developmental interventions is Lazarus's (1976) BASIC ID model, adapted for children by Keat (1979). Orton (1997) discussed the usefulness of observation by teachers and counselor, ideally in several home and school settings, that focuses on learning style, attention span, mood and affect, expression of emotions, and interactions with parents, teachers, and peers. Semrud–Clikeman (1995) suggested observing not only the client but also the client's peers to make behavioral comparisons. Semrud–Clikeman also recommended observing the parent–child interaction, which can be helpful in forming treatment goals and strategies and also in assessing how various behaviors may be affecting the parent–child relationship. Schmidt (1996), however, cautioned that conclusions based on informal procedures, like those based on more formal procedures, should be viewed in conjunction with other assessment data.

Formal, structured assessment might involve psychological and educational tests, including intelligence, aptitude, and achievement instruments (Thompson & Rudolph, 2000), personality and self-concept scales, and developmental inventories (Vernon, 1993). Also commonly used are behavioral checklists or rating scales, with attention to presence, frequency, duration, and severity of specific behaviors.

Clinicians involved with third-party reimbursement have to refer to the *Diagnostic and Statistical Manual of Mental Disorders* (DSM–IV) (American Psychiatric Association, 1994). For organizing and communicating clinical information, this volume presents a standardized format based on a multiaxial system of assessment. Indeed, all counselors should be familiar with the DSM–IV diagnostic terminology and with common diagnoses among children and adolescents (Geroski, Rodgers, & Breen, 1997), including attention deficit/hyperactivity disorder, post-traumatic stress disorder, conduct disorder, depressive disorders, and anorexia nervosa. When young clients show symptoms of depression, counselors with solid knowledge of this diagnosis can, for example, administer an instrument specifically designed to assess depression (e.g., Beck, 1987; Reynolds, 1987,

1989) or make informal inquiries with specific symptoms in mind. Assessment is vital not just to diagnosis but also to developing appropriate interventions (Semrud–Clikeman, 1995). Counselors should be prepared to provide referrals, based on their assessments, to other service providers when appropriate (Schmidt, 1996).

Gathering More Information

A trusting relationship between counselor and client, regardless of the client's age, is the hallmark of effective counseling, although theoretical approaches differ regarding when "the problem" and information about it become the focus in this relationship. Carlson (1990) suggested a direct approach for obtaining information from the client when working with other-referred children. Thompson and Rudolph (2000) concurred, noting that the counselor can acknowledge whatever information the referral source has provided and indicate readiness to discuss the situation.

When interviewing children, listening is a more important skill than questioning (Hughes & Baker, 1990). One of the purposes of an initial session is to show the child that he or she is in a safe environment and will be listened to, so that a bond can develop. Some children form bonds easily and talk readily about their feelings and concerns. Others require some time before they feel safe enough to share confidences (Herlihy, 1993; Semrud–Clikeman, 1995). Counselors may face resistance if they try to push a child, forcing attention on "therapeutic issues." Beginning counselors in particular might feel defensive and frustrated when a child "just doesn't want to talk" (Herlihy, 1993, p. 66). When a child answers a question, many counselors tend to follow the response with another question. More effective is to paraphrase or summarize, as those strategies encourage expanding on the previous response (Thompson & Rudolph, 2000). The less counselors intrude, the more children will tell them (Greenspan, 1981). Children "intuitively trust and open up to those who like and understand them" (Thompson & Rudolph, 2000, p. 149). Erdman and Lampe (1996) warned against becoming impatient when rapport is delayed. Abused children, for instance, may be alert to the possibility of deception (Bugental, Shennum, Frank, & Ekman, 2001) and therefore slow to trust a counselor.

In general, the counselor has to be open to young clients' needs and concerns, paying attention to what the child is expressing and exploring how to help with that expression without having a rigid agenda for a session and without making judgments ("This isn't at all what she needs to deal with"). When a counselor reflects feelings accurately ("You seem happy about that"; "You sound sad today"; "I sense that you're worried about your dad"), young clients feel heard. In instances when a child assumes incorrectly that "the problem" should be obvious to a counselor, such as in situations of self-referral to a school counselor, the counselor can say, "I'm guessing that there's something you would like to talk to me about. Could you help me out, because I'm not sure what it is?"

The value of counselors' patience in getting information and of an approach that does not immediately follow an agenda can be seen in the following account.

Matthew, age 10, was being bullied at school. He came to see the school counselor because his teacher noticed that he was not doing his schoolwork and was unresponsive in class. Neither she nor Matthew's parents were aware of any cause for this. In meeting with the counselor, Matthew seemed shy and nervous, perhaps even frightened. While he and the counselor put a puzzle together, they talked about the people he lived with, his teacher, his dog, and what he did when he could do anything he wanted. He then worked with some clay. As he did so, the counselor asked him if he wondered what counselors do. In response to Matthew's affirmative head nod, the counselor said, "Kids can talk to counselors about anything they wonder about, or think about, or are upset about. Counselors are good listeners. But what kids say is up to them." Matthew then chose some markers and began to draw designs on a paper. As he drew, the counselor made nonevaluative statements about the colors and shapes.

When the counselor prepared to send Matthew back to class, she told him that she enjoyed talking with him and would like to do that again sometime. Matthew, however, seemed reluctant to leave, and took another sheet of paper to draw on. Suddenly, with tears welling in his eyes, he told her about the bullying. "That sounds scary," the counselor said. Matthew told her he was afraid his father and older brother would call him a sissy and said he knew his parents were going to fight over what he should do. He said his older brother punched him regularly to "teach me not to be a wimp."

"You don't feel very good about that," the counselor replied, responding with empathy to his sad, serious expression. Matthew admitted that he felt angry and hurt. In the next session, they interacted further, always with the counselor following Matthew's lead, validating his feelings, and asking open-ended questions to become informed about sequences and situations related to the bullying.

The following account of a school counselor's work with Maya illustrates the value of effective listening and the use of a structured activity.

Maya's teacher referred the 10-year-old to the school counselor because the teacher noticed dark circles under Maya's eyes and observed that she had a flat affect. Maya and the counselor began by exploring the toys in the counseling office and conversing about Maya's siblings, her friends, and her interests. During a subsequent get-acquainted activity involving completing sentence stems ("When I was little . . . ;

now . . . ."), Maya said, "When I was little, I was afraid of monsters; now I'm afraid of the dark." She added, "I'm really afraid of the dark!"

Further conversation revealed sleep problems, fears about accidents, fears about death, and nonvalidation of her fears by her parents. The counselor normalized Maya's fears by saying, "Many kids are scared of the dark—or of something. That's okay. There's nothing wrong with you. I wonder what we can do to help you with your fear of the dark." They decided that Maya would ask her parents for a flashlight and for them to read her a calm story before bedtime. The counselor expressed confidence that, with practice, Maya would get better and better at being able to deal with her fears. They agreed that Maya would return in a week to tell the counselor how her "practicing" was going.

With Maya's knowledge and permission, the counselor met a few days later with Maya's mother. During their meeting he normalized the fears, engaged the mother in an exploration of coping strategies for Maya, and explored other possible sources of anxiety. The mother reported that she had been on the phone a great deal lately, talking with relatives about Maya's cousin's recent accident and hospitalization. The counselor noticed the mother's use of "awfulizing language" and gently explored with her the possibility that catastrophizing and negativity in "scary" family talk might be having an impact on Maya. Maya's mother said she had been overprotective of Maya since the accident and might be anxious herself at bedtime.

At the conclusion of the conversation, the counselor sent the mother a message of confidence, saying, "I'm sure you'll figure out how to help Maya relax at bedtime and how to let her know that you will be there to take care of her. We get smarter and smarter about these things." As a result of this discussion, the counselor was more informed, although he planned not to discuss the cousin's accident in subsequent sessions until or unless Maya brought it up.

Teachers and administrators frequently expect school counselors to "fix" a classroom behavior problem quickly, perhaps in just 15 minutes! When a quick solution seems possible, and best, the counselor may apply a brief-counseling model (see Chapter 5). The counselor may decide, however, that the best course initially is simply to work on establishing a relationship. Unpressured interaction, even for a few minutes a few times a week, can be a key to other "progress." An apparently no-agenda approach, including reframing of the presenting problem, might get the attention of a reluctant child. This approach was used in the following scenario of a child who had just been removed from a physical education class because of problematic behavior:

> You look like an interesting kid, and I like interesting kids. They're usually nice to get to know. Sometimes they're full of surprises, and

> that makes my work interesting, and that's good. Sounds as if
> you've got some spunk. Think I'm right? Maybe we can just hang
> out here for a while and get a start on knowing each other.

Clark (1993) offered a helpful example of a situation in which a counselor's interventions were premature in response to pressure from parents and teachers. Even the counselor's self-disclosure seemed to be too intimate, because a relationship had not been sufficiently established. Here, as with many other clients, it was important to "trust the counseling process and remain solidly focused on the relationship" (p. 25).

Asking Questions

Garbarino and Stott (1989) recommended, in working with preschoolers, that counselors use the child's name and the child's terms in their questions; rephrase, not repeat, questions that the child does not understand; avoid time-sequence questions; not ask a question following every answer the child gives; and use questions that are only slightly longer than the sentences the children use. Park (2001) found that, during interviews with child witnesses, developmentally appropriate questions elicited accurate responses, whereas questions beyond the cognitive capabilities of the children created difficulties with accuracy.

Thompson and Rudolph (2000) pointed out that adults' questions often reflect curiosity rather than a desire to help; that questions can be used to judge, blame, or criticize; that "why" questions are often associated with blame; and that children easily fall into a pattern of answering and then waiting for the next question. Thompson and Rudolph, as well as Lamb, Sternberg, Orbach, Esplin, and Mitchell (2002), acknowledged that direct questions can be appropriate for gaining factual information or clarification but noted that open-ended questions generate more information and promote spontaneous expression. Open-ended questions also generate more accurate responses in children within and across interviews (Fivush, Peterson, & Schwarzmueller, 2002) and fewer contradictions across multiple interviews than do closed questions, particularly questions that provide options or are suggestive (Lamb & Fauchier, 2001).

Accuracy also may be compromised over time by parental pressures or misleading questioning (Henderson, 2001). According to one study (Waterman, Blades, & Spencer, 2001), children may answer closed questions (requiring a yes/no response) even when questions are unanswerable, while readily acknowledging that they do not know the answer to questions requiring specific details. In their examples of open inquiry, Evans, Hearn, Uhlemann, and Ivey (1998) offered the following question stems: "Could you help me understand . . ."; "What do you feel like doing when . . ."; "Can you tell me more about . . ."; "How do you feel about . . ."; "What do you . . ."; "What sorts of things . . . ." (pp. 39–50).

Establishing a Relationship and Developing a Focus

Using Media

Many children, and even some adolescents, benefit by having "something to fiddle with" in the counselor's office. Every counselor working with young clients should have available an array of developmentally appropriate toys, materials for creative expression, drawing paper and good-quality markers, and puzzles for clients who feel the need to be distracted from the intensity of the situation at hand, need something to diminish their self-consciousness, or need media to help with expression. (See Chapter 4 for a discussion of play therapy.)

Aaron, age 13, appeared nervous when he arrived for his first counseling session. He made no eye contact with the counselor and responded with only monosyllables when she tried to engage him in light conversation. The counselor knew that Aaron's family had recently been traumatized by his violent father. To help Aaron feel at ease, she moved a shallow tub of Legos between them and began to construct something, inviting Aaron to do the same. Soon it was just Aaron who was involved with the Legos.

After some small talk, the counselor said, "I understand that your life has been difficult lately. But I don't know much about it. What should I understand to get an idea of what it's been like?" Aaron continued to keep his hands busy with the Legos as he gradually became engaged in dialogue, talking about his fears as an oldest child trying to protect his siblings. His comments were incisive. Although he still made no eye contact, he seemed less self-conscious and more able to concentrate on his feelings and thoughts when his hands were busy.

* * *

Play media were essential during the first session with Sonja, age 9, who had been diagnosed with attention-deficit/hyperactivity disorder (ADHD) and was reported to be increasingly disruptive in the classroom. The counselor asked Sonja if she would like to sit with her on the floor and play with dolls and miniature dishes. As Sonja played, they talked quietly about her interests and what she liked to do with her parents, who had been divorced for 2 years.

The counselor said, "It sounds as if you and your parents have worked it out so you can be with both of them every week. How's that going for you?" Sonja was articulate and calm when talking about the divorce but was agitated and tearful when talking about her mother's new baby. Playing seemed to help her concentrate and express her feelings instead of being overwhelmed by them. She lapsed momentarily into baby talk but stayed focused on the issue of the baby and her relationship with her mother.

Sonja's counselor made no mention of the 9-year-old's play during the session. Regardless of the purpose of play media, it is important not to make evaluative judgments about the quality of constructions, drawings or play. Adolescents, especially, are often so concerned about evaluations of what they are doing that the process ceases to be either expression or distraction. Children's artwork should be viewed only in conjunction with their other behaviors. Although drawings can be revealing, they also can simply be creative expression for the sake of creative expression. In addition, having a creative outlet and having something to be busy with can help to build the counseling relationship with a child or adolescent (Orton, 1997). Sometimes, of course, the content of the drawings may provide basic information about family members, portray school relationships, or convey requests. For example, one 6-year-old, unsolicited, drew his preferred custody arrangement during a counseling session.

Giving Clients Feedback About Themselves

De Jong and Berg (1998) discussed the potential therapeutic benefit of giving "reality-based" compliments throughout sessions in the interest of building hope and confidence. Particularly when counseling is directed toward finding solutions, mentioning the client's past strengths and successes is important: "Useful past experiences are those in which the client either thought about or actually did something that might be put to use in resolving the current difficulties. These experiences are the client's past successes" (p. 31).

Children need to receive information and feedback about themselves. Affirming children is never inappropriate, and timely, credible comments help to build the client–counselor relationship. The value of accurate, positive feedback is clearly apparent in the following vignette, shared by a veteran counselor.

Talia, age 15, had been sexually abused by an older boy several years before coming to see me. Nothing had been done at the time. Talia's parents were ashamed and blamed her. The message she received was, "It's your fault; there's something wrong with you." That key information was incorrect. I told Talia what should have happened. I told her that she was not bad or wrong. Her family just didn't know what to do about what had happened. They were afraid, so they reacted in a wrong way. It made sense that she was upset. It also made sense that they had misunderstood.

I then described a hypothetical scene in which Talia's mother had behaved appropriately. In this scene, Talia told her mom what had happened, and her mom rocked, comforted, and soothed her, listened to her story, told her it was not her fault, and told her that she would protect her and get her help. In the scene, Talia's mom called the police, and the police talked to both Mom and Talia to get all the pertinent information. The police then arrested the boy, and Talia's mom took her to their family doctor, who helped them. Every day Talia's mom rocked her and told her it wasn't her fault and that she wasn't a bad person.

I encouraged Talia to imagine that scene every day and to rock herself, since she was too big to be rocked by her mother now. But she could get hugs from her mom—real hugs. She reported the next week that she and her mom had had their first sustained conversation ever about the incident. They had both cried and hugged, and she felt she might be able eventually to understand and forgive her mother.

By providing Talia with accurate feedback and affirming her, the counselor helped her to make sense of a troubling situation and empowered her to move forward.

Unconditional Affirmation

Unconditional positive regard, congruence, and empathy are essential to all counseling relationships (Orton, 1997). Counselors using a nondirective approach are most likely to use the unconditional positive regard espoused by Rogers (1957) and to refrain from moralizing, making judgments, diagnosing, or focusing on solutions. By focusing on the possibilities within that child/adolescent, these therapists work "to free up those possibilities so that the child can continue on her or his journey of development" (Semrud–Clikeman, 1995, p. 102).

According to Thompson and Rudolph (2000), children are more sensitive than adults to others' feelings and attitudes. In the example of Talia, she appeared to benefit from the counselor's affirmation and unconditional acceptance. In discussing application of Rogers' person-centered approach to working with children, Thompson and Rudolph noted that, although some situations require counselors to take an active role, "even young children can distinguish between positive and negative behaviors and are able to choose the positive once the counselor has established an open dialogue in which feelings and emotions can be aired and conflicts resolved" (p. 149). This approach is most effective when clients teach their counselors about their problem situations, with the counselor practicing active listening and using summary and reflection statements. In this way, the counselor communicates that the client is worth hearing and understanding.

Many times, children and adolescents need only to have someone "stand beside them" during a difficult period. A teen who was sexually abused as a child might not be ready to talk at length about it but may need someone to offer uncritical acceptance. A child experiencing his parents' divorce may need reassurance that his feelings are normal and that he is a worthy human being. A depressed adolescent may be unable to name the problem, but a counselor can provide some stability and affirmation. Counselors who are constrained by managed care probably have less opportunity to "stand" with complexly distressed young clients over an extended time than do school counselors, who usually must connect more briefly but have opportunities to connect informally and frequently. Despite their constraints, however, agency counselors, too, can offer important support. I have observed numerous instances in and out of school settings in which children and adolescents survived extended periods of suicidal ideation while leaning periodically on a counselor and later experienced spontaneous resolution as young adults.

Telling the Truth

Thompson and Rudolph (2000) discussed the dilemma that counselors face when children seem to be exaggerating to gain attention or sympathy. Directly challenging a statement or story may interfere with maintaining a trusting relationship, especially if all or part of the story is true. One strategy is to use immediacy, saying, for example, "That story bothers me. It seems like a strange thing to happen. I'll have to think about that one." A response like this gives the child a chance to alter the story while avoiding a direct challenge. Other effective responses include these: "Which parts of that story do you think I should think about the most?" "I need to have you tell me more about that"; "I'll bet some people might think that was strange for someone your age," all of which offer opportunity for the child to expand or retract.

Counselor Self-Disclosure

Counselors should be judicious in their use of self-disclosure with children and adolescents, striking a therapeutically effective balance between rigid self-distancing and careless, unthinking, and unnecessary self-disclosures (Renik, 1999). Counseling should stay focused on the young client and not be displaced onto the counselor. The use of immediacy—offering personal reactions to client comments or behaviors in the present—is usually an appropriate form of self-disclosure. In contrast, self-disclosure of personal experiences usually does not enhance the interaction or the relationship, although well-timed self-disclosure of experiences may not enhance the interaction or the relationship, but well-timed and pertinent sharing may help a child or adolescent focus concretely and stimulate discussion (Evans et al., 1998). It may be tempting to say, "When I was your age," or "I once had a similar experience," but, especially with adolescents, high-quality active listening is better (Nichols, 1995). Few adolescents believe that anyone else, particularly someone older than they are, could have had an experience similar to theirs (Elkind, 1981). Young clients need an objective, nonjudgmental listener who validates their experience as unique and important. They might actually view counselor disclosure as "not listening." At-risk children and adolescents in particular appreciate a stable listener who is not self-absorbed.

A "One-Down" Position

By taking a one-down position, the counselor can elicit information from young clients while empowering them. Counselors do not know the child's or adolescent's world, and they will not learn about it from an authoritative one-up position. More effective is this: "Teach me about . . . [your life; your sadness; being 13; your sleep problems]." Clients then can "show the counselor that they know more about their lives than their counselors do" (Thompson & Rudolph, 2000, p. 134). Counselors are trained to explore the phenomenological world of all clients, including children and adolescents. In these explorations, being "clueless" can be extremely helpful. Comments such as the following can be effective in eliciting information about their clients' world:

"I can't imagine what it's like to be 9 years old and have your mom tell you that she and your dad are going to get a divorce."
"Help me understand what going to the hospital to visit your dad is like."
"I'm not in your world, so I don't know what kinds of drugs are out there. What should adults understand about drugs these days?"
"Maybe you could take me down to the auto-mechanics room and show me around. I'm really not very smart about cars."

When telling about their world, children and adolescents might need help finding words to describe their feelings. Comments such as the following might help:

"If I were in your shoes, I'd probably be feeling a little scared."
"That sounds really confusing."
"I think if someone were teasing me like that, I might get very angry."
"Some kids I've known have felt sad when that happened to them."

Using "Process" Questions

Process-oriented comments and questions, which look at internal and external processes, are important in dealing with awkward moments, revelations, expressions of intense feelings, moments of insight, counselor "error," and silences. Examples include these:

"What was it like to make that powerful statement?"
"Tell me how that felt—to be quiet."
"What were you thinking just now?"
"What feelings do you have now—after all that hard work?"
"What was it like to challenge me like that?"
"How did that feel, making such a mature observation?"
"Tell me about what just happened in here. Did I invade your space a bit?"
"I didn't say that very well. What did that sound like to you?"

Processing helps to punctuate moments in the counseling relationship and significant moments of personal growth. It also can provide the client with the opportunity to explore his or her feelings, and it can stop long narratives and reestablish focus on feelings or a presenting issue, as in this instance: "I'd like to put a period at the end of what you've told me so far. I can see that it was disturbing to talk about what happened. What were you feeling as you told me that?"

Using Structured Exercises

Although using structured exercises (Peterson, 1993, 1995; Vernon, 1998a, b, c) can be effective with all children and adolescents, it is especially helpful with reluctant clients. Counselors can overuse and abuse structure, of course, but well-crafted pencil-and-paper or oral activities such as the following have great potential for building trust, eliciting information, helping shy and unassertive children and adolescents "find words to say," and providing information about ability and development:

1. Sentence stems (e.g., "I'm probably most myself when I . . . .") (Peterson, 1993, p. 19)
2. Open-ended questions (e.g., "What would your life be like if you suddenly were to become an achiever?")
3. Checklists (for parent or child, including statements such as, "My child seems rested each morning when he/she begins the day"; "I often feel uncomfortable at school.")
4. Continuum exercises (e.g., "On a scale of 1 to 10, how much do you agree with the following statements?") (Peterson, 1995)
5. Stress-sorters (Peterson, 1993, p. 158)
6. Role-plays (e.g., "You be yourself, and I'll pretend I'm a bully in gym class. Let's practice with some of the strategies we've been talking about.")
7. Written scenarios presenting problematic situations such as date rape, aggressive behavior, or not being appropriately assertive (Peterson, 1995, p. 146)
8. Decision-making dilemmas (Vernon, 1993, p. 28)
9. Self-rating sheets (e.g., "My mother thinks I am . . . ."; "My father thinks I am . . . ."; "My teachers think I am . . . ."; "My friends think I am . . . ."; "I think I am . . . .") (Peterson, 1993, p. 119)
10. Self-monitoring exercises (Vernon, 1993, p. 30)
11. Role-exploration exercises (Peterson, 1995, p. 94)
12. Diaries, logs, and journals; self-composed songs, poems, and stories (Vernon, 1993, pp. 27–28)
13. "Word-movies" (Spees, 2002)

Developmentally appropriate activities provide a good beginning for self-exploration and also can be used throughout the counseling relationship to raise clients' awareness of self and others and assist in problem solving.

Special Considerations When Working With Adolescents

Adolescents require approaches different from those used with younger children. Trust is often harder to achieve with adolescents than with children. Rapport may be more tenuous. "What's the angle?" they wonder. Moments of "chatting" may be productive when joining with an adolescent client, especially when unexpected personal connections occur. Some adolescents, however, may be suspicious of such "unbusiness-like" conversation. A counselor educator, who was serving as the counselor in a small school for at-risk students, once confided that, after chiding one of his graduate students for "just chatting" in a supervised session at an agency, he found himself chatting at length with a previously resistant adolescent male at the school. The counselor educator self-consciously reminded himself to focus on the issue he had planned to address. But they had stumbled into a discussion of motorcycles, about which both had considerable knowledge, and the adolescent became animated. Several minutes later the counselor successfully used a "biker" metaphor to access an important issue, and he reported improved behavior and responsiveness in the adolescent thereafter.

Agency and school counselors I have interviewed indicate that it is important for counselors to be interested in adolescents personally but not to be patronizing. When they come to counseling, many adolescents feel they have been "written off" by family, teachers, administrators, and perhaps even peers. Therefore, they must feel that they are being taken seriously, respected, and not judged by the counselor. They want to be accepted unconditionally—no matter how weird they are trying to be. They also do not like being "pushed." Direction, when it comes, is accepted much more readily when they think it is *their* idea, not the counselor's.

During sessions, wise counselors react to comments and behaviors by being respectful, nonreactive, collaborative, and not argumentative. In addition, they respect adolescents' need for personal space and individual expression. These counselor behaviors might be new for adolescents, who may be used to mutually "walking on eggshells" with adults. The following examples of counselor responses illustrate low reactivity and respect:

"I stole a Toyota once." (Counselor: "So what was going on in your life when you stole the Toyota?")

"Like when you came to our class and talked about violence with a guy you're going out with? That's happened to me." (Counselor: "I'm so sorry that you had that experience. It may have been hard to tell me that, but I'm glad you did. Do you feel like talking about it?")

"Sometimes I feel so bad that I get scared at how bad I feel." (Counselor: "That sounds frightening—to feel that bad. Tell me more about that. What do you think about? What's scary?")

Verbal "bombshells," such as those in the previous examples, may be meant to test counselors personally or to find out whether something actually can be talked about. For the counselor, good listening requires hard work and low emotional reactivity (Nichols, 1995). The counselor's poise and attentive, low-reaction responses can help young clients know that difficult issues can be addressed.

Perhaps, quite unlike the high reactivity the client experiences at home, the counselor's poise, attention, affirmation, and validation will lead to trust. Poise, however, does not preclude a counselor from saying, "Wow! That sounds like a very difficult situation." In fact, such a statement can serve as powerful validation. Poise also means remembering to check out the possibility of suicidal ideation when hearing statements like the last of the above examples—if not immediately, then after a feelings-reflection and/or open-ended question.

Because adolescents sometimes are used to adults judging them and leaving them, counselors also need to demonstrate that they are there "for the long haul." Authority figures in the adolescents' lives may have been capricious and inconsistent and may have modeled displaced anger, scapegoating, mood instability, and unhealthy coping. Counselors must be careful not to mimic the ineffective and problem-creating behaviors of adult figures in their clients' lives, including emotional enmeshment, high reactivity, and rejection. When counselors do not behave in ways the adolescents are used to in adults, it can be a corrective emotional experience (Semrud-Clikeman, 1995).

All adolescents are moving through uncertain territory, one part of which is the process of differentiating from parents. Counselors can acknowledge and normalize the discomfort and uncertainty that adolescents often experience during that process. Corrective information can be provided in the safety of a counseling session, as in the following example involving a 17-year-old girl:

Client: "I did what you said. I told my dad I wanted to talk about seeing my boyfriend [outside of school]. He grounded me for a month."

Counselor: "Your dad may be scared for you, and he might not know how to protect you except by being very strict and keeping you at home. But that was a good thing you did—asking to talk to him. I'm glad you believe that talking can be helpful. I hope you'll be able to talk with him about things like this sometime. I'm sorry you were grounded."

Working Together Toward Change

Developing Interventions

Developing interventions, should not be a haphazard enterprise. Reynolds (1993) emphasized the need for careful planning, design, implementation, and evaluation. After exploring the presenting problem with the client, the counselor begins to plan the interventions, designing them based on current goals, awareness of unsuccessful previous interventions, counselor skills, client ability and developmental level, client learning style, and time constraints. Implementation might entail homework assignments. At the time of implementation, however, the counselor may need to make adjustments to the intervention as a result of timing and lack of client readiness. Later, evaluation should involve a systematic, deliberate appraisal of the intervention. Myrick (1997) suggested asking questions such as: "What did you like best about what you did?" "If you were to change things, what would you do differently?" (p. 154).

School counselors, in particular, often are called on to solve students' problems. Myrick (1997) presented a systematic problem-solving model consisting of four questions that can be asked in an interview:

1. What is the problem?
2. What have you tried?
3. What else could you do?
4. What is your next step?

Myrick acknowledged that the presenting problem may not be the real problem, but it nevertheless is a place to begin. When a child presents with multiple problems, Myrick cautioned against "flooding the person by focusing on all of them" (p. 172). Instead, he suggested encouraging the child to select a few of the problems to work on and to take a few steps with them. Osborn (1991) also warned that concrete thinkers may need help through role-play, Gestalt methods, and examples and illustrations when struggling with concepts, contradictions, and alternatives.

Thompson and Rudolph (2000) recommended following problem definition by clarifying the young client's expectations. Eventually, no matter what problem-solving model is followed, the counselor puts to use what he or she has learned previously while working with the client (Clark, 1993), applying patterns and themes heard and observed, helping the young client gain insight (Orton, 1997), and, depending on theoretical approach, focusing on goals and the "next step." According to Myrick (1997), "It is assumed that a first and next step will trigger other related positive behaviors, if a next step is carefully planned" (pp. 152–153). Thompson and Rudolph (2000) noted that those subsequent behaviors are more likely if the client has made a commitment to try a problem-solving idea.

Some authors have advocated brief-counseling approaches for use in the schools (Bruce & Hopper, 1997; Littrell, Malia, & Vanderwood, 1995; Myrick, 1997). Indeed, a study by Littrell, Malia, and Vanderwood (1995) found that a single-session brief counseling model was effective. Brief therapy is discussed in detail in Chapter 5. Vernon (see Chapter 6) discusses the effectiveness of rational–emotive behavior therapy with children and adolescents. Both of those approaches work well with young clients because, among other reasons, they are brief and fit with the clients' developmental conceptualization of time. For young clients, what is a problem today may not be a problem tomorrow.

Interventions applied during this stage of the counseling process may encompass a wide variety of developmentally appropriate approaches, including play therapy, bibliotherapy, therapeutic writing, music, art, and structured experiences, some of which were referred to earlier in this chapter. Chapter 3 provides a more detailed discussion of appropriate interventions for working with children and adolescents.

Giving Advice

The public perception of counselors is that they are advice-givers, and with young clients it indeed is often tempting to offer advice. Thompson and Rudolph (2000) urged counselors to resist this temptation:

> Counselors who believe in the uniqueness, worth, dignity, and responsibility of the individual and who believe that, given the proper conditions, individuals can make correct choices for themselves are reluctant to give advice on solving life's problems. Instead, they use their counseling knowledge and skill to help clients make responsible choices of their own and, in effect, learn how to become their own counselor. (p. 44)

These authors emphasized the danger of creating dependency and overconformity in young clients as a result of encouraging them to rely on adults to make decisions for them. According to Erdman and Lampe (1996), "advising or offering solutions may convey a lack of confidence in the child's ability to solve problems" (p. 376).

When clients, even young children, feel in charge of their own growth, they are more likely to continue to grow, sustain their exploration independently, and find their own strengths and strategies in the future. Counselors can empower young clients by affirming their strengths and by stepping back periodically and explaining to the client "what just happened," while minimizing the counselor's role. In the case of 9-year-old Sonja, whose case was introduced earlier in this chapter, the counselor might say this:

> I'm really impressed with what you just did. You said something that was very, very important, and you said it in grown-up language. You told me how you felt—that you didn't feel very good about the new baby. That was beautiful. I'm surprised, because I didn't know you could do that. You didn't whine, and you didn't get upset. You just said it! I asked a question that you could have answered any way you chose. And you knew how to do it. That's so important to be able to tell people exactly what you feel. When you need to do that again, you'll be ready. How did it feel to tell me that?

Here-and-Now Focus

Myrick (1997) distinguished between here-and-now and then-and-there comments during the counseling process. The former relate to what is happening in the present between the counselor and the client; the latter refer to feelings and events in the past. Here-and-now counselor statements help the client to explore matters in depth and are likely to be intense, intimate, and personal. They are potentially threatening but also are powerful and exciting. Then-and-there counselor statements can be used to diffuse the intensity of the present moment and also may be appropriate at the outset of counseling, as they are less threatening. Here-and-now statements can be effective in dealing with resistance: "Tell me what you're feeling right now. I'm sensing a reaction to what I said."

Affirming Resilience

Counselors also can empower young clients by affirming their resilience, described by Higgins (1994) as an "active process of self-righting and growth," being "able to negotiate significant challenges to development, yet consistently 'snap back' in order to complete the important developmental tasks that confront them as they grow" (p. xii). Resilience can mediate the effects of difficult circumstances. No one may have noticed a child's strengths in this regard, yet these strengths could be crucial to his or her day-to-day survival. A counselor who notices these strengths and speaks confidently of their place in "a better future" offers optimism at a critical time during development. After noting client strengths, a counselor's saying "I know you'll figure it out" can be powerfully affirming, besides expressing a belief about human potential in general. Factors of resilience include the following, based on representative literature (Beardslee & Podorefsky, 1988; Cesarone, 1999; Farrell, Barnes, & Banerjee, 1995; Garmezy, Masten, & Tellegen, 1984; Herrenkohl, 1994; Higgins, 1994; Katz, 1997; Rak & Patterson, 1996; Smith, 1995; Tschann, Kaiser, Chesney, & Alkon, 1996; Werner, 1995):

1. Qualities of temperament
2. Personal characteristics
3. Buffering family conditions
4. Affectional ties that encourage trust, autonomy, and initiative
5. Self-understanding
6. Faith that one's actions can make a positive difference in one's life
7. Environmental supports in the form of mentors, parental surrogates, and role models for coping
8. Intelligence and exceptional talents
9. The desire to be different from the parents.

A counselor may have a long-term impact on children or adolescents simply by being a stable, caring figure who acknowledges their difficult circumstances and has confidence in them. In general, counselors will have credibility if comments are based on information and observations from sessions, as in this situation:

I n what you've told me today, I've noticed many things that make me very hopeful for you. You have a grandma you can count on. You've found ways to get other adults to pay attention to you and help you. You think well. You're a survivor. You "make sense" of complicated situations. And your mom took good care of you before she died, when you were very young. All of those things are good in your life, and they help to make you strong. That's why I'm very hopeful for you.

At the same time, counselors may have to point out that, although certain "survival skills" may have been essential in the past, they now might interfere with relationships. For example, lying might have been necessary to avoid beatings, manipulation might have been critical to engaging helpful adults, bottling emotions might have ensured short-term calm in the family, self-medicating through substances might have dulled pain, and aggressive behavior might have offered some self-protection. But these behaviors now might be contributing to problems at home, at school, with friends, in relationships, or on the job. Reframing the problematic behaviors into the more affirmative perspective of "using your intelligence" offers a functional view of them, probably quite different from other adults' feedback. Then, helping young clients to understand that their behaviors are no longer effective might generate openness to strategies for making positive changes.

Closure

Referral

After careful attention to the scope of the problem, to responses to current interventions, and to what would be best for the child or adolescent (Semrud–Clikeman, 1995), a counselor may determine that his or her counseling competence or institutional resources are not adequate to meet a child's or adolescent's needs. In such cases, referral to other services, such as substance abuse or mental health facilities, residential treatment centers, or social services, is in order. The counselor is responsible for organizing information to ensure a smooth transition and to provide parents or guardians with accurate information about the referral site and services offered (Schmidt, 1996).

Termination

Counseling ends for many reasons. Insurance and personal finances may be factors. The school term might be over, or school children might move to a new school level, district, or city. Parents or the child may call a halt to counseling for a variety of reasons. A counselor may make a referral to another professional.

Some children and adolescents simply do not return after intake, or they discontinue treatment with no explanation. Christy (2001) found that low family income and history of truancy or runaway behaviors was associated with self-termination. The focus here, however, is on situations in which counselors can facilitate termination of young clients that is satisfactory to counselor and client alike.

Often, the counseling relationship is a powerful presence in the lives of young clients, and they become anxious as the counseling process draws to a close. For children for whom change has meant upheaval or for whom endings have meant abandonment, termination of counseling may be especially difficult. Therefore, the counselor should prepare the young client for the end of counseling in advance of the final session, whenever possible. The counselor should help the client process his or her feelings associated with the ending, perhaps arranging some sort of ritual to mark it, and should reassure the client that he or she will remain in the counselor's thoughts. By doing so, the counselor communicates an important message: The counseling process has been a significant experience, and the client has been worthy of it. Semrud–Clikeman (1995) noted that agitation, anger, and anxiety are normal reactions to termination. However, they should be explored to determine if termination is premature or calls for more processing, particularly when termination is initiated by the counselor.

As termination nears, various issues can be addressed. When both client and counselor will remain in proximity and the counselor will be available, the client can be made aware that future counseling can be arranged if needed. Based on the client's progress in counseling, the counselor can make predictions about his or her continued success and potential developmental challenges—the latter to prepare the client for "normal stumbling." Progress made during the sessions can be noted and celebrated, with the counselor emphasizing what the client did for himself or herself. The relationship between counselor and client can be affirmed and validated. The counselor can model the expression of genuine feelings about terminating a relationship and also can model saying good-bye. Some counselors ask children or adolescents how their leave-taking should be concluded. Semrud–Clikeman (1995) has used the "graduation" metaphor with young clients, explaining that endings reflect "success, not just loss" (p. 144). At the end of the final meeting with a preadolescent, the counselor might say something like this:

I've really enjoyed working with you. You've done a lot of hard work over the past few weeks, and I respect that very much. I'll remember you as having lots of interesting parts that go together to make someone really beautiful—like pieces of cloth that make a quilt. Some pieces are velvety-soft, some rough and nubby, some of cotton, some wool, some corduroy. I've seen lots of different pieces in you. I thank you for sharing those with me.

What do you think you'll remember from our conversations together? What has been helpful?

I imagine there will be times when you'll worry that things will go back to the way they were when things were bad—like if you have to move again. That will be normal to worry. But you've worked hard here, and I know you'll remember some of the things you've learned about yourself. And you'll remember all the things you did to survive your last move and what you can do again. [The counselor then would list them.] If you ever feel you need to talk to a counselor again, don't hesitate to be in touch with me, if you're here, or with another counselor.

What would be the best way to say good-bye right now? You can choose. I'm open to a handshake, a hug, a smile, a "good-bye," or whatever.

When concluding counseling with clients of any age, the counselor may have unsettling thoughts and feelings, including thoughts about endings and loss. This may be especially true when the clients are children and adolescents. The feelings arise because the counseling relationship was satisfying and productive and also because the counselor knows that the young client may continue to be vulnerable in a complex and troublesome environment. The caring counselor consequently may have anxiety about the loss of counseling support for the child. Helping professionals need to monitor themselves during these transitions, validating their own feelings and needs and paying attention to boundary and dependency issues. When working with children and adolescents, counselors also can consider that termination is not a final step, as young clients have considered their issues only at their particular developmental stage (Oaklander, 1997).

In some cases, counseling is better phased out gradually by increasing the length of time between sessions than ended more abruptly. The counselor also may schedule occasional "check-up" visits to monitor progress, particularly in school settings.

Summary

When working with children and adolescents, as with adults, counselors must pay attention to ethical and legal concerns. In addition, they need to assess physical, emotional, social, and cognitive development, as well as the family system, school context, and social milieu. As counseling continues, they need to build rapport, develop focus, plan, implement, and assess intervention strategies, and prepare the client for termination. Building a relationship with children and adolescents is a process different from developing a relationship with adults. Toys, manipulatives, and other media may be used as "language" or to mitigate emotional intensity. Structured exercises also may be used effectively in building a relationship and also in eliciting information and exploring issues.

The process of building a relationship may in itself result in therapeutic gain. By actively listening, giving feedback, providing corrective information, and generating corrective emotional experiences, counselors can model important relationship skills and affirm client strengths and resilience. Counselors should assume that significant adults in the lives of their young clients will be involved in the counseling process at some point.

References

Achenbach, T. (1990). Conceptualizations of developmental psychopathology. In M. Lewis & S. Miller (Eds.), *Handbook of developmental psychopathology (pp. 3–13).* New York: Plenum Press.

American Association for Marriage and Family Therapy. (1991). *AAMFT code of ethics.* Washington, DC: Author.

American Counseling Association. (1995). *Code of ethics and standards of practice.* Alexandria, VA: Author.

American Psychiatric Association. (1994). *Diagnostic and statistical manual of mental disorders* (4th ed.). Washington, DC: Author

American Psychological Association. (1995). *Ethical principles of psychologists and code of conduct.* Washington, DC: Author.

American School Counselor Association. (1992). Ethical standards for school counselors. *The ASCA Counselor, 29*(3), 13–16.

Axline, V. (1969). *Play therapy* (rev. ed.). New York: Ballantine Books.

Beardslee, M. D., & Podorefsky, M. A. (1988). Resilient adolescents whose parents have serious affective and other psychiatric disorders: Importance of self-understanding and relationships. *American Journal of Psychiatry, 145,* 63–69.

Beck, A. T. (1987). *Beck depression inventory.* New York: Psychological Corp.

Bolton, J. E. (2000). Attachment theory and family systems theory: An integrative approach to treating childhood anxiety. *Dissertation Abstracts International, 61*(4–B), 2191.

Bradley, L. J., & Gould, L. J. (1999). Individual counseling: Creative interventions. In A. Vernon (Ed.), *Counseling children and adolescents* (pp. 65–95). Denver: Love Publishing.

Bruce, M. A., & Hopper, G. C. (1997). Brief counseling versus traditional counseling: A comparison of effectiveness. *School Counselor, 44,* 171–184.

Buchanan, C. M., & Waizenhofer, R. (2001). The impact of interparental conflict on adolescent children: Considerations of family systems and family structure. In A. Booth & A. C. Crouter (Eds.), *Couples in conflict* (pp. 149–160). Mahwah, NJ: Erlbaum.

Bugental, D. B., Shennum, W., Frank, M., & Ekman, P. (2001). True lies: Children's abuse history and power attributions as influences on deception detection. In V. Manusov & J. H. Harvey (Eds.), *Attribution, communication behavior, and close relationships. Advances in personal relations* (pp. 248–265). New York: Cambridge University Press.

Carlson, K. (1990). Suggestions for counseling "other-referred" children. *Elementary School Guidance and Counseling, 24,* 222–229.

Cesarone, B. (1999). Fostering the resilience of children. *Childhood Education, 75,* 182–184.

Chapman, C. R. (2000). Ethnic match and depression. *Dissertation Abstracts International, 61*(5–B), 2815.

Christy, V. F. (2001). Factors associated with premature termination of psychotherapy in children and adolescents. *Dissertation Abstracts International, 61*(12–B), 6698.

Clark, A. J. (1993). The defense never rests. In L. B. Golden & M. L. Norwood (Eds.), *Case studies in child counseling* (pp. 13–26). Upper Saddle River, NJ: Prentice–Hall.

Corey, G., Corey, M. S., & Callanan, P. (1998). *Issues and ethics in the helping professions* (5th ed.). Pacific Grove, CA: Brooks/Cole.

De Jong, R., & Berg, I. K. (1998). *Interviewing for solutions.* Pacific Grove, CA: Brooks/Cole.

Elkind, D. (1981). *Children and adolescents. Interpretive essays on Jean Piaget* (3rd ed.). New York: Oxford University Press.

Erdman, P., & Lampe, R. (1996). Adapting basic skills to counsel children. *Journal of Counseling & Development,* 74, 374–377.

Evans, D. R., Hearn, M. T., Uhlemann, M. R., & Ivey, A. E. (1998). *Essential interviewing: A programmed approach to effective communication.* Pacific Grove, CA: Brooks/Cole.

Farrell, M. R., Barnes, G. M., & Banerjee, S. (1995). Family cohesion as a buffer against the effects of problem-drinking fathers on psychological distress, deviant behavior, and heavy drinking in adolescents. *Journal of Health and Social Behavior, 36,* 377–385.

Ferris, R., & Linville, M. (1988). The child's rights: Whose responsibility? In W. Huey & T. Remley, Jr. (Eds.), *Ethical issues in school counseling* (pp. 20–30). Alexandria, VA: American School Counselor Association.

Fivush, R., Peterson, C., & Schwarzmueller, A. (2002). Questions and answers: The credibility of child witnesses in the context of specific questioning techniques. In M. L. Eisen & J. A. Quas (Eds.), *Memory and suggestibility in the forensic interview* (pp. 331–354). Mahwah, NJ: Erlbaum.

Garbarino, J., & Stott, E. (1989). *What children can tell* us. San Francisco: Jossey–Bass.

Garcia, M., & Peralbo, M. (2000). Culture, acculturation, and perception of family relationships (Cultura, aculturacion y percepcion de las relaciones familiares). *Infancia y Aprendizaje, 89,* 81–101.

Garmezy, N., Masten, A. S., & Tellegen, A. (1984). The study of stress and competence in children: A building block for developmental psychopathology. *Child Development, 55,* 97–111.

Geroski, A. M., Rodgers, K. A., & Breen, D. T. (1997). Using the DSM–IV to enhance collaboration among school counselors, clinical counselors, and primary care physicians. *Journal of Counseling & Development,* 75, 231–239.

Gitlin–Weiner, K., Sandgrund, K., & Schaefer, C. (Eds.) (2000). *Play diagnosis and assessment* (2nd ed.). New York: John Wiley & Sons.

Golden, L. B. (1993). Help! But don't get close. In L. B. Golden & M. L. Norwood (Eds.), *Case studies in child counseling* (pp. 39–49). Upper Saddle River, NJ: Prentice–Hall.

Golden, L. B., & Norwood, M. L. (1993). *Case studies in child counseling.* Upper Saddle River, NJ: Prentice–Hall.

Greenspan, S. I. (1981). *The clinical interview of the child.* New York: McGraw-Hill.

Gumaer, J. (1984). *Counseling and therapy for children.* New York: Free Press.

Gustafson, K. E., & McNamara, J. R. (1987). Confidentiality with minor clients: Issues and guidelines for therapists. *Professional Psychology: Research and Practice, 18,* 503–508.

Hailparn, D. F., & Hailparn, M. (2000). Parent as saboteur in the therapeutic treatment of children. *Journal of Contemporary Psychotherapy, 30,* 341–351.

Hansen, J. C., Rossberg, R. H., & Cramer, S. H. (1994). *Counseling: Theory and process* (5th ed.). Boston: Allyn & Bacon.

Henderson, A. L. (2001). The role of parental pressures and interviewing techniques on children's eyewitness reports. *Dissertation Abstracts International, 61*(9–B), 4985.

Herlihy, B. (1993). Mandy: Out in the world. In L. B. Golden & M. L. Norwood (Eds.), *Case studies in child counseling* (pp. 63–73). Upper Saddle River, NJ: Prentice–Hall.

Herrenkohl, E. C. (1994). Resilient early school-age children from maltreating homes: Outcomes in late adolescence. *American Journal of Orthopsychiatry, 64,* 301–309.

Herring, R. D. (1997). *Counseling diverse ethnic youth.* Ft. Worth, TX: Harcourt Brace.

Higgins, G. O. (1994). *Resilient adults.* San Francisco: Jossey–Bass.

Huey, W. C. (1996). Counseling minor clients. In B. Herlihy & G. Corey (Eds.), *ACA ethical standards casebook* (5th ed., pp. 241–250). Alexandria, VA: American Counseling Association.

Huey, W. C., & Remley, I. P. (1988). *Ethical & legal issues in school counseling.* Alexandria, VA: American School Counselor Association.

Hughes, J. N., & Baker, D. B. (1990). *The clinical child interview.* New York: Guilford.

Ivey, A. E. (1986). *Developmental therapy.* San Francisco: Jossey–Bass.

Ivey, A. E., Ivey, M. B., & Simek–Morgan, L. (1997). *Counseling and psychotherapy: A multicultural perspective* (4th ed.). Boston: Allyn & Bacon.

Katz, M. (1997). Overcoming childhood adversities: Lessons learned from those who have "beat the odds." *Intervention in School & Clinic, 32*(4), 205–210.

Keat, D. L. (1979). *Multimodal therapy with children.* New York: Pergamon.

Kottman, T. (1990). Counseling middle school students: Techniques that work. *Elementary School Guidance and Counseling, 25,* 138–145.

Kottman, T. (1993). Billy, the teddy bear boy. In L. B. Golden & M. L. Norwood (Eds.), *Case studies in child counseling* (pp. 75–88). Upper Saddle River, NJ: Prentice–Hall.

Kottman, T. (1995). *Partners in play: An Adlerian approach to play therapy.* Alexandria, VA: American Counseling Association.

Kranz, P. L., & Lund, N. L. (1993). Axline's eight principles of play therapy revisited. *International Journal of Play Therapy, 2*(2), 53–60.

Lamb, M. E., & Fauchier, A. (2001). The effects of question type on self-contradictions by children in the course of forensic interviews. *Applied Cognitive Psychology, 15,* 483–491.

Lamb, M. E., Sternberg, K. J., Orbach, Y., Esplin, P. W., & Mitchell, S. (2002). Is ongoing feedback necessary to maintain the quality of investigative interviews with allegedly abused children? *Applied Developmental Science, 6,* 35–41.

Landreth, G. L. (1991). *Play therapy: The art of the relationship.* Muncie, IN: Accelerated Development.

Lazarus, A. A. (1976). *Multimodal behavior therapy.* New York: Springer.

Littrell, J. M. (1998). *Brief counseling in action.* New York: Norton.

Littrell, J. M., Malia, J. A., & Vanderwood, M. (1995). Single-session brief counseling in a high school. *Journal of Counseling & Development, 73,* 451–458.

Melton, G. B. (1991). Socialization in the global community: Respect for the dignity of children. *American Psychologist, 46,* 66–71.

Minuchin, P. (2001). Looking toward the horizon: Present and future in the study of family systems. In J. P. McHale & W. S. Grolnick (Eds.), *Retrospect and prospect in the psychological study of families* (pp. 259–278). Mahwah, NJ: Erlbaum.

Moran, H. (2001). Who do you think you are? Drawing the ideal self: A technique to explore a child's sense of self. *Clinical Child Psychology & Psychiatry, 6,* 599–604.

Mosley–Howard, G. S., & Burgan Evans, C. (2000). Relationships and contemporary experiences of the African American family: An ethnographic case study. *Journal of Black Studies, 30,* 428–452.

Muro, J. J., & Kottman, I. (1995). *Guidance and counseling in the elementary and middle schools: A practical approach.* Madison, WI: Brown & Benchmark.

Myrick, R. D. (1997). *Developmental guidance and counseling: A practical approach* (3rd ed.). Minneapolis: Educational Media.

National Association of Social Workers. (1996). *Code of ethics.* Washington, DC: Author.

Nichols, M. P. (1995). *The lost art of listening.* New York: Guilford.

Nock, M. K., & Kazdin, A. E. (2001). Parent expectancies for child therapy: Assessment and relation to participation in treatment. *Journal of Child & Family Studies, 10,* 155–180.

Oaklander, V. (1997). The therapeutic process with children and adolescents. *Gestalt Review, 1,* 292–317.

O'Brien, P., & Burnett, P. C. (2000). Counselling children using a multiple intelligences framework. *British Journal of Guidance and Counseling, 28,* 353–371.

Orton, G. L. (1997). *Strategies for counseling with children and their parents.* Pacific Grove, CA: Brooks/Cole.

Osborn, D. (1991). A return to Piaget: Guidelines for counselors. TACD *Journal, 19*(2), 13–19.

Papilia, D. E., Olds, S. W., & Feldman, R. D. (1998). *Human development* (7th ed.). Boston: McGraw Hill.

Park, L. (2001). The child witness of sexual abuse: Recognizing developmental differences and creating a forum for eliciting accurate testimony. *Dissertation Abstracts International, 62*(2–B), 1117.

Peterson, J. S. (1993). *Talk with teens about self and stress: 50 guided discussions for school and counseling groups.* Minneapolis: Free Spirit.

Peterson, J. S. (1995). *Talk with teens about feelings, family, relationships, and the future: 50 guided discussions for school and counseling groups.* Minneapolis: Free Spirit.

Peterson, J. S. (1999). Gifted—through whose cultural lens? An application of the postpositivistic mode of inquiry. *Journal for the Education of the Gifted, 22,* 354–383.

Ponterotto, J. G., Gretchen, D., & Chauhan, R. V. (2001). Cultural identity and multicultural assessment: Quantitative and qualitative tools for the clinician. In L. A. Suzuki, J. G. Ponterotto, & P. J. Meller (Eds.), *Handbook of multicultural assessment* (2nd ed., pp. 67–69). San Francisco: Jossey-Bass.

Rak, C. E., & Patterson, L. F. (1996). Promoting resilience in at-risk children. *Journal of Counseling & Development, 74,* 368–373.

Remley, T. P. (1988). The law and ethical practices in elementary and secondary schools. In W. C. Huey & T. R. Remley, Jr. (Eds.), *Ethical & legal issues in school counseling* (pp. 95–105). Alexandria, VA: American Counseling Association.

Remley, T. (1990). Counseling records: Legal and ethical issues. In B. Herlihy & L. Golden (Eds.), *Ethical standards casebook* (pp. 162–169). Alexandria, VA: American Counseling Association.

Renik, W. (1999). Das ideal des anonymen analytikers und das problem der selbstenthuellung. *Psyche: Zeitschrift Fuer Psychoanalyse und Ihre Anwendungen, 53,* 929–957.

Reynolds, S. (1993). Interventions for typical developmental problems. In A. Vernon (Ed.), *Counseling children and adolescents* (pp. 51–82). Denver: Love Publishing.

Reynolds, W. M. (1987). *Reynolds adolescent depression scale (RADS).* Odessa, FL: PAR.

Reynolds, W. M. (1989). *Reynolds child depression scale (RCDS).* Odessa, FL: PAR.

Ritchie, M. H. (1994). Counselling difficult children. *Canadian Journal of Counselling, 28,* 58–68.

Rogers, C. R. (1957). The necessary and sufficient conditions of therapeutic personality change. *Journal of Counseling Psychology, 21,* 95–103.

Salo, M. M., & Shumate, S. G. (1993). Counseling minor clients (Vol. 4). In T. Remley, Jr. (Series Ed.), *The ACA legal series.* Alexandria, VA: American Counseling Association.

Sampson, D. T., Sato, T., & Miyashita, K. (1993). The three-generation triangle: A non drama. In L. B. Golden & M. L. Norwood (Eds.), *Case studies in child counseling* (pp. 133–154). Upper Saddle River, NJ: Prentice–Hall.

Savin–Williams, R. C., & Diamond, L. M. (1999). Sexual orientation. In W. K. Silverman & T. H. Ollendick (Eds.), *Developmental issues in the clinical treatment of children* (pp. 241–258). Needham Heights, MA: Allyn & Bacon.

Schmidt, J. J. (1996). *Counseling in schools: Essential services and comprehensive programs* (2nd ed.). Boston: Allyn & Bacon.

Semrud–Clikeman, M. (1995). *Child and adolescent therapy.* Boston: Allyn & Bacon.

Shamir, H., DuRocher Schudlich, T., & Cummings, E. M. (2001). Marital conflict, parenting styles, and children's representations of family relationships. *Parenting: Science & Practice, 1,* 123–151.

Smith, J. (1995). Temperament and stress resilience in school-age children: A within-families study. *Journal of the American Academy of Child and Adolescent Psychiatry, 34,* 168–179.

Spees, E. K. (2002). Word movies: Strategy and resources for therapeutic storytelling with children and adolescents. *Annals of the American Psychotherapy Association, 5*(1), 14–21.

Stromberg, C., and colleagues in the Law Firm of Hogan & Hartson of Washington, DC. (1993, April). Privacy, confidentiality and privilege. *The Psychologist—Legal Update.* Washington, DC: National Register of Health Service Providers in Psychology.

Sue, D. W., Ivey, A. E., & Pedersen, R. B. (1996). *A theory of multicultural counseling and therapy.* Pacific Grove, CA: Brooks/Cole.

Suzuki, L. A., Ponterotto, J. G., & Meller, P. J. (Eds.). *Handbook of multicultural assessment: Clinical, psychological, and educational applications* (2nd ed.). San Francisco: Jossey–Bass.

Swenson, L. C. (1993). *Psychology and law for the helping professions.* Pacific Grove, CA: Brooks/Cole.

Thompson, C. L., & Rudolph, L. B. (2000). *Counseling children* (5th ed.). Pacific Grove, CA: Brooks/Cole.

Tschann, J. M., Kaiser, R., Chesney, M. A., & Alkon, A. (1996). Resilience and vulnerability among preschool children: Family functioning, temperament, and behavior problems. *Journal of the American Academy of Child and Adolescent Psychiatry, 35,* 184–192.

Turley, D. L. (1993). Frederika: Wrapped in burgundy wool. In L. B. Golden & M. L. Norwood (Eds.), *Case studies in child counseling* (pp. 187–209). Upper Saddle River, NJ: Prentice–Hall.

Vernon, A. (1993). *Developmental assessment & intervention with children & adolescents.* Alexandria, VA: American Counseling Association.

Vernon, A. (1998a). *The passport program.* A *journey through emotional, social, cognitive, and self-development, grades 1–5.* Champagne, IL: Research Press.

Vernon, A. (1998b). *The passport program: A journey through emotional, social, cognitive, and self-development, grades 6–8.* Champaign, IL: Research Press.

Vernon, A. (1998c). *The passport program: A journey through emotional, social, cognitive, and self-development, grades 9–12.* Champaign, IL: Research Press.

Vernon, A. (2002). *What works when with children and adolescents: A handbook of individual counseling techniques.* Champaign, IL: Research Press.

Wagner, C. (1981). Confidentiality and the school counselor. *Personnel and Guidance Journal, 51,* 305–310.

Waterman, A. H., Blades, M., & Spencer, C. (2001). Interviewing children and adults: The effect of question format on the tendency to speculate. *Applied Cognitive Psychology, 15,* 521–531.

Werner, E. E. (1995). Resilience in development. *Current Directions in Psychological Science, 4*(3), 81–85.

Wright, L. (1990). The social and nonsocial behavior of precocious preschoolers during free play. *Roeper Review, 12,* 268–274.

Using Innovative Techniques
for Counseling Children
and Adolescents

Loretta J. Bradley, L.J. Gould, and C. Bret Hendricks

M aria comes to counseling and just sits. Despite many verbal attempts by the counselor, Maria remains unresponsive. José comes to counseling and quickly tells the counselor, "I don't like counseling." Martha comes to counseling and essentially tells the counselor that she doesn't have a problem. Instead, Martha says that the real problem is her family. John comes to counseling, and says in essence, "Fix me if you can."

What is the common denominator with these four clients? The thing they all share is that they do not want to be in counseling. Despite the best verbal techniques the counselor might use, more than verbal techniques are likely needed to help these clients. In essence, the clients have come to counseling with the attitude that they do not want to be in counseling, and they have little, if any, intention of helping counseling succeed. Maria, José, Martha, and John are not unique.

Most counselors have had to counsel children and adolescents who do not want to be in counseling. Although verbal techniques are important, many children and adolescents need different types of interventions. This chapter focuses on innovative, creative techniques in counseling.

The helping professions have used innovative techniques utilizing music, drawing, and literature for centuries (Frostig & Essex, 1998; Pardeck, 1995). The Romans used poetry as a means of calming troubled persons, and the ancient Egyptians played and listened to music to treat the mentally ill (Gladding, 1999). In recent times counselors have become more and more interested in innovative, expressive techniques incorporating art and music because these methods facilitate insight and communication in the counseling process. Expressive techniques encourage originality and allow freedom of expression, which in turn facilitates identification of feelings and encourages self-awareness (Jensen, 2001). Music, drawing, storytelling, and drama enable the client to express feelings and thoughts that otherwise might be unidentified.

Regardless of the counseling approach or theory used, counselors often encounter challenges when working with youth, in part because the developmental levels of children and adolescents limit their ability to express themselves verbally. Often, children have not reached the level of cognitive development that allows for spontaneous introspection or the ability to express themselves. Furthermore, they often have limited attention spans, which results in their becoming easily bored or distracted. For these reasons, using developmentally appropriate interventions is critical.

This chapter describes counseling interventions applicable to children and adolescents: art, bibliotherapy, guided imagery, games, music, puppets, role-playing and drama, storytelling, metaphors, and therapeutic writing. In addition, interventions are suggested for specific problems common in children and adolescents, such as low self-esteem, anger and aggression, grief and loss, and stress and anxiety.

Art

Children have difficulty verbally communicating their needs because they have not yet developed the skills and coping mechanisms of adults (Webb, 1999). Art therapy techniques facilitate the expressions of children and adolescents, allow clients to express anger and hostility with less guilt, and enable clients to perceive themselves and those around them more clearly (Kwiatkowska, 2001). Art therapy techniques also allow the counselor to examine the client's inner language, thereby giving the therapist and the client increased insight (Lev–Wiesel & Daphna–Tekoha, 2000).

Gladding (1995) described art therapy techniques that have been utilized with diverse populations and concluded that these techniques can transcend cultural boundaries. Art therapy techniques have been found to be especially useful in treating a variety of child/adolescent problems including trauma, grief, depression, stress, and low self-esteem (Chapman, Morabito, Ladakakos, Schreier, & Knudson, 2001; Webb, 1999). Art is both relaxing and soothing. Furthermore, art facilitates the manipulation of various media and can lubricate verbal communication of thoughts and feelings (Rubin, 1988). Rubin noted that "art, like talk, is simply a way to get to know each other, another mode of communication" (p. 181). In using art, counselors should permit clients to select the medium they want to use, and the counselors' suggestions should be limited to technical areas.

Art media should not be limited to drawings. Other effective methods include sculpture using clay, soap, or other media. Collages using construction paper or pictures from magazines and paintings are also effective. At the end of any session in which art therapy techniques are used, counselors should allow time for the client to describe and discuss his or her work (Sontag, 2001). Because some children are concerned that their art products will not be good enough, counselors must stress the importance of the progress, not the product or artistic skill (Dalley, 1990).

Counselors must be aware of ethical considerations unique to the use of art therapy techniques. A client's artwork always must be viewed as "symbolic speech" and must be given the same consideration as any other form of speech (Hammond & Gantt, 1998). Consequently, the artwork the client produces should be accorded the same protection and consideration as all other client communications. As in any counseling relationship, the client's right to privacy and confidentiality should be observed and protected.

Descriptions of several specific art interventions follow. Depending on the client's age and developmental level, some adaptation may be necessary.

Color Your Life (O'Connor, 1983)

Purpose: To identify feelings associated with life

Materials: A large sheet of plain white paper and any type of coloring instruments (paint, crayons, chalk, pencils); available colors must include yellow, green, blue, black, red, purple, brown, and gray

Procedure:

1. Ask the client to pair an emotion or feeling with a color. If the client seems to be having trouble, the counselor may offer a prompt, such as, "What feeling might go with the color red?"
2. Have the client continue to pair emotions with color. The most common associations are red/anger, purple/rage, blue/sad, black/very sad, green/jealous, brown/bored, gray/lonesome, and yellow/happy. Or the child might pair orange with excitement, pink with femininity, and blue-green with masculinity. Combinations are limited only by the client's knowledge of feelings

and colors, imagination, and ingenuity. Usually, however, the counselor should limit the associations to eight or nine pairs.

3. Once the pairs are established, give the client a sheet of white paper. Ask him or her to fill the paper with colors to show the feelings he or she has had during his or her life. The counselor might ask, "How much of your life has been happy? Color that much of your paper yellow."

4. Explain that the client is to color the paper in whatever designs he or she wishes until it is completely covered in colors. Encourage the client to verbalize thoughts and feelings during the activity.

Lines of Feeling (Gladding, 1995)

Purpose: To gain insight into affect by representing emotions nonverbally

Materials: White paper and colored pencils

Procedure:

1. Instruct the client to identify several feelings that he or she had about an event or during a significant time period. Next, ask the client to use colored lines on a piece of paper to depict these emotions. As examples, a smooth blue line might represent a calm feeling, and a jagged red line might represent an angry feeling.

2. Discuss with the client what the lines mean in relation to his or her emotions and what other lines he or she might draw to represent different emotions.

Windows (Gladding, 1995)

Purpose: To help the client examine where he or she is presently focusing

Materials: Plain white paper and pencil

Procedure:

1. Instruct the client to draw a window on a sheet of white paper.

2. Explain that this is a window on his or her life. Ask the client to "look" through the window and draw what he or she sees. (Some clients will be looking out, others in; this is not important.)

3. After the drawing has been completed, explore what the client is focusing on in the present and what he or she wants to see for the future.

Serial Drawing Technique (Allan, 1988)

Purpose: To discuss and process feelings about issues

Materials: Plain white paper and pencil with no eraser

Procedure:

This technique may be nondirective, directive, or partially directive, depending on the client's ability to engage in the process.

1. Ask the client to draw on the sheet of white paper a picture about what is bothering him or her (nondirective). If the client seems unable to use his or her own initiative, suggest a subject based on your assessment of his or her problem (directive).
2. After the client has completed his or her drawing, ask if the drawing tells a story. Also ask about any observations he or she made during the drawing process.
3. If the client demonstrates that a specific symbol has special relevance, ask him or her to redraw it every four to six sessions, allowing enough time to elapse for the client to process changes in attitude or relationships.

Squiggle Drawing Game (Nickerson, 1983)

Purpose: To encourage creativity and self-expression

Materials: Plain white paper and pencil

Procedure:

1. Draw a squiggle on the piece of white paper with a felt-tip pen and give the paper to the client.
2. Ask him or her to make the squiggle into a picture.
3. When the drawing is finished, ask the client to tell a story about the drawing. This technique is often used with resistant or reluctant children.

Bibliotherapy

Literature has been integrated into counseling for many years and in a variety of ways. It has been used to help establish relationships with clients, explore clients' lifestyles, promote clients' insight, and educate and reorient clients (Jackson, 2000). Bibliotherapy refers to a process designed to help individuals solve problems and better understand themselves through reading (Pardeck, 1995). Bibliotherapy techniques can help children and adolescents in many ways (Gladding, 1999, Pardeck, 1995). For example, although younger clients might be unable to verbalize their thoughts and feelings, they often gain insight as they identify with characters or themes presented in literature. Bibliotherapy techniques also may be used to explore relationships, deal with unfinished business, alleviate depression, and enhance school achievement (Nugent, 2000; Quackenbush, 1991).

Bibliotherapy techniques are best used to promote interaction and exploration on important issues and concerns while providing ample opportunity for feedback (Schumacher, Wantz, & Taricone, 1995). Young clients may accept themselves as they accept fictional characters. Or the reverse could be the case: The fiction may produce anxiety in which the children condemn and reject the characters. Therefore, the counselor should exercise caution when implementing these techniques by using appropriate interventions that will facilitate positive communication and therapeutic interventions.*

School counselors may wish to consult with the school librarian to select books for the library and to keep abreast of new books available dealing with students' concerns and problems. National bookstore chains, too, have extensive bibliotherapy selections.

Using Storybooks

Purpose: To encourage the client to discuss and relate to the story themes

Materials: Assorted books and stories related to the client's problem area (for example, *The Worst Day of My Life,* by Bill Cosby)

Procedure:

1. Allow the client to select a book or story from a prepared list of literature, or have the books and stories available for the client to view.
2. Give the client time to read the book or story he or she selected, or read it to him or her, depending on the age of the client and length of the selection.
3. Focus on the literature. Ask the client to tell the story, with special attention to the characters and action.
4. Ask about the client's perceptions of the characters' behaviors and feelings. Help the client identify alternatives to and consequences of the story.
5. Focus on the client's reality. Encourage the client to personalize and relate to the themes in the story.
6. With the client, evaluate the effectiveness of the characters' behaviors and discuss how the client could apply effective behaviors to his or her situation.

Super Action Heroes

Super Action Heroes is adapted from work presented by Jackson (2000).

Directions: Using the client's favorite comic books, make a list of action heroes (e.g., Superman, Spiderman, Batman, Wonderwoman). Ask the client to list at least three characteristics that describe these "superheroes." After the client has identified these characteristics, ask the following questions:

1. Name one person who has made a positive difference in your life. Why?
2. Name some people whom you admire and tell me why you admire them.
3. What makes someone a superhero?

---

*Paperbacks for Educators in Washington, Missouri (1-800- 227-2591), and the Self-Esteem Shop (1-800-251-8336) publish several comprehensive catalogs identifying books appropriate for use with children and adolescents on topics such as abuse, body image, divorce, family problems, fears, friendship, illness, loss, school problems, self-esteem, sexuality, stress, teen problems, and values.

4. Who would you consider a "real live" superhero?
5. How hard is it to name positive characteristics about someone?
6. What is a role model?
7. What impact do role models have on our lives?
8. How should you choose role models?
9. Could you be someone's hero? Why or why not?

Brian, an 11-year-old, has come to see Ms. Peary, the school counselor, because he is failing two subjects. Brian is usually a good student, but lately he has not been completing his assignments. When Brian arrives at Ms. Peary's office, he sits in a chair across the room from Ms. Peary and appears very withdrawn. After Brian is seated, Ms. Peary asks him what he wants to discuss with her, but he doesn't respond. After several minutes, she asks if he likes to read comic books. She tells Brian that she keeps several comic books, including Superman, Wonderwoman, and Spiderman, in her office. Brian responds that he likes to read comic books, especially Superman. "Superman is cool," he says.

Ms. Peary shows Brian a Superman comic book and tells him that they can read the book together during the counseling session. While reading the comic book, Ms. Peary points out that Superman always helps people and does good for others. Brian agrees and adds that Superman does what is right because he has Kryptonite, a special material that enables him to do superhuman things. Ms. Peary agrees and asks Brian what he would do if he had Kryptonite. Brian states that he would help his grandmother who has been sick lately. "I would use the stuff to make grandmother feel better so she could get out of the hospital."

Brian goes on to say that he has been very worried about his grandmother, and because of this worry he has not been finishing his schoolwork. Ms. Peary suggests that, even though Kryptonite is not available, Brian still can do something to help his grandmother while she is in the hospital. Ms. Peary invites Brian to brainstorm things he might be able to do, and he identifies several things, including sending her cards to let her know that he is thinking of her, calling her at her hospital room, and visiting her at the hospital after school. Brian decides that he would like to make the card first, so Ms. Peary says he can work on it during his counseling session. As Brian leaves the session, he says he is already feeling better just knowing that he can do something to help cheer his grandmother while she is sick.

After Brian leaves, Ms. Peary reflects on the session and realizes that the comic book was an important catalyst for helping Brian to share his worry about his grandmother. In turn, she now understands why Brian's grades have gone down. As Ms. Peary processes this session, she concludes that if she had not introduced the comic book, Brian probably would not have shared his worries in this session.

Guided Imagery

Guided imagery is a structured, directed activity designed to increase expression, personal awareness, and concentration through inducing and processing mental images (Myrick & Myrick, 1993). Myrick and Myrick noted that clients are familiar with imagery because they use it in their daily lives. For example, everyone can daydream and visualize outcomes that may be positive or negative. When counseling adolescents, guided imagery can be used to clarify emotional problems and blocks, reduce anxiety and fear, produce behavioral changes, and enhance self-concept (Omizo, Omizo, & Kitaoka, 1998). Guided imagery allows children to experience life events in a therapeutic environment. Imagery may be used in problem solving, to reexperience and resolve past situations, or to fantasize about future possibilities (Witmer & Young, 1987). Through mental images, individuals can explore situations and rehearse skills needed to accomplish successful resolutions in "real life."

Guided imagery, sometimes called guided fantasy, involves inducing relaxation, imagining or experiencing the actual fantasy, and processing the fantasy (Skovholt, Morgan, & Negron–Cunningham, 1989). When using guided imagery, the counselor evokes three types of images (Witmer & Young, 1985):

1. Spontaneous images such as daydreams, fantasies, creative thinking, and contemplation, in which the counselor gives direction of content.
2. Directed images, in which the counselor gives the client a specific image to concentrate on or react to.
3. Guided imagery, which combines spontaneous and directed images by giving the client a starting point and allowing him or her to fill in the actions or ambiguous situations.

The counselor should be cautious when using guided imagery techniques. Although imagery is an important technique, some schools and state licensure laws prohibit the use of imagery by counselors. Counselors are therefore strongly encouraged to check policies, procedures, and laws pertaining to guided imagery.

Myrick and Myrick (1993) suggested a procedure for using guided imagery. The counselor's first step is to create a script. In creating a script or "scripting," the counselor selects words that evoke a mood. For example, the counselor might ask the client what place the client thinks of as "peaceful" or "tranquil." Having obtained this information, the counselor writes a script evoking this place and describing scenes related to that which the client has previously described.

Scripts do not have to be long or extremely detailed, although they do have to be descriptive.

The script is written before the client arrives for the session. During the session the counselor sets the mood by introducing the activity and helping the client relax. After the client is relaxed, the counselor speaks softly and smoothly with appropriate pauses, allowing the client to create mental images. After the client creates the images, the counselor asks the client to notice details of the created images so the client might recall these later. The counselor brings closure to the experience by finding a stopping place that does not disrupt the mood. At the end of the session, the counselor discusses the experience with the client and asks him or her to describe the experience and the feelings it evoked. The step-by-step technique is as follows:

1. The counselor makes sure the room is quiet and has a comfortable chair or a carpeted floor on which the client can sit or lie. The counselor should use a calm, soothing voice at all times, emphasizing that the client is in control of the process.
2. The counselor starts the basic guided imagery technique by helping the client relax, perhaps suggesting that the client close his or her eyes and breathe slowly and deeply. The counselor could say: "Concentrate on your breathing . . . in . . . out . . . in . . . out. . . . Feel the tension flow out of your body." If the client seems to have trouble relaxing, the counselor could try some tense/relax exercises.
3. When the client has relaxed, the counselor begins the guided imagery. The exercises should be simple at first. The counselor might suggest that the client allow his or her mind to become blank, like an empty TV or movie screen.

In step 3, the counselor could ask the client to imagine a single object—something familiar, such as an orange. The client could imagine how it looks, how it feels, how it smells, how the juice runs out when it is cut. The object should not be threatening to the client. Images of nonthreatening animals are sometimes useful in the imagery process. Henderson (1999) suggested a technique in which the client utilizes animal imagery associated with photographs of wild animals. In this technique the counselor asks the client to look at pictures of animals and then close his or her eyes and imagine feelings associated with these animals. After the client identifies feelings associated with pictures of the wild animals, the counselor asks how the client felt during the exercise and what the experience was like for him or her.

Games

Games serve a variety of functions in counseling. Friedberg (1986) noted that games are "appropriate interventions for various children's problems" (p. 12) and posited that they are helpful in working with externalizing disorders (aggression, impulsivity, attention disorders) and internalizing problems (depression, anxiety). According to Friedberg, games are particularly helpful with resistant children, verbally deficient children, resistant children who are in denial, and anxious and inhibited children. Games can be used to teach new behaviors, facilitate verbalization, and address specific concerns on which a child or adolescent is working. For example, a client who is having difficulty with problem solving would benefit by playing Who Knew That Problem Solving Could Be This Much Fun? (*Childswork, Childsplay,* 1998), and a young adolescent struggling with relationship and sexuality issues could benefit by playing Crossroads: A Game on Teenage Sexuality and Relationships (*Childswork, Childsplay,* 1998).

Counselors are encouraged to be creative and design their own board games. A simple game to help young clients express their feelings can be developed by stapling four paper plates to the middle of a large sheet of tagboard. On one plate draw a happy face and place a yellow dot beside it. On another plate draw an angry face and put a red dot beside it. On the third plate draw a sad face and place a blue dot beside it. On the last plate draw a worried face and label it with a green dot. Next place a path of 20–25 colored dots (red, blue, green, and yellow, in random order) around the edge of the tagboard. The client and counselor take turns rolling a die and moving a marker the designated number of dots. When a player lands on a dot, the player talks about a time he or she has experienced the feeling corresponding to the color of the dot (e.g., red/angry) (Vernon, 2002).

Friedberg (1986) suggested that games are more effective when they are incorporated into counseling sessions rather than being presented at the beginning or end of a session. Friedberg also noted that games are most effective when they are tailored to individual problems. Nickerson and O'Laughlin (1983) identified the following guidelines for selecting games to be used in counseling:

1. The game should be familiar or easy to learn.
2. The game should be appropriate for the client's age and developmental level.
3. The game should have clear, inherent properties related to the therapeutic goals of counseling.

Frey (1986) discussed three categories of games:

1. Interpersonal communication games.
2. Games for specialized populations.
3. Games with specific theoretical orientations.

Games have both advantages and disadvantages in the counseling process. Gaming formats are familiar and nonthreatening; therefore, they are effective in establishing rapport with children and adolescents. Further, games have diagnostic value because the counselor may observe a variety of behaviors, thoughts, and feelings as the game is played. In addition, games can enhance clients' egos by allowing clients to receive positive feedback, gain a sense of mastery, and indulge in a pleasurable experience. Games also permit clients to test reality by playing different roles and selecting solutions in a safe environment. Finally, games allow clients to come to terms with objects and people and learn to work within a system of rules and limits (Frey, 1986; Friedberg, 1996; Nickerson & O'Laughlin, 1983).

Friedberg (1986) identified some disadvantages with using games in counseling. If the games are used in an artificial and stilted manner, they do not enhance the counseling process. Also, inflexible game play disconnected from the client's problems is ineffective and may reflect avoidance of difficult and painful topics. Complicated games with a myriad of rules are likely to be counterproductive because they can be confusing. Older children and adolescents may find games condescending. Therefore, counselors must consider the developmental appropriateness of any game they are considering using in counseling.

As mentioned, counselors can create their own games. Posterboard can be used for the gameboard and cards, and checkers or small toys may be used as markers. Commercially developed games may be found in catalogs such as *Childswork/Childsplay.** In addition, games often are available at professional conferences. The following games, "Me Too" and "Soup Cans," can be played with items that are obtained easily and inexpensively.

Me Too

This game can be used as an individual or a group technique. With individual clients, the counselor writes statements on separate index cards that relate to identified problems. For example, if a child is having problems with his or her parents, topics for the cards might include statements such as: "Sometimes I feel sad when I see my father." "Sometimes I feel angry when I see my mother." If the client agrees with each statement as each card is shared, he or she says, "Me too." Then the counselor helps the client discuss and process these statements.

A variation of this game can be used in a group setting. The counselor explains the game by saying, "When you hear someone say something with which you identify say, 'Me too!'" For example, a member of the group might say, "My name is Amanda, and math is my favorite class." Anyone in the group who agrees with the class preference stands up and says, "Me too!" This game is a good icebreaker, especially for new members of the group.

Soup Cans

For the Soup Cans activity you will need several clean soup cans with the labels removed. In place of the labels, the counselor attaches on the front of the soup can a picture representing a family member. The picture may be drawn, or it may

---

*Genesis Direct, Inc., 100 Plaza Dr., Secaucus, NJ 07094-3613; website: www.Childswork. com.

come from a magazine. For example, if the client comes from a family that has a mother, father, and brother, three soup cans are needed to represent each member of the family.

The counselor explains to the client that they are going to play a game involving the soup cans, some tokens, and a few questions. The counselor develops approximately 10–12 questions individualized to address the client's presenting problem. For example, if the child feels neglected, the counselor might initiate questions around belonging or inclusion, such as: With whom would you like to spend more time? If you could go to your favorite movie, with which family member would you choose to go? If the client replies, "I want to spend more time with Mom," the client is instructed to drop a token inside the can with the mother's picture on it. This game continues until all questions have been asked and all tokens have been dispersed into the soup cans.

The counselor should have the questions written prior to the counseling session, and each of the tokens should be labeled with numbers corresponding to the questions. In this way, after the questions have been asked, the counselor can match the token number with the respective question. This game can be revealing by showing the family member(s) with whom the client wants to spend time and also family member(s) the client wants to avoid.

A variation of this game might be to include peers at school. If, for example, the child feels isolated from his or her friends at school, the pictures on the soup can could represent classmates. The questions could be posed to ascertain why the child feels isolated or omitted from activities with peers.

Activity Books and Worksheets

Activity books are a valuable resource for counselors because they provide a format that is adaptable, flexible, and nonthreatening. Activity books are widely available and easy to obtain. In addition, techniques from activity books may be adapted for use with children representing a variety of developmental levels and ages (Schumacher, Wantz, & Taricone, 1995). The purpose of activity books is to provide counselors with therapeutic worksheets that clients may complete during a counseling session or outside a counseling session as "homework." These worksheets enable the child or adolescent to gain stronger awareness and understanding of issues pertinent to topics encountered in counseling.

Some activity books, such as the *Student's Workbook for Exploring the Spiritual Journey* (Atkinson, 2001), deal with specific areas such as spirituality. Other activity books provide topics on broader areas. For example, the *Passport Series: A Journey through Emotional, Social, Cognitive, and Self-Development* (Vernon, 1998a, b, c) consists of worksheets on many topics including anger management, feelings, self-esteem, social skills, and cognitive development. Other activity books that counselors find useful are *Getting Along With Others* (Jackson, Jackson, & Monroe, 2002) and *Thinking, Feeling, and Behaving for Children*

(Vernon, 1989). An example of a worksheet activity from the *Passport Series: A Journey through Emotional, Social, Cognitive, and Self- Development* (Vernon, 1998a, pp. 217–219) is provided below.

Solutions for Bad Feelings

Solutions for Bad Feelings is appropriate for use with first grade through fifth grade and is designed to enable children to identify effective ways of dealing with sad feelings. The first step in this group activity is to have the participants divide into pairs. The counselor then hands out a worksheet to each pair of students. The counselor explains that the worksheets are dealing with sad situations, and their job is to help the child in the situation feel less sad. After reading the first situation, the counselor allows a short time for the pairs to discuss what they could do to deal with the sad feelings. They may write this on the worksheet or simply talk about the ideas. The paired participants then are asked to share their ideas with the whole group. Some examples of the situations described on the worksheets are:

- Carlos's dog, 8 years old, just got run over by a car. What would you suggest to help Carlos feel less sad?
- Annie's grandma fell and broke her leg. She is in the hospital. What would you suggest to help Annie feel less sad?
- Theresa's best friend is moving to another town. What could you suggest that might help Theresa feel less sad?

The activity book also includes content questions to be used for discussion and personalization questions that facilitate participants' self-awareness and encourage personal application of the activity. Examples of content questions (related to a feelings worksheet) are: Do you think that everyone feels sad about the same things? Were you surprised at the number of different ideas that you came up with to deal with sad feelings? Do you think that it is possible to feel less sad about sad situations if you find some good ways to help you deal with them? Examples of personalization questions are: Have you tried any of the ideas that were suggested today? If so, which ones have worked best for you? Of the ideas presented today, which ones would you like to try the next time you feel sad?

Music

Adolescents spend an average of 3 hours per day listening to music (Gladding, 1999; Jensen, 2001). Music alleviates feelings of depression, anxiety, loneliness, and grief, and it clarifies developmental issues and identity. Music plays an important role in healing and nurturing and is considered an effective adjunct to counseling with children and adolescents (Newcomb, 1994). For example, music is used in counseling to increase affective awareness, intensify understanding, reduce anxiety, and increase verbal disclosure (Jensen, 2001). Gladding (1992) described music as "therapeutic to the verbal approaches to counseling" (p. 14), and Newcomb (1994) suggested that music is an ideal approach for clients who have difficulty expressing themselves verbally.

Counselors may use music-listening exercises in counseling to reduce depression and increase self-concept (Hendricks, 2000). Music often is used in conjunction with other techniques to elicit memories, fantasies, and visual imagery. Songs help to teach children about their feelings, cope with their fears, and gain self-understanding. Although many music techniques are designed for group work, they can be adapted for individual counseling (Hendricks, 2000; Hendricks, Bradley, Robinson, & Davis, 1997). In addition, counselors have found that background music in the counseling environment enhances positive mood, increases self-disclosure, and decreases negative self-talk (Jensen, 2001). Overall, music has been found to be therapeutic. Suggestions for counseling interventions using music are provided in the following paragraphs.

Music Listening

In Music Listening the counselor has the client select a song that has strong personal meaning for him or her. Together, the counselor and the client listen to the music. Afterward, the counselor asks the client questions about the feelings and thoughts that the song evoked and way(s) that the feelings and thoughts contribute to the client's present life functioning. For example, a song describing friendship might elicit feelings of comfort and pleasure for the client. The client then would identify ways by which these feelings could be helpful in combating stress and anxiety about friendships or any other applicable situation. This technique gives insight to both the client and counselor about the client's life situation, history, and functioning.

Reframing

In Reframing, the therapist and the client generate new, positive, cognitive understandings or frames of reference for a given situation or experience. For example, a client who is having difficulty understanding a curfew time might reframe his or her misunderstanding to focus on the parents' concern for their child's safety. Following identification of the reframe, the client is asked to find a piece of written or recorded music that describes some of the feelings that have been identified in the process of the reframe. The client and the counselor then listen to the music. Following this, the client talks about why he or she chose the music and what feelings the music evoked.

My Own Song

For the My Own Song technique, young clients make up a short song about something that is bothering them or occurring in their lives. Creating songs increases self-awareness and emotional release, and it facilitates problem-solving and coping skills.

Songs as Lessons

In using Songs as Lessons, the counselor selects a song with a positive, useful message. The song may be one that is currently popular or one expressly written for children, such as Bowman's (1985) *I Have Lots of Feelings and They're OK.* After teaching the children the song, the counselor invites the children to stand and sing the song. Movement and gestures may be incorporated to go along with the lyrics. For example, in Bowman's song, children might jump when singing "jump" or bring a finger and thumb together when singing "they're okay." After the children sing the song, the counselor leads a discussion about the feelings identified in the song.

Music Collage

In Music Collage the counselor gives the client access to a tape recorder and asks him or her to tape enough short (5–20 seconds) segments of songs that have personal meaning to create a 3- to 5-minute music collage. When the collage is finished, the counselor facilitates a discussion of how the music is meaningful and what feelings it evokes. This activity is especially effective with adolescents.

Music and Color

In the Music and Color activity, the client is asked to listen to a piece of recorded music that has personal meaning. Then the client is asked to visualize colors they associate with the music. After the colors are identified, the client is asked to discuss the colors and explain what the colors might represent.

Melinda is a 15-year-old female in ninth grade. Until recently she has been a high-achieving student. Currently she is failing two subjects, and Ms. Johnson, her school counselor, is concerned. Ms. Johnson asks to see Melinda, and Melinda reluctantly agrees. During the session Melinda is withdrawn and sullen. To build rapport, Ms. Johnson asks Melinda if she likes to listen to music. Melinda says she enjoys music and describes her favorite song, which Ms. Johnson asks her to bring to the next session. At that session, Melinda brings a recording of the song, "A Change Would Do You Good" (Sheryl Crow). Melinda plays the song on a compact disc player, and she and Ms. Johnson listen to the music together. After the song is played, Ms. Johnson asks Melinda to describe what the song means to her.

Soon Melinda is describing the lyrics with animation. The lyrics refer to the positive aspects of change and the ways that routine can be stifling. Melinda begins to talk about her own routine and how she is bored much of the time. She states that a change would do her good. When Ms. Johnson asks her about school, Melinda replies that school is "boring" and teachers should change the way(s) they do things. Specifically, she says that her biology class is not "fun" and the teacher should do more interesting things.

Ms. Johnson inquires about what would make biology class more interesting for Melinda, and she says she would like to study subjects such as butterflies and moths. Ms. Johnson encourages Melinda to talk with Mr. Teeter, and Ms. Johnson engages Melinda in a role-play about how to do this effectively.

At this point Melinda begins to talk excitedly about the ways she could collect information for the project and present the project to the class. She proudly says she could be the "insects expert" in her class. Ms. Johnson sees for the first time that Melinda is excited about her school-work and enthusiastic about completing a project. In the next session, Melinda reports that she has talked to Mr. Teeter, who agreed that a but-terfly project was "just what the class needs" and that Melinda can be the leader of this project that will involve the entire class.

As Ms. Johnson and Melinda begin to set new goals, Melinda's enthu-siasm about school builds. For reinforcement, Ms. Johnson asks Melinda to play the piece of music she originally brought to counseling. As she plays the song a second time, Melinda proudly announces that it has become her "theme song" and that she is more than ever convinced that "change can do you good."

Puppets

Puppets are effective in counseling children and are especially useful in estab-lishing trust and rapport (Carter, 1998). Puppet play allows young clients to dis-place their feelings about significant others onto the puppets (Bromfield, 1995). Through this displacement the puppets offer physical and psychological safety that facilitates self-expression about problematic events and situations. In addi-tion, children may project onto puppets the feelings they consider unacceptable in themselves, or they may use puppets to gain mastery over situations in which they feel they have no control.

Counselors using puppets must be skilled in the mechanics of operating them. Whether the counselor uses simple sock puppets or more elaborate designs, operating the puppet requires a certain amount of physical dexterity and practice. Therefore, some advanced preparation is necessary. Selection of the puppets depends upon practicality and the client's needs (Carter, 1998).

During puppet play, counselors need to continually assess the client's anxi-ety level and note the significance of what is occurring (Bromfield, 1995). Clients must be allowed to set the pace of puppet play, and, equally important, puppet play should be at an appropriate developmental level (Johnson, 1997). Puppet theater illustrates the use of puppets.

Puppet Theater (Irwin, 1991)

Materials: 15–20 puppets (handmade or purchased) to stimulate children's interest and offer a real choice; puppet stage

Categories: Realistic family (father, mother, sister, brother—black and white), royalty (king, queen, knight, lady, prince, princess), occupations (police officer, nurse, teacher, firefighter, cowboy, mail carrier), animals (tame and wild), monsters (devil, witch, ogre, skeleton).

Procedure:

1. Introduction: Ask the child if he or she would like to tell a story using puppets as the characters. Emphasize that each child should decide whether he or she wants to play and that the story may be on any subject they choose.
2. Selection: Invite the child to choose the puppets he or she wants to use.
3. Warm-up: Invite the child to take the puppets he or she has chosen to the area behind the puppet stage and introduce the characters for the show. Introducing the puppets helps the child prepare for the story. If the child seems to be having trouble getting started, ask open-ended questions about the characters, such as, "And this is …" or "This seems to be a cowboy. Tell me about him."
4. The play: After the introductions, say, "And now, the story." Most children will be intrigued enough to begin on their own. Observe the plot and action. If the child seems to be stuck at some point, comment on the "five Ws" of construction (who, what, where, when, why).
5. Post-play interview with the characters: Speak directly to the puppets. This interview helps to clarify the plot and themes of the story—what did/did not happen, meanings, and motivations. The focus on the puppets extends the make-believe.
6. Post-play interview: Invite the child to talk directly about the experience. Ask what stimulated his or her choice of puppets or story and if anything similar has happened in real life. This interview gives the counselor an opportunity to assess the capacity for self-observation, defenses, strengths, weaknesses, and coping mechanisms.

Role-Play

The use of drama in counseling involves spontaneous, highly personalized improvisation. Clients may choose a role that represents themselves, others in their life, or symbolic character types. The counselor gains information from the way in which the client plays the role. Drama encourages safe expression of strong feelings, both positive and negative, and allows clients to learn from externalizing experiences. In addition, role-play encourages social interaction, learning, awareness, creativity, and spontaneity (Edwards & Springate, 1995). At the same time, these techniques function as a medium for dialogue and narrative (Chesner & Hahn, 2002). With groups, drama is useful in facilitating interaction among group members and has many uses in establishing and maintaining rapport (Cattanach, 1997). Counselors may use costumes to facilitate role-play and aid children in switching roles (passive to aggressive, strong to weak, good to bad).

Role-play provides clients with a way to rehearse new skills and practice stressful situations without undue stress (Thompson, 1996). Role-play may be initiated in several ways. The counselor could give the client a dilemma and ask the client to act it out. The situation may be one that the client has or has not experienced or one that he or she is anxious about. For example, the counselor might suggest a situation in which an adolescent has a conflict with a parent. In this situation, the adolescent might role-play ways to initiate a conversation with the parent about the conflict. The adolescent could play both the roles of self and parent as means of achieving insight. This type of role-play gives clients opportunities to practice strategies and increase their coping abilities (Akande, Akande, & Odewale, 1994).

Another form of role-play is role reversal. The child or adolescent may be asked to play the role of someone significant in his or her life (parent, sibling, teacher) with whom the client is having difficulty. Similarly, Hackney and Cormier (1996) suggested a role-play in which the young client plays two parts: the public self and the private self. This type of role-play encourages clients to confront aspects of their own personality and behavior.

Empty Chair Dialoguing (Okun, 1987)

Empty Chair Dialoguing, influenced by Gestalt therapy constructs, is an example of the way that drama and role-play may be integrated into a counseling relationship. This type of role-play is especially valuable in helping children and adolescents deal with conflict situations.

Materials: Two chairs

Procedure: The client speaks to an empty chair as if it is someone in his or her life (parent, sibling, friend, teacher). If a child has difficulty speaking to an empty chair, the counselor may have the child speak to a stuffed animal.

Antonio is a shy eighth-grader new to his school. Several of his teachers have noticed that Antonio is not making friends and avoids getting involved in school activities. The school counselor, Mr. DiBrito, is concerned that Antonio is feeling alienated from the other students and asks him to stop by his office. After talking with Antonio about his previous school, Mr. DiBrito determines that Antonio had been shy in that environment as well. He asks Antonio, "If things here at school could be different, what would you change?" Antonio thinks a minute and then answers, "I'd be one of the guys . . . involved in sports and school stuff." "What do you think keeps you from being that way?" Mr. DiBrito asks. Antonio looks at the floor and says, "I just don't know what to say or do. I get tongue-tied and make an idiot of myself. So it's easier not to say anything."

Mr. DiBrito assures his young client that many adolescents feel self-conscious and adds that it seems like Antonio's self-consciousness is really getting in his way. The counselor takes a piece of paper and divides it into three columns. At the top of the first column, he writes "Activity." On the second he writes, "Positive Results." On the third column he writes, "Negative Results." He hands the paper to Antonio and says, "I want you to list in the 'Activity' column at least five things you would like to do. Then, in the appropriate columns, list at least three possible good results from each activity and three possible bad results. Bring this paper back to our next session."

At the next session, Antonio shows the counselor his list. His list of activities includes joining the computer club and talking with another student. Mr. DiBrito asks, "Antonio, if you were to talk to another student, which one would you choose, and what would you like to say?" Antonio thinks for a minute and then says he would like to talk to Tom, who is in his history class and on the football team.

"Antonio, can you pretend that Tom is sitting in this empty chair and imagine saying something to him?" asked Mr. DiBrito. He goes on to explain that sometimes when people are having problems talking to someone, they find it easier to do it in real life if they practice it first. Antonio seems a little dubious but agrees to try. He looks at the empty chair and says, "Hi, Tom. My name is Antonio, and I just moved here. I went to the game yesterday and thought you played really well."

When he finishes speaking, Mr. DiBrito tells him that it is a good beginning and encourages him to continue talking. Antonio looks at the empty chair again and talks more about the game. Over the next several sessions, they repeat this empty chair dialoguing, branching out to other students Antonio says he wants to meet, and they set goals for him to practice in real life.

Several weeks later, Mr. DiBrito notices Antonio hanging out in the lunchroom with a small group of students. Later in the month, Antonio stops by Mr. DiBrito's office and tells him he is getting along well with his schoolmates and has even joined the computer club.

Storytelling

Storytelling, used as a means of communication for centuries, provides a way for individuals to express their identities (Miles, 1993). Storytelling is a powerful means for exploring painful experiences and can be used effectively with children and young adolescents to help them gain personal understanding and self-acceptance. Stories can be about a myriad of subjects: the client, the client's family, events in the client's life, fictional characters from books, cartoons, television, or movies, or characters the child has invented. The only limit to the topic of a story is the imagination of the client or the counselor.

Mutual Storytelling Technique

The Mutual Storytelling technique, described by Gardner (1979), has been used effectively with depressed and suicidal children and is most appropriate for children between the ages of 9 and 14 years (Kottman & Skyles, 1990).

Materials: Tape recorder

Procedure:

1. Ask the child if he or she would like to work with you to make a tape of a make-believe TV or radio show in which the child is the guest of honor.
2. Turn on the tape recorder and make a few brief statements of introduction. To help put the child at ease, ask the child to state his or her name, age, school, and grade.
3. Then ask the child to tell a story. Most children will start immediately, but some need time to think or need help getting started. If the child needs help, ask him or her about interests, hobbies, family, and the like.
4. While the child tells his or her story, take notes on the story's content and possible meaning.
5. After the child has finished the story, ask if it might have a moral lesson. Also ask for more details or information about specific items.
6. Comment about the story, such as how good (exciting, interesting, unusual, etc.) it was.
7. Turn off the tape recorder and discuss the child's story with him or her to get the information you need to prepare your own version of the story. Have the child determine which figures in the story represented him or her and which represented significant others in his or her life, what symbols the child used, and the overall "feel" of the setting and atmosphere of the story. Take into account the emotional reactions the child showed while telling the story. Use the moral lesson the child stated in selecting the story's theme. Consider healthier resolutions or adaptations to problems than those in the story.
8. Turn on the tape recorder and tell your story, which should involve the same characters, settings, and initial situation as the original story but have a

better resolution of conflict. In the story, identify alternatives to problems and indicate that behavior can change. The story should emphasize healthier adaptations.

9. Turn off the tape recorder and ask the client if he or she would like to hear the complete story.

Metaphors

Counselors frequently use metaphors in counseling children and adolescents. Metaphors add richness to description and provide memorable symbols for the child (Bowman, 1995). Metaphors often are used to describe individual or group characteristics, processes, and products in terms familiar to the child. In addition, metaphors help the client understand experiences that are not easily described in literal terms. Metaphors are abundant in children's literature, fairy tales, cartoons, movies, and television shows that contain important social and emotional lessons. Metaphors are useful in expressing empathic understanding of a problem (such as shyness), presenting feedback (using an object to both compliment the positive aspects of behavior and confront the negative aspects of behavior), and giving affirmations (emphasizing personal strengths rather than specific behaviors) (Bowman, 1995).

1. Determine the client's preferences (favorite cartoons, games, hobbies, animals, etc.).
2. From previous counseling sessions, determine the client's problem areas, challenges, and personal strengths. Assess the client's primary sensory learning style (visual, auditory, kinesthetic).
3. Construct a story that interweaves this information. Keep the story short and to the point.
4. Do not interpret or explain the story to the client. Help the client explore new possibilities (different endings, etc.) by bringing the story back to reality.

Movies as Metaphors

Movies provide a wealth of metaphoric illustrations. Many movies that are familiar to children and adolescents could be selected. Because the story of the *Wizard of Oz* is familiar to most adolescents, it can illustrate metaphors relating to substance abuse. In the *Wizard of Oz,* Dorothy has three friends: the Lion, the Scarecrow, and the Tin Man. These friends could represent the Serenity Prayer. In the Serenity Prayer the participant asks for "the serenity to accept the things I cannot change" (Tin Man), "the courage to change the things that I can change" (Lion), and "the wisdom to know the difference" (Scarecrow). After the metaphoric relationships are identified, the counselor could ask clients if they can accept the things they cannot change. This might be to accept that one's parents are divorcing or that a grandparent has died. The counselor could also ask the client if he or she understands what cannot change.

Another example of metaphor occurs when Toto bites Elmira Gulch, who later becomes the Wicked Witch. This incident leads to Dorothy having trouble with the law. The counselor could use this example (dog bites) to say that little things can lead to big problems. Then the client could be asked if little things have occurred that led to big problems. The counselor also could ask if he or she has had family members who have been in trouble with the law. Later in the story, the Wicked Witch pursues Dorothy relentlessly. This could symbolize the way that addiction pursues someone. During the pursuit, the flying monkeys attach themselves to Dorothy, illustrating the Alcoholic Anonymous adage of "having a monkey on my back." The counselor could ask if the client has ever had a "monkey on your back." If the client answers yes, the counselor might explore this further.

Regarding family roles, the Munchkins could exemplify enablers who falsely believe that Dorothy has special powers. Like so many enablers, the Munchkins say, "Don't do this and don't do that," but they never come up with concrete, specific examples. In addition, the Wizard could illustrate the role of the sponsor who helps give meaning to the Serenity Prayer by finding existing positive qualities in Dorothy's friends and by giving encouragement so that these qualities can be seen. The Good Witch also illustrates the role of the sponsor by showing Dorothy that the answers to the questions she has are within herself, and that ultimately, there's no place like home.

The sponsor can help addicts see that the answers to the questions they ask are self-evident, and that "home" is a state of mind about feeling comfortable with oneself. Finally, the counselor could ask the client who he or she is most like, the Scarecrow, the Lion, or the Tin Man (Allison, personal communication, February 7, 2002).

The *Wizard of Oz* is not the only movie that has metaphorical messages. Other examples of movies rich in metaphor are *Star Wars, The Fellowship of the Ring, Spiderman, Lilo and Stitch,* and *Mulan.* These movies and others may effectively be used by the counselor to illustrate many points and assist clients in clarification of issues.

Therapeutic Writing

Writing has been used for decades to help individuals develop perspective (Vernon, 1997). In counseling, writing enhances awareness by helping clients organize their thoughts and feelings, providing cathartic emotional release, and contributing to personal integration and self-validation. Writing is particularly beneficial for adults and older children. Further, counselors often find that writing can be used effectively with young children, if the writing is simplistic. In using this technique with younger children, ages 3–5, the counselor may serve as the recorder (Vernon, 1997). Examples of therapeutic writing include:

- *Correspondence,* which may be used when the client is unable or unwilling to sustain a verbal dialogue with another person.
- *Journal writing,* which may be a stream of consciousness or structured in some manner.
- *Creative writing, prose, or poetry,* which may be used to clarify projections, explore problems and solutions, or fantasize.
- *Structured writing,* including making lists, writing instructions, responding to open-ended sentences, or filling out questionnaires or inventories.

In any writing technique, the client should be told that grammar, style, spelling, punctuation, and neatness are not important.

Autobiography

Autobiographies can describe a specific aspect of one's life, or they can cover the entire lifespan. Autobiographies help clients express feelings, clarify concerns, and work toward resolving problems. In developing an autobiography, the counselor might suggest that the young client try to organize his or her life into 2-year intervals and write about that. For older children, the intervals might be 3–4 years. Although the counselor doesn't want to stifle or interrupt creativity with younger children, some structure may be helpful. The counselor might begin by suggesting that clients tell where and when they were born and anything they might remember during the first two years of their life.

Lifeline

For the Lifeline technique, the counselor asks the client to draw a long line across a large sheet of paper and place a symbol of a baby at one end of the line to indicate birth. The client is to place symbols above (good events) or below (challenging events) the line to indicate when the best or most challenging things occurred. The client is asked to write/describe these events beneath each symbol. The counselor then discusses with the client the various events that happened in his or her life.

Outer/Inner Exercise

For the Outer/Inner Exercise, the counselor asks the client to draw a line down the middle of a sheet of paper, making two columns, then label the columns "outer" and "inner." The outer column represents memorable events that occurred at a particular point in time. The inner column represents the client's feelings in relation to these events. The client is to complete the columns, which serve as a stimulus for discussion. For example, if the client states that he or she moved at a certain time, that would go in the outer column. The feelings the client associates with the move would be in the inner column. The counselor should help the client continue to process the feelings associated with words in the columns.

Uninterrupted, Sustained, Silent Writing

For this writing technique, the counselor should ask the client to write down everything that comes to mind until the counselor tells him or her to stop. A typical time period is 3–5 minutes. At the end of the exercise, the counselor and the client discuss this writing. For example, if the client wrote words related to negative feelings (sad, mad, scared), the counselor could explore with the client why he or she has these feelings and try to set goals enabling the client to change these feelings. If the client wrote about positive feelings, the counselor could talk with the client about where these feelings came from and devise strategies to sustain them.

Multicultural Techniques

Children and adolescents who are aware of multicultural issues are more tolerant and less critical of others (Moses, 2002). They are less likely to create negative stereotypes and more likely to be tolerant of differences between persons. The following techniques may be used to create and enhance multicultural awareness in children and adolescents.

What's in a Name?

What's in a Name can be used in either individual or group counseling. It is an easy exercise in which clients tell how they received their first name. For example, a client might say, "I'm David, and I was named David because my father's favorite Biblical character was David." Another client might say that she was named Maria because the family has a tradition of naming the oldest daughter Maria. This exercise can be helpful in identifying important family dynamics such as religion, values, traditions, family histories, and cultural awareness.

Diversity Bingo

Purpose: To encourage the clients to become more aware of diversity

Type of Activity: Group

Supplies: Pencil, paper, and bingo card with 25 squares

Directions: As in bingo, the first person to complete *all* squares wins. In playing Diversity Bingo the counselor asks the client to find someone in the group who meets one of the following criteria and write that person's name in the box. As with any game of bingo, the first client to complete all squares wins the game. The first square is a "free" square, so the client focuses on the remaining 24 bingo squares, which ask questions such as: Who in this group:

1. Was born before 1995?
2. Has parents or grandparents who lived outside the USA?
3. Has met someone who is a Native American?
4. Has met someone who is African American?
5. Has met someone who is Hispanic American?
6. Has met someone who is Asian American?
7. Knows someone who was born outside the USA?
8. Knows someone who is older than 75 years?
9. Has visited a country outside the USA?
10. Knows someone who has a physical challenge?

These questions provide examples. The counselor should tailor the questions to meet clients' needs.

Dream Catcher

Dreams are an integral part of the world of children and adolescents. The technique of Dream Catcher is borrowed from Native American culture, which emphasizes that dreams can be good or bad. Native Americans have a tradition of keeping a dream catcher in their home, usually in the bedroom, so that during the night the dream catcher can catch both good and bad dreams. According to tradition, the good dreams know how to slip out of the dream catcher's web and escape by way of the feather attached to the dream catcher. In contrast, the bad dreams do not know how to get out of the web, so they remain caught in the web until the next morning, when they perish at the first light of dawn.

The Dream Catcher technique offers an opportunity for clients to discuss their dreams. Counselors may use this technique to elicit both good and bad feelings and, in addition, allay fears associated with dreams. Further, this technique offers a good opportunity to involve parents in the counseling process.*

Purpose: To identify feelings associated with dreams

Materials: Pipe cleaners (usually two) large enough to make a circle having a 2–4 inch diameter

String or thread long enough to make a web inside the pipe cleaners

A feather 1–3 inches long

Colorful threads, pipe cleaners, and feathers seem to appeal to children.

---

*Dream Catchers can be purchased from Billy Ashley, in Albuquerque, New Mexico, at 505-237-2276.

Procedure:

1. Construct the dream catcher.
2. Ask the client to describe a dream that he or she has had.
3. Ask the client to pair an emotion or feeling with the dream.
4. Talk with the client about the role of the dream catcher in catching the bad dreams and freeing the good dreams.
5. Have the client talk more about the dream mentioned in item #1.
6. Focus on the reality of the dream.
7. With the client, talk about how having a dream catcher in his or her room might be helpful.
8. Follow up on the role of the dream catcher in future counseling sessions.

Multicultural Circle

Multicultural Circles may be used in either individual or group counseling. As the counselor names certain topics/issues, the client moves to the center of the circle if he or she identifies with the topic or issue. For example, the counselor might say, "Please move to the center of the circle if you . . .

1. Are a Native American.
2. Have a family member who is Hispanic.
3. Have lived in a country other than the USA.
4. Have parents with a physical challenge.
5. Are younger than 10 years old.
6. Are older than 10 years .
7. Have parents who are divorced.

After each item is called (e.g., item #1) the counselor says, "If you're a Native American, please move to the center of the circle. "The counselor allows sufficient time, then asks each person to move out of the center before continuing with item #2. The procedure continues through item 7. Then the counselor helps the participants process the thoughts and feelings evoked by this experience.

Although this exercise is conducted most often in a group setting, it can be used with individual clients. Also, variations can be conducted around various topics. For example, if the counselor is working with a client on anger management, the questions would focus on anger. The counselor might say, "If you tend to hit someone when you get angry, please move to the center of the circle. Item #2 might be, "If you count to 10 when you're angry, please move to the center of the circle." Regardless of the topic, this technique is powerful in helping clients see with what/whom they identify and associate.

"You Are Dealt a Hand in Life"

Purpose: To increase awareness of diversity and challenge stereotypes that clients may have

Materials: Two decks of cards shuffled together (one red deck and one blue deck of cards)

Procedure: This technique, which may be used with individuals or groups, is especially effective with adolescents. The counselor deals four cards randomly to each client and asks them to keep the cards face down. Each of the cards has a multicultural connotation; however, the client is not told the interpretation(s) until after the cards have been dealt.

After all clients have received the cards, the counselor explains that the cards create a profile of the client based upon the combination of the cards dealt. The card dealt first refers to gender. For example, if the first card dealt to the client is red, the client is a female, and if the card is blue, the client is a male. The second card refers to height. If the second card dealt is a club, the client is taller than 6' 6". If the second card is a heart, the client is 6' tall. A diamond indicates that the client is 5' 2" tall, and a spade indicates that the client is under 5' 2" tall. The third card indicates age. This is determined by totaling the amount on the face cards. For example, an ace = 1 point, a king = 10, a queen = 10, a jack = 10. If the card is a 2, 3, 4, 5, 6, 7, 8, 9, or 10, the value is the face value on the card (e.g., 2 = 2 points, 9 = 9 points). If the total points are an odd number, the client is 39 years of age or younger. If the total is an even number, the client is 40 years or older.

The fourth category in the profile is that of physical challenge. If the rank of the fourth card dealt to the client is an ace, king, or queen, the person has a debilitating long-term disease that causes physical impairment, such as multiple sclerosis or cerebral palsy. If the rank of the card is a jack or 10, the client has a weight issue. If the rank of the card is 9, 8, or 7, the client has a physical appearance issue. If the rank of the card is 6, 5, or 4, the client has an eating issue, and if the rank of the card is 3 or 2, the client has a fashion issue.

The counselor discusses the profiles. For example, after the profile is obtained from the cards that have been dealt, the counselor may ask the client the following questions as if the client fit that profile:

1. What do you think about the profile you obtained?
2. Based on the profile, what do you think is the most positive aspect of your life?
3. What is the least positive aspect of your life ?
4. What is your great hope for the world?

5. If you could change one of the cards you were dealt, which card would it be? Explain.

Interventions for Specific Problems

Self-Esteem

Low self-esteem is a prevalent problem in children and adolescents. In a child's environment, low self-esteem can be debilitating because it contributes to violence, low academic performance, substance abuse, and teenage pregnancy. In addition, low self-esteem contributes to adolescent suicide, which is the second leading killer of adolescents, following accidents (Bracken, 1996). Parents and other adults sometimes inadvertently foster low self-esteem by putting too much emphasis on school performance or peer relationships. There are many techniques, such as the following, that assist in building self-esteem.

Accomplishments

The counselor asks the client to make a list of the client's accomplishments for the day. First the client is to list the big items, then the medium items, and finally the small items. The counselor should help the client put the spotlight on what *was* accomplished and have the client acknowledge each accomplishment as a success (Carter–Scott, 1989).

How To Be, How Not To Be

The counselor asks the client to title one piece of paper "How To Be" and another "How Not To Be." The client will have about 10 minutes to list on the papers everything he or she can remember that significant adults (parents, teachers) have told him or her about how to behave. When the client has completed the lists, the counselor discusses what he or she has been taught, to determine if the child is dwelling on negatives and mistakes. The counselor discusses the positives and successes from the lists and stresses the need to put more energy into success than failure (Frey & Carlock, 1989).

Magic Box

In the Magic Box activity, the counselor asks the client to place a mirror in any type of box so it will reflect the face of whomever looks inside. The counselor says to the client, "I have a magic box that will show anyone who looks inside the most important person in the world." Then the counselor asks the client who he or she thinks is the most important person in the world and invites the client to look inside the box. After the client looks into the box, the counselor comments on the client's reaction and asks the client what he or she thought when seeing himself or herself. The counselor explains that the box is valuable because it allows the client to see himself or herself as a special person (Canfield & Wells, 1976).

USA

For this USA technique the counselor labels a paper bag "USA" and places inside it five strips of paper, each with one of the following terms written on it: school performance, peer relationships, sports, music/drama, jobs or chores, son or daughter. When the client discusses his or her failures, the counselor hands the client the paper bag. The counselor introduces the concept of unconditional self-acceptance, which means accepting yourself as a worthwhile person and not rating yourself as either "all good" or "all bad." The client is invited to open the bag, take out the strips of paper, and rate himself or herself 1 (low) to 5 (high) in each area. The counselor encourages the client to think about performance in these areas over time, rather than one or two isolated incidents. The client is encouraged to share the ratings, and the counselor emphasizes that all of these dimensions contribute to who he or she is and that what he or she may judge as poor in one area does not make him or her a bad person, that we are all people who perform better in some areas than others and it is important to accept ourselves unconditionally with strong and weak points (Vernon, 2002).

Positive Mantra

The counselor asks the client to close his or her eyes and repeat the following sentence: "No matter what you say or do to me, I'm still a worthwhile person." Although the Positive Mantra exercise seems simple, it can have a profound impact when done repeatedly. Each time the client begins the sentence, the counselor asks him or her to imagine the face of someone who has put him or her down in the past. The counselor instructs the client to stick out his or her chin and repeat the sentence in a strong, convincing voice. After the client has become familiar and comfortable with the sentence, the counselor interjects statements such as, "You're stupid . . . ugly . . . lazy" (whatever the client says was directed to him or her), while the client responds with, "No matter what you say or do to me, I'm still a worthwhile person" (Canfield & Wells, 1976).

Lifeboat

The Lifeboat game can be used in individual or group counseling. The counselor tells the client that he or she is in a lifeboat and the lifeboat cannot handle that many people at a time. Therefore, to avoid sinking, someone must leave the boat. The counselor asks the client to discuss the unique talents he or she has to justify why he or she should remain in the boat. This exercise is valuable in helping the client recognize his or her unique contributions and in bolstering self-esteem, especially with older children and adolescents.

Pride Line

In the Pride Line activity, the counselor makes a positive statement about a specific area of the client's behavior. For example, the counselor might say, "I'd like you to tell me something about your free time that you're proud of." Then the counselor instructs the client to say, "I'm proud that I . . . ." Specific behavioral areas that might be highlighted include homework, schoolwork, sports, music, something the client owns, a habit, an accomplishment, or something the client has done for someone else. For example, if a client says she is proud of going to basketball practice every day, the counselor talks to her about what an accomplishment this is, and that she should be proud of this accomplishment.

What If

The counselor asks the client What If questions: "What if your bike could talk? What do you think it would say about you?" The "talking item" could be a toothbrush, a bed, a dog, a TV, a school desk, a coat, or anything the child might recognize. Through the use of projection, this activity allows the client to become aware of his or her feelings about self. An alternative technique is to substitute people in the client's life for the objects. Whether this alternative can be used effectively depends on how trusting and open the client is and on the strength of the therapeutic relationship between the counselor and the client.

Anger and Aggression

Children and adolescents often have trouble finding acceptable ways to express negative emotions and behaviors. Inappropriate expression of anger often results in discipline problems and difficulties with interpersonal relationships. The following techniques are helpful in working with children and adolescents who have problems with anger and aggression.

Tear It Up

The counselor gives clients something they can tear up, such as old telephone books, magazines, or newspapers. The counselor instructs the client to verbalize angry thoughts and feelings as they Tear It Up. As an example, the client might verbalize anger about having a conflict with a peer while he is tearing up the phone book.

Nerf Balls

The counselor gives the client several Nerf balls to throw across the room. Small objects that will do no damage (rubber balls, plastic figures, beanbags) may be substituted. This exercise allows the client to externalize anger in a safe way and at the same time attach a physical action to the feeling. For example, the client might think of several things that make her angry and then throw the ball across the room (yard).

Punch It Out

Clients can rechannel anger and aggression by hitting, punching, or kicking a pillow or a punching bag. Punch It Out provides an acceptable way of releasing the pent-up anger. It is helpful to point out to clients that when they are angry, they often have "hot thoughts" (thoughts that trigger the anger). After they have calmed down, the counselor helps them identify "cool thoughts" (thoughts that aren't as upsetting). The counselor helps them make a plan to think cool thoughts when they begin to get angry.

Parallels with Animals

Parallels with Animals is a good activity for young children who are unable to display their anger. For example, the counselor could ask, "How does a dog act when it is angry?" Then the counselor growls and barks like a dog and asks the child to join in. Other animals that might be used are bears, tigers, lions, and cats. This technique also may be used with other emotions such as happiness, sadness, and loneliness.

Reframing

When a client says, "I hate my mom because she won't let me do the things I like," ask the client to reframe the statement into an "I love" statement such as, "I love my mom because she cares enough to set limits." Reframing can be applied to self-concept statements as well. For example, "I'm too lazy to get my homework done" can be reframed into, "I get so involved in interesting things that I choose to do that I sometimes forget my homework."

Stress and Anxiety

Stress is triggered by various sources, some of the most frequent of which involve school problems, family problems, and personal problems. To help clients reduce stress, the counselor must identify the areas that are causing them to be anxious. Once the stressors have been identified, relaxation exercises and paradoxical techniques may be helpful in reducing the stress and anxiety. Some relaxation and paradoxical techniques are as follows.

Basic Relaxation

The counselor instructs the client to close his or her eyes. The counselor says, "Begin to relax by breathing evenly and slowly. Think of your feet. Feel your feet as they begin to relax. Ignore any worries, anxieties, or thoughts that come to you, and concentrate on keeping your breathing even and slow. Now think of your legs. Feel your legs relax." The counselor continues through the trunk of the body, back, arms, neck, and head. After about 10 minutes, the counselor leads the client back to the counseling room by saying, "Now that you have relaxed, sit quietly for a moment. Now open your eyes." This technique may be used to induce meditation by having the client repeat a meaningless word again and again (Thompson, 1996).

Special Place Relaxation

The counselor asks the client to imagine a special place that belongs only to him or her. The counselor says, "Imagine being in that place that is yours. Tell me what you see around you." After the client describes the special place, the counselor asks the client to describe his or her feelings about the place. Then the counselor discusses how the special place helps him or her relax and points out that the client may "go there" when the stress level gets uncomfortable. If the client has trouble imagining a special place, the counselor might suggest a quiet lake, the mountains, or floating on clouds (St. Denis, Orlick, & McCaffrey, 1996).

Paradoxical Intervention (adapted from Thompson, 1996)

The counselor might consider using the Exaggeration technique with clients who worry excessively. The counselor asks the client to exaggerate a thought or behavior that is disruptive and instructs him or her to set aside a specific time each day to worry about everything. For example, the counselor might get the client to agree to write down daily worries that arise and revisit them at 5:00 p.m. every day. Often, when 5:00 p.m. arrives, the problem is no longer a major concern.

For clients who fear speaking out in class, ask them to sit in the back of the room and say nothing at all. By exaggerating the behavior, clients are confronted with how they react in certain situations and the consequences of that behavior.

Grief and Loss

When someone significant in their life dies or when they experience a loss such as divorce or moving, children and adolescents may feel abandoned, angry, sad, or guilty. For most young people these feelings are confusing and disturbing. To help clients deal with grief and loss, the counselor helps them identify and try to deal with their feelings. Interventions that work well with grieving children and adolescents include bibliotherapy, music, art, writing poetry, and identifying and resolving unfinished business through journaling. Additional techniques include the following.

Saying Good-Bye

The counselor asks the client if he or she would like to tell anything to the person who is gone. If the client is unable to think of anything to say, the counselor might consider a short story about death (divorce, moving, etc.). If the client is unable to verbalize his or her feelings, the counselor might consider using the *empty chair* technique described earlier in this chapter (Thompson, 1996).

Letter Writing

The counselor invites the client to write a letter to the person who has died (moved, left), describing what he or she misses the most about that person and how life is different without him or her. The counselor informs the client that he or she has the choice of whether to share the letter with the counselor or anyone else (Thompson, 1996).

Creating a Tape

The counselor invites the client to compile a tape of songs that were especially meaningful to the person who left or died, or songs the client thinks this person would have enjoyed. For example, if a child's grandmother dies, the child might create a tape of songs that were a part of the generation in which the grandmother lived. The counselor then might talk with the client about the songs and what the songs meant or might have meant to the grandmother. The client may or may not choose to share the tape (Schoen, personal communication, March 18, 1998).

Making a Collage

The counselor encourages the client to collect pictures or small memorabilia representing the person who left or died, and use these materials to make a collage of memories (Vernon, 1997). For instance, if a child has fond memories of her uncle taking her to the circus, the child might make a collage of pictures that depict the circus. The counselor then discusses with the client how the visit to the circus made her happy and how these memories provide a source of comfort to her.

Summary

The counselor can call upon a wide spectrum of therapeutic techniques and interventions in the areas of art, bibliotherapy, guided imagery, games, music, puppets, role-play/drama, storytelling, and therapeutic writing. In addition, interventions can be used with specific problem areas, including low self-esteem, anger and aggression, stress and anxiety, and grief and loss. Although the techniques and interventions discussed here are directed mainly to children and adolescents in individual counseling, most may be adapted for use in group settings.

Familiarity with a variety of interventions and techniques allows the counselor to select those that most closely match the child's or adolescent's developmental level. Counselors working with elementary school children should avoid interventions or techniques that are too difficult, too complex, or too advanced for the age group with which they are working. The opposite is also true: Using techniques with adolescents that are appropriate for young children may offend or bore adolescents. At one end of the continuum, paradoxical interventions or techniques that depend on writing and verbal skills might well be too complex for young children and will merely confuse them. At the other end of the continuum, board games might not be appropriate for some adolescents.

Counselors must recognize that some children and adolescents are responsive to counseling and others are reluctant and hostile to counseling. Some require innovative techniques that also provide a means of deepening understanding, increasing affective awareness, and gaining insight into the client's personal world. If the children and adolescents enjoy these activities, it facilitates their ability to engage in counseling and resolve their problems.

References

Akande, A., Akande, B., & Odewale, F. (1994). Putting the self back in the child: An African perspective. *Early Child Development and Care, 105,* 103–115.

Atkinson, D. (2001). The student's workbook for exploring the spiritual journey. *American Journal of Health Education, 32*(2), 112–115.

Allan, J. (1988). Serial drawing: A Jungian approach with children. In C. E. Schaefer (Ed.), *Innovative interventions in child and adolescent therapy* (pp. 98–132). New York: Wiley.

Bowman, R. (1985). *Kid songs: Music for counseling children.* Unpublished manuscript, Department of Educational Psychology, University of South Carolina, Columbia.

Bowman, R. (1995). Using metaphors as tools for counseling children. *Elementary School Guidance and Counseling, 29,* 206–216.

Bracken, B. A. (Ed.) (1996). *Handbook of self concept: Developmental, social, and clinical considerations.* Oxford, England: John Wiley.

Brand, A. G. (1987). Writing as counseling. *Elementary School Guidance and Counseling, 21,* 266–275.

Bromfield, R. (1995). The use of puppets in play therapy. *Child and Adolescent Social Work Journal, 12*(6), 435–444.

Canfield, J., & Wells, H. C. (1976). *100 ways to enhance self-concept in the classroom: A handbook for teachers and parents.* Boston: Allyn & Bacon.

Carter, R. (1998). The selection and use of puppets in counseling. *Professional School Counseling, 1,* 50–53.

Carter–Scott, R. (1989). *Negaholics.* New York: Fawcett.

Cattanach, A. (1997). *Children's stories in play therapy.* London: Jessica Kingsley Publishers.

Chapman, L. M., Morabito, D., Ladakakos, C., Schreier, H., & Knudson, M. (2001). The effectiveness of art. Interventions in reducing post-traumatic stress disorder symptoms in pediatric trauma patients. *Art Therapy: Journal of the American Art Therapy Association, 18,* 100–104.

Chesner, A., & Hahn, H. (Eds.) (2002). *Creative advances in group work.* Philadelphia: Kingsley.

Childswork, Childsplay. (1998). King of Prussia, PA: Center for Applied Psychology. (resource catalog)

Dalley, T. (1990). Images and integration: Art therapy in a multi-cultural school. In C. Case & T. Dalley (Eds.), *Working with children in art therapy* (pp. 161–198). London: Tavistock/Routledge.

Edwards, C., & Springate, K. (1995). Encouraging creativity in childhood classrooms. *Dimension of Early Childhood, 22,* 9–12.

Frey, D. E. (1986). Communication boardgames with children. In C. E. Schaefer & S. E. Reid (Eds.). *Game play: Therapeutic use of childhood games* (pp. 21–39). New York: Wiley.

Frey, D., & Carlock, C. J. (1989). *Enhancing self-esteem* (2nd ed.). Muncie, IN: Accelerated Development.

Friedberg, R. D. (1986). Cognitive-behavioral games and workbooks: Tips for school counselors. *Elementary School Guidance and Counseling, 31,* 11–19.

Frostig, K., & Essex, M. (1998). *Expressive arts therapies in schools: A supervision and program development guide.* Springfield, IL: Thomas.

Gardner, R. A. (1979). Mutual storytelling technique. In C. E. Schaefer (Ed.), *The therapeutic use of child's play* (pp. 313–321). New York: Jason Aronson.

Gladding, S. (1992). *Counseling as an art: The creative arts in counseling.* Alexandria, VA: American Counseling Association.

Gladding, S. (1995). Creativity in counseling. *Counseling and Human Development, 28,* 1–12.

Gladding, S. (1998). *Counseling as art: The creative arts in counseling (2nd ed.).* Alexandria, VA: The American Counseling Association.

Gumaer, J. (1984). *Counseling and therapy for children.* New York: Free Press.

Hackney, H. L., & Cormier, L. S. (1996). *The professional counselor: A process guide to helping* (3rd ed.). Boston: Allyn & Bacon.

Hammond, L. C., & Gantt, L. (1998). Using art in counseling. *American Journal of Art Therapy, 38,* 20–26.

Henderson, S. J. (1999). The use of animal imagery in counseling. *American Journal of Art Therapy, 38,* 20–26.

Hendricks, B. (2000). A study of the use of music therapy techniques in a group for the treatment of adolescent depression. *Dissertation Abstracts International, 62,* 107.

Hendricks, B., Bradley, L. J., Robinson, B., & Davis, K. (1997). Using music techniques to treat adolescent depression. *Journal of Humanistic Education and Counseling, 38,* 39–46.

Irwin, E. (1991). Drama: The play's the thing. *Elementary School Guidance and Counseling, 21,* 276–283.

Jackson, N. F., Jackson, D. A., & Monroe, C. (2002). *Getting along with others: Teaching social effectiveness to children.* Champaign, IL: Research Press.

Jackson, T. (1995). *Activities that teach.* Salt Lake City: Red Rock Publishing.

Jackson, T. (2000). *Still more activities that teach.* Salt Lake City: Red Rock Publishing.

Jensen, K. L. (2001). The effects of selected classical music on self-disclosure. *Journal of Music Therapy, 38,* 2–27.

Johnson, S. (1997). The use of art and play therapy with victims of sexual abuse: A review of the literature. *Family Therapy, 24,* 101–113.

Kottman, T., & Skyles, K. (1990). The mutual storytelling technique: An Adlerian application in child therapy. *Journal of Individual Psychology, 46,* 148–156.

Kwiatkowska, H. (2001). Family art therapy: Experiments with new techniques. *American Journal of Art Therapy, 40,* 27–39.

Lev–Wiesel, R., & Daphna–Tekoha, S. (2000). The self-revelation through color technique: Understanding client's relationships with significant others through the use of color. *American Journal of Art Therapy, 39,* 35–41.

Miles, R. (1993). I've got a song to sing. *Elementary School Counseling and Guidance, 28,* 71–75.

Moses, M. S. (2002). *Embracing race: Why we need race-conscious education policy.* Williston, VT: Teachers College Press.

Myrick, R. E., & Myrick, L. S. (1993). Guided imagery: From mystical to practical. *Elementary School Guidance and Counseling, 28,* 62–70.

Newcomb, N. S. (1994). Music: A powerful resource for the elementary school counselor. *Elementary School Guidance and Counseling, 29,* 150–155.

Nickerson, E. T. (1983). Art as a therapeutic medium. In C. E. Schaefer & K. J. O'Connor (Eds.), *Handbook of Play Therapy* (pp. 251–258). New York: Wiley.

Nickerson, E. T., & O'Laughlin, K. S. (1983). The therapeutic use of games. In C. E. Schaefer & K. J. O'Connor (Eds.), *Handbook of play therapy* (pp. 234–250). New York: Wiley.

Nugent, S. A. (2000). Perfectionism: Its manifestations and classroom based interventions. *Journal of Secondary Gifted Education, 11,* 215–221.

O'Connor, K. J. (1983). The color-your-life technique. In C. E. Schaefer & K. J. O'Connor (Eds.), *Handbook of play therapy* (pp. 251–258). New York: Wiley.

Okun, B. F. (1987). *Effective helping, interviewing and counseling techniques (3rd ed.).* Pacific Grove, CA: Brooks/Cole.

Omizo, M. M., Omizo, S. A., & Kitaoka, S. K. (1998). Guided affective and cognitive imagery to enhance self-esteem among Hawaiian children. *Journal of Multicultural Counseling and Development, 26,* 52–62.

Pardeck, J. (1995). Bibliotherapy: Using books to help children deal with problems. *Early Child Development and Care, 106,* 75–90.

Quackenbush, R. L. (1991). The prescription of self help books by psychologists: A bibliography of selected bibliotherapy resources. *Psychotherapy, 28,* 671–677.

Rubin, J. A. (1988). Art counseling: An alternative. *Elementary School Guidance and Counseling, 22,* 180–185.

Schumacher, R. B., Wantz, R. A., & Taricone, P. E. (1995). Constructing and using interactive workbooks to promote therapeutic goals. *Elementary School Guidance and Counseling, 29,* 303–309.

Skovholt, T. M., Morgan, J. L., & Negron–Cunningham, H. (1989). Mental imagery in career counseling and life planning: A review of research and intervention methods. *Journal of Counseling and Development, 67,* 287–292.

Sontag, M. (2001). Art as an evaluative tool: A pilot study. *Art Therapy: Journal of the American Association of Art Therapy, 18,* 37–43.

St. Denis, T. M., Orlick, I., & McCaffrey, W. (1996). Positive perspectives: Interventions with fourth grade children. *Elementary School Guidance and Counseling, 31,* 52–63.

Thompson, R. A. (1996). *Counseling techniques: Improving relationships with others, ourselves, our families, and our environment.* Philadelphia: Taylor and Frances.

Vernon, A. (1989). *Thinking, feeling and behaving for children: An emotional education curriculum.* Champaign, IL: Research Press.

Vernon, A. (1997). Special approaches to counseling. In D. Capuzzi & D. Gross (Eds.), *Introduction to the counseling profession* (2nd ed., pp. 235–254). Needham Heights, MA: Allyn & Bacon.

Vernon, A. (1998a). *The Passport program: A journey through emotional, social, cognitive, and self development, grades 1–5.* Champaign, IL: Research Press.

Vernon, A. (1998b). *The Passport program. A journey through emotional, social, cognitive, and self-development, grades 6–8.* Champaign, IL: Research Press.

Vernon, A. (1998c). *The Passport program: A journey through emotional, social, cognitive, and self-development, grades 9–12.* Champaign, IL: Research Press.

Vernon, A. (2002). *What works with children and adolescents: A handbook of individual counseling techniques.* Champaign, IL: Research Press.

Webb, N. B. (1999). *Play therapy with children in crisis: Individual, group, and family treatment.* New York: Guilford.

Witmer, J. M., & Young, M. E. (1985). The silent partner: Uses of imagery in counseling. *Journal of Counseling and Development, 64,* 187–190.

Witmer, J. M., & Young, M. E. (1987). Imagery in counseling. *Elementary School Guidance and Counseling, 22,* 5–16.

Chapter 4

Play Therapy

Terry Kottman

Play therapy is an approach to counseling young children in which the counselor uses toys and play as the primary vehicle for communication. The rationale for using toys and play as the modality of communication stems from the belief that young children (under the age of 12)

> have relatively limited ability to verbalize their feelings and thoughts and to use abstract verbal reasoning. Most of them lack the ability to come into a counseling session, sit down, and use words to tell the therapist about their problems. . . . Children can come into sessions and use toys, art, stories, and other playful tools to communicate with the therapist. (Kottman, 2001, p. 4)

Because play is the natural language of young children, it can be used as a modality for working out problems and communicating with others. This makes play therapy an essential method for counseling children younger than 12 years of age (Thompson & Rudolph, 2000). This chapter presents parameters for determining whether play therapy approaches are appropriate for clients, goals for the play therapy process, and descriptions of how to set up an "ideal" play therapy space and how to choose toys and play materials that can be therapeutic to children. The various theoretical approaches to play therapy will give the reader an understanding of the various styles this counseling approach can take.

Appropriate Clients for Play Therapy

Although some play therapists work with adults (Frey, 1993; Ledyard, 1999; Peyton, 1986), most play therapy clients are children between the ages of 3 and 12. When working with older elementary-age children, preadolescents, and young teens, the counselor might wish to ask whether the client would be more comfortable sitting and discussing his or her situation or playing with toys. The counselor can extend the usual age range of play therapy by adding toys aimed at older children, such as craft supplies, carpentry tools, office supplies and equipment, and more complex games or games designed for specific therapeutic interventions (James, 1997; Kottman, 2001; Kottman, Strother, & Deniger, 1987).

Several syntheses of play therapy research (Bratton & Ray, 2000; LeBlanc & Ritchie, 1999; Ray, Bratton, Rhine, & Jones, 2001) have provided support for the effectiveness of play therapy as a therapeutic intervention with many different presenting problems. The professional literature includes many anecdotal reports of the therapeutic benefits of the approach. These reports support the efficacy of play therapy as an intervention with children and adolescents who exhibit the following behavioral or emotional difficulties: aggressive, acting-out behavior (Fischetti, 2001; Johnson & Clark, 2001; Kottman, 1993; Smith & Herman, 1994); attachment disorder (Benedict & Mongoven, 1997; Jernberg & Booth, 1999); attention deficit-hyperactivity disorder (Kaduson, 1997; Reddy, Spencer, Hall, & Rubel, 2001); conduct disorders and severe behavior disorders (Cabe, 1997; O'Connor, 1993; Reid, 1993); depression (Briesmeister, 1997); enuresis and/or encopresis (Briesmeister, 1997; Cuddy–Casey, 1997); specific fears and phobias, such as fear of hospitalization or separation anxiety (Kottman, 2002; Knell, 2000; Lyness–Richard, 1997); and selective mutism (Barlow, Strother, & Landreth, 1986; Cook, 1997; Knell, 1993b).

The professional literature also contains anecdotal and empirical support for the idea that play therapy can be helpful to children who are struggling with life circumstances of: abuse and/or neglect (Allan & Lawton–Speert, 1993; Costas & Landreth, 1999; Doyle & Stoop, 1999; Hall, 1997; Lovatt, 1999; Pelcovitz, 1999; Strand, 1999; Tonning, 1999; Tyndall–Lind, 1999; Van de Putte, 1995); adoption

(Kottman, 1997); divorce of parents (Cangelosi, 1997; Robinson, 1999); family violence (Nisivoccia & Lynn, 1999; Tyndall–Lind, Landreth, & Giordano, 2001; VanFleet, Lilly, & Kaduson, 1999; Webb, 1999); grief issues (Bluestone, 1999; LeVieux, 1994; Perry, 1993; Tait & Depta, 1994); hospitalization (Kaplan, 1999; Webb, 1995); chronic or terminal illness (Boley, Ammen, O'Connor, & Miller, 1996; Boley, Peterson, Miller, & Ammen, 1996; Goodman, 1999; Jones & Landreth, 2002; Kaplan, 1999; Ridder, 1999; VanFleet, 2000); and severe trauma, such as caused by war, earthquakes, car wrecks, and kidnapping (Fornari, 1999; Joyner, 1991; Shelby, 1997; Shen, 2002; Webb, 1999; Williams–Gray, 1999).

When deciding whether a specific client is appropriate for play therapy interventions, the play therapist should consider the following factors related to the child and his or her issues (Anderson & Richards, 1995):

1. Can this child tolerate, form, and utilize a relationship with an adult?
2. Can this child tolerate and accept a protective environment?
3. Does this child have the capacity to learn new methods of dealing with the presenting problem?
4. Does this child have the capacity for insight into his or her behavior and motivation?
5. Does this child have the capacity for insight into the behavior and motivation of others?
6. Does this child have the capacity for sufficient attention and/or cognitive organization to engage in therapeutic activities?
7. Is play therapy the most effective and efficient way to address this child's problems?

In addition, Anderson and Richards (1995) recommended that the play therapist consider the following questions related to his or her own situation and skills:

1. Do I have the necessary skills to work with this child? Is consultation or supervision available if I need it?
2. Is my practice setting devoid of barriers (e.g., not enough space, funding issues, inadequate length of treatment allowed) that might interfere with effective treatment of this child?
3. If effective therapy for this child will involve working with other professionals, can I work within the necessary framework?
4. Is my energy or stress level such that I can fully commit to working with this child?

If the answers to all of these questions are yes and the counselor has no unresolved personal issues that will have a negative impact on his or her ability to work with this child and his or her family, he or she may decide to work with the child. At that point, the counselor must explain to the child's parent(s) and/or teachers what play therapy is and how it can be helpful. As part of this process, the counselor should work with the parent(s) and teachers on the specific goals for the play therapy process.

Counselors have to be able to work with children from diverse cultures (Coleman, Parmer, & Barker, 1993; Glover, 2001; Kao & Landreth, 2001; Kottman, 2001; Schaefer, 1998). In working with multicultural populations in play therapy, counselors must (a) include materials and toys that convey respect for and understanding of a variety of different cultures and ethnic groups; (b) understand the role of play, art, and storytelling in a variety of different cultures and ethnic groups; (c) be aware of the values, customs, beliefs, and traditions of a child's culture; (d) seek to become more knowledgeable about other cultures and ethnic groups; and (e) work to find a "match" between a child's cultural background and the techniques used with that child in the play therapy process (Coleman et al., 1993).

Goals of Play Therapy

Many children who come to play therapy have a negative self-concept and little confidence in their own abilities. They frequently believe they are worthless. They may think they are unable to contribute anything positive to relationships and unable to take care of their own needs. One goal of play therapy is to build up children's sense of self-efficacy and competence by encouraging them to do things for themselves and make decisions for themselves in the playroom. By showing genuine concern, empathic understanding, and consistent positive regard, the play therapist can further counteract the negative images about self and others that children have incorporated into their worldviews.

Most children who come to play therapy also have relatively weak problem-solving and decision-making skills. Another important goal in the play therapy process is to increase their abilities in these areas and to help the children learn to accept responsibility for their own behavior and decisions.

Typical goals of play therapy include the following:

1. Enhance the client's self-acceptance, self-confidence, and self-reliance.
2. Help the client learn more about himself or herself and others.
3. Help the client explore and express feelings.
4. Increase the client's ability to make self-enhancing decisions.
5. Provide situations in which the client can practice self-control and self-responsibility.
6. Help the client explore alternative perceptions of problem situations and difficult relationships.
7. Help the client learn and practice problem-solving skills and relationship-building skills.
8. Increase the client's "feeling vocabulary" and formation of emotional concepts.

In addition to these broad therapeutic goals, counselors may have set specific goals for a specific client that depend on the counselor's theoretical orientation and the client's presenting problem (Kottman, 2001).

Setting Up a Play Therapy Space

A counselor who wants to use play therapy as an intervention approach with children can do so no matter what kind of space is available. Landreth (1991) described an "ideal" space for play therapy, but even a small corner of a school cafeteria can work as long as others are not using it at the same time to ensure client confidentiality. The most important element of the play therapy setting is the counselor's personal feeling of being comfortable (James, 1997; Kottman, 2001, 2003). If the counselor feels safe, happy, and welcome in the space, so will the children with whom he or she works.

Certain factors, however, can contribute to having an optimal play therapy space. Landreth (1991) described an "ideal" play room as:

1. Measuring approximately 12 feet by 15 feet, with an area of between 150 and 200 square feet. This size allows a child room to move freely but is still small enough so the child will not feel overwhelmed or be able to stray too far from the play therapist.
2. Having privacy so the children can feel comfortable revealing information and feelings without worrying about others overhearing them.
3. Having washable wall coverings and vinyl floor coverings so children can make messes without worrying or feeling guilty.
4. Having many shelves for storing toys and play materials within easy reach of children.
5. Having shelves that are securely attached to the walls so no one can accidentally or purposefully topple them.
6. Containing a small sink with cold running water.
7. Having some countertop space or a child-size desk with a storage area for artwork.
8. Having a cabinet for storing materials such as paint, clay, and extra paper.
9. Having a marker board or chalkboard (either attached to a wall or propped on an easel).
10. Having a small bathroom attached to the main room.
11. Being fitted with acoustical ceiling tiles to reduce noise.
12. Having wood or molded plastic furniture designed to accommodate children. It is also helpful to have some furniture designed for the counselor, parents, and teachers.
13. Having a one-way mirror and equipment for observing and videotaping sessions.
14. Being located in a place where noise during the session will not present a major problem to others in the building.

Toy Selection and Arrangement

Landreth (1991) suggested that the toys and play materials selected for play therapy should:

■ Allow for a broad range of emotional and creative expression by children
■ Capture the interest of children in some way
■ Facilitate verbal and nonverbal investigation and expression by children
■ Encourage mastery experiences for children.

He also stressed that the toys be sturdy and safe. The toys and play materials chosen should help children:

■ Establish positive relationships with the counselor (and with other children in groups)
■ Express a wide range of feelings
■ Explore and/or reenact actual experiences and relationships
■ Test limits
■ Increase self-control
■ Enhance understanding of self and others
■ Improve self–image

There are many different philosophies of toy selection, based on different theoretical orientations. Kottman (2001, 2003) provided a relatively generic list of toys and play materials that a counselor could use to stock an "ideal" playroom. She suggested that the playroom should have toys that represent each of five distinct categories:

1. Family/nurturing toys
2. Scary toys
3. Aggressive toys
4. Expressive toys
5. Pretend/fantasy toys.

Children can use the family/nurturing toys to build a relationship with the counselor and to explore family relationships. They also can use these toys to represent real-life experiences. Family/nurturing toys include, among others, a dollhouse and dolls of different ethnicities (with removable clothing and bendable bodies if possible), baby clothes, a cradle, animal families, a warm soft blanket, people puppets, stuffed toys, sand in a sandbox, several pots and pans, dishes and dinnerware, empty food containers, and play kitchen appliances (such as a sink and a stove).

Scary toys are included in the playroom to allow children to express their fears and learn to cope with them. These toys can be plastic or rubber snakes, rats, monsters, dinosaurs, sharks, insects, dragons, alligators, and "fierce" animal puppets (such as wolf, bear, and alligator puppets).

The purpose of aggressive toys is to encourage children to express anger and aggression symbolically, to give them symbolic means to protect themselves from objects of fear, and to explore their need for control in various situations. These toys could include a bop bag, toy weapons (such as play guns, swords, and knives), toy soldiers and military vehicles, small pillows for pillow fights, foam bats, plastic shields, and handcuffs.

While playing with expressive toys, children can give voice to their feelings, enhance their sense of mastery, practice problem-solving skills, and express their creativity. These materials could include an easel and paints, watercolors, crayons, markers, glue, newsprint, Play-Doh® or clay, fingerpaints, scissors, tape, egg cartons, feathers, materials for making masks, and pipe cleaners.

The purpose of pretend/fantasy toys is to allow children to express their feelings, explore a wide range of roles, experiment with varied behaviors and attitudes, and act out real-life situations and relationships. These toys can include masks, costumes, magic wands, hats, jewelry, purses, a doctor kit, telephones, blocks and other building materials, people figures, zoo and farm animals, puppets and a puppet theater, a sandbox, trucks and construction equipment, kitchen appliances, pots, pans, dishes, dinnerware, and empty food containers.

Of course the playroom does not have to include all of these different toys. With one or two toys from each category, the counselor can provide an effective vehicle for communication. Children are highly creative, and they will make the toys they need if they don't see them in the room—by pretending one of the available toys is something else (e.g., a crayon can easily become a magic wand, a gun, or dinnerware) or by constructing them from play materials (e.g., making a doll or a dish from construction paper or pipe cleaners).

A number of authors have suggested that toys and play materials should be returned to approximately the same place after every session (e.g., James, 1997; Kottman, 2001, 2003; Landreth, 1991). This structured placement helps to establish that the play therapy setting is a place where the child can count on predictability and consistency. By arranging the toys and play materials by category (e.g., placing all family toys together), the counselor will make clean-up easier and will help children remember where to locate specific toys. Counselors who do not have stationary playrooms can accomplish the same consistent and predictable arrangement by placing the toys in a specific order on the floor or a table in the space that is currently the "playroom" (Kottman, 2001). Some play therapists pick up the toys after the child has left the playroom (Axline, 1969; Landreth, 1991); others work with the child to clean up the room before the end of the session, using the cleaning-up process as a time for continuing to build a collaborative partnership with the child (Kottman, 2003).

Basic Play Therapy Skills

Most play therapists, regardless of their theoretical orientation, use several generic, basic skills. These skills, described in the following sections, include tracking, restating content, reflecting feelings, returning responsibility to the child, using the child's metaphor, and limiting (Kottman, 2001).

Tracking

Tracking involves describing the child's behavior to the child to convey that what the child is doing is important. The ultimate purpose is to build a relationship with the child by communicating caring and a feeling of connection (Kottman, 2001).

When using tracking, the counselor should avoid labeling objects. An object that looks like a snake to the counselor can be a whip, a tightrope, a slingshot, or any of a number of other things to a child. The counselor has to keep the description of the behavior relatively vague. A behavior that looks like jumping off a chair to the counselor can, in the child's imagination, be leaping out of a burning building, parachuting out of an airplane, jumping over a river filled with poisonous snakes, or any of many other actions. By using pronouns such as "this," "that," "them," "it," and "those" instead of specific nouns, and by using vague descriptions such as "moving over there" and "going up and down" instead of specific verbs such as "jumping" or "flying," the counselor allows the child to project his or her own meaning on the toys and on the actions in the playroom.

Some children will impose their own vision of the world on things in the playroom despite the descriptions the counselor offers. Many others will simply agree with whatever the counselor says rather than asserting their own version of how things are, or they will disagree with whatever the counselor says rather than giving the appearance of complying with the counselor's version of how things are. In any case, children need to have their freedom for self-expression reinforced. Avoiding labeling is one means to that end.

The following interactions illustrate the skill of tracking:

Leonard:	(Picks up a mouse and has it hop up and down on the head of a cat.)
Mr. Hawkins:	"That one is moving up and down on the other one."
Leonard:	(Buries a snake underneath the sand.)
Mr. Hawkins:	"You put that under there."
Leonard:	(Rocks a doll.)
Mr. Hawkins:	"You're moving that back and forth."
Leonard:	(Picks up handcuffs and examines them.)
Mr. Hawkins:	"You're checking those out."
Leonard:	(Carefully arranges animal figures on the floor.)
Mr. Hawkins:	"You know just where you want to put those."

Restating Content

Restating content involves paraphrasing the child's verbalizations. Just as with tracking, its purpose is to build a relationship with the child (Kottman, 2001). By conveying to the child that what he or she has to say is important, the counselor conveys concern and understanding.

To avoid sounding like a parrot, the counselor must use his or her own words and intonations. But the counselor must use vocabulary that the child understands; otherwise, this strategy will not help the child to feel understood.

The following interactions illustrate the skill of restating content:

Steve:	(Starting to hit the bop bag.) "I'm going to hit him and beat him up."
Mrs. Barry:	"You really want to get him."
Steve:	"You seem like a nice person. Can I come in here every day?"
Mrs. Barry:	"You think I might be a person you can like, and you wish you could come here once a day."
Steve:	"I got an A on my math test, but I got an F on my spelling test."
Mrs. Barry:	"You did really well on your math test, but not so well on your spelling test."
Steve:	"We went to my grandma's house this weekend to visit her because she is sick."
Mrs. Barry:	"Your grandmother isn't feeling well, so you went to see her."

Reflecting Feelings

By reflecting the child's feelings and the child's feelings projected onto toys or objects in the playroom, the counselor can deepen the counselor–client relationship and at the same time help the child express and understand his or her emotions, learn more about interactions with others, and expand his or her affective vocabulary (Kottman, 2001). With words such as, "You seem kind of sad today," the counselor can reflect the child's feelings directly. By saying, "It seems like you're disappointed, Miss Kitty," or "The kitty seems really disappointed right now," the counselor can reflect the feelings of the toys and other objects in the playroom.

To help children learn to take responsibility for their own feelings, the counselor should avoid using the phrase "makes you feel." Instead, the counselor should simply state the feeling by saying, "You feel . . . ."

The counselor must watch for both the surface, obvious feelings and the underlying, deeper feelings (Kottman, 2001; Muro & Kottman, 1995). In play therapy, deeper feelings sometimes are expressed through the toys and other objects in the playroom. For example, watching a child play with a cat and mouse, a counselor may observe that at first the cat seemed happy that he could catch the mouse, but then he almost seemed disappointed that the mouse didn't run faster.

The counselor also should look for patterns and interactions between children's behavior in the playroom and information he or she has about situations outside the playroom. For example, when Sam comes into the playroom and kicks the toys, he might appear to be simply angry. The counselor, however, knows that Sam's dog died over the weekend and suspects that Sam also may be feeling sad and lonely. When reflecting deeper, less obvious emotions, the counselor should use a tentative formulation. By not imposing his or her own viewpoint on the child, the counselor reduces the possibility of evoking a defensive reaction.

When reflecting feelings, as at all other times, the counselor must adjust his or her vocabulary to the child's developmental level (Muro & Kottman, 1995). Most preschoolers, kindergarteners, and first-graders seem to recognize four main feeling states: sad, mad, glad, and scared. With these children, the counselor, at least initially, should usually use only these words and simple synonyms for them when reflecting feelings.

Children in second and third grades typically have a wider range of feeling vocabulary but still might not comprehend or express feelings that are more subtle. Sometimes children in these grades have a more extensive receptive vocabulary than expressive vocabulary. That is, they may understand words such as frustrated, disappointed, and jealous even though they might not use these words regularly. The counselor can work to expand the affective vocabulary of these children by using a variety of feeling words to describe more subtle affective states.

Some fourth-, fifth-, and sixth-graders have relatively sophisticated feeling vocabularies. With these children the counselor might decide to switch to "talk therapy" or use more structured activities and games rather than using play therapy.

The following interactions illustrate the skill of reflecting feelings:

Max:	(In an angry voice.) "I got into trouble again, and I can't go to the play with the rest of my class."
Ms. Lilja:	"Sounds like you're mad because you got into trouble. I'll bet you're feeling kind of disappointed about not getting to go to the theater with the other kids."
Max:	(Moving an airplane up and down, dive-bombing a cluster of soldiers.) "Hahahaha!! I got you. You can't ever hurt me again."
Ms. Lilja:	"He's excited that he got all of them. Sounds like he feels like he will be safe from now on."
Max:	(Using the dolls in the dollhouse, he has the parents yell at each other and at the children. He moves the smallest doll so it is lying underneath the bed.)
Ms. Lilja:	"Seems like it's kind of scary when those bigger ones yell and fight."

Max:	"This was really fun. Can I come again tomorrow? I like it in here a lot better than in my classroom."
Ms. Lilja:	"You sound really happy. It feels safe and fun in the playroom, and you wish you could come again tomorrow instead of going to class."

Returning Responsibility to the Child

Returning responsibility to the child is a play therapy strategy designed to increase children's self-reliance, self-confidence, and self-responsibility (Kottman, 2001; Landreth, 1991; Muro & Kottman, 1995). It also can help them practice decision making, give them a sense of accomplishment, and increase their feelings of mastery and control. The counselor can return responsibility for executing behaviors (e.g., "I think you know how to open the lid to the sandbox yourself,") or for making decisions (e.g., "You can decide what to paint").

In the playroom, children are capable of making most decisions that come up, so counselors usually should return the responsibility for making decisions back to the children. When returning responsibility to a child, however, the counselor has to consider whether the child is capable of actually accomplishing the task (Kottman, 2001, 2003; Muro & Kottman, 1995). Children can be discouraged if an adult tells them that they can do something that they truly cannot do. If the counselor is not sure whether the child can execute the behavior, he or she can suggest that they work as a team to accomplish the goal or can ask the child to tell the counselor "how to do it." With both strategies, the counselor lets the child control the execution and does not take responsibility for the behavior from the child.

Several different techniques can be used for returning responsibility to a child (Kottman, 2001). The counselor can use a direct approach—simply telling the child that he or she is capable of executing the behavior or making the choice. The counselor also can use a less direct approach, returning responsibility to the child by using (a) tracking, restatement of content, or reflection of feelings; (b) the child's metaphor; (c) minimal encouragers or ignoring the child's desire for assistance, or (d) the "Whisper Technique" (Landreth, 1984, personal communication). The following interactions illustrate these techniques.

Martina:	"Will you put this furniture in the dollhouse?" (asking for help with the execution of a behavior and with a decision)
Mr. Chuppi:	"I think you can do that for yourself." (direct response)
	"You want me to put the furniture in the dollhouse for you." (indirect response; restatement of content)
	"You sound worried that you might not put the doll furniture where it is supposed to go." (indirect response; reflection of feelings)

"Hmm. . . ." (indirect response; minimal encourager, ignores child's request)

(In a whisper.) "Where do you think this piece should go?" (indirect response; "Whisper Technique")

Martina: "What is this?" (asking for help with a decision)

Mr. Chuppi: "In here, it can be anything you want it to be." (direct response)

"I bet you can figure out what you want it to be." (direct response)

"Mmmmmmmm.... What could it be?" (indirect response; minimal encourager)

"You are curious about what that could be." (indirect response; reflection of feelings)

"You want me to tell you what that is." (indirect response; restatement of content)

Martina: (Using the mouse puppet, brings a pair of scissors and some yarn to the counselor and says in a squeaky voice.) "Make me some nice red hair." (asking for help in executing a behavior)

Mr. Chuppi: "Martina, I'll bet you can make the mouse some hair without any help from me." (direct response)

"Ms. Mouse, I think you can figure out how to make some nice red hair for yourself." (indirect response; using child's metaphor)

"Let's work together to make some hair for Ms. Mouse." (Whispers.) "What shall we do first to make her some hair?" (indirect response; "Whisper Technique")

(Not taking the scissors and the yarn.) "You want to hand those things to me because you want me to make some hair for the mouse." (indirect response; tracking)

Using the Child's Metaphor

Much of the communication in play therapy takes the form of metaphor, with the child expressing feelings, thoughts, and attitudes and indirectly telling the story of his or her situation and relationships through the words and actions of various toys (Kottman, 2001). Sometimes the counselor will be able to discern the "hidden" meaning in the play; at other times the meaning will be a mystery. The counselor's willingness to "use" the metaphor is much more important than his or her ability to interpret it. "Using a metaphor" means that the counselor tracks, restates content, reflects feelings, and returns responsibility through the child's story without imposing his or her own interpretation of the meaning of the story. The counselor must exercise self-restraint and avoid "breaking" the metaphor by going outside the story to the "real" world.

During the following interaction, the counselor uses the child's metaphor to track, restate content, reflect feelings, and return responsibility to the child:

Jake:	Brings a stuffed puppy to the counselor and puts it in her lap. "Woof, woof! I'm a puppy, and my name is Little Puppy."
Ms. Rohlf:	"Sounds like you want to tell me who you are, Little Puppy."
Jake:	Brings a big plastic dinosaur and puts it next to the puppy. Moving the dinosaur, Jake makes growling noises. He then takes Ms. Rohlf's hand and puts it over the puppy.
Ms. Rohlf:	"The dinosaur seems kind of fierce, Little Puppy. You look like you're feeling scared and wanting to find a safe place."
Jake:	Moves the puppy's head and front paws out from under the counselor's hand toward the dinosaur. The puppy barks at the dinosaur, and the dinosaur yelps and runs away. Jake laughs.
Ms. Rohlf:	"Woo! Even though you were kind of scared, Little Puppy, you came out and barked at that dinosaur to let him know you wanted him to go away. It worked. You took care of yourself."

Limiting

Limiting, or setting limits in the playroom, protects the child and the counselor from harm, increases the child's sense of self-control and self-responsibility, and enhances his or her sense of social responsibility (Ginott, 1959; Kottman, 2001, 2003; Landreth, 1991). Appropriate limits in play therapy are those intended to keep the child from (a) physically harming himself or herself, other children, and/or the counselor; (b) deliberately damaging the play therapy facility or play materials; (c) removing toys or play materials from the play therapy setting; (d) leaving the session before the scheduled time; and (e) staying in the session after the time limit has expired. Imposing other limits (e.g., not aiming the toy gun at the therapist, not pouring water into the sandbox, not jumping from the furniture onto the floor) depends on the individual counselor and his or her setting and clientele.

Counselors seldom come into the first session with a long list of rules outlining "appropriate" playroom behavior. Most counselors wait to set a limit until a child is about to break one of the playroom rules. In this way, the counselor can avoid inhibiting the timid, withdrawn child or challenging the acting-out child who likes to get into power struggles.

Many different strategies can be used for setting limits in play therapy (Kottman, 2001). One widely used method, developed by Ginott (1959), involves the following four steps:

1. Reflecting the child's wishes, desires, and feelings (e.g., "You're really mad and would like to shoot me with the dart gun.").
2. Stating the limit in a nonjudgmental manner, using a passive voice formulation (e.g., "I'm not for shooting at people.").

3. Redirecting the child to more appropriate behavior (e.g., "You can shoot the dart at the target or the big doll.").
4. Helping the child express any feelings of anger or resentment at being limited (e.g., "I can tell you're really mad that I told you I'm not for shooting at people.").

Another method of setting limits, described in Kottman (2003), involves engaging the child in redirecting his or her own inappropriate behavior. This process also has four steps:

1. Stating the limit in a nonjudgmental way that reflects the social reality of the play therapy setting (e.g., "It's against the playroom rules to shoot darts at people.").
2. Reflecting the child's feelings and making guesses about the purpose of his or her behavior (e.g., "You're feeling kind of mad at me, and you want to show me that I can't tell you what to do.").
3. Engaging the child in redirecting his or her behavior by asking for suggestions of more socially appropriate behavior choices (e.g., "I'll bet you can think of something you can shoot that won't be against the playroom rules."). In many cases, the child will come to an agreement with the counselor about appropriate behaviors and will abide by that agreement, and the counselor will have to take no further action. If the child chooses to break the agreement, however, the counselor would move to the fourth step.
4. Setting up logical consequences that the child can enforce (e.g., "We need to think of a consequence just in case you decide to shoot the dart at me again. What do you think would be a fair consequence?"). Consequences might be to lose the privilege to play with the toy, to have to sit quietly for several minutes, to lose the privilege to play with certain other playroom materials, or another logical consequence.

Theoretical Approaches to Play Therapy

The many different theoretical approaches to play therapy range on a continuum from nondirective to directive (Kottman, 2001). The following are brief descriptions of several selected approaches: child-centered play therapy, which represents the nondirective end of the continuum; Adlerian and cognitive–behavioral play therapy, both of which combine nondirective and directive elements and represent the middle of the continuum; and Theraplay, which represents the directive end of the continuum.

Child-Centered Play Therapy

In developing nondirective, child-centered play therapy, Virginia Axline (1947, 1969, 1971) applied the basic concepts of client-centered therapy (Rogers, 1959).

Axline (1969) delineated the following principles for practitioners of client-centered play therapy:

1. The therapist must build a warm, friendly, genuine relationship with the child, facilitating a strong therapeutic rapport.

2. He or she must be utterly accepting of the child and have no desire for the child to change.

3. The therapist must develop and maintain a permissive environment that encourages the child to feel free in exploring and expressing emotions.

4. The therapist must constantly attend to the child's feelings and reflect them in a way that encourages the child to gain insight and increase his or her self-understanding.

5. The therapist must always respect the child's ability to solve problems if the child has the opportunity and the necessary resources. Part of this process is remembering that the child must be completely responsible for decisions about whether and when to make changes.

6. The therapist must always follow the lead of the child in the play therapy process. The responsibility and privilege of leading the way belong solely to the child.

7. The therapist must be patient with the therapy process and never attempt to speed it up.

8. The therapist must set only those limits essential for connecting the play therapy to reality.

In the words of Landreth and Sweeney (1997), child-centered play therapy is

> a philosophy resulting in attitudes and behaviors for living one's life in relationships with children. It is both a basic philosophy of the innate human capacity of the child to strive toward growth and maturity and an attitude of deep and abiding belief in the child's ability to be constructively self-directing. (p. 17)

Practitioners have found that children's behavior in child-centered play therapy goes through five distinct phases (Landreth & Sweeney, 1997).

1. Children use play to express diffuse negative feelings.

2. Children use play to express ambivalent feelings, usually anxiety or hostility.

3. Children again express mostly negative feelings, but the focus has shifted to specific targets—parents, siblings, or the therapist.

4. Ambivalent feelings (positive and negative) resurface but now are targeted toward parents, siblings, the therapist, and others.

5. Positive feelings predominate, but the child expresses realistic negative attitudes in appropriate situations.

In child-centered play therapy, the counselor "maintains an active role in the process of play therapy, not in the sense of directing or managing the experience but by being directly involved and genuinely interested in all of the child's feelings, actions, and decisions" (Landreth, 1991, p. 99). The counselor's main function is to provide the child with the core conditions of unconditional positive regard, empathic understanding, and genuineness. Client-centered play therapists believe that by communicating acceptance and belief in the child, they can activate the child's innate capacity for solving problems and moving toward optimal living.

Child-centered play therapists depend on the skills of tracking, restating content, reflecting feelings, returning responsibility to the child, and setting limits. They avoid skills that lead the child in any way, including interpretation, design of therapeutic metaphors, bibliotherapy, and other more directive techniques.

Adlerian Play Therapy

In using Adlerian play therapy (Kottman, 1993, 1994, 1997, 2003), counselors combine the principles and strategies of Individual Psychology with the basic concepts and skills of play therapy. They conceptualize clients through Adlerian constructs and communicate with them through toys and play materials.

Adlerian play therapy has four phases (Kottman, 2003):

1. The counselor builds an egalitarian relationship with the child, using tracking, restating content, reflecting feelings, returning responsibility to the child, encouraging, limiting, answering questions, and cleaning the room together.
2. The counselor, using the play interaction, the child's metaphors, and art techniques, gains an understanding of the child's lifestyle and how the child sees himself or herself, others, and the world.
3. The counselor, based on hypotheses he or she has formulated from the information gathered in the second phase, helps the client gain insight into his or her lifestyle, using metaphors, stories, metacommunication, artwork, role-playing, and so forth.
4. The counselor provides reorientation and reeducation for the client, which may involve helping the child learn and practice new skills and attitudes.

In Adlerian play therapy, consultation with parents and teachers is essential. The process is parallel to the play therapy process. In the first phase, the counselor builds a relationship with the important adults in the child's life. During the second phase, the counselor explores the adults' lifestyles and their perception of the child's typical ways of interacting with others. Based on an understanding of the child and the adults in his or her life, during the third and fourth phases the counselor helps parents and teachers gain insight into the child's patterns and their own lifestyles and teaches parenting skills.

Cognitive–Behavioral Play Therapy

Cognitive–behavioral play therapy (CBPT), developed by Susan Knell (1993a, 1993b, 1994, 1997), is an approach to play therapy that combines cognitive and behavioral strategies within a play therapy delivery system. Using interventions derived from cognitive therapy and behavior therapy, cognitive-behavioral play therapists integrate play activities with verbal and nonverbal communication.

Knell (1994) delineated six specific principles essential to CBPT:

1. The counselor involves the child in the therapy through play. The child is an active partner in the therapeutic process.
2. The counselor examines the child's thoughts, feelings, fantasies, and environment. Rather than being client-focused, CBPT is problem-focused.
3. The counselor helps the child develop more adaptive thoughts and behaviors and more effective strategies for solving problems.
4. CBPT is structured, directive, and goal-oriented.
5. The counselor uses specific behavioral and cognitive interventions that have empirical support for efficacy with specific problems.
6. The counselor designs interventions using baseline and follow-up measurements of behavior to provide empirical support for treatment effectiveness.

Cognitive–behavioral play therapy has four stages (Knell, 1993a, 1994):

1. Assessment
2. Introduction/orientation to play therapy
3. A middle stage
4. Termination.

During the assessment, stage the counselor employs formal and informal instruments to gather baseline data about the child's current level of functioning, the child's development, the presenting problem, the attitude of the parent(s) and the child toward the presenting problem, and their understanding of it (Knell, 1994). As part of this process, the counselor may use parent report inventories, clinical interviews, play observation, cognitive/developmental scales, and projective assessment methods (Knell, 1993a, 1994).

In the next phase, the introduction/orientation to play therapy, the counselor gives the parent(s) an initial evaluation of the child based on the data gathered during the assessment stage, and then they collaborate on devising a treatment plan that includes outcome goals and treatment strategies (Knell, 1993a, 1994).

During the middle stage of CBPT, the counselor combines play activities and interactions with specific cognitive and behavioral intervention techniques (including modeling, role-playing, and behavioral contingency) to teach children more adaptive behaviors for dealing with specific situations, problems, issues, or stressors (Knell, 1993a, 1994). In addition, the counselor uses strategies that will help the child generalize his or her new skills to situations and settings in the "real" world. One of the main functions of the counselor during this phase is to compare the child's current functioning with his or her baseline functioning and assess the child's progress toward therapeutic goals.

During the termination stage, the counselor helps the child develop plans for coping with various situations after counseling ends. The counselor uses behavioral techniques to reinforce changes in the child's thinking, feeling, and behaving and encourages the child to practice strategies for generalizing the progress he or she has made in the playroom to other relationships.

Theraplay

As defined by Koller and Booth (1997), Theraplay is an engaging, playful treatment method

> modeled on the healthy interaction between parents and their children. It is an intensive, short-term approach that actively involves parents—first as observers and later as co-therapists. The goal is to enhance attachment, self-esteem, trust, and joyful engagement and to empower parents to continue, on their own, the health-promoting interactions of the treatment sessions. (p. 204)

Healthy parent-child interactions serve as the model for the directive Theraplay dimensions of structure, challenge, intrusion/engagement, and nurture. Play therapists following this approach use activities and materials that facilitate these dimensions to remedy problems in the attachment process that create intrapersonal and interpersonal struggles for children (Jernberg & Jernberg, 1993).

Counselors exhibit the dimension of structure by setting limits and clear rules for safety and by employing experiences that have a beginning, a middle, and an end (e.g., singing games) and activities designed to define body boundaries (Jernberg & Booth, 1999). The dimension of challenge is facilitated by, for example, helping the child take an age-appropriate risk to strengthen the child's sense of mastery and self-confidence (Jernberg & Booth, 1999). The counselor exhibits the dimension of intrusion/engagement when, for example, he or she engages the child in playful, spontaneous interactions to show the child that the world is fun and stimulating and that other people can be simultaneously exciting and trustworthy. To facilitate the nurture dimension, the counselor initiates interactions designed to soothe, calm, quiet, and reassure the child by meeting his or her early, unsatisfied emotional needs. Such interactions include feeding, making lotion handprints, swinging the child in a blanket, and so forth.

Theraplay is directive, intensive, and brief. Usually, the counselor meets first with the parents for an initial interview and assessment of the parent/child relationship, using the Marschak Interaction Method (MIM) (Marschak, 1960). They then meet again so the counselor can explain the Theraplay philosophy, begin to build rapport with the parents, give feedback from the initial assessment, and develop a treatment plan in collaboration with the parent(s). This session is followed by 8 to 12 Theraplay sessions involving the child and parents, lasting a half hour each (Koller, 1994; Koller & Booth, 1997).

In the standard arrangement for Theraplay work, each session has two different counselors. The Theraplay counselor works directly with the child, and the interpreting counselor works directly with the parents. During the entire 30 minutes of the first four Theraplay sessions and the first 15 minutes of each of the remaining sessions, the parents and the interpreting counselor observe the interactions of the child and the Theraplay counselor from behind a one-way mirror or from a corner of the playroom. The interpreting counselor describes to the parents what is happening between the Theraplay counselor and the child and suggests ways in which the parents can use the Theraplay dimensions demonstrated in the sessions in their everyday interactions with the child. Starting with the fifth Theraplay session, the parents and the interpreting counselor join the child and the Theraplay counselor in the play during the last 15 minutes of each session so the parents can practice the Theraplay dimensions under the supervision of the counselors.

In the first session with the child, the Theraplay counselor communicates through demonstration and/or explanation the rules of Theraplay (Koller, 1994):

1. The therapist is in charge of the session.
2. Sessions are fun.
3. Sessions are active.
4. Sessions are predictable and structured.
5. Sessions never involve physical hurting.

The Theraplay counselor is constantly active and directive. He or she does not talk much. Instead, action is the focus of all Theraplay sessions. The Theraplay counselor plans activities and materials designed to facilitate the various dimensions for each session and are tailored specifically to the needs of the individual child. The counselor decides how much time during the session to spend on each dimension, based on the problems and interactional patterns of the child and his or her family. During the session, the counselor may change or adapt some of the activities in response to the child's attitude and/or reactions to the therapeutic process (Jernberg & Booth, 1999; Koller & Booth, 1997).

The interpreting counselor's role is both verbal and directive. During each Theraplay session, he or she explains to the parents the interaction between the child and the Theraplay counselor, makes suggestions to the parents of activities that could help the child at home, comments on how specific Theraplay dimensions could enhance the parent–child relationship, coaches the parents when they participate in activities, and provides support and encouragement when the parents begin to incorporate the Theraplay dimensions in their parenting.

Pedro, a 7-year-old Latino male, was brought to play therapy by his parents, Mr. and Mrs. Rodriguez, who had concerns about his behavior. Pedro's parents reported that he always expected to have his own way, throwing hour-long tantrums if his whims were not indulged. Mr. and Mrs. Rodriguez reported that they had probably spoiled Pedro, especially before the birth of his 1-year-old sister. They had always tended to give in to Pedro's demands, especially when he had tantrums in public.

In the first several play therapy sessions, Pedro exhibited behavior typical of a child newly introduced to a playroom. He played briefly with many of the toys, exploring the room and the play and art materials. As he did this, his play therapist, Carol, tracked Pedro's behavior (told him what he was doing), restated content, and reflected his feelings. She had to limit him several times when he wanted to pour sand on the floor and when he started to fling paint at the easel. He argued with Carol about why he should get to do whatever he wanted, but she was firm, reflecting his feelings, and he finally acquiesced with the limits.

By the third session, Carol had noticed themes in Pedro's interaction with her and in his metaphors of needing to be powerful and in control in his play. He frequently chose to use a lion puppet to represent himself. The lion, whom he named Leo, was bossy and domineering with the other puppets, played by Carol. As Carol used the Whisper Technique to let Pedro control the play, he always directed her to have the other puppets do whatever Leo wanted. When Carol chose not to use a whisper to find out what she was supposed to do next and had a kitten puppet ignore Leo's demands, Pedro first used the puppet to berate the kitten and then remonstrated with Carol, telling her she was "always supposed to check with me." When she reflected his feelings of being angry and wanting to be in charge in the playroom, he replied, "Sure, I was mad. I should always be in charge everywhere, and it makes me mad when people don't remember that."

Several times in subsequent sessions, Pedro had tantrums in the playroom when Carol limited his behavior. Because his behavior during these tantrums did not constitute a threat to anyone's safety or to the contents of the playroom, Carol chose to simply reflect his feelings, hoping that he would feel heard and understood. Because she did not want to reinforce this behavior, she remained firm in the limit, without conveying disapproval for his behavior.

In Sessions 4 through 20, Carol continued to work with Pedro on his feelings of entitlement through his metaphors and in his relationship with her. She consistently limited his inappropriate behavior, tracked, restated content, returned responsibility to him, and made interpretations about his perceived need for control. Sometimes she chose to use the Whisper

Technique and sometimes she chose to make her own decisions about how to play. Her goal was for Pedro to become more comfortable with sharing power with others, to find that he could be safe even when he was not in control, to learn skills for communicating about his feelings and desires using words rather than tantrums.

She designed several therapeutic stories about the difficulties Leo the lion got into with his controlling behavior and used the metaphor of his troubles to suggest other ways of interacting with others. Pedro liked these stories so much that he and Carol collaborated on an illustrated book chronicling the life and times of Leo. Pedro gradually started making suggestions for ways by which Leo could get his way without losing friends or hurting other animals' feelings. Carol also consulted with Pedro's parents, teaching them to use more consistent limits and to resist the temptation to let their son have his way when he had a tantrum.

By Session 20, Carol recognized, based on feedback from Mr. and Mrs. Rodriguez and Pedro's teacher and her own observation of Pedro's behavior in play therapy sessions, that Pedro was ready for termination. His behavior had improved significantly. His temper tantrums were reduced from one or two per week to one every other week or so. She and Pedro started a countdown—making a chart so that they could mark off the next two weeks as their final sessions. As is typical with most children, Pedro "replayed" many of the themes from his entire course of play therapy, concluding the last session by looking at Carol, smiling, and saying, "What would you like to do for our last 10 minutes? You can be the boss in here for right now."

Training and Experience

Counselors cannot learn how to effectively conduct play therapy simply by reading books or attending a workshop or two. This approach to counseling children requires an entirely different mindset than talk therapy. To make the paradigm shift from thinking about words and verbal interactions as the primary modality for communication to thinking about play and toys as the primary modality for communication takes concentrated training and practice. The Association for Play Therapy and the Canadian Association for Child and Play Therapy/International Board of Examination of Certified Play Therapists provide guidelines for registration or certification as a professional play therapist that include educational requirements and clinical experience.

Summary

Play therapy is an approach to counseling young children that uses toys and play materials as the primary vehicle of communication. The choice of play as a treatment modality is based on children's natural affinity toward toys and play materials and their developmental inability or limitations to an abstract discussion of issues and relationships. The professional literature provides both empirical and anecdotal support for using play therapy as a therapeutic intervention with a wide range of emotional and behavioral problems and life situations. In deciding whether a specific client is appropriate for play therapy intervention, the counselor must consider a number of factors related to the child and his or her situation and family, as well as a number of factors related to himself or herself and his or her skills, issues, and work setting.

The ideal playroom contains many different toys and play materials, but the most important factor in creating and effectively using a play therapy space is the counselor's own sense of comfort and appropriateness. Personal preference and beliefs about people and how they develop and move toward mental health will dictate the counselor's choice of play therapy skills and his or her theoretical approach. Basic play therapy skills include tracking, restating content, reflecting feelings, returning responsibility to the child, using the child's metaphor, and limiting. Theoretical approaches to play therapy include child-centered play therapy, Adlerian play therapy, cognitive–behavioral play therapy, and Theraplay.

References

Allan, J., & Lawton–Speert, S. (1993). Play psychotherapy of a profoundly incest abused boy: A Jungian approach. *International Journal of Play Therapy, 2*(1), 33–48.

Anderson, J., & Richards, N. (1995, October). *Play therapy in the real world: Coping with managed care, challenging children, skeptical colleagues, time and space constraints.* Paper presented at first annual conference of Iowa Association of Play Therapy, Iowa City.

Axline, V. (1947). *Play therapy: The inner dynamics of childhood.* Boston: Houghton Mifflin.

Axline, V. (1969). *Play therapy* (rev. ed.). New York: Ballantine.

Axline, V. (1971). *Dibs: In search of self.* New York: Ballantine.

Barlow, K., Strother, J., & Landreth, G. (1986). Sibling group play therapy: An effective alternative with an elective mute child. *School Counselor, 34,* 44–50.

Benedict, H., & Mongoven, L. (1997). Thematic play therapy: An approach to treatment of attachment disorders in young children. In H. Kaduson, D. Cangelosi, & C. Schaefer (Eds.), *The playing cure: Individual play therapy for specific childhood problems* (pp. 277–315). Northvale, NJ: Jason Aronson.

Bluestone, J. (1999). School-based peer therapy to facilitate mourning in latency-age children following sudden parental death: Cases of Joan, age 10½, and Roberta, age 9½, with follow-up 8 years later. In N. B. Webb (Ed.), *Play therapy with children in crisis* (2nd ed., pp. 225–251). New York: Guilford.

Boley, S., Ammen, S., O'Connor, K., & Miller, L. (1996). The use of the color-your-life technique with pediatric cancer patients and their siblings. *International Journal of Play Therapy, 5*(2), 57–78.

Boley, S., Peterson, C., Miller, L., & Ammen, S. (1996). An investigation of the color-your-life technique with childhood cancer patients. *International Journal of Play Therapy, 5*(2), 41–56.

Bratton, S., & Ray, D. (2000). What the research shows about play therapy. *International Journal of Play Therapy, 9*(1), 47–88.

Briesmeister, J. (1997). Play therapy with depressed children. In H. Kaduson, D. Cangelosi, & C. Schaefer (Eds.), *The playing cure: Individual play therapy for specific childhood problems* (pp. 3–28). Northvale. NJ: Jason Aronson.

Cabe, N. (1997). Conduct disorder: Grounded play therapy. In H. Kaduson, D. Cangelosi, & C. Schaefer (Eds.), *The playing cure: Individual play therapy for specific childhood problems* (pp. 229–254). Northvale, NJ: Jason Aronson.

Cangelosi, D. (1997). Play therapy for children from divorced and separated families. In H. Kaduson, D. Cangelosi, & C. Schaefer (Eds.), *The playing cure: Individual play therapy for specific childhood problems* (pp. 119–142). Northvale, NJ: Jason Aronson.

Coleman, V., Parmer, T., & Barker, S. (1993). Play therapy for multicultural populations: Guidelines for mental health professionals. *International Journal of Play Therapy, 2*(1), 63–74.

Cook, J. A. (1997). Play therapy for selective mutism. In H. Kaduson, D. Cangelosi, & C. Schaefer (Eds.), *The playing cure: Individual play therapy for specific childhood problems* (pp. 83–115). Northvale, NJ: Jason Aronson.

Costas, M., & Landreth, L. (1999). Filial therapy with non-offending parents of children who have been sexually abused. *International Journal of Play Therapy, 8*(1), 43–66.

Cuddy–Casey, M. (1997). A case study using child-centered play therapy approach to treat enuresis and encopresis. *Elementary School Guidance and Counseling, 31*, 220–225.

Doyle, J., & Stoop, D. (1999). Witness and victim of multiple abuses: Case of Randy, age 10, in a residential treatment center, and follow-up at age 19 in prison. In N. B. Webb (Ed.), *Play therapy with children in crisis* (2nd ed., pp. 131–163). New York: Guilford.

Fischetti, B. (2001). Use of play therapy for anger management in the school setting. In A. Drewes, L. Carey, & C. Schaefer (Eds.), *School-based play therapy* (pp. 238–256). New York: John Wiley and Sons.

Fornari, V. (1999). The aftermath of a plane crash—helping a survivor cope with deaths of mother and sibling: Case of Mary, age 8. In N. B. Webb (Ed.), *Play therapy with children in crisis* (2nd ed., pp. 407–429). New York: Guilford.

Frey, D. (1993). 1 brought my own toys today! Play therapy with adults. In T. Kottman & C. Schaefer (Eds.), *Play therapy in action: A casebook for practitioners* (pp. 589–606). Northvale, NJ: Jason Aronson.

Ginott, H. G. (1959). Therapeutic intervention in child treatment. *Journal of Consulting Psychology, 23*,160–166.

Glover, G. (2001). Cultural considerations in play therapy. In G. Landreth (Ed.), *Innovations in play therapy: Issues, process, and special populations* (pp. 31–41). Philadelphia: Brunner–Routledge.

Goodman, R. (1999). Childhood cancer and the family: Case of Tim, age 6, and follow-up at age 15. In N. B. Webb (Ed.), *Play therapy with children in crisis* (2nd ed., pp. 380–406). New York: Guilford.

Hall, P. (1997). Play therapy with sexually abused children. In H. Kaduson, D. Cangelosi, & C. Schaefer (Eds.), *The playing cure: Individual play therapy for specific childhood problems* (pp. 171–196). Northvale, NJ: Jason Aronson.

James, O. (1997). *Play therapy: A comprehensive guide.* Northvale, NJ: Jason Aronson.

Jernberg, A., & Booth, P. (1999). *Theraplay* (2nd ed.). San Francisco: Jossey–Bass.

Jernberg, A., & Jernberg, E. (1993). Family Theraplay for the family tyrant. In T. Kottman & C. Schaefer (Eds.), *Play therapy in action: A casebook for practitioners* (pp. 45–96). Northvale, NJ: Jason Aronson.

Johnson, S., & Clark, P. (2001). Play therapy with aggressive acting-out children. In G. Landreth (Ed.), *Innovations in play therapy: Issues, process, and special populations* (pp. 323–333). Philadelphia: Taylor & Francis.

Jones, E. M., & Landreth, G. (2002). The efficacy of intensive individual play therapy for chronically ill children. *International Journal of Play Therapy, 10*(2), 117–140.

Joyner, C. (1991). Individual, group and family crisis counseling following a hurricane: Case of Heather, age 9. In N. B. Webb (Ed.), *Play therapy with children in crisis* (pp. 396–415). New York: Guilford.

Kaduson, H. (1997). Play therapy for children with attention-deficit hyperactivity disorder. In H. Kaduson, D. Cangelosi, & C. Schaefer (Eds.), *The playing cure: Individual play therapy for specific childhood problems* (pp. 197–228). Northvale, NJ: Jason Aronson.

Kao, S., & Landreth, G. (2001). Play therapy with Chinese children. In G. Landreth (Ed.), *Innovations in play therapy: Issues, process, and special populations* (pp. 43–49). Philadelphia: Brunner–Routledge.

Kaplan, C. (1999). Life threatening blood disorder: Case of Daniel, age 11, and his mother. In N. B. Webb (Ed.), *Play therapy with children in crisis* (2nd ed., pp. 356–379). New York: Guilford.

Knell, S. (1993a). *Cognitive–behavioral play therapy.* Northvale, NJ: Jason Aronson.

Knell, S. (1993b). To show and not tell: Cognitive–behavioral play therapy. In T. Kottman & C. Schaefer (Eds.), *Play therapy in action: A casebook for practitioners* (pp. 169–208). Northvale, NJ: Jason Aronson.

Knell, S. (1994). Cognitive–behavioral play therapy. In K. O'Connor & C. Schaefer (Eds.), *Handbook of play therapy: Vol 2. Advances and innovations* (pp. 111–142). New York: Wiley.

Knell, S. (1997). Cognitive–behavioral play therapy In K. O'Connor & L. M. Braverman (Eds.), *Play therapy theory and practice: A comparative presentation* (pp. 79–99). New York: Wiley.

Knell, S. (2000). Cognitive-behavioral play therapy for childhood fears and phobias. In H. Kaduson & C. Schaefer (Eds.), *Short-term play therapy for children* (pp. 3–27). New York: Guilford.

Knell, S., & Moore, D. (1990). Cognitive–behavioral play therapy in the treatment of encopresis. *Journal of Clinical Child Psychology, 19,* 55–60.

Koller, T. (1994). Adolescent Theraplay. In K. O'Connor & C. Schaefer (Eds.), *Handbook of play therapy: Vol 2. Advances and innovations* (pp. 159–188). New York: Wiley

Koller, T., & Booth, P. (1997). Fostering attachment through family Theraplay. In K. O'Connor & L. M. Braverman (Eds.), *Play therapy theory and practice: A comparative presentation* (pp. 204–233). New York: Wiley.

Kottman, T. (1993). The king of rock and roll. In T. Kottman & C. Schaefer (Eds.), *Play therapy in action: A casebook for practitioners* (pp. 133–167). Northvale, NJ: Jason Aronson.

Kottman, T. (1994). Adlerian play therapy. In K. O'Connor & C. Schaefer (Eds.), *Handbook of play therapy: Vol. 2. Advances and innovations* (pp. 3–26). New York: Wiley.

Kottman, T. (1997). Building a family: Play therapy with adopted children and their parents. In H. Kaduson, D. Cangelosi, & C. Schaefer (Eds.), *The playing cure: Individual play therapy for specific childhood problems* (pp. 337–370). Northvale, NJ: Jason Aronson.

Kottman, T. (2001). *Play therapy: Basics and beyond.* New York: Guilford.

Kottman, T. (2002). Billy, the teddy bear boy. In L. Golden (Ed.), *Case studies in child and adolescent counseling* (3rd ed., pp. 8–20). Columbus, OH: Merrill Prentice Hall.

Kottman, T. (2003). *Partners in play: An Adlerian approach to play therapy* (2nd ed). Alexandria, VA: American Counseling Association.

Kottman, T., Strother, J., & Deniger, M. (1987). Activity therapy: An alternative therapy for adolescents. *Journal of Humanistic Education and Development, 25,* 180–186.

Landreth, G. (1991). *Play therapy: The art of the relationship.* Muncie, IN: Accelerated Development.

Landreth, G., & Sweeney, D. (1997). Child-centered play therapy. In K. O'Connor & L.M. Braverman (Eds.), *Play therapy theory and practice. A comparative presentation* (pp. 17–45). New York: Wiley.

LeBlanc, M., & Ritchie, M. (1999). Predictors of play therapy outcomes. *International Journal of Play Therapy, 8*(2), 19–34.

Ledyard, P. (1999). Play therapy with the elderly: A case study. *International Journal of Play Therapy, 8*(2), 57–75.

LeVieux, J. (1994). Terminal illness and death of father: Case of Celeste, age 5. In N. B. Webb (Ed.), *Helping bereaved children: A handbook for practitioners* (pp. 81–95). New York: Guilford.

Lovatt, D. (1999). Ecosystemic play therapy with maltreated children. *Masters Abstracts International, 37*(2).

Lyness–Richard, D. (1997). Play therapy for children with fears and phobias. In H. Kaduson, D. Cangelosi, & C. Schaefer (Eds.), *The playing cure: Individual play therapy for specific childhood problems* (pp. 29–60). Northvale, NJ: Jason Aronson.

Marschak, M. (1960). A method for evaluating child-parent interaction under controlled conditions. *Journal of Genetic Psychology, 97,* 3–22.

Muro, J., & Kottman, T. (1995). *Guidance and counseling in the elementary and middle schools: A practical approach.* Dubuque, IA: Brown & Benchmark.

Nisivoccia, D., & Lynn, M. (1999). Helping forgotten victims: Using activity groups with children who witness violence. In N. B. Webb (Ed.), *Play therapy with children in crisis* (2nd ed., pp. 74–103). New York: Guilford.

O'Connor, K. (1993). Child, protector, confidant: Structured group ecosystemic play therapy, In T. Kottman & C. Schaefer (Eds.), *Play therapy in action: A casebook for practitioners* (pp. 245–282). Northvale, NJ: Jason Aronson.

Pelcovitz, D. (1999). Betrayed by a trusted adult: Structured time-limited group therapy with elementary school children abused by a school employee. In N. B. Webb (Ed.), *Play therapy with children in crisis* (2nd ed., pp. 183–202). New York: Guilford.

Perry, L. (1993). Audrey, the bois d'arc, and me: A time of becoming. In T. Kottman & C. Schaefer (Eds.), *Play therapy in action. A casebook for practitioners* (pp. 5–44). Northvale, NJ: Jason Aronson.

Peyton, J. (1986). Use of puppets in a residence for the elderly. *Nursing Homes, 35,* 27–30.

Ray, D., Bratton, S., Rhine, T., & Jones, L. (2001). The effectiveness of play therapy: Responding to the critics. *International Journal of Play Therapy, 10*(1), 85–108.

Reddy, L., Spencer, P., Hall, T., & Rubel, E. (2001). Use of developmentally appropriate games in a child group training program for young children with attention-deficit/hyperactivity disorder. In A. Drewes, L. Carey, & C. Schaefer (Eds.), *School-based play therapy* (pp. 256–276). New York: John Wiley and Sons.

Reid, S. (1993). It's all in the game: Game play therapy. In T. Kottman & C. Schaefer (Eds.), *Play therapy in action: A casebook for practitioners* (pp. 527–560). Northvale, NJ: Jason Aronson.

Ridder, N. (1999). HIV/AIDS in the family: Group treatment for latency-age children affected by the illness of a family member. In N. B. Webb (Ed.), *Play therapy with children in crisis* (2nd ed., pp. 341–355). New York: Guilford.

Robinson, H. (1999). Unresolved conflicts in a divorced family: Case of Charlie, age 10. In N. B. Webb (Ed.), *Play therapy with children in crisis* (2nd ed., pp. 272–293). New York: Guilford.

Rogers, C. (1959). A theory of therapy, personality, and interpersonal relationships as developed in the client-centered framework. In S. Koch (Ed.), *Psychology: A study of a science. Study L Conceptual and systematic: Vol. 3. Formulation of the person and social context* (pp. 184–256). New York: McGraw Hill.

Schaefer, C. (1998). Critical issues for the next millennium. *Association for Play Therapy Newsletter, 17*(1), 1–5.

Shelby, J. (1997). Rubble, disruption, and tears: Helping young survivors of natural disaster. In H. Kaduson, D. Cangelosi, & C. Schaefer (Eds.), *The playing cure: Individual play therapy for specific childhood problems* (pp. 143–170). Northvale, NJ: Jason Aronson.

Shen, Y.–J. (2002). Short-term group play therapy with Chinese earthquake victims: Effects on anxiety, depression, and adjustment. *International Journal of Play Therapy, 10*(2), 43–64.

Smith, A., & Herman, J. (1994). Setting limits while enabling self-expression: Play therapy with an aggressive, controlling child. *International Journal of Play Therapy, 3*(1), 23–36.

Strand, V. (1999). The assessment and treatment of family sexual abuse. In N. B. Webb (Ed.), *Play therapy with children in crisis* (2nd ed., pp. 104–130). New York: Guilford.

Tait, D., & Depta, J. (1994). Play therapy group for bereaved children. In N. B. Webb (Ed.), *Helping bereaved children: A handbook for practitioners* (pp. 169–185). New York: Guilford.

Thompson, C., & Rudolph, L. (2000). *Counseling children* (5th ed.). Pacific Grove, CA: Brooks/Cole.

Tonning, L. (1999). Persistent and chronic neglect in the context of poverty—When parents can't parent: Case of Ricky, age 3. In N.B. Webb (Ed.), *Play therapy with children in crisis* (2nd ed., pp. 203–224). New York: Guilford.

Tyndall–Lind, A. (1999). Revictimization of children from violent families: Child-centered theoretical formulation and play therapy treatment implications. *International Journal of Play Therapy, 8*(1), 9–25.

Tyndall–Lind, A., Landreth, G., & Giordano, M. (2001). Intensive group play therapy with child witnesses of domestic violence. *International Journal of Play Therapy, 10*(1), 53–84.

Van de Putte, S. (1995). A paradigm for working with child survivors of sexual abuse who exhibit sexualized behaviors during play therapy. *International Journal of Play Therapy, 4*(1), 27–49.

VanFleet, R. (2000). Short-term play therapy for families with chronic illness. In H. Kaduson & C. Schaefer (Eds.), *Short-term play therapy for children* (pp. 175–193). New York: Guilford.

VanFleet, R., Lilly, J.P., & Kaduson, H. (1999). Play therapy for children exposed to violence: Individual, family and community interventions. *International Journal of Play Therapy, 8*(1), 27–42.

Webb, J. (1995). Play therapy with hospitalized children. *International Journal of Play Therapy, 4*(1), 51–60.

Webb, N. B. (1999). The child witness of parental violence: Case of Michael, age 4, and follow-up at age 16. In N. B. Webb (Ed.), *Play therapy with children in crisis* (2nd ed., pp. 49–73). New York: Guilford.

Williams–Gray, B. (1999). International consultation and intervention on behalf of children affected by war. In N. B. Webb (Ed.), *Play therapy with children in crisis* (2nd ed., pp. 448–470). New York: Guilford.

Chapter 5

Brief Counseling With Children and Adolescents: Interactive, Culturally Responsive, and Action-Based

John M. Littrell and Kirk Zinck

Several years ago we attended an entertaining evening performance by the humorist Tom Bodett. He told about his personal adventures that began after he left college. As it turned out, Tom offered us, beyond entertainment, useful insights for conceptualizing counseling with children and adolescents.

Tom opened his act by reaching into a small wooden box on the table and pulling out a stack of 12 pink cards, each labeled with a key word or phrase. As he explained how a bolt of electricity passed through his body when he climbed to the top of a telephone pole, he threw the cards into the air. Large, pink snowflakes descended to the stage. Tom asked members of the audience to come on stage and randomly point to specific cards. As each person pointed to a card, Tom picked it up, reflected for a moment, and told the story associated with the words written on that card. By evening's end, no more pink cards remained on the floor. Tom had told 12 stories, one for each card.

He explained how a bolt of some sort often strikes us. The bolt produces both entrance and exit wounds. Between its entrance and exit, the bolt jumbles and tumbles things out of order. For Tom, tossing the cards into the air represented a bolt that created chaos. Reassembling the cards in a new manner was a creative act made possible by the cooperation of Tom and his audience. The parts of Tom's larger story had been reassembled, in this case by random chance. Each of us in the audience heard the disjointed short stories, and we successfully wove them into a coherent larger one. Tom and the audience had experienced together the breaking of a pattern and then worked cooperatively to create new ones.

Just like the cards scattered over the floor, the order and meaning of life often are strewn about when a bolt hits. The children and adolescents with whom counselors work have entrance and exit wounds—divorcing parents, physical abuse, suicide of friends, blended families, eating disorders, and so forth. They commonly are struggling with typical developmental problems such as peer relationships, identity issues, and achievement, to name but a few. When we ask children and adolescents to tell us their stories, they do so in blown-apart fragments, similar to the way Tom Bodett told his story. Unlike the pieces of a shattered vase, which can be put back together like the pieces of a jigsaw puzzle, the fragments that Tom shared and that our clients share are fragments of meaning that must be put together in a new way.

The children and adolescents we see are struggling with familiar patterns that have been blown apart. Crisis bolts create chaos. Our job as counselors is to assist children and adolescents in creating new and more workable patterns from the shattered fragments of meaning. Tom Bodett's performance provided a model for how, regardless of the entrance and exit wounds, the fragments of meaningful patterns can be collected, reassembled, reorganized, fashioned, constructed, molded, shaped, and understood in many different ways.

Tom Bodett's performance provided two insights that counselors might find useful in helping children and adolescents.

1. Counselors can view the material that clients bring us as fragments of formerly meaningful patterns—often small patterns that once worked but no longer do. Meaningful patterns have exploded in clients' lives; the usefulness of the patterns has been shattered. Young people are asking for assistance in helping them put together new patterns that will work in their lives. They want help in putting back what the bolt has jumbled beyond their abilities to repair, to mend, to make whole once again. Initially, clients are unaware that the bolt has rendered a return to the former way of life impossible, and part of our challenge is to help youth begin the process of creating new patterns.
2. Life's patterns can be put together in many ways. Tom began by using a random disruption approach. He assumed that as his audience listened to his stories, we would be able to refashion a larger and more coherent story. Tom's act of throwing the cards and then presenting the small stories in a random

fashion guaranteed that the larger story would be reconstructed anew. Brief counseling avoids the randomness of thrown cards, but it echoes Tom's approach in that it breaks away from traditional ways of approaching clients' stories, which often are linear and chronological.

In this chapter we continue the exploration of how to help children and adolescents by focusing on eight defining characteristics of brief counseling. We then illustrate these characteristics as they manifest themselves in three counseling cases.

Eight Characteristics of Brief Counseling

Brief counseling is (a) time-limited, (b) solution-focused, (c) action-based, (d) socially interactive, (e) detail-oriented, (f) humor-eliciting, (g) developmentally attentive, and (h) relationship-based. These eight characteristics define brief counseling as a unique approach (Littrell, 1998). When counselors holistically integrate these eight characteristics into their practice, they can help clients more swiftly alleviate their discomfort and reach their desired states (Littrell, Malia, & Vanderwood, 1995).

Brief Counseling Is Time-Limited

School counselors always have been constrained by having a limited time within which to do counseling, yet the counseling models presented in graduate school programs often do not reflect the reality of the schools in which counselors will work. Today, managed care has affected the mental health counseling field in a similar way. The briefness we are referring to ranges from a single 10-minute session to five sessions. The brief counseling approach is designed to produce effects in a limited amount of time.

Brief Counseling Is Solution-Focused

All solutions are temporary because life continues to present new challenges. Yet, brief counselors find that focusing on solutions is a more productive way to approach issues than is dwelling on problems. Seeking solutions generates and mobilizes people's resources and inspires hope. Therefore, brief counselors emphasize what works rather than what does not work in clients' lives.

In brief counseling, counselors assist clients by focusing on three areas: (a) exceptions to the problem (Selekman, 1993), (b) untapped resources, and (c) goals (Littrell & Angera, 1998; Zinck & Littrell, 2002). By emphasizing what clients do that works, on instances when clients are not stuck, brief counselors help clients discover how every so often they engage in patterns that are exceptions to their problem states (De Jong & Berg, 1998). Effective interventions accent successful exceptions to encourage clients to do more of what works.

Because exceptions to problems are a potent source of information, brief counselors repeatedly ask such questions as: "When is this not a problem for you?" "How did you do that?" Often clients are amazed when they think about the times their problems were nonexistent or diminished. Usually they have dwelled exclusively on the problem parts of their lives and have failed to notice when problems have not occurred.

Brief counselors also guide clients toward their futures. Counselors and clients set concrete goals as a way of clarifying clients' desired states. The concreting process shows clients that the future is fluid and that many futures are possible. As new choices become evident, clients begin to experience freedom from being stuck. For some clients, setting goals is a liberating experience, and they know what they need to do to reach the goals. For other clients, goal setting is a scary experience because they cannot see how to achieve the goals they have helped to set. These clients would benefit from tapping their unused resources.

Clients often are unaware of the multitude of internal and external resources they possess that they can use to move from their present state to future states. Identifying resources assists clients in believing they can achieve their goals. Brief counselors are experts in helping clients tap their resources.

Brief Counseling Is Action-Based

Brief counselors believe that "client talk" does not equal "client action," and that action is needed in the client's life before change will occur. Therefore, brief counselors often provide clients with new experiences as quickly as possible. These new experiences let clients know that new patterns of behavior are possible, and hope emerges. Two highly effective methods to provide clients with new experiences are giving directives and assigning tasks.

Brief Counseling Is Socially Interactive

Clients and those around them powerfully influence one another in reciprocal ways. Brief counselors utilize these reciprocal interactions by tapping into need-satisfying qualities of socially supportive relationships. Changes come about more readily when other people support them. Brief counselors help clients utilize other people in the change process.

Brief Counseling Is Detail-Oriented

The power of patterns often lies in their details. Rather than asking for details of what is not working in a client's life, brief counselors ask for details about what is working, what the client wants, and what will get the client to his or her goal. Brief counselors are intrigued by details of their clients' resources, strengths, abilities, and talents and how these will be brought to bear on creating and maintaining new patterns. In short, brief counselors explore in detail what already works, clients' desired states, and methods to reach those desired states.

Brief Counseling Is Humor-Eliciting

The indexes of counseling books seldom contain the words "fun," "humor," and "laughter." The notion that counseling always must be serious is, we believe, a serious mistake. Because pain is a common response to problems, counselors and clients often have assumed that pain must continue during the process of moving toward solutions. In brief counseling, counselors focus less on the pain and more on life-enhancing elements. Attention to the latter tends to bring forth the healing forces of laughter and humor, which are strong indicators of clients' strengths.

Brief Counseling Is Developmentally Attentive

Many of the bolts that hit clients are aspects of developmental growth. Transitions have a way of jumbling and tumbling clients' lives. Brief counselors step back from clients' struggles and listen for the developmental themes and challenges. This larger perspective assists counselors in helping clients to construct new solutions that are ecologically sound for the clients' developmental stage.

Brief counselors help clients meet the psychological human needs of love/belonging, power, freedom, and fun (Glasser, 1986). They help clients meet their needs for love/belonging by emphasizing the socially interactive nature of counseling (Littrell, Zinck, Nesselhuf, & Yorke, 1997). They help clients meet their needs for power by highlighting the clients' internal and external resources. They stress freedom by having clients continually make their own choices rather than go on living by the dictates of their internalized "shoulds" or continue to respond unassertively to others' unreasonable demands. Finally, they help clients meet their need for fun by eliciting humor to solve problems and find solutions. Brief counselors recognize that clients' solutions work best when developmental perspectives and needs are acknowledged and embraced.

Brief Counseling Is Relationship-Based

A facilitative counseling relationship contributes considerably more to the success of counseling than do the techniques counselors use (Sexton, Whiston, Bleuer, & Walz, 1997). Brief counselors, of course, possess and use skills specific to brief counseling, but even more important, they make sure they do not neglect their relationship with their clients. Caring for clients, counselor genuineness, and empathic understanding are not simply frills added to brief counseling techniques. They form a foundation of effective brief counseling.

Case Studies

The eight characteristics of brief counseling intertwine to form a unique counseling approach, as illustrated in the case study we have titled "Sneaky Poo Revisited." In this case, John Littrell used a brief counseling framework to help a parent help her young son acquire urinary and bowel control.

Sneaky Poo Revisited

Many times, counselors do not have the opportunity to meet with a client for more than a few sessions. Brief counseling is a precise tool that has proven helpful in working within severely limited timeframes. The case described here lasted only one session with three follow-up phone calls; the total time was about 1 hour. The third phone conversation indicated that the goals of this very brief counseling intervention had been met. This case illustrates all eight characteristics of brief counseling (Littrell, 1998).

The brief counseling framework used in the case was developed by the Mental Research Institute (MRI) (Fisch, Weakland, & Segal, 1982; Watzlawick, Weakland, & Fisch, 1974). The MRI model has four steps (Watzlawick et al., 1974):

1. A clear definition of the problem in concrete terms
2. An investigation of solutions the client has attempted so far
3. A clear definition of the concrete change to be achieved
4. The formation and implementation of a plan to produce this change.

John Littrell added to step 2 an exploration of exceptions to the pattern (de Shazer, 1988) and identification of the client's strengths (Littrell, 1998).

Definition of the Problem

On the phone Melody asked if she could consult with me about her 4-year-old son, Randy, and we set up a time to meet. During the opening moments of our counseling session, I explained to Melody the basic four-step MRI counseling framework. I then asked a question to elicit information about how Melody saw the problem. The wording of the question "What are the most important aspects of this situation that I should be aware of?" was deliberately chosen to caution the client not to tell me every detail. The question prompted Melody to sift through her understanding and provide the most essential information rather than offer excruciating details. I acknowledged her thoughts and feelings about the situation but avoided spending too much time talking about them.

Melody told me that Randy still "messed" (wet and soiled) his pants regularly, a problem his 9-year-old sister had never experienced. This "messing" pattern was not of much concern to Randy, but it was a source of embarrassment and worry to his mother. In Melody's mind it was Randy, not she, who had the problem. One of the questions asked in the MRI framework is: Who is the customer? Another wording could be: Who is willing to work on the concern? Although Melody perceived the person with the problem to be her son, it was she who expressed the worry and concern. I therefore treated Melody, the parent, as the person who would be most willing to work on the problem; she was my client.

Attempted Solutions, Exceptions, and Strengths

We entered the second stage of the MRI framework: What are the client's attempted solutions? I added a solution-focused question that pinpointed exceptions: When is this not a problem? I learned that Melody had been an expert in designing attempted solutions, but, unfortunately, none of them had yet worked. Her most ingenious method had been to invent a game called "Potty Jeopardy." When Randy looked as if he were about to mess his pants, Melody immediately took him to the bathroom and had him sit on the toilet. If he proceeded to go, she offered profuse praise. Although clever in idea, Potty Jeopardy did not in practice change Randy's behavior. If Melody did not notice that Randy looked as if he should be heading to the bathroom, he made no attempt to go to the bathroom prior to messing his pants.

I asked Melody about exceptions to Randy's pattern. Melody could think of only two. In examining these in more detail, we discovered that occasionally Randy realized that something didn't feel quite right and he headed to the bathroom. Melody had picked up on this exception and subsequently talked to Randy about how he should go to the bathroom whenever he felt uncomfortable in that way. Melody's attempt to build on the exception met with additional failure.

Brief counselors are continually looking for clients' strengths. Two of Melody's stood out prominently. First, she was doggedly persistent. Regardless of the frustrating problem situation, she persevered in her efforts. She continued to look for solutions, illustrated by her seeking help from me. Second, Melody had a delightful sense of humor, as evidenced by her inventing Potty Jeopardy. When I pointed out both of these strengths to Melody, she beamed.

Goal Setting

Within 10 minutes of starting our session, Melody and I began to make concrete her desired outcome. We acknowledged that Randy did not seem too interested in changing his behavior. Therefore, we conceptualized my role as that of a consultant who would assist Melody in designing more options to bring about a change in Randy's behavior. Melody had to be more effective in "talking" a language that would make more sense to Randy and that would begin to convince him to change. From what Melody said, humor seemed to be an effective tool for communicating with Randy, but apparently Potty Jeopardy was not quite the right way.

Intervention

Brief counselors do not limit themselves when thinking about ways of creating new patterns that will help clients reach their goals. As Melody talked, I remembered a fascinating description I had read in Michael White and David Epston's (1990) *Narrative Means to Therapeutic Ends,* of how a therapist had helped a child overcome encopresis. The therapist had assisted 6-year-old Nick in defeating Sneaky Poo, who had a tendency to leave an "accident" or have an "incident."

I did not clearly remember all of the details in the case of Sneaky Poo, but I did remember that the child had been taught to recognize that Sneaky Poo would come when he was least expecting it and soil the boy's pants. The therapist had taught the boy to recognize when Sneaky Poo was coming and to defeat him by going to the bathroom.

Based on my recollection of the Sneaky Poo case, I talked with Melody about an action-based intervention to achieve her goal. I suggested that perhaps her son needed to be a better detective (an age-appropriate task) to discover clues of when Sneaky Poo was coming. With those clues, he could solve the mystery and catch Sneaky Poo.

In addition, I suggested that a detective would have to know what Sneaky Poo looked like before he left "brown balls and yellow water" in Randy's pants. I added, "Perhaps you and your son can draw a picture of what Sneaky Poo looks like." Because of her sense of humor and that of her son, Melody thought he might really go for this idea. Working together, Melody and I planned the details. We discussed in detail how she could carry out this assignment with Randy. The next day I spoke briefly on the phone with Melody, who related the following:

> I talked with Randy last night, and he was really excited about being a detective. I asked him what clues he would spot if Sneaky Poo were around. That's when Randy really surprised me. I had been saying to Randy that if he felt "pressure," that was a message to head to the bathroom. Randy told me that one of the clues would be that it felt "itchy." Then it hit me. I had been using my way of talking, but it hadn't made any sense to him. So now I started using his language of "itchy" to make more sense to him.

Melody and her son seemed to be on the right track, so I went to a bookstore and purchased an age-appropriate children's book about a small bear who acted as a detective looking for clues. I sent the book to Melody with a written homework assignment. My note said, "I suggest that you read this book to your son to prepare him to be the best detective in the world as he looks for clues." Melody wrote back, saying that the book and the idea sounded great.

A week later Melody and I talked on the phone for about 15 minutes. During the conversation, she said:

> After I received the book you sent, I decided to work with Randy by drawing a picture of Sneaky Poo. My daughter Sarah, Randy, and I had a picnic in the park, and I brought along crayons and paper. Sarah wanted to make a drawing, too, and that was all right with Randy. All three of us drew Sneaky Poo, and then we voted on which drawing looked the most like Sneaky Poo. We all agreed that Sarah's drawing won the prize. It was a brown figure with scary hands, and it was standing in a pool of yellow water. We were all laughing and having a good time.

> Then, last night I read to Randy the children's book you had given me. He really liked it. We were just about done reading when Randy looked at me and said, "I think Sneaky Poo is coming." He went to the bathroom by himself. I was so pleased with him. When he came back into the room, I said, "You're really getting to be a great detective." He just smiled the biggest smile.

A follow-up phone call a month later confirmed that Randy had continued to be a "great detective." Melody said she was much more relaxed now that Randy had learned a needed skill. They had kept the picture of Sneaky Poo so it could serve as a back-up reminder if needed, but for now it was simply being stored out of sight in Randy's dresser drawer.

Discussion

As shown in the following list, all eight characteristics of brief counseling found expression in Sneaky Poo Revisited. The characteristics appeared not as separate elements but, instead, as part of a coherent and systematic framework.

1. *Time-limited:* We met for only one session with three follow-up phone calls. The total time was less than 1 hour.
2. *Solution-focused:* Melody and I focused on (a) the key exceptions to the problem that Randy had exhibited, (b) Melody's resources of humor and persistence, and (c) Melody's goals.
3. *Action-based:* My directives to make a drawing, read a book, and search for clues all served to have Melody and Randy doing something about the situation.
4. *Socially interactive:* Melody involved not only Randy but also Randy's sister in the solution.
5. *Detail-oriented:* The drawing of Sneaky Poo, the instructions to find clues, and the avoidance of "brown balls and yellow water" in Randy's pants are all details focusing on solutions, not the problem.
6. *Humor-eliciting:* Melody's description of Potty Jeopardy and the family activity of drawing Sneaky Poo added warm humor to a frustrating problem.
7. *Developmentally attentive:* Recognizing Randy's need to master a developmental task and using the age-appropriate detective book and accompanying task to look for clues, indicated an attention to developmental stages.
8. *Relationship-based:* Even though I never saw Randy or his sister, I did establish and maintain a solid working relationship with Melody. She used her relationship skills within the family to assist Randy in creating a new, age-appropriate pattern.

Expert in Self-Defeating Behavior

In this case, which we have titled "Expert in Self-Defeating Behavior," Kirk Zinck assisted an adolescent to overcome acting-out behavior in the community and self-defeating behavior at home. As in Sneaky Poo Revisited, this case unmistakably includes all eight characteristics of brief counseling, employs the MRI model, and explores exceptions to the problem.

Definition of the "Problem"

Scott Randall, a 15-year-old high school sophomore, arrived for the first of four counseling sessions scowling and belligerent. He recently had been caught vandalizing property in the community, and he was failing in school. At home, family members perceived Scott as the catalyst for many family arguments. The referring therapist labeled Scott as troubled, disruptive, and a bully. After attempting family therapy with little success, the therapist believed Scott would benefit from individual counseling and referred him to my private practice.

Presession consultations with the referring therapist and Scott's father revealed that Scott lived with his father and a 14-year-old sister. The mother had abandoned the family when the children were very young, leaving Mr. Randall to raise the children. Like other single parents, Mr. Randall encountered many challenges in raising his children, yet the family had been close and enjoyed a stable history until the children entered adolescence. As the children began to differentiate themselves from the family unit, they intensified their competition for parental attention and access to family resources, such as allowances, telephone time, and rides to activities. By the time they entered family therapy, chaotic family arguments were occurring nightly.

The family members had additional stressors as well. Mr. Randall had recently become a new teacher in the community. The children's mother had reappeared, pressured the children to visit her, and then continually changed the dates of the planned visitations. Scott's problems drew embarrassing scrutiny from the community, and one vocal community member called him "emotionally troubled." A police officer conferred with the family after Scott's activities had resulted in several minor legal problems and community members had begun to question Mr. Randall's abilities as a parent. The attention embarrassed this new teacher, who worked with the children of the community members who were questioning him.

Typical of adolescents who are referred to counseling, Scott was a client whom others wanted to be "fixed." The first 20 minutes of the intake session included Scott and his father, and for the remaining minutes I spoke with Scott alone. Although, in the early part of the session, Mr. Randall discussed many problems, he voiced the most concern about his son's drop in grades and loss of interest in school. He believed that resolving school-related issues was a key to resolving other concerns. Only later in the session did I discover that Scott shared his father's concerns. I noticed that even though Scott was angry with his father for "making me attend counseling," the father and son tempered their disagreements with humor and affection.

Because of Scott's overall anger, I spent a considerable portion of the first session joining with him to develop a working coalition, even as we progressed in problem and goal definition. Having been labeled, blamed, and identified as "the problem" in his previous therapy, my client proceeded cautiously. "Burned" by past experience, Scott stoutly maintained his guard, and I wondered how long it would be before he lowered it.

To assist Scott in becoming a voluntary client, I explored his concerns and interests. What did he define as problems in his life? What was his preferred way of being? I especially focused on exceptions to problems—times when problems were not present. We explored his non-problem times and discovered what was different about those times. My concentrating on exceptions to problems reminded Scott that problems occur within a context. Much of the time Scott was problem-free, volunteering at his church, working with a neighbor, a truck driver, on the maintenance of his "rig," and "partnering up" with his father in a number of outdoor adventures.

Soon I discovered that Scott was sensitive and intense and had frequently sought his father's guidance and support as he matured and developed and as he coped with the developmental and environmental stressors he had described. His needs competed with those of his sister, who had aligned herself with their father to counter the intensity of Scott's demands and to ensure parental attention for herself. Scott had few tools for coping with this coalition and for effectively meeting his needs. Being labeled a "bully" and "troubled" only added to Scott's frustration, for these labels suggested that he had no viable alternatives to aggression and acting out. Further, they served to keep Scott stuck in destructive behaviors. We quickly discarded the labels.

Historically, Scott performed well as a student. Upon entering adolescence, however, this changed. In his attempts at developing independence, Scott had made a number of poor decisions that resulted in his receiving low grades and getting into trouble in school and in the community. The family's handling of the situation increased Scott's resistance to authority and his rejection of basic family and social values. Although Scott's motives were developmentally appropriate, his attempted solutions were clearly failing.

The respectful stance of brief, solution-focused counseling provided an important means of joining with Scott and eliciting his collaboration in the counseling process. Keeping in mind Glasser's (1986) formulation of needs, I turned to Scott's interests, values, and preferences. My own goals with Scott were threefold: (a) to build rapport and trust, (b) to relieve him from being held solely responsible for family difficulties, and (c) to enhance his sense of power, belonging, freedom, and fun within the context of counseling. We had a pleasant and meaningful, if guarded, conversation.

Attempted Solutions, Exceptions, and Strengths

Scott's description of his homework difficulties revealed that he had started to follow a pattern of attempted solutions that did not work. Each evening when Scott was supposed to be studying, his sister checked up on him. When she found her brother doing something besides homework, she reported this information to their father, who then would yell at Scott. From the sidelines, Scott's sister criticized Scott, and without fail a family fight erupted. Attempting to beat the coalition aligned against him, Scott began to stubbornly and with increasing resistance refused to complete or turn in homework assignments. As a consequence, his grades declined. At report card time, Scott's father reprimanded him and restricted him to the house.

As a developing adolescent who felt the need for power and control over situations, Scott found the father–sister collusion to be intolerable. His solution was to intensify his oppositional behavior and turn routine homework into an ongoing power struggle. This solution was a failing one.

Another of Scott's attempted solutions had been to yell back at his sister and father and to hit her—actions that earned him the title of "bully." He also retaliated against the family by sneaking out of the house at night and by involving himself in minor theft and vandalism. Learning of Scott's nighttime activity from a police officer dismayed and embarrassed his father and sister.

Following our discussion of attempted solutions, I talked with Scott about exceptions to his problem behavior (see Walter & Peller, 1992). An exploration of non-problem times revealed that Scott performed well in school when his sister did not check and report on him. We also discovered a major exception to his avoidance of homework. During a 2-week period when his sister was away from home, Scott had completed his homework without prompting.

Scott's description of life in his family, school, and peer group provided valuable information about his strengths. Within his narrative I heard many embedded personal strengths and talents. I stressed Scott's strengths by offering statements such as, "I'm amazed at your resourcefulness" and "You know, I like your sense of humor and how you can laugh at the absurdity of your situation, even as you recognize its seriousness." This acknowledgment made Scott's competencies known to us both and indirectly linked them to his natural ability to change, grow, and resolve adversity. Scott stated that he was capable of being a successful student and that he preferred to achieve good grades.

Goal Setting

In attempting to define the problem, Scott surprisingly expressed a strong interest in school. In keeping with a brief, solution-focused approach, I set aside other concerns I had been asked to address by the referring therapist and Mr. Randall and attended to Scott's homework-related problems. Clinical experience and research support the idea that, regardless of the complexity of a problem, a small behavioral change often is sufficient to bring about rapid, profound, and lasting change for an individual or a family (de Shazer, 1988; Furman & Ahola, 1992; O'Hanlon & Weiner–Davis, 1989). Accordingly, I expected that a simple change in Scott's approach to his homework problem would ignite an ongoing process that would lead to the elimination of other problem behaviors. Scott and

I spent the rest of the session defining and talking about his problems related to homework.

During our short second session, Scott and I co-authored a simple goal: a reduction in family conflicts regarding homework. I assigned a formula task (de Shazer & Molnar, 1984) to engage Scott in rediscovering his own power. I asked him to notice those times when he felt motivated to do schoolwork and to think about what was different about those times. We concluded the second session within 20 minutes.

Interventions

With Scott's permission and in his presence, I briefed his father at the end of each session about what was discussed. I had emphasized Scott's competence, intelligence, and humor. At each briefing I asked Mr. Randall, "What have you noticed Scott doing in the past week that you would like to see him continue?" I also discussed some "new attribute" that I had discovered during each session. For example, after the second session I remarked, "I'm fascinated with Scott's ability to concentrate on the task at hand. I suspect this comes in very handy in school. Have you noticed Scott exhibiting this ability at home?"

Thus, I seeded for both father and son the expectation of change. I also modeled for Mr. Randall the skill of noting and commenting upon Scott's attributes and the changes he had made (O'Hanlon & Weiner–Davis, 1989). Parental affirmation is important to an adolescent. This indirect intervention seemed to strengthen the expectation of change.

In our third counseling session Scott and I brainstormed novel approaches to the homework problem. We also evaluated Scott's past successes and advice that Scott had received from friends and teachers regarding potential solutions. The solution we came up with was overcompliance. Scott would endeavor to complete his homework early in the evening to short-circuit his sister's checking up on him and avoid the ensuing family arguments. Past experience indicated that as long as Scott finished his homework, his father, despite his offers to help and concern about grades, did not scrutinize the homework but simply accepted it as done correctly. As part of the solution, Scott decided to act as if he wanted to do his homework. By acting in this way, he would defeat the sister's motivation for interfering. The fact that Scott was capable and infrequently needed assistance worked in favor of this intervention.

Scott's sense of humor added a twist to his strategy of overcompliance. Scott's father liked to relax and watch TV in the evening. Scott decided it would be fun to insist that his father help him with homework during that time. Scott reasoned that Mr. Randall would soon tire of being asked to be involved with his son's homework, especially if Mr. Randall believed that Scott was completing the work.

Next, we brainstormed alternatives to fighting with his sister and father. We came up with some fun and creative alternatives, but no specific plan evolved from our discussion. Eventually I suggested an intervention task that Scott thought he could accomplish (de Shazer, 1988). I said to Scott, "The next time you are told to do your homework, do something different from what you usually do. Make it funny or creative. Have fun doing it. Notice the changes that occur so you can describe them to me the next time we meet" (Littrell, 1998). This open-ended task allowed Scott to determine his actions. Scott's creativity and sense of humor took over, and he generated some interesting possibilities that provided us a good laugh and offered a form of mental rehearsal. For example, Scott speculated on the disruptive effect that reporting that he had completed his homework early in the day would have upon his sister's nightly checking-up routine.

Scott also considered demanding his father's undivided attention and assistance during the entire homework session, and he speculated upon the family's reaction if he were to start his homework sessions by directing his sister to check on him, at which point he would provide her with an "official statement" to report to their father. As his enthusiasm regarding the possibilities grew, Scott proposed some absurd activities that were quite funny, though impractical. As we ended the session, I encouraged Scott to continue brainstorming and to choose the best idea. I cautioned him to create a plan that would not be harmful or hurtful to himself or to anyone else.

As we began our fourth session, Scott said he had, indeed, overcomplied in meeting his father's stated expectation that he do his homework. Starting early every evening, he had asked his dad for help. Scott's compliance and requests for assistance interrupted his father's TV watching and relaxation time. Scott pushed the assignment by turning off the TV while announcing, "Dad, you said you would help me with my homework." The relationship between father and son was such that Scott's request and action did not provoke an angry response from his father. After all, his father had emphasized the importance of homework and had worked hard to get Scott to complete it. The family patterns showed positive change almost immediately. This success motivated Scott to continue pursuing the assigned task and his homework with enthusiasm.

After 4 days of steady effort and requests for help, Scott's father had stopped directing him to do his homework. In a humorous turn of events, when Scott's sister reported to her father about Scott's activities while he was doing his homework, her comments were met with an exasperated and firm response, "Mind your own business!" More important, Scott's requests for his father's help evoked, "Scott, just do the work and show it to me when you're done." Mr. Randall had hit his saturation point. In the meantime, Scott was redeveloping the habit of completing and turning in homework.

Scott and I enjoyed a good laugh in that in 4 days he had accomplished a major change in the family pattern surrounding homework. I encouraged Scott to continue doing his homework to avoid reemergence of the old pattern—the tattling sister, demanding father, and family fights. The idea of frustrating his sister pleased Scott, as did meeting his father's expectations. The time Scott set aside for homework became constructive. Scott reported relief. He was able to set his own pace, do his homework when he was ready to complete it, and be undisturbed in the process. Scott had reclaimed power and freedom. We mutually agreed that counseling should end.

After four weekly sessions, counseling was terminated with the suggestion that if Scott ever desires a "tune-up" session, he could return for a session or two. The term "tune-up" is one I use for times when a client has reverted to an old pattern and needs a boost to resume his or her newly learned ways of being. As with a car, a "tune-up" session gets things running smoothly again. Adolescents easily relate to this metaphor.

Six weeks after the initial intervention, Scott reported in a follow-up phone call that he was continuing to do his homework nightly; his sister no longer interfered, and his father infrequently inquired about it. In addition, Scott's grades had improved. At the quarterly grading period, Scott's marks met his preferred self-image as a student as well as his father's expectations. During parent–teacher conferences, three teachers remarked to Mr. Randall on the positive change in Scott's academic and behavioral performance. Hearing their comments met Mr. Randall's desire to be seen as a competent parent with a well behaved and academically capable adolescent son. It also served to strengthen the father–son relationship.

Discussion

Following termination of counseling, ongoing contact with Scott and his family occurred periodically within our small community. Through brief chats I learned that Scott's grades had continued to improve. He found an interesting after-school job and was avoiding trouble. Scott eventually graduated from high school with a B+ average. The family considered this an important and meaningful accomplishment.

The intervention described in this case had a significant impact on Scott and his family, initiating ongoing and positive changes. The family reorganized to acknowledge and balance the needs of all members. Subsequently, Scott and his sister successfully negotiated the necessary and developmentally appropriate transition from adolescence into young adulthood. When problems arose within the family, they were dealt with in a manner that allowed coping or resolution as a unit. In particular, Scott and his sister reestablished their former closeness and mutual support, which allowed them to cope with some confusing and painful events that followed the reentry of their mother into their lives.

As summarized in the following list, all eight characteristics of brief counseling were evident in this case.

1. *Time-limited:* We met for four sessions and had one follow-up phone call.
2. *Solution-focused:* Scott and I focused on (a) key exceptions to the problem, (b) his resources of humor, academic capability and persistence in carrying out tasks, and (c) his goal.

3. *Action-based:* The intervention involved Scott doing his homework.

4. *Socially interactive:* Though the focus was on Scott, family relationships were restructured and strengthened as some dominant assumptions were challenged and a focus on solutions was encouraged.

5. *Detail-oriented:* Scott's strengths were explored in detail, as were exceptions to the problem. The intervention was carefully planned, with the purpose of allowing Scott to paradoxically involve his father so his father would become less involved. Another purpose was to decrease his sister's negative involvement.

6. *Humor-eliciting:* Scott's sense of humor was utilized in designing a paradoxical intervention.

7. *Developmentally attentive:* The intervention attended to both family and individual development as Scott was making a major developmental transition and the balance in the parent-child relationship was shifting (Becvar & Becvar, 1996). Especially important in this case were Scott's adolescent struggles with identity and role confusion within the family.

8. *Relationship-based:* Quickly the scowling and belligerent young man who was my client changed his mind about what the nature of our relationship would be. I believe that careful listening and demonstrated respect for Scott's feelings and qualities allowed us to develop a positive working relationship, and that our relationship, in turn, challenged Scott to believe and behave in new ways.

Carving a Mask

In our final case, "Carving a Mask," Kirk Zinck once again works with an adolescent, one who is struggling with how to grieve in a culturally sanctioned manner. As with the other two cases, all eight characteristics of brief counseling are present, and the MRI model is employed. The major challenge is to design culturally responsive interventions that are culturally appropriate.

Cultural Bias

Culture is a complex concept, yet the basic definition offered by Morris and Robinson (1996) will suffice for this discussion. They defined culture as "a frame of reference from which we encounter ourselves, the world, and life" (p. 51). Predominant counseling practices are firmly rooted in the values of European–American middle-class culture (Lee, 2001). Norms by which behavior and attitudes are interpreted adhere to European–American values, with little tolerance for cultural practices that differ from that dominant paradigm. Limitations imposed by this viewpoint may introduce cultural bias into the counseling relationship. Cultural bias also results from common practices such as ignoring the influence of culture upon our clients, assigning people to a cultural group based on their appearance, or generalizing certain behaviors and beliefs to all members of a cultural group, with little allowance for variation among individuals and subgroups

(Garrett, 1999; Lee, 2001; Thomason, 1991). In short, a culturally biased world-view confines normative behavior and attitudes within the parameters of a specific culture. It ignores variations in context, history, level of acculturation, and life experience among a group of people (Garrett, 1999). In contrast, a culturally responsive worldview allows for variation among the members of any group.

The European–American paradigm is founded upon several assumptions about what is normal and socially desirable. Accepting these assumptions may inhibit one's sensitivity to cultural norms, traditions, and beliefs of other cultural groups. Morris and Robinson (1996) included, among these assumptions, individualism; small, independent family structures; highly verbal communication; material goods as symbolic of power and status; deemphasis on heritage; a culture-specific view of determinants of "normal" behavior; and highly structured use of time. To these we would add emotional expression (Constantine & Gainor, 2001), open self-disclosure, and the rapid development of trust (Garrett, 1999; Thomason, 1991).

Lee (2001) suggested that people seeking to remedy cultural bias begin with a self-examination of their "cultural blind spots" (p. 262). Many cultural belief systems contradict the European–American worldview. Typical differences include valuing interdependence and connection among all members of the group, viewing independence as detrimental to communal welfare, the prominent use of observation and nonverbal means of communication (Garrett, 1999; M. Malchoff, personal communication, May 15, 2002), and a concept of family as extending beyond biological and nuclear boundaries. Time, viewed as a commodity in European–American culture, is considered plentiful and "impossible to waste" in many cultures (Garrett, 1999; Morris & Robinson, 1996; Thomason, 1991). Further, the temporal focus of problem solving may fall upon immediate circumstances instead of past or future behavior (Garrett, 1999; Morris & Robinson, 2001; Thomason, 1991).

Expression of emotions also varies. While much of European–American society values cathartic expression in counseling and promotes open self-disclosure, less dominant cultures may lack the words to describe strong emotions, and emotional restraint may be the expected norm (Constantine & Gainor, 2001). Trust is earned over an extended time, despite one's title or position (A. Seville, personal communication, June 10, 2001; Garrett, 1999; Morris & Robinson, 1996).

Cultural Responsiveness

Culturally responsive counseling includes interventions that are matched to the client's cultural orientation. Yet, research has demonstrated that three aspects of the counseling process are more important than providing culturally matched interventions (Constantine, 2001a; 2001b; Garrett, 1999; Duncan & Miller, 2000): (a) the counselor–client relationship, (b) the provision of developmentally appropriate interventions, and (c) counselor flexibility in setting a context, defining problems, and developing solutions.

Matching interventions to culture involves learning about a client's expectations of counseling and his or her beliefs about what conditions are necessary for change. Matching may involve appropriately pacing the session, learning and observing cultural norms or taboos, consulting with traditional healers, and incorporating pertinent rituals within the counseling process. A counselor must take time to learn which practices and beliefs regarding problems, healing, and change are important to the client. Clients from minority cultures face a need to resolve problems in ways that fit both their own culture and the dominant culture (Garrett, 1999). To achieve effective problem resolution, cross-cultural clients must develop "bicultural competencies."

The counselor–client relationship is the foundation upon which change is co-constructed. According to Duncan and Miller (2000), this relationship accounts for 30% of the contribution to change. Anderson's (1997) collaborative language systems (CLS) is effective across many cultures. In CLS the relationship is primary, as counselor and client co-create new meanings through a therapeutic conversation that promotes change. Constantine (2001a) found that theoretical orientation aside, a counselor whom clients perceive as empathic "is likely to develop effective working relationships with these individuals, resulting in potentially beneficial counseling outcomes" (p. 343). Empathy is the communication of caring and understanding regarding another person's experiences (Constantine, 2001b).

Developmentally appropriate interventions consider a person's stage of development, intellectual functioning, and attention span (Vernon, 2002). These interventions are collaborative in nature and may involve supportive others such as parents, teachers, family members, or friends. This fits the interdependent character of many nondominant cultures in which problem resolution is accomplished in a communal context (Constantine, 2001a). Garrett (1999) emphasized the importance of developmental intervention. His work with Native American youths established that the passage through adolescence was marked by commonalities with other distinct cultures and the developmental match of counseling interventions was much more important than a cultural match.

Counselor flexibility refers to the ability to incorporate a variety of conceptualizations and treatment strategies with diverse client populations. Constantine (2001b) found that flexibility makes an important contribution to cross-cultural effectiveness.

A final aspect of cultural responsiveness is multicultural competence, which is enhanced by high levels of multicultural training (Constantine, 2001a, 2001b) and the counselor's ability to acknowledge and understand the normality and significance of interdependence and ecological connectedness among cultural groups, that fall outside of the European–American paradigm.

Making Brief Counseling Culturally Responsive

Much of the aptitude to effectively respond in cross-cultural contexts rests in a counselor's ability to look beyond dominant cultural assumptions (Lee, 2001), to develop a strong relationship with clients (Duncan & Miller, 2000, Garrett, 1999; Thomason, 1991), and to be flexible (Constantine, 2001a, 2001b; Constantine & Gainor, 2001; Thomason, 1991). Empathic skill (Constantine 2001a; 2001b; Duncan & Miller, 2000) and cross-cultural training (Constantine 2001a; 2001b) are also important. These attributes are the foundation upon which the counselor can modify and adapt his or her approach to make it culturally responsive. As a process of seeking solutions that fit for the individual, brief counseling is readily adapted to meet the needs of clients from varied cultures. Four of the eight characteristics of brief counseling (Littrell, 1998) are especially pertinent to creating a culturally responsive approach: being socially interactive, developmentally attentive, detail-oriented, and relationship-based. In its attention to these factors, brief counseling is also culturally responsive.

The socially interactive aspect of brief counseling enables the counselor to match interventions to the interdependence of many cultural groups. It emphasizes defining and incorporating support and affirmation from the people who inhabit the client's world. The brief counselor often asks, "Who will be the first to notice a change and comment upon it?" or "What potential solutions have other people suggested to you?" These kinds of questions lend themselves to developing and involving a community of concerned persons (Freedman & Combs, 1996) in resolving a problem.

As a developmentally attentive intervention, brief counseling addresses problems at the client's level of understanding and capability. Flexibility is found in the attention to details regarding what has worked or is working for the client, what might work, and what will get the client to his or her goal. In bringing a client's unique resources to bear upon a problem each intervention is "custom-tailored". One size does not fit all. Finally, because the counselor–client relationship is the foundation for all effective counseling, the brief counselor takes special care to nurture a strong and positive relationship with the client.

Definition of the "Problem"

Myron was stunned. He had just learned of his grandfather's death. This 14-year-old Alaskan Native student was in foster care in a city. Removed from immediate contact with his village and the traditional guidance of village elders, Myron sought me out. As he began coping with his grandfather's death, Myron sought support and assistance to determine how to appropriately acknowledge his grandfather, his family, and his village. In most native communities, elders guide their people through the unique blend of cultural traditions and spiritual practices associated with mourning. Removed from his village, Myron was isolated from the benefit of this guidance, as well as other communal practices.

As his school counselor, I had enrolled Myron upon his arrival in the city. Intimidated and shy, he entered a school with a student population three times larger than his village. His foster parent had asked me to look after him, and I did so willingly. Unfortunately, court-ordered foster placement in the city left him far more isolated from the world and the people he knew. His home was a small village where 95% of the inhabitants are native and most are related by blood or marriage. Far from major settlements or roads, the village is seasonally accessible by boat, small plane, or snow machine. In his present circumstances, someone he could connect with—even a relative stranger of a different culture—was important. Myron and I did connect, and over 3 months our relationship had developed into a caring camaraderie.

Over the course of four counseling sessions, Myron and I addressed his distress and grief. We looked for ways of expression that were, for him, culturally appropriate. In his world, when a villager dies, people pull together in support of the immediate family and honor the deceased through established rituals and traditions. As a group, Myron's people share many commonalities, yet villages or small group of villages in close proximity are cultures unto themselves. Language, traditions, and religious practices vary considerably. My cultural responsiveness as a counselor did not equate to knowledge of practices specific to a village. Thus, part of the task ahead was for the two of us to call upon his memories of village traditions and to identify knowledgeable people in his present context to guide him.

Myron and I defined the problems posed by the death of his grandfather: attending the funeral, avoiding trouble, and honoring his deceased grandfather. Many native communities function as an extended family. The death of a village elder brings obligations and traditions that all villagers must observe. Removed from the guidance of village elders, Myron was confused regarding how to appropriately honor and mourn the deceased grandfather.

Attempted Solutions

When he arrived at my office that morning, Myron did not explain what he wanted. He was distressed about his grandfather's passing and bewildered about how to respond. He expressed a desire to return to his village for the funeral but did not ask for assistance. He indicated that he did not hold much hope that he would be allowed to travel back to his village, given his legal status. Seeking out the counselor was an attempt to come to terms with his dilemma and stoically verbalize his distress and grief in a supportive, private context. Direct attempts at a solution had been minimal, and Myron had not discussed this situation with his foster parents. Had he been among his own people, a direct request for assistance would have been unnecessary. The villagers would have simply responded to Myron's needs.

Thus, Myron's initial response in not making any specific requests was culturally congruent, yet it was unworkable in the predominantly European–American cultural context of his foster care placement. This impacted the problem resolution. Presenting problems often have a rich history of contemplated, suggested, and attempted solutions to consider when counselor and client join to construct a workable solution, but Myron and I had to quickly develop a solution through brainstorming and networking with other people, given that we had 2 days to make things happen if Myron were to attend the funeral.

Goal Setting, and Exceptions to the Problem

Having participated in a joint definition of the problems that Myron faced, I facilitated exploration of possible goals. Drawing upon Myron's experience and memories of similar situations in his past, we brainstormed goals in the three problem areas. Myron and I identified who must be contacted for permission to attend the funeral and determined how to approach them and request permission and funding to travel.

If permitted to attend the funeral, a related problem presented itself. He had been placed in therapeutic foster care through the juvenile justice system because he was in trouble in his village. Part of the trouble stemmed from his using alcohol. Returning to his home would place Myron in a context where he would encounter all the old temptations to drink and engage in other illegal activity. Focusing on the probability that he had also resisted temptation (exceptions to the problem), I inquired about times when Myron had avoided getting into trouble in the village. He responded by describing times when certain people had positively influenced him, and he went on to identify individuals who helped him avoid trouble and households he could visit, where abstinence or moderate drinking were the norm and young people did not consume alcohol.

Finally, we brainstormed ways by which Myron could receive guidance and support on how to appropriately express his loss, his love for his grandfather, and an ongoing (spiritual) connection. In the village, he would have received this guidance automatically. Yet, in the context of his foster placement, culturally responsive guidance was not available. Because Myron would be in the village only a few days, we attempted to identify people who could provide ongoing and culturally responsive support after the funeral and upon his return to the foster placement.

Interventions

Our next step was to develop an action plan. Myron would request permission to travel home and attend the funeral. We listed the appropriate people to contact: foster parents, parole officer, and case worker. We reviewed what Myron would say to each person. I suggested to Myron that he request his foster mother's assistance with making these contacts. As a part of the intervention, Myron and I collaboratively planned how he would avoid trouble in the village. He briefly practiced explaining this plan as we anticipated that his parole officer and case worker would inquire about this. Finally, Myron and I discussed making arrangements with his teachers for his absence. Having secured Myron's agreement to make up missed schoolwork, I agreed to talk with his teachers about Myron's possible absence.

Time was short, and we had to move quickly to put the plan into action. Myron phoned his foster mother from my office and explained his desire to attend the funeral. He requested her immediate assistance in contacting the parole officer and the case worker. His foster mother agreed to help. We ended our session and agreed to meet the next morning.

By the next day, Myron and his foster mother had made the necessary contacts and secured permission and funding for him to make a 3-day trip. During a 30-minute session Myron and I reviewed how he would avoid trouble. We also reviewed his agreement to make up missed schoolwork after I informed him that his teachers would provide make-up work and assistance upon his return. We developed a plan for exiting a situation if uncontrolled drinking or some other form of potential trouble were to develop while he was in the village.

Myron, his foster mother (by phone), and I developed a behavioral contract. To solidify and make his intent to avoid trouble "public" (Anderson, 1997), Myron agreed to describe the contract to a trusted uncle and two other supportive people upon his arrival in the village. Making an agreement public tends to elicit communal support and increase a client's commitment to act accordingly (Freedman & Combs, 1996). Myron departed for his village early in the afternoon.

Following his return from the funeral, Myron and I met for a 20-minute session. He reported feeling relieved and grateful that he had been allowed to return to his village. During his visit, Myron avoided trouble by requesting support from key people in the village and reviewing our behavioral contract. It had not been necessary to extract himself from a situation where trouble was developing, because he conscientiously chose his associations and activities. We celebrated Myron's success with a handshake and some affirming statements.

While Myron's return to the village satisfied his need to participate in a communal expression of grief, he wanted to honor his grandfather's memory with a personal expression. Recalling our earlier conversation regarding who could provide culturally appropriate guidance, Myron decided to seek advice from his art teacher. Although the teacher was from an Alaskan Native culture that differed from Myron's, he was knowledgeable and sensitive to the broad cultural issues of native students in general. The teacher and Myron determined that it would be appropriate for Myron to carve a traditional wooden mask to be placed at the gravesite when Myron again would return to his village. The teacher offered to provide artistic and spiritual guidance, as traditional masks tend to become personal and powerful expressions of spiritual connections.

In a final 20-minute check-in 2 weeks later, Myron reported feeling satisfied and peaceful with the process of carving a mask. Because I often visited the art room to talk with students and admire their art, I observed Myron's mask in progress. Myron also reported that his teachers had helped him catch up on what he had missed during his absence.

Over the remaining academic year, I saw Myron informally in the hallways during lunch and between classes, in art class, or when he dropped by my office to chat or share a joke. Upon completing his court-ordered rehabilitation, Myron returned to his village with mask in hand.

Discussion

Culture is a way of knowing the world. It is a perspective that is temporally, contextually, and interactionally determined (H. Anderson, personal communication, April 12, 2001; Gergen, 2000). Brief counseling is adapted to individual needs because clients' perceptions guide problem definition, intervention, and action. One aspect of cultural responsiveness is to adopt a "not knowing" stance such that the counselor is always in the process of becoming informed (Anderson, 1997). This allows clients to educate the counselor regarding their unique needs and ideas and theories about what makes change happen and what it looks like. This respectful stance and the emphasis on facilitating client-generated solutions make brief counseling effective across cultural settings.

Cultural responsiveness also included attention to Myron's speech patterns—a deliberate pace typical of rural natives—that cued me to be less verbal and slow down. As a friend of mine explained, "We native people take time to gather our thoughts before we speak" (M. Malchoff, personal communication, May 22, 2002). In comparison to non-native cultures, responses come slowly and the counselor must be comfortable allowing significant periods of silence. Responses usually are succinct. Among many native people, "Words are spiritually potent, generative, and . . . engaged in the continuum of the cosmos, not neutral and disengaged from it" (Suzuki & Knudtson, 1992, p. 78). Words are carefully considered before being spoken.

Another responsive aspect of the intervention was recognizing that grieving may be culturally specific. Myron sought to grieve in ways that fit with his culture and satisfied what he knew and felt to be appropriate. Linking Myron with a native elder (the art teacher) provided some culturally informed guidance.

Further adaptation was necessary in planning for the influence of the village community upon Myron. While traditional counseling centers on individuals or family units, most Alaskan Native societies are communal in nature, with a powerful involvement of the community in child rearing that obligates all adults to model, protect, and correct. Although not all act responsibly, a core of adults generally assume broad parental responsibility. In jointly planning Myron's stay in his village, we addressed this communal influence in two ways: first, potentially problematic interactions were identified and a plan was developed to avoid or move away from them; second, Myron agreed to seek out and interact with people who would affirm and support his efforts to avoid trouble and guide him in the healthy expression of grief.

This case is a specific example of using brief counseling in a cross-cultural context. It demonstrates that brief counseling can be successfully adapted to fit clients from a non-Western culture. Cultural responsiveness required little modification of the model itself. Of major importance was that cultural responsiveness was linked to the quality of the relationship between counselor and client (Duncan & Miller, 2000; Littrell, 1998).

As shown in the following list, all eight characteristics of brief counseling found expression in Carving a Mask. Once again, the characteristics appeared not as separate elements but as part of a coherent and systematic framework.

1. *Time-limited:* We met for four sessions; the total time was less than 2.5 hours.
2. *Solution-focused:* Rather than looking to the past, the sessions revolved around what Myron wanted and how he could act in the here-and-now to attain his goals. We focused on (a) his knowledge of cultural practices and expectations, (b) identifying people who could assist him in realizing his goals of being present at the funeral and expressing grief in a culturally appropriate way, and (c) developing and acting upon a goal.
3. *Action-based:* The intervention involved rapid problem and goal definition and the immediate creation of a plan. To achieve his goals, Myron was active. He persuaded others to let him travel, negotiated how to stay sober, attended the funeral, carved a mask, and delivered the mask to his grandfather's grave.
4. *Socially interactive:* Throughout the intervention the focus was on interdependence. Myron had to involve other people in several contexts (e.g., key people in his village) to realize his multifaceted goal. Rather than left to chance, this support was deliberately utilized.
5. *Detail-oriented:* As we worked together, Myron and I developed a detailed plan of action that met the unique requirements of his culture. Attention to detail highlights the flexibility of brief counseling, as each intervention is tied to the individual, and in this case to communal needs and expectations. Individual tailoring resulted in a culturally responsive intervention.
6. *Humor-eliciting:* Humor was not used in this intervention. Yet, the relationship bonds that Myron and I drew upon were founded in part upon shared humor in our prior interactions.
7. *Developmentally attentive:* The intervention attended to the needs of a young man in transition between early and mid-adolescence. It was culturally attentive because it allowed Myron to participate in an important community ritual, taking his place as a man in the village setting, and meeting the appropriate expectations that he would be present and participating. The process also balanced direction and empowerment, supporting Myron's assuming an active role in resolving the problem, so that it became an interaction in which he developed new skills and competencies.
8. *Relationship-based:* Key to any successful counseling is a working relationship between the client and the counselor. Myron and I had developed a bond prior to this intervention. I had talked with Myron informally, assisted him in negotiating an unfamiliar context, and inquired about his welfare. This early relationship-building led Myron to seek my assistance and support at a time of sorrow and confusion.

Summary

Clinical judgment must always enter into the choice of counseling approaches, and brief counseling is but one of many tools in counselors' repertoire. At times it may be a most appropriate tool; at other times it may be most inappropriate.

When brief counseling is used, the counselor enhances the dignity of children and adolescents by his or her insistence on persistently accentuating their strengths rather than their weaknesses. Brief counselors build on what works rather than wallowing in what does not. They point clients toward the future, not the irretrievable past. They find the humor in life even as they and their clients struggle to effect change.

Brief counseling offers overwhelmed counselors a possible solution to the recurring question: Where do I find the time to help so many people and not burn out? Counselors using a brief counseling tend to be energized by an approach focusing on what works. In turn, clients respond by living up to the expectations of change because they have been challenged to use their resources. By the very nature of life, children and adolescents get hurt in many different ways. Brief counseling functions as an effective tool for creating new patterns when old ones have been damaged. As a bonus, brief counseling seems to help in less time than other approaches.

References

Anderson, H. (1997). *Conversation, language, and possibilities: A postmodern approach to therapy.* New York: Basic Books.

Becvar, D. S., & Becvar, R. J. (1996). *Family therapy: A systemic integration.* Boston: Allyn & Bacon.

Constantine, M. G. (2001a). Multicultural training, self-construals, and multicultural competence of school counselors. *Professional School Counseling, 4*(3), 202–208.

Constantine, M. G. (2001b). Theoretical orientation, empathy, and multicultural counseling competence in school counselor trainees. *Professional School Counseling, 4*(5), 342–349.

Constantine, M. G., & Gainor, K. A. (2001). Emotional intelligence and empathy: Their relation to multi-cultural counseling knowledge and awareness. *Professional School Counseling, 5*(2), 131–138.

De Jong, P., & Berg, I. K. (1998). *Interviewing for solutions.* Pacific Grove, CA: Brooks/Cole.

de Shazer, S. (1988). *Clues: Investigating solutions in brief therapy.* New York: Norton.

de Shazer, S., & Molnar, A. (1984). Four useful interventions in brief family therapy. *Journal of Marital and Family Therapy, 10,* 297–304.

Duncan, B. L., & Miller, S. D. (2000). *The heroic client: Doing client-directed, outcome-informed therapy.* San Francisco: Jossey–Bass.

Erickson, E. H. (1963). *Childhood and society.* New York: W. W. Norton.

Fisch, R., Weakland, J. H., & Segal, L. (1982). *The tactics of change: Doing therapy briefly.* San Francisco: Jossey–Bass.

Freedman, J., & Combs, G. (1996). *Narrative therapy: The social construction of preferred realities.* New York: W.W. Norton.

Furman, B., & Ahola, T. (1992). *Solution talk: Hosting therapeutic conversations.* New York: W. W. Norton.

Garrett, M. T. (1999). Soaring on wings of the eagle: Wellness of Native American high school students. *Professional School Counseling, 3*(1), 57–65.

Gergen, K. J. (2000). *An invitation to social construction.* Thousand Oaks, CA: Sage.

Glasser, W. (1986). *Control theory in the classroom.* New York: Harper & Row.

Lee, C. C. (2001). Culturally responsive school counselors and programs: Addressing the needs of all students. *Professional School Counseling, 4*(4), 257–262.

Littrell, J. M. (1998). *Brief counseling in action.* New York: W. W. Norton.

Littrell, J. M., & Angera, J. J. (1998). A solution-focused approach in couple and family therapy. In J. D. West, D. L. Bubenzer, & J. R. Bitter (Eds.), *Social construction in couple and family counseling* (pp. 21–53). Alexandria, VA: American Counseling Association.

Littrell, J. M., Malia, J. A., & Vanderwood, M. (1995). Single-session brief counseling in a high school. *Journal of Counseling and Development, 73*(4), 451–458.

Littrell, J. M., Zinck, K., Nesselhuf, D., & Yorke, C. (1997). Integrating brief counselling and adolescents' needs. *Canadian Journal of Counselling, 32*(2), 99–110.

Morris, J. R. & Robinson, D. T. (1996). A review of multicultural counseling. *Journal of Humanistic Education and Development, 35*(1), 50–61.

O'Hanlon, W. H., & Weiner–Davis, M. (1989). *In search of solutions: A new direction for psychotherapy.* New York: W. W. Norton.

Selekman, M. D. (1993). *Pathways to change: Brief therapy solutions with difficult adolescents.* New York: Guilford Press.

Sexton, T. L., Whiston, S. C., Bleuer, J. C., & Walz, G. R. (1997). *Integrating outcome research into counseling practice and training.* Alexandria, VA: American Counseling Association.

Suzuki, D. & Knudtson, P. (1992). *Wisdom of the elders: Sacred native stories of nature.* New York: Bantam Books.

Thomason, T. C. (1991). Counseling Native Americans: An introduction for non-Native American counselors. *Journal of Counseling and Development, 69,* 321–327.

Vernon, A. (2002). *What works with children and adolescents: A handbook of individual counseling techniques.* Champaign, IL: Research Press.

Walter, J., & Peller, J. (1992). *Becoming solution-focused in brief therapy.* New York: Brunner/Mazel.

Watzlawick, R, Weakland, J. H., & Fisch, R. (1974). *Change: Principles of problem formulation and problem resolution.* New York: W. W. Norton.

White, M., & Epston, D. (1990). *Narrative means to therapeutic ends.* New York: W. W. Norton.

Zinck, K., & Littrell, J. M. (2002). A peaceful solution. In L. Golden (Ed.), *Case studies in child and adolescent counseling* (3rd ed., pp. 108–117). Upper Saddle River, NJ: Merrill/Prentice–Hall.

Applications of
Rational–Emotive Behavior Therapy
With Children and Adolescents

Ann Vernon

Daily, helping professionals work with children who have problems ranging from normal developmental concerns that seem major to the child to serious issues that can result in behavioral or emotional maladjustment. Although most children successfully overcome these problems and master their developmental tasks with minimal adult guidance, some children cannot cope and do not receive the kind of help they need before serious disturbances occur. Therefore, it behooves professionals to preventively, as well as therapeutically, employ the most appropriate approaches and interventions to help children and adolescents deal with their developmental and situational stressors.

This chapter describes applications of rational-emotive behavior therapy (REBT) to childhood problems, emphasizing both preventive and remedial approaches to treatment. Helping professionals who work with children and adolescents are increasingly practicing REBT because it is a viable approach that helps young clients get better as well as feel better (DiGiusepppe, 1999; Ellis & Wilde, 2002; Vernon, 2002; Wilde, 1995).

Rational–Emotive Behavior Therapy: An Overview

Rational–emotive behavior therapy, developed by Albert Ellis in 1955, combines cognitive, emotive, and behavioral techniques in an active–directive therapeutic process (Ellis, 1995, 2001; Ellis & Dryden, 1997). Although most research, theory, and practice in REBT has addressed the adult population, the professional literature also contains reports applying REBT to children (Bernard & Joyce, 1984; DiGiuseppe, 1999; Ellis & Bernard, 1983; Ellis & Wilde, 2002; Vernon, 1997, 2002; Waters, 1982; Wilde, 1992, 1995). The increasing emphasis on children has resulted in the development of a number of rational-emotive educational materials that can be used preventively (Bernard, 2001; Vernon, 1989a, 1989b, 1989c; 1997, 1998a, b, c; 2002).

According to REBT theory, cognition is the most important determinant of emotion, as several authors have succinctly stated: "We feel what we think" (Walen, DiGiuseppe, & Dryden, 1992; Vernon, 20002; Wilde, 1992). The primary goals of REBT are to help people think and feel better and begin to act in self-enhancing ways that will help them attain their personal goals and lead happier and more fulfilling lives (Ellis, 2001; Walen, DiGiuseppe, & Wessler, 1992). For counselors to help clients accomplish these goals using REBT, they must understand the major ideas of REBT theory, as follows.

1. In developing REBT, Ellis created and expanded on a schema to conceptualize the nature of emotional disturbance (Ellis, 1995, 1996, 2001; Ellis & Dryden, 1997; Walen et al., 1992). REBT theory posits that as people attempt to fulfill their goals, they eventually encounter an activating event (A) that blocks the goal. People have beliefs about the activating event, and these beliefs directly influence how they feel and act (C). Thus, the activating event does not create the emotional and behavioral consequence (C), but the beliefs (B) about the event contribute to the emotional consequence. These beliefs may be rational ones that contribute to attaining goals and to having moderate, healthy emotions, or they may be irrational beliefs that lead to disturbed emotions and inhibit attaining goals and satisfaction in life (Dryden & Ellis, 2001). If the emotional and behavioral consequences are strongly negative, the irrational beliefs contributing to these emotions and behaviors must be disputed (D) to help clients develop effective new beliefs (E) and effective new feelings (F).

2. Irrational beliefs derive from a basic "must" (Dryden & Ellis, 2001). They represent demanding and unrealistic perceptions of how things should be,

statements of blame directed at oneself and others, "awfulizing" statements that exaggerate the event, and the inability to tolerate frustration (Ellis, 1996; Walen et al., 1992). To eliminate these thinking patterns, the counselor initiates a process known as *disputing,* which involves challenging the client's irrational beliefs through rigorous questioning and rational self-analysis, utilizing a wide variety of cognitive, emotive, and behavioral techniques (Ellis & Dryden, 1997; Dryden & Ellis, 2001). The goal of disputation is to help people adopt more adaptive rational beliefs, characterized by a more flexible, nonabsolutistic viewpoint (Macaskill, 1995). If this procedure is effective, irrational beliefs are replaced with rational ones and disturbing emotions and self-defeating behaviors are minimized or eliminated (Ellis & MacLaren, 1998).

3. REBT is designed as a self-help, educative therapy. A primary goal is to teach people how to get better rather than simply feel better (Ellis, 2001; DiGiuseppe, 1999; Vernon, 2002), which Ellis (2001) claimed can be achieved by persistently using a variety of emotional, behavioral, cognitive, and philosophical methods. He noted that REBT practitioners emphasize skill acquisition, which distinguishes this form of therapy from others (Ellis, 1995; Grieger & Woods, 1993; Vernon, 2002).

4. REBT is a comprehensive form of therapy, not simply a patch work approach to problem solving. It deals with the irrational beliefs that perpetuate the problem so that lasting change can be achieved. Counselors help clients maintain change through the use of homework assignments, bibliotherapy, and various self-help materials (Ellis & MacClaren, 1998).

Applications of REBT With Children and Adolescents

Helping professionals working with children and adolescents have used rational-emotive behavior therapy to teach positive mental health concepts and the skills to use these concepts (DiGiuseppe, 1999; Vernon, 1997, 2002). The approach is used extensively in schools in the United States, Australia, England, and Western Europe as both a therapeutic and a preventive treatment (Vernon, 1997). It also has been applied in child guidance clinics, community mental health facilities, and private practice on an individual and small-group basis (Ellis & Dryden, 1997). It has been employed successfully with children and adolescents for a variety of problems, including anger, disruptive behavior, school phobia, fears, aggression, low self-concept, test anxiety, interpersonal relationship problems, impulsivity, cheating, withdrawal, lack of motivation, underachievement, and depression (Bernard, 1991; Bernard & Joyce, 1984; Vernon, 2002; Wilde, 1992).

REBT can be used in two ways with children and adolescents. For school-age children who are not in counseling, REBT can be used preventively through rational–emotive education to enhance socioemotional growth and teach rational thinking skills (Bernard, 2001; DiGiuseppe, 1999; Vernon, 2002). For children who have been referred to a counselor, social worker, or school psychologist for a specific problem, REBT can be used individually or in small groups to address the problem (DiGiuseppe, 1999; Vernon, 2002).

Some people wonder how applicable REBT is with young children, because of their limited ability to cognitively process concepts, but experience has shown that one can model rational thinking skills for children of any age. The only limiting factor is the counselor's creativity in adapting REBT to the child's level. According to DiGiuseppe (1999), REBT can be used with children from as young as 5 years of age, but developmental stage must be considered. (DiGiuseppe, 1999; Vernon, 2002). DiGiuseppe (1999) noted that children who have reached the concrete operational stage of thinking are better able to deal with the logic associated with disputing, in contrast to younger children, who respond better to problem-solving strategies and rational coping statements.

More than 35 years ago, Wagner (1966) argued that REBT is superior to other therapeutic approaches when working with children. He enumerated the following advantages, which REBT practitioners continue to support today (Vernon, 1997; Wilde, 1992):

1. REBT makes immediate direct intervention possible when it is needed to deal with school problems.
2. The basic principles can be easily understood, applied, and adapted to children of most ages and intelligence levels.
3. REBT typically takes less time than other therapies, permitting more effective use of the counselor's time.
4. REBT helps children learn to live in their own environment; it teaches them to deal realistically with what they can and cannot change in their lives. Given that children and adolescents do not have control over many of the events that happen to them, this approach is empowering.

Vernon (2002) expanded on these advantages and identified the following additional reasons why REBT is an excellent approach with this poplulation:

5. REBT helps kids "get better," not just feel better, by addressing the core irrational thinking patterns that cause emotional upset.
6. REBT incorporates many techniques and concepts that help children move beyond their concrete thinking tendencies that can be problematic, because when they think in this manner, children fail to consider alternatives, they adopt rigid and arbitrary notions, and they are prone to overgeneralization.
7. REBT teaches behavioral and emotional self-control by teaching the connections between thoughts, feelings, and behaviors.
8. REBT advocates using a wide variety of cognitive, emotive, and behavioral techniques to teach the basic principles.

9. REBT is effective because it immediately addresses the problem. This is important because children's sense of time is so immediate and their problems are often so pressing that they require swift intervention.

10. REBT can be incorporated in schools in a variety of ways, including individual and small group counseling, emotional education programs, and workshops for parents and school personnel.

DiGiuseppe, Miller, and Trexler (as cited in Vernon, 1997) noted that school-age children are capable of acquiring knowledge of rational-emotive principles and that modifying their self-verbalization or irrational self-statements can have a positive effect on their emotional adjustment and behavior.

The Counseling Relationship

Although Ellis himself prefers an active-directive therapeutic style with most clients (Ellis, 2001; Ellis & MacLaren, 1998), he does not dogmatically insist that there is only one type of relationship between counselor and client, and he stressed that the extent to which a counselor is active-directive is a choice (Dryden & Ellis, 2001). Recognizing that all REBT therapists do not share Ellis's preference for an active-directive style (Ellis & Dryden, 1997), Dryden (1996) encouraged REBT counselors to be flexible. He and Ellis concurred that it is possible to vary the style and adhere to the theorietical principles at the same time. It is important to determine which therapeutic style is most effective for an individual client (Yankura & Dryden, 1997). This is particularly critical with children, and it usually is necessary to employ a wider variety of techniques, to have patience, and to be less directive (Vernon, 1997; 2002). As Bernard and Joyce (1984) indicated, "The relationship the REBT practitioner builds with a young client is oftentimes a necessary precondition for change" (p. 183).

In working with young clients, the counselor should use concrete examples extensively (Vernon, 2002) and generously intersperse humor, warmth, and praise (Bernard & Joyce, 1984). It also is important to use the language of the child and to limit the number of "bombarding" questions. Because children often do not refer themselves for counseling, they may feel uncomfortable. Therefore, the counselor must be friendly, honest, and relaxed to let children see how he or she can help them change some things that might be bothering them (Vernon, 1999). The counselor also might do well to engage the client in some get-acquainted activities such as playing a game, drawing a picture, or completing some unfinished sentences as a way of establishing rapport. In addition to what has been discussed, one of the best relationship-building techniques is to be a good listener (Vernon, 1997).

With young clients, particularly adolescents, resistance to counseling is common, in part because they often are referred by others and don't think they have a problem (DiGiuseppe, 1999; Vernon, 2002). Because they may come to counseling feeling defensive, the best strategy for the counselor is to be straight-forward about the problem as he or she understands it: "I understand that you are here because you have some problems getting along with your parents." Simplifying the problem is also helpful, since many adolescents are afraid they are "crazy." Sometimes adolescents become more willing to open up if the counselor discusses their problem as a hypothetical problem that another teenager had. For example, the counselor might say, "I've worked with some kids who really resent being told what to do. Is that how you feel?" In all counseling relationships, it is important to establish mutual goals toward which the counselor and the client will work together to solve the youth's problems (DiGiuseppe, 1999).

Problem Assessment

Because of children's range of behavioral and emotional problems, professionals must examine the frequency, intensity, and duration of the symptoms to determine the extent of the problem and how extensive the intervention has to be. It is also important to consider whether the child's problem is representative of his or her age-group and whether the child's emotions and behaviors are normal expressions or atypical responses. In REBT, problem assessment determines which emotions and behaviors are problematic, as well as the irrational beliefs that perpetuate the problem.

Assessing Irrational Beliefs

As stated previously, the three core irrational beliefs are demanding, self-downing, and low-frustration tolerance. Waters (1982, p. 572) expanded on these three basic beliefs and identified the following irrational beliefs common in children:

1. It's awful if others don't like me.
2. I'm bad if I make a mistake.
3. Everything should always go my way; I should get what I want.
4. Things should come easy to me.
5. The world should be fair, and bad people must be punished.
6. I shouldn't show my feelings.
7. Adults should be perfect.
8. There's only one right answer.
9. I must win.
10. 1 shouldn't have to wait for anything.

Waters (1981, p. 6) enumerated irrational beliefs for adolescents:

1. It would be awful if my peers didn't like me. It would be awful to be a social loser.
2. I shouldn't make mistakes, especially social mistakes.
3. It's my parents' fault I'm so miserable.

4. I can't help it. That's just the way I am, and 1 guess I'll always be this way.
5. The world should be fair and just.
6. It's awful when things don't go my way.
7. It's better to avoid challenges than to risk failure.
8. 1 must conform to my peers.
9. 1 can't stand to be criticized.
10. Others should always be responsible.

Just because a problem exists does not automatically mean that irrational beliefs are causing the negative feelings and behaviors. The way to discern this is to note the emotional intensity and behavioral reaction. For example, it is entirely reasonable for a young client to be sad if his or her best friend moves out of the neighborhood. For a short time the client may be listless or cry occasionally, and this is normal. But if he or she stays in the bedroom, refuses to eat, and cries for days on end, the child probably is thinking that this is the worst thing that could ever happen, that new friends cannot replace this one, and that this situation is unbearable. In this case, the irrational beliefs would be contributing to the more extreme emotional upset.

In assessing irrational beliefs, it is important to distinguish between feeling sad, disappointed, regretful or irritated, and feeling very depressed, guilty, angry. If these latter feelings, or other strong negative emotions or unproductive or self-defeating behaviors are present, they emmanate from irrational beliefs.

Krista, a high school junior, came to the school counselor upset and angry because she had not been nominated for the National Honor Society (NHS). When the counselor asked her to talk more about what was upsetting her, Krista said it wasn't fair for certain others to be selected if she wasn't. She "knew" she was being discriminated against because of her clothes and her hairstyle. She was certain that not being nominated for NHS would ruin her chances for a college scholarship. She didn't know how she could face her friends again, because they'd now think less of her.

The counselor acknowledged Krista's anger and upset feelings. Then, to help Krista become aware of some of her irrational beliefs, the counselor asked her if she knew for a fact that she had not been nominated because of her hair and clothes or if there could be some other reason. Krista begrudgingly replied that she didn't know this for a fact, but it just had to be her hair and clothes, because she met all the other criteria and certainly was more qualified than some of the others who had been chosen.

Next the counselor asked if meeting all the criteria was a guarantee that a person would be chosen. Wasn't it a selective process? To this, the young woman replied, "But it's not fair that I didn't get picked."

In turn, the counselor said, "I understand that it would be preferable if things were fair and you had been selected. But don't some unfair things happen in the world? How much control did you have over this event?"

After discussing these questions, they began to talk about Krista's tendency to overgeneralize, evidenced here in her comment about not being able to get a scholarship because of the NHS situation. The counselor asked, "Do you know others who have gotten scholarships and weren't in the National Honor Society?" When Krista answered affirmatively, the counselor asked why she thought a different procedure would apply to her. Krista admitted that she probably could still get a college scholarship, but she also wanted to be in National Honor Society.

In response, the counselor questioned Krista about why she thought her friends would reject her because she hadn't been selected. Were they all members? And just because she wasn't chosen, did that make her any less of a person? Krista responded that she probably was exaggerating, because not all of her friends were in the National Honor Society and probably wouldn't care that much. But she felt ashamed because she was excluded.

The counselor pointed out that feeling ashamed for not being selected must mean that Krista felt she was no good. Even though she hadn't been chosen for this honor, had she received others honors because of her accomplishments? Krista responded affirmatively, but said that she wanted this honor.

The counselor acknowledged Krista's feelings and pointed out that a preference is a rational belief. She explained that Krista's demanding that she be able to control others is an irrational belief and that by demanding that something she can't control be a certain way, Krista was creating negative feelings for herself. If she can't control other people, the only thing she can control is how she responds to the situation. By the end of the session, Krista admitted that she was not as angry and that she probably had been blowing the problem a bit out of proportion.

The irrational beliefs in this case created excessive negative feelings for Krista. Without help in disputing them, she might have continued to feel angry at the "unfairness" of the situation and depressed about the implications of not having been selected. As it was, she still felt unhappy and upset, but those are normal, rational emotions for the situation.

The goal in REBT is not to eliminate emotion but, rather, to help dispute the irrational beliefs so that moderate, functional emotions replace the intensely negative ones and permit constructive problem solving. When assessing problems from an REBT perspective, the counselor does not encourage the child or adolescent to describe the situation in great detail. Elaboration is unnecessary. More

important, the counselor must get a brief ser
ents the activating event, and then to assess tl
quences. The nature of the emotional conseq
client's irrational beliefs. For example, anger r
self or others); guilt and depression often are tie
ety and panic usually are the predominant emotio
tion tolerance.

To detect a client's irrational beliefs, the REB
criminately to everything the client says. When an ad
a date . . . I'm a social misfit," the statement represent
alize and also is indicative of self-downing. Or, when a   .re to get
picked as class president; if I don't, it will be terrible,"   .ue is making an
absolutistic demand. Statements such as, "I can't stand having to take tests; it's
too hard to study, and it's boring" clearly indicate low frustration tolerance—the
irrational belief that "things should come easily for me; I shouldn't have to work
too hard at anything."

The counselor also must bear in mind that the evaluative component, or the
core irrational belief of self-downing, demanding, or low frustration tolerance, is
what makes a thought problematic. To get a grasp on the evaluative component,
the counselor often has to help a child extend his or her thoughts.

A sixth grader was extremely upset because he hadn't been invited to
spend the night at a friend's house. When the counselor asked the
child what he was thinking that made him so upset, he replied that it
must mean that this friend didn't like him. Rather than dispute this overgeneralization—that the friend might like him but might have other reasons for not including him—the counselor asked, "And what does that say
about you?" To which the child replied, "That there must be something
wrong with me; I must not be good enough for him."

The core belief has to do with the child's self-put-downs. The statement was not simply an overgeneralization about not being invited.
Questions such as, "And . . . ?"And so . . . ?" "And what does that mean?"
"Because . . . ?" will help the counselor dig deeper to get to the client's
core beliefs.

Also, distinguishing between practical and emotional problems is important
in assessment (Vernon, 2002). All too often, counselors center on practical problems—realistic difficulties that involve lack of skills for dealing with the problem—and forget to deal with the emotions behind the problems, which are generated by irrational beliefs. For example, a counselor working with an adolescent
who never does her homework often will focus on ways to help the client get the
homework done. A common strategy is to generate a list of good solutions. Many
times, however, the adolescent will fail to follow through. Why? Because the

...selor didn't deal with the adolescent's frustration, which stemmed from her irrational beliefs: "I shouldn't have to work this hard at something that's so boring and irrelevant; I can't stand to do this stupid work."

Or take the example of a young child who repeatedly failed to take his medication at school. His parents and teachers couldn't understand why he didn't remember to take it, and they devised various strategies to assist him. But nothing they suggested had a long-lasting effect until this young person dealt with his feelings of shame and embarrassment about having to take medication, which he thought made him "different and less than" others. Until he understood that taking medication didn't make him a bad person, the problem continued. By assessing and addressing both the emotional and practical problems, practitioners are better able to get to the heart of the issue.

Assessing Common Emotional Problems

The following discussion examines common emotional problems of children and adolescents from a cognitive perspective. Recognizing the irrational beliefs that accompany intense, unhealthy, negative emotions is a necessary step in designing appropriate interventions and in getting to the root of the problem.

Anger

Numerous children and adolescents are referred to counselors because their anger gets in the way of constructive problem solving (Wilde, 1995). Counselors need to help young clients realize that anger that results in aggression, characterized by rage and hate, is an upsetting, unhealthy anger. In contrast, healthy anger takes the form of disappointment or irritation and often results in appropriate assertive behavior.

The irrational beliefs that precipitate unhealthy anger are demands: "Things should go my way; people should act like I say they should; things should be easy" (Wilde, 1995). Events that trigger anger in children and adolescents include being teased, ignored, or attacked by others; being thwarted, criticized, or imposed upon; or perceiving things as unfair. Anger commonly escalates and the child loses behavioral control.

Event:	One of her girlfriends told Shannon that her boyfriend was in the lunchroom with another girl.
Irrational beliefs:	"He shouldn't do this to me; he's dumping me for her; this is awful and I can't stand it."
Resulting feeling:	Anger
Behavioral consequence:	Shannon yelled at her boyfriend, creating a scene; he got angry and ignored her. Had Shannon stopped to analyze the situation, she might have seen that her boyfriend had every right to be with another girl, and

his being with another girl didn't necessarily mean that something was wrong with their relationship. Because she was making assumptions and awfulizing about this situation, however, she allowed her anger to escalate, which created more problems because he responded to her anger.

Fear and Anxiety

Anxiety is typical in children and adolescents, in part because their level of comprehension about events tends to be limited (Vernon, 1997). Ellis and Bernard (1983) discussed two kinds of fear that children have. Most common are *external fears,* such as fear of the dark, ghosts, animals, and so forth. *Internal fears* related to one's inadequacies are defined as *anxiety.* Anxious children and adolescents worry about what the future will bring and imagine danger when there is none, or at least, very little. Children who become anxious in competitive situations often feel inadequate, thinking how awful it will be if they fail. Frequently, their anxiety gets in the way of their performance and leads to low self-esteem. Children who worry excessively often do not live for the present because they are so busy thinking about what might happen.

Leslie was in kindergarten, soon to be in first grade. A perfectionist, she felt badly whenever she made a mistake. She was worried about going into first grade—afraid that her teacher wouldn't like her and would yell at her for making mistakes, afraid that the work would be too hard and she wouldn't know how to do it, and afraid that other kids would think she was stupid. Even though Leslie was a bright little girl, she was not able to stop worrying. As a result, she had stomachaches and couldn't sleep at night. Her parents referred her to the school counselor.

Since first grade was rapidly approaching, the counselor suggested that she help Leslie write down all of her worries on separate slips of paper. Then she had Leslie pick out a puppet and asked her to pretend that the puppet was the Worrywart. The counselor explained to Leslie that this Worrywart, which the counselor would hold, was going to help Leslie with her worries. The Worrywart believed that, sometimes, the more we worry about something, the worse it seems. She instructed Leslie to hold out one of the papers to the Worrywart and tell the Worrywart the worry written on it. The counselor explained that the Worrywart would listen and try to help Leslie get rid of the worry so she (the Worrywart) could "gobble it up" and Leslie wouldn't have to worry about it any longer. The exchange went like this:

Leslie to Worrywart: "I know my teacher won't like me."

Worrywart: "How do you know? Just because you think your teacher this year doesn't like you, don't you think next year's teacher can be different?"

Leslie:	"Well, I'm just worried that she won't like me."
Worrywart:	"Well, do you suppose she might like you? Don't you think maybe this teacher could like you?"
Leslie:	"Well, maybe. I just worry about it."
Worrywart:	"What good does it do to worry about it? Will it make the teacher be nicer?"
Leslie:	"No, I guess not. Maybe I don't have to worry so much about that. I suppose she could be nicer than my kindergarten teacher. But I'm scared I'll make mistakes and the teacher and other kids will think I'm dumb."
Worrywart:	"Well, have you ever made a mistake before? (Leslie nodded her head). When you did, did anyone tell you you were dumb because you made that mistake? (Leslie shook her head no). And even if they did, does that mean you're dumb? For example, if your new puppy forgets to grab his chew bone when he comes inside, does that mean he's dumb, or does that mean he just forgot?"
Leslie:	"It means he just forgot."

The dialogue went on in this way, with the counselor demonstrating some simple disputing to help this young client deal with her worries. At the conclusion of the session, Leslie let the Worrywart "gobble up" her worries because she wasn't as worried about these things anymore.

Depression

With children, as with adults, feelings of hopelessness, helplessness, and lack of control are often associated with depression. Seligman (1995) suggested that irrational thinking is a major contributor to depression and indicated that depressed children see bad events as permanent, incorrectly blame themselves when bad things happen, and fail to look at negative events as situationally specific. Wilde (1996) identified several specific irrational beliefs that contribute to depression: "I'm no good and will never amount to anything; I can't do anything right; there's no way out; nobody could love me, because I'm worthless."

A compounding problem related to childhood depression is that, unlike adults, children often express depression behaviorally by acting out (Vernon, 2002). If adults are not sensitive to the possibility that acting out may mask depression, they might respond to the surface behavior in a punitive way, which in turn often results in greater frustration, anger or depression for the young client. The counselor must keep this in mind when working with young people and depression.

Ned had just had a very bad argument with his girlfriend and, depressed, came to see the counselor. He said that life wasn't worth living if he couldn't be involved in this relationship. He felt that he must be no good if she didn't want to see him and that he could never be happy again.

The counselor helped Ned see that one argument did not necessarily mean that the relationship was over. And even if it was, was Ned certain that he could never be happy again? As the counselor challenged Ned to think about why he could never be happy again if this one person was not in his life, Ned began to acknowledge that he probably could be happy, but not as happy as he would be with her. Ned also began to understand that even if this young woman rejected him, it didn't mean that he was not a good person; he was the same person regardless of whether she rejected him.

After dealing with the irrational beliefs that had created his depression, Ned still felt unhappy about the argument, but he was able to put the problem into better perspective. Had he not uncovered and dealt with his irrational beliefs, the depression could have escalated into some self-defeating behavior or even suicide.

Individual Counseling Interventions

After building the relationship and assessing the problem, the REBT counselor begins to help young clients resolve their emotional and behavioral problems. The goal of REBT is to teach clients that they have the power to change how they think, which in turn affects how they feel and behave. Waters (1981, p. 1) specified the following goals of REBT for young children:

1. Correctly identify emotions.
2. Develop an emotional vocabulary.
3. Distinguish between helpful and hurtful feelings.
4. Differentiate between feelings and thoughts.
5. Tune in to self-talk.
6. Make the connection between self-talk and feelings.
7. Learn rational coping statements.

Older children and adolescents can be taught to use the ABCs of REBT as well as more sophisticated forms of disputing the awfulizing, demanding, and self-downing beliefs. The extent to which the counselor directly "teaches" the goals depends on the counselor, the child, and the problem. My preference is to integrate the goals into the session in a more indirect manner rather than to structure the session with more direct emphasis on teaching the REBT concepts.

Upon being asked what problem she wanted to work on during the session, 14-year-old Keisha said that she hated school, that all of her teachers were awful, and that she absolutely wasn't going to do any work because all of the subjects were boring. To help Keisha put the problem in perspective, the counselor drew a continuum line and asked Keisha to rate each of her subjects on a 1 (awful, can't stand it) to 10 (wonderful) basis. In doing so, Keisha identified only one subject as being truly awful, two as being about in the middle, and one that was almost a "10." When the counselor pointed this out to Keisha, she seemed rather surprised, and the counselor discussed the concept of "awfulizing" and overgeneralizing. The counselor pointed out that in reality all of Keisha's subjects weren't awful but that she was upsetting herself by focusing on the one that was terrible and by demanding that all of her classes had to be exciting for her to tolerate them.

The counselor asked Keisha to think back to previous years: Were all of her classes wonderful and exciting? If not, how had she tolerated them? Together they identified some self-talk that Keisha could choose to employ, such as: "This teacher is so boring, but I guess I'd better figure out how to stand it or I'll flunk the course, and I don't want that to happen."

Before the session ended, the counselor asked Keisha to say what she had learned during the session, and the counselor gave her the homework assignment of identifying two things that were "tolerable" about each of her classes that week. In addition, Keisha was to try to dispute her tendencies to awfulize about her subjects by recalling the self-talk messages she and the counselor had identified.

This case illustrates a number of techniques frequently used in REBT sessions. First, the counselor introduced the session by asking the adolescent to specify a problem she wanted to discuss. The question helped to direct the session and also conveyed the notion that there was "work" to be done. Second, a concrete activity was used to effectively illustrate the problem of overgeneralizing and awfulizing. Third, homework was assigned to reinforce the concepts learned in the session.

Some children and adolescents referred by parents and teachers will not specify a problem they want to work on. In these instances the counselor can try to involve them in activities designed indirectly to help them deal with the issues.

Matt was referred by his teacher because he tended to misinterpret and overreact to comments made by others. His overreactions sometimes led to aggressive behavior. If confronted about the aggressive behavior, Matt became defensive. Armed with this information provided by the teacher, the counselor decided to involve Matt in a game similar to Concentration to introduce the idea of facts versus beliefs and then to illustrate the importance of checking out the facts before reacting to others' comments. They did these things in the first session.

In the next session, they played a game similar to tic-tac-toe, called Facts and Beliefs (Vernon, 1989a) that reinforced the ideas presented in the first session and helped Matt understand how his misinterpretations were actually beliefs, not facts. Matt now had a foundation of information that he could draw on and was more receptive to working directly on the problem. The techniques used in this case helped to build rapport and introduced and explained key REBT concepts related to the child's problem.

These techniques can be used initially to introduce concepts. They also can be used strategically throughout the counseling sessions to make an idea more explicit for children and adolescents.

Antonio and Dave, two fourth graders, were referred to counseling because Dave would tease Antonio and Antonio would respond with fists flying. All attempts to dispute Antonio's demands about how Dave should act did little good. Dave continued to tease Antonio, and the more Antonio reacted to the teasing, the more victorious Dave felt. The counselor attempted to work with the two boys together, but Dave wasn't motivated to change. Therefore, the counselor suggested to Antonio that maybe Dave was really doing Antonio a favor because, even though Antonio didn't like the teasing, the experience showed him that he could survive it and he probably would never run into such a terrible tease again. In fact, the counselor said, Antonio had learned some important lessons that maybe he should tell other children with similar problems.

Antonio then began working on a book called *How To Get Along With Friends.* He and the counselor identified ways to tolerate teasing, ways to get along with a difficult person, and what to do to make yourself reasonably happy even though you can't change the other person. In making the book, Antonio was able to reframe the situation somewhat and concentrate on ways he could tolerate what he had considered to be an intolerable situation.

With very young children, two useful techniques are (a) to teach rational coping self-statements, and (b) to challenge beliefs and behaviors with empirical questions (adapted from Vernon, 1983, p. 473). For example, a child who is fearful of the water can be taught to repeat a rational coping statement such as this: "Even though I'm afraid of the water, there really isn't anything to be afraid of. The water isn't that deep, and there are people here to watch me." The child also can be helped to understand that some fear is natural but that he or she will miss out on a lot by not trying new things. This can be achieved through challenging questions.

Child: "But I'm afraid to swim. The water is cold."

Counselor: "How do you know it's cold if you haven't gotten in yet?"

Child: "Well, I just think it is."

Counselor: "So maybe it isn't as cold as you think. Does it look as if the other children think it's too cold to have fun?"

Child: "I guess not."

Counselor: "Well, it must not be too bad or the other children would be shivering, wouldn't they? What else is bothering you about going swimming?"

Child: "What if I get in too deep and think I'll drown and no one is there to save me?"

Counselor: "Well, let's look around. How many teachers and helpers are walking around supervising?

Child: "There are four teachers or helpers."

Counselor: "That's right. And do you see the rope where some of the other children are standing? That rope shows children how deep they can go before it gets dangerous. Do you see anyone going beyond the rope?"

Child: "Not now. But what if some kids did go outside the rope?"

Counselor: "I bet if they went outside the rope, the teacher would blow a whistle and make them come back. What do you think?"

Child: "I don't know. I suppose the teacher would make them get back. I'm still sort of scared, though."

Counselor: "It's okay to be scared, but what's the worst thing you think would happen if you got in the water for just a few minutes?"

Child: "I would drown."

Counselor: "Well, since you've been watching the other kids swim, has anyone drowned?

Child:　　　　"No."

Counselor:　　"And you said that there are lots of adults around to help if that would happen. So, since the kids look like they're having fun, and you know how far you can go and still be safe because the rope is there, what do you think about getting in for a few minutes and seeing for yourself what it's like?"

Child:　　　　"Well, I guess I'll try it."

After children try a new experience, it is important to discuss whether it was as bad as they had thought it would be and how they "talked to themselves" to get through it. This type of discussion increases the likelihood that they will apply the coping strategies in future situations.

Other methods that are effective in individual sessions with children and adolescents include "experiments," role-playing, and bibliotherapy.

Damien, a young adolescent, was creating a lot of stress for himself because he thought he had to be perfect. To illustrate the point that perfection is next to impossible, the counselor asked Damien to juggle tennis balls. He had a great deal of difficulty doing this, and he and the counselor discussed the fact that only a few professional people can do something like juggling very well, and even they make a mistake occasionally. They also talked about what making mistakes said about Damien as a person. Was he a total failure because he didn't do everything perfectly? After a while, Damien was able to realize that, generally, he did most things well, and that if he didn't do something well, he wasn't a loser.

During the session, Damien said that some of his stress came from the pressure he felt from his dad. When the counselor asked Damien to identify specific indicators of that pressure, Damien's responses indicated that he might be making some assumptions about his dad's thoughts and feelings. The counselor described the difference between a fact and an assumption, and then they role-played different ways Damien could "check out" his assumptions with his dad. At a follow-up session, Damien stated with some relief that when he did check out his assumptions, his dad clearly stated that, although he expected Damien to do his best, he didn't expect perfection.

Another effective strategy for helping children, especially those dealing with fear and anxiety, is rational-emotive imagery. In adapting adult REBT techniques for use with children, Huber (1981) introduced the concept of the "hero." Children are asked to identify their fear and the circumstances under which this fear arises. They then are asked to think of a hero, such as the Incredible Hulk, Wonder Woman, or Spider Man, and to imagine that this hero is experiencing the same fearful sequence of events they have experienced. Next, the children are asked to imagine that they are the hero who can approach a situation without fear. This type of imagery can be useful to children when they encounter similar fearful circumstances in the future.

Another useful strategy is to involve the client in creating rational limericks or songs to demonstrate the disputing process or other REBT concepts (Vernon, 2002). These are fun to create, and they serve as a concrete way to remember what has been discussed during the counseling session. The following limerick was developed to help a child deal with her anger:

When I am mad
I say and do things that are bad
And later I regret it
But people can't forget it
So then I am lonely and sad

So when I am mad
I need to think that things aren't so bad
Then I can run or scream but not hit
And not act like a firecracker that was lit
And then I won't be so lonely and sad.

When working with young children, the activities that are used must convey REBT concepts in a concrete manner. With older children and adolescents, direct disputation of irrational beliefs is possible but often should be followed up with the introduction of an image or with an experiment that reinforces the concept and its retention. For instance, an adolescent with numerous irrational beliefs learned to dispute them in counseling. To reinforce the disputing process, the counselor suggested that when he caught himself beginning to think irrationally, he should imagine a bug zapper with his irrational beliefs being "zapped" away. The young man reported that this worked really well and in a short time he was thinking more rationally on a routine basis.

One of the reasons this theory is so applicable to children and adolescents is that it embraces a wide variety of cognitive, behavioral, and emotive strategies in the intervention (Vernon, 1997). These techniques can be used to help children identify and dispute irrational beliefs, deal with troublesome emotions and behaviors, and develop effective new coping strategies. For a detailed description of numerous developmentally appropriate REBT interventions for young clients, the reader is referred to *What Works When with Children and Adolescents: A Handbook of Individual Counseling Techniques* (Vernon, 2002).

Rational-emotive therapy can be applied to individual clients in school and agency settings and, further, the concepts can be used readily in classroom and small-group counseling settings with rational-emotive education (REE).

Rational-Emotive Education

Because of the educational nature of rational-emotive behavior therapy, its principles can be easily and systematically incorporated into a classroom or small-group setting to facilitate attitudinal and behavioral changes. Used in this manner, the primary emphasis is on prevention, although groups may have a problem-solving remedial focus. The major goal of rational-emotive education (REE) is to help children and adolescents understand, at an early age, the general principles of emotional health and how to apply these principles to help them deal more effectively with the challenges they encounter in the process of growing up.

Classroom Applications

In the classroom setting, rational-emotive education typically is implemented through a series of structured emotional education lessons that are experientially based, allowing for student involvement and group interaction. Several REE programs have been developed, and their lessons have been used extensively throughout the United States and abroad (Bernard, 2001; Knaus, 1974; Pincus, 1990; Vernon, 1989a, 1989b, 1989c; Vernon, 1998a, 1998b, 1998c). These programs emphasize the following:

1. *Feelings:* A critical component of the lessons is learning to understand the connections between thoughts, feelings, and behaviors. Also important are to develop a feeling vocabulary, to learn to deal with emotional overreactions, to assess the intensity of feelings, and to develop appropriate ways to express feelings. REE stresses the importance of recognizing that feelings change, that the same event can result in different feelings, depending on who experiences it and how they perceive it, and that it is natural to have feelings.

2. *Beliefs and behaviors:* REE emphasizes differentiating between rational and irrational beliefs, understanding the connection between beliefs and behaviors, and discriminating between facts and beliefs. Teaching children to challenge irrational beliefs is key.

3. *Self-acceptance:* REE stresses the importance of developing an awareness of personal weaknesses as well as strengths, learning "who am I?" is not to be equated with what one does, and understanding that people are fallible human beings who need to accept their own imperfections.

4. *Problem solving:* Teaching children to think objectively, tolerate frustration, examine the impact of beliefs on behaviors, and learn alternative ways of problem solving are crucial problem-solving components. This is achieved in REE by teaching children to challenge REE and use new behavioral strategies.

The lessons begin with a short stimulus activity, such as an imagery activity, a problem-solving task, an art activity, bibliotherapy, a simulation game, writing a rational story, or completing a worksheet. The stimulus activity is designed to introduce the concept specified in the lesson objective and lasts 15–25 minutes depending on the age of the children and the time allotment. Following the activity, students engage in a directed discussion about the concept introduced in the stimulus activity.

This discussion is the most important part of the lesson and is organized around two types of questions:

1. *Content questions,* which emphasize the cognitive learnings from the activity.
2. *Personalization questions,* which help the students apply the learnings to their own experiences.

The discussion usually lasts 15–25 minutes, again depending on the age of the children and the time period.

The goal of these lessons is to teach the principles of rational thinking and to apply the concepts to common concerns and issues that children encounter in the course of normal development.

Example of REE Lesson

This lesson, for fourth graders, is about how to handle a typical developmental problem—being teased. The activity was taken from *The Passport Program: A Journey Through Social, Emotional, Cognitive, and Self-Development* (Grades 1–5) (Vernon, 1998a).

Tease Tolerance

Objective: To learn effective ways to deal with feelings about being teased.

Materials: An ugly mask, a hand mirror, and paper and pencil for each child for the follow-up activity.

Procedure:

1. Put on the mask. Invite the children to tell you how you look. Solicit words such as ugly, dumb, terrible, and so forth.
2. Next ask the children how they might feel if someone calls them names such as ugly, dumb, terrible, and so on.
3. Tell the children that you are going to help them learn that if someone calls them names or teases them, they don't have to have to have bad feelings. That doesn't mean they will like being teased, just that they don't have to be very upset about it. The technique called Tease Tolerance goes like this:
   ▪ Someone calls you a name, like "ugly pig."
   ▪ You look in the mirror and ask yourself: "Am I ugly? Am I a pig?"
   ▪ If the answer is no, you say to yourself: "I'm not ugly, and I'm not a pig because I don't have pink skin and a snout. So if I'm not what they say I am, why get upset?"

◼︎ If the answer is yes (you are what they say you are), you still don't have to get upset about it because it may be just one or a few people who are saying these things, and it doesn't mean you are a no-good kid just because someone calls you a name.

◼︎ Have a pair of children demonstrate the technique. In front of the group, have one child tease or call the other child a name. Then help that child practice the Tease Tolerance technique just described.

◼︎ Repeat this procedure with several volunteers, then discuss the content questions and personalization questions.

Discussion

Content Questions

1. If someone calls someone else a name, does that mean it's true?
2. What is the Tease Tolerance technique?
3. Even if what someone teases you about is true (like if they say you are stupid in math and you don't get good grades in math), what can you tell yourself so you won't get so upset?

Personalization Questions

1. Have you ever been called names before? If so, how did you feel about it?
2. Have you ever used the Tease Tolerance technique? If so, did it work for you?
3. Have you used other things to handle your feelings about being teased? (Invite sharing of ideas).

Follow-up Activity

Have the children write a story about when they have been teased. Have them write two endings for the story. In the first ending, have them write about what they did (or might have done) that would not be a good way to handle their feelings about teasing. In the second ending, have them write about what they did or could have done to handle their feelings about teasing in a better way. Provide opportunities for them to share the stories with others.

Application

The information learned from REE lessons can be applied to current problems and can provide a foundation of knowledge and insight to draw on when future difficulties arise. To illustrate, a third grader participated in the activity just described, Tease Tolerance. A week later he told his teacher that a classmate had called him a dumb, stupid beetlebrain and that he was very upset. By referring to the activity, the teacher helped the student see that, although it was a fact that someone had called him these names, where was the evidence that what this classmate had said about him was true?

The teacher encouraged this student to use the strategies he had learned in the REE activity from the previous week. After doing this, the student said he was less upset and better able to tolerate the teasing because he realized that the names the classmate had used did not apply to him. Because the teacher had the lesson to refer to, this intervention took only a short time and was an effective way to help this young boy who otherwise might have continued to be upset about this situation.

REE certainly will not eliminate all problems. But this preventive approach will equip children with information that may minimize the extent of a problem or help them reach new understandings and resolutions by using foundation concepts that serve as "tools."

Emotional education lessons can be implemented regularly with children at primary and secondary levels. The topics should be presented sequentially with core ideas introduced and reinforced as developmentally appropriate. For sequentially based lessons the reader is referred to *Thinking, Feeling, Behaving: An Emotional Education Curriculum for Children* (Vernon, 1989c) and *Thinking, Feeling, Behaving: An Emotional Education Curriculum for Adolescents* (Vernon, 1989b), The *Passport Programs* (Vernon, 1998a, 1998b, 1998c), and *Program Achieve* (Bernard, 2001).

Small-Group Applications

Two types of rational–emotive group counseling are (a) problem-centered, and (b) preventive.

The Problem-Centered Group

In the problem-centered group, members raise their current concerns and are taught to apply REBT principles for problem resolution by the group leader as well as by group members. Group members learn from the problems they themselves present and also by observing how other members' problems are addressed (DiGiuseppe, 1999). The group leader also may use didactic methods to teach the ABCs of REBT, disputational skills, and problem-solving strategies as appropriate. Major objectives include modeling rational attitudes and helping group members apply REBT basic ideas. As members learn the concepts, they are involved in group interaction, and members work to help the individual presenting the problem apply REBT principles.

The Preventive Group

The REBT group that emphasizes prevention is similar to rational–emotive education except that the process occurs in small groups of 6 to 10 members. In this type of group, the focus is on children's normal developmental difficulties. Groups may be organized around topics such as perfectionism, self-acceptance, interpersonal relationships, dealing with frustration, or problem-solving strategies. These group sessions are structured around an activity with a specific objective, and the children are encouraged to interact and exchange ways in which they can apply concepts from the lesson to their lives.

Another way to conduct this type of group is to organize a series of six to eight sessions, with each session addressing a different topic related to REBT concepts. For example, sessions might deal with teaching a feeling vocabulary, understanding the thought–feeling connection, identifying irrational beliefs, becoming more rational by learning to challenge beliefs, understanding that no one is "all good or bad," and learning that everyone makes mistakes. All of these concepts can be presented through activities designed to capture the group members' interest, while at the same time helping them to learn rational concepts. Much of the material that has been developed for classroom applications is applicable to small-group sessions.

In both types of REBT groups, the group leader must develop rapport, create a climate of acceptance, and give positive reinforcement for rational behavior and for learning rational–emotive skills. DiGiuseppe (1999) advised that it is best to group children by age, because having children who differ in age by more than 3 years in the same group makes it too difficult for the counselor to address all the issues and keep the attention of all members.

Summary

Rational–emotive behavior therapy can be used effectively with children and adolescents both therapeutically and preventively. Given the typical developmental milestones that children must master and the increasing stressors of contemporary society, helping professionals must concentrate on children's socioemotional development and provide therapeutic approaches that deal with children's immediate concerns and also help them develop coping skills so they can solve problems independently.

Although Knaus (1974) summarized the goal of RET almost 25 years ago, his words still provide the best summary I have found of the primary purpose of this approach. He wrote:

> Permitting a youngster to down himself or herself, and to become afflicted with needless anxiety, depression, guilt, hostility, and lack of discipline, and then taking that individual later in life and attempting to intensively "therapize" him or her in one-to-one encounters or small groups, is indeed a wasteful, tragically inefficient procedure. Far better, if it can be truly done, is to help this youngster to understand, at an early age, some of the general principles of emotional health and to teach him or her to consistently apply these principles to and with self and others. This is now one of the main goals of RET. (p. xii)

Rational–emotive behavior therapy is increasingly being used with children and adolescents to help them "get better," not just "feel better." Professionals concerned with helping today's youth will find this counseling approach extremely viable with young clients.

References

Bernard, M. E. (1991). *Using rational-emotive therapy effectively: A practitioner's guide.* New York: Plenum Press.

Bernard, M. E. (2001). *Program achieve: A curriculum of lessons for teaching students how to achieve and develop social–emotional–behavioral well-being* (Vols. 1–6.). Laguna Beach, CA: You Can Do It! Education.

Bernard, M. E., & Joyce, M. R. (1984). *Rational-emotive therapy with children and adolescents.* New York: Wiley.

DiGiuseppe, R. (1999). Rational emotive behavior therapy. In H. T. Prout & D. T. Brown, *Counseling and psychotherapy with children and adolescents: Theory and practice for school settings* (pp. 252–293). New York: John Wiley & Sons.

Dryden, W. (1996). *Rational emotive behavioural counselling in action* (2nd ed.). London: Sage.

Dryden, W., & Ellis, A. (2001). Rational emotive behavior therapy. In K. S. Dobson (Ed.), *Handbook of cognitive behavioral therapies* (pp. 295–347). New York: Guilford Press.

Ellis, A. (1995). Fundamentals of rational emotive behavior therapy for the 1990's. In W. Dryden (Ed.), *Rational emotive behaviour therapy* (pp. 1–30). London: Sage Publications.

Ellis, A. (1996). *Better, deeper, and more enduring brief therapy: The rational emotive behavior therapy manual.* New York: Brunner/Mazel.

Ellis, A. (2001). *Overcoming destructive beliefs, feelings, and behaviors.* Amherst, NY: Prometheus Books.

Ellis, A., & Bernard, M. E. (1983). Rational–emotive approaches to the problems of childhood. In A. Ellis & M. E. Bernard (Eds.), *Rational–emotive approaches to the problems of childhood* (pp. 3–36). New York: Plenum.

Ellis. A., & Dryden, W. (1997). *The practice of rational–emotive therapy.* New York: Springer.

Ellis, A., & MacLaren, C. (1998). *Rational emotive behavior therapy: A therapist's guide.* Atascadero, CA: Impact Publishers.

Ellis, A., & Wilde, J. (2002). *Case studies in rational emotive behavior therapy with children and adolescents.* Columbus, OH: Merrill Prentice Hall.

Grieger, R. M., & Woods, P. J. (1993). *The rational–emotive therapy companion: A clear, concise, and complete guide to being an RET client.* Roanoke, VA: Scholars Press.

Huber, C. H. (1981). Cognitive coping for elementary age children. *RET Work, 1,* 5–10.

Knaus, W. J. (1974). *Rational–emotive education: A manual for elementary school teachers.* New York: Institute for Rational Living.

Macaskill, N. D. (1995). Educating clients about rational emotive therapy. In W. Dryden (Ed.), *Rational emotive behavior therapy: A reader* (pp. 42–52).

Pincus, D. (1990). *Feeling good about yourself: Strategies to guide young people toward more positive, personal feelings.* Carthage, IL: Good Apple.

Seligman, M. (1995). *The optimistic child.* New York: Houghton Mifflin.

Vernon, A. (1983). Rational–emotive education. In A. Ellis & M. E. Bernard (Eds.), *Rational–emotive approaches to the problems of childhood* (pp. 467–483). New York: Plenum.

Vernon, A. (1989a). *Help yourself to a healthier you: A handbook of emotional education exercises for children.* Minneapolis: Burgess.

Vernon, A. (1989b). *Thinking, feeling, behaving: An emotional education curriculum for adolescents.* Champaign, IL: Research Press.

Vernon, A. (1989c). *Thinking, feeling, behaving: An emotional education curriculum for children.* Champaign, IL: Research Press.

Vernon, A. (1997). Applications of REBT with children and adolescents. In J. Yankura & W. Dryden (Eds.,), *Special populations of REBT—A therapist's casebook* (pp. 11–37). New York: Springer.

Vernon, A. (1998a). *The Passport Program: A journey through social, emotional, cognitive, and self-development* (grades 1–5). Champaign, IL: Research Press.

Vernon, A. (1998b). *The Passport Program: A journey through social, emotional, cognitive, and self-development* (grades 6–8). Champaign, IL: Research Press.

Vernon, A. (1998c). *The Passport Program: A journey through social, emotional, cognitive, and self-development* (grades 9–12). Champaign, IL: Research Press.

Vernon, A. (1999). Applications of rational emotive behavior therapy with children and adolescents. In A. Vernon (Ed.), *Counseling children and adolescents* (2nd ed.) (pp. 140–157). Denver: Love Publishing.

Vernon, A. (2002). *What works when with children and adolescents: A handbook of individual counseling techniques.* Champaign, IL: Research Press.

Wagner, E. E. (1966). Counseling children. *Rational Living, 1,* 26–28.

Walen, S. R., DiGiuseppe, R., & Dryden, W. (1992). *A practitioner's guide to rational-emotive therapy.* (2nd) (pp. 15–35). New York: Oxford University Press.

Walen, S. R., DiGiuseppe, R., & Wessler, R. L. (1992). *A practitioner's guide to rational–emotive therapy.* New York: Oxford University Press.

Waters, V (1981). The living school. *RET Work, 1,* 1–6.

Waters, V (1982). Therapies for children: Rational–emotive therapy. In C. R. Reynolds & T. B. Gutkin (Eds.), *Handbook of school psychology.* New York: Wiley.

Wilde, J. (1992). *Rational counseling with school-aged populations: A practical guide.* Muncie, IN: Accelerated Development.

Wilde, J. (1995). *Anger management in schools: Alternatives to student violence.* Lancaster, PA: Technomic Publishing.

Wilde, J. (1996). *Treating anger, anxiety, and depression in children and adolescents: A cognitive–behavioral perspective.* New York: Taylor and Francis.

Wilde, J. (2001). Interventions for children with anger problems. *Journal of Rational–Emotive and Cognitive–Behavior Therapy, 19* (3), 191–197.

Yankura, J., & Dryden, W. (Eds.). (1997). *Special applications of REBT A therapist's casebook.* New York: Springer.

Chapter 7

Counseling With
Exceptional Children

Shari Tarver-Behring and Michael E. Spagna

C hildren and adolescents with disabilities are an extremely heterogeneous group of diverse learners, each with unique learning strengths and needs. Often misunderstood and frequently less served by the counseling profession, these children and adolescents need counseling services just as much as, if not more than, other children (McDowell, Coven, & Eash, 1979). Federal legislation makes it imperative that all counselors who work with children and adolescents, even those not working within public school settings, be knowledgeable about the identification of and services for those with disabilities. In addition, all counselors have a professional and ethical responsibility to facilitate conditions that promote the full potential for all individuals, including exceptional groups (Baker, 1992; Holmgren, 1996; Maes, 1978; Seligman, 1985). As knowledge and experience are obtained for this population, counselors can serve children and their families more fully as intended by legal and professional guidelines.

Most counselors will encounter in their practice children and adolescents with disabilities. According to the U.S. Department of Education (2000), approximately 9% of the school-age population is classified as having a federally recognized disability and, therefore, receiving special education and/or related services. This figure does not include gifted children, who also are significantly different from the norm and are in need of identification, curricular modifications, and counseling interventions (Silverman, 1993). Nor does it include students with disabilities who do not qualify for special education but may be eligible for other educational and counseling services.

Despite the number of children and adolescents with disabilities, counseling professionals historically have had limited contact with this population for a variety of reasons. Some counselors lack confidence and training to serve these groups. Some are uncomfortable around people with disabilities. Others have incorrect information about or prejudices toward those with exceptional needs (Tucker, Shepard, & Hurst, 1986). In addition, because services to children and adolescents with disabilities are most often delivered by special education personnel within public schools, counselors may believe that their skills are not needed for these groups (Tarver Behring, Spagna, & Sullivan, 1998). Most counselors, however, do have many of the skills needed to work with these children and their families, such as communication strategies, a background in human development, and experience with an array of therapeutic techniques (Cochrane & Marini, 1977).

Counselors can prepare themselves to serve exceptional groups in several ways. As a first step, they must clarify their feelings and attitudes about working with children and adolescents who have disabilities. Pity, low expectations, repulsion to physical abnormalities, misinformation, and other biases can preclude effective counseling (Baker, 1992). Correct information and direct experience can facilitate accurate awareness and acceptance of these groups. In addition, counselors must obtain knowledge and training for working with specific groups with exceptional needs (Tarver Behring et al., 1998; Tucker et al., 1986). They can obtain this knowledge through training about federal and state guidelines, counseling workshops, consultation, supervision, current therapeutic literature, and community resources.

This chapter presents a brief legislative history of special education, including the most recent changes in the laws and definitions. This is followed by a discussion of identifying characteristics of children with sensory, physical, neurological, and developmental disabilities and a range of counseling approaches that have proven beneficial for specific groups of children and youth with disabilities.

Overview and History of Special Education

Taking the lead from the civil rights movement of the 1950s, which initiated the process of dismantling racial discrimination, parents of children with disabilities decided in the 1960s and early 1970s that they could achieve better services for their children if they were to take an activist stance and force public schools that previously had segregated students with disabilities to allow their children access to services. Until that time, schools had routinely denied admission to public education for students with a range of different disabling conditions.

Largely because of this public activism, two federal laws were passed that drastically changed this situation: Section 504 of the Rehabilitation Act of 1973 and Public Law 93–380 (Education of the Handicapped Amendments of 1974). These laws, for the first time in modern history, prohibited discrimination by federally funded organizations based on the existence of a disability (Section 504) and required services to be put in place for students with disabilities (PL 93–380). They also laid the foundation for the landmark piece of legislation known as Public Law 94–142, which was enacted in 1975.

PL 94–142 provided access to public education for all students ages 3 through 21 with disabilities. Since its enactment, the law has been reauthorized twice, as Public Law 101–476 (the Individuals with Disabilities Education Act) in 1990 and as Public Law 105–17 (also known as the Individuals with Disabilities Education Act), IDEA, in 1997. The original law included six provisions, each designed to allow for a free and appropriate public education for students with disabilities:

1. *Child find.* Schools were required to seek out all students with disabilities located within the boundaries of a given local plan area (usually a district).

2. *Nondiscriminatory assessment.* Students suspected of having disabilities were to receive a comprehensive and nondiscriminatory assessment to determine their eligibility for special education and/or related services.

3. *Individualized education program.* Based on a comprehensive assessment, students found eligible for special education and/or related services were to have an individually designed educational program put in place addressing their specific educational needs.

4. *Least restrictive environment.* Students were to receive, to the maximum extent possible, education with peers not having disabilities and were to be removed from general education classes only when a multidisciplinary team deemed these classes more restrictive to a given student's specific educational program.

5. *Due-process safeguards.* Guidelines to ensure that parents and schools are equal partners in the education of students with disabilities (prior to passage of PL 94–142, schools often made unilateral decisions concerning educational placement and instructional delivery).

6. *Parental involvement.* Parents were to have equal input into all educational decisions affecting their children and had the right to refuse educational placements and services if they so desired.

All of these provisions have been kept intact through the aforementioned reauthorizations of PL 94–142. In addition, eligibility was expanded to children from birth through 3 years of age. The most recent reauthorization, PL 105–17, reflects a number of changes that warrant attention: Children and youth with disabilities, once exempt from statewide and districtwide testing, now are required to participate in all assessment programs; there has been a shift toward full inclusion, which ensures greater participation of students with disabilities in the general education classroom, with the individualized education program (IEP) as the mechanism to ensure the greatest possible inclusion; parent participation in all eligibility and placement decisions has been increased; alterations have been made in the way assessments, required as part of referral procedures, are conducted; broader emphasis has been placed on transition planning; there now is support for voluntary mediation as a means of resolving family–school disputes concerning placement and educational programming issues; and specific guidelines have been included to address discipline and behavior issues of students with disabilities (National Information Center for Children and Youth with Disabilities [NICHCY], 1997).

Categories of Exceptional Children

As explained earlier, federal law ensures a free and appropriate public education for students with disabilities. According to the Individuals with Disabilities Education Act of 1997, children who fall within the following 13 categories of exceptionality are eligible to receive special education and related services: specific learning disabilities, speech and language impairments, emotional disturbance, mild mental retardation, developmental delay, multiple disabilities, hearing impairments, visual impairments, deaf–blindness, orthopedic impairments, other health impairments, traumatic brain injury, and autism.

The Commission on Excellence in Special Education (U.S. Department of Education, 2002) has recommended that these 13 eligibility categories be grouped into three major types of disorders (sensory disabilities, physical and neurological disabilities, and developmental disabilities) to facilitate the assessment and identification procedures often associated with students with disabilities.

History of Section 504 of the Rehabilitation Act

Some children who do not qualify for specific special educational categories under the Individuals with Disabilities Education Act are eligible for educational modifications and services under Section 504 of the Rehabilitation Act of 1973. According to Yell and Shriner (1997), the Rehabilitation Act of 1973 is in essence a civil rights act that protects the rights of persons with disabilities in settings where federal funds are received, such as public schools. Section 504 specifically protects students in educational settings whose disabilities do not adversely affect their educational performance leading to inclusion in a special educational category but who still require reasonable accommodations in the instructional setting to receive an appropriate education.

Under Section 504, a qualified person with disabilities is someone who has a physical or mental impairment that substantially limits one or more major life activities (walking, seeing, hearing, speaking, learning, etc.), who has experienced the impairment for some time, and who is perceived as currently exhibiting the impairment. Students eligible for reasonable educational modifications under Section 504 include those with attention deficit/hyperactivity disorder, communicable diseases, behavioral disorders, physical disabilities, chronic asthma, and diabetes, among others. Educational modifications include reduced or modified classwork assignments, different approaches in testing, providing a teacher's aide, having the student sit in the front row, instituting a behavioral modification plan, providing for building and program accessibility, and providing the student the use of a computer and technical aids. In addition, students who have met the definitions of qualified disabilities are eligible to be evaluated and to receive a written plan describing placement and services (Slenkovich, 1993).

Culturally Diverse Students in Special Education

Although the goal of special education is to promote academic and social/emotional success for *all* students, historically these services were not always offered to students in a fair and culturally equitable manner. Students from diverse cultural backgrounds have long been overrepresented in special education programs. The practice of dumping students from minority backgrounds, non-middle-class environments, and non-English-speaking families into segregated, special education classrooms was documented more than 30 years ago (Dunn, 1968). Educational reform and federal legislation have made great strides to create more equitable and effective special education services; however, diverse students are still disproportionately represented in the present-day special education system. According to a recent study by the American Youth Policy Forum and the Center on Educational Policy (2002), African American, American Indian, and Latino students are referred and placed in special education programs at a higher rate than Asian and European American students.

Cultural inequity in special education referral and placement continues for a variety of reasons: (a) unfair assessment procedures (Padilla & Medina, 1996; Hamayan & Damico, 1991), (b) inadequate teacher training in culturally sensitive methodology (Echevarria & Graves, 1998), (c) cultural mismatch of the learner with classroom materials and context (Vogt & Shearer, 2002), (d) lack of diversity within the assessment team (Harry, 1992), and (e) stereotypical expectations of lower performance toward certain groups by school professionals (Oswald, Coutinho, & Best, 2000). In addition, school failure and special education referral may be attributable to other cultural variables, such as language differences (Genesee, 1994), the adverse effects of poverty on school performance and study habits (Smith, 2001), and cultural differences in students' and teachers' behavioral expectations (Patton & Townsend, 1999).

In the last decade the educational field has identified a number of promising practices to correct these inequities. These include:

- Preservice training for teachers and specialists in culturally and linguistically appropriate educational practices (Echevarria & Graves, 1998)
- Culturally sensitive screening and consultation about alternative solutions in the general education classroom (Tarver Behring & Ingraham, 1998)
- Intervening with educational supports when academic risk factors are first evident in students (Echevarria, 2002)
- Culturally fair assessment for special education needs (Ridley, Li, & Hill, 1998)
- Culturally sensitive and inclusive school-based programs to support the academic and social success for all students (American Youth Policy Forum and the Center on Educational Policy, 2002).

Counselors can promote culturally equitable special education services by advocating for, and participating in, practices such as those just described.

History of Gifted Education

In 1972 the U.S. Department of Health, Education, and Welfare submitted a report to Congress that identified giftedness as an area of exceptionality and recommended that gifted students receive special services, including counseling. Several federal laws since have been passed that have outlined services for the gifted population. PL 103–382, enacted in 1994, continues to support research and programming for the gifted and talented and encourages the use of these resources for all students as well.

Since then, the definition of giftedness has changed from a description of a unitary trait into a description of a complex group of talents influenced by culture, age, experience, and sociometric status, and sometimes hidden by variables such as learning disabilities (Gagne, 1985; Shaklee, 1997; Silverman, 1993; Sternberg & Davidson, 1986). Currently, the federal definition for giftedness is:

> Children and youth with outstanding talent who perform or show the potential for performing at remarkably high levels of accomplishment when compared with others of their age, experience and environment. These children and youth exhibit high performance capability, or excel in specific academic fields. They require services not ordinarily provided by the schools. Outstanding talents are present in children and youth from all cultural groups, across all economic strata, and in all areas of human endeavor. (Ross, 1993, p. 28)

Gifted education programs historically were designed to match the child's educational needs to a continuum of services similar to the design of special education, such as pullout programs and gifted classrooms. Funding for gifted education, however, has become increasingly limited in most states, resulting in a severe decrease in educational services available for gifted children and youth. In addition, gifted children are more frequently being fully included in the general education classroom, similar to special education students, often with teachers who lack the time, skills, and resources to adequately serve the gifted (Shaklee, 1997).

Students With Developmental Disabilities

Students with developmental disabilities, according to the Commission on Excellence in Special Education (U.S. Department of Education, 2002), include those having specific learning disabilities, speech and language impairments, emotional disturbance, mild mental retardation, and developmental delay. The categories of specific learning disabilities, emotional disturbance, and mild mental retardation are explored in more detail in the following discussion, which addresses the cognitive, academic, adaptive, social, perceptual-motor, and language functioning of students with these types of developmental disabilities.

Categories of Students With Developmental Disabilities

Specific Learning Disabilities

Children and adolescents who have been identified as having specific learning disabilities usually are eligible for special education and related services only if they exhibit average intellectual functioning. This eligibility criterion has created a great deal of controversy, as children and adolescents with above-average intellectual functioning also may benefit from services in certain areas. In direct comparison to students with mild mental retardation, who have global deficits in the areas of memory and attention, individuals with specific learning disabilities have difficulties in an encapsulated area or areas of cognitive functioning (e.g., phonemic awareness), which are referred to as *psychological processing deficits.* These deficits cause academic difficulties and result in achievement significantly below expectations given average intellectual capacity. The incidence of children and adolescents with specific learning disabilities has been reported at 4.5% for the 50 states and Washington, DC, for ages 6–21 during the 1999–2000 school year (U.S. Department of Education, 2001).

Adaptive functioning in students with specific learning disabilities, similar to cognitive ability, is relatively intact. Even though these children and adolescents might exhibit dependency on teachers and parents, they have learned in many instances how to compensate for the impact their disabilities have on life outside of school.

According to Henley, Ramsey, and Algozzine (1993), students with specific learning disabilities, similar to those with mild mental retardation, have low self-esteem and generally a poorly defined self-concept. Even more than individuals with mild mental retardation, these students want to be accepted by peers without disabilities, so much so that they place themselves particularly at risk for gang involvement, breaking the law, and substance abuse.

Students with specific learning disabilities may have absolutely no deficits in perceptual–motor functioning. If their specific learning disability does affect this area of functioning, however, as in individuals who have dysgraphia, their gross and fine-motor skills may be so involved that even beginning handwriting skills might be affected.

In the area of language functioning, children and adolescents with specific learning disabilities may experience any of a multitude of difficulties in both receptive and expressive language. These deficits in language functioning might be evidenced by an inability to follow oral directions, to ask appropriate questions, to interact with peers socially, and so forth. Dysnomia, a type of specific learning disability that involves the inability to retrieve and express vocabulary, results in tip-of-the-tongue difficulties.

Cultural sensitivity should be considered in screening and referring students because a number of racial/ethnic subgroups have been misidentified for specific learning disabilities because of language differences, cultural mismatches in educational methodology, learning difficulties related to poverty, and teachers-versus-students cultural differences in behavioral expectations (American Youth Policy Forum and the Center on Educational Policy, 2002).

Emotional Disturbance

Cognitively, students with emotional disturbance usually are characterized as having at least low-average to average intellectual functioning and do not exhibit psychological processing deficits. According to the federal definition:

(i) The term [emotional disturbance] means a condition exhibiting one or more of the following characteristics over a long period of time and to a marked degree that adversely affects a child's educational performance:

(A) An inability to learn that cannot be explained by intellectual, sensory, or health factors.

(B) An inability to build or maintain satisfactory interpersonal relationships with peers and teachers.

(C) Inappropriate types of behavior or feelings under normal circumstances.

(D) A general pervasive mood of unhappiness or depression.

(E) A tendency to develop physical symptoms or fears associated with personal or school problems.

(ii) The term includes schizophrenia. The term does not apply to children who are socially maladjusted, unless it is determined that they have an emotional disturbance. (IDEA, 1997, sec. 300.7[4])

Students with emotional disturbance experience academic failure as a direct result of emotional problems or internalized and/or externalized behaviors that impact their performance. For example, students who have severe depression or suicidal ideation most certainly will encounter academic difficulties; pupils who are engaged in continuing behavioral outbursts (e.g., kicking other students) also will incur educational consequences—especially if they are suspended or expelled. Indeed, students with emotional disturbance often have discipline problems. The incidence of children and adolescents with emotional disturbance has been reported at 0.7% for the 50 states and Washington, DC, for ages 6–21 during the 1999–2000 school year (U.S. Department of Education, 2001).

As a result of their behavioral outbursts or generalized withdrawal, pupils with emotional disturbance tend to have poor relationships with their peers without disabilities. Like students with specific learning disabilities, they usually suffer from poor self-concept and low self-esteem. Often, their behaviors elicit negative reactions in peers, teachers, and parents that result in nonacceptance. As a result, these students are particularly susceptible to outside influences and are at risk for substance involvement, gang-related activity, and so forth.

Perceptual–motor skills and language functioning in this group are generally considered intact. But profane language and other behavioral outbursts resulting from emotional problems or socialized aggression can severely limit the interaction of these students with others.

As seen with the category of specific learning disabilities, African American students have been identified as having emotional difficulties at a higher rate than other cultural groups. Students from all cultural backgrounds must be understood and evaluated for emotional disorders in a culturally fair and appropriate manner (American Youth Policy Forum and the Center on Educational Policy, 2002).

Mild Mental Retardation

The incidence of mild mental retardation is approximately 1% in the 50 states and Washington, DC, for ages 6–21 during the 1999–2000 school year (U.S. Department of Education, 2001). Causes of mental retardation range from organic factors, such as Down syndrome, to environmental factors, such as fetal alcohol syndrome, malnutrition, and several known maternal infections (e.g., rubella).

Children and adolescents who have been identified as having mild mental retardation are determined eligible for special education and related services in accordance with federal law: "Mental retardation means significantly subaverage general intellectual functioning, existing concurrently with deficits in adaptive behavior and manifested during the developmental period, that adversely affects a child's educational performance" (IDEA, 1997, sec. 300.7[6]). As a direct result of their subaverage cognitive functioning, these children and adolescents generally learn at a slower pace than their peers without disabilities (Henley et al., 1993). They also avoid attempting new tasks and use inefficient learning strategies when faced with new tasks. In addition to having subaverage intellectual functioning, to be found eligible for special education and related services, these children and adolescents must be assessed as having below-average adaptive behaviors. Some poor adaptive behaviors found in students with mild mental retardation are poor self-help skills, low tolerance, low frustration and fatigue levels, and moral judgment commensurate with cognitive functioning.

Generally speaking, students with mild mental retardation are delayed in terms of social and emotional functioning. They usually exhibit lower levels of self-esteem and a more unfavorable self-concept than their peers without mental retardation. Because of their negative view of themselves, adolescents with mild mental retardation are overly susceptible to negative peer influences. Consequently, they might agree to experiment with foreign substances such as narcotics or to participate in gang-related activities in an attempt to gain peer acceptance (Polloway, Epstein, & Cullinan, 1985).

Perceptual-motor and language functioning also are significantly delayed in children and adolescents with mild mental retardation. This below-average functioning particularly affects their ability to participate fully in physical education activities and negatively curtails their ability to communicate socially and interact with students without mild or moderate mental retardation.

African American students have been found to be identified in this category at a much higher rate than other racial/ethnic groups. All students should be screened, referred, and assessed for services with particular attention to approaching the needs of students in a culturally sensitive and fair manner (American Youth Policy Forum and the Center on Educational Policy, 2002).

Counseling Students with Developmental Disabilities

Several general guidelines are useful for counselors serving children and adolescents with developmental disabilities and their families. Of utmost importance, counselors must understand the characteristics and needs of these groups. Also crucial is familiarity with the criteria for qualifying for special educational categories and services, as outlined earlier, and familiarity with the rights of parents and children pertaining to these services. Counselors should advocate for culturally sensitive screening and consultation about alternative solutions in the general education classroom prior to referral and placement in special education (Tarver Behring & Ingraham, 1998). Counselors also should support and participate directly in educational supports when academic difficulties are first evident (Echevarria, 2002). Counselors, too, must have general knowledge of the culturally fair methods and instruments for assessing children and youth in various categories.

Once an exceptional need has been identified, counselors may help by providing parents with referrals for various services, such as educational evaluations and services within the public school setting; health screenings; neurological evaluations; psychiatric assessments for medication; speech and language services, physical therapy, and career and vocational resources, both at school and in the community; specialized family counseling services; and support groups. Counselors then can consult with teachers, special educational personnel, parents, and community sources to plan educational and social interventions in a coordinated manner.

Planning should center on specific educational, behavioral, and emotional disabilities rather than abstract diagnostic categories (Westman, 1990). The student (especially if he or she is an adolescent) should be included in decision making about educational and therapeutic plans whenever possible. By including the child, he or she becomes educated about his or her strengths and weaknesses and feels mastery in helping to decide how to meet his or her special needs. Whenever possible, children and adolescents with mild and moderate disorders should be fully included in the general education classroom with appropriate modifications to allow for optimal educational and social opportunities.

Counselors also can help to promote social and emotional adjustment for children and adolescents with developmental disabilities (Tarver Behring et al., 1998). A number of sourcebooks are available offering intervention strategies, describing social skills programs, and listing therapeutic books for counselors to use with these children and adolescents, as well as with their parents and teachers (Albrecht, 1995; Bloomquist, 1996; Pierangelo & Jacoby, 1996; Rosenberg & Edmond–Rosenberg, 1994; Sinason, 1997; Smith, 1991). In the school setting, counselors can assist the child or adolescent with developmental disabilities by consulting with teachers about social skills strategies and programs for the entire class. For example, through the guidance of counselors, teachers can act as role models by showing respect for all students and can help the class generate ground rules for classroom communication and give positive feedback to students without disabilities who are engaging in social interaction or academic activities with classmates with disabilities.

Both within and outside the school setting, counselors can work directly with children and adolescents with developmental disabilities through individual and group counseling on key social and emotional areas of difficulty, such as low self-esteem. Counselors can help these children and adolescents to build positive self-esteem by modeling appropriate ways to express feelings, teaching them how to think of alternative solutions to a problem, empowering these youngsters to be involved in decision making about themselves, creating opportunities for them to learn positive behavior through rewards and recurring successful experiences, providing them with accurate information about the disability, and identifying others with the disability who have succeeded (Pierangelo & Jacoby, 1996).

Counselors also can work with the entire family on acceptance, goal setting, and rewards for success in the home to promote optimal conditions for these children and adolescents to reach their fullest potential. In addition, counselors can work with the family to facilitate the emotional adjustment of all family members by encouraging positive feelings for one another within the family, discussing how to balance attention for each child in the family, and specifying methods for support and stress reduction for the parents.

Counseling Students With Specific Learning Disabilities

Children and adolescents with specific learning disabilities need remedial services that target specific areas of functioning. Many of their other developmental areas are entirely normal and may even be areas of strength. These areas can be encouraged to promote overall adjustment in these individuals. Because most of the difficulties these children and adolescents experience are in academic areas, it is important to include teachers as team members when planning services for this group.

Federal law mandates inclusion in the general education classroom of children and adolescents with specific learning disabilities to the fullest extent possible. Therefore, counselors need to have contact with general education teachers and the resource specialists who provide specialized services to students with learning disabilities both inside and outside of the classroom (Tarver Behring & Spagna, 1997; Tarver Behring et al., 1998). Counselors can consult with teachers about specific techniques (e.g., teaching the sequential-step approach to math problems, using repetition, teaching outlining techniques, and instructing students in the use of memory aids), classroom modifications (e.g., administering oral tests, using computers, audiotaping lectures, reducing assignments, and allowing extended time to complete work), and motivational approaches (e.g., employing internal and external reinforcers, token economies, and contracts for adolescents) that fit each student's special needs (Westman, 1990). Counselors who are less skilled in these interventions can team with the resource specialist to offer these services to the general education teacher. The partnership between special education and general education teachers is necessary for successful full inclusion, but it often does not happen without an advocate, because of time constraints, scheduling differences, and the differing roles of school personnel (Eichinger & Woltman, 1993).

Social adjustment might be an additional area of need for students with specific learning disabilities, either because of weaknesses in social perception or of being viewed as different as a result of academic difficulties. Counselors can help teachers to be role models for the rest of the class in promoting social success for students with learning disabilities and can help them facilitate supportive peer activities such as peer pairing, cooperative work groups, and classroom social skills programs (Tarver Behring et al., 1998). When providing services to adolescents who are fully included in the general education classroom teachers should be discrete because of the importance of peer acceptance at this age.

Children and adolescents with specific learning disabilities also can benefit from having tutors outside of school to help with homework and test preparation. In addition, the tutors can help to reduce stress between the parents and child involving completion of academic activities and help the parents to further understand their child's or adolescent's educational needs (Westman, 1990).

If attention difficulties are present in combination with specific learning disabilities, counselors can recommend that parents consult with a psychiatrist about the possibility of prescribing stimulant medication for children who have not responded to other techniques (Barkley, 1995). Counselors, too, can work directly with children to help reduce their low self-esteem and with adolescents about identity their issues and long-term career planning, in individual and group counseling settings. Finally, counselors can offer support to parents in relation to specific difficulties and demands in the home: tutorial services to reduce parents' stress surrounding schoolwork demands; assistance in developing schedules to help parents who are frustrated because of their children's lack of organization; and referral of children to social organizations to address parents' concerns about their children's low self-esteem, social status, and long-term educational and career adjustment (Westman, 1990).

Counseling Students With Emotional Disturbance

Children and adolescents with emotional disturbance are most in need of stable, supportive environments that offer emotional nurturance, clear behavioral rules, and limits (Thompson & Rudolph, 1988). To maximize the effectiveness of treatment, counselors should be familiar with the various emotional and behavioral disorders of childhood and adolescence from both an educational and a psychological perspective (American Psychological Association, 1994; Individuals with Disabilities Education Act, 1997).

At school, students with emotional disturbance can benefit greatly in educational and emotional/social areas alike from inclusion in general education programs and activities when their inclusion is planned properly (Colvin, Karmeenui, & Sugai, 1994; Keenen, 1993). Counselors can help parents advocate that educational strategies and behavioral plans for their child are developed and fully implemented in the general education classroom setting. Because counselors have expertise in assisting with social and behavioral adjustment, they can consult with teachers about how to be appropriate role models, how to pair children with peer mentors in classroom activities, and how to identify ground rules for communication and behavior for the whole class (Kramer & Wright, 1994).

Counselors can provide teachers with social skills strategies and programs for the classroom that focus on problem solving, conflict resolution, anger management, and friendship making (Tarver Behring et al., 1998). For example, an elementary age child with emotional disturbance can benefit from clear classroom rules, rewards and consistent consequences; journaling about feelings; bibliotherapy; discrete prompts from the teacher, such as a gentle touch, to help the child be aware of inappropriate behavior before it escalates; brainstorming various solutions and consequences about friendship problems; being paired with a high social-status peer mentor in school activities; working on goal-oriented projects; and participating in activities with other children in areas in which he or she can be successful. Counselors can provide guidance in all of these areas.

Counselors also may be called upon to provide any of a number of counseling services that are critical for the adjustment of children and adolescents with emotional disturbance. Counselors working with these children and their families should have training in crisis counseling, the mandated reporting laws for child abuse, suicidal behavior, and intent to harm others, to name just a few essential areas, so they can be of assistance to students, parents, and teachers in these areas if needed. Counselors also can offer behavioral strategies and parent training to parents. Especially helpful for parents of adolescents with emotional disturbance is training in creating and using contracts that clearly specify limits, rules, expected behaviors, privileges, and consequences for inappropriate behaviors.

Even though families may contribute to the behavioral and emotional disorders of children and adolescents when discipline is harsh or inconsistent, a child's difficulties often are caused less directly by the parenting style alone than by a negative cycle in which the parents lack coping skills and strategies to deal with the youngster's difficult temperament (Patterson, 1986). Therefore, family therapy is strongly recommended to resolve anger and negative interaction patterns in the family. Individual and group counseling can be beneficial with children and adolescents who have mild and moderate emotional problems. Through individual counseling, the counselor can build a therapeutic, supportive relationship and work to change the child's or adolescent's negative self-image, depressed or anxious feelings, or relationship difficulties with peers. Group counseling can help the child or adolescent learn to express feelings more appropriately and can help the child or adolescent develop a positive self-concept, improve social skills and academic performance, and increase motivation. Planning educational and career goals with adolescents, parents, and teachers can provide positive alternatives to help the adolescent with a mild and moderate emotional or behavioral disorder toward long-term adjustment (Kauffman, 1997).

Counseling Students With Mild Mental Retardation

Students with mild mental retardation must meet criteria generally aligned with the widely accepted definition of mental retardation proposed by the American Association on Mental Retardation (AAMR, 1992), which states:

> Mental retardation refers to substantial limitations in present functioning. It is characterized by significantly subaverage intellectual functioning, existing concurrently with related limitations in two or more of the following applicable adaptive skill areas: communication, self-care, home living, social skills, community use, self-direction, health and safety, functional academics, leisure and work. Mental retardation manifests before age 18. (p. 1)

Because they experience developmental delays in most areas of functioning, children and adolescents with mild mental retardation require multiple services. Counselors can help to coordinate school, home, and community services for all areas of need. In the school setting, children and adolescents with mild and moderate mental retardation will benefit in educational and social areas alike by being fully included in the general educational program (Stevens & Slavin, 1991). Counselors, therefore, often work with parents, special educators, and teachers to advocate for appropriate educational modifications and resources in the general education classroom. They can help teachers to promote social adjustment for these students by providing guidance in incorporating peer modeling, self-reliance, age-appropriate social behavior, and friendship-making skills into classroom activities (Tarver Behring et al., 1998). They can promote tolerance of differences in peers without disabilities through social skills programs, integrated counseling groups, and classroom modeling and discussion (Frith, Clark, & Miller, 1983; Gottlieb, 1980; Salend, 1983). Further, they can teach behavioral modification, token economy, and contingency contracting strategies to teachers and parents to assist them in helping the students develop appropriate academic, social, and self-help behaviors (Cochrane & Marini, 1997).

Although the value of counseling with this group is controversial because of the students' cognitive limitations, it seems reasonable that counselors can offer individual and group counseling focusing on self-esteem, self-expression, and behavioral rehearsal, which are all typical areas of need (Thompson & Rudolph, 1988). Counselors can help parents understand and encourage their child's or adolescent's abilities and help the parents cope with the stresses of parenting a disabled child. For adolescents, special attention should be given to their developing independent living skills and to educational and vocational planning.

Three of Anthony's teachers contacted his school counselor concerning his academic difficulties. They reported that Anthony struggled with decoding words when reading orally, did not know basic math facts, had difficulty with reasoning and problem-solving skills, and exhibited poor social skills when interacting with his eighth grade classmates. Although his teachers described Anthony as a "good kid," they reported that he was falling behind in classroom and homework assignments, had become increasingly defiant in classes, was openly berating other students, and was not responding to the teacher's redirection prompts. According to Anthony's parents, he seemed to have become more apathetic about school, no longer expressed interest in academic subjects, and had gradually become resistant to finishing homework assignments of any sort. The parents noticed that over the past several weeks he had become more withdrawn and easily agitated when they asked him what was bothering him. His parents reported that he had few friends and seemed to be vulnerable to falling in with the wrong crowd.

The counselor referred Anthony for testing and consideration for special education and related services by a multidisciplinary team that included the previously mentioned teachers, the resource specialist, and the school counselor. The team found that Anthony had specific learning disabilities and qualified for assistance by the resource specialist. The team then designed a program for fully including Anthony in the general education classroom with resource support. The resource specialist worked with Anthony's teachers in the classroom to identify specific instructional modifications. He also would work with Anthony in the resource room for one class period each day on academic areas of need.

The team included counseling as a designated instructional service on the individualized education program. Anthony would attend a social skills group offered by the school counselor for other adolescents his age. In this group the participants learned social problem-solving skills. For example, they learned how to identify a problem, how to brainstorm a solution, and how to evaluate the outcome. The group members then role-played the problem and the identified solutions and discussed other problems that could arise with this situation and how they might solve them.

In addition, the school counselor offered to assist Anthony's teachers with social skills strategies in the classroom, such as locating a peer mentor to help Anthony with difficult academic work. Further, with the help of the school counselor, the resource teacher and the classroom teachers formed a team with the parents to plan a home-school academic program. This system allowed the resource specialist to offer academic, organizational, and communication strategies for home and school. The team designed a plan in which Anthony would daily record homework and schoolwork assignments in a notebook and, upon completion, his teachers would check it off. The homework assignments also would be checked off by Anthony's parents, who would reward Anthony upon completion of his homework.

As another intervention, the family hired a tutor to work with Anthony once a week. This relieved tension between the parents and Anthony stemming from the schoolwork issue. The parents also decided to attend short-term counseling with Anthony at a community agency to better understand and support Anthony's needs and to allow him to work individually with the counselor on self-esteem. Finally, Anthony joined a baseball team, which gave him the opportunity to experience success and provided a healthy social outlet.

Following these interventions, the parents and teachers reported to the school counselor that Anthony was completing his academic work, was less frustrated, and was more socially adjusted. They noted that he recently had developed several positive relationships with friends. As a final intervention, the school counselor asked the career counselor at school to meet with Anthony to develop long-range academic and career goals that would help Anthony reach his full potential.

Students With Physical and Neurological Disabilities

According to the Commission on Excellence in Special Education (U.S. Department of Education, 2002), students with physical and neurological disabilities include students having orthopedic impairments, other health impairments, traumatic brain injury, multiple disabilities, and autism. The categories of orthopedic impairments and multiple disabilities are described in more detail next, addressing the cognitive, academic, adaptive, social, perceptual–motor, and language functioning of students who have these forms of physical and neurological disabilities.

Categories of Physical and Neurological Disabilities

Students With Orthopedic Impairments

The incidence of orthopedic impairments is approximately 0.1% in the 50 states and Washington, DC, for ages 6–21 during the 1999–2000 school year (U.S. Department of Education, 2001). Federal law describes children and adolescents with orthopedic impairments in the following manner:

> Orthopedic impairment means a severe orthopedic impairment that adversely affects a child's educational performance. The term includes impairments caused by congenital anomaly (e.g., clubfoot, absence of some member, etc.), impairments caused by disease (e.g., poliomyelitis, bone tuberculosis, etc.), and impairments from other causes (e.g., cerebral palsy, amputations, and fractures or burns that cause contractures). (IDEA, 1997, sec. 300.7[8])

Musculoskeletal impairments usually result in severe restriction of movement, typically affecting both gross- and fine-motor movements, as a result of stiffening of joints, inflammation of bones, degeneration of muscle fiber and bone structure, and muscle atrophy resulting from lack of use. In addition to influencing range of motion, severe musculoskeletal impairments can cause children and adolescents to become extremely embarrassed and frustrated because they are so dependent on others for assistance. These impairments include arthrogryposis multiplex congenita (also known as Pinocchio syndrome due to the wooded appearance of the individuals affected), osteogenesis imperfecta (also known as brittle bone disease), juvenile rheumatoid arthritis, and muscular dystrophy.

Spinal cord impairments, as the name implies, involve a disabling condition whereby the spinal cord is severed or injured resulting in anything from incoordination to partial to full paralysis below the point of nerve damage. Children and adolescents with severe spinal cord injuries may also suffer from a variety of skin, urinary, and respiratory infections, insensitivity to heat and cold, and inability to control bowel and bladder functions. Severe spinal cord impairments include spina bifida and spinal muscular dystrophy.

Cerebral palsy and several seizure disorders are considered orthopedic impairments that can result in severe physical difficulties. As opposed to spinal cord impairments, cerebral palsy involves dysfunction of the brain and nervous system (not including the spinal cord) that results in difficulty with gross- and fine-motor skills, attention, eye-hand coordination, and so forth.

Students With Multiple Disabilities

According to the U.S. Department of Education (2001), 0.2% of the school-age population in the United States is considered to have multiple disabilities and, therefore, receives special education and related services. Although it is easy to think of multiple disabilities as an accumulation of several of the categories covered so far, in fact, students who have multiple disabilities experience difficulties that are magnified beyond a simple analysis of the sum of the parts. The combinations of disabilities are endless. Mild mental retardation, for example, can co-occur with cerebral palsy, with a variety of orthopedic impairments such as those already presented, with a range of severe behavior disorders, as well as with visual and/or hearing impairments. Emotional disturbance can also coexist with a full range of physical, visual, and/or hearing impairments.

Counseling Students With Physical and Neurological Disabilities

The best approach for counselors involved with children and adolescents who have physical and neurological disabilities is to work closely with the multidisciplinary team of the school's special educational personnel, physicians, community specialists, and personnel from governmental services, such as vocational counselors, who provide the primary services to these students. These experts can determine the student's strengths and needs and how best to offer support. Counselors can consult with these personnel and assist parents in understanding, accessing, and advocating for programs that will help their child or adolescent to reach their fullest potential.

Counselors also can offer parents individual, group, or family counseling involving issues of grief surrounding their child's disability, issues of guilt, and issues of hopelessness in viewing their child's future (Thompson & Rudolph, 1988). By the time the child with physical and neurological disabilities reaches age 16, a transition plan should be in place as a part of the child's individualized education program, offering support in work, home, recreation, and community activities and promoting optimal long-term adjustment (Downing, 1996).

Counseling Students With Orthopedic Impairments

In counseling with children and adolescents who have orthopedic impairments, the client's strengths as well as disabilities must be recognized. Frequently, individuals who associate with these children and adolescents overlook their strengths by assuming deficits in all domains based upon the child's physical appearance. Often, the low self-esteem of these children and adolescents derives as much from having unrecognized strengths as from self-consciousness resulting from a physical disorder. In addition to supporting the child's strengths and helping the child to work with his or her disability, the counselor can assist parents in advocating for appropriate assessment and services at school and through community resources.

These children and adolescents should be included to the maximum extent possible to allow for optimal educational, self-care, vocational, and social opportunities (Downing, 1996). Counselors can coordinate services with other specialists to help parents and teachers reorganize physical environments, remove barriers, and obtain special equipment to facilitate inclusion in all areas of life. Counselors also can help parents and teachers avoid overprotectiveness and assist these children and adolescents in reaching their full potential (Thompson & Rudolph, 1988).

Counseling Students With Multiple Disabilities

To coordinate services for children or adolescents with multiple disabilities, the counselor must understand disabilities in multiple areas and has to work with all involved parties. Most of the previous suggestions apply to counseling members of this group and their families, depending on which combinations of disabilities are present. Counselors can assist parents by advocating for school and community services, requesting appropriate modifications and aids, and offering supportive counseling. They also can help the students directly in the areas of self-esteem, self-help, and social skills if they have a high enough level of communication and cognitive functioning. Finally, counselors should help develop, with the parents and IEP team, a plan to promote the long-term adjustment of these children and adolescents in multiple areas.

Rosa, a 3-year-old Hispanic female, had been identified as having multiple disabilities. Her parents reported that the mother had contracted rubella during the second trimester of her pregnancy and that her labor was long and difficult. According to the parents, they first suspected that something was wrong when they returned home from the hospital just after Rosa was born. The father stated that Rosa did not appear to recognize the parents and did not respond to environmental noises such as a toy's rattle.

After a year and a half, the family pediatrician confirmed that Rosa had profound hearing and visual impairments. The pediatrician recommended that the family contact a local counselor who might be able to suggest services for Rosa. That counselor invited the parents to a support group for parents of young children with multiple disabilities. The counselor also referred the family to a regional center, where an intervention program was designed for them by professionals specializing in vision and hearing impairments.

The parents began implementing a variety of the recommended approaches to address the increasingly apparent language delays in Rosa. At a 6-month follow-up visit at the regional center, the parents indicated that Rosa's communication skills were slowly developing and that Rosa acknowledged their presence and responded to specific structured stimuli. The following year, the counselor referred the family to a public preschool program designed specifically to meet the needs of deaf–blind children. There, an individualized education program was developed for Rosa, to be reviewed annually and to continue as Rosa entered elementary school.

The parents reported that they were extremely happy with the intervention program at the preschool and noted dramatic improvements in Rosa's interaction and communication skills. The family was invited to stay in contact with the counselor as needed in the future.

Students With Attention Deficit/Hyperactivity Disorder

Attention deficit hyperactivity disorder (ADHD) is a high-incidence disorder of children in the United States and a common reason for referral for special services. It is believed to occur in 10%–20% of children and adolescents and appears more frequently in males than females (Barkley, 1990; Rief, 1993; Silver, 1992). The *Diagnostic and Statistical Manual of Mental Disorders* (DSM–IV) defines the disorder as the presence of developmentally inappropriate hyperactivity, inattention, and impulsivity that is evident in the child by age 7 and leads to clinically significant impairment in social, academic, or occupational functioning across two or more settings, such as home and school (American Psychological Association, 1994). Inattention includes behaviors such as difficulty in sustaining task-related attention, listening, following instructions, and organization; distractibility; and forgetfulness. Hyperactivity/impulsivity includes fidgeting, out-of-seat behavior, restlessness, overactivity, excessive talking, interrupting others, difficulty awaiting one's turn, and responding impulsively to questions.

Categories of Students With ADHD

Three subtypes of ADHD are now recognized in the DSM–IV:

1. ADHD, Predominately Inattentive Type: six or more inattentive symptoms but fewer than six hyperactive–impulsive symptoms are present.

2. ADHD, Predominately Hyperactive–Impulsive Type: six or more hyper-active–impulsive symptoms but fewer than six inattentive symptoms are present.
3. ADHD, Combined Type: six or more inattentive symptoms and six or more hyperactive–impulsive symptoms are present.

Without treatment, ADHD symptoms often persist throughout adolescence and adulthood; with treatment, the symptoms often decrease (Barkley, 1990). According to a theory developed by Barkley (1995), a delay in the development of behavioral inhibition could be the primary cause underlying all of the symptoms of ADHD.

The cause of ADHD is unclear. A variety of factors are associated with ADHD. Neurological variables and hereditary influences are the most likely factors. Diet and environmental toxins do not seem to significantly contribute to the presence of ADHD (Barkley, 1990).

Children and adolescents with ADHD may or may not qualify for educational services. Although these children and adolescents frequently have some form of academic difficulty, such as attentional or organizational problems, their achievement problems aren't always severe enough to fall into a special education category. Children and adolescents with ADHD qualify for special education services when the ADHD occurs in combination with another disability, such as a specific learning disability, or when the ADHD symptoms are so severe that achievement is delayed to the extent that the child or adolescent qualifies for the special education category entitled *other health impairment.*

Frequently, children and adolescents with ADHD qualify under Section 504 guidelines for educational modifications; that is, they exhibit symptoms that affect learning to the extent that reasonable educational modifications are required, such as implementation of a behavioral management program, placement in a small, highly structured classroom, counseling, and the administration of medication (Zirkel & Gluckman, 1997). Classroom modifications and interventions for the child and adolescent with ADHD usually are necessary regardless of whether the child qualifies for specific educational services.

Children who have ADHD often are first identified at school, where their behavioral problems stand out in contrast to other children. To accurately assess for ADHD, DuPaul and Stoner (1994) recommended that the initial screening be followed by multiple assessment techniques such as rating scales, behavioral observations, and evaluation of academic and organizational skills in both home and school settings.

Counseling Children and Adolescents With ADHD

Multiple interventions are recommended for effectively treating the child or adolescent with ADHD (DuPaul & Stoner, 1994). Barkley (1995) recommended that naturalistic interventions such as behavioral modification, cognitive strategies, teacher consultation, and social skills training be implemented at home and at school before considering the use of stimulant medication, which sometimes results in side effects. Stimulant medication has been found to be especially beneficial with more severe cases of ADHD (Barkley, 1990).

Behavioral Modification

One of the most effective treatments that counselors can use to change behavior in children with ADHD is behavioral modification (Barkley, 1990). With this approach, counselors can teach parents positive reinforcement strategies that can increase the child's task-related attention and activity and decrease his or her disruptive behavior in the home. Ideally, preferred activities rather than concrete rewards should be used as reinforcement; frequent and specific behavioral feedback should be given; and redirection and/or mild consequences should be used following inappropriate behavior (DuPaul & Stoner, 1994).

Cognitive Behavioral Training

The cognitive behavioral training approach focuses on teaching self-control through strategies such as self-monitoring, self-instruction, and self-reinforcement. With the *self-monitoring* strategy, the child or adolescent with ADHD uses self-reminder statements to increase awareness and control of his or her behavior when direct feedback is not available (Taylor, 1994). With the *self-instruction* strategy, the child learns to follow a set of self-directed instructions for completing class work. *Self-reinforcement* operates on a principle similar to self-monitoring—teaching the child ways to praise himself or herself or to give himself or herself a reward, such as a checkmark on a behavioral chart following positive behavior when external reinforcers are unavailable. Research indicates that these approaches typically are effective only for the specific situation in which they were taught and do not continue without the ongoing monitoring and encouragement of a counselor, parent, or teacher; therefore, cognitive behavioral training should be used in combination with other interventions and not as the only treatment strategy (Barkley, 1995).

Teacher Consultation

Counselors can consult with teachers to set up school-based interventions for children and adolescents with ADHD. These include the use of behavioral techniques, such as modeling, token economies, and home–school reward systems. Other classroom strategies include adapting instruction to highlight the main idea, giving the students prompts to respond, teaching the students to use organizers, working with them in small groups, using visual aids, and teaching problem-solving strategies (Kling, 1997). Teachers also should offer structure, supervision, and support in classroom activities (Taylor, 1994).

Social Skills Training

Programs that promote social adjustment can be beneficial for helping children and adolescents with ADHD. Social skills interventions for this population, however, should always be planned for specific settings, as social skills training does not automatically generalize to new social situations for the child or adolescent with ADHD (Barkley, 1990). Among the social problems that children and adolescents with ADHD exhibit are aggression, impulsive or intrusive conversational style, poor social problem solving, excessive talking, limited self-awareness, emotional overreactivity, and bossiness when initiating interactions (Guevremont, 1992). These social problems may lead to peer rejection and lower self-esteem, further complicating social adjustment.

Several general social skills instructional programs are available for counselors to use with children or adolescents with ADHD individually, in groups, or in classroom settings (Bender, 1997). One effective social skills program specifically designed for adolescents with ADHD targets methods for joining social exchanges, conversational skills, conflict resolution, and anger control (Guevremont, 1990). This program also involves peer models, strategies for maintaining social success, and cognitive strategies.

Stimulant Medication

Counselors can recommend screening for medication for the child or adolescent with ADHD. Two medications that have been found to improve behavioral, academic, and social functioning on a short-term basis are Ritalin and Cylert (DuPaul & Barkley, 1990). Initial research indicated that 70%–80% of hyperkinetic children responded positively to initial doses of stimulant medication, with the most notable improvement seen in the area of attention span (Barkley, 1977). But not all children and adolescents with ADHD respond to this medication, and some may experience side effects. For these reasons, careful screening for the severity of ADHD must be done to determine if drug administration is warranted. If medication is prescribed, it must be accompanied by ongoing drug monitoring by qualified physicians and child psychiatrists.

Although early research failed to show that stimulant medications improved academic performance in hyperkinetic children as measured by standardized tests (Barkley & Cunningham, 1978), more recent studies have indicated improvements in assignments and test scores in adolescents with ADHD taking stimulant medication (Pelham, Vodde–Hamilton, Murphy, Greenstein, & Vallano, 1991). Most interventions for ADHD, including cognitive interventions (Barkley, 1989), behavioral therapy (Gomez & Cole, 1991), and parent training (Horn, 1991), seem to be more effective for improving behavior in children and adolescents with ADHD, especially when ADHD is severe, when these interventions are used in combination with stimulant medication.

Family Counseling

Families with a child or an adolescent with ADHD can benefit from counseling for difficulties linked to having a family member with this disorder. For example, the parents and ADHD child may develop co-dependency as the parents try to establish normalcy through solving problems, organizing work, directing impulse control, completing tasks, and guiding social situations for the child who has difficulty in these areas. In addition, the family might experience stress directly related to the child's difficulties. For instance, the child's impulsivity and overactivity may keep the family in a constant state of arousal, and the child's inattention may require the parents' hypervigilance and repeated reminders (Bender, 1994). Adolescents with ADHD may lie, steal, skip school, and exhibit similar antisocial behaviors (Barkley, 1990).

A number of family interventions are available for helping a family with a child or adolescent with ADHD (Barkley, 1995; Bender, 1994). Through family counseling, the counselor can help all family members to acquire knowledge, understanding, and strategies for coping with the child or adolescent with ADHD without neglecting the needs of other family members. For example, parents can learn to channel their child's energies into productive activities that allow the child to attain success. Further, the counselor can help the family envision a positive future for the child by informing the parents and child of college academic and vocational options and services available for adolescents with ADHD.

Support Groups

Parents of children and adolescents with ADHD can benefit from support groups that target stress, guilt, and co-dependency issues. Parents find comfort when they realize that they are not alone in their feelings. The support group meetings can include lectures, demonstrations, question-and-answer sessions, or informal discussions. Counselors can help parents locate a recognized support group, such as CHADD (Children and Adolescents with Attention Deficit Disorder) or ADDA (Attention Deficit Disorder Association).

Counselors also can facilitate their own local ADHD parent-support groups. These groups often are organized around specific topics. A session on prescribed medications, for example, could feature discussion by a qualified speaker or a group of experts having different points of view. Other topics might focus on how parents can help their children with ADHD in specific problem areas, such as anger control. A session on anger control might involve teaching parents to role-model appropriate anger for their child, to encourage their child to self-monitor anger, and to administer rewards to the child for the appropriate expression of anger (Taylor, 1994).

Parenting Programs

Parent education programs are available for counselors to use with parents of children with ADHD. These include the Barkley Parent Training Program

(Barkley, 1990), the Patterson Parent Training Program (Newby, Fischer, & Roman, 1991), and Forehand and McMahon's Parent Training Program (Forehand & McMahon, 1981). All of these programs cover ADHD behaviors and related parenting skills, methods for consistent, positive consequences for positive behaviors, and punishment through time-out for negative behaviors.

Parents can learn to use behavioral charts with younger children. The charts list three or four target behaviors in the home, and the children earn reinforcers each time the child performs a positive behavior. With adolescents, behavior can be managed through behavioral contracts negotiated with the teenager that specify ways to earn social activities and age-appropriate rewards (such as use of the family car).

Direct Counseling

Individual and group counseling can be offered to children and adolescents with ADHD to help them with issues of self-esteem and self-control. These individuals often feel low self-worth as a result of repeated negative feedback about their behavior. Among the therapeutic books available for use in counseling children with ADHD are *I Would If I Could* (Gordon, 1992) and *Putting on the Brakes* (Quinn, 1992). And games and other activities targeting ADHD behaviors are available for the counseling setting (Taylor, 1994). Group counseling can help these children and youth feel less different and more supported. Adolescent groups can promote the identification of positive role models and can help members set long-range goals as a tool for seeing themselves as having the potential for success. To help children and adolescents with ADHD maintain attention and behavior during direct counseling, structured, time-limited sessions and more directive approaches are recommended.

Jordan Devine, a 6-year-old boy, recently entered kindergarten. His teacher, Mrs. Warner, contacted Jordan's parents soon after the school year began, because of his behavior. She expressed concern that Jordan was not able to stay in his seat, did not pay attention to simple instructions, blurted out responses rather than waiting to be called on, did not complete his work, was distracted by classroom wall displays, grabbed objects from his classmates, and at times became aggressive toward his peers. Mrs. Devine agreed that she had observed many of these behaviors at home, and Mr. Devine said he had similar problems himself as a child.

The school psychologist referred the family to a counselor who worked with children with ADHD. With the counselor's assistance, the teacher and parents agreed to a home–school behavioral program for Jordan, in which he would be rewarded in both settings for complying with specific rules in the classroom. The teacher would give him a star for each of four rules he complied with: complete work in class, keep our hands to ourselves, raise our hands before talking, and stay in our seat. At home, he would receive a sticker whenever he earned at least three stars.

The counselor also consulted with the teacher about classroom modifications, such as minimizing distractions in the classroom, cuing on-task behavior, structuring class time to direct Jordan to specific activities, and modifying instruction to short, specific tasks with frequent breaks, thereby reducing the need for long-term attention. The counselor encouraged the parents to request that these modifications be put into a written modification plan under the guidelines of Section 504, which would be reviewed annually at school.

Further, the counselor also provided the teacher with a social skills program for the entire class, to assist other children having social problems, to avoid singling out Jordan. In addition, the counselor provided the parents with parent training and short-term therapy to teach them specific parenting skills, such as the use of a home behavioral chart, to provide them with support, and to help reduce their stress generated by Jordan's behavior. Finally, the counselor gave the parents information about the CHADD parent support group in their area.

After these interventions were tried, behavioral improvement was measured. Difficulties in paying attention and impulsive behavior, such as blurting out answers, still were evident. The counselor provided the parents with a referral to a child psychiatrist, and Jordan was placed on a low-dose trial of Ritalin. The counselor worked with Jordan and his parents to help Jordan understand the purpose of the medication. To help answer Jordan's questions, the counselor read Jordan the book, *Otto Learns About His Medication* (Galvin, 1988), and Jordan's parents read it again with Jordan at home when additional questions arose. The counselor also taught Jordan some simple cognitive behavioral strategies for monitoring his own behavior. These included a self-reward strategy in which Jordan would put a checkmark on a card every time he raised his hand without talking in class. At the end of the day, Jordan would earn a superhero sticker from his teacher for every 10 marks on his card.

Following these interventions, Jordan's symptoms improved. With parent permission, the teacher and counselor asked the school psychologist to keep track of Jordan's academic progress and to evaluate the possibility of referral for special education services in the future.

Gifted Children and Adolescents

Even though PL 103–382 recognizes giftedness as an exceptional education category, no specific guidelines are available for serving gifted students. This puts them in a unique position relative to the other categories of exceptionality.

Challenges in Gifted Education

For several reasons, gifted children and adolescents are one of the most misunderstood and politically controversial groups that counselors serve. First, stereotypes abound about the gifted being socially isolated and emotionally unstable (Brody & Benlow, 1986; Solano, 1987). In truth, most gifted children and adolescents are as well adjusted as their nongifted peers when functioning in educational, social, and familial environments that are supportive of their giftedness (Gottfried, Gottfried, Bathurst, & Guerin, 1994; Nail & Evans, 1997). Some gifted children, however, have adjustment problems. Those who most frequently experience these problems are the highly gifted, whose emotional sensitivity, isolation, and perfectionism can interfere with their social adjustment (Brody & Benbow, 1986; Milgram, Dunn, & Price, 1993; Orange, 1997; Roedell, 1984); children who are twice exceptional, such as those who are gifted and have learning disabilities (Johnson, Karnes, & Carr, 1997); and gifted girls, who have been found to have difficulties in social status related to their high ability (Ludwig & Cullinan, 1984). Therefore, although giftedness often does not lead to social isolation or emotional instability, it also does not necessarily guarantee mental health. Giftedness must be viewed as a complex set of characteristics for each individual.

Second, and even more troubling, many refuse to view giftedness as an exceptional education category in need of appropriate educational programming, notwithstanding the law (Johnson et al., 1997). People frequently believe that other forms of exceptionality are more in need of educational services than is giftedness. This bias is related to the bigger issues within the existing educational system of not accepting the variation among individual learners and not providing academic and fiscal support equally to accommodate the educational process for each individual learner. Funding for gifted education has continued to decrease over the years in comparison to funding for other exceptional educational categories (Shaklee, 1997).

In addition, educational services for the gifted often are inadequate or nonexistent. Most gifted children and adolescents do not receive differentiated instruction and often are in class settings in which they already have mastered much of the curriculum (Ross, 1993).

Parents frequently must advocate for educational services for their gifted children, often in the face of considerable opposition from school personnel (Silverman, 1993). Parents also experience negative and unsupportive reactions from friends, relatives, and community resources when seeking appropriate services for their gifted children (Alsop, 1977). Similar to other exceptional children, gifted students may hide their abilities to avoid the negative stereotyping associated with being different (Ross, 1993). The mismatch between ability and services increases the potential of problems in adjustment such as underachievement, behavioral problems, and frustration.

A third challenge in education for this group is in the way in which giftedness is identified. The most frequently used indicator of giftedness is the intelligence quotient (IQ) in combination with student achievement and teacher nominations. This approach has been found to be unreliable, with teachers often nominating compliant children and adolescents over outspoken, underachieving, or difficult students who still may be deserving of gifted programs (Cioffi & Kysilka, 1997). In addition, European-American students are overrepresented by 30%–70% in gifted programs because of a biased assessment system based on the dominant culture (Richert, 1997). Further, some types of giftedness, such as musical and artistic giftedness, often are overlooked in identification (Shaklee, 1997).

For these reasons, the counselor must clearly understand the sociopolitical environment surrounding gifted clients, as well as the individual issues that lead these clients to counseling. Counselors, too, must be aware of methods for fairly identifying a range of giftedness (Shaklee, 1997). These include methods that assess intrinsic motivation (Gottfried & Gottfried, 1997), identify new types of giftedness, such as the gifted artist (Shaklee, 1997), and recognize cultural and contextual biases and more fairly include in the identification process students from culturally different backgrounds (Passow & Frasier, 1996). Finally, counselors must be prepared to educate parents of the gifted, support parents in response to negative reactions to their gifted children, and advocate with parents and teachers for appropriate services for gifted children and adolescents.

Counseling Gifted Children

Early literature about the psychological functioning of gifted children and adolescents identified their tendency to be overly sensitive or excitable. Dabrowski (1972) developed a model of overexcitability in five areas (psychomotor, sensual, intellectual, imaginational, and emotional) that frequently was used as a means of understanding difficulties with adjustment of gifted children. Tucker and Hafenstein (1997), however, redefined these areas as strengths that lead to positive adjustment, especially when supported by the children's environment.

Often, teachers and parents misunderstand areas of strength in a gifted child, thinking of them as problems, and do not realize that these patterns are normal and should be encouraged, especially when expressed appropriately. Orange (1997) described different subtypes of giftedness in adolescents that sometimes are perceived as dysfunctional, yet are more a reflection of the diversity within gifted groups. For example, the aggressive–independent subtype can be seen as confrontational and argumentative even though this behavior is more a reflection of self-sufficiency, inquisitiveness, and brightness than malicious intent. Clearly, counselors can help in a number of ways in promoting positive adjustment for gifted children and adolescents.

Adjustment in the Academic Environment

Counselors can assist with the student's academic adjustment by consulting with teachers, assisting parents in advocating for services with school administrators and teachers, and coordinating services and resources. Counselors can assist teachers, as well as the parents and gifted children or adolescents themselves, to acquire accurate knowledge and understanding of characteristics associated with giftedness, thereby increasing understanding and dispelling negative attitudes. Counselors also can assist parents in seeking appropriate and fair educational identification, programs, and services for their child.

Frequently, students who are not educationally stimulated become unmotivated, passive, and even despondent within general education. By advocating for appropriate services, parents and counselors may prevent or eliminate behavior problems that result from boredom and frustration stemming from an unchallenging curriculum. The counselor also can consult with general education teachers about classroom instructional methods that encourage gifted students' strengths. This intervention is especially needed today, as many teachers lack training in this area and specific programs for the gifted are often minimal because of lack of support and funding (Shaklee, 1997).

Some methods that counselors can suggest to teachers are team teaching with an intervention specialist; learning how to make the educational curricula and resources presently available in the school appropriately challenging for gifted students; finding professional development opportunities and mentors in the gifted area for teachers; facilitating home–school communication to support student learning; and identifying career and vocational opportunities and linking them with academic activities as early as elementary age (Ross, 1993). In addition, the counselor can facilitate college advisement and long-term career planning for gifted adolescents and can assist in identifying community resources and coordinating their services with the school.

Adjustment in the Home

Other counseling interventions can be directed to helping the child at home through family counseling, parent education, and parent consultation services. Parents can promote intellectual stimulation in the home, especially stimulation in response to the child's or adolescent's interests rather than directed or chosen by the parents (Feldman, 1986). Gifted children and adolescents should be encouraged and supported when they express interest in activities such as chess club, junior scientists, sports, educational books and television, and intellectually challenging projects in the home.

Another counseling intervention is to work with parents who feel inadequate in comparison to their gifted child or adolescent, to help them manage these feelings. Counselors also can help parents manage their feelings about the additional demands, sibling jealousy, and tension associated with the presence of the gifted child in the home. Further, counselors can teach parents (as well as teachers) basic behavioral strategies designed to maintain control and fairness with gifted and non-gifted children. Finally, counselors can provide supportive counseling and teach coping skills to help parents deal with the negative and unsupportive reactions of school personnel, community resources, and friends toward their seeking educational placement in the best interest of their children (Silverman, 1993).

Direct Counseling With the Gifted

When the counselor works directly with the gifted child or adolescent in individual or group counseling, several strategies are helpful. First, the counselor can teach cognitive strategies such as self-monitoring and self-discipline that can help gifted children and adolescents making good choices, especially as they typically need to feel a sense of power and participation in decision making. The counselor can further teach these students how to brainstorm an array of choices in a given situation instead of adhering to a rigid, all-or-nothing worldview.

Second, peer relationships will likely be positive when outlets such as that provided by group counseling are available for making friends who have similar abilities and interests. Because friendships are based on cognitive similarities, age differences frequently are present in friendships. Counseling also can promote understanding and acceptance of others with different abilities. Finally, the counselor can encourage self-awareness and acceptance of personal strengths, as well as weaknesses such as intolerance, frustration, and perfectionism, and offer methods by which gifted children can cope with negative reactions and jealousy from those who are not gifted (Silverman, 1993).

The gifted have a tendency to be perfectionistic. Although perfectionism can be a positive force toward great achievement (Roedell, 1984), it can have negative aspects, such as compulsiveness, over concern for details, rigidity, and a tendency to set unrealistically high standards. Counselors can help their gifted clients to set realistic short- and long-term goals, enjoy activities solely for pleasure, develop self-tolerance through the use of positive self-statements and exposure to less-than-perfect gifted role models, identify their strengths rather than limitations, and learn progressive relaxation or meditation techniques to counter the stressful aspects of perfectionism (Silverman, 1993).

Bibliotherapy can promote self-understanding for gifted students. A therapeutic book that can be used to help younger children understand and deal with issues of giftedness is *The Gifted Kids Survival Guide* (Galbraith, 1984).

Amy, an 11-year-old African American girl in the sixth grade, had achieved at uneven levels ever since entering school. She clearly seemed capable of exceptional work but sometimes rushed through assignments and made careless errors. In addition, Amy's teachers perceived her as challenging of authority because she shouted out answers in class, corrected mistakes the teachers made, and questioned the teachers' directives. Further, after finishing her classwork and before the rest of the class was done with theirs, Amy would wander around the classroom and talk to her peers.

Because Amy was seen as having behavioral problems and perhaps because she was an African American, her teachers had not recommended her to be assessed for the gifted program. Amy was well liked by her peers, even seen as a leader. Amy's parents enjoyed her brightness but were frustrated by the demands and challenges that Amy created in the home.

Amy and her parents met with a family counselor because of Amy's difficulties. The counselor recognized behavioral patterns often seen in gifted children and recommended that an assessment of Amy's cognitive and artistic abilities be requested from the school. Amy was found to be gifted in several areas, but she did not qualify for the school's criteria for giftedness because her grades were erratic and she lacked teacher nominations. The counselor advocated for Amy with the principal and Amy's sixth grade teacher to allow Amy to be enrolled in the gifted program on a trial basis. The counselor also consulted with the teacher about how to find resources at school that were intellectually more appropriate for Amy.

A gifted curriculum for sixth graders was initiated with Amy. The parents and teacher worked with the counselor to put Amy on a positive reward system at home and school. The goals were for Amy to complete her schoolwork accurately, take turns talking with her classmates and siblings, and, to prevent boredom, finish her work before starting another project, which, when possible, would be identified for her as soon as she completed her current activity.

Amy was delighted to be in the gifted program and developed higher self-esteem as she began to see herself as a role model rather than a child who was always in trouble. She completed her schoolwork and received excellent grades in both the general and gifted curricular activities. Because Amy had challenging material to engage her energies, her disruptiveness in class greatly diminished. The counselor met with Amy's parents and teacher to provide more information on the behaviors of gifted children, which helped them to reframe Amy's actions in a more positive light. Amy enjoyed the reward system and chose to continue the program even after she achieved all of the initial behavioral goals. Her parents met separately with the counselor to process their feelings about having a gifted child, to develop coping skills for negative reactions to Amy's giftedness, and to set realistic expectations for Amy, other children in the family, and themselves.

Summary

Exceptional children and adolescents comprise a diverse and complex group requiring a wide range of services according to their individual needs. Counselors must obtain information and training about educational laws, clinical and educational definitions, and appropriate interventions for children and adolescents who are gifted. The traditional counselor model is less effective with this population than is a broad-based service model in which the counselor creates a collaborative community with all individuals and resources necessary for the child or adolescent to experience success in every area of life to the greatest extent possible.

Counseling with children and adolescents with exceptional needs must be coordinated with educational services, medical and remedial specialists, family members, and the students themselves. Exceptional children and adolescents receive maximal benefits when comprehensive counseling services are offered in combination with a variety of other support services in the most normalized environment possible.

References

Albrecht, D. G. (1995). *Raising a child who has a physical disability.* New York: Wiley.

Alsop, G. (1997). Coping or counseling: Families of intellectually gifted students. *Roeper Review, 20,* 28–34.

American Association on Mental Retardation. (1992). *Mental retardation: Definition, classification, and systems of supports* (9th ed.). Washington, DC: Author.

American Psychological Association. (1994). *Diagnostic and statistic manual of mental disorders* (4th ed.). Washington, DC: Author.

American Youth Policy Forum and Center on Educational Policy. (2002). *Twenty-five years of educating children with disabilities: The good news and the work ahead.* Washington, DC: Author.

Baker, S. B. (1992). *School counseling in the twenty-first century,* New York: Merrill.

Balthazar, E., & Stevens, H. (1975). *The emotionally disturbed, mentally retarded.* Englewood Cliffs, NJ: Prentice–Hall.

Barkley, R. A. (1977). The effects of methylphenidate on various measures of activity level and attention in hyperkinetic children. *Journal of Abnormal Child Psychology, 5,* 351–369

Barkley, R. A. (1989). Attention-deficit hyperactivity disorder. In E. J. Mash & R. A. Barkley (Eds.), *Treatment of childhood disorders* (pp. 39–72). New York: Guilford.

Barkley, R. A. (1990). *Attention-deficit hyperactivity disorder: A handbook for diagnosis and treatment.* New York: Guilford.

Barkley, R. A. (1995). *Taking charge of ADHD.* New York: Guilford.

Barkley, R. A., & Cunningham, C. E. (1978). Do stimulant drugs improve academic performance of hyperkinetic children? A review of outcome research. *Journal of Clinical Pediatrics, 17,* 85–92.

Bender, W. N. (1997). *Understanding ADHD: A practical guide for teachers and parents.* Englewood Cliffs, NJ: Prentice–Hall.

Bloomquist, M. L. (1996). *Skills training for children with behavioral disorders: A parent and therapist guidebook.* New York: Guilford.

Bower, E. (1982). Defining emotional disturbances: Public policy and research. *Psychology in the Schools, 19,* 55–60.

Brimer, R. W (1990). *Students with severe disabilities: Current perspectives and practices.* Mountain View, CA: Mayfield.

Brody, L. E., & Benbow, C. P. (1986). Social and emotional adjustment of adolescents extremely talented in verbal or mathematics reasoning. *Journal of Youth and Adolescence, 15,* 1–18.

Cioffi, D. H., & Kysilka, M. L. (1997). Reactive behavior patterns in gifted adolescents. *Educational Forum, 61,* 260–268.

Cochrane, P V, & Marini, B. (1977). Mainstreaming exceptional children: The counselor's role. *School Counselor, 25,* 17–21.

Colvin, G., Karmeenui, E. J., & Sugai, G. (1994). Reconceptualizing behavior management and school-wide discipline in general education. *Education and Treatment of Children, 16,* 361–381.

Conroy, J. (1982). Trends in deinstitutionalization of the mentally retarded. *Mental Retardation, 15,* 44–46.

Dabrowski, K. (1972). *Psychoneurosis Is Not an Illness.* London: Gryf.

Donnellan, A., LaVigna, G., Zambito, J., & Thvedt, J. (1985). A time-limited intervention program model to support community placement for persons with severe behavioral problems. *Journal of the Association for Persons with Severe Handicaps, 10,* 123–131.

Downing, J. E. (1996). *Including students with severe and multiple disabilities in typical classrooms.* Baltimore: Paul H. Brookes.

Dunn, L. (1968). Special education for the mentally retarded: Is much of it justifiable? *Exceptional Children, 34,* 5–22.

DuPaul, G. J., & Barkley, R. A. (1990). Medication therapy. In R. A. Barkley (Ed.), *Attention-deficit hyperactivity disorder: A handbook for diagnosis and treatment* (pp. 573–612). New York: Guilford.

DuPaul, G. J., & Stoner, G. (1994). *ADHD in the schools: Assessment and intervention strategies.* New York: Guilford.

Echevarria, J. (2002, March 15). *The disproportionate representation of minority students in special education: Where do we go from here?* Paper presented at Oxford Round Table on Education and Human Rights at Oxford University, Oxford, England.

Echevarria, J., & Graves, A. (1998). *Sheltered content instruction: Teaching English language learners with diverse abilities.* Boston: Allyn & Bacon.

Education for All Handicapped Children Act of 1975 (PL 94–142), 20 U. S. C. 1400 et seq. (1977).

Eichinger, J., & Woltman, S. (1993). Integration strategies for learners with severe multiple disorders. *Teaching Exceptional Children, 26,* 18.

Feldman, D. (1986). *Nature gambit: Child prodigies and the development of human potential.* New York: Basic Books.

Forehand, R. L., & McMahon, R. J. (1981). *Helping the noncompliant child: A clinician guide to parent training.* New York: Guilford.

Frith, G. H., Clark, R. M., & Miller, S. H. (1983). Integrated counseling services for exceptional children: A functional, noncategorical model. *School Counselor, 30,* 387–391.

Gagne, F. (1985). Giftedness and talent: Reexamining a reexamination of the definition. *Gifted Child Quarterly, 29,* 103–112.

Galbraith, J. (1984). *The gifted kids' survival guide.* Minneapolis: Free Spirit.

Galvin, M. (1988). *Otto learns about his medicine.* New York: Magination.

Genesee, F. (1994). *Educating second language children: The whole child, the whole curriculum, the whole community.* New York: Cambridge University Press.

Gomez, K., & Cole, C. (199 1). Attention deficit hyperactivity disorder: A review of treatment alternatives. *Elementary School Guidance and Counseling, 26,* 106–114.

Gordon, M. (1992). *I Would If I Could.* DeWitt, NY: GCL.

Gottfried, A. E., & Gottfried, A. W. (1997). A longitudinal study of academic intrinsic motivation in intellectually gifted children: Childhood through early adolescence. *Gifted Child Quarterly, 40,* 179–183.

Gottfried, A. W, Gottfried, A. E., Bathurst, K., & Guerin, D. W. (1994). *Gifted IQ: Early developmental aspects.* New York: Plenum.

Gottlieb, J. (1980). Improving attitudes toward retarded children by using group discussion. *Exceptional Children, 47,* 106–111.

Grossman, H. (Ed.). (1983). *Classification in mental retardation.* Washington, DC: American Association on Mental Deficiency.

Guevremont, D. (1990). Social skills and peer relationship training. In R. A. Barkley (Ed.), *Attention deficit hyperactivity disorder: A handbook for diagnosis and treatment* (pp. 540–572). New York: Guilford.

Guevremont, D. (1992). The parent's role in helping the ADHD child with peer relationships. *CHADDER, 6,* 17–18.

Hamayan, E., & Damico, J. (1991). *Limiting bias in the assessment of bilingual students.* Austin, TX: Pro-Ed.

Harry, B. (1992). Restructuring the participation of African American parents in special education. *Exceptional Children, 59*(2), 123–131.

Henley, M., Ramsey, R. S., & Algozzine, R. (1993). *Characteristics of and strategies for teaching students with mild disabilities.* Boston: Allyn & Bacon.

Hill, J., Wehman, P, & Horst, G. (1982). Toward generalization of appropriate leisure and social behavior in severely handicapped youth: Pinball machine use. *Journal of the Association for Persons with Severe Handicaps, 6,* 38–44.

Holmgren, V S. (1996). *Elementary school counseling: An expanding role.* Boston: Allyn & Bacon.

Horn, W. (1991). Additive effects of psychostimulants, parent training, and self-control therapy with ADHD children. *Journal of the American Academy of Child and Adolescent Psychiatry, 30,* 233–240.

Individuals with Disabilities Education Act Amendments of 1997, PL 105–17, 105th Congress, 1st session.

Johnson, L. J., Karnes, M. B., & Carr, V. W. (1997). Providing services to children with gifts and disabilities. In N. Colangelo & G. A. Davis (Eds.), *Handbook of gifted education* (2d ed., pp. 516–528). Boston: Allyn & Bacon.

Kauffman, J. M. (1997). *Characteristics of emotional and behavioral disorders in children and youth.* Columbus, OH: Merrill.

Keenan, S. (1993, October). *Planning for inclusion: Program elements that support teachers and students with EIBD.* Keynote address at Council for Children with Behavioral Disorders Working Forum, "Inclusion: Ensuring Appropriate Services to Children/Youth with Emotional/Behavioral Disorders," Saint Louis, MO.

Kling, B. (1997). Empowering teachers to use successful strategies. *Teaching Exceptional Children, 30*(2), 20–24.

Kraemer, K., Cusick, B., & Bigge, J. (1982). Motor development, deviations, and physical rehabilitation. In J. Bigge (Ed,), *Teaching individuals with physical and multiple disabilities* (2d ed., pp. 12–14). Columbus, OH: Merrill.

Kramer, B., & Wright, D. (1994). *Inclusive educational workshop,* CA: Diagnostic Center.

Ludwig, G., & Cullman, D. (1984). Behavioral problems of gifted and nongifted elementary school boys and girls. *Gifted Child Quarterly, 28,* 37–39.

Maes, W. (1978). Counseling for exceptional children. *Counseling and Human Development, 10,* 8–12.

Matson, J., & DiLorenzo, T. (1986). Social skills training, mental handicap, and organic impairment. In C. Hollin & P. Trower (Eds.), *Handbook of social skills training: Clinical applications and new directions* (pp. 67–90). New York: Pergamon.

McDowell, W. A., Coven, A. B., & Eash, V. C. (1979). The handicapped: Special needs and strategies for counseling. *Personnel and Guidance Journal, 58,* 228–232.

Milgram, R. M., Dunn, R. S., & Price, G. E. (1993). *Teaching and counseling gifted and talented adolescents: An international learning style perspective.* Westport, CT: Praeger.

Morrow, L., & Presswood, S. (1984). The effects of self-control technique on eliminating three stereotypic behaviors in a multiply handicapped institutionalized adolescent. *Behavior Disorders, 9,* 247–253.

Nail, J. M., & Evans, J. G. (1997). The emotional adjustment of gifted adolescents: A view of global functioning. *Roeper Review, 20,* 18–21.

Newby, R., Fischer, M., & Roman, M. (1991). Parent training for families of children with ADHD. *School Psychology Review, 20,* 252–255.

National Information Center for Children and Youth with Disabilities (NICHCY). (1997). The IDEA amendments of 1997. *News Digest, 26,* 1–40.

Orange, C. (1997). Gifted students and perfectionism. *Roeper Review, 20,* 39–41.

Oswald, D., Coutinho, M., & Best, A. (2000). *Community and school predictors of over representation of minority children in special education.* Paper presented at Minority Issues in Education Conference, sponsored by Civil Rights Project at Harvard University, November 17, 2000, Cambridge, MA.

Padilla, A. M., & Medina, A. (1996). Cross-cultural sensitivity in assessment: Using tests in culturally appropriate ways. In L. A. Suzuki, P. J. Meiler, & J. G. Ponteretto (Eds.). *Handbook of multicultural assessment: Reexamination, reconceptualization, and practical application* (pp. 3–18). San Francisco: Jossey–Bass.

Passow, A. H., & Frasier, M. M. (1996). Toward improving identification of talent potential among minority and disadvantaged students. *Roeper Review, 61,* 212–219.

Patterson, G. R. (1986). Performance models for antisocial boys. *American Psychologist, 41,* 432–444.

Patterson, G. R., Reid, J. B., & Dishion, T. J. (1992). *Antisocial boys.* Eugene, OR: Castalia.

Patton, J., & Townsend, B. (1999). Ethics, power, and privilege: Neglected considerations in education of African American learners with special needs. *Teacher Education and Special Education, 22*(4), 276–286.

Pelham, W. E., Vodde–Hamilton, M., Murphy, D. A., Greenstein, J. L., & Vallano, G. (1991). The effects of methylphenidate on ADHD adolescents in recreational, peer group, and classroom settings. *Journal of Clinical Child Psychology, 20,* 293–300.

Pierangelo, R., & Jacoby, R. (1996). *Parents complete special education guide.* West Nyack, NY: Center for Applied Research in Education.

Polloway, E., Epstein, M., & Cullinan, D. (1985). Prevalence of behavior problems among educable mentally retarded students. *Education and Training of the Mentally Retarded, 20,* 3–13.

Powers, M. D. (1989). *Children with autism: A parent guide.* Bethesda, MD: Woodbine House.

Public Law 94–142 (1975). *Federal Register, 42,* 42474–42518.

Public Law 101–476 (1990). *Federal Register, 54,* 35210–35271.

Quinn, P. (1992). *Putting on the brakes.* New York: Magination.

Reich, R. (1978). Gestural facilitation of expressive language in moderately/severely retarded preschoolers. *Mental Retardation, 16,* 113–117.

Richert, S. (1997). Excellence with equality in identification and programming. In N. Colangelo & G. A. Davis (Eds.), *Handbook of gifted education* (2d ed., pp. 75–88). Boston: Allyn & Bacon.

Ridley, C. R., Li, L. C., & Hill, C. L. (1998). Multicultural assessment: Reexamination, reconceptualization, and practical application. *Counseling Psychologist, 26,* 827–911.

Rief, S. E. (1993). *How to reach and teach ADD/ADHD children.* West Nyack, NY: Center for Applied Research in Education.

Ritvo, E., & Freeman, B. (1977). *Definition of the syndrome of autism.* Washington, DC: National Society of Autistic Children.

Roedell, W. C. (1984). Vulnerabilities of highly gifted children. *Roeper Review, 6,* 127–130.

Rosenberg, M. S., & Edmond–Rosenberg, I. (1994). *The special education sourcebook: A teacher guide to programs, materials, and information sources.* Bethesda, MD: Woodbine House.

Rosenberg, S., Clark, M., Filer, J., Hupp, S., & Finkler, D. (1992). Facilitated active learner participation. *Journal of Early Intervention, 16,* 262–274.

Ross, R. O. (1993). *National excellence: A case for developing America's talent.* Washington, DC: U.S. Department of Education.

Salend, S. (1983). Using hypothetical examples to sensitize nonhandicapped students to their handicapped peers. *School Counselor, 33,* 306–310.

Seligman, M. (1985). Handicapped children and their families. *Journal of Counseling and Development, 64,* 274–277.

Shaklee, B. D. (1997). Gifted child education in the new millennium. *Educational Forum, 61,* 212–219.

Silver, L. B. (1992). *The misunderstood child.* New York: TAB Books.

Silverman, L. K. (1993). *Counseling the gifted and talented.* Denver: Love Publishing.

Sinason, V. (1997). *Your handicapped child.* Los Angeles, CA: Warwick.

Slenkovich, J. E. (1993). Compliance with Section 504 regulations: Is it wise? Is it possible? *School Advocate, 8,* 641–644.

Smith, D. (2001*). Introduction to special education: Teaching in an age of opportunity* (4th ed.). Boston: Allyn & Bacon.

Smith, S. L. (1991). *Succeeding against the odds: How the learning disabled can realize their promise.* New York: Penguin Putnam.

Solano, C. H. (1987). Stereotypes of social isolation and early burnout in the gifted: Do they still exist? *Journal of Youth and Adolescence, 16,* 527–539.

Sternberg, R. J., & Davidson, J. E. (Eds.). (1986). *Conceptions of giftedness.* New York: Cambridge University Press.

Stevens, R. J., & Slavin, R. E. (1991). When cooperative teaming improves the achievement of students with mild disabilities: A response to Tateyama-Smezek. *Exceptional Children, 57,* 276–280.

Tarver Behring, S. & Ingraham, C. L. (1998). Culture as a central component to consultation: A call to the field. *Journal of Educational and Psychological Consultation, 9,* 57–72.

Tarver Behring, S., & Spagna, M. E. (1997). School counselors as chance agents toward full inclusion. *Arizona Counseling Journal, 21,* 50–57.

Tarver Behring, S., Spagna, M. E., & Sullivan, J. (1998). School counselors and full inclusion for children with special needs. *Professional School Counselor, 1,* 51–56.

Taylor, J. F. (1994). *Helping your hyperactive/attention deficit child.* New York: Prima.

Thompson, C. L., & Rudolph, L. B. (1988). *Counseling Children.* Pacific Grove, CA: Brooks/Cole.

Tucker, B., & Hafenstein, N. L. (1997). Psychological intensities in young children. *Gifted Child Quarterly, 41,* 66–75.

Tucker, R. L., Shepard, J., & Hurst, J. (1986). Training school counselors to work with students with handicapping conditions. *Counselor Education and Supervision, 26,* 56–60.

U.S. Congress. (1994). *Improving America—Schools Act of 1994* (Public Law 103–382). Washington, DC: Author.

U.S. Department of Education. (1995). *Seventeenth annual report to Congress on the implementation of the Individuals with Disabilities Education Act.* Washington, DC: Author.

U.S. Department of Education (2000). *Twenty-second annual report to Congress on the implementation of the Individuals with Disabilities Education Act.* Washington, DC: Author.

U.S. Department of Education (2001). *Twenty-third annual report to Congress on the implementation of the Individuals with Disabilities Education Act.* Washington, DC: Government Printing Office.

U.S. Department of Education (2002). *A New Era: Revitalizing special education for children and their families.* Washington, DC: Government Printing Office.

U.S. Department of Health, Education, and Welfare. (1972). *Education of the Gifted and Talented.* Washington, DC: Author.

Vogt, M. E., & Shearer, B. (2002). *The reading specialist's evolving and emerging roles: A sociocultural perspective.* Boston: Allyn & Bacon.

Westman, J. C. (1990). *Handbook of learning disabilities: A multisystem approach.* Boston: Allyn & Bacon.

Yell, M. L., & Shriner, J. G. (1997). The IDEA Amendments of 1997: Implications for special and general education teachers, administrators, and teacher trainers. *Focus on Exceptional Children, 30,* 1–20.

Zirkel, P. A., & Gluckman, B. (1997). ADD/ADHD students and Section 504. *Principal,* May 1997, 47–48.

Counseling Culturally
and Ethnically Diverse Youth

Roberto Clemente

The concept of multiculturalism is an evolving construct that first captured the attention of professional counselors when "The Culturally Encapsulated Counselor" (Wrenn, 1962) was published. Previous to Wrenn's findings, the fields of sociology and anthropology had stressed the importance of the concept of culture as part of the collective behavior of human beings. Up to that point, however, culture had not transcended those fields and had impacted the counseling field minimally.

Members of the counseling profession realized that culture could not be ignored as an instrumental variable during the counseling experience. The definition of culture has evolved from a simple categorization of ethnic groups (Bennet, 1990; Meadows, 1991) into a complex and ever evolving construct that encompasses multiple dimensions of daily living (Carter & Qureshi, 1995; Pedersen,

Draguns, Lonner, & Trimble, 2002). There are many definitions that attempt to encompass all areas of culture, and perhaps no definition is comprehensive enough to include all its dimensions. Nevertheless, we must define the meaning of culture so we can understand the dynamics of underrepresented ethnic groups in the United States. According to Vontress (Pedersen et al., 2002), culture is defined as

> a way of life or the totality of the individual artifacts, behaviors, and mental concepts transmitted from one generation to the next in a society. It is visible and invisible, cognitive and affective, conscious and unconscious, internal and external, rational and irrational, and coercive and permissive at the same time. This conception of culture implies that it is generally out of sight and out of mind. People do not think about it. They take it for granted. (p. ix)

The best way to conceptualize the construct of culture is to compare it to the air we breathe, the food we eat, or the language we speak. They are not noticed unless they are removed from us. To put it simply, the lifestyle of individuals is dictated by the beliefs and principles established by their culture.

This chapter exposes counselors to the unique challenges presented by young clients who belong to various underrepresented ethnic groups in the United States. First I provide a framework of self-awareness for counselors to understand the complexities of their own culture and ethnicity and how it positively or negatively affects the level of competency when working with children and adolescents in multiethnic scenarios. Next I provide a knowledge base about selected ethnic groups and their chief characteristics. This is followed by a series of multiethnic case vignettes illustrating various culturally and nonculturally responsive interventions to help readers develop awareness and understanding about working with multicultural ethnic clients. Finally, I suggest some ways to become a social advocate for multiethnic children and adolescents.

Developing Cultural, Ethnic, and Racial Self-Awareness As a Counselor

The demographics within the United States are changing rapidly. If the number of people of color continues to increase at its present rate, it eventually will surpass the number of Americans of White European descent (Pedersen & Carey, 2003). But there is no direct correlation between the demographic figures and the number of counselors who belong to underrepresented groups in the field. Most counselors are members of the White European American majority. This situation poses a challenge to helping professionals who eventually will find themselves in multiethnic counseling relationships.

Traditionally, the way White European American professional counselors have been exposed to information regarding members of underrepresented ethnic groups has been by means of information that portrays cultures as monolithic entities (Canino & Spurlock, 2000). This monolithic description of cultures has been combined with international parameters that ignore the complex dynamics of children and adolescents growing up as members of an underrepresented group in the United States versus their native country of origin.

After years of being involved in the multicultural field as a school counselor and counselor educator, and of living a bicultural life daily, I have noticed that most White European American individuals have difficulty defining the meaning of their North American culture. Most important, they have difficulty defining the role of their own ethnicity and White racial identity in their daily lives and counseling interactions. To increase their cultural and ethnic–racial self-awareness, counselors must engage in ongoing self-exploration. If this does not occur before being exposed to children and adolescents from diverse backgrounds, the tendency is to evaluate youth from a critical stance in which the dominant culture dictates what is "normal, right, and acceptable" (Sciarra, 1999).

By foregoing self-exploration, counselors may be enticed to say, "Tell me how individuals of certain ethnic groups behave and I'll know how to help them." The implication of such a statement could be, "Give me the prescription to fix them because I have the right culture." Prior to the early 1980s, when Janet Helms's model of *White Racial Identity Development* (WRID) was developed, minimal consideration was given to "how the condition of being White influences Whites' psychosocial development" (Helms, 1990, p. 4). The underlying principle of Whites being aware of their own identity is the abandonment of intentional or unintentional racism and the development of a healthy White racial identity. In short, the White Racial Identity Development Model (Helms, 1984; 1990; 1995) contains the following stages:

1. *Contact.* Race is not important to White European Americans, and they are unaware of issues of racial identification and minimize the fact that their ethnicity has benefited them.
2. *Disintegration.* Beliefs and attitudes about the contact stage are challenged. The individuals involved try to convince themselves that racism does not exist and is not their fault.
3. *Reintegration.* Beliefs of White superiority are expressed passively or actively.
4. *Pseudoindependence.* There is some intellectual acceptance of the existence of racism along with a rationalization that the solution lies within the hands of the other groups, not Whites.
5. *Immersion/emersion.* Individuals learn about being White, and a positive racial identity is created.
6. *Autonomy.* Individuals welcome contact with multiple ethnic groups and are committed to keep growing as an ethnic entity.

The main focus of White European American counselors should be to strive for the final stage, *autonomy*. Although most counselors are among the White European American majority, members of underrepresented groups must engage in a similar process of self-exploration. Being a member of an underrepresented ethnic group does not automatically make an individual an expert in multicultural issues or free of biases and prejudices. For instance, African American counselors can use the Cross model as a platform to explore their racial identity (Cross, 1971, 1995; Ford, Harris, & Schuerger, 1993; Parharm, 1989). The revised Cross model contains two stages: (a) *preencounter,* and (b) *internalization.*

Those at the *preencounter* stage are said to give low precedence to racial issues. These individuals "lack an Afrocentric perspective and do not have a strong sense of value orientation, historical perspective, and worldview" (Cross, 1995, p. 104). During the *internalization* stage the person changes the amount of importance given to racial issues in conjunction with the primary group of identification. At this stage individuals become proactive toward Black pride, develop self-love, and gain a sense of connection and interaction towards the Black or African American community.

Similarly, and in a more generic way, members of other underrepresented groups are encouraged to go through the same process of self-exploration and cultural identity development. For instance, Atkinson, Morton, and Sue (1998) developed a five-stage *Generic Cultural Identity Development (CID) Model* for individuals who belong to diverse ethnic groups: (a) conformity, (b) dissonance, (c) resistance, (d) introspection, and (3) integrative awareness.

Individuals who assume a naïve acceptance of and preference for the dominant culture's values and beliefs are going through the *conformity* stage. At the *dissonance* stage the person starts experiencing conflictual perceptions and attitudes toward the dominant culture and his or her own culture. During the *resistance* stage, the individual evidences guilt, shame, and anger toward the dominant culture with a tendency to reject the dominant culture. Then the individual embarks on a quest of embracing and recovering what was lost from his or her original ethnic heritage. During the *introspection* stage the individual embraces the idea of developing a healthy self-identity and balance in his or her life. Finally, the *integrative awareness* stage is characterized by an appreciation of the majority culture, the individual's own ethnic heritage, and the integration of the best of both worlds.

Both the *White Racial Identity Development Model* (Helms, 1995) and the *Generic Cultural Identity Development Model* (Atkinson, Morton, & Sue, 1998) should not be seen as frameworks of operation from a linear perspective but, rather, as fluid operational models that may reflect patterns of reversal and progress in individuals.

Multiethnic Groups in the United States

Members of underrepresented ethnic groups are expected to constitute 50% of the U.S. population by the year 2050 (U.S. Bureau of the Census, 2000). These statistics highlight the importance of more inclusive and culturally responsive interventions for a growing number of young, diverse, ethnic clients (Atkinson, Morton, & Sue, 1998).

One of the major disadvantages of describing the main characteristics of selected underrepresented ethnic groups, regardless of the context (U.S., Australia, Canada, Brazil), is the tendency to stereotype *all* members of that group as if all of them are the same. The unique personality of every individual could be lost in the generic descriptors of the ethnic group. Consequently, the intent of the discussion here is to provide general characteristics or a synopsis of commonalities among members of certain ethnic groups *without ignoring their individual personalities* and the fluidity and changes in their culture of origin when in contact with the majority culture.

Although the U.S. population is highly diverse, only the main four ethnic groups, according to the U.S. Bureau of the Census, will be included here because of space constraints. Throughout the chapter, members of ethnic groups that do not belong to the White European majority will be characterized as members of underrepresented groups or multiethnic groups instead of *minorities,* because the term *minority* has derogatory connotations (Clemente, 2000).

African Americans

In 2000 the African American population of the United States was approximately 35 million (U.S. Bureau of the Census, 2000). The majority of this population is concentrated in the South with smaller numbers in the Northeast, West, and North Central regions. According to the U.S. Bureau of the Census (2000), the median income of African American families and individuals is below the national U.S. average; about 30% of African American individuals live below the poverty standard.

Central to the African American population are the effects of slavery, and how the mainstream population and the government have dealt with it has left ingrained scars and attitudes from which young children and adolescents still suffer. The racial labels utilized to depict individuals with African roots have evolved from derogatory terms to more culturally inclusive ones. For instance, members of this group have been called Colored, Negro, Black, Afro American, and African American (Cross, 1995; Smith, 1992). The progression of terms evolves from skin color to cultural heritage—empowering the person and rationalizing the group's distinctive cultural traits (Dana, 1993; Griffith & Baker, 1993; Pedersen & Carey, 2003). Nevertheless, we should ask the youth which term describes him or her better and not assume that the one used in the literature is the correct one.

Family

The concept of family among African Americans is fluid and nontraditional. By way of illustration, Paniagua (1998) noted that "both biological (e.g., parents, children, uncles, and sisters) and non-biological (e.g., friends, minister, and godfather) members are part of the family tree" (p. 20). Therefore, the "head" of the family is not necessarily the father; sometimes the mother plays that role. Also, older children can fulfill that role with the mother. This factor is of extreme importance when conducting family counseling and identifying the figures of power.

Religion and Spirituality

The role of the church has been instrumental in providing help to young African American clients. Determining church affiliation is the first step in establishing the religious background. According to Boyd–Franklin (1989), African Americans have reported affiliation with church denominations such as Baptist, African Methodist Episcopal, Church of God in Christ, Pentecostal, Apostolic, Presbyterian, Lutheran, Episcopal, Assembly of God, and Nation of Islam. In exploring the spiritual beliefs of young clients, it may be important to decide whether to include the minister or other church member in the counseling process.

Some African Americans believe in nontraditional approaches to medicine as an effective tool in dealing with physical, mental, and spiritual concerns (Baker & Lightfoot, 1993). By way of illustration, some believe that the cause of an illness is not just physical in nature but also the result of spiritual and evil elements. Also, African Americans commonly use herbs, natural remedies, and teas. Spiritualists and voodoo priests are involved with these nontraditional medical concerns (Baker & Lightfoot, 1993).

Linguistic Differences

The controversy revolving around the use of street language among youth transcends ethnic divisions. The media have termed this as Black English and gang language. Considering that most counselors are middle class and well educated individuals who use Standard English, the language factor is extremely important (Smitherman, 1995). Counselors cannot possibly know the meaning of all slang or connotations attached to the Black culture. Therefore, the counselor has every reason to inquire and explore the meaning or significance of certain terminology to enhance communication. By the same token, not all African American youth utilize Black English; they may use Standard English.

Time

Life for many urban African American adolescents is complicated by systemic problems of illiteracy, racism, and extreme poverty. They often assume adult roles such as the care of younger siblings and household duties at an early age (Belgrave, Chase–Vaughn, Gray, Addison, & Cherry, 2000). The combination of these issues and the traditional resistance toward mental health or school counseling services give the impression to counselors that African American youth have a different conceptualization of time. When young African American youth occasionally show up late to appointments or do not follow up with treatment interventions, these are not indicators of time management deficiencies but, instead, systemic variables.

Latinos (Hispanics)

According to the U.S. Bureau of the Census (2000), Latinos, or Hispanics, reached demographic parity with African Americans, or perhaps surpassed them if undocumented individuals are taken into account. An estimated 57 million Latinos will be residing in the United States by the year 2020, according to the current demographic growth rates (Dana, 1993; Marin & Marin, 1991). The median income for Latino families ($26,300) falls below the national median ($41,500) and below the $43,400 of White European American families (U.S. Bureau of the Census, 2000).

Latinos are the most diverse group of all ethnic groups because they also are members of most other ethnic/racial groups. For instance, there are Latinos of Asian, European, Middle Eastern, African, Native Indian, and Jewish backgrounds. Latinos come from far-flung places such as Cuba, Puerto Rico, Dominican Republic, Venezuela, Peru, Bolivia, Mexico, Honduras, Argentina, Uruguay, and Chile, among others. In this chapter the term *Latino* will be used to be consistent with most current literature, even though the debate continues about the usage of Hispanic versus Latino (Clemente, 2000; Fisher & Moradi, 2001).

Family and Respect (respeto)

The family is the center of the Latino culture. Decisions are considered and made within the family circle. Nuclear and extended family members are active participants in the youths' lives (Martínez, 1993). Others are considered to be family members even without a blood relationship—for example, the godfather (el padrino) and godmother (la madrina) (C. Vázquez–Pietri, personal communication, July 2002).

The concept of *respeto (respect)* is based on the view of men as the head of the family and the way children interact with adults (Paniagua, 1998). The *respecto (respect)* that children show to adults, parents, elders, and figures of authority demonstrates submission to the hierarchical order of the family and system.

Religion and Spirituality

Catholicism is the predominant religion among Latinos, although a considerable number are Protestants (Martínez, 1988; Comas–Díaz & Griffith, 1988). Religious beliefs are an integral part of the culture, and even though not all Latinos are devoted practitioners, they treat religion with respect. For instance, certain gender practices have their origin in folklore and religious beliefs. For women, the importance of being a virgin, and of being submissive, docile, emotional, and a caregiver of the family, has its origin in the belief that the Virgin Mary made similar sacrifices and she should be emulated. Again, these practices are contingent upon the extent of acculturation and level of education.

Linguistic Differences

The Spanish language tends to be the common denominator among Latinos, although they have language differences. For instance, in parts of Latin America, native indigenous languages such as Mayan and Tarrasco, not Spanish, are the primary language. According to Zuñiga (2003), "Each Latino group speaks Spanish with a cultural style that highlights group differences. Each group has many idioms and metaphors that belong strictly to that group, for example, Cubans and Puerto Ricans" (p. 240).

Counselors who are bilingual should explore differences in idioms, expressions, and meaning of regionalisms (Pérez Foster, 2001). In addition, if a youth client is bilingual, the counselor must discuss and assess the language preference to be able to serve the client more effectively.

Time and Fatalism (fatalismo)

Fatalism *(fatalismo)* has different connotations in different cultures. For Latinos, the idea of *fatalismo* differs by social class and disempowerment. At times it is related to God's will and destiny. An expression that Latinos typically use is, "If this happened to me, it's because it was God's will" (Neff & Hoppe, 1993; C. Vázquez–Pietri, personal communication, July 2002). Similarly, the concepts of time and fatalism are based on the concept of external locus of control; that is, individuals may feel that they do not have control over what happens to them. Depending on the extent of acculturation, they approach life in a relatively less structured fashion and with a present-oriented emphasis. Traditionally, sessions with Latino youth begin with an informal conversation about family, life, and other nontherapeutic issues.

Native Americans (First Generations or American Indians)

Native American tribes are diverse in regard to language, customs, religions, beliefs, and region of origin (Thompson, Walker, & Silk–Walker, 1993). For this reason, only the most general characteristics among most tribes are included in the discussion here. The Native American population is about 2.8 million (U.S. Bureau of the Census, 2000). As a total ethnic group, Native Americans are the most disadvantaged group with respect to education, living conditions, life expectancy, and socioeconomic status (U.S. Department of Health and Human Services, 1991).

Although *acculturation* should be the correct term, the reality of Native Americans in the United States has been one of "forced assimilation" and systematic obliteration of their culture, language, and religion (J. Buffalo, personal communication, June 2002). From the end of the 19th century until the 1970s, Native Americans suffered racial and cultural discrimination, living on reservations and receiving education in boarding schools (Jaimes, 1996). This reinforced the institutional–societal racism that isolated them from the mainstream.

At the same time, various Native American programs have served as collective empowerment instruments, enhancing the quality of life. The following federal programs provide evidence: the Indian Religious Freedom Act (1978), the Indian Self-Determination Act (1975), the Indian Child Welfare Act (1978), and the Indian Health Care Improvement Act (1976) (Goodluck, 1993; O'Brien, 1989; Walker & LaDue, 1986).

Family and Collectivism

The family and the tribe have precedence over the individual. This value is more prevalent among those who live on reservations and keep the traditions alive than among those who are not in contact with their roots (J. Buffalo, personal communication, June 2002). Native American families have a more democratic lifestyle than the authoritative way of life of Asians and Latinos. Decisions are made as a group, weighing points of view from all the relatives. Tribal leaders are involved in taking disciplinary actions (Ho, 1992).

Most Native American tribes do not necessarily embrace the concept of competition among themselves or against others. They do not espouse individualism and obtaining benefit for oneself without considering its effects on others. Ideas such as self-actualization, self-assertion, and self-interest should be carefully considered in a therapeutic center (J. Buffalo, personal communication, June 2002).

Religion

Native Americans are a greatly diverse ethnic group encompassing more than 512 tribes. Therefore, their religious beliefs are not necessary the same (Hamby, 2000), although "the spirit, mind, and body are all interconnected. Wellness is a disharmony between these elements" (Sue & Sue, 2003, p. 316).

The body, mind, and spirit must be considered during treatment. The counselor can assist the youth to identify which one of the elements is not in harmony. A client-centered approach seemed to be more effective with Native Americans (Garret and Wilbur, 1999). In this approach, if the clients generate their own ideas in terms of curative events and solutions, they take ownership of the process.

According to Paniagua (1998) "Native Americans treat time as a natural event and do not believe that time should control their natural way of living" (p. 82). Like Latinos, the event (situation) takes precedence over the concept of time (Sue & Sue, 1990; Pedersen & Carey, 2003).

Linguistic Differences and Communication Style

Unlike most European cultures, listening, to most Native Americans, is more important than talking. Nonverbal communication is of primary importance and at times takes precedence over verbal communication. For instance, avoiding eye contact and extending a soft handshake are signs of respect. The contrary could be said from a Eurocentric point of view (Thompson et al., 1993).

Time

Native American youth—depending on the level of acculturation, tribe or nation, and reservation or urban area—are present-oriented rather than future-oriented (Garret & Wilbur, 1999). Life is to be lived in the here-and-now with, and emphasis on, enjoying every daily activity. The idea of long-term or future planning must be approached with caution because it could be misinterpreted as an act of egoism that benefits only the individual and not the tribe.

Asian Americans

Like Latinos and Native Americans, the intradiversity among Asians is immense. Ordinarily, Asians are classified in three major clusters, Southeast Asians (Vietnamese, Cambodians, Laotians), Asian Pacific Islanders (Guamanians, Hawaiians, and Samoans), and North Central Asians (Asian Indians, Chinese, Koreans, Japanese, and Filipinos). According to the U.S. Bureau of the Census (2000) 12 million individuals of Asian descent are living in the United States. Southeast Asians are the most disadvantaged subgroup among Asians.

Family and Children

In general, and depending on the level of acculturation, Asian American wives and children demonstrate faithfulness to the family by being submissive to the father authority. When the level of assertiveness of White European women and children is compared with that of Asians, the Asians seem to be the less assertive of the two groups (Ho, 1992). The level of verbal and nonverbal communication reflects this behavior. For example, some Asian children appear passive, nonresponsive, and quiet during group activities in schools. This may send the wrong message to the instructors when, in reality, they are demonstrating politeness and attentiveness to those who share their views (Chung, 1992).

Religion, Public Restraints, Control, and Shame

Trying to understand the religious background of Asian Americans is complex and actually almost impossible because of the diversity among ethnic groups

(Buddhism, Hinduism, Islam, etc.). Most Asians, however, hold a holistic view regarding mind and body: "The mind and the body are considered inseparable" (Sue & Sue, 2003, p. 334). Instead of expressing spiritual and emotional concerns, Asians typically describe changes in appetite, physical fatigue, headaches, and lack of sleep (Toarmino & Chun, 1997).

As a norm, most Asians avoid talking about personal problems (physical, psychological, and financial) with people outside of the family circle (Sue, 1997). For that reason, the family is the center of the decision-making process and self-control is highly encouraged. This self-control is exercised especially in public settings regardless of the intensity of emotions. This is based on the idea of not calling oneself to the attention of others and being as nondisruptive as possible. Shame is used as a mechanism to enforce the family rules and norms, and serves as a psychological strategy with many emotional ramifications (Lowe & Mascher, 2001).

Linguistic Differences

Because Asian languages number in the dozens, counselors cannot have a command of a "generic" language (other than English) that permits communication with the various Asian groups. Nevertheless, "when most Asian American youth (depending on the level of acculturation) are exposed to verbal communication, they often look quiet and passive and go to a great deal of effort to avoid offending others" (Paniagua, 1998, p. 60). Depending on their command of the English language, the Asian-American youth might answer all questions affirmatively to be polite when they really cannot understand the counselor's questions or activities. Among Asian Americans, silence is a sign of respect, politeness, and willingness to maintain the conversation after making a short remark (Sue & Sue, 2003).

Time

Again, depending on their level of acculturation, Asian Americans put a strong emphasis on long-term activities; they are future-oriented. This principle does not fit in a counseling milieu (Paniagua, 1998). Asian youth should be informed that some problems do not have a quick solution, and the duration of counseling should be made clear (Sue & Sue, 2003).

Assessment and Evaluation

Once young clients are referred to a counselor's office, the automatic assumption is that something has to be corrected. Otherwise they would not be in the counselor's office. Children and adolescents are not referred to the school counselor when their academic performance is excellent, their social life is healthy, and their behavior is exemplary. Parents normally do not ask a counselor why their son or daughter is so well behaved and academically talented. Parents consult the school counselor when their children are not performing well academically, when their behavior is disruptive, when they have social or emotional problems, or when problems at home are taking a toll on the child.

One of the most difficult challenges for counselors is to determine whether the problems that young clients manifested are appropriate developmental reactions or are more dysfunctional or a psychopathological condition. If culture is part of the equation, making decisions becomes even more difficult. What criteria do counselors need to consider to make culturally appropriate evaluations?

Traditionally, mental health counselors rely on the DSM–IV–TR for diagnosis and to develop treatment plans. Although this diagnostic resource has expanded the section on culturally bound syndromes, it places clear limitations on how to interpret them if taken literally and not put in the context of acculturation. School counselors are less knowledgeable about severe mental health conditions because psychopathological conditions are not emphasized during their training (Pedersen & Carey, 2003). Despite differences in knowledge and training, all counselors struggle with the same question: "Is this behavior appropriate within the child's cultural parameters, or is it an abnormal behavior that should be evaluated and treated as in any other mainstream U.S. youth?"

Levels of Acculturation

The unique personality and developmental level of each young client must be taken into account, as well as the client's ethnic and cultural background. The impact of various levels of acculturation on the evaluation of each young client must be determined. Acculturation "may be defined in terms of the degree of integration of new cultural patterns into the original cultural patterns. This process of acculturation can be internal and external" (Paniagua, 1998, p. 8). Many agree with Paniagua's definition of acculturation and its implication in the counseling process (Dana, 1993; Grieger, Moyerman, & Forman, 1992; Whiton & Abercrombie, S., 2002).

The best strategy for determining whether culture is an important factor in evaluating young, diverse clients is to verify their level of acculturation. The following is a modified version of the *Brief Acculturation Scale,* developed by Burnam, Hough, Karno, Escobar, and Telles (1987) and cited in Paniagua (1998, p. 10). The original scale was modified to cover more areas and to make it more developmentally appropriate for younger clients while maintaining the simplicity of its use.

Instructions: Please check only one item from each of the following questions:

1. *My generation is:* (e.g., If my grandparents were the first to come to the United States, I am third generation).

    (a) First
    (b) Second

(c) Third

(d) Fourth

(e) Fifth

2. *The language that I prefer to use most of the time is*: (e.g., at home, with my friends)

(a) Mine only

(b) Mostly mine

(c) Both mine and English

(d) Mostly English

(e) Only English

3. *When not attending school, I like to spend my time:* (e.g., in the neighbor- hood, YMCA, sport and social activities)

(a) Only with friends of my own ethnic group

(b) Mostly with friends of my own ethnic group

(c) Within and between different ethnic groups

(d) Mostly with a different ethnic group

(e) Only with a different ethnic group

4. *I think of myself as being* _____ (e.g., Mexican, Vietnamese, Japanese, Cuban, Puerto Rican, Middle Eastern)

(a) All the time

(b) Most of the time

(c) Sometimes

(d) Never

5. *I am* _____ *to be* _____.

(a) proud/ (e.g., Mexican, Vietnamese, Japanese, Cuban, Puerto Rican, Middle Eastern)

(b) more or less okay/ (e.g., Mexican, Vietnamese, Japanese, Cuban, Puerto Rican, Middle Eastern)

(c) embarrassed/ (e.g., Mexican, Vietnamese, Japanese, Cuban, Puerto Rican, Middle Eastern)

(d) ashamed/ (e.g., Mexican, Vietnamese, Japanese, Cuban, Puerto Rican, Middle Eastern)

(e) humiliated/ (e.g., Mexican, Vietnamese, Japanese, Cuban, Puerto Rican, Middle Eastern)

This scale should not be used as a rigid classification of quantitative meas- urement and evaluation in which a "score" determines the level of acculturation. To the contrary, the counselor is encouraged to use the five basic questions to draw qualitative conclusions about the young client and to use these as a spring- board from which to elaborate upon and further explore areas related to culture and ethnicity. Thus, if the young client identifies more closely with the culture of origin than with the majority culture, the counselor should seriously take into account the knowledge base and information about the ethnic group to which the client belongs.

More important, the level of acculturation of the young client can be a strong indicator in ruling out "dysfunctional" behavior as established by the standards of the majority culture (Kim & Abreu, 2001). Also, resulting misconduct or inappropriate behavior could be a result of acculturation difficulties and not necessarily a reflection of cultural differences or "abnormal behavior." Especially in children, constructing an ethnic identity in a different cultural context could be fraught with frustration and disappointments (Roysircar–Sodowsky & Frey, 2003).

In addition to the modified Brief Acculturation Scale, multiple acculturation scales have been developed that could serve as sources of information, clarification, and rationalization of distinct behaviors and attitudes. The following is a list of ethnically specific acculturation scales:

Hispanic–Latinos

- *Short Acculturation Scale for Hispanic Yo*uths (SASH–Y) (Barona & Miller, 1994).
- *Acculturation Rating Scale for Mexican Americans–II* (ARSMA) (Cuellar, Arnold, & Maldonado, 1995).
- *Acculturation Scale for Mexican-American Children* (Franco, 1983).
- *The Bidimensional Acculturation Scale for Hispanics* (BAS) (Marín & Gamba, 1996).
- *A Children's Hispanic Background Scale* (Martínez, Norman, & Delaney, 1984).

Asian Americans

- *The Asian Values Scale* (Kim, Atkinson, & Yang, 1999)
- *The Suinn–Lew Asian Self-Identity Acculturation Scale* (SL–ASIA) (Ponterotto, Baluch, & Carielli, 1998).
- *Na Mea Hawaii–I: A Hawaiian Acculturation Scale* (Rezentes, 1993).

African Americans

- *The African American Acculturation Scale* (Landrine & Klonoff, 1994).
- *A Scale to Assess African American Acculturation* (Snowden & Hines, 1999).
- *Developmental Inventory of Black Consciousness* (Milliones, 1980).

American Indians (Native Americans)

- *Rosebud Personal Opinion Survey* (Hoffman, Dana, & Bolton, 1985).

Interventions and Modalities—Case Studies

The following case studies are fictitious multiethnic young clients with diverse issues that school or mental health counselors might be called upon to help their own clients who could be experiencing similar issues. These case studies can serve as a generic model or a guide for helping professionals. As has been reiterated throughout the chapter, however, every individual client is different, each with a unique personality, character traits, and acculturation levels that affect the counseling process.

The Case of Pablo Mayoral

A fictitious 16-year-old Mexican male, Pablo Mayoral, has a solid B average in high school. He has been living in California since his parents immigrated from Michoacán, México, 2 years before. Pablo recently was transferred to the mainstream student population as he finished the English as a Second Language (ESL) program. He has four younger siblings, all of whom are in school. His father is a field worker on a nearby farm, and his mother has a part-time job as a house cleaner.

Pablo demonstrates good ability in mathematics and computer sciences, as shown by his grades and state tests. His goal is to either drop out of school or finish high school and get a job in a meat-packing plant where some of his friends and relatives work. He wants to buy a "neat car" and help the family. During a classroom career guidance activity the school counselor compiled some personal information about the students and noticed the dichotomy in Pablo's career goals.

A Nonculturally and Developmentally Appropriate Intervention

The school counselor called Pablo to his office, where they explored his future academic and career goals. Also, the counselor administered various career and personality inventories similar to the Myers–Briggs and the Strong Inventory to gather more information. After getting the "whole picture," the school counselor indicated to Pablo that he must finish high school if he wants to have a "future" in this country. The counselor indicated that Pablo would be wasting his talent if he didn't pursue a career in mathematics or computer science.

The counselor did give Pablo the option of pursuing the non-college (vocational) track to "at least obtain a technical degree." Pablo left the office indicating that he would get back to the counselor during the next few weeks. After two weeks Pablo's being absent from school, a social worker visited his house and found that the family had moved without leaving a trace.

A Culturally and Developmentally Appropriate Intervention

Developmental considerations. For many adolescents, regardless of their ethnicity, career issues or college are not a priority at 16 years of age. At this point, many adolescents are concrete thinkers and do not consider long-term plans with regard to personal accomplishments. Enjoying the present is more important than the future. Pablo indicated that he wanted to get a job in order to buy a "neat car." This is a common dream of many adolescents and a rite of passage into adulthood and freedom.

Instead of invalidating his desire to drop out of school to buy a car, Pablo would have been better to normalize his need for freedom and independence that buying a car symbolizes. The counselor can introduce the possibility of doing that and completing high school by working at a part-time job.

Cultural considerations.   To make progress, including the family in the career counseling experience is vital. It is a good idea to contact the parents to ask for their opinion and explain the context of the situation. If the parents are fully informed, they can serve as allies, facilitating progress. Parents might need interpreters during the sessions. Counselors should avoid using Pablo or other family member as an interpreter. The counselor should obtain the assistance of a bilingual person who is not related to the family and who can remain objective during the interviews.

Gender considerations.   After his father, Pablo is the man of the house and feels a moral obligation to help the family financially. Therefore, Pablo wants to have his own things (e.g., a "neat car"), but at the same time understands that the family's immediate needs are money, food, and shelter. This creates a dilemma for Pablo that is not easily solved by imposing "long-term goals" that will not benefit the family immediately.

Acculturation considerations.   Pablo seems to have a fairly strong command of the language, according to the ESL and state tests. Mastering the language, however, is not equivalent to being fully acculturated. For this reason, his cognitive, emotional, and social acculturation process must be understood by using one of the acculturation scales listed in this chapter. By understanding his acculturation level, the counselor can devise a more culturally appropriate and individualized plan.

Contextual and historical considerations (U.S. versus Latin America). Providing for the family is a priority for most Latino immigrants. Education is not a priority because it does not put food on the table immediately. A recent immigrant from Latin America would not embrace the concept of obtaining an education and moving up on the socioeconomic ladder. Pablo had experienced sociopolitical and economic oppression for years in his home country. The concept of a middle class is unfamiliar for many Latin Americans. Although they realize that the United States has plenty of jobs, many do not envision a gradual escalation in the socioeconomic system.

The family fled without leaving a trace. This could indicate that the parents did not have appropriate documentation to be in the country. As a result, the "pressing attitude" of the counselor could have made the family suspicious, possibly precipitating the decision to move to a "safer" place. Understanding the dynamics of undocumented immigrants is an important issue in providing more culturally sensitive interventions.

Theories, modalities, and technique interventions (i.e., interpretation, family counseling, group counseling, plan of action). Family sessions during the first or second interviews are vital to the counseling process. Also, being directive and providing a tentative outcome or answer to the dilemma are important. Extreme nondirective interventions may be confusing and nonproductive to many Latinos who are used to dealing with authority figures as sources of information. Devising a provisional plan of action is always advised. Interventions that are extremely individualistic and negate the collective perception of Latino youth may not be effective.

Consultation and referral. If the counselor is unsure about how to proceed with such a cultural dilemma, the best alternative is to consult with the Latino Resource Center in the community, ESL teachers of the district, or professors at the nearest college.

Sensitivity training for students and staff. As evidenced by the culturally inappropriate intervention, the counselor's knowledge of the Latino culture is limited. Because the Latino population in the United States is steadily increasing, professionals and students alike must have opportunities to expand their knowledge and sensitivity.

General guidelines when working with Latino youth. The following generic suggestions may be applied while at the same time considering the uniqueness of each client.

1. Less acculturated Latino youth will expect a formal and professional relationship. Use your last name with a title, Mr., Mrs., Ms., or Miss.
2. Provide a tentative solution to the problem, and explain the counseling process and expectations.
3. Respect the client's worldview, especially when religious issues may be misperceived as fantasies or hallucinations.
4. Explore with the client the possibility of including family members in some of the sessions.
5. Approach the case from a systemic point of view, and consider environmental issues that may be affecting the youth's mental health, behavior, or academic performance (e.g., poverty, poor nutrition, or neighborhood crime).

6. Reassure the client that the sessions are confidential and that information will not be released to the Immigration and Naturalization Service (for undocumented clients) or similar agencies.

The Case of Dashira Johnson

Dashira Johnson, a fictitious 14-year-old African American female, recently moved with her mother, grandmother, and younger brother from an inner-city section of Chicago to a predominantly White European American small town in the Midwest. Her mother moved to this small town because her company offered a transfer with a substantial package of benefits. Even though Dashira had not had behavioral problems at school in Chicago, she knew "how to take care of herself"—she had acquired the street knowledge of an inner-city adolescent. She was heavily involved in a prestigious jumprope team and in a choir, both of which made the national semi-finals twice during the past 4 years.

When she was enrolled in the new school, Dashira learned that she was one of the few minorities attending that school. Most of the minority students were Native Americans and Latinos. After 4 months, Dashira demonstrated self-destructive behavior (fighting, confronting and challenging authority figures, cutting classes, destroying school property). Her GPA dropped below 2.0, and she did not meet the minimum state benchmarks for her grade level. The school counselor, resource teacher, and community-agency counselor were consulted to help Dashira.

A Nonculturally and Developmentally Appropriate Intervention

As a result of the behavioral problems Dashira manifested, the school counselor, resource teacher, and community-agency counselor agreed that she must undergo a behavioral plan: She would have to report to the school counselor once a day with a paper–pencil instrument filled by the homeroom teacher indicating her behavioral progress during the day. Dashira was banned from any extracurricular activities until her GPA and behavior would improve.

According to the resource teacher and community-agency counselor, Dashira was diagnosed with a conduct disorder or oppositional defiance disorder. She did not seem to be making progress and it was apparent that she did not feel like she belonged in this small town. She seemed to be acting out to provoke those in authority, and the resource teacher and counselor considered referring her to a psychiatrist who could prescribe psychotropic medication to alleviate the problem.

A Culturally and Developmentally Appropriate Intervention

Developmental considerations. To a certain extent, challenging authority figures and being resistant are trademark of adolescence. Before relocating, however, Dashira did not exhibit extreme acting-out behaviors, just typical adolescent rebellion. Therefore, the relocation and unwelcome feelings that Dashira perceived seemed to be psychosocial stressors that triggered the negative behaviors. Her behavior is not developmentally appropriate and most likely resulted from feeling estranged in a very different cultural setting.

Cultural considerations.   A person experiences cultural shock when people move from one country to another and also when they move to another region of the country. Dashira abandoned a lifestyle (the fast pace of the city) and also experienced for the first time in her life the concept of a "true numeral minority" in a place where she was one of the few people of color. If all these variables are added to the equation of developing self-concept, self-identity, and ethnic–racial identity as an adolescent, the outcome could be devastating.

Also, as in most underrepresented groups, including the family, at least in the initial sessions of the counseling experience, is vital to ensure a positive outcome. The counselor must normalize the resistance that Dashira experienced upon finding herself in a cultural setting in which her previous coping skills are no longer operational.

Gender considerations.   The search for a social life and a clique that accepts her are appropriate developmental behaviors for a female adolescent. Dashira found herself alone and without a support group. Dashira now must find a role model to help her understand that it will take some time to succeed in a different environment, but it is possible.

Acculturation considerations.   To complete Dashira's cultural profile, her acculturation level must be explored to evaluate her degree of ethnic identity. Because Dashira needs to feel that she is part of the "in crowd" at school, she may be having ethnic identity issues (negation and blaming her ethnicity for her failure and problems). As a result, administering a brief acculturation scale is advisable.

Contextual and historical considerations.   Dashira possibly was displacing some anger based on negative racial experiences. The counselor must explore and normalize her unique personal experiences. Validating these experiences lays the groundwork for a more productive relationship. Ignoring the racial history and struggle between African Americans and individuals of White European descent would be offensive and discouraging to her. The counselor has to gain her trust and acceptance and help her understand that not all people of White European descent are racists.

Theories, modalities, and technique interventions (interpretation, family counseling, group counseling, plan of action).   The mother and grandmother must be consulted and probably included in the initial two sessions. Interpreting the "negative behaviors" by means of a theory could be a hazardous approach if the behaviors are not analyzed in light of the ethnic and cultural context. Similarly, the DSM–IV–TR must be used with caution, always considering the *culturally bound syndromes*. For instance, Dashira's negative behaviors could be entirely appropriate in an inner-city context in which people have to take matters in their own hands by means of physical force when threatened.

Because she felt threatened and isolated by the environment and cultural circumstances, Dashira used the coping skills that had worked for her in the past. Instead of overanalyzing what is "wrong" with her, the counselor should exploit her strengths and assets. Dashira was involved with a jumprope team and choir, so, in conjunction with the music teacher and the P.E. teacher, the counselor could devise strategies to enhance these areas of potential.

Consultation and referral. An African American minister, or perhaps a diversity group sponsored by a community agency, could serve as sources of information and inspiration. Counselors who belong to an underrepresented ethnic group in the community and who understand the racial dynamics of the area could also provide a strong network of support.

Sensitivity training for students and staff. Compared to other regions of the country, the Midwest has fewer African Americans. Including more activities related to African American history in the curriculum sets a welcoming and empowering environment for Dashira and also offers a great deal of knowledge to the staff and students.

General guidelines when working with African American youth. The following generic suggestions may be applied depending on the youth's socioeconomic and educational background:

1. If the youth is in the counseling office against his or her will, explore the apprehensive feelings about the counseling process.
2. If the counselor is not African American, discuss the presence of interracial discomfort.
3. Discuss inspiring role models who have succeeded, and explore the youth's positive areas rather than concentrating on past failures.
4. After the goals have been established, take a solution-focus and problem-solving approach.

The Case of Neshiri Noritaka

Neshiri is a fictitious 8-year-old Japanese female born in Oregon, the youngest of three children. Her sister is in middle school, and her brother is a freshman in high school. She lives in an upper middle-class neighborhood with her parents and grandparents. Her grandparents immigrated to the United States, where they found academic and financial success in this country after having been incarcerated in United States concentration camps during World War II. They still carry some resentment about this and have instilled a degree of distrust in their family. Neshiri's parents are both chemical engineers. Her siblings, who are highly successful students, are striving for similar careers. Lately, Neshiri has exhibited somatic symptoms (headaches, gastrointestinal discomfort, anxiety, physical pain, consecutive common colds).

Her teachers have reported that Neshiri's tolerance level and perfectionism at school have increased considerably. When she cannot solve a problem, puzzle, riddle, or mathematical exercise, she cries incessantly. Her grades have dropped significantly in the past 6 months, and her academic performance does not fall within the norm for her grade level. The teachers have noticed that she enjoys drawing and painting during recess.

A Nonculturally and Developmentally Appropriate Intervention

Neshiri's teachers previously worked with her siblings as they went through elementary school, and the teachers know that all of them are intelligent. Mrs. Johnson, the mathematics teacher, has constantly reminded Neshiri that she should imitate her siblings and follow in their footsteps. Thinking that Neshiri might have some form of learning disability, Mrs. Johnson referred Neshiri to the counselor, who requested that the resource teacher administer a battery of evaluations to test her suspicions.

After talking with the teacher, the counselor consulted with the nurse regarding the somatic symptoms. The teacher contacted Neshiri's parents to discuss her concerns. When the teacher and the counselor met with the parents, they were highly offended by insinuations that Neshiri does not have adequate academic ability, and she threatened to pull Neshiri out of the school.

A Culturally and Developmentally Appropriate Intervention

Developmental considerations.   At 8 years of age, Neshiri is a concrete operational thinker. She is able to classify people and situations. At this stage she approaches situations without considering multiple solutions, because she lacks abstract thinking skills. Therefore, it seems that she has not been able to cope with pressures from various angles and has somatized her concerns. Developmentally she is coping to the best of her capacities.

Cultural considerations.   The school staff members have ignored cultural variables. First, academic performance in Neshiri's family, and in many Asian American families, is viewed as a sign of success. Neshiri's parents seem to have high expectations for their children, and poor performance in school shames Neshiri and the whole family. It may be easier for Neshiri to blame her body rather than her academic deficiencies for her failure.

Gender considerations.   As is the case in Latino families, females may be subject to parental authority and may have strict social standards depending on the level of acculturation. This is a socially constructed role that seems to be of extreme importance in Neshiri's case.

Acculturation considerations.   To rule out culture as an important factor, the level of acculturation must be explored. Depending on Neshiri's level of acculturation, the counselor and teachers should pursue interventions that fit with the Japanese culture. For instance, the counselor and the teachers need to normalize Neshiri's feelings of failure and shame. At the same time, the school counselor should use positive reframing interventions to counterbalance her negative emotions. Also, the school counselor needs to lead her to find the balance between collective and individual expectations.

Contextual and historical considerations.   In the United States, some people of Japanese descent were subjected to cultural and social shame and persecution during their incarceration decades ago after WW II. Consequently, many Japanese Americans feel a desperate need to prove their worth and national loyalty by being highly productive.

Neshiri's family seems to be imposing a lot of pressure on their children to earn a high social position. In addition, the grandparents have instilled distrust of the system—an area that the counselor should explore with Neshiri and the family. Not all individuals of Japanese descent experienced the phenomenon of persecution and incarceration in the United States, but, based on Neshiri's case, it is a factor that should be examined.

Theories, modalities, and technique interventions (interpretation, family counseling, group counseling, plan of action).   As is true with any other underrepresented ethnic group, the counselor must use the DSM–IV–TR with caution and always consider the *culturally bound syndromes*. Within a Japanese cultural framework, Neshiri's reactions seem to be typical of a highly competitive Japanese student. However, extreme somatization may cause negative long-term effects. Although she indeed may have a learning disability or a medical condition, the cause could be the excessive pressure she feels from her parents and school staff who promote high standards. Also, she may be more creatively oriented than mathematically inclined. If Neshiri is not able to verbalize her concerns, art therapy and play therapy might be less threatening interventions. Also, games, rather than talk therapies, are more appropriate at this stage of cognitive development.

Also, interviewing her parents and exploring their expectations could provide indicators of her current behaviors. If the parents seem to be exerting a considerable amount of pressure that Neshiri is not capable of dealing with, the family must be included in the counseling process. Basic principles of family therapy, such as triangulation, systemic pressure, and enmeshment, can be utilized during the meetings with the parents. All counseling interventions must be used in light of Japanese cultural beliefs (respect for authority and privacy). The focus should be on positive aspects of their parenting styles instead of the deficiencies. Also, modeling and teaching based on a solution-focused model of family counseling is advisable.

Consultation and referral. Understanding what is culturally appropriate for normally functioning individuals who belong to the same culture complements the assessment process. Consulting professionals who belong to the same culture and have had similar experiences could enhance the outcome. In particular, community agencies and college student associations can be rich sources of information. Some of these agencies might be able to provide strategies on how to present an academic concern or learning disability to Japanese parents without giving the impression that her daughter is "crazy." Or they could offer specific ways to present counseling as a developmental and preventive intervention, not as a mental health disability.

In addition, some Asian and international student associations have produced handouts for students and parents on how to handle academic pressures and maintain a healthy life. These could well be more credible sources for the parents because they have been developed by individuals with the same cultural background and the same needs.

Sensitivity training for students and staff. The teachers seem to be comparing Neshiri's academic performance to that of her siblings. This could be based on the family's successful academic history or on the stereotypical image of the "perfect Asian American minority" held by educators who work with these children. The staff must understand that not all Asian Americans are academically gifted and that all individuals have unique talents regardless of ethnicity.

General guidelines when working with Asian American youth. The following generic suggestions should take into account the youth's acculturation level and past experiences:

1. Adopt an active role, but let the youth evaluate the options and make his or her own decisions.
2. Explore the role of interdependence (from an Asian position) and independence (from a North American position) in the youth's life.
3. Emphasize the importance of confidentiality.
4. If the youth experiences institutional racism or discrimination, assume the role of an advocate.

The Counselor as Social Advocate for Multiethnic Youth

In conjunction with exploring racial and ethnic identity, counselors should engage in proactive activities that enhance their multicultural sensitivity and demonstrate their commitment to diversity before making systemic changes. Following are some ways by which counselors may engage in a dynamic process of multicultural involvement.

1. Read literature, watch movies, and attend plays with participants and themes from other cultures.

2. Establish a yearly plan in which you consciously become an advocate for an oppressed group. Engage in social, cultural, and community committees, as well as focus groups, that take a stand against oppression, discrimination, and racism.

3. Before working with a client from a cultural–ethnic group with which you are not familiar, develop a list of all the stereotypes, biases, and negative concepts you may hold against this group. Research the history of the ethnic group in the United States. Before meeting the client, evaluate your counseling interventions in light of the negative biases you developed.

4. Create your own cultural genogram, and use it as a source of connection with other ethnic groups. To develop empathy and compassion, try to find similarities among negative practices experienced in the past.

5. Post a copy of the Bill of Rights in your office as a reminder to yourself and your clients.

6. Prior to setting any counseling intervention, try to imagine yourself in the position of your young client and how your life might have been different if you were African American, Latino/Latina, Asian, Native American, or Eskimo.

7. Be aware of your own defense mechanisms and always question whether you have invested the best of your knowledge and time in your client.

8. Do not be a silent supporter. Protest, complain, and demonstrate your disgust when you hear slurs and unacceptable language against members of underrepresented ethnic groups. Be an advocate, and use your professional position and education as mechanisms to advance equality.

9. Learn a second language, preferably a language used by the largest number of multicultural youth in your community. Find groups in which to practice the new language.

10. Reach out and try to form durable and significant relationships with members of underrepresented ethnic groups. Do not wait for them to invite you; take the initiative yourself. Make connections with members of your clients' family.

11. Attend church and community activities to demonstrate your support and interest for underrepresented ethnic groups.

12. Decorate your office with multicultural artifacts that represent various ethnic groups.

13. Monitor and evaluate your verbal and body language, especially when facing difficult situations. After every session, learn to conduct self-evaluations with a member of an underrepresented ethnic group.

14. Find a colleague who can serve as a confidant and consultant with expertise in multicultural issues. Consult whenever you are puzzled about certain ethnic and cultural practices.

The Counselor's Office: A Multicultural and Welcoming Environment

If anyone is asked what a soothing and healing place looks like, most people, regardless of cultural origin, would describe natural scenes such as the ocean and the soothing sound of the waves crashing against the rocks, the soft sound generated by a gentle stream in the country, or breathtaking views of imposing mountains or beautiful fields planted with crops. For this reason, people take "healing" vacations. and look for contact with nature.

At some point during our counseling training, we may have lost perspective of the basic principles of healing and haven't seriously considered the context in which the healing occurs. A typical counseling office, for example has a file cabinet, a bookshelf, diplomas and certificates hanging on the wall, inexpensive pieces of art, bright light, several chairs, a clock, and a tissue box. What should be a healing environment becomes an artificial and perhaps uncomfortable place that might not be conducive to relaxation and self-disclosure. Although an artificial environment may be the norm for some people, it is not necessarily appropriate for young multiethnic clients.

Because the experience of multiethnic young clients is diverse and sometimes difficult, counselors must create an ideal environment that can be associated with a safe haven. Following are suggestions on how to create a curative environment:

1. *Decoration, furnishings, and equipment.* Although the presence of diplomas and certificates enhances the counselor's professional image, a delicate balance should be sought between friendly artwork and professional emblems. Art that represents nature, space, freedom, hope, and relaxation may enhance the counseling process. Natural elements such as wooden ornaments, plants, and a small fish tank are appropriate. Wooden, as opposed to metal, furniture, as well as a sofa, promote relaxation.
2. *Aroma.* The human brain is highly influenced by certain fragrances, and certain behavioral experiences are connected to the sense of smell (Vroon, 1997). Taking this into account, soft herbal, citrus, and vanilla scents contribute to a comfortable environment.
3. *Space.* Provide space for children to play, paint, and lie on the floor. Also, the way furniture is arranged can communicate status, quality of relationships, and frivolity or warmth (Whiton & Abercrombie, 2002). And take into account the concept of personal space. Depending on the client's gender, age, and level of acculturation, the physical distance between the counselor and the client may vary.

4. *Sound, color, and light.* Deafening and loud sounds provoke anxiety and discomfort, whereas musical elements and natural sounds contribute to a peaceful and healing atmosphere (Wigram, Pedersen, & Blonde, 2002). For this reason, it maybe helpful to incorporate a small water fountain that mimics the soft sound of a stream. Like the power of sound, light, and color to stimulate the visual modality, a room that is too bright and is lit by artificial fluorescent lights is not as conducive to self-discovery as the use of pastel colors and soft lighting (Ker, 1982).

The Counselor as Social Advocate for Multiethnic Youth at the Community Level

As in any other workplace, counselors should integrate multicultural activities into the general curriculum, as well as into the principles and mission statement of the institution. To do this and ensure an atmosphere that promotes social advocacy for multiethnic youth, the administration and staff should be engaged as active participants. To incorporate multicultural activities at the systemic level:

1. Revise the counseling literature, books, pamphlets, manuals, films, and other related material to reflect diversity.
2. Contact artists from multiethnic groups, and work with them to revamp the physical environment and climate of the school or agency to make it more welcoming to young clients from diverse backgrounds.
3. Develop group counseling interethnic activities that are not reactive to ethnic tensions but instead are proactive and promote a better ethnic climate.
4. Form a teacher advisory group to help revise the curriculum and to infuse multicultural principles into the curriculum.
5. Re-label signs to reflect several different languages.
6. Establish a series of multicultural activities rather than celebrating diversity only on certain days (Cinco de Mayo, Martin Luther King Day, etc.).
7. Evaluate divisive symbols with pejorative connotations that may create ethnic tension.
8. Develop counseling procedures that invite young multiethnic clients to report discriminatory practices to teachers, administrators, and counselors.
9. Remind other counseling staff members and teachers to avoid scheduling important activities on religious holidays of underrepresented ethnic groups.
10. Make the most of the strengths and richness of diverse young clients by initiating diversity activities such as talent shows or potlucks with multiethnic foods.
11. Observe the development of ethnic cliques among staff as well as youngsters. Although it is natural to gravitate toward one's own ethnic group, promote integration instead of segregation.

Summary

The counseling profession has been influenced by the societal changes reflected in the demographic growth and diversification of the U.S. population. Immigration patterns and generational growth have altered the balance between members of the White European population and underrepresented ethnic groups. Because of these demographic dynamics, school and agency counselors should explore their own ethnic identity to increase their level of effectiveness in working with multiethnic youth.

Sensitivity to developmental and acculturation considerations is a critical quality of competent counselors. Acquiring a knowledge base with respect to diverse groups in this country provides the foundation for culturally competent counselors. Considering the environment as a healing factor must be part of that restructuring. Counselors should apply cultural considerations at the individual level, become social advocates, and be actively involved in multiethnic activities in the community.

References

Atkinson, D. R., Morton, G., & Sue, D. W. (1998). *Counseling American minorities* (5th ed.). Boston: McGraw-Hill.

Baker, F. M., & Lightfoot, O. B. (1993). Psychiatric care of ethnic elders. In A. C. Gaw (Ed.), Culture, ethnicity, and mental illness (pp. 517–552). Washington, DC: American Psychiatric Press.

Barona, A., & Miller, J. A. (1994). Short Acculturation Scale for Hispanic Youths (SASH–Y): A preliminary report. *Hispanic Journal of Behavioral Sciences, 16,* 155–162.

Belgrave, F. Z., Chase–Vaughn, G., Gray, F., Addison, J. D., & Cherry, V. R. (2000). The effectiveness of a culture and gender specific intervention for increasing resiliency among African American pre-adolescent females. *Journal of Black Psychology, 26,* 133–147.

Bennett, C. (Ed.). (1990). *Comprehensive multicultural education.* Boston: Allyn & Bacon.

Boyd-Franklin, N. (1989). *Black families, therapy: A multisystems approach.* New York: Guilford.

Burnam, M. A., Hough, R. L., Karno, M., Escobar, J. I., & Telles, C. A. (1987). Acculturation and lifetime prevalence of psychiatric disorders among Mexican Americans in Los Angeles. *Journal of Health and Social Behavior, 28,* 89–102.

Canino, I. A., & Spurlock, J. (2000). *Culturally diverse children and adolescents: Assessment, diagnosis, and treatment* (2d ed.). New York: Guilford Press.

Carter, R. T., & Qureshi, A. (1995). A typology of philosophical assumptions in multicultural counseling training. In J. G. Ponterotto, J. M. Casas, L. A. Suzuki, & C. M. Alexander (Eds.), *Handbook of multicultural counseling* (pp. 239–262). Thousand Oaks, CA: Sage.

Chung, D. K. (1992). Asian cultural commonalities: A comparison with mainstream American culture. In S. M. Furuto, R. Biswas, D. K. Chung, K. Murase, & F. Ross-Sheriff (Eds.), *Social work practice with Asian Americans* (pp. 27–44). Newbury Park, CA: Sage.

Clemente, R. (2000). Cultural identity and bilingualism of Latinos in an Anglo American context. *Hispanic Outlook of Higher Education, 11* (1), 27–28.

Comas–Díaz, L. & E. E. H. Griffith (Eds.) (1988). *Clinical guidelines in cross-cultural mental health.* New York: John Wiley.

Cross, W. E. (1971). The Negro-to-Black conversion experience. *Black World, 20*, 13–27.

Cross, W. E. (1995). The psychology of Nigrescence. In J. G. Ponterotto, J. M. Casas, L. A. Suzuki, & C. M. Alexander (Eds.), *Handbook of multicultural counseling* (pp. 93–122). Thousand Oaks, CA: Sage.

Cuellar, I., Arnold, B., & Maldonado, R. (1995). Acculturation Rating Scale for Mexican Americans–II: A revision of the origingal ARSMA scale. *Hispanic Journal of Behavioral Sciences, 17*, 275–304.

Dana, R. H. (1993). *Multicultural assessment perspectives for professional psychology*. Boston: Allyn & Bacon.

Franco, J. N. (1983). An acculturation scale for Mexican–American children. *Journal of General Psychology, 108*, 175–181.

Ford, D. Y., Harris, J., & Schuerger, J. M. (1993). Racial identity development among gifted black students: Counseling issues and concerns. *Journal of Counseling and Development, 71*, 409–417.

Fisher, A. R., & Moradi, B. (2001). Racial and ethnic identity: Recent developments and needed directions. In J. G. Ponterotto, J. M. Casas, L. A. Suzuki, & C. M. Alexander (Eds.), *Handbook of multicultural counseling* (pp. 341–370). Thousand Oaks, CA: Sage.

Garret, M. T., & Wilbur, M. P. (1999). Does the worm live in the ground? Reflections on Native American Spirituality. *Journal of Multicultural Counseling and Development, 27*, 193–206.

Goodluck, C. T. (1993). Social services with Native Americans: Current status of the Indian Child Welfare Act. In H. P. McAdoo (Ed.), *Family ethnicity: Strength and diversity* (pp. 217–226). Newbury Park, CA: Sage.

Grieger, I., Moyerman, D. R., & Forman, B. D. (1992). Acculturation and adjustment: A meta-analytic study. *Hispanic Journal of Behavioral Sciences, 14*, 163–200.

Grieger, I., & Ponterotto, J. G. (1995). A framework for assessment in multicultural counseling. In J. G. Ponterotto, J. M. Casas, L. A. Suzuki, & C. M. Alexander (Eds.), *Handbook of multicultural counseling* (pp. 357-374). Thousand Oaks, CA: Sage.

Griffith, E. E. H., & Baker, F. M. (1993). Psychiatric care of African Americans. In A. C. Gaw (Ed.), *Culture, ethnicity, and mental illness* (pp. 147–173). Washington, DC: American Psychiatric Press.

Hamby, S. L. (2000). The importance of community in a feminist analysis among American Indians. *American Journal of Community Psychology, 28*, 649–669.

Helms, J. E. (1984). Toward a theoretical explanation of the effects of race on counseling. A black and white model. *Counseling Psychologist, 13*, 695–710.

Helms, J. E., (Ed.). (1990). *Black and white racial identity: Theory, research, and practice*. Westport, CT: Greenwood.

Helms, J. E. (1995). An update of Helm's white and people of color racial identity models. In J. G. Ponterotto, J. M. Casas, L. A. Suzuki, & C. M. Alexander (Eds.), *Handbook of multicultural counseling* (pp. 181–198). Thousand Oaks, CA: Sage.

Ho, M. K. (1992). *Minority children and adolescents in therapy*. Newbury Park, CA: Sage.

Hoffmann, T., Dana, R., & Bolton, B. (1985). Measured acculturation and MMPI–168 performance of Native Americans. *Journal of Cross-Cultural Psychology, 16*, 243–256.

Jaimes, M. A. (1996). American racism: The impact on American-Indian identity and survival. In S. Gregory & Sanjek (Eds.), *Race* (pp. 41–61). New Brunswick, NJ: Rutgers University Press.

Kim, B. S. K, & Abreu, J. M. (2001). Acculturation measurement: Theory, current instruments, and future directions. In J. G. Ponterotto, J. M. Casas, L. A. Suzuki, & C. M. Alexander (Eds.), *Handbook of multicultural counseling* (pp. 394–424). Thousand Oaks, CA: Sage.

Kim, B. S. K., Atkinson, D. R., & Yang, P. H. (1999). The Asian Values Scale: Development, factor analysis, validation, and reliability. *Journal of Counseling Psychology, 46*, 342–352.

Landrine, H., & Klonoff, E. A. (1994). The African American Acculturation Scale: Development, reliability, and validity. *Journal of Black Psychology, 20*, 104–127.

Lowe, M. S., & Mascher, J. (2001). The role of sexual orientation in multicultural counseling. In J. G. Ponterotto, J. M. Casas, L. A. Suzuki, & C. M. Alexander (Eds.), *Handbook of multicultural counseling* (pp. 755–778). Thousands Oaks: Sage.

Marín, G., & Gamba, R. J. (1996). A new measurement of acculturation for Hispanics: The Bidimensional Acculturation Scale for Hispanics (BAS). *Hispanic Journal of Behavioral Sciences, 18,* 297–316.

Marín, G., & Marín, B. V. (1991). *Research with Hispanic populations.* Newbury Park, CA: Sage.

Martínez, C. (1988). Mexican–Americans. In L. Comas–Díaz & E. E. H. Griffith (Eds.), *Clinical guidelines in cross-cultural mental health* (pp. 182–203). New York: John Wiley.

Martínez, R. E. (1993, August). Minority label "dehumanizing" [Letter to the editor]. *San Antonio Express News*, p. 5B.

Martínez, R., Norman, R. D., & Delaney, H. D. (1984). A children's Hispanic background scale. *Hispanic Journal of Behavioral Sciences, 6,* 103–112.

Meadows, F. B. (1991). Getting to the bottom to understand the top. *Journal of Counseling and Development, 70,* 72–76.

Milliones, J. (1980). Construction of a Black consciousness measure: Psychotherapeutic implications. *Psychotherapy: Theory, Research, and Practice, 17,* 175–182.

Moyerman, D. R., & Forman, B. D. (1992). Acculturation and adjustment: A meta-analytic study. *Hispanic Journal of Behavioral Sciences, 14,* 163–200.

Neff, J. A., & Hoppe, S. K. (1993). Race/ethnicity, acculturation, and psychological distress: Fatalism and religiosity as cultural resources. *Journal of Community Psychology, 21,* 3–20.

O'Brien, S. (1989). *American Indian tribal governments.* Norman: University of Oklahoma Press.

Paniagua, F. A. (1998). *Assessing and treating culturally diverse clients: A practical guide.* Thousands Oaks, CA: Sage.

Parham, T. A. (1989). Cycles of psychological Nigrescence. *The Counseling Psychologist, 17,* 187–226.

Pedersen, P. B., & Carey, J. C. (2003). *Multicultural counseling in schools.* Boston: Allyn & Bacon.

Pedersen, P. B., Draguns, J. G., Lonner, W. J., & Trimble, J. E. (2002). *Counseling across cultures* (5th ed.). Thousand Oaks, CA: Sage.

Pérez Foster, R. M. (2001, April). When immigration is trauma: Guidelines for the individual and family clinician. *American Journal of Orthopsychiatry, 71*(1), 153–170.

Ponterotto, J. G., Baluch, S., & Carielli, D. (1998). The Suinn–Lew Asian Self–Identity Acculturation Scale (SL–ASIA): Critique and research recommendation. *Measurement and Evaluation in Counseling and Development, 31,* 109–124.

Ponterotto, J. G., Casas, J. M., Suzuki, L. A., & Alexander, C. M. (Eds.).(2001). *Handbook of multicultural counseling.* Thousand Oaks, CA: Sage.

Rezentez, W. C. (1993). Na Mea Hawai'I: A Hawaiian acculturation scale. *Psychological Reports, 73,* 383-393.

Roysircar–Sodowsky, G., & Frey, L. L.(2003). Children of immigrants: Their worldviews value conflicts. In Pedersen, P. B., & Carey, J. C. (Eds.), *Multicultural counseling in high schools: A practical handbook* (pp. 61–83). Boston: Allyn & Bacon.

Sciarra, T. D. (1999). *Multiculturalism in counseling.* F. E. Peacock Publishers.

Smith, T. W. (1992). Changing racial labels: From "colored" to "Negro" to "Black" to "African American." *Public Opinion Quarterly, 56,* 496–544.

Smitherman, G. (1995). *Black talk.* Boston: Houghton Mifflin.

Snowden, L. R., & Hines, A. M. (1999). A scale to assess African American acculturation. *Journal of Black Psychology, 25,* 36–47.

Sue, D. (1997). Multicultural training. *International Journal of Intercultural Relations, 21,* 175–193.

Sue, D. W., & Sue, D. (1990). *Counseling the culturally different: Theory and practice* (2nd ed.). New York: John Wiley.

Sue, D. W., & Sue, D. (2003). *Counseling the culturally diverse: Theory and practice.* (4th ed.). New York: John Wiley.

Thompson, J., Walker, R. D., & Silk–Walker, P. (1993). Psychiatric care of American Indians and Alaska Natives. In A. C. Gaw (Ed.), *Culture, ethnicity, and mental illeness* (pp. 189–243). Washington, DC: American Psychiatric Press.

Toarmino, D., & Chun, C. A. (1997). Issues and strategies in counseling Korean Americans. In C. C. Lee (Ed.), *Multicultural issues in counseling* (2d ed., pp. 233–254).

U.S. Bureau of Census (2000). *2000 Census of Population. General Population Characteristics.* Washington, DC: U.S. Government Printing Office.

U.S. Department of Health and Human Services. (1991). *Health status of minorities and low-income groups: Third edition.* Washington, DC: Health Resources and Services Administration, U.S. Department of Health and Human Services.

Vroon, P. (1997). *Smell: The secret seducer.* New York: Farrar, Strauss and Giroux.

Walker, R. D., LaDue, R. (1986). An integrative approach to American Indian mental health. In C. B. Wilkinson (Ed.), *Ethnic psychiatry* (pp. 143–199). New York: Plenum.

Whiton, S., & Abercrombie, S. (2002). *Interior design and decoration.* Upper Saddle River, NJ: Prentice Hall.

Wigram, T., Pedersen, I. N., & Bonde, L. O. (2002). *A comprehensive guide to music therapy: Theory, clinical practice, research, and training.* Philadelphia, PA: Jessica Kingsley Publishers.

Wrenn, C. G. (1962). The culturally encapsulated counselor. *Harvard Educational Review, 32,* 444–449.

Zuñiga, M. E. (2003). Cultural competence with Latino Americans. In Lum, D. (Ed.), *Cultural competent practice: A framework for understanding diverse groups and justice issues* (pp. 238–260). CA: Brooks/Cole.

Counseling Children and Adolescents with Special Needs

William McFarland and Toni Tollerud

As they grow up, children and adolescents find themselves in many circumstances over which they have little control. These circumstances can influence the healthy development of young people in a variety of negative ways. All young people have the potential to become "at risk" and are influenced by pressures from family, school, peers, and society (Capuzzi & Gross, 2000). As they attempt to deal with these pressures, children and adolescents often make choices that result in new problems such as substance abuse, gang involvement, sexually transmitted diseases, and pregnancy. Early intervention can help young people successfully deal with the challenges and life circumstances they encounter. Understanding how young people respond to situations that are out of their control—such as a parent who drinks too much or parents who become divorced—is essential for practitioners who want to help children and adolescents respond to these life events with healthy coping strategies.

In this chapter we discuss problems over which children and adolescents have little choice. These issues bring difficulties, pain, and sorrow that can keep young people from functioning effectively in their world. We explore the family circumstances of divorce, adoption, blended families, and what counselors need to know to work effectively with children and adolescents to create resilient behaviors. In addition, we explore grief and loss, living with alcoholic parents, growing up gay or lesbian, eating disorders, and helping children and adolescents cope with the psychological effects of terror attacks. The emphasis for counselor intervention is the presentation of an empowerment model intended to develop and enhance resilient behaviors in young clients.

Resilience

Resilience is the ability to adjust to special problems and achieve positive outcomes. It is

> the capacity of those who are exposed to identifiable risk factors to overcome those risks and avoid negative outcomes such as delinquency and behavior problems, psychological maladjustment, academic difficulties, and physical complications. (Rak & Patterson, 1996, p. 368)

Hollister–Wagner, Foshee, and Jackson (2001) described resiliency as "the ability of individuals to survive and thrive despite exposure to negative circumstances" (p. 445). According to Hauser, Vieyra, Jacobson, and Wertreib (1985), "Only a minority of at-risk children . . . experience serious difficulties in their personality development" (p. 83). Reporting on an earlier study by Werner (1984), Werner and Smith (1992) explained the results of a longitudinal study of more than 200 children. Werner followed her research subjects for 32 years. As children, the participants in her study experienced poverty, perinatal stress, family discord, divorce, parental alcoholism, and parental mental illness. By 18 years of age, one third of these children were described as competent young adults who "loved well, worked well, and expected well" (Werner, 1984, p. 69). By age 32, most of those who had problems coping as adolescents had become more effective and competent in adult roles.

Similarly, in a narrative analysis study, Hauser (1999) reported that resilient young adults had experienced more helplessness, rage and lower self-esteem as adolescents but that these subjects developed special strengths that compensated for their serious difficulties as adolescents. These strengths included increased coherence, self-reflection, increased discourse, and exploited resources. Jew and Green (1998) found that resilient individuals are those who learn to cope with stress more appropriately by utilizing skills such as appraising a situation, processing the experience, attaching meaning to it, and incorporating the person's belief system into the experience.

Characteristics of Resiliency

In their review of the literature, Rak and Patterson (1996) listed the following seven personality traits as protective factors that distinguish resilient children from those who become overwhelmed by problems:

- an active approach toward problem solving
- an ability to gain others' positive attention
- an optimistic view of their experiences even while immersed in suffering
- an ability to maintain a positive vision of a meaningful life
- an ability to be alert and autonomous
- a tendency to seek novel experiences
- a proactive perspective.

Werner (1984) proposed the following four protective factors of resilient children:

- both a pronounced autonomy and a strong social orientation
- sociability coupled with a sense of independence
- hobbies and creative interests as sources of self-esteem
- engaging in acts of helpfulness.

Hollister–Wagner, Foshee, and Jackson (2001) detailed protective factors as:

- having a close relationship with an adult
- high value of religion
- self-esteem
- relationship competence
- good communication skills
- ability to deal with anger constructively

Besides personality traits, buffering factors distinguish resilient children from nonresilient children. For example, protective factors within the family operate when children receive support from caregivers other than parents or have access to role models outside of the family. The critical point for counselors is that protective factors, including the child's temperament, alternative sources of support in the family, and mentoring by role models in the community, can help children overcome adversity and mature into successful adults.

Interventions

As children cope with difficult situations, they develop the following resiliencies (Wolin & Wolin, 1993):

- insight: the ability to figure things out

■ independence: being able to do for oneself
■ relationships: finding support and mentoring outside the family
■ initiative: figuring out strategies to stay safe
■ humor: laughing at adverse circumstances
■ creativity: expressing feelings through artistic expression
■ morality: a promise not to do what has been done to them

These resiliencies develop in phases. The resiliency of insight might be evident in young children as they sense something about the family situation; in adolescents it may be the ability to know something about the family situation; and in adults it could be the ability to understand something about the family situation. For example, when living with a violent alcoholic parent, young children may read facial expressions of the adults or older children in the family the morning after the parent has been intoxicated and violent. They notice that the family atmosphere has changed. Adolescents in this situation would notice the change in family atmosphere and also figure out that the cause was the intoxicated parent abusing the other parent. Adults in this situation would know about the destructive conflict in the family and also understand the parents' significant issues and problems.

As the counselor listens to young clients relate their stories of stress and pain, he or she can reframe these experiences as resiliencies or strengths. For example, adolescents who don't want to go home immediately after school because it might not be safe may spend time in the school library or with friends. This strategy clearly demonstrates insight and initiative because the teenager knows that going home might pose danger and takes actions to stay safe. The counselor can encourage the continued development of these strategies and reframe the situation as one of building resilience.

Counselors working in the schools can teach resiliency skills through classroom guidance lessons or in small-group counseling sessions. Examples include training in conflict resolution, interpersonal skills, assertion training, problem solving, and rational-emotive education. Elementary and middle school counselors could use the game *Bounce Back: A Game That Teaches Resiliency Skills* (Childswork/Childsplay, 2002) to build resiliency skills in children and teens. Arman (2002) described a six-session brief group counseling model to increase the resiliency of students with mild disabilities. The topics for the group sessions were: setting group norms, educating students about resiliency, identifying dependable and trustworthy people in the lives of the students, appreciating the need for high expectations, involvement in meaningful community or school-related activities, and wrapping up unfinished business.

Miller (1999) argued that racial socialization and racial identity are protective factors that can promote resiliency in African American adolescents as well as other minority groups. Racial socialization refers to raising physically and emotionally healthy children who are Black in a society in which being Black has negative connotations. Parents socialize their children regarding racial issues such as prejudice, thereby creating a buffer against a hostile environment. Racial socialization helps to build a racial identity that Helms (1990) defined as "one's perception that he or she shares a common racial heritage with a particular group" (p. 3). A well developed racial identity can help minority adolescents overcome the stigma of negative social stereotypes.

Counselors can apply solution-focused counseling with their young clients (Murphy, 1997; Walter & Peller, 1992). This counseling approach assumes that clients have the assets to set and reach goals. The counselor assists clients in revealing what they are already doing that can help them achieve their goals. Combining resiliency models with the solution-focused approach to counseling enables the counselor to empower children and adolescents in their struggle to adjust to challenging life events.

In addition to a solution-focused counseling approach, counselors can use their knowledge of resiliencies when consulting with parents and teachers regarding the adjustment of their clients. Counselors can point out the resiliencies the children possess and suggest ways by which teachers, parents, or other family members can help to develop those resiliencies.

By reframing difficult, stressful situations in terms of the development of resiliencies and by working to enhance protective factors within children, within their families, and within the school and community, counselors can tilt the balance for these young clients from vulnerability to resiliency. Counselors can play a critical role in facilitating the development of competent, successful, resilient children.

Counseling Children and Adolescents in Nontraditional Families

The family is a major contributor to the development of children. Problems may be present in the *internal* functioning of the family, such as the way people communicate within the family or the rules it follows and, *externally,* based on the family structure. Certainly, children growing up in the traditional two-parent family are subject to difficulties, but children and adolescents in families with nontraditional structures are much more prone to self-defeating behaviors (Capuzzi & Gross, 2000; Goldenberg & Goldenberg, 1996). In addition, children may have problems stemming from both internal dynamics and external circumstances (Fincham, 1994). Children who are having difficulty and acting out at-risk behaviors may be doing so as a result of dysfunctional family dynamics (Palmo & Palmo, 1996).

The traditional definition for family clearly is no longer applicable. We now readily acknowledge and accept diversity in how families are constituted and what special needs they have. More than half of all marriages end in divorce

(Seibert & Willetts, 2000). Children and adolescents who lack resilience may become casualties in these families. As their family structure goes through new phases, these children are susceptible to a variety of self-defeating behaviors and special problems.

Counseling Children and Adolescents of Divorce

Ever since World War II, the divorce rate in the United States has been increasing dramatically. In the 40 years between 1960 and 2000, the divorce rate in the United States has tripled. The National Center for Health Statistics (U. S. Bureau of the Census, 2000) estimated that more than 1.14 million divorces took place in 2000. As many as one third to one half of the adolescent population is affected by divorce, and approximately 18 million, or one in four children, are currently living in single-parent homes (Fields, 2001).

Divorce signifies major changes in the lives of children and adolescents, usually accompanied by stress. To understand the complete impact of divorce on children, we might view it as a chain of events rather than a single stressful crisis. The chain of events begins with marital conflict prior to the divorce, leading to the pain and confusion of the divorce itself, and concluding with the aftermath of the divorce, which may involve geographical relocations, loss of peer relationships, significant changes in socioeconomic status, redefining parental relationships, and possible remarriage of one or both parents. Research has suggested that children of divorce are much more likely to have relationship problems and school problems (DeLucia–Waack & Gerrity, 2001).

Characteristics

Most children and adolescents face the following issues to varying degrees (Wallerstein & Kelly, 1996):

- *Fear.* Children of divorce often believe that if their parents' marriage can be terminated, so can the parent–child relationship. The children may worry about who will provide food, shelter, clothes, and protection for them.
- *Sadness or feelings of loss.* Children of divorce may show depressive symptoms manifested by changes in sleeping and eating patterns, difficulty in sustaining attention, and dramatic emotional swings. Most children desire contact with the absent parent, and many children hold on to the hope that their parents will reconcile.
- *Loneliness.* Because divorced parents often are preoccupied with their own needs during the divorce, they may overlook their children's needs. With only one parent in the household, children sometimes are left alone or with a caregiver.
- *Rejection.* Children of divorce may feel the noncustodial parent is rejecting them, regardless of whether this is true. Because the custodial parent may

have less time for the children, the children may feel rejected by that parent as well.

▬ *Conflicting loyalties.* Many children of divorce report wanting to maintain a relationship with both parents, while parents often pressure the children to be loyal to only him or her and not the other parent. The result is parents' competing for the support and loyalty of their children and even enlisting the children in an alliance against the other parent. Parents also commonly persuade grandparents and other relatives to pressure the children to take sides in the parental dispute, which results in feelings of confusion and guilt.

▬ *Anger.* Children of divorce may be angry because they are expected to fill the role of the absent parent and fulfill physical and emotional responsibilities beyond their capabilities. They may be angry with their parents for breaking up the family and forcing them to adjust to new circumstances.

Within 2 to 3 years after the divorce, most parents and children adjust to their new life (Dacey & Kenny, 1997). How well children adjust depends on a number of factors. The first factor is the *cumulative stress* children experience following a divorce (Hetherington, as cited in Dacey & Kenny, 1997). They have more stress if there is a great loss of income in the household, a significant change in methods of discipline, or a move to a new location and school. If the divorce was destructive rather than benevolent, it could amplify these problems (Spencer & Shapiro, 1993).

The second factor affecting children's adjustment is *temperament and personality.* If children are able to easily adapt to change prior to the divorce, adjustment to the divorce may not be as difficult and children can develop personal assets to use in dealing with subsequent stressful life events. For children who already have difficulty adjusting to change, the divorce can be damaging and destructive (Dacey & Kenny, 1997).

The third factor affecting adjustment to the divorce is *the child's age.* Adolescents are better able than younger children to understand the causes and consequences of the divorce because of their ability to think more abstractly. With peer contacts outside the family, adolescents also may have developed a better support system than younger children. In their review of the literature of the effects of divorce on children, Thompson and Rudolph (1996) stated:

> Preschoolers (ages 3 to 5) have only a vague understanding of the family situation. . . . They often feel frightened and insecure, experience nightmares, and regress to more infantile behaviors. School-age children, who have more advanced cognitive and emotional development, see the situation more accurately; however, children ages 6 to 8 often believe the divorce was their fault. . . . And children this age often hold unrealistic hopes for a family reconciliation. . . . Age 9 to 12 is a time when children are developing rapidly and rely on their parents for stability. They may become very angry with

the parent they blame for the divorce or may take a supportive role as they worry about their troubled parent. Because of their anxiety, they may develop somatic symptoms, engage in troublesome behaviors, or experience a decline in academic achievement. (pp. 414–415)

The fourth factor affecting adjustment to the divorce is *gender.* The father most often is the one who leaves the home, and the effects are more negative for males than females (Dacey and Kenny, 1997). Hetherington (1991), however, concluded that many girls from divorced families develop adjustment problems similar to boys. Wallerstein (1987), too, noted that adolescent girls from divorced families often had difficulty relating to males during adolescence, were afraid of being hurt by their boyfriends, and worried that their future marriages wouldn't last.

Interventions

Wallerstein and Blakeslee (1996) described six psychological tasks that children of divorce must resolve. As children and adolescents work through these tasks, they can become more resilient. These tasks provide a framework for counselor interventions.

1. *Acknowledging the reality* of *the marital rupture.* Younger children often fantasize about and deny the reality of the family break-up. Counselors can consult with the parents and encourage them to discuss the divorce with their children. The parents may need to learn ways to be supportive. Counselors can listen to children's concerns, validate their feelings, and develop lists of topics the children may want to explore with their parents. Pardeck and Pardeck (1993) suggested having older children compose a "Dear Abby" letter describing their family situation. They also suggested that younger children might use pictures and words cut from magazines to create a collage describing their family situations. Support groups also provide a viable vehicle for dealing with a variety of issues relative to the divorce.

2. *Disengaging from the parental conflict and distress and resuming customary pursuits.* Counselors can recommend to parents that they maintain familiar routines and continue to encourage involvement in school and extracurricular activities. Counselors may encourage the use of structured procedures to ensure that homework is completed and study time is scheduled.

3. *Resolution of loss.* Resolving the many losses that children of divorce experience may be the most difficult task, according to Wallerstein (1987). The counselor can encourage the absent parent to maintain contact with the children and also assist clients to develop connections with other adults outside the family who can offer support. Group counseling with other children who have worked through some of these loss issues might be helpful as well.

To help children cope with the losses resulting from divorce, Morganett (1994) addressed the following goals in an eight-session group-counseling intervention for children from divorced families:

- Help children realize that others have the same feelings about divorce.
- Help children realize that others have new families and feelings about these new families.
- Help children understand that they are not to blame for the divorce.
- Help children identify their feelings about the divorce.
- Help children express their feelings about the divorce.
- Help children understand the issues around remarriage.
- Help children understand and manage stress.

Similarly, Spencer and Shapiro (1993) described a 10-session group counseling treatment program for adolescents from divorced families in which clients addressed issues such as self-esteem, trust, problem solving, personal rights, conflict resolution, and remarriage.

4. *Resolving anger and self-blame.* Counselors may need to correct the cognitive distortions that children often have about the divorce. Using puppets is a good way for young children to project and express their feelings. Another excellent technique is bibliotherapy, in which young people can read about others who have experienced what they are going through. This helps them understand the divorce and identify with issues and feelings of the characters in the story (Pardeck & Pardeck, 1993). Useful books include, among others, *Don't Fall Apart on Saturdays* (Moser & Melton, 2000), *My Mother's House, My Father's House* (Christiansen, 1990), *Chevrolet Saturdays* (Boyd, 1995), and *The Squeaky Wheel* (Smith, 1990).

5. *Accepting the permanence of the divorce.* Counselors may have to work with children who relentlessly hold firm to the idea that their parents will reconcile. Again, group counseling with other students who have worked through this issue may be helpful. Counselors may use expressive and creative techniques to help children understand the changes that have taken place in their family structure. For example, the counselor can ask children to draw their families before the divorce and after the divorce. The counselor places "feeling words" on 3×5 cards and asks the children to place the card on the picture of the family member that best describes their feelings toward that person.

6. *Achieving realistic hope regarding relationships.* Adolescents who have experienced parental divorce may struggle with creating satisfying intimate relationships. Counselors can use cognitive–behavioral techniques to help these teens realize the irrationality of their fears. Counselors can challenge their clients' thoughts through questions such as: Where is the proof that . . . ? Is it true that . . . ? Does it make sense that because you experienced . . . it means . . . ?

For example, because their families were extremely conflicted, some clients fear that any conflict in a relationship is unhealthy, and therefore they avoid conflict at all costs. Counselors can assist teenagers to realize that not all conflict is destructive and that constructive conflict can enhance rather than destroy relationships. Behavioral rehearsal of constructive conflict-resolution skills, such as active listening, assertion, brainstorming, and problem solving, may help adolescents build and maintain more satisfying relationships.

For children in elementary school, DeLucia-Waack and Gerrity (2001) suggest a group-counseling intervention that addresses the following goals:

- bring the divorce situation into the real world of the child so he or she can cope with the reality of the situation;
- normalize the common experiences and feelings of the child;
- create a safe and supportive environment so each child can talk about the divorce;
- help each child label, understand, and express their feelings;
- develop new coping strategies and skills;
- and emphasize that the divorce is not the child's fault.

Pedro–Carroll, Sutton, and Wyman (1999) suggested similar goals emphasizing group support and training in social competence as key factors in working with children. In their research study on using a group experience for children to address issues around divorce, results showed that the children demonstrated less anxiety and fewer adjustment problems in the classroom (Pedro–Carroll, Sutton & Wyman, 1999). School-based interventions suggested by Richardson and Rosen (1999) advocate for the involvement of the classroom teacher as a part of the intervention.

Counselors can facilitate the development of resiliency in children and adolescents who have experienced divorce by helping them resolve psychological tasks (Wallerstein & Blakeslee, 1996). The more resilient they are, the more likely they will be able to function successfully and not resort to unhealthy ways of coping with the potentially devastating effects of parental divorce. Resiliency is especially important with this issue because, as Goldenberg and Goldenberg (1996) noted, within 3 years of the divorce, three-fourths of the women and five-sixths of the men remarry, creating a blended family. Children and adolescents in these new family structures may benefit from counselor interventions again to help them adjust to another set of circumstances.

Counseling Children and Adolescents in Stepfamilies and Blended Families

The stepfamily represents a substantial portion of families in the United States; one third of children will live in a stepfamily before they reach adulthood (Coleman, Ganong, & Fine, 2000) and the 2000 Census reported that nuclear families now make up less than 25% of U. S. households. Visher and Visher (1996) defined a stepfamily, as "a household in which there is an adult couple, at least one of who has a child by a previous relationship" (p. 3). Other authors referred to this family structure as the blended family (Becvar & Becvar, 1993; Fenell & Weinhold, 1997; Lambie & Daniels–Mohring, 1993). Blending is a more positive concept that seems to fit the resiliency model in a proactive perspective in that it implies an active approach toward addressing difficulties and using problem-solving techniques toward healthy adjustment for all participants. Lambie and Daniels–Mohring suggested that once the remarriage happens, the focus turns to the efforts of blending the two families into one.

Working with blended families requires a unique understanding utilizing approaches different from the traditional family (Kelly, 1996; Visher & Visher, 1996). Blending can cause difficulties within the family on a variety of levels. A major issue is the desire for the new members of the family to reconstitute a traditional family structure. This wish for "instant readjustment," in which members believe that once the remarriage takes place, everyone will live "happily ever after," is a myth for the blended—and, for that matter, any—family (Becvar & Becvar, 1993).

The reconstituted family faces many challenges resulting from the complex and confusing circumstances of becoming a blended family. Visher and Visher (1996) identified 16 characteristics of the blended family, as compared to a nuclear family. Walsh (1992) suggested 20 major issues that blended families encounter as they blend. He organized these issues into four topical categories, noting that these issues impact children and adolescents because what happens in the family affects all members.

Characteristics

The first category, *initial family issues,* occurs early in the development of the blended family unit. The ability to cope with these initial family issues depends on the age of the children at the time of the remarriage. Younger children usually adjust more easily than adolescents do, and adolescents have more difficulty when the stepparent is not the same sex as the teenager (Fuller, 1988). Issues may revolve around loyalty, in which a child believes that loving anyone other than the biological parent is disloyal. Children also may worry that the new stepparent is trying to take away the love from the biological parent. This fear may cause parents to be competitive or to undermine the other family members' relationships.

Children and adolescents also may need time to deal with the loss and grief still present from the divorce. Attachment issues and the loss of significant others can further disrupt children's development, or they may hold on to a fantasy that their biological parents will reconcile and the original family will be a unit again (Walsh, 1992).

For adolescents who are coping with these initial family issues, the remarriage may challenge their own development around identity, sexuality, and the need for individuation from the family (Visher & Visher, 1996). Issues of attachment can become complicated as they seek to become more independent at a time when the new family is working to bond and attach. Watching their new parents act out the rituals of love may be embarrassing and conflictual and may impact the development of their own dating and peer relationships.

Some children and adolescents who have been living in single-parent households have served in parental roles, shouldering responsibility and playing prominent roles in their families. Although the remarriage may be a source of relief, it also may demote youngsters from positions of power they previously held in their families. Finally, the remarriage may cause problems around parenting time with the noncustodial parent, feelings of rejection, and the potential of moving the family to a new location.

The second category, *developing family issues,* surfaces after initial formation of the blended family (Walsh, 1992). As they cope with these developing family issues, children and adolescents deal with potentially difficult family dynamics such as discipline, role assignments within the family, sibling conflict, competition for time with the noncustodial parent, and moving between families for visits. In addition, the reconstituted family members bring into the new family most of the personal issues from the former marriage and divorce, such as grief and loss issues, insecurity, low selfesteem, and anger.

In the third category, *feelings about self and others,* Walsh (1992) noted that children and adolescents are influenced by society's concept of remarriage. For example, the school system often reinforces the conflict and hurt feelings by its insensitivity to issues such as parent/teacher conferences, graduations, and other events. Classroom assignments that deal with drawing or talking about parents or family can become stressful for these children and adolescents. Being called or labeled as a member of a "stepfamily" still represents a negative image in U. S. society. Children and adolescents may be forced to keep their feelings hidden, which can result in anger, low self-esteem, and guilt. Children who feel stress in the new family may act out in school or have difficulty concentrating. If the new parents conceive children of their own, this introduces another factor. Often this new child, living with both biological parents, receives most of the attention and affection in the family, leaving stepchildren to feel less valued.

The fourth category is *adult issues that relate to the new family* (Walsh, 1992). Financial concerns such as child support and alimony, competition with the noncustodial parent, continuing conflicts between biological parents, and conflict in parenting styles in the remarried family can put young people in the middle. For example, who will pay for college may become a bitter fight, creating stress for adolescents. Also, as adolescents begin to mature and become young adults, their personal values and beliefs about love, marriage, and their future families may be strongly influenced by having lived in a blended family situation. These young adults may be much more sensitive and critical about how they build their future and how they intend to rear their own children.

Interventions

Counselors who work with children and adolescents in families of divorce and blended families can help them with their concerns about loss, loyalty, and lack of control (Visher & Visher, 1996). Lack of control can impact adolescents by increasing the risk of anger or depression stemming from the inability to control their environment. In a survey conducted by Lutz (1983), children ages 12–19 identified several issues that were most stressful for them:

- hearing their biological parents argue and put each other down
- inability to see the other parent
- feeling caught in the middle between biological parents
- fighting within the stepfamily
- adjusting to rules and discipline set by the stepparent.

Costa and Stiltner (1994) outlined an 11-session group-counseling intervention for junior high students whose family situations had changed through divorce and remarriage. The sequence of topics is as follows; with some topics requiring more than one session:

1. Generate group guidelines and acquaint members.
2. Create and share lifelines.
3. Clarify values by reading and discussing prepared statements about family change.
4. Discuss bibliotherapy assignments.
5. Create and discuss a family coat of arms.
6. Learn and use empathic assertion skills.
7. Summarize thoughts and feelings about the group experience.

Counselors need to provide a basis for emotional support in which their young clients have a safe place to express their feelings and have them validated. For example, Cobia and Brazelton (1994) described procedures using kinetic family drawings with children in remarriage families, in which the counselor asks clients to draw a picture of everyone in their family, including themselves, doing something. Counselors should ask their clients to include family members from both households. After the children have completed the drawings, the counselor asks clarifying questions to explore the issues the drawings suggest.

Robson (1993) recommended group interventions for adolescents in remarriage families. She endorsed the use of creative drama, role-play, and videotape playback to facilitate the expression of feelings about family issues and to promote problem solving by the adolescent clients.

Counselors also can ask clients to keep journals and record their thoughts and feelings about the transition to a blended family. Within the counseling sessions children and adolescents can develop insights about their issues, work on troublesome relationships, and gain some control over their lives by identifying and employing effective coping strategies.

Counselors also must deal with loss issues of children and adolescents in blended families. Either the death of a parent or divorce has preceded the formation of the blended family, and often this major loss is exacerbated by other loss issues such as moving, loss of household income or economic status, loss of friends and extended family, and loss of familiar routines and family rituals.

Counselors have to help children and adolescents in blended families overcome their feelings of helplessness. Counselors can help them explore developmentally appropriate behaviors such as visiting old friends, getting involved in extracurricular activities at school or in the community, finding private space in the home, or asking for one-on-one time with the birth parent without the presence of the stepparent or stepsiblings. Allowing children and adolescents to make choices can lead to a sense of independence, freedom, and control in one's life. Children can read books about blended families. Good resources include *Louie's Search* (Keats, 2001), *Like Jake and Me* (Jukes, 1987), *When a Parent Marries Again* (Heegaard, 1993*), All Families Are Different* (Gordon & Cohen, 2000*), Daddy's New Baby* (Vigna, 1982), and *All Kinds of Families* (Simon, 1987*)*.

Counselors also must be willing to get involved and join with the family members in understanding the frustrations of each person's role within the blended family unit (Fenell & Weinhold, 1997). Because the newly formed parental subsystem is unfamiliar with becoming a blended family, the counselor should be willing to intervene and work with the parents. Many times, the adults in the family put unrealistic expectations on the children or are so consumed with their own issues of adjustment that they do not support the children through this transitional time.

Advocating for young clients helps adults recognize children's unique needs and also assists them in developing appropriate solutions and options that empower the family. Kirby (1997) suggested that school counselors have an important role in establishing communication between all those involved in the child's life including stepparents, adoptive parents, social workers, and school personnel. In addition, the counselor can suggest parenting strategies or introduce family meetings to open up communications among all members of the blended family. Interventions such as these can lead to greater self-confidence in children and adolescents, enabling them to adjust in healthy ways to the new blended family.

In dealing with adolescents, counselors need to keep in mind that being in the blended family may complicate the normal developmental changes that adolescents are experiencing. Adolescents who seemed to be adjusting well to the blended family at first may later exhibit anger, acting-out behavior, or withdrawal. Helping stepparents know what behavior is typical for adolescents can be helpful. Counselors can diminish crisis situations to normal developmental passages and allow adolescent clients to talk about their feelings and concerns.

Counselors can suggest books to help adolescents gain insights about themselves. Good resources include: *Step Kids: A Survival Guide for Teenagers in Stepfamilies* (Getzoff & McClenahan, 1984); *Stepliving for Teens: Getting Along with Stepparents and Siblings* (Block & Bartell, 2001); *Finding Your Place: A Teen Guide to Life in Blended Family* (Leibowitz, 2000); *Step Trouble: A Survival Guide for Teenagers with Step Parents* (Coleman, 1993); and *How to Win as a Stepfamily* (Visher & Visher, 1991).

In their efforts to become independent, adolescents struggle with their search for identity, as well as their need to separate from their family. If the blended family is being formed simultaneously, this can cause conflicts for adolescents who feel pressured to join with the family at the same time they should be developing a sense of autonomy. Adolescents need to see where they can take control in their lives and take on more resilient behaviors in handling their world.

Finally, adolescents may develop problems involving sexuality. They may withdraw from step-siblings or even stepparents in reaction to their emerging sexual feelings. At the same time, discussing one's sexuality may be taboo in the family. Counselors should bring up the subject in counseling and help adolescents explore their feelings about their sexuality. Counselors may work with the adolescent and his or her significant adults to discuss the importance of peer relationships, dating, and trust.

Knowing that students live in blended families can be helpful in addressing classroom problems, academic failures, and personal or social problems. School counselors must work toward normalizing the blended family, along with all types of families, in the school. Teachers should be informed about children and adolescents from blended families so they can be sensitive to issues such as parent conferences, sending home notes, step-siblings, and academic or behavioral problems (Lambie & Daniels–Mohring, 1993). Programs and developmental guidance lessons can address diverse families and assist children and adolescents in developing understanding and tolerance of peers from various families.

Crosbie–Burnett and Pulvino (1990) outlined a classroom program for elementary, middle, and high school students about children in nontraditional families. Workshops for teachers and administrators may help break down stereotypes and biases about divorce and blended families so schools will be safe, friendly places to promote a healthy and effective education for all students.

Counseling Children and Adolescents Who Are Adopted

A positive characteristic of adoptive families is that the household usually is headed by an adult couple. Children who are aware that they have been adopted might have issues related to abandonment, family attachment, and loyalty (Jarratt, 1994). In addition, children who are adopted may feel insecure, angry, guilty, and blame themselves or their biological parents (Lambie & Daniels–Mohring, 1993). The circumstances surrounding the adoption have a strong impact on children and adolescents. In many cases, children are adopted because of unwanted pregnancies, abuse or neglect, or circumstances that have depleted all the family's emotional and economic resources. The new family might provide a healthier, more stable environment that makes adjustment easier for the adoptee. An important aspect in adjustment is the adoptee's' feelings of belonging in the adopting family. Children studied by Benson, Sharma, and Roehikepartain (1994) who had been adopted developed good coping strategies and grew into happy, successful adolescents.

Conversely, Dickman (1992) reported that school success can be greatly diminished for adopted children, and Brodzinsky, Schechter, and Henig (1992), as cited in Kizner and Kizner (1999), believed that a disproportionate number of children who are adopted experience psychological distress. To address the needs of these children and adolescents, Kizner and Kizner (1999) and Zurkle, Peterson, and Collins–Marotte (2001) suggested assertive interventions by school counselors through school-based interventions.

Characteristics

Adjustment is complex and varies according to age (Brodzinsky & Schechter, 1992). Children who are adopted before they are old enough to be in school go through little adjustment because they do not understand exactly how they are different. Counseling may be beneficial with the adoptive parents, however, to help them deal with their possible infertility issues and bonding with the adopted child. Parents also may need to consider how they want to address the adoption issue as their adopted children get older and enter school.

At the point when they enter school, children become more capable of understanding the meaning of adoption. Brodzinsky and Schechter (1992) suggested that during this phase parents tell children about the adoption and create a safe environment where they can feel free to ask questions. Helping them feel that they belong in this family and that they are "chosen" assists with their adjustment.

As later childhood approaches and children move from concrete thinking to more abstract reasoning, they are better able to understand that being chosen into a family also means that another family rejected them. At this point children become aware of the loss they sustained. They may react with feelings of uncertainty and insecurity, as well as anger at the parents who "gave me up." They may want to know more about their birth family and the circumstances surrounding the adoption. Children at this phase may be sensitive and aware of their feelings of loss and grief (Brodzinsky & Schechter, 1992).

As children approach adolescence, their adoption may add to the normal problems of development and growth. Adolescents typically are struggling with issues of identity formation (Erikson, 1968). These issues are confounded for adopted adolescents who are searching for answers to "Who am I?" Because they do not live with their birth parents, they may look different from their adoptive parents and siblings, be unaware of their medical histories, and have questions about their biological parents. Brodzinsky and Schechter (1992) indicated that, in addition, the normal fears and confusion of adolescence may be exacerbated and adolescents may worry about their adoptive family rejecting them.

Sexuality may become another issue for adopted adolescents. For those who were given up by their birth mother because of a teen pregnancy or unwanted pregnancy, involvement in a sexual relationship may stir up many feelings. Benson et al. (1994) compared sexual behaviors of adopted and nonadopted adolescents and found no differences. Sorosky, Baran, and Pannor (1989), however, found that adopted female adolescents acted out sexually. Those authors concluded that some adopted female adolescents desired to become pregnant to identify with their birth mothers and to connect with a blood relative, their own child.

Interventions

Dealing with children and adolescents who have been adopted means being aware that at critical periods in their growth and development, new issues and concerns may surface around the adoption. For example, adopted children who are adjusting well may find that at the onset of adolescence, they suddenly face major problems relating to the adoption. Parents and counselors may not understand why problems are emerging now when they were absent previously. Janus (1997) suggested that normal problems might be intensified for children and adolescents who have been adopted. The older the child at the time of placement, the greater is the probability that the child will have behavioral and emotional difficulties (Zirkle, Peterson, & Collins–Marotte, 2001). Lambie and Daniels–Mohring (1993) recommended working with the whole family to assist with the healthy adjustment of adopted children. Zirkle, Peterson, and Collins–Marotte, 2001 suggested school-based interventions that include the following:

- consultation with teachers
- group work for students who are adopted
- individual counseling, especially around issues of grief, loss, and intimacy
- coordination of mental health services with the school programs in a "wrap-around" approach

When selecting interventions, the counselor should, of course, consider the child's age.

If adopted children are referred for counseling as preschoolers, working with the parents may be more helpful. Common issues with the parents may center on infertility, parenting skills, and setting realistic expectations. Adopted children often are only children, and parents may have unrealistic expectations for them (Lambie & Daniels–Mohring, 1993). Parents also may lack general knowledge of child development, discipline, and boundaries.

An area that can be complicating during this period is the open adoption. In an open adoption the birth parent or parents are involved with the adoption family before, during, and after the adoption (Janus, 1997). Although this can have advantages, it may create problems around child-rearing practices, and confusion as children try to understand how they have two sets of parents.

As adopted children begin to understand what makes them different, they realize that they have had a loss in their life. When working with these children, counselors should help them deal with the issue of being different and the feelings related to loss. Adopted children may have problems with establishing trust, low self-esteem, and fear of being rejected (Lambie & Daniels–Mohring, 1993). They need to know that they belong, have support, and feel a sense of stability. Counselors can engage adopted children in the therapeutic process using a variety of techniques that are developmentally appropriate for the age level. These include drawing, journaling, storytelling, incomplete sentences, role-play, puppets, and play therapy. Listening to their "story," affirming their feelings, and offering support can facilitate adopted children's adjustment.

Counselors should also involve the family at this point, encouraging the parents to discuss aspects of the adoption openly with children. Jarratt (1994) warned of the potential damage to children who are not involved in learning about their past and the circumstances around the adoption. Counselors also may need to assist with adjustment issues for adopted children in school. Adopted children may have difficulty drawing a family tree or talking about their parents, for instance.

Counselors also may need to assist children and their parents in understanding biases or mistaken assumptions that teachers may have regarding adopted children. School counselors can offer assistance to teachers and lead inservice workshops to increase educators' awareness and understanding. Ng and Wood (1993), among others, have developed resource materials on adoption for use by educators.

Group counseling can be helpful in working with adopted children (Kizner & Kizner, 1999; Morganett, 1990, 1994). Myer, James, and Street (1987) offered ideas for a classroom meeting approach based on Adlerian principles. Kizner and Kizner (1999) proposed a 12-session group counseling unit for children, supporting the belief that children need help in understanding their thoughts and feelings about adoption. Group counseling allows children who have common experiences to feel normal, to share their stories with others who can understand them, and to gain support in knowing they are not the only one who has been adopted.

In counseling adolescents, the picture becomes more complicated because of the physical, social, and emotional changes characteristic of adolescence, which can trigger feelings about being adopted. As adolescents struggle with their self-identity, they question their heritage, are concerned with looks, worry about their intelligence, and wonder about health problems they might have inherited from their birth parents. This can be frustrating if are unable to find answers to these questions.

Counselors need to create safe places for adolescents wh
their feelings surface. Counselors need to help these clients
sion. Interventions can allow adolescents to tell their stori
insights and understandings about their lives. Encouraging t
about their questions, concerns, and feelings also can be he.
apy. Assisting teens to recognize where they can take control of their lives anu
relate effectively to their adoptive family, friends, and, in some cases, their birth
parents, can lead to healthy adjustment.

Older adolescents may raise issues about sexuality and family planning for
the future. Counselors can help these clients explore healthy alternatives and values about family, marriage, and rearing children.

Adopted adolescents may want to search for or meet their birth parents
(Krueger & Hanna, 1997). This can be traumatic, especially if these clients are
immature or harbor anger and resentment. They may exhibit external behaviors
such as signs of stress, inability to sleep, trouble concentrating, inability to eat,
irritability, or acting out in school. Counselors can help adolescents sort through
their feelings, provide support, and help them identify issues involved in meeting
the birth parent(s), as well as processing the effects of the meeting after it has
taken place. In all cases, the role of counseling should be to help adolescent
clients gain insight and awareness that will lead to better coping strategies, self-
understanding, and healthier interactions.

Counseling Children and Adolescents of Alcoholic Parents

In the United States, an estimated 14 million adults abuse or depend on alcohol;
9.6 million children under age 17 are living with an adult who is abusing alcohol;
and one in every four children is exposed to alcohol abuse or dependence in the
family, sometime before the age of 18 (Grant, 2000). Based on these statistics,
Post and Robinson (1998) indicated that there is a greater risk in every developmental area for school-aged children of alcoholics. This research continues to
support the findings of Frymier (1992) regarding the effects of alcohol on student
behavior. Frymier reported that:

- 23% of children and adolescents with a parent who drank excessively had
  been suspended from school, in contrast to 5% of those whose parents were
  not alcoholic.
- 32% with an alcoholic parent used alcohol, whereas only 4% of those whose
  parents were not alcoholic used alcohol.
- 28% of the students with an alcoholic parent had low grades in school, compared to 13% of students who did not have an alcoholic parent.
- 31% of those with an alcoholic parent had been retained in grade, and 14%
  of those who did not have an alcoholic parent had been retained in grade.
- 33% of the students with a parent who drank too much reported low self-
  esteem, compared to 12% of students who did not have an alcoholic parent.

As children and adolescents with alcoholic parents or caregivers work through developmental tasks, they experience circumstances that interfere with normal development and encounter challenging problems in trying to adjust to their family situation. Post and Robinson (1998) suggest that the stress involved in alcoholic families results, for example, in increased physical, mental, social, and emotional difficulties.

Characteristics

When counselors work with children of alcoholic parents, several themes may be evident, including role reversal, low self-esteem, and role confusion (Ackerman, 1983; Black, 1991). The children may seem grown-up and extremely mature, maybe more so than their parents. These children have learned to curb many childhood behaviors as they try to anticipate their parents' reactions, which may be unpredictable and inconsistent. These children sometimes appear extremely responsible, competent, and high-achieving and display no outward signs of distress. Having lived their early years behaving like adults, these children later describe their experience as "growing up without a childhood."

Children from alcoholic families may believe that something is wrong and shameful about their families and, therefore, mistakenly conclude that something is wrong and shameful with *them*. These children might compare their family situation to families of their peers and decide that their own family is inferior. They don't see the same turmoil in those other families as they routinely experience in their own (O'Rourke, 1990). Children who live with alcoholic parents have role confusion because they are expected to be mature and adultlike at home but are treated as typical children or adolescents by their teachers and peers. Determining when to act like a grown-up and when to allow themselves to be a child can be difficult.

After interviewing children of alcoholic parents, Dundas (2000) reported that the participants described a coping strategy to avoid getting too close to their alcoholic parents. The students adopted a physical, cognitive, and affective distancing strategy when interactions with the parent were intrusive and overwhelming. Dundas argued that this may be a necessary coping strategy for these students.

In her research, Skibbee (2001) noted that adolescent boys experience more stress than girls when being raised by an alcoholic parent, either mother or father. The boys in her study had lower self-esteem scores and higher depression scores, and they reported greater family disruption and lower levels of family rituals than the girls did. In their study of 103 Danish children of alcoholic parents, Christensen and Bilenberg (2000) reported that daughters of alcoholics were more impaired than sons of alcoholics, as measured by the Child Behavior Check List (CBCL). They concluded that children of alcoholics (COAs) should be regarded as a risk group but with heterogeneous consequences in response to parental alcoholism.

Wegscheider (1989) described four roles that children in alcoholic families commonly assume to maintain the balance of the family system:

1. family hero
2. scapegoat
3. lost child   *Roles*
4. mascot.

Family Hero. The family hero is usually the oldest child in the family. "Heroes" believe they can push the family toward "normalcy" by being overly responsible (Glover, 1994). Parents may reinforce these behaviors in their children, living their lives vicariously through the hero's achievements. The nonalcoholic parent may turn to their oldest children for emotional support, relying on them to meet their need for intimacy.

"Heroes" feel burdened because of the overwhelming pressure to perform and appear flawless. These children may be lonely and isolated, fearful of allowing anyone to get close and discover the great "cover-up." The hero's world is one of perfectionism, isolation, emotional numbness, constantly being on the alert, and feeling hopeless. They realize that no amount of achievement will correct the fundamental source of the family's dysfunction—alcohol abuse by the parent.

Scapegoat. Scapegoats are targets in the family. They are blamed for the family's stress and dysfunction. The scapegoat draws the attention of the parents away from each other. Rather than the adults focusing their attention on their abuse of alcohol, they direct their time and effort toward managing the misbehavior of children in the scapegoat role (Wegscheider, 1989). Parents do not define their alcohol abuse as the source of the family's dysfunction. Instead, they target the scapegoat as the cause of the stress in the family.

These children and adolescents may live out this self-fulfilling prophecy by engaging in troublesome behaviors such as acting-out in school, running away, or engaging in drug use or promiscuous sexual behavior. They typically feel angry, rejected, and hurt. Counselors may become frustrated as they try to enlist the help of reluctant parents in working with these children, because some parents feel threatened by possible loss of children in the scapegoat role. Without a scapegoat, parents might be compelled to examine their own dysfunctional behavior.

Lost Child. The "lost child" is commonly the middle child. Lost children feel confused because no one is explaining the reasons for the turmoil, violence, and stress in the family (Wegscheider, 1989). They feel lost as to how they fit in the family or what is expected of them as they try to cope. These children and adolescents may be shy, withdrawn, and reluctant to reach out to others for support. This family role actually may be more about *not* having a role in the family.

Mascot. The youngest child often assumes the mascot role. In this role children are shielded from the effects of the parent's alcoholism (Wegscheider, 1989).

These children may not have the opportunity to become aware of the issues the family is struggling to manage. Because mascots tend to be overindulged by their caregivers, they take on the behaviors of the family jokester or clown. Children in the mascot role may attempt to capture and hold the attention of adults and peers. Acting silly to control situations is common in children and adolescents in the mascot role.

Interventions

Children from alcoholic homes feel powerless to influence the fundamental cause of the family's dysfunction—the parents' drinking. Counselors can help their clients understand that, even though they cannot control their parent's drinking, they can manage their own behaviors, feelings, and attitudes in healthy ways.

Group counseling is an effective way for counselors to assist children of alcoholics (Wilson & Blocher, 1990). O'Rourke (1990) recommended a series of 8 to 12 weekly 1-hour sessions. She also recommended limiting the group to 12 members who are no more than 2 or 3 years apart in age. To reduce the stigma surrounding the group, the parents were notified that their children were to participate in a personal growth group. They were sent a list of topics to be covered during the sessions, and they gave permission for the children to participate. O'Rourke (1990) suggested the following six themes with sample activities for group counseling:

- Explore feelings by learning to name, communicate, and manage uncomfortable feelings.
- Build self-esteem by constructing "superman" capes on which group members write affirmations for each other and show family pictures and memorabilia to indicate that everyone is unique and special.
- Develop coping skills by keeping small notebooks with important phone numbers of relatives, hospitals, and Alateen, and rehearse safe ways out of stressful situations.
- Manage stress by using soft music, guided imagery, and relaxation exercises.
- Rehearse decision making by using a balance scale with blocks to add up the pros and cons of a decision.
- Encourage primary relationships through involvement in activities in the school and community to bond with adults or other children.

Arman and McNair (2000) also suggest a 9-week group approach that promotes resiliency and coping strategies such as taking control and choosing ways to respond.

Webb (1993) recommended the following cognitive behavior techniques for working with children of alcoholics:

1. *Modeling.* In the group setting the counselor can arrange for clients to interact with peers who have good interpersonal skills, such as listening to others,

expressing their thoughts, feelings, and wishes, and being able to give appropriate feedback to other group members.

2. *Thought-stopping.* Children of alcoholic parents may be preoccupied with self-defeating thoughts. Counselors can teach these clients how to identify and interrupt their thoughts. This may be done in either individual or group counseling.

3. *Cognitive restructuring.* Counselors can teach children of alcoholics how to replace self-defeating thoughts with more positive thoughts, how to identify distorted thinking, and how to recognize the relationship among thoughts, feelings, and behaviors.

Another approach to working with children of alcoholic parents is for the counselor to determine which role children may be filling in the family and then to identify the resiliencies that role may enhance. For example, children in the hero role may develop the resiliency of initiative, in which they gain a sense of competence by focusing on achievement at school or other interests (Wolin & Wolin, 1993). To strengthen this resiliency, counselors can encourage them to become successful and competent and also help them manage their unhealthy drive for perfection.

Children in the role of scapegoat may have developed the resiliency of insight concerning the families' troubles (Wolin & Wolin, 1993). Counselors can encourage these children to see things for what they are and also help them develop strategies to manage their behavior and emotions that are not self-defeating.

Children in the role of lost child often develop the resiliency of morality, quietly deciding not to act in hurtful ways toward others (Wolin & Wolin, 1993). Counselors can encourage their sense of not wanting to harm others and also help them build bridges to people outside the family who can offer support and guidance.

Mascots develop a sense of humor to cope with threatening emotions and may use humor to diffuse dangerous situations in the home (Wolin & Wolin, 1993). Counselors can encourage the humor and at the same time help these children to identify and appropriately express other feelings. The challenge for counselors is to identify and reinforce resiliencies that may accompany these family roles and also intervene to help the children avoid self-defeating behaviors associated with these same roles.

Even though a majority of children of alcoholics do well, a greater proportion of them exhibit emotional and behavioral problems than children who don't live with alcoholic parents (Ambert, 1997). Counselors can aid these children and adolescents to become more resilient, and behave in ways that are not self-defeating, through individual counseling in which children can experience trust and safety; in group counseling wherein the sense of difference and isolation can be diminished and new skills acquired and practiced; by referring families for counseling with a family therapist; and, in the case of young children, through the use of play therapy, which allows for expression of thoughts and feelings without threatening self-worth. The long-term effects of these interventions can be more than just their survival in a dysfunctional family; they may become resilient adults who are stronger rather than psychologically damaged.

Counseling Grieving Children and Adolescents

Children and adolescents often do not have the opportunity to grieve because many adults do not understand how they react to loss and, therefore, deny them the opportunity to discuss their grief. Many of the social rituals for grieving, such as funerals, were developed to meet adults' needs, and children and adolescents often are not permitted to participate in those activities (Swihart, Silliman, & McNeil, 1992).

An estimated 2% of children are bereaved before the age of 18 (Kmietowicz, 2000). In one study, 63% of college students reported experiencing the death of a peer while in high school (Swihart, Silliman, & McNeil, 1992). The leading cause of deaths for children is accidents, and as they move into the teen years, homicides and suicides also are leading causes of death (Anderson, 2002), suggesting that a peer's death is often unexpected and the circumstances of the death are often violent. Manifestations in adolescents who experience a loss in this manner include irritability, sleep disturbance, anxiety, difficulty concentrating, guilt, and depression (Thompson, 1993).

Other losses common in the lives of children and adolescents include the death of grandparents, parents, siblings, and teachers. Children and adolescents also experience grief through the death of a pet.

Characteristics

Children's ages and levels of cognitive development influence their understanding of death. During the *preoperational stage* of development (ages 2–7) children exhibit magical thinking and egocentricity, are unable to distinguish between thoughts and deeds, and cannot comprehend the irreversibility of death. Therefore, children at this developmental level may believe they caused the death of a loved one because they had a fight with that person. Children may believe that if they wish the person back to life, it will happen, or they may wonder how the deceased can breathe or eat while confined in a coffin (N. B. Webb, 1993). Adults, unaware of these typical developmental characteristics, may be confused, embarrassed, or hurt by the child's reaction to the loss.

During the *concrete operational stage* of development (ages 7–11), children demonstrate reduced egocentricity and greater ability for reasoning. These children understand that death is irreversible but may not believe it could happen to them (N. B. Webb, 1993). Their understanding of time permits them to place the inevitability of their own death in the distant future. These children believe that death happens mainly to the elderly and sick. They might personify death as skeletons and ghosts.

By the age of 9 or 10, or shortly before they reach formal *operational thinking,* which begins around age 11 or 12, children perceive death as irreversible, inevitable, and universal (N. B. Webb, 1993). These children begin to understand concepts of spirituality and life after death. Although age references cannot be taken too literally because they describe only general patterns, the critical point is that children's conception of death progresses over the years from an immature to a mature understanding and will have an impact on the way they grieve the loss.

Grief is a process rather than an emotion (Wolfelt, 1983), and children do grieve. According to N. B. Webb (1993), however, their grief is different from adult grief because of their

— immature cognitive development, which impacts their understanding about the irreversibility, universality, and inevitability of death
— limited capacity to tolerate emotional pain
— limited ability to verbalize their feelings
— sensitivity about behaving different from their peers who are not experiencing a loss.

Counselors have to help family members understand that children's grief is different from adult grief.

N. B. Webb (1993) suggested that, when children have experienced a loss, counselors do an assessment to help these children understand how they are experiencing their grief. The assessment involves three groups of factors:

1. Individual factors
2. Factors related to the death
3. Family, social, and religious/cultural factors.

When assessing *individual factors,* counselors should consider the child's age, developmental level, and temperament. In assessing temperament, the counselor is concerned with how children approach routine and stressful life events. For example, children who have approached new situations with difficulty probably will experience more stress in response to a loss than those who approach new situations more comfortably. Though past coping and adjustment may not predict precisely how children will cope with current stress, well adjusted children are likely to have less difficulty in adjusting to the loss than those who don't deal well with routine daily stresses.

Other individual factors the counselor can assess are the overall psychological, social, and school functioning by ratings on the global assessment of functioning of the *Diagnostic and Statistical Manual*—IV, Axis V; medical history, because children who are ill have diminished resources for grieving; and past experience with death or loss, as cumulative losses impact the grief response. To measure the impact of losses, counselors also can use *The Loss Inventory* (Wolfelt, 1983), which covers loss ranging from death to having to share a room.

The second group consists of *factors related to the death itself.* The first of these is the type of death: anticipated or sudden; preventable; if pain, violence, or trauma accompanied the death; and any stigma surrounding the death. For example, if a child was playing with a friend yesterday, and the friend was killed today in an automobile accident, the child likely will feel more anxiety than if a friend who had a terminal illness died and death had been anticipated.

Another factor associated with the death that should be assessed is contact with the deceased: whether the child was given the opportunity to participate in rituals surrounding the death, including being present at the death, viewing the body, attending ceremonies, or visiting the grave. N. B. Webb (1993) recommended that children be given the choice of attending these rituals after having been told about what these entail. A related factor is the expression of good-bye. Children may benefit from doing something concrete such as writing a poem or placing flowers at the grave.

In addition, the relationship to the deceased is important. The closer the relationship to the person who died, the more of an impact the death is likely to have. Finally, one must consider grief reactions—the feelings the child described or what the family observed about the child, including signs of sadness, anger, confusion, guilt, or relief.

The third area for assessment involves *family, social, religious, and cultural factors.* Family factors include how the family perceives the death and to what extent children are involved in the family's mourning rituals (N. B. Webb, 1993). Some families believe in shielding children from pain, and adults in some families do not express their feelings about the death. In other families adults and children mourn together. In the social area, the counselor can assess the reaction of bereaved children's friends and peers. When children experience a loss, their friends may treat them differently, resulting in stress because of their desire to fit in.

In the religious and cultural area, the counselor may benefit from knowing what the children have been taught either formally or informally. The counselor should attempt to obtain a sense of their religious beliefs about death, life after death, and their thoughts and feelings about those ideas. The counselor may not obtain all of this information. Nevertheless, learning as much as possible will aid the counselor in understanding the ways in which specific children experience grief.

Normal mourning entails pain, sadness, grief, anger, and guilt (Furman, 1974). Bowlby (1980) identified four phases in the grieving process:

1. Numbing (lasting a few hours to a few weeks)
2. Yearning and searching (lasting from months to years)
3. Disorganization and despair
4. Reorganization.

Mourning may become more complicated if children have more than one stressor, such as the divorce of the parents along with the death of a family member. In mourning the loss of an intact family, such as in the case of a divorce, children get confused because they are mourning the loss of a parent who is not dead.

Sometimes the counselor has difficulty distinguishing between normal grief and symptoms of post-traumatic stress disorder (PTSD) (N. B. Webb, 1993). The criteria for a PTSD diagnosis include a distressing experience (such as a death or divorce), reexperiencing the traumatic event (commonly upon the anniversary of the loss), avoiding trauma-related stimuli/numbing (forgetting circumstances that surround the loss), increased arousal (becoming irritable), and symptoms that have persisted for at least 1 month. Counselors will better understand the grief responses of children and adolescents if they can describe the child's grieving process as normal grief, complicated grief, or post-traumatic stress disorder.

Interventions

Worden (1991) offered the following guidelines for counselors to help young clients work through a grief situation and come to resolution:

- Help survivors actualize the loss. Helping them talk about the facts surrounding the loss can facilitate this.
- Help them to identify and express feelings such as anger, guilt, anxiety, and helplessness.
- Assist survivors to live without the deceased. Helping them make decisions and solve problems can facilitate this.
- Facilitate emotional withdrawal from the deceased by encouraging them to form new relationships.
- Allow them time to grieve by explaining that grief takes time and anniversaries of the loss may be particularly painful.
- Interpret normal behavior by reassuring survivors that these new experiences are common for people in similar situations.
- Allow for individual differences by reassuring them that not everyone grieves in the same way and that there may be dramatic differences in the same family.
- Provide continuing support by making yourself available at least for the first year following the loss.
- Examine the child's defenses and coping styles. After trust has developed, help the survivors examine their coping style and evaluate its effectiveness.
- Identify any pathology and make an appropriate referral. Some survivors need special interventions to cope with the loss.

The tasks of children's grief are different from the tasks of adult grief. N. B. Webb (1993) claimed:

> The child may not understand the finality and irreversibility of death until age 9 or 10, so the goal of saying a final good-bye may not be

realistic until the child is older. Similarly, when a child has lost a parent, he/she may need to retain a relationship with that deceased parent, in fantasy, as a source of comfort and ego integrity. . . . The psychological tasks of bereaved children take a considerable span of time for completion, even in the best circumstances extending for many years following the death. So the notion that delayed or prolonged grief constitutes "pathology" is not applicable to children. (pp. 45–46)

Baker, Sedney, and Gross (1992) described the grief process in bereaved children as a series of psychological tasks to accomplish over time. Counselors can use these tasks to structure interventions. The tasks for the early phase of grief for children are concerned with gaining an understanding of what has happened. Many children use self-protective mechanisms to protect against being overwhelmed by emotions relating to the loss. Psychoeducational guidance for the entire family in this phase is appropriate. Counselors can encourage significant adults to explain the circumstances of the loss so children's questions are answered.

Cooper (1999) reported that grieving children tend to recall dreams more frequently than nongrieving children do. She therefore encourages counselors to introduce the topic of dreams in individual and group counseling sessions with grieving children. Cooper points out that counselors frequently discuss nightmares that children have but may overlook asking them about dreams that lack elements of fear. She suggests that these dreams may be a safe starting point for a child to begin examining his or her feelings.

Counselors might give parents resources explaining how to talk about death with children. Good sources include *Talking About Death: A Dialogue Between Parent and Child* (Grollman, 1990), *Life & Loss: A Guide to Help Grieving Children* (Goldman, 1994), *Helping Children Cope with Death* (Schuurman, Hoff, Spencer, and White, 1997), and *Thirty-Five Ways to Help a Grieving Child* (Barrett, Spencer, Schuurman, and Hoff, 1999). Parents should be cautioned about how children might react to this information. For example, to avoid pain, children may not want to talk about the loss, or after hearing about the loss, they may continue with normal tasks such as play while showing no apparent impact. Parents need to know that this is normal.

By providing information and answering questions, including an explanation of their own feelings surrounding the loss, parents can encourage development of the resiliency of insight in their children. Because children also may better understand death by reading, counselors can use bibliotherapy with bereaved children. Good sources include *The Fall of Freddie the Leaf* (Buscaglia, 2002), *Nana Upstairs and Nana Downstairs* (Depaola, 2000), *The Saddest Time* (Simon, 1992), and *After a Suicide: A Workbook for Grieving Kids* (Lindholm, Schuurman, & Hoff, 2001).

Tasks in the middle phase of grief include accepting and reworking the loss and tolerating the psychological pain associated with the loss. Counselors can use a variety of individual counseling techniques with children, including:

— incomplete sentence stems such as, "The memory that I like best of my loved one is when we . . ." "I'm glad my loved one and I got to . . ."
— helping the counselor write a story about grief, drawing a memory of the deceased person, or drawing a picture of what they remember about the funeral
— writing about happy and sad memories of the deceased and keeping these stories and drawings in a book
— writing a letter to the deceased person expressing their feelings
— keeping a journal in which they record thoughts and feelings about the loss.

Bereavement groups are suited to the tasks of the middle phase of grief (Haasl & Marnocha, 1990a, 1990b). Children who experience a loss may feel different from their peers, so being a member of a bereavement group allows them to be with others in a similar situation, which reduces their sense of being different. Groups composed of children at different stages of the grieving process are especially beneficial because middle-phase children tend to be more likely to rework their own loss when they hear how children at later stages have coped.

Morganett (1994) outlined an eight-session, group-counseling intervention for bereaved children. It is designed to help children realize that others have experienced loss, to label and express feelings about the loss, to say good-bye to a deceased person, to understand that funerals are not to be feared, to understand the stages of grief, to understand the causes of death, and to express sympathy to a grieving person.

Tasks of the late phase of grief for children include consolidating of the child's identity and resuming normal developmental tasks. These children can be resources for children in the early phases. Offering support to other children in the earlier phases of grief can help children in the later phases to integrate the loss they suffered and begin getting on with their lives (Yalom, 1985). Counselors can use bibliotherapy, selecting books that describe how the characters resume their lives after a loss. A good resource for counselors is *How to Go on Living When Someone You Love Dies* (Rando, 1991), which lists books, films, and tapes that can be used with bereaved children and adolescents.

In her study of 1,802 adolescents faced with unresolved grief and seeking counseling, Nambi (2000) reported that bereaved adolescent boys manifest more delinquency than bereaved adolescent girls, bereaved adolescent girls manifest more psychological problems in general and more depression in particular than adolescent bereaved boys, and younger bereaved adolescents manifest more psychological problems than their older counterparts. She argued that teachers, counselors, parents, and police need to see the early warning signs and begin preventive interventions to treat grieving adolescents.

Counselors and adults must realize that children and adolescents cannot be protected from loss. To try to shelter or protect children is futile. Instead, an approach that involves calmly presenting the reality of the situation, answering questions honestly, helping them find support so they don't feel different, and acknowledging that their grief will be different from adults' grief will assist them in dealing with loss in ways that build resiliency.

Counseling Gay and Lesbian Youth

Counselors have overlooked the needs of gay and lesbian youth because homosexuality formerly was viewed strictly as an adult issue. Adolescent homosexuality has been explained as merely experimental behavior by youths who later will become heterosexual (Remafedi & Blum, 1986). Ryan and Futterman (1998) asserted that since the 1990s, lesbian, gay, and bisexual youth have moved from invisibility to an awareness of the development of sexual identity in childhood and adolescence.

Gay and lesbian youth experience identity conflict as they try to discover who they are in a predominantly heterosexual society (Marinoble, 1998). They struggle to cope with a variety of issues including isolation, as most adolescents try to keep their orientation hidden; family issues such as parental rejection; health risks such as AIDS, drug and alcohol abuse, and suicide; and educational issues, because many schools do not promote tolerance and acceptance of homosexuality (Cooley, 1998). Gay and lesbian youth most likely will need assistance in coping with these difficult situations.

Characteristics

Gay and lesbian youth are four times more likely than other teens to attempt suicide. Suicide attempts by lesbian and gay youth range from 20% to 42% of the population, in comparison to a rate for heterosexual high school students of 8% to 13% (Ryan and Futterman, 1998). Increased suicide rates for gay and lesbian teens are affected by factors that inhibit the development of a positive gay identity, such as emotional deprivation, physical or sexual abuse, stress, and prejudices. Lesbian and gay youth, for example, often report chronic stress as a result of verbal or physical abuse, or harassment from family members or peers.

Homosexual identity itself does not cause suicide. "They are not high-risk because they are lesbian or gay; it is a result of hatred and prejudice that surround them" (Cook, 1991, p. 1). Because most gay and lesbian youth lack positive adult models and support systems, they can easily conclude that they have little hope of becoming happy or productive adults (Owens, 2001).

Previously, gays and lesbians remained less vocal because their survival depended on separating their social, professional, and emotional lives. Today's generation of gay and lesbian youth have an opportunity to live fully integrated lives.

Ryan and Futterman (2001b) reported that the average age of self-identification has been decreasing. Gay and lesbian adults indicated that their self-identification occurred between the ages of 19–23, lesbian and gay adolescents reported self-identification at age 16. Self-identification at a younger age means greater stress, more negative social pressure, and greater need for support. Because students are struggling with these critical issues at these ages, the school counselor must be prepared to assist them appropriately.

Approximately 20% of acquired immunodeficiency syndrome (AIDS) cases in the United States are young men and women in their 20s (Vare & Norton, 1998). Because people with HIV are typically asymptomatic for 7 to 10 years prior to the AIDS diagnosis, they most likely were infected during their teens. AIDS is the seventh leading cause of death among individuals aged 14 to 23 (Vare & Norton). More than half of the adolescents with AIDS are young gay males and bisexual men.

Gay and lesbian youth encounter academic and social problems in school. They have increased social risk factors including high school dropout, and a sense of social isolation and loneliness contributes to their difficulty at school (Remafedi & Shelby (1998). They often lack peer-group identification because they withdraw from typical adolescent peer-group experiences. Socializing with either gender is difficult because if they date the opposite sex, they could be discovered, and acting toward same-sex friends in any way that demonstrates intimacy also might lead to discovery. The result is isolation and feeling like "I'm the only one" and "I don't fit in anywhere."

In their qualitative study of gay and lesbian teenagers, Omizo, Omizo and Okamoto (1998) identified four categories of concerns:

1. Confusion and not being understood
2. Fear and negative reactions from others
3. Concerns about the future
4. Internalized hostility.

Homophobia and unsupportive social institutions affect the emotional and social development of these youths. Most gay and lesbian adults have been targets of anti-gay verbal abuse or threats. The average high school student hears anti-gay remarks 25 times a day, and teachers who hear these remarks fail to respond to them most of the time (Callahan, 2001). Nearly 17% of reported hate crimes were motivated by a bias toward the victim's sexual orientation (U.S. Department of Justice, 2001). Ryan and Futterman (2001a) reported, "Surveys of bias-related experiences among adult lesbian and gay men show that during their lifetimes, more than half had experienced some kind of violence because of their sexual orientation" (p. 6). A survey of more than 4,000 students reported in the *Youth Risk Behavior Study* (Massachusetts Department of Education, 1995) that gay males and lesbians were five times more likely than their heterosexual peers to skip school out of fear for their safety.

Gay adolescents quickly learn that knowledge of their sexual orientation may have a negative effect on their treatment by family, friends, and social institutions such as schools, churches, and employers. But several recent court cases, as well as changes in the federal Title IX Guidelines prohibiting sex discrimination, have created a clear duty for school districts to protect gay and lesbian students from sexual harassment (McFarland & Dupuis, 2001). School administrators now must ensure that gay and lesbian students are provided a safe educational environment, and ignoring this type of sexual harassment could be very costly.

To remain hidden, these youths engage in various coping behaviors. They sometimes date the opposite sex even though they are not erotically or emotionally attracted to their dates. They may avoid gym class. Some vocally denounce homosexuality as a way to prove to others that they are not gay. Young lesbians even become pregnant in some cases to prove they are heterosexual. Still other youths turn to casual sex with strangers so they can separate or keep their sexuality hidden from other facets of themselves. For gays and lesbians, the result of all these coping behaviors can be a sense of inferiority and worthlessness and a tearing apart of the person rather than integrating their sexual orientation into their identity.

Interventions

Counselors working in the school setting can address the needs of gay and lesbian youth through the components of a developmental guidance program (McFarland, 1993). Educational information about gay and lesbian topics that has been developed for English, history, and social studies classes can be shared with all students (Lipkin, 1992). Curriculum materials such as Project 10 (Urbide, 1991) address issues such as challenging the myths and stereotypes surrounding homosexuality, exploring issues related to families of gay and lesbian youth, and correcting misinformation about homosexuality.

All students can be given the opportunity to learn about homosexuality through contact with positive gay and lesbian adult role models. Reading lists of positive books regarding gay and lesbian lives can be made available. Good resources for individuals who want to learn more include:

Bi Any Other Name: Bisexual People Speak Out (Hutchings & Kaahumanu, 1991)

Challenging Lesbian and Gay Inequalities in Education (Epstein, 1994)

Children of Horizons: How Gay and Lesbian Teens are Leading a New Way Out of the Closet (Herdt & Boxer, 1995)

Dangerous Liaisons: Blacks, Gays, and the Struggle for Equality (Brandt, 1999)

Gay Parents, Straight Schools: Building Communication and Trust (Casper & Schultz, 1999)

One Teacher in Ten: Gay and Lesbian Educators Tell Their Stories (Jennings, 1994)

Piece of My Heart: A Lesbian of Colour Anthology (Silvera, 1991)

School's Out: The Impact of Gay and Lesbian Issues on America's Scho
(Woog, 1995)

Straight Parents, Gay Children: Inspiring Families to Live Honestly and with Greater Understanding (Bernstein, 1999)

Strong Women, Deep Closets: Lesbians and Homophobia in Sport (Griffin, 1998)

Families: A Celebration of Diversity, Commitment, and Love (Jenness, 1990)

Free Your Mind: The Book for Gay, Lesbian, and Bisexual Youth and Their Allies (Bass and Kaufman, 1996)

The Shared Heart: Portraits and Stories Celebrating Lesbian, Gay, and Bisexual Young People (Mastoon, 2001).

Support groups provide an opportunity for developing social skills, discussing the meaning of sexuality, sharing information, and socializing (Muller & Hartman, 1998). Effective support groups for gay and lesbian youth need not focus on in-depth exploration of psychological issues but, rather, on developmental issues such as decision making and elevating their self-esteem. Muller and Hartman (1998) outlined a 15-session group counseling intervention for sexual-minority youth. Group sessions include relationships with parents, stages in the coming-out process, coping with homophobia, clarifying values, adult male and female homosexual speakers, and field trips to gay and lesbian community centers.

Teachers and parents may need information and support as they try to understand the issues of gay and lesbian youth. Parents of gay and lesbian youth may be served through support groups such as Parents and Friends of Lesbians and Gays (PFLAG), where they can discuss their concerns with other parents in similar situations. Inservice programs can be developed to educate the school and agency staff about gay and lesbian youth (National Education Association, 1991). Counselors should be aware of appropriate referral sources within their communities for serving gay and lesbian youth and their families.

Although models of homosexual identity development vary, the general pattern seems to be one of moving from early awareness, through confusion, to an initial embracing of the gay identity, and finally to an affirmation of the gay identity (Troiden, 1989). Gay and lesbian youth may have fewer traumas as they construct their identities if they view their development and its challenges as opportunities for enhancing resiliencies (Wolin & Wolin, 1993). For example, when parents are informed about their child's homosexuality, they commonly experience shock, disappointment, grief, or denial. Because parents may be preoccupied with their own adjustment, gay or lesbian youth might need to develop supportive relationships outside the family.

Contact with other gay and lesbian youths and adults can be critical in establishing a positive identity. And gay and lesbian youth need access to accurate information about homosexuality so they can acquire insight about their thoughts, feelings, and behaviors and work through their confusion resulting from the presumption of heterosexuality. Counselors can facilitate the development of ʜ as insight and relationships in gay and lesbian youth so they may ...uccessful adults who are secure in their sexual orientation and limitless possibilities for their future.

ʜildren and Adolescents With Eating Difficulties

ʜat children and adolescents face regarding eating are staggering ...ting problems can shatter lives and even kill. Children and adolescents get caught in and succumb to destructive cultural messages about body weight. These messages can become an obsession that fills young people with shame, depletes their energy, and inhibits them from normal development and feelings of success.

According to Wright (2000), "The standard for body size and weight is socially determined. It is a cultural phenomenon that demands that the current ideal physique is slim" (p. 197). When children become indoctrinated by messages such as this, they begin to fear food and, in essence, quit eating for fear of becoming fat. Other children "fail to thrive because of the social shame they endure for being large" (Berg, 1997, p. 15).

From messages they see and hear in the media, in society, and from adults, children and adolescents develop the irrational belief that, to be accepted and successful, they must be thin; to be fat is to fail. Consequently, eating disorders have increased rapidly over the last 30 years (Wright, 2000). Scott and Sobczak (2002) differentiate between disordered eating problems that are problematic, such as fear of being fat, bingeing, restrictive dieting, and compulsive exercise from clinical, more serious issues including anorexia, bulimia, and binge eating.

More than half of adults are dieting at any given time. An estimated two thirds or more of high school girls are dieting, and many more are undernourished (Berg, 1997). Results of the National Eating Disorders Screening Project, as reported by Austin, Ziyadeh, Keliher, Zachary, and Forman (2001), found that 30% of high school girls and 16% of high school boys participated in disordered eating behaviors including bingeing, vomiting, fasting, compulsive exercise, and consuming laxatives and diet pills. Children as young as third grade speak of "watching my weight." Counselors who intend to work with children and adolescents must be knowledgeable about the risk factors in this population.

Characteristics

Poor eating habits in children and adolescents set the stage for more severe eating disorders such as anorexia nervosa (self-imposed starvation) and bulimia (cyclic bingeing and purging of food). Adolescents are at high-risk for developing eating disorders that seem to interact with the stress, anxiety, and vulnerability that coincide with puberty and maturation. In addition to age, Wright (2000) identified some risk factors associated with eating disorders, as follows:

▪▪▪ *Gender.* More females than males report anorexia and bulimia, although males also are susceptible, especially to suffering from bulimia. Girls who previously were open to many options for careers and futures suddenly are placing an inordinate amount of energy into how they look rather than developing their identity, as well as developing peer attachments.

■ *Socioeconomic level.* The popular view permeating U.S. society has suggested that anorexia and bulimia tend to affect people from the middle to upper-middle socioeconomic class, and obesity is associated with lower status. This is more of a myth that is perpetuated because families with resources tend to get help and treatment more often (Scott & Sobczak, 2002); "eating disturbances are equally common among all socioeconomic and ethnic groups" (p. 13).

■ *Family characteristics.* Families with eating disorders tend to have other dysfunctional patterns such as alcoholism, emotional disorders, and dysfunctional conflict (Kog & Vandereychen, 1985).

Certain social norms are also associated with eating disorders. Our inability to nurture our youth fuels the problem (Berg, 1997). For example, adolescent girls are taught early that, to be acceptable, they must sacrifice parts of themselves. The message sent to them is that they will be judged by appearance and thinness, not talent, creativity, or ability. Girls use these unrealistic standards to judge their suitability for belonging and acceptance by their peers, including boys. This causes girls to develop a false self, one that is culturally based and the one they present in public (Pipher, 1994). The media saturate girls in how to do this, with emphasis on makeup, clothing, and weight. At the same time, the real issues that girls struggle with, such as careers, sports, hobbies, and maturity, are played down (Pipher, 1994). Boys, too, are caught in this unnurturing web. They are taught to be "macho," take control, and exploit femaleness.

Children and adolescents who have eating difficulties present several different eating patterns to counselors. Berg (1997) organized eating patterns, as well as the effects of negative eating on normal development and relationships, into three categories: normal eating, dysfunctional eating, and eating disorders. Counselors can assess their clients' eating patterns according to these three categories:

Normal Eating.   Children with normal eating patterns (Berg, 1997) tend to eat regularly throughout the day, eat for nourishment as well as social reasons, and report feeling good about eating. Their weight is acceptable within a wide range of normal weight.

Disordered Eating.   Disordered eaters are involved in a more chaotic, irregular eating pattern, skipping meals and overeating at others. They eat for reasons other than nourishment, such as shaping the body, reducing stress or anxiety, boredom, or loneliness. Children and adolescents who exhibit disordered eating behaviors may develop physical symptoms such as feeling tired, lacking energy, or appearing apathetic. Their growth may be retarded or the onset of puberty delayed (Berg, 1997)

Disordered eating is often linked to other serious at-risk behaviors such as use of drugs, alcohol, and tobacco, unprotected sex, dating violence, and even suicide (Scott & Sobczak, 2002). Mentally, these students tend to be less alert and able to concentrate, which can influence school performance negatively. They may lose interest in friends and school and isolate themselves. They may have mood swings and become easily upset or irritable. Dieting impairs a person's ability to think and to learn effectively (U.S. Department of Health and Human Services, Office on Women's Health, 2000). As their dysfunctional eating habits escalate, they may develop an eating disorder (Berg, 1997).

Eating Disorders.   Nearly 10% of high school students have some kind of eating disorder. Adolescents with eating disorders report eating for purposes other than nourishment or enjoyment. They are motivated by external or internal controls such as stress, anger, or pain.

Omizo and Omizo (1992) summarized the physical symptoms of anorexia and bulimia as including extreme weight loss, hair loss, edema (swelling), skin abnormalities, lethargy, and discoloration of teeth. They reported behavioral signs as including frequent trips to the bathroom, avoidance of snack foods, abnormal eating habits, frequent weighing, substance abuse, and social avoidance. These researchers reported common psychological signs as low self-esteem, external locus of control, feelings of helplessness, depression, anxiety, anger, perfectionism, and overconcern with body size.

Clients who have severe eating disorders should be under a physician's or psychiatrist's care because the mental focus of these adolescents is incapacitated by the inability to think rationally and clearly, memory loss, and obsessing. Victims may spend more than 90% of their waking time focusing on food, hunger, and weight issues (Berg, 1997).

In a study conducted by the National Center for Health Statistics (Centers for Disease Control and Prevention, 1997), the prevalence of overweight children has increased by 80% in children and 100% in adolescents. Although some children and adolescents become overweight because of genetic reasons, the most frequent reason cited is that children are less active. Based on the cultural pressure to be thin, overweight youngsters often develop shame and hatred for their bodies. Dieting should be discouraged as a meaningful intervention because most of the time it is unsuccessful and actually does more harm than good to students.

Interventions

Scott and Sobczak (2002) offered a new approach to working with children and adolescents, stating, "To resist dieting and eating disorders, people must embrace their bodies as they are, and pursue lifestyle changes that include healthy eating and exercise" (p. 15). In this "Body Positive's Body Aloud" approach, Scott and Sobczak suggested five principles to prevent eating disorders:

1. Help the young person find his or her own solutions to problems with eating and body image. Counselors need to listen actively, ask appropriate questions, and honor the student's experiences and perceptions.
2. Help young people say no to dieting. Instead, encourage students to eat healthy for life. Allow students to reclaim their own natural physiological cues that tell them when to eat and when to stop.
3. Help children and adolescents to feel shame-free about their bodies and to care for their bodies by promoting health no matter what their size.
4. Help students to decode their "I feel fat" messages. Every time children say this about themselves, they pay an awful price that leads to discouragement and despair. Create a supportive and safe environment for students.
5. Support multidimensional change in the lives of students. This includes the need to talk with teachers, students, parents, and health providers to improve the environment that young people are living in.

In working with children and adolescents with eating difficulties, a wide variety of treatments can be effective (Wright, 2000). Individual counseling, as well as group and family counseling, seems to help. The more severe the eating problem, the more difficult is the treatment. Recovery can be slow and difficult, and relapse is common (Wright, 2000).

To assess of an eating problem, especially an eating disorder, the services of a physician are needed. Collaborating with the medical expert can assist the counselor in understanding medications and proper diets and watching for side effects. If the medical condition of the person is severe, close monitoring or even hospitalization may be necessary.

Counselors need to develop a strong therapeutic relationship with the client and work to establish trust and support. Eclectic approaches (Wright, 2000), behavioral approaches (Thompson & Rudolph, 1996), and family approaches (Kog & Vandereychen, 1985) are helpful in treating eating disorders. To be effective, treatment interventions must be directed to the behavioral, cognitive, emotional, and interpersonal difficulties of children and adolescents. For example, initial assessments might look at the internal messages they are telling themselves about eating, weight, and body size.

Counselors may have to challenge the irrational beliefs inherent in clients' thinking about body image and self-esteem. Determining how they handle stress and emotions also provides insight into possible dysfunctional behaviors. The counselor's goal is to increase clients' awareness so they can express their feelings and develop resiliency, as well as positive coping strategies. Counselors might start a disordered-eating support group to complement individual counseling with these young clients (Omizo & Omizo, 1992). In a group, members often feel less alone with their symptoms and they can receive feedback from peers. Group members can challenge each other's beliefs and values while offering support for each other during their recovery. Group sessions should challenge stereotypical thinking about traditional female and male role behavior, encourage sharing fears about sexuality and adulthood, and teach social competency skills to deal with peer, parent, and societal pressures.

Parenting skills may have to be addressed so parents can help to set realistic expectations for their children and adolescents. Parents can help to debunk the pressure from media, peers, and the culture regarding gender role differences for their sons and daughters so their children do not have to compromise their development of a true self (Pipher, 1994).

Counselors who work with this population have to be informed, skilled, and creative. They have to address the role of prevention and early intervention with eating difficulties. For example, school counselors and teachers should be trained in how to detect early signs of potential eating problems (Omizo & Omizo, 1992; Wright, 2000). Students who are having eating difficulties should be referred to the school counselor and specialists early, when interventions can be most effective. Schools can also become proactive in addressing

> the obsession with thinness and scorn for large people. The pressure, the harassment is all there—between students, between teachers, in the classrooms, and in the halls. (Berg, 1997, p. 225)

School counselors or other trained specialists can develop and conduct educational guidance programs to inform students, break down stereotypes, and build self-esteem.

Rhyne–Winkler and Hubbard (1994) outlined a framework for a school wellness program that includes parent and staff involvement, assessment, classroom guidance, and a small-group counseling component. Jensen–Scott and Delucia–Waack (1993) described developmental guidance programming in junior and senior high schools for eating disorders and weight management.

School personnel also must be cognizant of the particular risk factors for students who are cheerleaders, drill team members, wrestlers, track team members, and gymnasts. These students already live in a society that encourages perfectionism and competitiveness, in which weight and appearance are critical to survival, success, and worth. Educational and prevention programs should include these groups of students and others in building awareness and providing early intervention for those who are struggling with early symptoms (Wright, 2000). The National Association for Anorexia Nervosa and Associated Disorders (ANAD) is a good resource.

Counselors need to keep in mind the influence of media on the developing self-concept and self-esteem of children and adolescents. When working with this population, counselors must be open to the possibility of eating difficulties and confront these issues with young clients. If the issues young clients bring into counseling are severe, counselors must refer them or seek consultation to provide effective interventions.

Responding to School-Age Children and Adolescents Affected by Terrorist Acts

Students of all ages who witness, experience, or hear about acts of terrorism are likely to incur severe psychological effects. Children in the United States who had never witnessed an attack on their country before September 11, 2001, had no frame of reference for that event or how to respond. The early television coverage of the attack on the World Trade Centers included images of airplanes crashing into skyscrapers and people jumping to their deaths from the burning buildings. Before parents or day-care workers realized what was being shown on television, young children had seen these horrific pictures. Counselors working with children need to use their skills to provide opportunities for children and adolescents to openly discuss their concerns and stresses that can develop after a traumatic event such as a terrorist attack.

Characteristics

Although it is difficult to predict a precise reaction to a devastating event such as a terror attack, children and adolescents will have some likely responses. First a traumatic event can impact children's assumptions about how safe and secure their world is. Secure children become frightened children. Denial is another typical initial reaction to trauma. While in denial, they may appear to be unaffected by what is going on around them. Other common reactions include nightmares, sleep disturbances, and changes in eating patterns. Some children regress emotionally or act younger than their chronological age. Parents may notice that their children are more clinging and unhappy or more demanding of parental time and attention. Some families see increased levels of aggression and violence in their children. Children also may complain of headaches, stomachaches, or sweating (National Association of School Psychologists, 2001).

Fear may be the major reaction—fear about the safety of themselves and their families or the threat of further terrorism. Media coverage may magnify their sense of danger. Another emotional response in children is loss of control as they realize that neither they nor adults can control the attackers. Many children and adolescents will react with anger, maybe blaming people in other countries for the attacks. Another emotional response is the loss of trust and sense of security as a result of the unsettling effect of the attack on the child's sense of stability. Children who have relatives or friends where the attack occurs develop a feeling of uncertainty as they worry about the safety of their friends (American School Counselor Association, 2002).

Some children and adolescents will act out traumas through repeated dreams or in the way they play. Other children will react by withdrawing from people or refusing to talk about their irritability, anger, sadness, fear, or guilt. Many children will be reluctant to initiate a conversation about the event, and others will talk sporadically about it, concentrating on certain aspects of the tragedy. They will avoid any activities that remind them of the event.

Children and adolescents may react to acts of terrorism by losing interest in school and showing poor concentration in activities that normally interest them. Because children react to how their caregivers respond to the events, students will be disturbed to the extent they see disturbance in adults. Symptoms will vary, and the more severe symptoms could indicate that a student is experiencing post-traumatic stress disorder or depression (National Association for School Psychologists, 2001).

Interventions

To help their school-age clients cope with reactions to a terrorist act, counselors' main goal is to help children and adolescents describe the impact the event has had on them. Asking questions is more important than giving advice. Counselors can reassure them about how safe they really are and point out that people are available to assist them and be near to them as they work through the impact of this event. As counselors conduct discussions with students, they should give clear messages about the inappropriateness of showing disrespect to any people involved. Counselors can shift the focus to the negative effects of hatred and intolerance.

Other recommendations for counselors who work with children and adolescents are (American School Counselor Association, 2001):

- Provide support, rest, comfort, food, and an opportunity to play or draw.
- Clarify issues they are confused about.
- Provide emotional labels for the children's reactions.
- Tolerate regressive symptoms in a time-limited fashion.
- Permit the children to talk and act it out; address distortions; acknowledge the normalcy of their feelings and reactions.
- Encourage them to express fear, anger, sadness, and other emotions in your supportive presence.
- Offer to help the children let their parents know how they are feeling.
- Encourage them to allow time to work through their responses to the event and to grieve.

Counselors can suggest to parents how they can be helpful to their children as they cope with this event. Some suggestions that could be made to parents are (American School Counselor Association, 2001):

- Tolerate regression.
- Give special indulgences, extra nurturing.
- Help children put their words to what this means to them.

▮ Don't feed their fears—don't give them additional things to worry about.

▮ Limit their exposure to television coverage.

▮ Keep them from becoming engulfed in seriousness all the time. Encourage normal routine activities including play.

Juhnke (2002) described the Adapted Family Debriefing Model for school students, which was developed as an assessment and intervention method specifically for school-age children and adolescents exposed to violence. This process first requires a debriefing with a group of the students' parents (usually fewer than 12), then a joint student–parent debriefing. The primary goals of the parent session are to inform the parents of possible symptoms their children may exhibit, to offer referral sources, and to explain the parental role as validating their children and normalizing the children's concerns.

During the joint student–parent debriefing, two circles are formed. Five or six students sit in the inner circle and the parents sit behind their children. The model prescribes three roles for team members.

1. The *leader* explains the debriefing process, creates a supportive atmosphere, identifies those experiencing excessive levels of emotional discomfort, and directs the other team members via hand signals to intervene with distraught students or parents. The leader discusses with the students and parents normal reactions, as well as more severe symptoms.

2. *Co-leaders* add comments to support the leader. The primary role of the co-leaders is to offer immediate support to students and parents who become emotionally distraught.

3. The *doorkeeper* prevents nonparticipants from entering the session and distraught students or parents from bolting from the session.

The seven steps in the debriefing process are:

1. *Introduction.* The team leader identifies members of the team and establishes rules for the debriefing experience, explains confidentiality and the purposes of the debriefing as: to help student survivors of terrorism to better understand their feelings, increase their coping skills, and gain solace.

2. *Fact-gathering.* The leader may begin by asking what the students saw on television. The emphasis is on the students telling the facts of what each participant saw or encountered. At this stage the team does not ask participants to describe their feelings.

3. *Thought.* This is a transitional step from cognitive to affective responses. The leader asks questions to elicit students' thoughts at the time the terrorist act occurred.

4. *Reaction.* Participants' share their reactions to the terrorist act by discussing the most difficult or surprising part of seeing or hearing about the incident. This is the step where strong emotions are expressed.

5. *Symptom.* The leader facilitates the group's movement from the affective step back to the cognitive domain. The leader may ask about any physical, cognitive, or affective symptoms anyone in the group has experienced since the violent episode. Symptoms might include nausea, trembling hands, inability to concentrate, or feelings of anxiety. The leader might ask for a show of hands of those who have experienced any of these symptoms.

6. *Teaching.* The leader normalizes symptoms described by the participants. Possible future symptoms, such as reccurring dreams of being attacked, are briefly described. The leader will inquire about what the participants have done to help them handle the situation. Young children might report active fantasy such as a cartoon hero protecting them. Older students might report turning to peers for support.

7. *Re-entry.* The leader asks group members to mention any other concerns or thoughts they have, and then the debriefing team makes a few comments about the group's progress or visible group support. The team might distribute a handout for students and one for adults discussing common reactions or symptoms.

Juhnke recommended that after the session, team members should mingle with parents and children, serve refreshments, and pay particular attention to those who appear shaken. Those experiencing severe distress should be encouraged to meet individually with a counselor. Counselors can offer critically important services to children and their families as they attempt to cope with effects of overwhelming violent acts.

The Case of Joshua

Joshua's mother, who had divorced her husband a year ago, brought 15-year-old Joshua to the counselor. She and her former husband had joint custody of Joshua and less than a month previously, her former husband was killed in an automobile accident. The mother was concerned about the effects of these events on Joshua, who refused to speak about his emotions.

Although Joshua did not self-disclose to the counselor during the initial session, he and his mother agreed to have six sessions with the counselor. During the next session Joshua was unresponsive when the counselor asked him about his father's death. The counselor empathized how difficult that must be and then asked Joshua about his parents' divorce.

Joshua said that his parents had been fighting for years prior to the divorce and that he felt awkward admitting that he was relieved when they separated because the fighting stopped. While his parents were working out the separation, he felt forgotten because no one took an interest in him. He said he felt sad and lonely. He was living with his mother and visiting with his father one weekend a month, and was unhappy because he wanted to see more of his father.

The counselor asked Joshua if he had questions about the divorce that he still wanted to ask his mother. Joshua responded that he understood that his parents just couldn't get along and he realized that the divorce might have been best for everyone. He was able to talk with a favorite uncle about his parents and all their problems.

To help Joshua explore his feelings about the divorce, the counselor asked him to describe the feelings about the divorce, how he dealt with those feelings, and what he said to himself that helped him deal with these feelings. The counselor validated Joshua's emotions and explained that adolescents typically feel this way during a divorce. To focus on his strengths, the counselor asked Joshua to write down three things he liked about himself and describe them in detail. The counselor complimented Joshua on his insight about his parents' divorce, his initiative in developing self-statements to cope with this difficult situation, and the supportive relationship with his uncle. The counselor pointed out that not all teenagers could do these things.

In later sessions Joshua indicated that he was worried that if he developed a relationship with someone, it could be as conflictual as his parents' relationship. The counselor asked Joshua to remember a conflict he had with his parents that was resolved to everyone's satisfaction. This helped Joshua realize that he had successfully compromised with his parents over curfew hours. When the counselor asked him how he did that, he said he listened, reminded himself to stay calm, and told himself that it was all right to "give in just a little." The counselor told Joshua that he could use those same skills in working through conflicts with friends. The counselor's use of this solution-focused approach empowered Joshua to further develop his skills at conflict resolution.

During the sixth session the counselor asked Joshua if he wanted to contract for another six sessions. Joshua and his mother agreed to additional counseling sessions. During their next meeting the counselor asked Joshua about his goals for counseling. Joshua responded that he wanted to talk about his father's death. Since his father's death, he had been having trouble sleeping, couldn't concentrate on his schoolwork, and was feeling sad. Joshua had been with his dad only two days before the accident, and he felt shocked when he was told his father had died.

The counselor asked Joshua if he had attended his father's funeral, and Joshua said he had. The counselor asked what his thoughts and feelings were at the funeral. Joshua said he felt sad, cried, hurt inside, and wished he had said some important things to his father while he was alive. The counselor assessed Joshua's mourning as complicated rather than normal because of his parents' recent divorce and the unexpectedness of his father's death.

The counselor suggested as a homework assignment that Joshua write a letter to his father telling him the things he wished he had said. The counselor and Joshua wrote the first few sentences during the counseling session. Joshua brought the completed letter to their next meeting and read the letter to the counselor, who reflected the themes and feelings. Joshua cried as he read the letter. The counselor gave him a book, *How It Feels When a Parent Dies* (Krementz, 1988) and asked him to read several of the interviews with children and adolescents who had lost a parent.

During their next session, the counselor asked Joshua how his thoughts, feelings, and experiences were similar to those of the people in the book. Joshua realized that his reactions to his father's death were similar to those of other people his age. The counselor asked Joshua to complete another homework assignment, which involved writing a final letter to his father to say good-bye and listing ways he could remember his father. When Joshua returned for his sixth session, he read the good-bye letter to the counselor, who reflected its themes and feelings. Joshua said he would remember his father by always carrying his picture in his wallet.

During this session the counselor complimented Joshua on his creativity and his ability to express honest feelings, and then asked Joshua if he wanted more counseling sessions to talk about his father. Joshua responded "no" but indicated that his mother was going to remarry and he was worried. The counselor asked Joshua if he would contract for six more sessions, and he and his mother agreed.

Joshua explained that since his father's death, his mother expected him to be the "man of the house." He felt angry about all the responsibility, but he also liked "having more say around the house." He could decide when to go to bed, how much television to watch, and no one except his mother could tell him what to do. He was worried that when his mother would remarry, his stepfather would try to "run my life." The man his mother planned to marry had a daughter, older than Joshua, and Joshua was concerned that she would "take over the house." The counselor empathized with his story, validated his feelings, and encouraged Joshua to keep a personal journal to record his thoughts, feelings, and questions about the remarriage. The counselor asked Joshua if he would agree to the counselor's informing Joshua's mother about his concerns. Joshua agreed to the counselor's speaking with his mother.

The counselor told the mother that Joshua had concerns about his impending role in the blended family and suggested that she explain to Joshua the roles of everyone in the new family—especially who would be responsible for discipline. The counselor explained to her that, as a typical adolescent, Joshua may be confused and angry as he tries to figure out how "close" or how much "space" he needs from people in the stepfamily. The counselor pointed out that it is normal for adolescents to struggle with strong emotions such as anger, helplessness, jealousy, guilt, and fear as they give up the special role they had prior to the remarriage.

Later in counseling with Joshua, the counselor gave him the book, *Stepliving for Teens: Getting Along with Stepparents and Siblings* (Block & Bartell, 2001). The counselor discussed the book with him, encouraged him to investigate additional activities at school to develop new interests, helped him develop a list of topics to discuss with his mother, and discussed the results of those dialogues between Joshua and his mother. Although still feeling he might be "betraying my real dad," Joshua was becoming less anxious and fearful about the new step-family.

During their final session the counselor asked Joshua if he wanted additional counseling sessions. Joshua indicated that he had one issue he was afraid to talk to his mother about and was terrified that his new stepfather would not react well to the "problem." With his mother's approval, Joshua contracted for six more sessions with the counselor.

Joshua informed his counselor that he had "some funny feelings." When the counselor asked him to talk more about them, he indicated that, unlike most of his friends, he didn't get "turned on" by girls but that when he thought about other boys, he got "all hot and bothered." He said this seemed all wrong, and he tried hard to hide what happens, even cutting gym class so his friends won't notice how excited he gets. The counselor empathized with his confusion and embarrassment, demonstrated a nonjudgmental attitude, and encouraged Joshua to talk more about his confusion. The counselor was careful not to label Joshua.

Joshua himself first used the word "gay." The counselor asked Joshua if he knew what the word means. Joshua said it means men who "do it with other men." The counselor asked him how he felt about that, and Joshua said he wasn't sure. He had read something in a newspaper that gay people wanted to be allowed to get married. The counselor asked how he felt about that idea, and Joshua indicated that if two people really loved each other and could have a more peaceful marriage than his parents did, maybe it was all right. The counselor normalized Joshua's feelings, saying it was common for teenagers to feel attractions to both same-sex and opposite-sex people and that, although most people develop an attraction to the opposite sex, maybe 10% or so develop attractions for people of the same sex. The counselor asked Joshua if he were interested in more information. Joshua indicated that he was.

The counselor provided Joshua with several books including *Understanding Sexual Identity: A Book for Gay and Lesbian Teens and Their Friends* (Rench, 1990) and *Two Teenagers in Twenty* (Heron, 1993). During the next several counseling sessions Joshua discussed his reaction to the books, saying he felt he had much in common with the gay teenagers in the stories. Joshua was beginning to believe that he was gay. He had read in the newspaper that the local university had a gay and lesbian student support group, open to any teenager, and he was planning to "check this out."

The counselor asked Joshua to visualize approaching the building where the group was meeting, then entering the building, finding the room, and introducing himself to the people there. As he imagined this scenario, Joshua felt scared. The counselor explained relaxation techniques using deep breathing and encouraged Joshua to visualize the scenario. When he felt himself getting tense, he could use his deep breathing to relax.

Joshua returned from the meeting excited, saying he was surprised to see so many "normal-looking" people there. None of them looked like what his classmates said gay people were like. Joshua was becoming more certain that he was gay, and he was feeling better about the label. Over the next several sessions, the counselor asked Joshua to explore issues around

— "coming out" to his family, weighing the pluses and minuses
— sexual behavior and his thoughts and feelings about abstinence and safer sex
— dating and what he wanted in a partner
— how he would conduct himself in a relationship

As Joshua acquired more information and continued his contacts with positive role models, the counselor noticed that he became more certain of his identity and more planful and thoughtful about how to safely manage the stigma of a gay identity.

During their final session the counselor asked Joshua to summarize what he considered the most important aspects of their work over the 6 months of counseling. Joshua indicated that he was glad he had an opportunity to say good-bye to his father, blend into the new stepfamily without "too much trouble," and discover "who I really am."

The counselor shook Joshua's hand one last time, wished him well, and invited him to return if he felt the need. The counselor was inspired by this young person's incredible life, as he had encountered major issues beyond his control, faced them, and moved toward becoming a resilient, integrated, competent, and successful adult.

Summary

Many children and adolescents encounter traumatic situations as they grow up. These youths are challenged to adjust to issues over which they can exercise little control. Counselors may not be able to understand all the issues these young clients face: what they face going home to an impulsive, violent, alcoholic parent; what it is like to have the family split apart by divorce; adjusting to a new stepfamily; the challenge of answering the question, "Who am I" while confused and scared about sexual orientation.

By applying appropriate developmental assessment and interventions (Vernon, 1993, 2002), counselors can help these young clients cope with difficult life events in self-enhancing rather than self-defeating ways. The initial challenge for counselors is to empower these clients to survive stressful and often traumatic events and conditions. The greater challenge—and the one that will ultimately prove more beneficial for clients—is for the counselor to identify resilient traits in these youths and use interventions that will enhance their strengths. Clients may not be aware, and may not initially accept the notion, that they have developed remarkable assets in response to overwhelmingly stressful situations. Therefore, counselors have to be patient and persistent in assuring these young clients that, in addition to their pain, they are acquiring and enhancing aspects of themselves that can assist them to become successful adults.

Counselors may develop a refreshing new attitude toward their work with these children and adolescents as they shift their emphasis from centering strictly on the problem and what is wrong to identifying resiliencies and the positive aspects these clients are pulling from these experiences. Counselors will be empowering their young clients, and counselors themselves may feel empowered, as they observe with wonder the strengthening of these young people that results from their personal trials and challenges.

References

Ackerman, R. J. (1983). *Children of alcoholics: A guidebook for educators, therapists, and parents.* Holmes Beach, FL: Learning Publications.

Ambert, A. (1997). *Parents, children, and adolescents.* New York: Haworth Press.

American School Counselor Association (2001). Crisis management: Supporting students, staff, and parents. Retrieved June 10, 2002, from http://www.schoolcounselor.org/contnet.cfm?L1=1000L2=50

American School Counselor Association (2002). Response to terrorism. Retrieved June 10, 2002, from http://www.school counselor.org/content.cfm?L1=1000L2=48

Anderson, R. N. (2002). *Deaths: Leading causes for 2000.* National vital statistics reports *50*(16). Hyattsville, MD: National Center for Health Statistics.

Arman, J. F. (2002). A brief group counseling model to increase resiliency of students with mild disabilities. *Journal of Humanistic Counseling, Education, and Development, 41,* 120–128.

Arman, J. F., & McNair, R. (2000). A small-group model for working with elementary school children of alcoholics. *Professional School Counseling, 3*(4), 290–293.

Austin, B., Ziyadeh, N., Keliher, A., Zachary, A. & Forman, S. (2001). Screening high school students for eating disorders: Results of a national initiative. *Journal of Adolescent Health, 28*(2), 96.

Baker, J. E., Sedney, M. A., & Gross, E. (1992). Psychological tasks for bereaved children. *American Journal of Orthopsychiatry, 62*(1), 105–116.

Barrett, M.R., Spencer, D.W., Schuurman, D. L., & Hoff, J.S. (1999). *Thirty-five ways to help a grieving child.* Portland, OR: Dougy Center for Grieving Children.

Bass, E., & Kaufman, K. (1996). *Free your mind: The book for gay, lesbian, and bisexual youth and their allies.* New York: HarperCollins.

Becvar, D. S., & Becvar, R. J. (1993). *Family therapy: A systemic integration* (2d ed.). Boston: Allyn & Bacon.

Benson, P L., Sharma, A. R., & Roehikepartain, E. C. (1994). *Growing up adopted: A portrait of adolescents and their families.* Minneapolis: Search Institute.

Berg, E. M., (1997). *Afraid to eat.* Hettinger, ND: Healthy Weight Publishing Network.

Bernstein, R. (1999). *Straight parents, gay children: Inspiring families to live honestly and with greater understanding.* New York: Thunder Mouth Press.

Black, C. (1991). *It will never happen to me.* New York: Ballentine Books.

Block, J. D., & Bartell, S. S. (2001). *Stepliving for teens: Getting along with stepparents and siblings.* East Rutherford, NJ: Penguin Putnam Books.

Bowlby, J. (1980). *Attachment and loss: Vol. 3. Loss.* New York: Basic Books.

Boyd, C. (1995). *Chevrolet Saturdays.* New York: Macmillan.

Brandt, E. (Ed.) (1999). *Dangerous liaisons: Blacks, gays, and the struggle for equality.* New York: New Press.

Brodzinsky, D. M., Schechter, M. D., & Henig, R. M. (1992). *Being adopted: The lifelong search for self.* New York: Doubleday.

Brodzinsky, D. M., & Schechter, M. D. (1992). *Being adopted: The lifelong search for self.* New York: Doubleday.

Buscaglia, L. (2002). *The fall of Freddie the leaf* (anniversary ed.). New York: Henry Holt & Company.

Callahan, C. (2001). Protecting and counseling gay and lesbian students. *Journal of Humanistic Counseling, Education and Development, 40*(1), 5–10.

Capuzzi, D., & Gross, D. R. (2000). *Youth at risk: A prevention resource for counselors, teachers, and parents* (3d ed.). Alexandria, VA: American Counseling Association.

Casper V., & Schultz, S. (1999). *Gay parents, straight schools: Building communication and trust.* New York: Teachers College Press.

Centers for Disease Control and Prevention. (1997). Update: Prevalence of overweight among children, adolescents, and adults—United States, 1988–1994. *Morbidity and Mortality Weekly Report, 46,* 198–202.

Christiansen, C. B. (1990). My *mother's house, my father's house.* New York: Atheneum.

Christensen, H. B., & Bilenberg, N. (2000). Behavioral and emotional problems in children of alcoholic mothers and fathers. *European Child & Adolescent Psychiatry, 9*(3), 219–226.

Cobia, D. C., & Brazelton, E. W (1994). The applications of family drawing tests with children in remarriage families: Understanding familial roles. *Elementary School Guidance and Counseling, 29,* 129–136.

Coleman, W. L. (1993). *Step trouble: A survival guide for teenagers with stepparents.* Center City, MD: Hazelden Information & Educational Services.

Coleman, M., Ganong, L., & Fine, M. (2000). Reinvestigating remarriage: Another decade of progress. *Journal of Marriage and the Family, 62*(4), 1288–1307.

Cook, A. I. (1991). *Who is killing whom?* (Monograph, Respect All Youth Project, Issue Paper 1). Washington, DC: Federation of Parents and Friends of Lesbians and Gays.

Cooley, J. J. (1998). Gay and lesbian adolescents: Presenting problems and the counselor's role. *Professional School Counseling, 1,* 30–34.

Cooper, C. A. (1999). Children's dreams during the grief process. *Professional School Counseling, 3*(2), 137–140.

Costa, L., & Stiltner, B. (1994). Why do the good things always end and the bad things go on forever? A family change counseling group. *The School Counselor, 41,* 300–304.

Crosbie–Burnett, M., & Pulvino, C. J. (1990). Children in nontraditional families: A classroom guidance program. *The School Counselor, 37,* 286–293.

Dacey, J., & Kenny, M. (1997). *Adolescent development.* Boston: McGraw–Hill.

DeLucia–Waack, J. L., & Gerrity, D. (2001). Effective group work for elementary school-age children whose parents are divorcing. *The Family Journal: Counseling and Therapy for Couples and Families, 9*(3), 273–284.

Depaola, T. (2000). *Nana upstairs and Nana downstairs* (reissue ed.). New York: Puffin.

Dickman, G. E. (1992). Adoptees among students with disabilities. *Journal of Learning Disabilities, 25,* 529–531, 543.

Dundas, I. (2000). Cognitive/affective distancing as a coping strategy of children of parents with a drinking problem. *Alcoholism Treatment Quarterly, 18*(4), 85–98.

Eichberg, R. (1991). *Coming out: An act of love.* New York: Plume.

Epstein D. (Ed.) (1994). *Challenging lesbian and gay inequalities in education.* New York: Taylor & Francis.

Erikson, E. (1968). *Identity: Youth and crisis.* New York: Norton.

Fairchild, B., & Hayward, N. (1981). *Now that you know.* New York: Harcourt, Brace, Jovanovich.

Fenell, D. L., & Weinhold, B. K. (1997). *Counseling families* (2d ed.). Denver: Love Publishing.

Fields, J. (2001). *Living arrangements of children: Fall 1996.* Current Population Reports (pp. 70–74). Washington DC: U. S. Census Bureau.

Fincham, F. D. (1994). Understanding the association between marital conflict and child adjustment: Overview. *Journal of Family Psychology, 8,* 123–127.

Frymier, J. (1992). *Growing up is risky business, and schools are not to blame.* Bloomington, IN: Phi Delta Kappa.

Fuller, M. (1988). Facts and fictions about stepfamilies. *Education Digest, 54*(2), 52–54.

Furman, E. (1974). *A child's parent dies.* New Haven, CT: Yale University Press.

Getzoff, A., & McClenahan, C. (1984). *Step kids: A survival guide for teenagers in stepfamilies.* New York: Walker and Co.

Glover, J. G. (1994). The hero child in the alcoholic home: Recommendations for counselors. *The School Counselor, 41,* 185–190.

Goldenberg, L., & Goldenberg, H. (1996). *Family therapy: An overview* (4th ed.). Pacific Grove, CA: Brooks/Cole.

Goldman, L. (1994). *Life & loss: A guide to help grieving children.* Muncie, IN: Accelerated Development.

Gordon, S., & Cohen, V. (2000). *All families are different.* Amherst, NY: Prometheus Books.

Grant, D. F. (2000). Estimates of U. S. children exposed to alcohol abuse and dependence in the family. *American Journal of Public Health, 90*(1), 112–115.

Griffin P. (1998). *Strong women, deep closets: Lesbians and homophobia in sport.* Champaign, IL: Human Kinetics Publishers.

Grollman, E. A. (1990). *Talking about death: A dialogue between parent and child.* Boston: Beacon Press.

Haasl, B., & Marnocha, J. (1990a). *Bereavement support group program for children: Leader manual.* Muncie, IN: Accelerated Development.

Haasl, B., & Marnocha, J. (I 990b). *Bereavement support group program for children: Participant workbook.* Muncie, IN: Accelerated Development.

Hauser, S. T. (1999). Understanding resilient outcomes: Adolescent lives across time and generations. *Journal of Research on Adolescence, 9*(1), 1–24.

Hauser, S. T., Vieyra, M. A., Jacobson, A. M., & Wertreib, D. (1985). Vulnerability and resilience in adolescence: Views from the family. *Journal of Early Adolescence, 5*(l), 81–100.

Heegaard, M. (1993). *When a parent marries again: Children can learn to cope with family change.* Chapmanville, WV: Woodland Press.

Helms, J. E. (1990). *Black and white racial identity: Theory, research, and practice.* New York: Greenwood Press.

Herdt, G., & Boxer, A. (1995). *Children of Horizons: How gay and lesbian teens are leading a new way out of the closet.* Boston: Beacon Press.

Heron, A. (Ed.). (1993). Two *teenagers in twenty.* Boston: Alyson Publications.

Hetherington, E. M. (1991). Families, lies, and videotapes. *Journal of Research on Adolescence, 1,* 323–348.

Hollister–Wagner, G. H., Foshee, V. A., & Jackson, C. (2001). Adolescent aggression: Models of resiliency. *Journal of Applied Social Psychology, 31*(3), 445–466.

Hutchings, L., & Kaahumanu, L. (eds.) (1991). *Bi any other name: Bisexual people speak out.* Boston: Alyson Publications.

Janus, N. G. (1997). Adoption counseling as a professional specialty area for counselors. *Journal of Counseling and Development, 75,* 266–274.

Jarratt, C. J. (1994). *Helping children cope with separation and loss* (rev.). Boston: Harvard Common Press.

Jenness, A. (1990). *Families: A celebration of diversity, commitment, and love.* New York: Houghton Mifflin.

Jennings, K. (1994). *One teacher in ten: Gay and lesbian educators tell their stories.* Boston: Alyson Publications.

Jensen–Scott, R. L., & Delucia–Waack, J. L. (1993). Developmental guidance programming in junior and senior high schools: Eating disorders and weight management units. *The School Counselor, 41,* 109–119.

Jew, C. L., & Green, K. E. (1998). Effects of risk factors on adolescents' resiliency and coping. *Psychological Reports, 82,* 675–678.

Jukes, M. (1987). *Like Jake and me.* New York: Knopf.

Juhnke, G. (2002). Intervening with school students after terrorist acts. ERIC/CASS Resources for Helping Youth and Adults with Traumatic Events. Retrieved June 10, 2002, from http://ericcass.uncg.edu/juhnke

Keats, E. (2001). *Louie's search.* New York: Scholastic.

Kelly, P. (1995). *Developing healthy stepfamilies: Twenty families tell their stories.* New York: Harrington Park Press.

Kelly, R (1996). Family-centered practice with stepfamilies. *Families in Society, 77*(9), 535–544.

Kirby, K. M. (1997). A school counselor's guide to working with children adopted after infancy: Jason's story. *Elementary School Guidance and Counseling, 31*(3), 226–238.

Kizner, L. R., & Kizner, S. R. (1999). Small-group counseling with adopted children. *Professional School Counseling, 2*(3), 226–229.

Kmietowicz, S. (2000). More services needed for bereaved children. *British Medical Journal, 7239,* 893.

Kog, E., & Vandereychen, W (1985). Family characteristics of anorexia nervosa and bulimia: A review of the research literature. *Clinical Psychology Review, 5,* 159–180.

Krementz, J. (1988). *How it feels when a parent dies.* New York: Knopf.

Krueger, M. J., & Hanna, E J. (1997). Why adoptees search: An existential treatment perspective. *Journal of Counseling and Development, 75,* 195–202.

Lambie, R., & Daniels–Mohring, D. (1993). *Family systems within educational contexts.* Denver: Love Publishing.

Leibowitz, J. (2000). *Finding your place: A teen guide to life in a blended family.* New York: Rosen Publishing Group.

Lindholm, A. B., Schuurman, D. L., & Hoff, J. S. (2001). *After a suicide: A workbook for grieving kids.* Portland, OR: Dougy Center for Grieving Children.

Lipkin, A. (1992). *Strategies for the teacher using gay/lesbian-related materials in the high school classroom* (Gay/Lesbian Secondary Schools Curriculum Project). Cambridge, MA: Harvard Graduate School of Education.

Lutz, P. (1983). The stepfamily: An adolescent perspective. *Family Relations, 32,* 367–375.

Marinoble, R. M. (1998). Homosexuality: A blind spot in the school mirror. *Professional School Counseling, 1,* 4–7.

Massachusetts Department of Education. (1995). *Youth risk behavior study.* Boston: Author.

Mastoon, A. (2001). *The shared heart: Portraits and stories celebrating lesbian, gay, and bisexual young people.* New York: HarperCollins Children's Books.

McFarland, W. P. (1993). A developmental approach to gay and lesbian youth. *Journal of Humanistic Education and Development, 32,* 17–29.

McFarland, W.P. & Dupuis, M. (2001). The legal duty to protect gay and lesbian students from violence in school. *Professional School Counseling, 4*(3), 171–179.

Miller, D.B. (1999). Racial socialization and racial identity: Can they promote resiliency for African–American adolescents? *Adolescence, 34*(135), 493–502.

Morganett, R. S. (1990). *Skills for living: Group counseling activities for young adolescents.* Champaign, IL: Research Press.

Morganett, R. S. (1994). *Skills for living: Group counseling activities for elementary students.* Champaign, IL: Research Press.

Moser, A. & Melton, D. (2000). *Don't fall apart on Saturdays!: The children's divorce–survival book.* Kansas City, MO: Landmark Editions.

Muller, L. E., & Hartman, J. (1998). Group counseling for sexual minority youth. *Professional School Counseling, 1,* 38–41.

Murphy, J. (1997). *Solution-focused counseling in middle and high schools.* Alexander, VA; American Counseling Assocation.

Myer, R., James, R. K., & Street, T. (1987). Counseling internationally adopted children: A classroom meeting approach. *Elementary School Guidance and Counseling, 22,* 88–94.

Nambi, J. (2000). Resiliency and vulnerability among bereaved adolescents: A study of the susceptibility of bereaved adolescents to delinquency, social, psychological, and school problems. *Dissertation Abstracts International, 60*(8–B), 4240. (University Microfilms No. 0419–4217)

National Association of School Psychologists. (2002). Children's reaction to trauma: Suggestions for parents. Retrieved June 10, 2002, from http://www.naspcenter.org/safe_schools/trauma

National Center for Health Statistics. (1997, November). *NHANES 111.* Washington, DC: U. S. Department of Health and Human Services/U. S. Department of Agriculture, Life Sciences Research Office, Interagency Board for Nutrition Monitoring and Related Research.

National Education Association. (1991). *Affording equal opportunity to gay and lesbian students through teaching and counseling. A training handbook for educators.* Washington, DC: NEA.

Ng, N. S., & Wood, L. (1993). *Understanding adoption: A guide for educators.* Palo Alto, CA: FAIR.

Omizo, M. M., Omizo, S. A., & Okamoto, C. M. (1998). Gay and lesbian adolescents: A phenomenological study. *Professional School Counseling, 1,* 35–37.

Omizo, S. A., & Omizo, M. M. (1992). Eating disorders: The school counselor's role. *The School Counselor, 39,* 217–224.

O'Rourke, K. (1990). Recapturing hope: Elementary school support groups for children of alcoholics. *Elementary School Guidance and Counseling, 25,* 7–115.

Owens, R. E. (2001). Counseling with lesbian, gay, and bisexual youth. *The Prevention Researcher, 8*(1), 9–13.

Palmo, A. J., & Palmo, L. (1996). The harmful effects of dysfunctional family dynamics. In D. Capuzzi & D. Gross (Eds.), *Youth at risk* (2d ed., pp. 37–58). Alexandria, VA: American Counseling Association.

Pardeck, J. T., & Pardeck, J. A. (1993). *Bibliotherapy: A clinical approach for helping children.* Yverdon, Switzerland: Gordon and Breech.

Patricia, S. (1998). *Isolated and invisible: Gay, lesbian, bisexual and transgendered youth.* (Report for the South Fraser Regional Health Board, March 1988). British Columbia, Canada: *3,* 28.

Pedro–Carroll, J. L., Sutton, S. E., & Wyman, P. A. (1999). A two-year follow-up evaluation of a preventative intervention for young children of divorce. *School Psychology Review, 28*(3), 467–476.

Pipher, M. (1994). *Reviving Ophelia.* New York: Ballantine Books, Random House.

Post, P., & Robinson, B. E. (1998). School-age children of alcoholics and non-alcoholics: Their anxiety, self-esteem, and locus of control. *Professional School Counseling, 1*(5), 36–40.

Rak, C., & Patterson, L. E. (1996). Resiliency in children. *Journal of Counseling and Development, 74,* 368–373.

Rando, T. A. (1991). *How to go on living when someone you love dies.* New York: Bantam.

Remafedi, G. C. & Shelby, P. (1998). Isolated and invisible: Gay, Lesbian, Bisexual and transgendered Youth. Report for South Fraser Regional health board, March 1998. (Report No. 6028728) Canada: British Columbia 1998-03-00.

Remafedi, G. J. (1999). Suicide and sexual orientation: nearing the end of controversy? *Archives of General Psychiatry, 56*(10), p. 885–886.

Remafedi, G. J., & Blum, R. (1986). Working with gay and lesbian adolescents. *Pediatric Annals, 15,* 773–783.

Rench, J. E. (1990). *Understanding sexual identity: A book for gay and lesbian teens and their friends.* Minneapolis: Lerner Publications.

Rhyne–Winkler, M. C., & Hubbard, G. T. (1994). Eating attitudes and behavior: A school counseling program. *The School Counselor, 41,* 195–198.

Richardson, C. D., & Rosen, L. A. (1999). School-based interventions for children of divorce. *Professional School Counseling, 3*(1), 21–26.

Robson, B. E. (1993). Changing family patterns: Developmental impacts on children. In J. Carlson & J. Lewis (Eds.), *Counseling the adolescent* (pp. 149–166). Denver: Love Publishing.

Ryan, C., & Futterman, D. (1998). *Lesbian and gay youth: Care and counseling.* New York: Columbia University Press.

Ryan, C., & Futterman, D. (2001a). Experiences, vulnerabilities, and risks of lesbian and gay students. *The Preventative Researcher, 8*(1), 6–8.

Ryan, C., & Futterman, D. (2001b). Lesbian and gay adolescents: Identity development. *The Preventative Researcher, 8*(1), 1–5.

Schuurman, D. L., Hoff, J. S., Spencer, D.W. & White, C. (1997). *Helping children cope with death.* Portland, OR: Dougy Center for Grieving Children.

Scott, E. & Sobczak, C. (2002). *Body aloud! Helping children and teens find their own solutions to eating and body image problems.* Berkeley, CA: The Body Positive.

Seibert, T. M., & Willetts, M. C. (2000). Changing family forms. *Social Education, 64*(1), 42–47.

Selin, J. (1995). *Sex, death, and the education of children: Our passion for ignorance in the age of AIDS.* New York: Teachers College Press.

Silvera, M. (Ed.). (1991). *Piece of my heart: A lesbian of colour anthology.* Toronto: Sister Vision Press.

Simon, N. (1987). *All kinds of families.* Niles, IL: Whitman.

Simon, N. (1992). *The saddest time* (Reprint). Niles, IL: Whitman.

Skibbee, D.B. (2001). The relationship between parental mental health, family rituals, family environment, and the resiliency of adolescents of alcoholic parents. *Dissertation Abstracts International, 62*(1–B), 565. (University Microfilms No. 0419–4217)

Smith, R. K. (1990). *The squeaky wheel.* New York: Delacorte Press.

Sorosky, A. D., Baran, A., & Pannor, R. (1989). *The adoption triangle.* San Antonio, TX: Corona.

Spencer, A. J., & Shapiro, R. B. (1993). *Helping students cope with divorce.* West Nyack, NY: Center for Applied Research in Education.

Swihart, J., Silliman, B., & McNeil, J. (1992). Death of a student: Implications for secondary school counselors. *The School Counselor, 40,* 55–60.

Thompson, C. L., & Rudolph, L. B. (1996). *Counseling children.* Pacific Grove, CA: Brooks/Cole.

Thompson, R. A. (1993). Posttraumatic stress and posttraumatic loss debriefing: Brief strategic intervention for survivors of sudden loss. *The School Counselor, 41,* 16–21.

Troiden, R. R. (1989). The formation of homosexual identities. *Journal of Homosexuality, 17,* 43–73.

Urbide, V. (1991). *Project 10 handbook: Addressing lesbian and gay issues in our schools.* Los Angeles: Friends of Project 10.

U. S. Bureau of the Census. (2000). *Statistical abstract for the United States.* Washington, DC: U. S. Department of Commerce.

U.S. Department of Health and Human Services, Office of Women's Health. (2000). *BodyWise Handbook.* Washington, DC.

U.S. Department of Justice, Federal Bureau of Investigation. (2001). *Hate crime statistics: 1999.* (FBI Uniform Crime Reports), Washington, DC: Government Printing Office.

Vare, J. W., & Norton, T. L. (1998). Understanding gay and lesbian youth: Sticks, stones, and silence. *Clearing House, 71*(6), 327–331.

Vernon, A. (1993). *Developmental assessment & intervention with children & adolescents.* Alexandria, VA: American Counseling Association.

Vernon, A. (2002). *What works when with children and adolescents: A handbook of individual counseling techniques.* Champaign, IL: Research Press.

Vigna, J. (1982). *Daddy's new baby.* Niles, IL: Whitman.

Visher, E. B., & Visher, J. S. (1991). *How to win as a stepfamily* (2d ed.). New York: Taylor and Francis.

Visher, E. B., & Visher, J. S. (1996). *Therapies with stepfamilies.* New York: Brunner/Mazel.

Wallerstein, J. S. (1987). Children of divorce: Report of a ten-year follow-up of early latencyage children. *American Journal of Orthopsychiatry, 57*(2), 199–211.

Wallerstein, J. S., & Blakeslee, S. (1996). *Second chances.* New York: Ticknor & Fields.

Wallerstein, J. S., & Kelly, J. (1996). *Surviving the breakup: How children and parents cope with divorce.* New York: Basic Books.

Walsh, W. M. (1992). Twenty major issues in remarriage families. *Journal of Counseling and Development, 70*(6), 709–715.

Walter, J. L., & Peller, J. E. (1992). *Becoming solution-focused in brief therapy.* New York: Brunner/Mazel.

Webb, N. B. (1993). *Helping bereaved children: A handbook for practitioners.* New York: Guilford.

Webb, W. (1993). Cognitive behavior therapy with children of alcoholics. *The School Counselor, 40,* 170–177.

Wegscheider, S. (1989). *Another chance: Hope and health for the alcoholic family* (2d ed.). Palo Alto, CA: Science and Behavior Books.

Werner, E. E. (1984). Resilient children. *Young Children, 40,* 68–72.

Werner, E. E., & Smith, R. S. (1992). *Overcoming the odds: High risk children from birth to adulthood.* Ithaca. New York: Cornell University Press.

Wilson, J., & Blocher, L. (1990). The counselor's role in assisting children of alcoholics. *Elementary School Guidance and Counseling, 25,* 98–106.

Wolfelt, A. (1983). *Helping children cope with grief.* Muncie, IN: Accelerated Development.

Wolin, S., & Wolin, S. (1993). *The resilient self: How survivors of troubled families rise above adversity.* New York: Villard.

Woog, D. (1995). *School's out: The impact of gay and lesbian issues on America's schools.* Boston: Alyson Publications.

Worden, J. W. (1991). *Grief counseling and grief therapy: A handbook for the mental health practitioner.* New York: Springer.

Wright, K. S. (2000). The secret and all-consuming obsessions: Anorexia and bulimia. In D. Capuzzi & D. Gross (Eds.), *Youth at risk* (pp. 8–153). Alexandria, VA: American Counseling Association.

Yalom, I. (1995). *The theory and practice of group psychotherapy* (4th ed.). New York: Basic Books.

Zirkle, D. S., Peterson, T. L., & Collins-Marotte, J. (2001). The school counselor's role in academic and social adjustment of late-adopted children. *Professional School Counseling, 4*(5), 366–369.

Counseling At-Risk Children
and Adolescents

*Ellen Hawley McWhirter,
Rachel E. Shepard, and Marcy C. Hunt-Morse*

W e live in a complex, ever-changing society. In recent years numerous social, demographic, and economic factors have weakened the ability of families to provide healthy and developmentally appropriate environments for their children. Poverty and economic instability have led to some families' living in substandard housing with inadequate nutrition in neighborhoods plagued with crime and violence. Social changes and new technologies have dramatically affected the marketplace, changing family circumstances and creating new sets of influences and experiences for children and adolescents. Marital transitions and changes in family composition (such as increases in the numbers of single-parent, step-, blended, and foster families), the presence and temptation of drugs, the increasing number of media figures who model sexual permissiveness, irrational risk-taking, and the use of violence to cope with frustration and anger have contributed to a societal context that provides fewer supports and resources than in the past and is significantly more challenging for young people to negotiate (McWhirter, McWhirter, McWhirter, & McWhirter, 2004).

As adults, we must find a way to respond to these risks and better support our youth. Statistics indicate that the challenges faced by youth today are greater than those of previous generations. For example, as documented in McWhirter et al. (2004), more adolescents are experimenting with drugs at a younger age, with many having their first experiences with drugs prior to age 15. Although overall crime victimization rates have decreased since 1993, U. S. adolescents are twice as likely as adults to be victims of serious violent crimes, including aggravated assault, rape, robbery, and homicide (Forum on Child and Family Statistics, 2002). In 1999, youth ages 12–18 were victims of about 2.5 million crimes at school, including 186,000 serious violent crimes (National Center for Education Statistics, 2001).

Among industrialized countries the United States is last in protecting our children against gun violence: U.S. children under age 15 are 12 times more likely to die from gunfire than children in 25 other industrialized countries combined (Children's Defense Fund, 2001). Children today have fewer adults helping them develop skills such as responsibility and self-discipline, and much of the adult contact for adolescents is via television, with adults displaying aggression, self-centeredness, superficiality, and poor communication skills on a routine basis. Indeed, today's children and adolescents are plagued by a multitude of risks that can have a deleterious effect on healthy development. These risk factors are discussed in this chapter.

Poverty as a Major Risk Factor

More and more children and adolescents are experiencing the effects of poverty along with the related and cumulative risks of poor physical health, low educational attainment, and psychological disorders. McLoyd (personal communication, April 6, 1998) identified four factors contributing to the deteriorating economic well-being of children in the United States.

1. Sluggish economic growth, which has stagnated and eroded income, especially among young families. Back-to-back recessions in the 1980s and 1990s, along with industry responses to foreign competition, have contributed to high rates of unemployment and job loss.
2. The significant loss of low-skill, high-wage jobs resulting from the decline in number of manufacturing industries and movement of manufacturing employment sites from urban to suburban areas and to Third World nations.
3. A cut in government benefits for children. For example, eligibility requirements for Aid to Families With Dependent Children (AFDC) have become more restrictive, decreasing the number of eligible children; welfare benefit

rates have not kept pace with inflation (between 1971 and 1983, for example, the real value of food stamps and AFDC decreased by 22%).

4. The real value of personal exemption on federal income taxes declined during the 1970s and 1980s while payroll taxes affecting lower income wage earners increased significantly.

Finally, McLoyd pointed to the increase in the number of children living with single mothers, especially never-married and teenage mothers. Single mothers have to rely on their own earnings to survive and, as a result, face a great risk of poverty. Of children living in female-headed homes, 40% are poor, compared to 8% of children living in two-parent homes (Forum on Child and Family Statistics, 2002). The economic plight of single-mother families continues to worsen as health factors, low skills, and the cost of child care decrease the ability of single mothers to find work. The proportion of poor children in working families is at a record high, with 77% of poor children living in families in which a family member worked at least part of the year, and more than a third of poor children lived in a family in which someone is employed full-time year-round (Children's Defense Fund, 2001).

Poverty experienced at younger ages has greater negative effects than poverty experienced later in life (McLoyd, 1998), and children under the age of 6 are at greater risk of being poor than older children, largely because their parents are younger and earn lower wages (Bronfenbrenner, McClelland, Wethington, Moen, & Ceci, 1996). Although the majority of poor children in the United States are of European ancestry, 30.6% of Black children, 28% of Hispanic children, and 14.4% of Asian and Pacific Island children live in poverty, compared to 12.9% of White children (Children's Defense Fund, 2001).

The effects of poverty are multifaceted and often devastating. Poor families living in high-poverty communities are disadvantaged by less accessibility to jobs, high-quality public and private services (e.g., child care, parks, and community centers), and informal social supports (McLoyd, 1998). Children's health, education, later employment, and future earnings are strongly influenced by the socioeconomic status (SES) of their families. In comparison to middle-SES children, lower-SES children are more likely to have experienced neonatal damage, be underweight and malnourished, have vision and hearing problems, be neglected and uncared for, and experience untreated illnesses (Haveman & Wolfe, 1994). Lower-SES children may experience chaotic living environments and be socially isolated from extended support systems. Further, low-SES is predictive of juvenile delinquency (Straus, 1994). Finally, poverty correlates strongly with increased family stress, school failure, and other problems. Although some children from poor families will succeed despite their disadvantages, children living below the poverty line are more likely to have difficulty in school, to become teen parents, and, as adults, to earn less and be unemployed more frequently (Forum on Child and Family Statistics, 2002).

The effects of economic deprivation on parent–child relations can be traumatic. Children and adolescents tend to be unsympathetic to the difficulties of their parents resulting from economic pressures. Instead of placing the blame for their parents' unemployment on external, uncontrollable factors, adolescents are likely to blame their parents, calling them inept or unskilled. Thus, economic deprivation may create a distorted perception of reality and, in turn, lead to an adolescent's acting out and demonstrating other detrimental behaviors including juvenile delinquency (J. J. McWhirter et al., 2004).

Local Contexts of At-Risk Behavior

In addition to the broader systemic and societal factors already discussed, local contexts can contribute greatly to the difficulties of young people. Our focus here is on family and school environments.

The Family Context

Much of the theory that guides our understanding of family systems and functioning reflects the dominant European American culture. Bearing that in mind, counselors must explore a family's norms, values, and practices within the family's cultural context, tailoring their application of family systems theories to the individual family. Given the large within-group differences for any ethnic minority group, and the variation within European American subgroups as well, counselors cannot make any assumptions about the cultural appropriateness of specific interventions.

To understand the nature of the stresses on families and the dysfunction within families that place children at risk, one first must have a clear understanding of characteristics of healthy families. From a family-systems perspective, a healthy family is an open system that interacts with the environment and is capable of adaptation and flexibility. Within this open system the family is able to maintain the stability necessary to allow the development of individual and separate identities, and family members make accommodations to environmental changes as necessary. In contrast, a closed system is isolated from and does not respond to the environment and is less receptive than an open system to external stimuli.

J. J. McWhirter et al. (2004) have suggested that parenting behavior in a healthy family falls near the middle on three dimensions of child rearing:

1. The permissiveness–restrictiveness dimension, which reflects control and power in the parents' behaviors
2. The hostility–warmth dimension, which reflects levels of support and affection that parents give to children
3. The anxious/emotional involvement–calm detachment dimension, which reflects the emotional engagement or connectedness of the parent.

In contrast, parenting in troubled families tends to be inconsistent and to fall near the extremes on these three dimensions.

Changing Family Structure

Divorce affects large numbers of families in the United States. One in four children lives with only one parent, one in 24 lives with neither parent, and one in 60 will see their parents divorce in any given year (Children's Defense Fund, 2001). Compounding the stress of changes in the nuclear family, extended family support from grandparents, aunts, uncles, and cousins is no longer as available to the vast majority of young people as it was in the past. Only about 5% of American children see a grandparent regularly (Hamburg, 1995).

One result of the rising divorce rates is the increasing probability that children will be part of a blended family, in which one or both parents marries someone who brings children to the relationship. Although new social networks may be available to children and families when parents remarry, shifting family structures may also add variability in family experience, produce alienation, and not provide the type of secure base in which children can grow and develop in healthy ways, thus serving to place children and adolescents at risk (J. J. McWhirter et al., 2004). Indeed, children in blended families face a number of challenges that at times bring them considerable discomfort. The entire family must adjust to a whole new set of expectations, procedures, and interactions. This is stressful for the children, and the new spouses, and the rate of divorce in second marriages is even higher than in first marriages.

Because most parents in single- and dual-parent households work outside of the home, many children are responsible for taking care of themselves after school and on school holidays. Although this circumstance can teach children independence and responsibility, the after-school experience of many latchkey children is characterized by boredom, fear, and loneliness (J. J. McWhirter et al., 2004). Latchkey children may feel alienated and resentful of their isolation and are at risk for accidents, crime victimization, poor school performance, and committing vandalism or other forms of delinquency in the absence of parental monitoring and supervision (Goyette–Ewing, 2000; Flannery, Williams, & Vazsonyi, 1999).

Dysfunctional Families

Dysfunction in the family context is stressful for children, as well as adults, and may lead to serious behavioral and other problems. The dysfunctional family environments that are most likely to lead to problems for youth are those characterized by substance abuse, domestic violence, child abuse and neglect, and parental psychopathology (J. J. McWhirter et al., 2004). Substance abuse by an adult caregiver puts children at higher risk for abuse and neglect, but even in the absence of abuse or neglect, parental alcoholism puts children at risk for developing alcoholism themselves, for entering into relationships with alcoholics, and for poor emotional and social adjustment. Their adjustment problems may include hyperactivity, relationship difficulties, aggression, depression, truancy, and drug abuse.

Violence between spouses is also strongly related to severe problems in children. Witnessing family violence is detrimental to a child's development, weakening his or her self-esteem and confidence (Straus, 1994) and increasing his or her vulnerability to stress disorders and other psychological difficulties. In addition, growing up in a violent environment increases the probability that the child will engage in violent and abusive behavior as an adolescent or an adult (American Psychological Association, 1996).

Child Abuse

Child abuse, including physical and emotional abuse, neglect, and sexual abuse, also places children at severe risk for future problems. Physical violence against children can range from hair-pulling and slapping to severe beatings. Some of the behaviors that constitute verbal and emotional abuse are harsh criticism and ridicule, withholding of affection, irrational punishment, and inconsistent expectations (Gershoff, 2002). Gay and lesbian youth are at particular risk for verbal and physical abuse by family members (J. J. McWhirter et al., 2004).

Neglect is defined as the failure of a parent to safeguard the health, safety, and well-being of a child. Neglected children may not be fed and bathed regularly, may be left unattended, or may be ignored by caregivers. About 3 million reports of possible maltreatment are made to child protective service agencies each year, and the actual incidence of abuse and neglect is estimated to be three times higher than the number reported to authorities. Of 870,000 substantiated reports in the year 2000, 63% of child victims suffered neglect, 19% were physically abused, 10% were sexually abused, and 8% were psychologically maltreated (U.S. Department of Health and Human Services, 2002).

Homicide is one of the top five causes of death among children under age 12, and nine young people under the age of 20 die from homocide every day in the United States (Children's Defense Fund, 2001). Among young adolescent African American girls, homicide is the leading cause of death (Gillis, 1998). Indeed, reports of family violence have increased dramatically over the past two decades (Emery & Laumann–Billings, 1998). Although extreme violence accounts for only a small percentage of cases reported to authorities, a number of researchers believe that the incidence of severe abuse in families is rising and that community disintegration, increased poverty, increased use of illegal drugs, and increased overall violence are strong contributing factors (Emery & Laumann–Billings, 1998).

Emery and Laumann–Billings (1998) noted that social service agencies spend most of their resources investigating reports of abuse and have few resources left for providing interventions that support families and reduce the recurrence of family violence. Interventions for family violence may be supportive or coercive. Supportive programs attempt to reduce violent behavior within families and may include individual and/or group therapies for victims and perpetrators, couples therapy, parent training, family therapy, and home-visitation programs. In addition, supportive programs may use a combination of methods, such as behavioral interventions, stress management, and relationship skills training. Coercive interventions include removal of children from the home, termination of parental rights, early adoption, and mandatory arrest, even in cases in which the victims do not wish arrest to occur. The optimal type of intervention depends upon the specific characteristics of the abuse situation.

Child sexual abuse (CSA) is a specific form of violence that may occur in dysfunctional families. Definitions of sexual abuse vary widely but can include both contact abuse (e.g., fondling) and noncontact abuse (e.g., genital exposure), as well as rape or attempted rape (Vogeltanz, Wilsnack, Harris, Wilsnack, Wonderlich, & Kristjanson, 1999). Estimates of the incidence and prevalence of the sexual abuse of children vary widely, depending upon the definitions of sexual abuse and the population sample. In any case, sexual abuse occurs within all cultures, races, and types of families (Kenny & McEachern, 2000).

Vogeltanz et al. (1999) surveyed a nationally representative sample with regard to ethnicity and found a prevalence rate for CSA in women of 15.4% to 32.1%, depending on the criteria used to define CSA and the interpretation of missing data. In the majority of sexual abuse cases, the abuser is known to the victim and the rates of intrafamilial abuse in this study were 40%. In more than half of the cases the first occurrence of CSA was before age 12, and about one-third occurred before age 9 (Vogeltanz et al., 1999).

The consequences of family violence are a function of the nature, frequency, intensity, and duration of the act; victim characteristics; the nature of the relationship between the abuser and the victim (e.g., parent–child); the response of others to the abuse; and other correlates of the abuse such as family chaos (Emery & Laumann–Billings, 1998). The consequences include physical injury, increased risk of psychological problems, acute and post-traumatic stress disorders, and more subtle psychological effects.

The effects of stranger abuse may be very different than the effects of abuse by someone who is known and trusted. When the abuser is someone they know, children are placed in a position of isolation and powerlessness, their trust having been violated by an adult who is supposed to be taking care of them. Within this context they have extreme difficulty understanding what has happened to them, saying no, and disclosing the abuse (Peake, 1987).

Child sexual abuse is recognized as a predictor of many physical and psychological problems (Vogeltanz et al., 1999). In a review of the literature on the sequelae of child sexual abuse, Berkowitz (1998) described numerous problems in individuals who have been sexually abused, including severe depression, eating disorders, anxiety disorders, substance abuse, somatization, post-traumatic stress disorder, and dissociative identity disorder, as well as psychosexual dysfunction, prostitution, adolescent pregnancy, a number of medical conditions, and difficulties with interpersonal relationships (Berkowitz, 1998).

Child physical and sexual abuse is associated with higher suicide rates. Girls with a history of CSA are three times more likely to develop psychiatric and substance abuse disorders than girls with no such history (Kendler et al., 2000). A history of sexual or physical abuse seems to increase the risk of disordered eating behaviors for adolescent girls and boys alike (Neumark–Szteiner, Story, Hannan, Beuhring, & Resnick, 2000). Young girls who are sexually abused are more likely to develop eating disorders as adolescents, perhaps because of higher levels of emotional distress that may be linked to their abuse experiences, and disordered eating behaviors reflect efforts to cope with those emotional difficulties (Wonderlich et al., 2000). Adolescents with a history of sexual abuse seem to have lower levels of impulse control and are significantly more likely to engage in high-risk sexual behavior, placing themselves at risk for HIV infection and other sexually transmitted diseases (Brown, Lourie, Zlotnick, & Cohn, 2000).

Important consequences for counselors to bear in mind are that children may feel stigmatized as "different" because of their abuse experiences and may feel isolated from their peers. Children often are not believed when they disclose sexual abuse, are blamed for the abuse, are threatened by their perpetrators, and come to believe that they are to blame for the abuse, which leads to intense feelings of guilt and shame (Wolf, 1993). The case of Julia, presented at the end of this chapter, provides an overview of how a counselor might respond to sexual abuse issues.

The School Context

Among the elements that characterize healthy school environments are strong instructional leadership, a curriculum that emphasizes academics, a collaborative atmosphere among teachers and staff members, a sense of commitment and a feeling of belonging among students, and student discipline that is fair, clear, and consistent (J. J. McWhirter et al., 2004; Taylor, Pressley, & Pierson, 2000). If a school is to be truly effective, community support is important. The level of community support depends, in large part, on the community's "social capital"—the network of nuclear and extended families, the neighborhood and church community, and social services and other community agencies—united in beliefs and values regarding, among other things, the nature and role of education (J. J. McWhirter et al., 2004). Deficient social capital in present-day society constrains school systems, as does the lack of financial support for educational systems.

Strong correlations have been found between school difficulties of young people and the kinds of serious problems that are the topics of this chapter. Although educators may have little power to change the familial and social living situations of at-risk youth, they do have the power to create a learning environment that reduces risk and promotes positive adjustment. Teacher/staff climate and student climate are two important components of such an environment (J. J. McWhirter et al., 2004). Common characteristics of the teacher/staff climate in effective schools are collegiality and collaboration among staff members, community support, autonomy, and strong leadership. Indicators of a healthy student climate include positive self-concept and self-esteem among students, support for the development of student decision-making and problem-solving skills, structures that facilitate and encourage the self-monitoring of behavior and school progress, and promotion of an attitude of shared responsibility for learning.

Peer Interactions

Schools that systematically promote positive peer interactions through mediation programs, violence-prevention curricula, life-skills curricula, and the like, are likely to have an influence on peer group behavior. *Peer cluster theory* suggests that the attitudes, beliefs, and behaviors of peer groups are the dominant influences on drug use and other behavior problems in adolescents (Beauvais, Chavez, Oetting, Deffenbacher, & Cornell, 1991; Oetting & Beauvais, 1987). The dynamics of peer clusters help to explain the failure of many prevention and intervention programs targeted at changing the behavior of at-risk adolescents: When adolescents return to their original peer cluster after treatment, they are subject to the same pressures to conform as they were prior to treatment.

The work of Dishion, McCord, and Poulin (1999) suggests that interventions that place adolescents with significant behavior problems in proximity may increase the incidence of disruptive behavior, as students learn from and imitate each other. In schools with a poor student climate, peers can influence one another in negative ways through coercion and manipulation. In schools that promote a positive school climate, peer influences are usually positive as well, with peers providing one another with support, companionship, advice, and opportunities to successfully resolve conflicts.

School Environment

School size, structure, and philosophy also have an influence on the learning environment. Smaller schools can increase the sense of community and personal identity for students. Classroom structures can help students feel a sense of empowerment, safety, and influence over their environment, enhancing their acceptance and appreciation of differences, creativity, and personal autonomy, which in turn may lead to improvements in mental health and the overall quality of learning. Curricula that include social skills training, problem solving, and critical thinking can be highly beneficial to at-risk students (J. J. McWhirter et al., 2004).

Entry into adolescence often coincides with the emergence of problems such as lower academic motivation, lower self-concept, higher rates of truancy, and greater inattentiveness in class (Eccles & Midgley, 1989; Eccles, Midgley, &

Adler, 1984; Eccles et al., 1993). For girls, the onset of adolescence has been associated with depression and loss of vitality, resilience, and sense of self (Brown & Gilligan, 1992). Eccles et al. (1993) argued that these difficulties arise, in part, as a response to a mismatch between school environments and adolescent developmental needs. Specifically, an adolescent's needs for increasing independence, autonomy, and responsibility are often met at school with fewer opportunities for exercising independence and autonomy.

According to Eccles et al. (1993), when students enter junior high school, they typically are confronted with changes in task structure, grouping practices, evaluation techniques, motivational strategies, locus of responsibility for learning, and quality of teacher–student relationships that are counter to their developmental needs. They found, for example, increased use of social-comparison techniques, fewer opportunities for autonomous behavior, and lower teacher perceptions of their own efficacy for teaching. In addition, those authors found that classwork in junior high required lower-level cognitive skills than in the years prior to junior high. They also found that when levels of teacher efficacy and support did not decrease in the transition from the middle grades to junior high school, student motivation did not decline. These findings attest to the importance of school structure to student health.

Gender Role Socialization

The influence of gender role socialization also may contribute to school problems for girls. Research by Gilligan (1982) suggests that girls respond differently than boys to classroom environments. For example, girls tend to prefer cooperative over competitive learning situations, whereas the opposite is true for boys. Ample research indicates that teachers tend to pay less attention to girls than boys, hold lower academic expectations for girls, and provide less effective feedback to girls than to their male classmates. These discrepancies are even greater for girls of color. A curriculum tailored to the learning styles and socialization patterns of boys may result in lower self-esteem, less independence, declining ambition, and self-defeating career choices in girls (AAUW, 1989).

According to the American Association of University Women (AAUW, 1998), although the gap between girls and boys in the number of math and science courses they take seems to be diminishing in recent years, gender differences remain in the kinds of courses taken, with boys more often taking advanced courses. In the area of technology, girls show less self-confidence about computers and less frequent use of computers, and they are less likely to enroll in advanced computer courses than boys are. A new gender gap seems to be emerging in the area of computer science (AAUW, 1998).

School Dropout

Another negative consequence of problems in school structure and climate is school dropout. A dropout is defined as a student who leaves school before his or her program of study is complete—that is, before graduation and without transferring to another school. According to current research, the dropout rate in many states is as high as one in four students, and the problem likely is even more pronounced in large cities (J. J. McWhirter et al., 2004). Identified risk factors for dropping out of school include low academic motivation, a history of problems with school authorities and/or police, frequent absences, pregnancy or marriage, being poor and having to work, family problems, substance-abuse problems, being members of a minority group, or having fallen two or more years behind grade level. Thus, the young people who are most likely to drop out of school are those already at risk, and dropping out of school, on the whole, compounds their difficulties.

Dropping out of school leads to economic and social consequences such as lower earning potential, unemployment, dissatisfaction with self and the surrounding environment, and lack of opportunities (J. J. McWhirter et al., 2004). A potential problem for efforts to prevent dropout was revealed in a study showing that commonly cited risk factors (e.g. family background, previous school experiences, personal/psychological characteristics, and adult responsibilities) were not effective predictors of dropping out (Gleason & Dynarski, 2002), a finding that has implications for dropout prevention programs.

School Violence

The National Association of School Security Directors has estimated that 12,000 armed robberies, 270,000 burglaries, 204,000 aggravated assaults, and 9,000 rapes occur in primary and secondary schools each year. In the 1993–94 school year, 12% of all elementary and secondary school teachers (341,000) were threatened with injury by a student from their school, and 4% (119,000) were physically attacked by a student (NCES, 2001). Further, school vandalism costs many millions of dollars every year in property damage. Fighting and intimidation among students are also increasing, with estimates indicating that one in seven children are either bullies or victims of bullies in grade schools and approximately 4.8 million schoolchildren in the United States are threatened by the violent or aggressive behavior of other students.

Violence within schools and local communities creates a climate of fear for young people. Girls may respond by dissociating during school, often appearing to be daydreaming; however, their responses are becoming more similar to those of boys, with an increase of aggressive and impulsive behaviors (Gillis, 1998). Boys and girls alike report having experienced sexual harassment in school, and girls are more likely to report being negatively affected by the experience (AAUW, 1998).

Students ages 12 through 18 experienced 2.5 million incidents of violence at school in 1999; of these, 186,000 were serious violent crimes such as aggravated assault, rape, robbery, and sexual assault (Kaufman et al., 2001). With regard to handgun violence, the Children's Defense Fund (2001) reported that nine young people under age 20 die every day in the United States from handgun injuries. According to a report issued by the David and Lucille Packard Foundation (2002) each year, more than 3,000 youths under age 20 are killed and more than 18,000 are injured by firearms in the United States each year. School shootings in Colorado, Oregon, and elsewhere have received national attention in the past several years, creating a climate of uncertainty for children, parents, and teachers.

A Framework for Prevention and Intervention

Factors contributing to the development of conduct disorders, substance abuse, pregnancy and sexually transmitted diseases, and depression in youth and adolescents are numerous and diverse. Because families, schools, communities, and society clearly play a role in the development and maintenance of these problems, models of prevention and intervention must be comprehensive if they are to produce lasting effects. In general, counselors will be most effective when they are involved in service delivery that goes beyond traditional individual interventions and involves programming that reaches large numbers of young people prior to the onset of severe problems as well as programming that links families, schools, and communities.

The comprehensive prevention/intervention framework presented by J. J. McWhirter et al. (2004) is described here. This framework involves three distinct continuums: the at-risk continuum, the approach continuum, and the context continuum.

At-Risk Continuum

The *at-risk continuum* reflects the degree to which children and adolescents are at risk for serious behaviors such as substance abuse, risky sexual activity, depression, violence, gang involvement, and conduct disorders. The continuum ranges from minimal risk to imminent risk. Young people characterized by minimal risk are those who enjoy "favorable demographics"; that is, they have a higher socioeconomic status, have positive family, school, and social interactions, and are exposed to only limited psychosocial and environmental stressors. Although they certainly are not invulnerable to problems, they have many buffers and supports for coping with their experiences.

Next on the continuum are young people at remote risk. These youths have less favorable demographic characteristics, such as lower socioeconomic status or less cohesive community life; they may be members of a family that is under stress, perhaps because of poverty, divorce, remarriage, or job loss. Family functioning may be affected by these demographic variables, and school and social interactions are less positive. The effects of these risky demographic characteristics are additive; the more of these demographic characteristics present, the greater is the risk of developing problems.

High risk is characterized by negative family, school, and social interactions (such as domestic violence and school performance problems), numerous stressors, and personal at-risk markers including negative attitudes, emotions, and skill deficiencies. Young people at imminent risk are those who, in addition to having several or many of the preceding characteristics, have developed "gateway" behaviors—behaviors that typically (though not inevitably) lead to more negative behaviors. Gateway behaviors include smoking (which may occur with or precede alcohol use, which may be a gateway to the use of illegal substances such as marijuana, cocaine, and other illicit drugs) and involvement in negative peer networks (which may lead to juvenile offenses, aggression, rejection by other peers, family distancing, and later to gang involvement and more serious offenses). J. J. McWhirtcr et al. (2004) defined "at-risk category" activity as behaviors that lead to violent and destructive behavior, substance abuse, unprotected sexual activity, and other severe problems. These behaviors are the primary concern in this chapter, though our emphasis on prevention requires that we address the risk factors that precede the development of these behaviors.

Approach Continuum

The *approach continuum* reflects the types of prevention and intervention approaches that are most appropriate for different levels of risk. Paralleling the at-risk continuum, it begins with universal approaches that correspond to minimal risk. *Universal approaches* are considered to be appropriate for all children, not just those who are presumed to be at risk, and they target all children in a given catchment area. An example is a life-skills curriculum that is implemented across all grades in a given school. In such a curriculum, developmentally appropriate personal, social, and cognitive skills in areas such as communication, conflict resolution, and problem solving are most effective when taught early and supported throughout elementary, middle, and secondary school.

Next on the continuum are *selected approaches,* which are aimed at groups of young people who share some circumstance or experience that increases their likelihood for developing problems in the future. Examples of selected programs are Head Start, which is directed toward low-income children, and school-based, small-group interventions for children whose parents are divorcing or divorced. Universal and selected programs are not mutually exclusive; in fact, overlap is often preferable. That is, children whose parents are divorcing would benefit from a school curriculum that promotes life skills such as communication plus participation in a small group specific to addressing their current experience.

Booster sessions, or follow-up sessions that review and reinforce components of universal and selected and target approaches, occupy the next space on the continuum. These are followed on the continuum by *indicated treatment approaches,* which are used with children and adolescents who are at imminent risk of serious problems or who have just begun to engage in serious problem behaviors. An adolescent who is considering suicide, has begun to skip classes, and is brought to counseling because he came home intoxicated, for example, would require an indicated treatment approach. The goals of treatment would include helping him to develop coping skills that would prevent him or her from committing suicide, from dropping out of school, and from developing a substance abuse problem.

At the end of the continuum are *second-chance programs,* designed for young people who already have engaged in severe problem behavior. They may, for example, regularly use alcohol or drugs, be pregnant, or be clinically depressed. Second-chance programs provide them with an opportunity to develop the skills and support they need to make different choices.

Context Continuum

Finally, the prevention and intervention framework incorporates a *context continuum,* which reflects the manner in which three important contexts—society/community, family, and school — are involved in early, broad-based prevention efforts, early intervention efforts that coordinate support and training activities, and treatment approaches that incorporate a variety of education, training, and counseling efforts. With respect to *society/community,* prevention involves improving economic conditions, increasing supplies of low-cost housing and child care, increasing job opportunities, providing an umbrella of community-based support services, and promoting prosocial norms and values.

With respect to the *family* context, prevention may involve providing culturally appropriate family-strengthening opportunities that increase interaction and communication between family members and increase support for families, as well as making available prenatal and health care programs. Parent training and other kinds of family support programs constitute early intervention, and family counseling and programs designed to address child abuse, neglect, and domestic violence are at the treatment end of the continuum.

Prevention in *schools* includes early compensatory programs such as Head Start and before- and after-school programs that provide safe, nurturing environments for children whose parents are not available at those times. Participation in quality after-school programs can have significant learning, career, social, and health benefits (Schwendiman & Fager, 1999). Prevention also includes generic programs infused in the curriculum that provide training in life skills such as decision making and social skills. Intervention includes target programs, such as those that provide specific social skills training for violent or aggressive young people. At the treatment end of the continuum are second-chance, school-based programs, such as alternative high schools and school-based health clinics that provide a variety of treatment services.

An Empowerment Model of Counseling

A given counselor in a given context might not be able to implement comprehensive prevention and intervention strategies. Advocacy for prevention programs is an important counselor responsibility (Keys, Bemak, Carpenter, & King-Sears, 1998; Lee & Walz, 1998; E. H. McWhirter, 1997, 2001), but individual counselors must implement other strategies for responding to the needs of children and adolescents in crisis. One such strategy is the empowerment model of counseling described by E. H. McWhirter (1994, 1997, 1998). This model incorporates a systemic perspective that recognizes the influence on children and adolescents of forces such as poverty, racism, sexism, heterosexism, broad economic policies that undermine family functioning, and sociopolitical issues. Many traditional counseling approaches do not address these aspects of context, as they were developed by White, middle-class theorists for a White, middle-class population (Katz, 1985; Sue & Sue, 1991).

Empowerment, according to E. H. McWhirter (1994), is

> the process by which people, organizations, or groups who are powerless or marginalized: (a) become aware of the power dynamics at work in their life context; (b) develop the skills and capacity for gaining some reasonable control over their lives; (c) which they exercise; (d) without infringing upon the rights of others; and (e) which coincides with actively supporting the empowerment of others in their community. (p. 12)

Thus, empowerment is a comprehensive process affecting people internally as well as in relation to others, to the community, and to society. It is a complex, lifelong process that involves critical self-reflection and action; critical awareness of the environment, especially of the power dynamics within the environment related to forces such as racism and national support for education; skill and resource recognition and development; connectedness with a community; and support for the empowerment of others.

The five core components (the five Cs) that make up the empowerment model of counseling are collaboration, context, critical consciousness, competence, and community (E. H. McWhirter, 1997, 1998).

Collaboration

The counselor–client relationship should be dynamic, characterized by a collaborative definition of the problem and the collaborative development of interventions and strategies for change. The ability of children and adolescents to define the problem varies, with definitions ranging from "I don't know what's wrong with me" to "I hate school" to "I want my mom and her boyfriend to stop fighting." What is most important is that young people are invited into the counseling process, that their experiences are validated, and that they are presumed to be knowledgeable about what is important to them. Even when young people are unable to articulate or even acknowledge a problem, letting them know that their opinions and feelings are important and that they are expected to influence the direction of their therapy can lay the groundwork for empowerment.

Collaboration implies a reduction in the traditional power differential between counselor and client and, at the same time, acknowledgment of the real power differences that are present. The counselor thus would acknowledge the authority associated with the client's role—for example, explaining that he or she is responsible for monitoring aspects of treatment compliance and initiating consequences for noncompliance. Despite the implications of acknowledging clients' authority on the therapeutic relationship, counselors must not pretend to be "equals." A final implication of the collaborative stance is that counselors recognize that they do not "empower others" but, instead, participate in the empowerment process or facilitate the empowerment of young people.

Context

The dynamics of power and privilege shape the young person's context and the context in which counselors provide services. These contexts include social forces and realities that extend well beyond the counseling room (e.g., social policies that undermine families, the decreasing numbers of two-parent households, discrimination, increasing violence displayed in media, inaccessible health care, decreased funding for education, and poor-quality schools) and the effects of these factors on care providers, families, and children.

In the empowerment model, counselors acknowledge the role of context in the young person's current situation or problem, including how the context serves to maintain or exacerbate the client's problems, and at the same time they recognize the client's options and responsibilities related to change. Thus, counseling with the goal of empowerment is inconsistent with victim-blaming; instead, it promotes proactive responses to situations.

For example, a young person in a dysfunctional family who has developed a sense of "badness" and internalized responsibility for parental discord and a host of other problems would be assisted in distinguishing responsibility for his or her own behavior and realistically assigning responsibility elsewhere. Counseling for empowerment implies that young people have the capacity to change, grow, act, and shape their environment despite contextual limitations.

Sometimes the context is so negative that even though the counselor is acutely aware of its influence, ideas for how to assist the child may be difficult to come by. But solutions do exist.

Ten-year-old Jeana was seen by one of the authors of this chapter (EHM) during her parents' custody battle. It appeared that her father, an alcoholic, was attempting to gain sole custody of Jeana just to punish her mother for initiating the divorce. At the time, Jeana's father had visitation rights and Jeana spent every other weekend and some weeknights with him. These visits were painful for her, as her father largely ignored her or belittled her when she attempted to engage him in activity or conversation. Jeana was not permitted to call her mother during these evenings and weekends, and she developed a tremendous amount of anxiety and fear in anticipation of the visits.

Jeana and her mother did not know how to make the situation better. The context was being shaped by the courts, and Jeana's father seemed to have a great deal of control as well. As one component of increasing Jeana's coping repertoire, the counselor suggested that Jeana make use of an imaginary shield to protect herself from her father's hurtful comments. She and Jeana identified the kinds of things that Jeana's father typically said and did that were hurtful, and then practiced the use of a "magic shield" that Jeana could activate by touching an invisible button on her left shoulder. When her father said something hurtful, Jeana would touch her left shoulder, an invisible shield would envelope her, and his hurtful words would bounce off the shield and fall to the ground. Safe inside her shield, Jeana would think about receiving a hug from her mother.

The technique seemed to work well. Though only 10 years old and not having control of most of the elements of her context, Jeana was able to modify her environment enough, using this technique, to alleviate a good portion of her anxiety.

Critical Consciousness

Critical consciousness is fostered by both counselor and client through two simultaneous processes: *critical self-reflection* and *power analysis.* Critical self-reflection involves increasing awareness of one's privilege, power, strengths, biases, and so forth. Privilege refers to one's status by virtue of membership in various groups that are viewed as "better" or as the standard against which others are judged. For example, a person who is White, male, of higher socioeconomic status, adult, or able-bodied occupies a position of privilege relative to a person who is not a member of one of these groups. When we practice critical self-reflection, we are honest with ourselves and others about our privileged status (without apology; guilt and pity don't empower anybody) and aware of how privilege influences our assumptions and experiences.

Power analysis involves examining how power, including the power of privilege, is used in a given context. For example, a counselor might focus attention on his or her own agency, considering how the use of power is manifested in the manner in which clients (children and adults, male and female, white clients and clients of color) are discussed or in how office space is allocated among staff members. For the counselor, power analysis further involves examining the effects of these factors on his or her behavior and on the behavior of others. Along the same lines, a counselor can facilitate an adolescent client's power analysis by examining with the child (a) school, home, and peer group "rules"; (b) consequences of violating the rules; (c) the nature and effects of the client's antidepressant medication; and (d) behavioral choices available to the client in the context of the client's health and school, peer, and family situation.

Counselors also facilitate critical self-reflection and power analysis with colleagues and within the community. A counselor might, for example, speak to a city council or other public forums about the long-term social and economic consequences of funding prison construction versus funding prevention programs, raising the community's critical consciousness. In addition, counselors actively seek feedback from their clients, as well as from supervisors and colleagues, and engage in ongoing efforts to educate themselves on issues and interventions that support their clients' power and control over their lives.

Competence

All young people have skills, resources, and experience to contribute to the counseling process. An important part of counseling for empowerment is to recognize and authentically appreciate these competencies. Counselors sometimes make the mistake of overlooking or underemphasizing the competencies of adolescents with multiple problems, focusing only on their deficits. They lose sight of how the destructive or self-defeating behavior of children and adolescents reflects their attempt to survive and protect themselves.

Also essential to counseling for empowerment is that the counselor recognize his or her own competencies and weaknesses. Counselors are unlikely to truly appreciate the strengths of others if they are unable to appreciate their own competencies, and they are unlikely to accept others' weaknesses without accepting their own. Indeed, the ACA code of ethics includes recognition of the limits of one's expertise as part of the counselor's responsibility (American Counseling Association Ethics Committee, 1995). The identification, development, and practice of relevant new skills and resources are important for clients and counselors alike. Facilitating the development of self-efficacy expectations will increase the likelihood that young people will attempt to practice those skills.

Community

Community may be defined in terms of family, peers, neighborhood, church groups, or other bonds. A sense of belonging to a community, and the ability to contribute to that community are critical for young people. We are communitary beings, and our potential for healthy development is greatest when we receive the nurturance, role modeling, identity, security, and encouragement provided by communities and also contribute something positive back to our communities. Both processes are fundamental to empowerment.

Rudolf Dreikurs (1964, 1967) built upon the work of psychologist Alfred Adler (1930, 1964) by noting that young people who misbehave are often seeking a way to contribute to and be valued by a community. Adler believed that all young people need a sense of belonging and an arena or group in which to contribute (Pryor & Tollerud, 1999; Sweeney, 1998). Families, schools, and communities can provide these arenas.

Garbarino and his colleagues (cited in Emery & Laumann–Billings, 1998) demonstrated that the extent of social cohesion and mutual caring in a community was the critical contextual distinction between impoverished families that abused their children and those that did not. Further, Furstenberg (1993) found that the ability to identify community organizations in which a family can participate, and the sense of being able to ask for help from others, distinguished maltreating from non-maltreating families. Counselors need to work with young people to help them understand their sense of community, the resources available in that community, and the extent and quality of their interactions with the community.

Often, young people in crisis do not experience a sense of community with any other groups in their environment or belong to communities that undermine their resources and abilities (e.g., a chaotic family, a gang that they join out of pressure rather than the desire to affiliate with its members, a competitive peer group). Counselors must be aware of potential new sources of community and assist clients in accessing or fostering community. School-based programs that promote positive social interactions, build communication skills, and foster a sense of shared identity are especially helpful to this end (Sinclair, Hurley, Evelo, Christenson, & Thurlow, 2002).

Clubs or organizations with a particular theme (e.g., an athletic or academic team; a social-justice club; a gay/lesbian student support group; a volunteer group for a local shelter) can provide a common goal that contributes to a sense of community. Counselors may have to help children develop the skills needed for drawing upon the community's support, because young people who are isolated may behave in ways that further their estrangement from others.

Finally, counselors can assist young people in identifying ways to support the empowerment of others in their community through mutual encouragement or shared goals. More specific and systemic means of contributing to others' welfare in a school context include school-based peer mentoring, peer tutoring, and peer mediation programs. The latter, for example, have been shown to contribute to less school violence (Araki, Takeshita, & Kadomoto, 1989; McCormick, 1988) and to have significant benefits for at-risk students who were trained as mediators (Araki et al., 1989; Blake, Wang, Cartledge, & Gardner, 2000).

Specific Disorders and Problems

The following discussion addresses a number of serious problems that place children and adolescents at great risk, including suicide and suicide attempts, teenage pregnancy and sexually transmitted diseases, conduct disorders, substance abuse, and clinical depression. Prevention and treatment interventions are suggested for each.

Suicide and Suicide Attempts

Incidence and Characteristics

In the United States, suicide is the third leading cause of death among adolescents, behind unintentional injury and homocide (Hoyert, Anas, Smith, Murphy, & Kochanek, 2001). Gay and lesbian adolescents also have high rates of suicide attempts and completions, primarily because of the effects of living in a homophobic society (Faulkner & Cranston, 1998). Overall, approximately 1 million young people attempt suicide each year in the United States, and estimates indicate that this number is increasing (Hoyert et al., 2001).

Among ethnic minority adolescents, Native Americans have the highest suicide rate, although there is variability across tribes. In Native American communities the high rates of suicide and attempted suicide have been attributed to acute acculteration stress, cultural conflict, and social disorganization (Institute of Medicine, 2002). The stress of these dilemmas has been shown to increase alcohol and drug abuse, depression or other psychopathology, and suicide behavior in this population (Beauvais, 1998).

Although reported suicide rates traditionally have been lower for African American youth than European American youth, findings from the National Center for Injury Prevention and Control (NCIPC, 2001) reported that between 1980 and 1995, suicide rates for African American male youth increased from 2.1 to 4.5 per 100,000, an increase of 114%, while for European American male youth the increase was only 5.4 to 6.4 per 100,000.

Some research also indicates higher rates of attempts and completed suicides for Hispanic adolescents than for European American and African American adolescents. A study of risky youth behaviors (Kann et al., 1998) reported that 13% of Hispanic adolescents had attempted suicide compared to 7% for European American and African American youth.

Females are three times more likely to attempt suicide than males; however, males are five times more likely to complete the suicide (Hoyert et al., 2001). Although females tend to use more passive, low-lethality methods (e.g., consuming alcohol and barbiturates, carbon-monoxide poisoning), whereas males are more prone to use violent and highly lethal methods (e.g., firearms, hanging), trends indicate that females are experimenting increasingly with more lethal methods (IOM, 2002). In the United States in 1998, firearms accounted for 61% of the suicides among youths (NCIPC, 2001). Youths who contemplate suicide often have had difficult adjustments or transitions evoking feelings of depression, aggression, abandonment, and sometimes anger and rage, leading to an impulsive reaction such as a threat to harm oneself.

A national school-based study of youth found high one-year prevalance rates for suicide attempts (7.7%), ideation (20.5%), and making a plan (15.7%) (Kann et al., 1998). Depression, in particular, has been found to affect approximately 30% of the adolescent population (Lewinsohn, Rohde, Seeley, & Fischer, 1993) and has been linked to suicidal thoughts, ideation, and behaviors in this population. The loss of a parent through separation, divorce, or death, losses of other family members or friends, and troubled relationships with significant others may evoke suicidal thoughts or attempts. Many suicidal youth come from families in which the parental system is dysfunctional or disintegrated.

When family interactions are characterized by anger, emotional ambivalence, and ineffective communication, young people are less likely to develop skills for coping effectively with their families and with their own negative affect. They may engage in aggression or withdrawal, reducing the likelihood that they will get nurturance and support from others in their environment. Progressive isolation, manifested in reduced communication with family mernbers and friends, may be a warning sign of potential self-destructive, suicidal behaviors (American Psychiatric Association, 1998).

Intrapersonal and psychological characteristics of children and adolescents that have been associated with suicide ideation include loneliness (e.g., peer rejection, isolation), impulsivity (e.g., low tolerance for frustration), risk-taking (e.g., daredevil reactions to stressors), low self-esteem (e.g., poor self-concept, a sense of worthlessness), faulty thinking patterns (e.g., negative beliefs about oneself, strictly dichotomous thinking patterns, decreased ability to solve problems), and alcohol or drug use. Counselors should be alert to the presence of these characteristics in young people, especially those who are undergoing difficult transitions.

Assessment

In assessing an adolescent's suicidality, a multifaceted approach is necessary. The clinical interview is an effective method of assessing the risk and lethality of the adolescent's ideation. Risk factors include a family history of suicide, any previous suicide attempts, substance abuse, anxiety, hopelessness and depression, current family problems, and other current stressors. Suicide ideation may be communicated in poems, journals, diaries, or artwork. Any signs of poor impulse control, acting out, or rage should be explored further, as should mood swings, changes in sleeping or eating patterns, evidence of cognitive constriction, acting-out behaviors in school, and statements such as, "I wish I were dead" or "I won't be around much longer." Self-report measures such as the Beck Depression Inventory (BDI) (Beck, Ward, Mendelson, Mock, & Erbaugh, 1961) may be helpful for assessing adolescent suicidality.

Prevention and Intervention

Suicide-prevention efforts should be directed to the underlying environmental and interpersonal characteristics linked to suicide, such as depression, lack of social support, poor problem-solving skills, and hopelessness. As noted earlier, schools are an excellent setting for primary prevention efforts (King, Price, Telljohann, & Wahl, 2000; McWhirter et al. 2004). A number of model programs are available to teach young people how to build their self-esteem, learn to problem-solve, develop a repertoire of social skills, manage their anger and anxiety, and learn ways to assert themselves positively (Johnson, 1999; Shure, 1999).

Follow-up or booster sessions that foster additional adaptive skills and competencies are critical to a program's long-term effectiveness. Garland and Zigler (1993) argue for the inclusion of family support programs as an important and effective adjunct to suicide-prevention efforts. The purpose of these programs is to empower families by teaching them new ways to cope with life's stressors, such as poverty, single parenthood, substance abuse, and teenage pregnancy.

An example of a family support program currently being implemented in schools across the country is the Family Resource Center. These centers provide a variety of services within the school setting, such as child care, parent training, adult literacy training, and parental support.

Early intervention efforts are aimed at minimizing the frequency and severity of the suicide ideation experienced by adolescents who exhibit some or all of the characteristics described earlier. Group screening processes are the easiest and least expensive method to identify those who may be at high risk for suicide, but these types of screenings are likely to produce a number of false positives, which can be upsetting to the misclassified youths (Garland & Zigler, 1993). To reduce the number of misclassified youths, Garland and Zigler (1993) have suggested that suicide-screening processes be nested in other health-related screening programs.

Schools may be reluctant to allow the screenings. One of us was involved in an attempt to conduct a suicide-ideation screening in a middle school as part of a research project (Metha & E. H. McWhirter, 1997). It took approximately 1 year to secure permission to enter one school district. When a suicide occurred just prior to the scheduled screening, permission for the screening was withdrawn; the school administrators feared that attention to the topic would result in copycat behavior.

In addition to screening, many researchers have emphasized the need for schools to develop interdisciplinary crisis teams that include teachers, school counselors, school nurses, parents, and others in the community (King, Price, Telljohann, & Wahl, 2000; Vidal, 1989). Such teams are responsible for a number of activities including (a) developing prevention and early intervention programs; (b) establishing networks with other mental health agencies in the community; (c) making educational presentations in the schools and community; and (d) keeping the programs up-to-date and running smoothly. Many schools have districtwide crisis-response teams that are prepared to respond to a variety of school-related tragedies, including suicide.

J. J. McWhirter et al. (2004) delineated four steps to be followed in managing a suicide crisis.

1. The school counselor should assess the lethality of the threat (e.g., existence of a plan, lethality of the plan, and feasibility of carrying out the plan).

2. The counselor and the adolescent should develop a written agreement estab-lishing that the client will contact the counselor before attempting suicide. The counselor also should provide the client with 24-hour emergency crisis line numbers as another support outlet.

3. The client must be monitored carefully and his or her behavior tracked closely for 1 to 3 days, depending on the severity of the risk. In cases in which the client will not agree to a contract or in which the counselor assesses the likelihood of an attempt to be high, the counselor may have to hospitalize or otherwise secure the safety of the client.

4. When the client is a child or an adolescent, the counselor has a legal and eth-ical responsibility to inform the client's parents when the counselor is aware of their child's threat of suicide. Thus, the counselor must explain to the child or adolescent the limits of confidentiality so he or she will not feel betrayed if the counselor makes a disclosure to parents.

Teen Pregnancy

Incidence and Characteristics

Each year, about 1 million girls in the United States become pregnant (Alan Guttmacher Institute, 1999). Although birthrates to adolescents have decreased since mid-century, the percentage of out-of-wedlock teenage births has soared, resulting in an increase in welfare dependence and persistent childhood poverty (Child Trends, 2001). Though most pregnant adolescents are 18 and 19 years old, 40% of this population are 17 years and younger (Annie E. Casey Foundation, 1999). The U. S. teen pregnancy rate is more than twice as high as that in other industrialized countries, even though U. S. teenagers do not exhibit significantly different patterns of sexual activity (National Campaign to Prevent Teen Pregnancy, 2001).

Compared to the early 1990s, teen birthrates have declined in each of the major race/ethnic groups. The birthrate for African American teens declined by 30% between 1991 and 1999, and for European American teens, 24%. The birthrates for Hispanic adolescent females was stable between 1991 and 1995 and increased slightly in 2000, but the overall rate declined 12% between 1995 and 2000 (Child Trends, 2001).

The likelihood that a teenage girl will engage in unprotected sex, become pregnant, and give birth is highly correlated with a number of risk factors: grow-ing up in a single-parent family, living in poverty or in a high-poverty neighbor-hood, having low attachment to and performance in school, and having parents with low educational attainment (Annie E. Casey Foundation, 1999; Moore, Miller, Glei, & Morrison, 1995). In addition to increasing the risk of teen parent-hood, these factors increase the likelihood of a number of other negative out-comes, such as poor school performance (low aspirations and low aptitude test scores), limited social-skill development, low economic earning potential, and increased probability of single parenthood (Jaffee, 2002).

If a young teen feels helplessly restricted in her educational options (e.g., feeling alienated at school), occupational options (e.g., lacking stable career prospects), and economic options (e.g., seeing the decline in low-skill, high-paying manufacturing jobs), she is less likely to perceive the birth of a child as a barrier to her future. Further, a family life maintained by poor interpersonal relationships, ineffective communication, and limited problem-solving skills may encourage a teen to turn elsewhere for nurturing relationships.

Adolescents who give birth to a child find their physical, social, educational, and career worlds altered significantly. Giving birth to an unwanted child affects the teen's socioeconomic status, educational attainment, health, and family development (Way & Leadbeater, 1999). Young teen mothers have an exceptionally low probability of completing their education and have poor employment prospects. They are three times more likely to drop out of school than are mothers who delay childbearing until they are in their 20s (Annie E. Casey Foundation, 1999).

In recent years more teen mothers have received their General Equivalency Diploma (GED), thereby completing high school, than in the past (Alan Guttmacher Institute, 1999). But even those teen mothers who complete high school, whether receiving a high school diploma or a GED, tend to have lower basic skills than teens who are not parents. Their lower skills, coupled with the responsibilities of parenting, further restrict these teens to the low-wage, welfare-dependent job market. Adolescent mothers are highly likely to be single parents and sole providers for themselves and their children. Those who do marry are likely to divorce within 5 years (J. J. McWhirter et al., 2004).

In addition to resulting in unplanned pregnancy, irresponsible and risky sexual behavior can have other serious consequences. Sexually transmitted disease (STD) rates are rising among teen populations; approximately one in four teens contract STDs every year (Kirby, 2000). Gay and lesbian youth who are rejected at home are more likely to run away, and runaways, in turn, are more likely to abuse substances and engage in prostitution (J. J. McWhirter et al., 2004). These young people are at high risk for HIV and other sexually transmitted infections (Savin–Williams, 1994). Chlamydia, an infection of the vagina or urinary tract, is the most frequently diagnosed STD among adolescents, and gonorrhea, genital warts, herpes, and syphilis also are common. STDs can be irreversible and in some cases (herpes and AIDS) are incurable.

Prevention and Intervention

Attention to the issue of teenage sexual activity has increased in recent years, as has the number of available prevention programs. Programs geared toward delaying or reducing the sexual activity of teenagers have focused on three prevention strategies (Kirby, 2000; Manlove et al., 2002):

1. Educating teens about sexual reproduction and contraceptive use (most effective when delivered prior to the onset of sexual activity);
2. Reinforcing values and teaching abstinence;
3. Building strong decision-making and social skills.

The most successful of these programs use a two-prong approach that takes into consideration the adolescents' developmental needs and their experience levels. For example, teaching abstinence is best for pre-teens and young adolescents who are virgins at the start of the program, whereas contraceptive information is most useful for older teenagers who are beginning or at least thinking about sexual activity.

Among high-risk teenagers, comprehensive health-oriented services seem to be the most promising avenue for decreasing pregnancy rates (Manlove et al., 2002). Important components of these coordinated preventive efforts are school-based comprehensive medical care and contraceptive services, social services, and parent education. Programs directed to enhancing social development through outreach and community service, in combination with career and life skills training, are also promising. These programs help adolescents build social and personal competencies in areas such as making decisions, being assertive, and having positive interactions with adults, and provide them with opportunities to contribute to the community. Both types of experiences can serve as building blocks for increasing adolescents' sense of self-sufficiency and self-esteem and for helping them to make responsible decisions about their sexuality.

Intervention programs that target teen parents provide for a broad array of services, such as education and job training, free child care, and other support services, in an effort to build the adolescents' life options. Manlove et al. (2002) argue, however, that these services are not enough by themselves. They call for stronger links between services for teen mothers and those for their children, that extend beyond infancy and the preschool years. The need for comprehensive programs that expand educational and occupational opportunities and educate young people about themselves and their bodies cannot be overestimated. If society does not actively engage in helping adolescents build a positive future, the problems of STDs and the cycle of children having children will continue.

Conduct Disorders

Incidence and Characteristics

Conduct disorder is a diagnostic label referring to a persistent pattern of behavior exhibited by children or adolescents that includes violation of others' rights and disregard for the major age-appropriate social norms. The DSM–IV (American

Psychiatric Association [APA], 1994) lists 15 criterion behaviors associated with conduct disorder. These behaviors fall into the following four categories:

1. Aggression against people and animals;
2. Destruction of property;
3. Deceitfulness or theft;
4. Serious violations of rules.

The presence of at least 3 of the 15 behaviors over the past 12-month period and at least 1 behavior over the past 6-month period, as well as clinical impairment of academic, social, or occupational functioning, constitute the diagnostic criterion for conduct disorder. Ratings of severity range from mild (few if any problems in excess of those required to make the diagnosis and the problems cause only minor harm to others) to severe (many conduct problems in excess of those required to make the diagnosis, or conduct problems cause considerable harm to others, such as serious physical injury, extensive vandalism or theft, or manifested in prolonged absence from home). The behavior associated with the diagnosis may be displayed across a variety of settings—home, school, community—or may be specific to a given setting.

Approximately 6% of children have conduct disorders. They are more common in boys than girls. The rate in boys in the general population ranges from 6% to 16%, and the rate in girls ranges from 2% to 9% (NMHA, 2000). Among both boys and girls, conduct disorder is one of the disorders most frequently diagnosed in mental health settings (Loeber, Burke, Lahey, Winters, & Zera, 2000). Conduct disorder develops along one of three routes:

1. Early onset, in which severe symptoms are present by preschool;
2. Late childhood or early adolescent onset, in which conduct problems but not aggression are present;
3. Middle to late adolescent onset and accompanied by substance abuse.

Early onset often is accompanied by additional diagnoses such as attention deficit disorder, and these young people are at a greater risk for persistent academic and peer-relationship problems. Numerous studies of general population and clinical samples have shown strong associations of childhood antisocial behaviors with attention deficit and hyperactivity symptoms and symptoms of anxiety and depression (Angold, Costello, & Erklanli, 1999).

Family psychopathology, including parental alcohol abuse and parental criminality, critical or coercive parenting, and socioeconomic disadvantage are strongly associated with increased risk of conduct disorders (Hill, 2002). Factors that reduce the likelihood of children and adolescents developing conduct disorders include intelligence; easy-going disposition; the ability to get along well with parents, siblings, teachers, and peers; doing well in school; having friends; and having a good relationship with at least one parent and with other important adults. Another factor that reduces the likelihood of conduct disorder is commitment and adherence to the values of others in the context of families, school, and peers (Conner, 2002).

Prevention and Intervention

Based on his review of the treatment efficacy literature for young people with antisocial behavior disorders, Conner (2002) identified the following key features of effective programs:

- They are multifaceted, targeting family supports and early childhood education.
- They are designed or modified for the ecological context of a specific community.
- They encourage collaboration among community, school, and mental health professionals.
- They target youth at risk rather than those already engaging in antisocial behaviors.
- They begin as early as possible (preschool or kindergarten) and are maintained over time (at least 2 years and often longer).

The prognosis for children with early-onset conduct disorder is poorer than that for other children with conduct disorders, especially when interventions commence long after onset. Aggressiveness combined with shyness (Farrington, 1987, 1989) or peer rejection (Andersson, Bergman, & Magnusson, 1989) appears to aggravate symptoms of conduct disorder in boys. For these children, as well as children with other types of conduct disorder, social-competency training can be helpful. In addition, parent training or education can serve an important function in preventing further behavior deterioration and in modifying the child's (and the parent's) current behavior.

Patterson, Reid, and Dishion (1992) argued that inconsistent discipline in the form of coercive parenting contributes to aggression and antisocial behavior in boys. Similarly, Webster–Stratton and Hancock (1998) recommended that parent-training include attention to inadequate or ineffective discipline; inadequate parental involvement, monitoring, or supervision of children; and negative modeling.

Finally, teachers often need assistance in dealing with conduct-disordered children. Already dealing with the heavy demands of growing class sizes and children with less home support and more substantial problems, teachers sometimes are tempted to utilize strategies that are effective in maintaining order for the short-term (e.g., removing the student from the classroom) but that fail to increase the likelihood of longer-term solutions (e.g., the student learning to behave appropriately while in the classroom).

School counselors are crucial in facilitating teachers' ability to work with conduct-disordered students in the classroom. Among the important roles the school counselor can play are: working with teachers and students to develop a consistent set of procedures and reinforcements, recommending appropriate assessment procedures when learning problems or other issues complicate the student's difficulties, coordinating interdisciplinary teams to provide the student and teacher with the support they need to continue pursuing their educational goals together, and providing encouragement to teachers and students.

In sum, interventions that are most likely to succeed begin early, include families and/or parents and teachers, deliver social-competency training for the young person with the conduct disorder, and facilitate the translation of new skills into home and school environments.

Substance Abuse and Addiction

Incidence and Characteristics

Substance abuse is defined in the DSM–IV (APA, 1994) as the pathological use of a substance that causes significant impairment in social, school, or occupational functioning. Common indicators are withdrawal from family or friends; change of friends; change in appearance; loss of initiative; drop in grades; emotional highs and lows; becoming more secretive; runaway attempts; defiance; and the disappearance of money, alcohol, or prescription drugs from the home. Important factors for the counselor to assess include frequency of use, quantity used, variety of substances used, consequences of use, context in which the substance(s) are used, and emotional state of the abuser.

Systematically conducted research on rates of substance use in children and adolescents is rare, but the information that is available is troubling. Based on a review of this research, J. J. McWhirter et al. (2004) reported that 80%–85% of high school students have used alcohol. According to the Forum on Child and Family Statistics (2002), 30% of high school seniors, 25% of 10th-graders, and 13% of 8th-graders report heavy drinking (i.e., at least five drinks in a row at least once in the previous 2 week period), and males are more likely than females to drink heavily. Alcohol is the most commonly used substance during adolescence and is associated with numerous serious consequences including motor vehicle accidents, injuries and deaths, school and work problems, and involvement in violent crime, either as offender or victim (Forum on Child and Family Statistics, 2002). Tobacco use during adolescence also is quite common, with many children experimenting with tobacco by age 9.

The use of both of these substances seems to be starting at earlier and earlier ages, and tobacco and alcohol are considered to be "threshold" substances that tend to lead to the use of illicit drugs. Regular cigarette smoking ranges from about 7% for 7th-graders to 19% for high school seniors, with differing rates between racial and ethnic groups. White students have the highest rates of smoking, followed by Hispanics and then African Americans (Forum on Child and Family Statistics, 2002).

Illicit drug use is reported by 26% of high school seniors, 23% of 10th-graders, and 12% of 8th-graders, with males more likely to use illicit drugs than females in each grade (Forum on Child and Family Statistics, 2002). Contrary to prevailing stereotypes, African American youths have lower rates of illicit drug use, as well as alcohol use, than do White and Hispanic youths, with 19% of African American, 25% of Hispanic, and 27% of White students reporting illicit drug use in the past month (Forum on Child and Family Statistics, 2002). Gay and lesbian youth are at high risk for substance abuse and alcoholism (Sullivan & Wodarski, 2002). As many as 50% of gay adolescents report the use of illicit substances, and 80% report using alcohol by their senior year of high school (Olsen, 2000). Counselors have to consider the social contexts that may play a part in placing these groups at greater risk for substance abuse and tailor their prevention and intervention efforts accordingly.

Social, personal, and peer group variables all contribute to substance abuse in youth. Social variables include prior experience with drugs (the best predictor of future use is prior use), social reinforcement by peers, media reinforcement of substance use as an appropriate solution to physical complaints, and the glamorization of substance use by the television and movie industries. Further, behavioral modeling by older siblings, parents, and peers increases the likelihood of drug use by adolescents, and family environments that are disruptive or disorganized tend to produce teens who are more likely to use drugs.

Families experiencing high levels of conflict are more likely to have low levels of parent–child involvement, poor parental monitoring, and higher association with deviant peers—all strong predictors of engagement in an array of problem behaviors, including substance use (Ary, Duncan, Duncan, & Hops, 1999). Personal factors that can lead to chemical dependency include a high level of self-criticism, chronic sense of failure, depression, and anxiety. These factors, combined with ineffective coping skills, may lead young people to use drugs to gain relief. Drug use also is motivated by pleasure-seeking and a desire for independence and autonomy.

Other personal factors associated with increased substance use are deviant behavior, the need for excitement and risk-taking, and low interpersonal trust. Finally, peer groups have a strong influence on adolescents' decisions to use drugs, as discussed in the framework of peer cluster theory (Beauvais et al., 1996; Oetting & Beauvais, 1987).

Drug use is associated with physiological, psychosocial, and legal consequences, which vary with the substance used. Most substances alter the user's sense of reality, judgment, and sensory perceptions because they interfere with central nervous system functioning and other bodily functions. Automobile accidents, drug overdoses, and long-term physical effects, such as lung cancer and severe impairment of internal organs, can result from the use of addictive substances. Psychosocial consequences of drug use during childhood and adolescence include early sexual involvement, early marriage, fewer educational opportunities, and unemployment.

Prevention and Intervention

A variety of prevention and treatment interventions have been developed to address substance use and abuse. Information-based preventive interventions are probably the most common strategy used in schools. For young people to be able to make positive decisions about whether to use drugs, the information provided must be relevant, accurate, and focus on increasing knowledge and fostering healthy attitudes. Two other ways to intervene with adolescents at risk for substance abuse are parent education and family therapy. Dishion and Kavanagh (2001) describe an ecological approach to family intervention for adolescent substance use, with the use of a multilevel approach in which each level of intervention builds on the previous level. Elements of this ecological approach include establishing family-based services in the school setting, which allows for collaboration between school staff and parents, and disseminating information to families that promote practices to discourage alcohol and drug use among youth.

Another level of intervention, the Family Check-Up, offers family assessment, professional support, and motivation to maintain current, positive parenting practices and alter disruptive practices. At this point, a menu of options is offered to parents of adolescents with problem behaviors, including brief family interventions, parent groups, behavioral family therapy, and case management services. The Family Check-Up focuses on engaging parents in treatment, promoting motivation to participate, and providing support and information to parents about how improved family management practices can protect children against risk and provide a context for healing (Dishion & Kavanagh, 2001).

Additional treatment approaches for adolescents include basic counseling strategies that do not involve medication, as well as drug-free programs, outdoor experiences, group therapy, brief or long-term individual therapy, and placement in therapeutic communities that attempt to resocialize the drug abuser using peer influence and group action in a structured, isolated, mutual-help environment. Other treatment options include residential adolescent treatment programs, day treatment programs, and aftercare programs. Schools may offer treatment programs, too.

All of these programs typically involve confronting the individual about his or her behavior. In addition, they emphasize the importance of taking responsibility and facing consequences for behavior, provide accurate education about drugs, teach skills for realistically evaluating both the costs and the benefits of drug use, and address the factors that have led to the substance use, including peer influences, family problems, low self-esteem, and poor interpersonal skills. School-based substance-abuse treatment programs also include assertiveness training, decision-making strategies, and discussion of peer group influences.

The programs that are most likely to be effective are those that address, in addition to the individual young person, the family and school contexts. School counselors who are familiar with community resources for treating substance abuse can provide valuable information and support to young people and families affected by substance problems.

Depressive Disorders

Incidence and Characteristics

Symptoms of major depressive disorder (MDD) include depressed mood, markedly diminished interest or pleasure in most activities, significant weight loss or gain, insomnia or hypersomnia, psychomotor agitation or retardation, fatigue, feelings of worthlessness or inappropriate guilt, diminished ability to concentrate, and recurring thoughts of death or suicidal ideation (APA, 1994). Symptoms of dysthymic disorder—a chronic sense of dysphoria that is less intense than MDD—include poor appetite or overeating, low energy or fatigue, low self-esteem, poor concentration or indecision, and feelings of hopelessness (APA, 1994).

Although efforts have been made to differentiate adolescent and adult depression, counselors often apply to children the criteria that have been developed to define adult depression without taking into account developmental considerations that may affect the etiology, course, and outcome of depression in children and adolescents (Cicchetti & Toth, 1998). Signs that may be associated with depression in children and adolescents include frequent physical complaints such as headaches, stomachaches, muscle aches or fatigue, school absence or poor performance in school, talking about running away or efforts to run away from home, outburts of anger, irritability or crying, boredom and lack of interest in previous activities, alcohol or substance abuse, heightened social sensitivity and difficulty in relationships, and fear of death (National Institute of Mental Health, 2000). Depression in children and adolescents is associated with anxiety disorders, disruptive behaviors, substance-abuse disorders, physical illnesses such as diabetes, and increased risk of suicidal behaviors (NIMH, 2000).

From a review of the epidemiological studies of major depressive disorder, Cicchetti and Toth (1998) found the prevalence of major depression in adolescence to be between 15% and 20%. Risk factors for the onset of depressive disorders include having a parent or other close relative with a mood disorder, severe stressors such as divorce in the family, traumatic experiences or a learning disorder, low self-esteem, low self-efficacy, a sense of helplessness and hopelessness, living in poverty, and being female (Beardslee & Gladstone, 2001). In their review of the literature, Aube, Fichman, Saltaris, and Koestner (2000) noted that research has consistently shown that the rate of female depression is twice that of males and that this difference emerges as early as adolescence. Certain characteristics of the feminine gender role in interpersonal functioning reflecting excessive caregiving and difficulties in being assertive may be linked to the gender differences in depression that emerge in adolescence (Aube et al., 2000).

The results of a longitudinal study of low-SES families showed that adverse early family environments, including maternal depression, abuse, deficits in supportive early care, and overall maternal stress are particularly associated with prepubertal-onset depression, whereas maternal depression is particularly associated with the development of depression in adolescent females, and lack of supportive early care is associated with adolescent depression in males (Duggal, Carlson, Sroufe, & Egeland, 2001). This finding is consistent with another study showing that mothers' history of depression was significantly associated with higher levels of depressive symptoms in their adolescents (Garber, Keiley, & Martin, 2002). Duggal et al. (2001) noted that the identification of such risk factors underscores the importance of early intervention to prevent depression in the children of lower-SES families.

We must not minimize depression during childhood and adolescence as being a part of a "phase." Depressive disorders are not normal developmental events, nor are they short-lived problems that will pass with time (Kovacs, 1989). Depressive episodes predict the development of recurring depressive disorder, as well as comorbid diagnoses, in particular anxiety disorders and alcohol or substance abuse, and suicide attempts (Cicchetti & Toth, 1998). Cicchetti and Toth (1998) point to the importance of understanding the complex developmental processes that contribute to the emergence of depressive disorders and of taking into account the interplay of the psychological, social, and biological components that are involved.

Further, as indicated earlier, we must consider the possibility that theories of and interventions for depression in adults may not be appropriately applied to depression in adolescents (Mueller & Orvaschel, 1997). For a treatment to be effective, the client's environment, attitude toward therapy, cognitive development, and maturity must be considered—factors that, clearly, are likely to be quite different for adolescents than adults. When working toward an understanding of depression in an adolescent, the counselor must consider issues of separation from family, creation of the adolescent's identity, interpersonal challenges the adolescent faces, such as the development of new peer groups and intimate relationships, and physical and cognitive milestones (Mueller & Orvaschel, 1997). Family factors that have been associated with developing and maintaining depression in adolescents include excessively rigid or lax family structure, low socioeconomic status, parental death, divorce, or separation, and child maltreatment (Cicchetti & Toth, 1998).

Finally, the school environment must be considered an important player in adolescents' psychological and academic adjustment, especially since depressive symptoms have been shown to increase during the middle school years (Cicchetti & Toth, 1998). School and peer issues can contribute to an environment in which depression can take root and grow (Goldman, 2001).

Prevention and Intervention

The treatment of adolescent depression requires that counselors alter adult treatments, making them developmentally appropriate for adolescents and consistent with the ways in which adolescents express depression (Mueller & Orvaschel, 1997). Psychotherapy seems to be a more promising approach than pharmacological approaches (Cicchetti & Toth, 1998; Mueller & Orvaschel, 1997). Nevertheless, Zito and Safer (2001) note a three- to fivefold increase between 1988 and 1994 in the prevalence of antidepressant treatment of youths aged 2–19, while research into the safety and efficacy of the use of these medications for pediatric populations lags behind the clinical use (Emslie & Mayes, 2001). Some studies have shown that newer antidepressant medications can be safe and efficacious for the short-term treatment of severe and persistent depression in young people (NIMH, 2000; Wagner & Ambrosini, 2001). After reviewing studies of specific psychotherapies for childhood and adolescent depression, Curry (2001) noted the demonstrated efficacy of cognitive behavior therapies (CBT) and interpersonal therapy (IPT) in reducing depression, but pointed to the need for research that investigates combined treatments such as CBT and medication, that includes depressed individuals with comorbid disorders, and that addresses all phases of a depressive episode to minimize relapse (Curry, 2001).

Cicchetti and Toth (1998) have pointed out that most studies have concentrated on middle- or upper-class youth and have not included youth of color, resulting in a need for research on treatment with diverse populations. Preventive, community-based programs that are supportive of healthy family relationships, that promote child competence, and that educate families about the effects of parental depression are needed to reduce the prevalence of depressive disorders (Cicchetti & Toth, 1998).

From the perspective of the prevention/intervention framework described by J. J. McWhirter et al. (2004), counselors working with depressed youth should implement prevention, early intervention, or treatment strategies that involve the family, the school, and the community. A family approach to prevention and treatment might include both family therapy and parent training that promote open and healthy communication, training in problem solving and conflict resolution, and training in active listening skills. When working with minority and majority culture families alike, family approaches must take cultural variables into account.

One of the authors of this chapter (R. S.) recently worked with "Tanya," a 14-year-old girl who was depressed. Individual therapy sessions focused on identifying and altering Tanya's negative patterns of thinking and helping her to develop coping strategies for dealing with painful feelings. The counselor also saw Tanya in joint sessions with her mother and older brother, sessions directed at changing some of their negative patterns of interaction and at increasing positive interactions and activities. Finally, Tanya received group counseling with other girls who were struggling with self-esteem and body-image concerns. These group sessions fostered Tanya's communication skills and lessened her sense of isolation.

Prevention and intervention in the school setting can include programs with specific topics, such as the group Tanya attended, or they may more generally focus on life-skills training. Prevention at the community level might be directed to reducing the social stigma associated with seeking treatment for a mental disorder, promoting increased awareness of the availability and effectiveness of treatments for depression (e.g., through free depression screenings), and educating the public about the consequences of depressive disorders and the importance of intervention (Cicchetti & Toth, 1998).

The Case Example of Julia

Julia, a 14-year-old Mexican American eighth grader, lives with her mother and two younger siblings, a sister, age 10, and a brother, 4. When Julia was 11, she was molested by her mother's boyfriend. He disappeared after the incident, and Julia did not disclose what happened until one month ago. Julia's mother, Trini, 32, has had ongoing problems with depression since prior to Julia's birth, and Julia frequently is left responsible for caring for her younger siblings when her mother is unable to function effectively.

Julia recently has begun to skip classes and is hanging out with a group of 17- and 18-year-olds. She has started drinking and experimenting with marijuana and speed, and she informed her mother that she plans to have sex with her 17-year-old boyfriend. Two weeks ago Julia ran away and stayed with her boyfriend's family for several days. She returned home, and Trini has brought her in for counseling, saying, "I don't know what to do with her anymore. Fix her." Julia came across as angry and resentful at this interference in her life and stated that she doesn't need counseling.

Given Julia's resentment and anger over being brought to see a counselor, it is critical to begin by validating her feelings about seeing a counselor. This is essential to laying the groundwork for the formation of a collaborative relationship. If Julia does not feel respected, the counseling relationship will not progress. To define the problem areas Julia believes to be most relevant, the counselor must gain an understanding of how Julia perceives her home life, school, and relationships.

Because Julia's home life has been riddled with problems and painful experiences, the counselor might work with her on understanding how the molestation and her mother's depression have affected Julia's current feelings, perceived options, and decisions. For example, talking about what it is like to live with a mother who does not get out of bed for several days straight and to be burdened with caring for younger siblings could help identify the factors that led to her decision to run away to her boyfriend's home.

The counselor's consideration of these contextual factors would convey to Julia at several levels that the counselor is not attempting to blame her for her behavior. Understanding the Mexican American culture, as well as sensitivity to cultural variation, Julia's ethnic identity, and the roles that culture and identity play in Julia's experience of the world, will also be an important component in establishing the relationship and working collaboratively.

Helping Julia consider how her life context has contributed to decisions she has made would be the beginning of power analysis. As Julia develops a growing sense of trust in the counselor, they could explore in increasing detail the situations Julia has experienced at home, the choices she has made, and the consequences of her choices. Fostering Julia's ability to step back from her behavior and consider alternative actions, consequences, and outcomes in her home, school, and peer contexts would help Julia develop the life skill of reflective decision making.

Because Julia has only recently made choices to change her peer group, to experiment with drugs and alcohol, and to potentially engage in sexual intercourse, she may not feel very secure in or satisfied with these choices, despite her defiant behavior toward her mother. The counselor and Julia could critically self-reflect on the effects of the decisions she has made, or plans to make, and further explore her sense of responsibility and self-efficacy for making different—or at least more reflective—choices concerning each of these issues. Julia still may decide to be sexually active, but if she first considers options and feels able to make her own informed choices instead of falling into decisions, she will be more likely to use measures to prevent pregnancy and STDs.

Julia has endured a tremendous amount of stress and has found ways to cope and survive. This demonstrates that she has a good deal of strength. The counselor should consistently provide feedback about Julia's strengths and resources and encourage her to acknowledge her many positive characteristics. Specific feedback is harder to dismiss than generalities—an important consideration when working with discouraged young people like Julia. Enhanced self-esteem may help Julia make more positive life choices about friendships, school, drug use, and her body.

After a strong foundation of trust is established, it might be appropriate to work directly on issues of sexual molestation. The six-stage model of rape response described by Remer (1986) is helpful for describing recovery from rape as well as other incidents of sexual violence. The counselor might explore these stages with Julia, tailoring the information to fit her context and developmental level.

Stage 1, *pre-rape,* refers to the social context existing at the time of the rape and includes all of the life experiences of the survivor, as well as the survivor's sex-role socialization and cultural norms. For Julia, this was the time prior to age 11. Her mother was often emotionally and physically unavailable even then, leaving Julia alone with her boyfriends on a number of occasions. Thus, even prior to the molestation, Julia often felt alone and vulnerable.

Stage 2, the *rape event,* involves the events immediately preceding, during, and after the rape. The survivor's perceptions, feelings, and behaviors, as well as the behaviors of the perpetrator, are important to explore. The counselor should be sensitive to the complexity of Julia's memory and her constructions of an event that happened 3 years earlier. Listening for indicators of self-blame is critical. The counselor also should explore with Julia how she coped with the molestation as it happened—perhaps by dissociating, pleading, struggling, or remaining motionless—and help Julia honor her own way of surviving this threatening and frightening situation.

Stage 3, *crisis and disorganization,* relates to the time period immediately after the rape or other incident, characterized by feelings of helplessness, shock, confusion, guilt, and numbness. The stage may last for hours or up to a year (Remer, 1996). Blaming reactions from others intensify the negativity of this time period and make healing more difficult. When Julia told Trini about the molestation during an argument, Trini initially reacted with anger, shouting, "So that's why he took off all of a sudden, you liar! What else did you do?" Subsequently Trini began feeling guilty but seemed unable to communicate effectively with Julia about her enormous sense of responsibility, shame, and self-directed anger.

The counselor could explore with Julia how the onset of her drinking and drug use coincided with her mother's negative reaction to the molestation, and work with Trini and Julia together to help them communicate about and cope with this difficult issue. Joint sessions might promote faster healing and prevent further deterioration of their relationship.

Stage 4, *outward satisfactory adjustment and denial,* reflects the survivor's attempt to return life to normal. The survivor utilizes avoidance strategies such as minimizing what happened, blocking out memory of the event, denying that the incident occurred, or repressing details of the experience. Although the client may express that she is "fine," symptoms such as depression and nightmares are common. Julia probably has been in this stage for a long time. Although she is able to describe what happened, she appears lethargic about it, presenting the attitude of, "It's no big deal—just the way it was."

Julia's more recent behavior suggests that she may be trying to prevent the onset of stage 5, *reliving and working through.* This stage begins when denial breaks down and may occur in response to a movie scene, a smell, a comment, or in response to some unidentifiable stimulus. In this stage the survivor relives the experience, often vividly, has flashbacks and intense nightmares, and reexperiences the crisis stage that occurred immediately after the incident.

Stage 6, *resolution and integration,* is characterized by integrating the experience into the survivor's life. The person no longer blames herself and accepts that the experience occurred and is a part of her personal history. The survivor appreciates her own personal strengths that helped her to survive the experience and frequently participates in organized efforts to prevent rape or to help other survivors. Many survivors recycle through stages 5 and 6 several times, each time achieving a higher level of integration and functioning. Teaching Julia about the stages of response might assist her in healing, by normalizing her reactions and providing a source of validation and hope.

Given that most of Julia's problems stem from her stressful home environment and, specifically, her relationship with her mother, the counselor should intervene on the family level. The counselor has to attend to Trini's concerns and find ways to actively encourage and support her in her parenting role. Parent training sessions or participation in a parent support group could allow Trini to build self-confidence in her ability to be an effective parent who is capable of caring for all three of her children. The parent group meetings might help Trini begin to develop a support network with other parents who have similar stresses of rearing an adolescent.

After assessing Trini's ethnic identity, the counselor should identify, if possible, parenting groups that involve other parents of the same ethnicity, which would help broaden Trini's experience of support and community. Based on what the counselor knows of Trini's depression, the counselor also should refer her for individual counseling to provide assessment and treatment. Trini likely would benefit significantly from having additional, individual social and emotional support. Further, the family might benefit from a series of family sessions that emphasize communication. Developing a family project that involves everyone and demonstrates support for Julia would be ideal. For example, the family could plan a small quincinera or 15th birthday celebration for Julia, with each family member contributing ideas, decorations, and homemade gifts.

Fostering in Julia a sense of belonging and of contributing to a community should be a vital component in this counselor's work. Julia has disengaged herself from the school community and has never felt a connection with the greater community in which she lives. Her grades have dropped significantly over the course of this school year as a result of her increasingly withdrawn behavior in school. As Julia develops a better sense of her strengths, she might be able to work with the counselor to identify ways to contribute to her school community.

Ultimately, Julia might be able to serve as a peer mediator or a peer counselor, helping other students in situations similar to hers to obtain the support they need. Engaging Julia in discussion about her future aspirations might help to identify ways for her to participate in the larger community. For example, if Julia is interested in children, the counselor could help her find volunteer opportunities at a women's shelter or in a Head Start classroom.

Helping Julia see the connection between her current educational activities and her future could be critical to preventing her from dropping out of school and might generate within Julia a new sense of autonomy and responsibility. The counselor may be able to serve as an advocate for Julia, meeting with the school counselor or teachers, and engaging in behavioral observations at Julia's school to understand her school experience better.

Julia also might benefit from group counseling and/or skills training focused on making positive life choices or learning problem-solving skills for negotiating difficult peer and family situations. Because Julia does not have an older sibling, the counselor could attempt to find a young Mexican American woman to serve as a mentor or "big sister." The women's center at the local community college, the Latino community center, or the local church might be able to assist the counselor in identifying potential mentors.

In these ways, Julia's counselor could integrate the five Cs of empowerment into the intervention. The counselor's intervention plan would be multifaceted, involving individual, family, and community approaches for building on Julia's strengths and providing the support, fostering the skills, and accessing the resources that would enable Julia to successfully negotiate the challenges of her life.

Summary

Working with children and adolescents in crisis can be difficult, and the counseling process is made more complex by the severity of the challenges young people face. Awareness of the complexity of the problems faced by today's youth, together with knowledge of the range of community and school programs and resources that are locally available, can help counselors deliver more comprehensive and effective interventions. Advocacy for broader social and policy change is a necessary adjunct to the direct work that counselors do with young people and will help lay the foundation for a better future.

References

Adler, A. (1930). *The education of children.* South Bend, IN: Gateway.

Adler, A. (1964). *Social interest: A challenge to mankind.* New York: Capricorn.

Allan Guttmacher Institute (1999). *Teen sex and pregnancy.* Washington DC: Author.

American Association of University Women. (1989). *Equitable treatment of girls and boys in the classroom,* Washington, DC: AAUW.

American Association of University Women, Educational Foundation (1998). Gender gaps: Where schools still fail our children. Retrieved July 28, 2002, from http://www.aauw.org/2000/GGES.pdf

American Counseling Association, Ethics Committee. (1995). ACA proposed standards of practice and ethical standards. *Guidepost, 36*(4), 15–22.

American Psychiatric Association (1998). *Let's talk facts about teen suicide.* Washington, DC: APA.

American Psychiatric Association. (1994). *Diagnostic and statistical manual of mental disorders* (4th ed.). Washington, DC: Author.

American Psychological Association, Presidential Task Force on Violence and the Family. (1996). *Violence and the family.* Washington, DC: APA.

Andersson, T., Bergman, L. R., & Magnusson, D. (1989). Patterns of adjustment, problems, and alcohol abuse in early adulthood: A prospective longitudinal study. *Development and Psychopathology, 1,* 119–131.

Angold, A., Costello, E. J., & Erkanli, A. (1999). Comorbidity. *Journal of Child Psychology and Psychiatry, 40,* 57–87.

Annie E. Casey Foundation (1999). *Why teens have sex: Issues and trends.* Baltimore: Author.

Araki, D., Takeshita, C., & Kadomoto, L. (1989). *Research results and final report for the Dispute Management in the Schools project.* Honolulu: University of Hawaii at Manoa, Program on Conflict Resolution.

Ary, D. V., Duncan, T. E., Duncan, S. C., & Hops, H. (1999). Adolescent problem behavior: The influence of parents and peers. *Behavior Research and Therapy, 37,* 217–230.

Aube, J., Fichman, L., Saltaris, C., & Koestner, R. (2000). Gender differences in adolescent depressive symptomatology: Towards an integrated social–develomental model. *Journal of Social and Clinical Psychology, 19*(3), 297–313.

Beardslee, W. R., & Gladstone, T. R. G. (2001). Prevention of childhood depression: Recent findings and future prospects. *Biological Psychiatry, 49,* 1101–1110.

Beauvais, F. (1998). American Indians and alcohol. *Alcohol Health and Research World, 22*(4), 253–259.

Beauvais, F., Chavez, E. L., Oetting, E. R., Deffenbacher, J. L., & Cornell, G. R. (1996). Drug use, violence, and victimization among White American, Mexican American, and American Indian dropouts, students with academic problems, and students in good academic standing. *Journal of Counseling Psychology, 43,* 292–299.

Beck, A. T., Ward, S. H., Mendelson, M., Mock, J., & Erbaugh, 1. (1961). An inventory for measuring depression. *Archives of General Psychiatry, 4,* 561–571.

Berkowitz, C. D. (1998). Medical consequences of child sexual abuse. *Child Abuse and Neglect, 22*(6), 541–550.

Blake, C., Wang, W. Cartledge, G., & Gardner, R. (2000). Middle school students with serious emotional disturbances serve as social skills trainers and reinforcers for peers with SED. *Behavioral Disorders, 25,* 280–298.

Bronfenbrenner, U., McClelland, R., Wethington, F., Moen, P., & Ceci, S. (1996). *The state of Americans: This generation and the next.* New York: Free Press.

Brown, L. K., Lourie, K. J., Zlotnick, C., & Cohn J. (2000). Impact of sexual abuse on the HIV-risk-related behavior of adolescents in intensive psychiatric treatment. *American Journal of Psychiatry, 157*(9), 1413–1415.

Brown, L. M., & Gilligan, C. (1992). *Meeting at the crossroads: Women's psychology and girls' development.* Cambridge, MA: Harvard University Press.

Child Trends, Inc. (2001). *Facts at a glance.* Washington, DC: Author.

Children's Defense Fund (2001). The State of America's Children Yearbook 2001. Retrieved July 10, 2001, from http://www.childrensdefense.org/keyfacts.htm

Cicchetti, D., & Toth, S. L. (1998). The development of depression in children and adolescents. *American Psychologist, 53*(2), 221–241.

Conner, D. F. (2002). *Aggression and antisocial behavior in childhood and adolescence.* New York: Guilford Press.

Curry, J. F. (2001). Specific psychotherapies for childhood and adolescent depression. *Biological Psychiatry, 49,* 1091–1100.

David and Lucille Packard Foundation (Spring/Summer 2002). Children, Youth and Gun Violence. *The Future of Children.* Author. Retrieved August 29, 2002, from http://www.futureofchildren.org/index.htm

Dishion, T. J., & Kavanagh, K. (2001). An ecological approach to family intervention for adolescent substance use. In E. F. Wagner & H. B. Waldron (Eds.), *Innovations in adolescent substance abuse interventions.* Oxford: Pergamon.

Dishion, T. J., McCord, J., & Poulin, F. (1999). When interventions harm: Peer groups and problem behavior. *American Psychologist, 54*(9), 755–764.

Dreikurs, R. (1964). *Children: The challenge.* New York: Hawthorne.

Dreikurs, R. (1967). *Psychology in the classroom.* New York: Harper & Row.

Duggal, S., Carlson, E. A., Sroufe, L. A., & Egeland, B. (2001). Depressive symptomatology in childhood and adolescence. *Development and Psychopathology, 13,* 143–164.

Eccles, J. S., & Midgley, C. (1989). Stage/environment fit: Developmentally appropriate class-rooms for early adolescents. In R. E. Ames & C. Ames (Eds.), *Research on motivation in education* (Vol. 3, pp. 139–186). San Diego: Academic Press.

Eccles, J. S., Midgley, C., & Adler, T. (1984). Grade-related changes in the school environment: Effects on achievement motivation. In I. G. Nicholls (Ed.), *The development of achievement motivation* (pp. 283–331). Greenwich, CT: JAI Press.

Eccles, J. S., Midgley, C., Wigfield, A., Buchanan, C. M., Reuman, D., Flanagan, C., & MacIver, D. (1993). Development during adolescence: The impact of stage environment fit on young adolescents' experiences in schools and in families. *American Psychologist, 48*(2), 90–101.

Emery, R. E., & Laumann–Billings, L. (1998). An overview of the nature, causes, and consequences of abusive family relationships: Toward differentiating maltreatment and violence. *American Psychologist, 53*(2), 121–135.

Emslie, G. J., & Mayes, T. L. (2001). Mood disorders in children and adolescents: psychopharmacological treatment, *Biological Psychiatry, 49*, 1082–1090.

Farrington, D. P. (1987). Epidemiology. In H. C. Quay (Ed.), *Handbook of juvenile delinquency* (pp. 33–61). New York: Wiley.

Farrington, D. P. (1989). Early predictors of adolescent aggression and adult violence. *Violence Victim, 4*(2), 79–100.

Faulkner, A. H., & Cranston, K. (1998). Correlates of same-sex sexual behavior in a random sample of Massachusetts high school students. *American Journal of Public Health 88*(2), 262–266.

Flannery, D. J., Williams, L. L., & Vazsonyi, A. T. (1999). Who are they with and what are they doing? Delinquent behavior, substance use, and early adolescents' after-school time. *American Journal of Orthopsychiatry, 69*(2), 247–253.

Forum on Child and Family Statistics (2002). America's children 2002: Key national indicators of well-being. Retrieved August 4, 2002, from http://www.childstats.gov/americaschildren/

Furstenberg, E. F. (1993). How families manage risk and opportunity in dangerous neighborhoods. In W. J. Wilson (Ed.), Sociology *and the public agenda* (pp. 231–258). Newbury Park, CA: Sage.

Garber, J., Keiley, M. K., & Martin, N. C. (2002). Developmental trajectories of adolescent' depressive symptoms: Predictors of change. *Journal of Consulting and Clinical Psychology, 70*(1), 79–95.

Garland, A. E., & Zigler, E. (1993). Adolescent suicide prevention: Current research and social policy implications. *American Psychologist, 48*(2), 169–182.

Gershoff, E. (2002). Corporal punishment by parents and associated child behaviors and experiences: A meta-analytic and theoretical review. *Psychological Bulletin, 128*, 539–579.

Gilligan, C. (1982). *In a different voice.* Cambridge, MA: Harvard University Press.

Gillis, A. M. (1998). School violence. *Outlook, 92*(1), 12–17.

Gleason, P., & Dynarski, M. (2002). Do we know whom to serve? Issues in using risk factors to identify dropouts. *Journal of Education for Students Placed at Risk, 7*(1), 25–41.

Goldman, W. T. (2001). Depression in children. Retrieved July 28, 2002, from http://www.keepkidshealthy.com/cgi-bin/MasterPFP.cgi

Goyette–Ewing, M. (2000). Children's after-school arrangements: A study of self-care and developmental outcomes. *Journal of Prevention & Intervention in the Community 20*(1–2), 55–67.

Hamburg, D. A. (1995). *A developmental strategy to prevent lifelong damage.* New York: Carnegie Corporation of New York.

Haveman, R., & Wolfe, B. (1994). *Succeeding generations.* New York: Russell Sage Foundation.

Hill, J. (2002). Biological, psychological, and social processes in the conduct disorders. *Journal of Child Psychology and Psychiatry, 43*, 133–164.

Hoyert, D. L., Anas, E., Smith, B. L., Murphy, S. L., & Kochanek, K. D. (2001). Deaths: Final data for 1999. *National Vital Statistics Reports 49*(8). Hyattsville, MD: National Center for Health Statistics. (DHHS Publication Number (PHS) 2001–1120).

Institute of Medicine (2002). *Reducing suicide: A national imperative.* Washington, DC: National Academy Press.

Jaffee, S. R. (2002). Pathways to adversity in young adulthood among early childbearers. *Journal of Family Psychology, 16,* 38–49.

Johnson, W. (1999). *Youth suicide: School's role in prevention and relapse.* Bloomington, IN: Phi Delta Kappa Educational Foundation.

Kann, L., et al. (1998). Youth risk behavior surveillance–United States 1997. *Journal of School Health 68*(9), 355–369.

Katz, J. (1985). The sociopolitical nature of counseling. *The Counseling Psychologist, 13*(4), 615–621.

Kaufman, P., Chen, X., Choy, S. P., Peter, K., Ruddy, S. A., Miller, A. K., Fleury, J. K., Chandler, K. A., Planty, M. R., & Rand, M. R. (2001). Indicators of school crime and safety: 2001. Washington, DC: U.S. Department of Education and Justice. Bureau of Justice Statistics (BJS) and the National Center for Education Statistics (NCES). Retrieved August 10 from http://nces.ed.gov/pubs2002/quarterly/winter01/q3-4.asp

Kendler, K. S., Bulik, C. M., Silberg, J., Hettema J. M., Myers, J., Prescott, C. A. (2000). Childhood sexual abuse and adult psychiatric and substance use disorders in women. *Archives of General Psychiatry, 57,* 953–959.

Kenny, M. C., & McEachern, A. G. (2000). Racial, ethnic, and cultural factors of childhood sexual abuse: A selected review of the literature. *Clinical Psychology Review, 20*(7), 905–922.

Keys, S. G., Bemak, E, Carpenter, S. L., & King–Sears, M. E. (1998). Collaborative consultant: A new role for counselors serving at-risk youths. *Journal of Counseling & Development, 76,* 123–133.

King, K. A., Price, J. H., Telljohann, S. K., & Wahl, J. (2000). Preventing adolescent suicide: Do high school counselors know the risk factors? *Professional School Counseling, 3*(4), 255–263.

Kirby, D. (2000). School-based interventions to prevent unprotected sex and HIV among adolescents. In J. L. Peterson & R. J. DiClemente (Eds.), *Handbook of HIV prevention* (pp. 83–101). New York: Kluwer Academic Press.

Kovacs, M. (1989). Affective disorders in children and adolescents. *American Psychologist, 44,* 209–215.

Lee, C. C., & Walz, G. B. (1998). *Social action.* Alexandria, VA: American Counseling Association Press.

Lewinsohn, P., Rohde, P., Seeley, J., & Fischer, S. (1993). Age-cohort changes in the lifetime occurrence of depression and other mental disorders. *Journal of Abnormal Psychology. 102,* 110–120.

Loeber, R., Burke, J. D., Lahey, B. B., Winters, A., & Zera, M. (2000). Oppositional defiant and conduct disorder: A review of the past 10 years, Part I. *Journal of the American Academy of Child and Adolescent Psychiatry, 39,* 1468–1484.

Manlove, J., Terry–Humen, E., Papillo, A. R., Franzetta, K., Williams, S., Ryan, S. (2002). *Preventing teenage pregnancy, childbearing, and sexually transmitted diseases: What the research shows.* Washington, DC: Child Trends.

McCormick, M. (1988). *Mediation in the schools: An evaluation of the Wakefield Pilot Peer Mediation Program in Tucson, Arizona.* Washington, DC: American Bar Association.

McLoyd, V. (1998). Socioeconomic disadvantage and child development. *American Psychologist, 53*(2), 185–204.

McWhirter, E. H. (1994). *Counseling for empowerment.* Alexandria, VA: American Counseling Association.

McWhirter, E. H. (1997). Empowerment, social activism, and counseling. *Counseling & Human Development, 29*(8).

McWhirter, E. H. (1998). An empowerment model of counselor training. *Canadian Journal of Counselling, 32*(1), 12–26.

McWhirter, E. H. (2001, March). Social action at the individual level: In pursuit of critical consciousness. In P. Gore & J. Swanson (chairs), *Counseling psychologists as agents of social change.* Paper presented at Fourth National Conference on Counseling Psychology, Houston, TX.

McWhirter, J. J., McWhirter, B. T., McWhirter, A. M., & McWhirter, E. H. (2004). *At-risk youth: A comprehensive response* (3d ed.). Pacific Grove, CA: Brooks/Cole.

Metha, A., & McWhirter, E. H. (1997). Suicide ideation, depression, and stressful life events among gifted adolescents. *Journal for the Education of the Gifted, 20*(3), 284–305.

Moore, K. A., Miller, B. C., Glei, D., & Morrison, D. R. (1995). *Early sex, contraception, and childbearing: A review of recent research.* Washington, DC: Child Trends.

Mueller, C. & Orvaschel, H. (1997). The failure of "adult" interventions with adolescent depression: What does it mean for theory, research, and practice? *Journal of Affective Disorders, 44,* 203–215.

National Campaign to Prevent Teen Pregnancy (2001, May). *Emerging answers: Research findings on programs to reduce teen pregnancy.* Washington, DC: Author.

National Center for Educational Statistics (2001). Nonfatal Teacher Victimization at School: Teacher Reports. Retrieved June 8, 2002, from http://nces.ed.gov/pubs2002/crime2001/10.asp?nav=3

National Center for Injury Prevention and Control (NCIPC) (2001). Web-based injury statistics query and reports system. Retrieved August 5, 2002, from http://www.cdc.gov/ncipc/wisqars

National Institute of Mental Health (2000). Depression in children and adolescents: A fact sheet for physicians. Retrieved July 28, 2002, from http://www.nimh.nih.gov/publicat/depchildresfact.cfm

National Mental Health Association (NMHA) (2000). Conduct disorder fact sheet. Retrieved August 7, 2002, from http://www.nmha.org/infoctr/factsheets/74.cfm

Neumark–Sztainer, D., Story, M., Hannan, P., Beuhring, T., & Resnick, M. (2000). Disordered eating among adolescents: Associations with sexual/physical abuse and other familial/psychosocial factors. *International Journal of Eating Disorders, 28*(3), 249–258.

Oetting, E. R., & Beauvais, E. (1987). Peer cluster theory, socialization characteristics, and adolescent drug use: A path analysis. *Journal of Counseling Psychology, 34*(2), 205–213.

Olsen, E. D. (2000). Gay teens and substance use disorders: Assessment & treatment. *Journal of Gay and Lesbian Psychotherapy, 3*(3–4), 69–80.

Patterson, G. R., Reid, J. B., & Dishion, T. J. (1992). *Antisocial boys.* Eugene, OR: Castalia.

Peake, A. (1987). An evaluation of group work for sexually abused adolescent girls and boys. *Educational and Child Psychology, 4*(3–4), 189–203.

Pryor, D. B. & Tollerud, T. R. (1999). Applications of Adlerian principles in school settings. *Professional School Counseling, 2*(4), 299–304.

Remer, P. (1986). *Stages in coping with rape.* Unpublished manuscript.

Savin–Williams, R. C. (1994). Verbal and physical abuse as stressors in the lives of lesbian, gay male, and bisexual youths: Associations with school problems, running away, substance abuse, prostitution, and suicide. *Journal of Consulting and Clinical Psychology, 62*(2), 261–269.

Schwendiman, J., & Fager, J. (1999, January). *After-school programs: Good for kids, good for communities.* Portland, OR: Northwest Regional Educational Laboratory.

Shure, M. B. (1999, April). Preventing violence: The problem solving way. *Juvenile Justice Bulletin,* 1–11.

Sinclair, M. F., Hurley, C. M., Evelo, D. L., Christenson, S. L., & Thurlow, M. L. (2002). Making connections that keep students coming to school. In B. Algozzine & P. Kay (Eds.) *Preventing problem behaviors: A handbook of successful prevention strategies* (pp. 162–182). Thousand Oaks, CA: Sage.

Straus, M. B. (1994). *Violence in the lives of adolescents.* New York: Norton.

Sullivan, M., & Wodarski, J. S. (2001). Social alienation in gay youth. *Journal of Human Behavior in the Social Environment, 5*(1), 1–17.

Sue, D. & Sue, D. W. (1991). Counseling strategies for Chinese Americans. In C. C. Lee & B. L. Richardson (Eds.), *Multicultural issues in counseling: New approaches to diversity* (pp. 79–90). Alexandria, VA: American Association for Counseling and Development.

Sweeney, T. J. (1998). *Adlerian counseling: A practitioner's approach* (4th ed.). Philadelphia: Taylor & Francis.

Taylor, B., Pressley, M., & Pearson, D. (2000). *Research-supported characteristics of teachers and schools that promote reading achievement.* Center for the Improvement of Early Reading Achievement.

U.S. Department of Health and Human Services, Children's Bureau (2002). National Child Abuse and Neglect Data System (NCANDS). Summary of Key Findings from Calendar Year 2000. Retrieved August 6, 2002, from http:// www.acf.dhhs.gov/programs/cb/publications/index.htm

Vidal, J. A. (1989). Establishing a suicide prevention program. *National Association of Secondary School Principals Bulletin, 70,* 68–71.

Vogeltanz, N. D., Wilsnack, S. C., Harris, T. R., Wilsnack, R. W., Wonderlich, S. A., & Kristjanson, A. F. (1999). Prevalence and risk factors for childhood sexual abuse in women: National survey findings. *Child Abuse and Neglect, 23*(6), 579–592.

Wagner, K. D., & Ambrosini, P. J. (2001). Childhood depression: Pharmacological therapy/treatment (pharmacotherapy of childhood depression). *Journal of Clinical Child Psychology, 30*(1), 88–97.

Way, N., & Leadbeater, B. (1999). Pathways toward educational achievement among African American and Puerto Rican adolescent mothers: Reexamining the role of social support from families. *Development and Psychopathology, 11,* 349–361.

Webster–Stratton, C., & Hancock, L. (1998). Training for parents of young children with conduct problems: Content, methods, and therapeutic processes. In J. M. Briesmeister & C. E. Schaefer (Eds.), *Handbook of parent training: Parents as co-therapists for children's behavior problems* (2d ed.). (pp. 98–152). New York: John Wiley & Sons.

Wolf, V. B. (1993). Group therapy of young latency age sexually abused girls, *Journal of Child and Adolescent Group Therapy, 3*(1), 25–39.

Wonderlich, S. A., Crosby, R. D., Mitchell, J. E., Roberts, J., Haseltine, B., Demuth, G. & Thompson, K. (2000). Relationship of childhood sexual abuse and eating disturbance in children. *Journal of the American Academy of Child and Adolescent Psychiatry, 39*(10), 1277–1283.

Zito, J. M., & Safer, D. J. (2001). Services and prevention: Pharmacoepidemiology of antidepressant use. *Biological Psychiatry, 49,* 1121–1127.

Small-Group Counseling

James J. Bergin

Small-group counseling with children and adolescents is becoming more popular in school and community settings (Myrick, 2002). Both group and individual counseling provide a facilitative environment characterized by trust, caring, acceptance, understanding, and support. Group counseling, however,
uniquely allows children and adolescents to be understood and supported by
peers as well as by the counselor. These interactions are especially valuable to
students whose primary concerns are in the areas of social interaction and self-
expression. Moreover, the group provides an excellent opportunity for young
people to observe and learn from one another. Behavior modeling teaches new
behaviors and also can be a powerful force in motivating group members to try
out alternative behaviors and practice specific skills such as stress reduction,
study, and social skills (Ehly & Dustin, 1989).

The group experience also can become a primary source of support for the individual because it creates an atmosphere in which potentials and skills can be discovered, explored, developed, and tested. Through group participation, members maximize the opportunity to help themselves and others (Grayson, 1989). Moreover, through helping others, an individual's own self-esteem and self-confidence can be increased" (Gladding, 2002).

This chapter provides a definition of group counseling and then covers the goals of group counseling with children and adolescents, stages of the group process, the counselor's role, and ethical considerations in group work with minors. The chapter also presents practical procedures for selecting participants, determining the size of the group, planning the number of sessions, establishing group rules, and planning for evaluation. The chapter concludes with a description of three types of counseling groups, with outlines of procedures and suggested resources for designing group activities.

Definition of Group Counseling

A useful definition of group counseling is offered by Gazda, Duncan, and Meadows (1967):

> Group counseling is a dynamic, interpersonal process focusing on conscious thought and behavior involving the therapy functions of permissiveness, orientation to reality, catharsis, and mutual trust, caring, understanding, acceptance, and support. The therapy functions are created and nurtured in a small group through the sharing of personal concerns with one's peers and the counselor. The group counselees are basically normal individuals with various concerns which are not debilitating to the extent of requiring extensive personality change. The group counselees may utilize the group interaction to increase understanding and acceptance of values and goals and to learn or unlearn certain attitudes and behaviors. (p. 306)

This definition underscores the concept that involvement in counseling creates a dynamic interactive process among peers and, as such, it can exert strong influences on the individual members in a number of ways:

1. The group's offer of caring, acceptance, and support for each member encourages mutual trust and sharing of individual concerns.
2. The group's orientation to reality and emphasis on conscious thought lead individuals to examine their current thoughts, feelings, and actions and to express them in a genuine manner.
3. The group's overt attempt to convey understanding to each member encourages tolerance and an accepting attitude toward individual differences in personal values and goals.

The group's focus on personal concerns and behavior encourages the individual to consider alternative ways of behaving and to practice them within the context of a supportive environment.

The definition also points out that members of counseling groups are normal individuals who have the ability to deal with their own concerns and do not have extensive personality problems. Instead, the members make educated choices about their personal behaviors. In addition to helping themselves, they, along with the counselor, can participate in the development of all group members.

Goals of Group Counseling With Children and Adolescents

The major goal of group counseling is to create the opportunity for individuals to gain knowledge and skills that will assist them in making and carrying out their own choices. The intent is to promote personal growth and resolve problems and conflicts. To this end, the group process engages individuals in activities that explore personal thoughts, feelings, attitudes, values, and interests and the way these factors influence personal choices. It also examines the individual's skills in communication, cooperation, and decision making, particularly as these skills pertain to interpersonal interaction and problem solving (Baker, 2000).

Group counseling is well suited to the needs of elementary, middle, and secondary school students. Developmentally, most children and adolescents lack the knowledge and skill needed to deal with all of the challenges of growing up. Much of the curriculum that covers these areas is addressed appropriately through large-group guidance activities. If students require additional assistance, more personalized information, or emotional support, group counseling provides an atmosphere that is highly conducive to remedial training, self-exploration, and peer support (Sandhu, 2001).

Group counseling also is a valuable supplement to individual counseling. Students who are being counseled individually may present problems and concerns that can be addressed best in a group context. For example, a student who has difficulty making decisions and committing to a course of action may benefit a great deal from a group experience addressing the tasks of communication and cooperative decision making. Similarly, young children who have difficulty articulating their thoughts and feelings, perhaps because of delayed language development, can enhance their vocabulary and expressive skills by participating in a "feelings" group. In addition, group counseling can be an effective supplement to individual counseling for students with behavior problems at home and at school (Vander Kolk, 1985).

Group counseling with children differs from group work with older students in some respects. Although the basic principles of group counseling apply to all ages, groups for young children must be adapted to their social, emotional, and intellectual development as well as their verbal communication skills (George & Dustin, 1988). Young children tend to feel most natural in play and activity groups because they are accustomed to acting out their needs as a way of expressing themselves (Gladding, 1998; Lifton, 1972). Small groups (two to four members) that use play media as the main vehicle for communication are often recommended for preschoolers and primary-grade youngsters (Kaduson & Schaefer, 2000). In his book *Group Counseling: A Developmental Approach,* Gazda (1989) provided a thorough description of these kinds of groups and the application of play therapy techniques in a school setting.

During the elementary and middle school years, children rapidly gain verbal ability, which enables them to participate readily in the verbal exchange that typifies most counseling groups. Hence, most groups in this age range use activities similar to those used with adolescents. Even though these students may be quite articulate and expressive, many require some training in social interaction, especially in functioning as a member of a group. Therefore, counselors in elementary and middle schools incorporate into group procedures the opportunity for participants to learn group roles and to practice active listening skills that will facilitate the group process. Some practitioners have developed specialized group activities targeting the acquisition of these skills for group participants (Bergin, 1991; Myrick, 2002).

Group counseling may be the preferred intervention for adolescents (Corey, 1999). Adolescents strongly desire peer acceptance and affiliation, and the group context affords them easy access to peer feedback and support. Moreover, the struggle for independence from authority and the preoccupation with self that characterize this developmental stage can make adolescents reluctant to seek individual counseling with an adult. Unlike younger children, who more readily trust counselors, adolescents tend to feel threatened by any suggestion that they seek counseling. The invitation to join a group and to work with peers is more appealing, as it reduces the chances of being put on the "hot seat"; at the same time, it increases the opportunity to relate with peers and gain their approval. Other than the additional emphasis on trust and peer acceptance, group counseling procedures with adolescents are generally the same as those used with adult groups.

Stages in the Group Process

Groups typically proceed through four stages: initial, transition, working, and termination.

Initial Stage

In the *initial* stage, activities are geared to bring about cohesion among group members. Icebreaker activities frequently are employed to introduce members to, and help them feel comfortable interacting with, other participants. This stage also involves discussion of the group's purpose and objectives as well as members' commitment to work with and help one another (Capuzzi & Gross, 2001).

The group agrees upon and establishes the rules. Each rule is clarified for the group to ensure understanding, especially concerning confidentiality. Once these issues have been clarified, the group sets about building rapport by demonstrating caring, attention, and a desire to know and understand one another. The trust that develops in the group allows group members to self-disclose and address their personal concerns through problem-solving techniques (the theme of the working stage).

Transition Stage

The group's movement from stage to stage is seldom smooth and uniform. Some individuals are ready to self-disclose before others, and many are reluctant to give up the warm feelings they experienced in the trusting atmosphere of the group. Hence, most groups go through a *transition* stage, during which members confront their own and others' reluctance to proceed, reiterate the group's purposes, and eventually recommit themselves to supporting one another to accomplish the group's objectives.

This stage is characterized by resistance. It may be in the form of avoidance behaviors such as coming late to sessions, failing to listen attentively to others, engaging in chitchat, or withholding ideas and opinions from the group. Or it may take the form of challenges to the counselor. Participants might question the "real" purposes of the group, why the members were chosen for the group, and how confidentiality can be guaranteed. The key ingredient in group success is trust. As individual members confront others' concerns in a caring and accepting manner, they reinforce other members' trust and commitment to the group's progress.

Working Stage

The group reaches the *working* stage when it addresses its primary purpose of helping individual members deal with their present concerns. These concerns may revolve around a developmental need, a situation, or an experience common to many or all group members, or it may be an issue of immediate concern to an individual. In any case, the manner in which the issue or concern manifests itself in the individual's life is unique. The group process assists individual members in clarifying their concerns and exploring alternative ways of achieving their personal goals. Activities such as role-playing and modeling afford group members the opportunity to express themselves, receive feedback from others, and observe, practice, and learn new ways of behaving, which they can choose to transfer to their environments outside the counseling group.

Termination

The major function of the final stage, *termination,* is to help members evaluate their progress toward personal goals during involvement in the group process. Members engage in self-evaluation, provide feedback to one another, and are reinforced for their participation in the group process. They formulate and discuss plans for implementing what each member has learned. Follow-up and evaluation arrangements also are made at this time.

The Counselor's Role

In groups for children and adolescents, the counselor is the primary facilitator of the group process. These groups often take place in the school setting, with the facilitator being the school counselor. Initially he or she assesses students' needs, defines the group purposes and objectives, identifies and selects prospective group members, arranges permission for members to join, organizes the schedule of sessions, plans the group activities, and arranges space for the group to meet. While carrying out these responsibilities, the counselor enlists the support of parents, school administrators, teachers, and other faculty members.

During the group process, the counselor concentrates on promoting the development of group interaction, establishing rapport among group members, leading the group progressively through all four stages, and encouraging individual members' self-exploration and personal decision making. The counselor guides the group as it discusses individual and joint concerns, models appropriate attending and responding behaviors, and reinforces members for supporting one another during their individual self-exploration. In addition, the counselor confronts resistance sensitively, redirects negative behavior, and encourages the group's efforts to become self-regulatory. The counselor safeguards the group's integrity by enforcing the rules the group establishes for itself.

After completion of the group process, the counselor evaluates the group as a whole and helps the group conduct an evaluation of the group process. After the final session, in which members assess their personal progress and contributions to the group, the counselor conducts a follow-up evaluation with the members to gain their opinions of the group's effectiveness. The counselor also contacts the teachers and parents of the members to get their impressions of the group's impact on members' functioning in settings outside of the group. *Group Counseling Techniques* (Corey, Corey, Callahan, & Russell, 1992) and *Group Counseling: Strategies and Skills* (Jacobs, Harvill, & Masson, 1998) give comprehensive explanations of group stages and group leadership techniques.

Ethical Considerations in Group Work With Minors

When engaging children and adolescents in the group counseling process, one of the counselor's primary responsibilities is to protect each client's welfare. Adult clients presumably have the ability to care for themselves and make wise choices regarding their present and future behavior. Minors, however, are dependent upon their parents or guardians to assist them in these matters. Therefore, the counselor has to accept ethical responsibility for advising children and adolescents of their rights to choose how they participate in the group process and deal with their personal feelings, beliefs, values, and behaviors.

Likewise, because parents and guardians normally have a deep interest in the welfare of their children, as well as being legally responsible for them, the counselor should collaborate with parents and keep them apprised of the children's progress and needs as revealed through the counseling group process (Schmidt, 2002). Other adults, such as teachers and school administrators, who actively participate in the child's growth and development also have ethical and legal rights to be informed of the counselor's work with group members, especially if the parents grant these other adults these privileges.

The counselor should prepare an information sheet describing the group process, purpose, activities, rules, and number of sessions to present to parents. Some counselors also request that parents give written consent allowing the child to participate in the counseling group. The counselor must clarify and emphasize the group rule regarding confidentiality. The group counseling context offers less assurance of maintaining confidentiality than does individual counseling, and the counselor cannot guarantee to the group anyone's confidentiality other than his or her own. Some group members may question whether the counselor is adhering to the rules of confidentiality when they know that he or she is consulting with their parents, teachers, and other adults. Therefore, during pre-group interviews and again in the first session, the counselor must explain the importance of maintaining confidentiality, inform members of the potential consequences of intentionally breaching it, and clarify the specific conditions under which he or she will reveal information about a member to parents, guardians, teachers, or others.

Corey and Corey (2001) presented a number of guidelines concerning the issue of confidentiality when working with minors. They recommend that the counselor ask participants to sign a contract agreeing to not discuss outside of the group what happens in the group, obtain written parental consent even when it is not required by state law, and scrupulously abide by school policies regarding confidentiality. Counselors must practice within the boundaries of local and state laws, especially laws regarding child neglect and abuse, molestation, and incest. Group leaders who videotape or audio-record sessions should inform members of the ways the recordings will be used and the manner in which their security will be maintained. Whether the recordings are being used for supervision of counseling interns or as a part of a research project, the counselor should obtain the parents' written permission to release the information (Vander Kolk, 1985). A thorough discussion of these issues as they pertain to counseling with groups of public school students can be found in the works of Herlihy and Corey (1997), Huey and Remley (1988), and Salo and Schumate (1993).

Logistics of Group Formation

In forming a group, logistical considerations include the selection of participants, a determination of how many to include, and the duration and number of group sessions. Also, the rules must be clearly defined.

Selecting Participants for the Group

Perhaps the most significant factor in the ultimate success of a group is the membership of the group itself. Group cohesion and productivity are most likely when members share a common goal and have the desire and ability to work cooperatively with one another. The counselor has to identify the common needs of prospective members and conduct interviews with potential group members to determine their interest in and suitability for group membership.

The counselor's assessment of student needs forms the basis for establishing goals for the group and its individual members (Ritchie & Huss, 2000; Vander Kolk, 1985). The counselor observes the students directly, interprets data from educational achievement tests and career-development inventories, analyzes students' self-reports, and accepts referrals from parents, teachers, and other professionals. Some authorities recommend conducting a systematic needs assessment of the entire school to identify the needs of a broad spectrum of students (Ohlsen, Horne, & Lawe, 1988; Worzbyt & O'Rourke, 1989). The results can be used to determine topics that would be especially helpful to address through group counseling, as well as to highlight the prevalence of issues and problems impacting specific groups within the student population. In addition, the counselor might give students self-referral forms on which they can describe their degree of interest in joining a group and the topics they would like to discuss. The counselor can use the self-referral information to construct special groups addressing the current concerns of these students while they are highly motivated toward self-improvement.

In determining students' needs, the counselor is advised to consult with parents and teachers and seek their collaboration throughout the group's existence. Observations of teachers and parents, and the data they supply by completing needs assessment surveys, can help the counselor pinpoint students' concerns and identify the abilities of prospective group members. Further, during consultation with parents and teachers, the counselor can address any concerns these people have about the group counseling process. Conducting orientation sessions for parents and teachers fosters their understanding of and support for the group counseling process (Duncan & Gumaer, 1980; Vernon & Al–Mabuk, 1995). At a minimum, the counselor should contact parents and teachers to arrange scheduling for the group sessions and to secure permission for students to be released from class to attend the group sessions.

Prior to being enrolled in the group, each prospective group member should be interviewed. The interview is intended to ascertain the student's willingness to work on self-improvement, desire to assist others in their efforts toward growth, commitment to the group's progress toward its goals, and compatibility with other group members. During the interview, the counselor explains the purpose and goals of the group, clarifying the reasons the individual was selected and describing the procedures, activities, and materials to be used in the group process (Gibson, Mitchell, & Basile, 1993). The counselor also defines the meaning of "confidentiality" (and the conditions under which it is broken) and specifies the time and space arrangements for the meetings, the duration and number of the group sessions, the group rules, and the requirements for membership. The counselor listens carefully to any questions, responds to each, and makes sure the questions are answered to the prospective member's satisfaction. Clarifying the group's purpose, goals, and process assures that the students (and their parents) can give informed consent to group membership.

During the first session, the counselor should discuss these issues again with all the group members and reiterate them throughout the group process as necessary, especially when group members are young children. From a legal standpoint, the counselor, if asking parents for written permission for their child's participation in the group, should provide parents with this information in writing. The information also can be used to create a "contract" that students sign to indicate that they understand the group's purposes and are committed to becoming part of it.

As noted earlier, the interview also allows the counselor to assess whether the individual is compatible with other group members and whether the group goals and physical setting are appropriate for the individual. According to Carroll and Wiggins (2001), the ingredients for good group composition include members' acceptance of one another, members' willingness to self-disclose, voluntary participation, and a balance of personal characteristics among group members. Individuals who are initiators, cognitive, expressive, other-oriented, and willing to risk self-disclosure should be included in the group to balance those who are primarily followers, reflective, quiet, self-oriented, and low risk-takers.

Creating a heterogeneous mix of minority and majority viewpoints, males and females, and various cultural backgrounds adds to the interchange of ideas. Including individuals who are better adjusted and more experienced with the group's major issues helps build cohesion in the group, and these members can be models for other members. Carroll and Wiggins (2001) urged counselors to be intuitive regarding a prospective member's effect on the potential interaction of all the members and to avoid selecting individuals who are unable to conceptualize or verbalize at the average level of functioning within the group. Consideration of level of functioning is especially important when working with groups of children.

Differences in physical maturation and verbal ability preclude some children's participation with peers or older children in group activities that demand strength, coordination, or verbal fluency. To avoid differences of this nature and to take advantage of students' natural preference for same-age companions, counselors tend to group elementary school students by grade level for counseling. This grouping also makes scheduling easier and allows group members to transfer what they learn in the group to their interactions within the school setting. During the middle school years, students sometimes express a strong preference for same-sex peers, so some counselors conduct separate counseling groups for boys and girls. Generally, however, heterogeneous grouping is acceptable for any age group and is recommended for adolescent groups in particular to promote better communication between the sexes.

Counselors should avoid including "best friends" or "worst enemies" in the same group, as these relationships can interfere with the group's efforts to be cohesive and maintain its focus. Similarly, students with severe disciplinary problems bring their own agenda to the group and can be highly disruptive. These individuals, as well as those who show a lack of concern for others, should be considered for individual counseling or some other strategy that emphasizes the consequences of antisocial behavior (Vander Kolk, 1985). Further, suicidal or severely depressed students who need immediate help might be better served by individual counseling and monitoring (Capuzzi & Gross, 2001; Lifton, 1972; Myrick, 2002).

Determining Size of the Group

In determining the number of members to include in the group, the leader's primary consideration is his or her ability to manage the group's interactions. With primary-grade youngsters engaged in play therapy, group size should be limited to three or four members. Groups for older children and adolescents usually have 6 to 8 members but can range from 5 to 10 members depending on the group's focus and the skills of the members and their counselor. A group of older children or adolescents with fewer than five members runs the risk of limiting the opportunities for individuals to interact with a variety of peers and benefit from a broader range of suggestions and support.

The counselor also must take into account student absenteeism. Young students are prone to childhood diseases, and absentee rates of at-risk students are often higher than those of their peers. Transience in the student population also portends dropouts. Expanding the group membership beyond 10, however, strains the counselor's ability to attend and respond to all the interactions in the group.

Larger groups can be managed by the counselor working with a co-leader, and some experts highly recommend co-leaders for smaller groups as well. By collaborating in planning and managing the group process, a co-leader helps the counselor broaden his or her skills as a leader. A thorough discussion of co-leadership is provided in Corey and Corey's (2001) book, *Groups: Process and Practice*.

Determining Length and Number of Group Meetings

Groups need time to warm up, to build cohesion, to address their problems, and to come to closure. To maintain continuity and momentum, groups ideally should meet weekly for 90 to 120 minutes per session. Counselors in public schools, however, often are restricted in the amount of time they can arrange for group counseling. Convincing teachers and parents to release students from class for an extended time each week is difficult, especially when state officials and the public pressure the schools to assume more accountability for student achievement. Further, once-a-week sessions often are disrupted by school special events and holidays.

Therefore, many school counselors arrange for their groups to meet for a normal class hour once or twice a week over 8 to 12 weeks. Groups for younger students usually meet for one or two 30-minute sessions each week, as this timeframe more closely fits their regular instructional class periods and their average attention spans.

Counselors have different preferences in scheduling. Some find that group continuity and momentum are enhanced by meeting more frequently over a shorter timeframe. This schedule might be especially advantageous for topic-specific groups directed at crises such as coping with suicide or dealing with a death or natural disaster. Developmental groups for elementary school students often are scheduled to meet daily for 2 weeks. Holding the sessions during a different class session each day minimizes the amount of time students miss a given instructional period (Myrick, 2002).

Setting Group Rules

Early on, the group should establish a set of clearly defined rules governing members' behavior. Members typically commit to:

- joining the group voluntarily
- attending and coming on time to all group sessions
- working on self-improvement
- helping others improve themselves
- maintaining confidentiality concerning what others say and do in the group
- obeying the rules the group adopts

The group might set additional rules either initially or as the need arises during the group process. Examples of group-specific rules include:

- only one person speaking at a time
- speaking directly to individuals
- listening and attending to the speaker
- participating in the group discussions
- dealing with the here-and-now

▓▓ no fighting or shoving
▓▓ no put-downs or verbal assaults

The number of rules established is determined by the counselor and the members. As guiding principles, each member must assume responsibility for choosing what he or she does and says in the group and each is committed to taking an active role in growth and maintenance of the group (Anderson, 1984). The counselor and the members are bound by the rules the group sets for itself, and they share responsibility for maintaining the rules. Only the counselor, however, has the right to remove someone from the group.

Evaluation

As part of the evaluation of the group process, the counselor should allow members to receive feedback from the group and should collect data that can be used to assess the group's perceived effectiveness. To facilitate member feedback, counselors often devote the last sessions (the termination stage) of the group to members' self-reflecting and to summarizing others' observed behaviors during the group process. Group members should be given time to assess how far they have progressed, to summarize their observations of other members' behaviors, and to make recommendations for their personal growth and that of other members.

The counselor should instruct members to evaluate their growth in terms of the group's stated purposes and encourage them to make positive comments and suggestions in their feedback to one another. Based upon this reflection and feedback, students can devise a personal plan of action that they can follow after the group terminates. Whenever possible, the counselor should arrange for the group to hold a follow-up meeting after a few months to allow members to discuss their progress in the personal plans they designed for themselves. If a meeting is not possible, the counselor should arrange to meet with members individually.

To determine the effectiveness of the group process itself, the counselor usually analyzes information he or she obtains from the members, their parents, and teachers. Information from the members regarding the group's effectiveness in meeting its goals is usually obtained during the follow-up session. The counselor may have a brief questionnaire or rating sheet that students fill out. Thompson and Rudolph (2000) recommended using the following evaluation instrument (developed by Bruckner and Thompson, 1987), which they suggest also may be used as a needs survey for future group sessions. The instrument contains six incomplete statements and two forced-choice items:

1. I think coming to the group room is _____.
2. Some things I have enjoyed talking about in the group room are _____.

3. Some things I would like to talk about that we have not talked about are
_____.

4. I think the counselor is _____.

5. The counselor could be better if _____.

6. Some things I have learned from coming to the group room are
_____.

7. If I had a choice, I (would) (would not) come to the group room with my class.

8. Have you ever talked with your parents about things that were discussed in the group? (yes) (no). (p. 398)

Change in student attitude can be ascertained by having members complete an attitude scale or survey prior to beginning the group process and again following termination. Examples of inventories that can be used in both pre- and post-group assessment are included in Morganett's (2002a, b) books, *Skills for Living: Group Counseling Activities for Young Adolescents,* and *Skills for Living: Group Counseling Activities for Elementary Students.* Similar procedures can be employed with parents and teachers to obtain their perceptions of students' new knowledge and skills targeted in the group. The counselor also may wish to interview these adults to discuss their observations of any changes in students' behaviors or attitudes following the group experience and to talk about any additional counseling needs or suggested follow-up interventions.

Types of Counseling Groups

Counseling groups for children and adolescents can be divided into three types: developmental, problem-centered, and topic-specific. Certain basic elements are common to all three types.

First, all groups must have a definite purpose, which the counselor clearly defines and states. Group purposes are defined and delineated in the goals and objectives the counselor prepares for the group process prior to selecting members. The goals may target the needs of an identified group of students who, for example, are deficient in certain academic, vocational, or interpersonal skills, or the goals may center on the expressed needs and interests of individual students. In either case, the goals direct the group process from its inception through post-group evaluation. The objectives clarify the goals by stating expected outcomes for members to derive from the group experience. The objectives also guide the counselor in selecting activities and discussion procedures to use during the group sessions and are the basis for evaluating how well the group attains its purposes (Furr, 2000).

Second, all three types of groups must have requirements for member participation and enforce rules for membership. Group members, screened from a pool, are expected to commit to the rules of conduct the group establishes and to be accountable to the group itself. If the group process takes place within an educational institution and the group members are minors, the group must operate within certain legal restrictions, organizational policies, and the expectations of parents, teachers, and school administrators.

Third, all three types of groups must include structured procedures. Each type of group proceeds through the same four stages of group development. For each type of group, the length of sessions and duration of the meetings are predetermined. Although the roles of the counselor and the members vary depending on the purpose of the group, the age and characteristics of the students, and the counselor's theoretical orientation, the counselor and the group collaborate through the structural procedures to bring about cohesion among the members and sustain an atmosphere of mutual trust, caring, understanding, acceptance, and support. This dynamic interaction is what provides the core structure for all of the group's activities.

The incorporation of structured activities into the group process is intended to be a stimulus for group interaction and self-reflection. The activities should not be used to limit the thoughts and expressions of group members or to substitute for lack of communication among group members. The leader is responsible for assuring that the group is meaningful and productive (Jacobs, 1992). The counselor's emphasis should be on helping members identify their unique personal reactions (thoughts, feelings, opinions, and values) as they emerge in the context of the group process in response to the stimulus each activity provides.

Developmental Groups

Developmental groups help children and adolescents meet the challenges of everyday, normal activity in the process of growing up. Like large-group guidance activities, they address the individual's need to gain knowledge and acquire skills in the areas of personal identity, interpersonal interaction, emotional and behavioral development, academic achievement, and career planning. These groups are oriented to growth and prevention rather than remediation and are directed toward developing specific behaviors and skills that will enhance the individual's ability to function independently and responsibly.

Although group membership is open to all students, it usually is targeted to children and adolescents who are developmentally delayed in comparison to their peers of the same ability levels and social and academic backgrounds. Prospective group members often are identified by parents or teachers, during consultation with the counselor, as students who are experiencing underachievement, absenteeism, tardiness, low self-esteem, or lack of social involvement with peers. In addition, individuals volunteer for developmental groups to enhance their skills or learn how to cope with what they currently are experiencing in the process of growing up.

The groups usually have a central theme related to the students' level of understanding, perceived needs, and developmental stage. Based upon "developmental milestones," described by Berk (1998), Vernon (1993, 1999), and other specialists in human growth and development, the counselor selects an issue for the group theme that is appropriate to the members' ages, abilities, and social/emotional maturity and is relevant to the developmental tasks at their stage of development (see Chapter 1 for a detailed description of developmental considerations). The group is designed to address the developmental needs of all individuals at this age level, to promote their personal growth regarding the issue, and to prevent problems with their dealing with the issue in the future.

Specific group themes vary according to age level, although the general issues may be continuous throughout childhood and adolescence. For example, a group dealing with interpersonal communication skills might be called "The Friendship Group" for younger students and deal primarily with identifying friendship behaviors and how to maintain them. For adolescents, the focus may still be on interpersonal relationships but within the context of dating, so the group might be called "Dating Conversation Made Easy." For younger students dealing with relationships with parents, the topics might have to do with separation anxiety and the children's fears about being away from parents, whereas an adolescent group would address how to negotiate the adolescents' need for independence and freedom with their parents without creating conflict. A feelings group for adolescents might focus on coping with mood swings during this period of development, whereas for young children the emphasis would be on learning to identify various feelings.

When establishing developmental groups for children and adolescents, the counselor must draw on his or her knowledge of, and sensitivity to, specific developmental issues. The counselor has to address the general issues related to a specific theme during the group and also must identify for inclusion in the group those students for whom these issues are a serious concern. For example, the counselor might regularly conduct a group for adolescents on getting along with parents but make sure to include in the group students who are beginning to have more severe problems dealing with their parents.

When analyzing student behavior, the counselor must use his or her skill in assessment and intervention techniques to distinguish between behavior caused by situational stressors and that resulting from developmental issues. For example, an adolescent whose academic performance is slipping and who appears uncharacteristically withdrawn in his or her social interactions may actually be caught up in personal identity issues rather than academic or social skills concerns. The student might have doubts about his or her competence or physical appearance and withdrawal may be the adolescent's way of avoiding possible academic failure or social rejection. Appropriate for this student would be a developmental counseling group that addresses these specific identity issues (not a group with a theme of "achievement motivation" or "improving social skills"). In the former type of group, the counselor can assist the individual in meeting his or her current "life challenges" and prevent the problem from becoming more severe. A concise, comprehensive examination of developmental issues and counselor assessment procedures and techniques is found in *Developmental Assessment and Intervention With Children and Adolescents* by Vernon (1993).

Developmental groups may teach specific skills such as assertiveness training or steps in problem solving. Or they may present models to help students understand their communication styles, as in transactional analysis groups (Thompson & Rudolph, 2000), or information about rational and irrational thinking (Vernon, 1989, 1998a, 1998b). Developmental groups frequently incorporate media such as videos, films, and books. Games, worksheets, simulations, and role-plays also can encourage discussion. Descriptions of developmental groups and small-group activities are available in the literature.

Developmental issues that can be addressed in groups for elementary school students include, among others:

- listening skills (interpersonal communication) (Pearson & Nicholson, 2000; Peyser & McLaughlin, 1997)
- dealing with feelings (Akos, 2000; Morganett, 2002a; Omizo, Hershberger, & Omizo, 1988; Phillips–Hershey & Kanagy, 1996; Vernon, 1998a)
- social skills and friendship (Kramer & Radey, 1997; Mehaffey & Sandberg, 1992; Reeder, Douzenis, & Bergin, 1997; Utay & Lampe, 1995; Vernon, 1998a)
- academic achievement (Campbell & Bowman, 1993; Paisley & Hubbard, 1994)
- self-concept (Garrett & Crutchfield, 1997; Morganett, 2002a; Wick, Wick, & Peterson, 1997)
- career awareness (Flanagan & Rosenberg, 1999; Parramore & Hopke, 1999; Rogala, Lambert, & Verhage, 1991)
- problem solving/decision making (Bergin, 1991; Vernon, 1998a; Wilde, 1996)

For secondary students, groups addressing the same developmental issues might focus on:

- communication and assertiveness training (Morganett, 2002b; Myrick, 2002)
- dealing with feelings and managing stress (Escamilla, 1998; Morganett, 2002b; Vernon, 1998b, c)
- social skills and making friends (Martin & Lehr, 1999; Morganett, 2002a; Thompson, 1998; Vernon, 1998b, c)
- achievement motivation and school success (Campbell & Myrick, 1990; Morganett, 2002b; Paisley & Hubbard, 1994)
- personal identity and self-esteem (Lee, 1987; Morganett, 2002b; Nims, 1998; Siccone & Canfield, 1993a, b; Vernon, 1998b, c)
- career exploration and planning (Pope & Minor, 2000; Rogala et al., 1991; Rosenbaum, 1994)
- problem solving/decision making (Hutchinson, 1996; LaFountain & Garner, 1996; Vernon, 1998b, c)

An example of a developmental group for adolescents is described on the following pages.

Developmental Group: Polishing My Self-Image

Group Goals:

■ To build group cohesion, cooperation, and communication
■ To develop an understanding of self-concept formation
■ To identify the effect of positive and negative reinforcement on self-esteem
■ To identify personal strengths and weaknesses
■ To develop a plan for enhancing personal self-image

Session 1:

Objectives:

■ To demonstrate cooperative behaviors
■ To make positive, reinforcing statements and suggestions to one another
■ To establish rules for the group

Procedure:

The counselor leads the group in a discussion of the group's purpose and goals and facilitates the establishment of group rules. Members sign the individual contracts negotiated in the initial counselor/student interviews. The contracts confirm the individual members' commitment to the group. Members then are paired and invited to participate in a "Who Are You?" icebreaker activity (Vernon, 2002). One member asks his or her partner, "Who are you?" and the partner answers. The questioning continues for 2 minutes. (Example: "Who are *you?" An eighth-grader.* "Who are you?" *Someone who likes rock-and-roll music.*) After 2 minutes the partners reverse roles. At the end of the activity, each member introduces his or her partner to the entire group and tells at least two things about the person that he or she discovered during the "Who Are You?" activity. Following this icebreaker activity, the counselor asks questions such as:

■ Did you learn anything about yourself by participating in this activity?
■ Did you learn anything about others?
■ What are you looking forward to in the next group session?

Session 2:

Objectives:

■ To describe personal strengths and weaknesses
■ To realize that all individuals have both strengths and weaknesses

Procedure:

The counselor gives each group member a journal and explains that members are to record in it their personal reactions to all of the group's activities and discussions. Members then complete a "Personal Coat of Arms" activity (Canfield, 1976), which requires them to think of symbols representing each of the following: a personal achievement, something they've recently learned to do, something they'd like to do better, a special talent, a weakness, and a bright idea they have had. They draw their symbols on a paper shield the counselor provides. The counselor asks members to display their shields and encourages each to explain the symbols he or she has drawn. The counselor can facilitate discussion by asking questions such as:

- Which symbol was the most difficult for you to think of?
- How did you feel when you shared your symbols?
- How did it feel to talk about your strengths?
- Did you feel like you were bragging or just telling it like it is?
- What was it like to share a weakness? Does having weaknesses mean you are not a good person? (The counselor should stress that everyone has strengths and weaknesses but that they don't affect a person's overall worth.)
- What did you learn about yourself in this activity?

Session 3:

Objectives:

- To describe personal characteristics using metaphors
- To explain how these metaphors describe their perceptions of themselves
- To state and describe their perceptions of one another using metaphors

Procedure:

The counselor explains and gives examples of metaphors. Members complete the metaphorical statement, "If I were a(n) _____, I would be a(n) _____, using an item of their choice from the following categories: *animal, building, home appliance, movie, car, book.* The counselor invites members to share their responses and offer additional positive metaphors about one another. The counselor asks each person who offers an alternative metaphor to explain his or her response.

The counselor then leads the group in discussing the following questions:

- Was it difficult to think of metaphors?
- What did you learn about yourself by identifying metaphors?
- What metaphors would you use to describe your best qualities as a friend? As a student? As a member of this group? As a worker?

Session 4:

Objectives:

■ To identify how self-concept develops
■ To identify ways in which self-worth is affected by positive and negative feelings

Procedure:

The group views the video *I Like Being Me: Self-Esteem* (Sunburst Communications, 1990). This tape describes the origins of self-worth, the ways feelings and beliefs about self-worth can be changed, and the ways positive and negative feelings affect self-worth. Afterward, the counselor reviews the major points covered and then leads the group in a discussion of self-worth. Comments and questions that stimulate discussion include:

■ Describe a time when you felt good about yourself.
■ Describe what it means to *value* yourself.
■ What can you do to change your feelings about yourself?

Session 5:

Objectives:

■ To identify the negative effects of "put-down" statements on self-esteem
■ To identify self-put-downs

Procedure:

The counselor directs the group in a "put-downs" activity (Vernon, 1989) in which volunteers read aloud negative statements such as, "Stupid idiot," "Dumb jerk," "Fat, ugly creep," and "Lazy good-for-nothing." The statements are read as though the reader is making them about himself or herself. The counselor then leads a group discussion about the effects of negative self-talk on a person's self-esteem. To stimulate discussion, the counselor asks questions such as:

■ What do you accomplish by putting yourself down?
■ What positive statements can you use to stop yourself from making personal put-downs?

Session 6:

Objective:

■ To describe positive statements and actions that can be used to stop negative self-talk

Procedure:

The counselor facilitates a group discussion of situations in which group members find themselves engaging in negative self-talk. The group identifies the put-down statements and then brainstorms positive, alternative statements and behaviors to reinforce feelings of self-worth and esteem. The counselor helps the group select some scenarios to role-play. First the members role-play the negative statements, then they role-play the situations using the positive statements they have proposed. To emphasize the concepts, the counselor can ask questions such as:

■ How did it feel when you made the positive statement instead of the put-down?
■ What positive statements can you use to keep yourself from making personal put-downs?

Session 7:

Objectives:

■ To identify personal goals for improving self-concept
■ To describe ways to achieve these goals

Procedure:

The counselor leads the group in a discussion of goal setting and then instructs members to develop a personal plan for self-improvement and write it in their journal. To help members develop goals and strategies, the counselor asks questions such as the following:

■ What goals do you want to set for yourself?
■ How do you need to change your behavior to meet these goals?
■ How can you encourage yourself when others put you down? When you make mistakes? When you don't seem to be making progress toward your goals?

Session 8:

Objectives:

■ To share what was learned during the group sessions
■ To give positive suggestions to others for accomplishing their personal goals

Procedure:

The counselor encourages members to share what they have learned with the group by reviewing and summarizing their journal entries. Members are invited to tell their plans for self-enhancement to the group. The counselor makes statements and asks questions that facilitate the group's sharing of suggestions for improving self-concept. The counselor and the group plan a follow-up session. To facilitate discussion during this session, the counselor asks questions such as:

- Which suggestions from the group can you use to help you reach your goals?
- How much progress do you think you can make toward meeting these goals before the group's follow-up session?
- How has this group been helpful to you?

Problem-Centered Groups

The problem-centered group is open-ended, and topics are determined by whatever is of concern to individual participants at the time of the meeting. The group members may all be working on different problems. Each member has the opportunity to receive the group's full attention to his or her individual concerns. Members' commitment to the group consists of agreeing to help others with their concerns and to foster problem-solving processes.

The emphasis is on here-and-now experiences of individual group members. They are encouraged to explore their problems, examine the alternatives open to them, consider the probable consequences of each alternative, and decide upon a course of personal action. The counselor and other group members attempt to empower the individuals to take action on their decisions by providing support, feedback, and the opportunity to practice new behaviors within the group. In addition, the counselor encourages members to try out new behaviors as homework between scheduled group meetings.

In schools, membership in problem-centered groups is open to all students, but members preferably should have skills in articulating personal concerns, skills in attending and responding to others, and some knowledge of their personal needs and aspirations. Intermediate, junior high, and senior high students, because of their level of maturation and social experience, are more likely to have these skills than are primary grade youngsters. Therefore, counselors may wish to establish problem-centered groups exclusively with older students. For younger children, play therapy techniques can be effective in promoting problem-solving skills. To facilitate communication in problem-centered groups, counselors might first involve students in developmental groups specifically designed to teach listening skills and cooperative behaviors that will enhance appropriate interaction in group-counseling activities.

The issues and concerns targeted in sessions of a problem-centered group are unique to the individuals who comprise the group. Each member is responsible for explaining to the group his or her specific problem and, with the group's assistance, for developing and implementing strategies to resolve the problem. Individuals selected for the group are chosen because they are committed to self-improvement and also because they have the desire and ability to help their peers. Thus, each individual's problem becomes an issue for the group. The counselor and other group members attempt to provide feedback to the individual who presented his or her problem, in a manner that the individual can understand and act upon. As Ehly and Dustin (1989) pointed out:

> When members help the individual identify a specific area of behavior that causes problems for the individual and for the other students, the problem seems real. What may have been seen as only something bothering a teacher now becomes the student's problem as group members indicate how much they also dislike the behavior. (p. 94)

Members of problem-centered groups are selected for a variety of reasons. Frequently they are referred by teachers and parents who are concerned about the individual's behaviors at home or at school. For example, these adults may hear the child complaining that "no one likes me" or notice that the child doesn't interact much with peers. Often individuals volunteer to join groups to focus on issues of special concern to them, such as resolving conflicts with parents or peers. Counselors invite some members to join a problem-centered group as a follow-up to individual counseling, especially if the individual's problems are interpersonal in nature. Counselors also may select some members specifically because they can articulate ideas and feelings, are effective problem solvers, and therefore can serve as good role models.

Because the group members usually are close in age and share the same school environment, their concerns tend to be similar, and common topics often emerge in the group sessions. Some of the topics typical of elementary school students are attitudes toward family members, conflicts with parental and school authority figures, relationships with friends, cliques within the peer group, and making the transition to middle/junior high school. Adolescents often are concerned about relationships with friends; dating and attitudes toward sex; dealing with teachers, homework, and school; balancing school and work commitments; preparing for the future in terms of career and post secondary education; and relationships with parents (Ehly & Dustin, 1989).

A sample outline for a problem-centered group follows. Additional examples and a comprehensive examination of strategies for conducting this type of group are found in *Elements of Group Counseling* by Carroll and Wiggins (2001); *Counseling and Therapy for Children* by Gumaer (1984); and *Working With Children and Adolescents in Groups* by Rose and Edelson (1987).

Problem-Centered Group

Group Goals:

■■■ To build group cohesion, communication, and cooperation
■■■ To define and analyze personal concerns

■ To generate solutions to personal concerns through problem solving
■ To establish personal plans of action to resolve problems
■ To accept responsibility for transferring what is learned in the group process to solving problems in one's personal life

Session 1:

Objectives:

■ To demonstrate cooperative behaviors
■ To establish group rules and develop group cohesion
■ To self-disclose concerns the individual wishes to address in the group

Procedure:

The counselor leads the group in discussing the group's purpose and goals and in establishing rules for the group. (Rules should be written on posterboard and displayed during each session.) Members sign the contracts they negotiated in the individual counselor/member interviews, which represent commitment to the group process. Individuals introduce themselves by sharing one thing that others can't tell by looking at them.

The counselor then employs an inclusion activity, "Group Logo" (Bergin, 1989), to begin to build group identity and promote cohesion. In this activity the members cooperate in drawing overlapping shapes on a large piece of posterboard. Together they agree upon a picture they see emerging from the lines they have drawn and then outline, color, and title the picture. The title and picture become the group's logo, which can be displayed throughout subsequent group sessions. Following this group-building activity, the counselor invites the students to identify personal concerns they want to bring up in subsequent sessions. The counselor can facilitate the group's discussion by asking questions such as:

■ Why do you think joining this group can be helpful to you?
■ How do you feel about the group logo?
■ How can you feel more comfortable in the group?
■ What are you looking forward to?

Sessions 2–8:

Objectives:

■ To identify individual problems
■ To brainstorm ways to solve these problems
■ To encourage self-disclosure of feelings, concerns, and opinions
■ To try out new behaviors and responses to problem situations through role-playing
■ To establish plans for resolving personal problems

Procedure:

Individual members identify their personal concerns and describe their thoughts, behaviors, and feelings about those problems. The group focuses on the here-and-now. Members respond to one another to clarify their feelings, perceptions, and concerns, and the counselor leads the group in brainstorming problem-solving behaviors. The members suggest alternative courses of action and identify and evaluate probable consequences of these proposed solutions. Role-playing may be used to try out alternative behaviors. The counselor also suggests homework assignments to help members try out new behaviors and encourages members to report the results during subsequent sessions. For closure, the counselor can initiate a round-robin sharing of an "I learned," an "I feel," or an "I will" statement relative to the issues discussed.

To stimulate dialogue, the counselor might briefly review and summarize what happened in the previous session and then ask group members to share how their problem-solving "plans" worked or how the problem has evolved since the last session. During the sessions, the counselor prompts members to speak directly to one another and links members by pointing out similarities in the problems, feelings, or experiences they describe.

The group must adhere to the rules it has established. The counselor must insist that members wait their turn and allow everyone to have the opportunity to speak. The counselor must allow reticent members to proceed slowly until they are comfortable with self-disclosure. The counselor can encourage the group by making statements such as:

■ I'd like to hear each of you give your opinion about what Jill has told us.
■ When Trent is ready, he will tell us more about his feelings.
■ Kara, you seem to understand how Andy and Chago are feeling. Can you tell us how your feelings are similar?

Sessions 9–10:

Objectives:

■ To share what was learned during group sessions
■ To share with the group personal goals and strategies for resolving the problems shared

Procedure:

The counselor initiates a discussion in which group members share what they have learned during the group process in regard to themselves and their personal problems. Each member defines a plan for applying the problem-solving skills learned in the group in his or her environment. To facilitate the discussion, the counselor might ask questions such as:

■ How do you feel about your problems right now?

■ What progress do you think you've made toward resolving the problems? What must you continue to do to resolve the problems?

■ What is the next step you need to take?

■ What things have you learned in this group that will help you reach your goals?

■ Members make positive statements, reinforcing one another for their communication and cooperation while in the group. The counselor and members then plan a follow-up session.

Topic-Specific Groups

Topic-specific groups are designed to meet the needs of individuals who are having difficulty with situational circumstances that create negative feelings and stress that interferes with normal functioning. These groups are similar to developmental groups in that new knowledge and skills are taught to the members, but topic-specific groups are formed to help members handle serious, immediate concerns rather than to help them resolve typical developmental problems. In topic-specific groups, members all share similar concerns about a given situation or condition. Because of the commonality of problems, topic-specific groups also have similarities to problem-centered groups, which center on open discussion about current issues.

In topic-specific groups, the group setting gives members the opportunity to understand the issue in more depth, to explore and express feelings, and to identify coping strategies. Group members learn that their feelings are normal, that their peers often feel the same way, and that they have options to help them deal more effectively with the problems and thereby reestablish personal autonomy and happiness. They also receive feedback and support from others who understand what they are experiencing because they have similar problems.

As in developmental groups, counselors facilitating topic-specific groups frequently use media and structured activities to stimulate discussion of the topic and present relevant information to the members. They may make extensive use of role-play and homework exercises to promote specific coping skills.

Although they are not primarily crisis intervention groups by design, topic-specific groups often arise out of crisis events such as a classmate's accidental death or suicide. In such instances, the immediate purpose of the group is to provide support to group members who are dealing with the crisis situation. Later, a follow-up group can be organized to help the members explore the incident more fully, as well as to explore any other concerns related to the larger issue, such as coping with death (Myrick, 2002).

Issues covered in topic-specific groups for children and adolescents include:

■ physical abuse (Baker, 1990; Brown, 1996)

■ grief and loss (Healy–Romanello, 1993; Lehmann, Jimerson, & Gaasch, 2001; Morganett, 2002a; Peterson & Straub, 1992)

- sexual abuse (de Young & Corbin, 1994; Karp & Butler, 1996; Newbauer & Hess, 1994; Powell & Faherty, 1990)
- aggressive behavior (Nelson, Dykeman, Powell, & Petty, 1996; Rainey, Hensley, & Crutchfield, 1997; Stewart, 1995)
- divorce and separation (Burke & Van de Streek, 1989; DeLucia-Waack, 2001; Hage & Nosanow, 2000; Kalter & Schreier, 1993; Morganett, 2002b; Omizo & Omizo, 1988; Tedder, Scherman, & Wantz, 1987; Yauman, 1991)
- fear and stress (O'Rourke & Worzbyt, 1996; Robinson, Rotter, Frey, & Vogel, 1992)
- children of alcoholics (Emshoff, 1989; McNair & Arman, 2000; Riddle, Bergin & Douzenis, 1997)
- suicide (Capuzzi, 1994; Morganett, 2002b; Peterson & Straub, 1992)
- teen parenting (Huey, 1987; Kiselica, 1994)
- adopted children (Kizner & Kizner, 1999)

Group membership usually is targeted at individuals who are having difficulty with a specific issue or are considered to be at-risk. Some members, however, may be chosen because of their past experience with the issue and their success in coping with it. These individuals can help stabilize the group atmosphere and build a sense of hope and confidence that the group process will lead to similar successes for all group members. They also serve as role models who exemplify the coping skills that group members desire. Further, counselors can provide powerful reinforcement by linking the models with targeted group members.

An outline for a topic-specific group for elementary school students who have trouble adjusting to divorce follows.

Topic-Specific Group: Support Group for Children of Divorce

Group Goals:

- To build group cohesion, cooperation, and communication
- To develop mutual support
- To correct misinformation about the causes of divorce
- To identify and express feelings about divorce
- To plan strategies for coping with divorce

Session 1:

Objectives:

- To establish rules for the group
- To demonstrate cooperative behaviors
- To develop group cohesion and commitment
- To state what members hope to achieve while in the group

Procedure:

The counselor leads the group members in a discussion of the purpose and goals of the group. The members then are asked to establish group rules and sign individual contracts, negotiated during counselor/client interviews, symbolizing the individual's commitment to the group. The counselor or a volunteer from the group writes the group rules on a large piece of posterboard for display throughout each session. The counselor then asks each member to introduce himself or herself to the group and initiates an icebreaker activity as follows:

The counselor distributes a magazine and a 9-inch square of tagboard to each student. Each student cuts out a picture describing himself or herself and pastes it on the tagboard. Then the students cut their tagboard into four to six pieces and put the pieces in an envelope. The students exchange envelopes, put the puzzles together, and share what they have learned about each other from the "people puzzle" (Vernon, 1980).

Following this activity, the counselor describes the goals of the group and invites the members to say what they would like to learn. Questions such as the following may stimulate this sharing:

▪ What do you want to learn while you are in this group?
▪ Now that you have heard everyone tell what they want to learn, what do you have in common?
▪ How did you feel about describing your goals to the group?

Session 2:

Objectives:

▪ To describe the changes that divorce has made on the family
▪ To identify similarities and differences in experiences with divorce

Procedure:

The counselor distributes paper and colored markers to group members and tells them that they will use this material for drawing pictures of their families and their homes. The counselor instructs the members to divide their paper into six spaces and draw pictures, one per space, to represent:

▪ their family
▪ a good time they've had with their family
▪ how their family has changed recently
▪ what they miss about the way their family used to be
▪ a good thing about the way their family is now
▪ how they feel about the way things are now

The counselor then asks each member to display his or her "family picture" and tell the group about it. Other members listen and then share their own experiences, which may be similar or dissimilar. The following questions can stimulate discussion:

- How did it feel to describe your family picture?
- What changes has divorce made in your family life?
- After hearing others in the group describe the changes in their lives, what changes do you think are similar for everyone?

Session 3:

Objectives:

- To encourage expression of feelings
- To learn to express feelings through pantomime
- To identify feelings common to all group members
- To identify ways to cope with negative feelings

Procedure:

The counselor leads the group members in an activity in which they express their feelings through pantomime. The counselor has the participants take a piece of paper labeled with a feeling word (such as "bored," "angry," "happy," "sad," "confused," "worried" or "frustrated") out of a sack and asks them to show how they look or act when they are feeling that way. Each group member is able to see the expressions on the other faces and identify with those feelings.

Following the pantomime, the participants are invited to draw out of the bag a piece of paper labeled with a situation, such as the following, and identify how they feel:

- Mom is angry with Dad (or Dad is angry with Mom).
- You are home alone.
- You don't get to see Mom or Dad very often.
- You think you're the cause of your parents' divorce.
- Your parents don't have as much time to spend with you.
- Your friend makes fun of your family.

The counselor encourages the group member drawing a card to verbalize his or her feelings and helps the group think of ways to cope with the feelings. Members describe what they do to relieve sad, angry, or lonely feelings. They are encouraged to brainstorm ways of coping by doing positive things. The counselor records on a large piece of posterboard all of the positive suggestions to use in later sessions. He or she then debriefs the activity by asking students:

- Was it hard to identify your feelings?
- Did others share similar feelings?
- What did you learn about ways to deal with negative feelings?

Session 4:

Objectives:

■ To learn that they are not the cause of divorce
■ To identify reasons that some parents divorce
■ To learn ways to cope with negative feelings caused by the changes that
   divorce brings

Procedure:

Members view the video *When Your Mom and Dad Get Divorced* (Sunburst
Communications, 1991), which reassures youngsters that they are not responsible
for divorce. The tape describes ways in which children affected by divorce can
help themselves feel better. The counselor facilitates discussion by asking the
group to respond to questions such as:

■ What are some reasons parents get a divorce?
■ Do children cause divorce?
■ Can children do anything to prevent divorce?
■ What positive things can children do to cope with the changes the divorce
   causes?

The counselor then displays the posterboard, listing the coping behaviors the
group brainstormed in session 3. The counselor asks the group to look at the
posterboard and determine which of the suggestions for coping with sad, lonely,
and angry feelings might be used to help them deal with feelings caused by
divorce.

Session 5:

Objectives:

■ To describe the negative situations that divorce causes
■ To listen to and reflect others' feelings

Procedure:

The counselor asks each group member to describe the divorce-related events that
"bother" him or her the most. The counselor then helps the group set up a role-
playing activity in which members can act out some of these events. Volunteers
take turns acting out problem events for the other group members, who then
attempt to help the individual clarify the reasons the events bother him or her the
most. The counselor and the other group members express their appreciation for
the individual's willingness to share his or her experiences and feelings with the
group. The counselor then asks questions such as:

■ Are your situations similar or dissimilar to others'?

■ How do you feel about discussing things that bother you?
■ Is it helpful to have others listen and understand?

Session 6:

Objectives:

■ To express concerns about divorce to a divorced adult
■ To simulate parent/child discussions about divorce
■ To identify strategies to cope with the changes precipitated by divorce

Procedure:

The counselor invites a divorced parent to attend the group session and respond to members' questions about divorce. The counselor emphasizes the importance of parent/child dialogue to help children and parents adjust to the changes in their lives resulting from the divorce.

Following the question-and-answer session, the counselor asks volunteers to use adult and child puppets to demonstrate situations precipitated by divorce that can be stressful for children. These situations could include:

■ talking with the custodial parent and the noncustodial parent about the divorce
■ meeting new adults in their parents' lives
■ adjusting to changes in the home environment
■ taking on new responsibilities that parents may place on the child

After each simulation, the counselor leads the group and guest in a discussion of the simulation. To facilitate the discussion, the counselor may ask questions such as:

■ What is the child feeling in this situation?
■ How does the parent feel?
■ How does the other adult feel?
■ What are the puppets saying and doing that make the parent and/or child feel bad?
■ How can they make each other feel better?
■ How can they make themselves feel better?

Session 7:

Objectives:

■ To state personal goals for coping with divorce
■ To identify strategies to help reach the goals
■ To identify people who can offer support after the group ends

Procedure:

Based upon work done in previous sessions, the counselor encourages and helps each individual make a plan for coping with his or her own problems relating to the divorce. The counselor leads the group in brainstorming a list of people such as peers, family members, clergy, and significant others who can provide support to group members. The counselor can facilitate these activities by asking the following kinds of questions:

- What things continue to upset you the most about divorce?
- When do you feel most upset?
- What can you do to feel better?
- What can other people do to help you?

Session 8:

Objectives:

- To express current feelings about the divorce
- To state what members have learned during the group sessions
- To offer support and encouragement to one another

Procedure:

The counselor distributes index cards to the participants and invites them to write the following on the cards:

- One thing you have learned from being in the group
- Something you can do about your negative feelings
- Someone who can help you if you need help
- One way you've changed because of the group

The counselor encourages members to share the statements they wrote on their cards and offer one another feedback and positive suggestions for coping. The group and the counselor plan a follow-up session. Then the counselor brings closure to the group by asking questions such as:

- How do you feel now compared to how you felt when you first became a member of the group?
- How have the other group members been helpful to you?
- What do you plan to do to help yourself between now and the group follow-up session?

Summary

Group counseling can be a valuable intervention in school as well as agency settings. Given the normal developmental concerns of children and adolescents and the more serious problems of many young people, counselors see group counseling as an efficient, effective, and viable approach for helping children and adolescents both remedially and preventively.

Group counseling can reach a larger number of individuals than one-to-one counseling, and it provides the added dimension of immediate feedback and support from peers. The major goal of group counseling is to offer members the opportunity to gain knowledge and skills they can use in decision making and problem solving about a wide variety of situational and developmental issues. In addition, group counseling helps members develop and refine their social skills.

The primary differences between group counseling with children and group counseling with adolescents involve the group members' verbal capacities and their ability to conceptualize problems based on their developmental level. For this reason, it is imperative to tailor group activities, topics, and methods to the targeted age level.

Although group counseling has many advantages, it is not intended to replace individual counseling or classroom guidance. Each form of counseling addresses different needs. In many cases, group counseling may be suggested to complement individual counseling. For example, an adolescent who is working individually with a counselor to deal with anger at a new step parent also may participate in a support group on blended families in which he or she can learn how peers are adjusting to similar family changes.

Group counseling is a powerful, strategic intervention for addressing problems and enhancing human development in both the agency and the school setting. The concepts covered in this chapter should aid counselors in both settings to effectively incorporate group work into their practices.

References

Akos, P. (2000). Building empathic skills in elementary school children through group work. *Journal for Specialists in Group Work, 25*(2), 214–223.

Anderson, J. (1984). *Counseling through group process.* New York: Springer.

Baker, C. (1990). *Development of an outreach group for children ages five through thirteen who have witnessed domestic violence* (Rep. No. CG 022 667). Fort Lauderdale, FL: Nova University. (ERIC Document Reproduction Service No. ED 325 737)

Baker, S. B. (2000). *School counseling for the twenty-first century* (3rd ed.). Upper Saddle River, NJ: Prentice-Hall, Inc.

Bergin, J. (1989). Building group cohesiveness through cooperation activities. *Elementary School Guidance and Counseling, 24,* 90–95.

Bergin, J. (1991). *Escape from pirate island* [Game]. Doyleston, PA: Mar*Co Products.

Berk, L. (1998). *Development through the life span.* Boston: Allyn & Bacon.

Brown, D. (1996). Counseling the victims of violence who develop posttraumatic stress. *Elementary School Guidance and Counseling, 30,* 218–227.

Bruckner, S., & Thompson, C. (1987). Guidance program evaluation: An example. *Elementary School Guidance and Counseling, 21,* 193–196.

Burke, D., & Van de Streek, L. (1989). Children of divorce: An application of Hammond's group counseling for children. *Elementary School Guidance and Counseling, 24,* 112–118.

Campbell, C., & Bowman, R. (1993). The "Fresh Start" support club: Small-group counseling for academically retained children. *Elementary School Guidance and Counseling, 27,* 172–185.

Campbell, C., & Myrick, R. (1990). Motivational group counseling for low-performing students. *Journal for Specialists in Group Work, 15,* 43–50.

Canfield, J. (1976). *100 ways to enhance self-concept in the classroom.* Englewood Cliffs, NJ: Prentice–Hall.

Capuzzi, D. (1994). *Suicide prevention in the schools: Guidelines for middle and high school settings.* Alexandria, VA: American Counseling Association.

Capuzzi, D., & Gross, D, (2001). *Introduction to group counseling* (3rd ed.). Denver: Love Publishing.

Carroll, M., & Wiggins, J. (2001). *Elements of group counseling. Back to the basics* (3rd ed.). Denver: Love Publishing.

Corey, G. (1999). *Theory and practice of group counseling* (5th ed.). Pacific Grove, CA: Wadsworth.

Corey, M., & Corey, G. (2001). *Groups: Process and practice* (6th ed.). Pacific Grove, CA: Brooks/Cole.

Corey, G., Corey, M., Callahan, R, & Russell, J. (1992). *Group counseling techniques* (2nd ed.). Pacific Grove, CA: Brooks/Cole.

DeLucia–Waack, J. L. (2001). *Using music in children of divorce groups: A session-by-session manual for counselors.* Alexandria, NC: American Counseling Association.

de Young, M., & Corbin, B. (1994). Helping early adolescents tell: A guided exercise for traumafocused sexual abuse treatment groups. *Child Welfare, 73,* 141–154.

Duncan, J., & Gumaer, J. (1980). *Developmental groups for children.* Springfield, IL: Charles C Thomas.

Ehly, S., & Dustin, R. (1989). *Individual and group counseling in schools.* New York: Guilford Press.

Emshoff, J. (1989). Preventive intervention with children of alcoholics. *Prevention in Human Services, 7*(1), 225–253.

Escamilla, A. (1998). A cognitive approach to anger management treatment for juvenile offenders. *Journal of Offender Rehabilitation, 27,* 199–208.

Flanagan, A. K., & Rosenberg, H. (1999). *Elementary career awareness through children's literature.* Chicago: Ferguson Publishing.

Furr, S. R. (2000). Structuring the group experience: A format for designing psychoeducational groups. *Journal for Specialists in Group Work, 25*(10), 29–49.

Garrett, M., & Crutchfield, L. (1997). Moving full circle: A unity model of group work with children. *Journal for Specialists in Group Work, 22*(3), 175–188.

Gazda, G. (1989). *Group counseling: A developmental approach* (4th ed.). Boston: Allyn & Bacon.

Gazda, G., Duncan, J., & Meadows, M. (1967). Group counseling and group procedures— Report of a survey. *Counselor Education and Supervision, 9,* 305–310.

George, R., & Dustin, D. (1988). *Group counseling: Theory and practice.* Englewood Cliffs, NJ: Prentice–Hall.

Gibson, R., Mitchell, M., & Basile, S. (1993). *Counseling in the elementary school: A comprehensive approach.* Boston: Allyn & Bacon.

Gladding, S. (1998). *Counseling as an art: The creative arts in counseling* (2nd ed.). Alexandria, VA: American Counseling Association.

Gladding, S. (2002). *Group work: A counseling specialty* (4th ed.). New York: Prentice–Hall.

Grayson, E. (1989). *The elements of short-term group counseling.* Washington, DC: St. Mary's Press.

Gumaer, J. (1984). *Counseling and therapy for children.* New York: Free Press.

Hage, S. M., & Nosanow, M. (2000). Becoming stronger at broken places: A model for group work with young adults from divorced families. *Journal for Specialists in Group Work, 25*(1), 50–66.

Healy–Romanello, M. (1993). The invisible griever: Support groups for bereaved children. *Special Services in the Schools, 8,* 67–89.

Herlihy, B., & Corey, G. (1997). *Boundary issues in counseling: Multiple roles and responsibilities.* Alexandria, VA: American Counseling Association.

Huey, W. (1987). Counseling teenage fathers: The "maximizing a life experience" (MALE) group. *School Counselor, 35,* 40–47.

Huey, W., & Remley, T. (1988). *Ethical and legal issues in school counseling.* Alexandria, VA: American Counseling Association.

Hutchinson, N. (1996). Group counseling intervention for solving problems on the job. *Journal of Employment Counseling, 33,* 2–19.

Jacobs, E. (1992). *Creative counseling techniques: An illustrated guide.* Odessa, FL: Psychological Assessment Resources.

Jacobs, E., Harvill, R., & Masson, R. (1998). *Group counseling: Strategies and skills* (3rd ed.). Pacific Grove, CA: Brooks/Cole.

Kaduson, H., & Schaefer, C. (Eds). (2000). *Short-term play therapy for children.* New York: Guilford Press.

Kalter, N., & Schreier, S. (1993). School-based support groups for children of divorce. *Special Services in the Schools, 8,* 39–66.

Karp, C., & Butler, T. (1996). *Activity book for treatment strategies for abused children: From victim to survivor.* Thousand Oaks, CA: Sage Publications.

Kiselica, M. (1994). Preparing teenage fathers for parenthood: A group psychoeducational approach. *Journal for Specialists in Group Work, 19,* 83–94.

Kizner, L., & Kizner, S. (1999). Small group counseling with adopted children. *Professional School Counseling, 2*(3), 226–229.

Kramer, L., & Radey, C. (1997). Improving sibling relationships among young children: A social skills training model. *Family Relations, 46*(3), 237–246.

LaFountain, R., & Garner, N. (1996). Solution-focused counseling groups: The results are in. *Journal for Specialists in Group Work, 21,* 128–143.

Lee, C. (1987). Black manhood training. *Journal for Specialists in Group Work, 12,* 18–25.

Lehmann, L., Jimerson, S., & Gaasch, A. (2001). *Mourning child grief support group curriculum: Middle childhood edition, grades 3–6.* Florence, KY: Bruner Rutledge.

Lifton, W. (1972). *Groups: Facilitating individual growth and societal change.* New York: Wiley.

Martin, C., & Lehr, J. (1999). *The START curriculum: An interactive and experiential curriculum for building strong character and healthy relationships in middle and high schools.* Minneapolis: Educational Media Corp.

McNair, R., & Arman, J. (2000). A small group model for working with elementary school children of alcoholics. *Professional School Counseling, 3*(4), 290–293.

Mehaffey, J., & Sandberg, S. (1992). Conducting social skills training groups with elementary school children. *School Counselor, 40,* 61–67.

Morganett, R. (2002a). *Skills for living: Group counseling activities for young adolescents* (2nd ed.). Champaign, IL: Research Press.

Morganett, R. (2002b). *Skills for living: Group counseling activities for elementary students* (2nd ed.). Champaign, IL: Research Press.

Myrick, R. (2002). *Developmental guidance and counseling: A practical approach* (4th ed.). Minneapolis: Educational Media.

Nelson, J., Dykeman, C., Powell, S., & Petty, D. (1996). The effects of a group counseling intervention on students with behavioral adjustment problems. *Elementary School Guidance and Counseling, 31,* 21–33.

Newbauer, J., & Hess, S. (1994). Treating sex offenders and survivors conjointly: Gender issues with adolescent boys. *Journal for Specialists in Group Work, 19,* 129–135.

Nims, D. (1998). Searching for self: A theoretical model for applying family systems to adolescent group work. *Journal for Specialists in Group Work, 23*(2), 133–144.

Ohlsen, M., Horne, A., & Lawe, C. (1988). *Group counseling* (3rd ed.). New York: Holt, Rinehart & Winston.

Omizo, M., Hershberger, J., & Omizo, S. (1988). Teaching children to cope with anger. *Elementary School Guidance and Counseling, 22,* 241–245.

Omizo, M., & Omizo, S. (1988). The effects of participation in group counseling sessions on self-esteem and locus of control among adolescents from divorced families. *School Counselor, 36,* 54–60.

O'Rourke, K., & Worzbyt, J. (1996). *Support groups for children.* Bristol, PA: Accelerated Development.

Paisley, R., & Hubbard, G. (1994). *Developmental school counseling programs: From theory to practice.* Alexandria, VA: American Counseling Association.

Parramore, B., & Hopke, W. (1999). *Early occupational awareness program.* Chicago: Ferguson Publishing.

Pearson, Z., & Nicholson, J. (2000). Comprehensive character education in the elementary school: Strategies for administrators, teachers, and counselors. *Journal of Humanistic Counseling, Education, and Development, 38*(4), 243–251.

Peterson, S., & Straub, R. (1992). *School crisis survival guide.* West Nyack, NY: Center for Applied Research in Education.

Peyser, S., & McLaughlin, M. (1997). *Character education activities for K–6 classrooms.* Minneapolis: Educational Media Corp.

Phillips–Hershey, E., & Kanagy, B. (1996). Teaching students to manage personal anger con-structive*ly. Elementary School Guidance and Counseling, 30,* 229–234.

Pope, M., & Minor, C. (Eds.). (2000). *Experiential activities for teaching career counseling classes and for facilitating career groups.* Columbus, OH: National Career Development Association.

Powell, L., & Faherty, S. (1990). Treating sexually abused latency age girls. *The Arts in Psychotherapy, 17,* 35–47.

Rainey, L., Hensley, E., & Crutchfield, L. (1997). Implementation of support groups in ele-mentary and middle school student assistance programs. *Professional School Counseling, 1*(2), 36–40.

Reeder, J., Douzenis, C., & Bergin, J. (1997). The effects of small-group counseling on the racial attitudes of second grade students. *Professional School Counseling, 1*(2), 15–18.

Riddle, J., Bergin, J., & Douzenis, C. (1997). The effects of group counseling on the self-concept of children of alcoholics. *Elementary School Guidance and Counseling, 31,* 192–203.

Ritchie, M., & Huss, S. (2000). Recruitment and screening of minors for group counseling. *Journal for Specialists in Group Work, 25*(2), 146–156.

Robinson, E., Rotter, J., Frey, M., & Vogel, K. (1992). *Helping children cope with fears and stress.* Ann Arbor, MI: ERIC Counseling and Student Services Clearinghouse.

Rogala, J., Lambert, R., & Verhage, K. (1991). *Developmental guidance classroom activities for use with the national career development guidelines.* Madison: University of Wisconsin, Vocational Studies Center.

Rose, S., & Edelson, J. (1987). *Working with children and adolescents in groups.* San Francisco: Jossey–Bass.

Rosenbaum, J. (1994). Experiences of adolescents participating in a developmental peer group counseling career programme. *Guidance & Counseling, 9*(5), 3–7.

Salo, M., & Schumate, S. (1993). Counseling minor clients. In T. Remley, Jr. (Ed.), *The ACA legal series* (Vol. 4). Alexandria, VA: American Counseling Association.

Sandhu, D., (Ed.). (2001). *Elementary school counseling in the new millenium.* Alexandria, VA: American Counseling Association.

Schmidt, J. (2002). *Counseling in schools: Essential services and comprehensive programs* (4th ed.). Boston: Allyn & Bacon.

Siccone, F., & Canfield, J. (1993a). *101 ways to develop student self-esteem and responsibility: Vol. 1.* Boston: Allyn & Bacon

Siccone, F., & Canfield, J. (1993b). *101 ways to develop student self-esteem and responsibility: Vol. 2.* Boston: Allyn & Bacon.

Stewart, J. (1995). Group counseling elementary school children who use aggressive behaviors. *Guidance & Counseling, 11*(1), 12–15.

Sunburst Communications. (1990). *I like being me: Self-esteem.* [Video]. Pleasantville, NY: Author.

Sunburst Communications. (1991). *When your mom and dad get divorced.* [Video]. Pleasantville, NY: Author.

Tedder, S., Scherman, A., & Wantz, R. (1987). Effectiveness of support group for children of divorce. *Elementary School Guidance and Counseling, 22,* 102–109.

Thompson, C., & Rudolph, L. (2000). *Counseling children* (5th ed.). Pacific Grove, CA: Brooks/Cole.

Thompson, R. (1998). *Nurturing an endangered generation: Empowering youth with critical social, emotional, and cognitive skills.* Bristol, PA: Accelerated Development.

Utay, J., & Lampe, R. (1995). Use of a group counseling game to enhance social skills of children with learning disabilities. *Journal for Specialists in Group Work, 20,* 114–120.

Vander Kolk, C. (1985). *Introduction to group counseling and psychotherapy.* Columbus, OH: Merrill.

Vernon, A. (1980). *Help yourself to a healthier you: A handbook of emotional education exercises for children.* Washington, DC: University Press of America.

Vernon, A. (1989). *Thinking, feeling, behaving: An emotional educational curriculum for adolescents.* Champaign, IL: Research Press.

Vernon, A. (1993). *Developmental assessment and intervention with children and adolescents.* Alexandria, VA: American Counseling Association.

Vernon A. (1998a). *The Passport Program: A journey through emotional, social, cognitive, and self-development/grades 1–5.* Champaign, IL: Research Press.

Vernon, A. (1998b). *The Passport Program: A journey through emotional, social, cognitive, and self-development/grades 6–8.* Champaign, IL: Research Press.

Vernon, A. (1998c). *The Passport Program: A journey through emotional, social, cogntive, and self-development/grades 9–12.* Champaign, IL: Research Press.

Vernon, A. (1999). *Counseling children and adolescents* (2nd ed.). Denver: Love Publishing.

Vernon, A. (2002). *What works when with children and adolescents: A handbook of individual counseling techniques.* Champaign, IL: Research Press.

Vernon, A., & Al–Mabuk, R. (1995). *What growing up is all about: A parent's guide to child and adolescent development.* Champaign, IL: Research Press.

Wick, D., Wick, J., & Peterson, N. (1997). Improving self-esteem with Adlerian adventure therapy. *Professional School Counseling, 1*(1), 53–56.

Wilde, J. (1996). The efficacy of short-term rational-emotive education with fourth-grade students. *Elementaty School Guidance and Counseling, 31,* 131–138.

Worzbyt, J., & O'Rourke, K. (1989). *Elementary school counseling: A blueprint for today and tomorrow.* Muncie, IN: Accelerated Development.

Yauman, B. (1991). School-based group counseling for children of divorce: A review of the literature. *Elementary School Guidance and Counseling, 26,* 130–138.

Chapter 12

Designing a Developmental Counseling Curriculum

Toni R. Tollerud and Robert J. Nejedlo

Think back to your school days and recall your school counselor. Do you remember the counselor's name? Under what conditions did you talk with the counselor? Do you remember the school having a counselor during all grades or just in high school?

For most adults, remembrances about a school counselor are vague or minimal. Often, they saw the counselor only to get help in setting up their schedule, to look at college information, or if they got into trouble. Indeed, many recollections of meetings with the counselor are negative. Quite rare is the recollection that the school counselor came to the students' classroom and did any kind of teaching or group activities to address students' developmental needs. Historically, counselors have followed a traditional format of counseling that has been reactive, remedial, and crisis-oriented. Counselors in some middle and high school settings have had to take on, in addition, the cumbersome administrative role of scheduler, which can consume much time and energy.

Fortunately, the days of the school counselor as disciplinarian, scheduler, and crisis counselor are in transition. As early as 1991, Ellis wrote:

> A new school of thought is emerging among educators and counselors. Unlike the reform movement of the past decade, this new movement takes full account of students' personal needs in formulating educational goals. Proponents of this school of thought recognize the close relationship between students' academic development and their personal growth; accordingly, they are seeking to place guidance at the heart of the educational process. (p. 70)

Work by Gysbers and Henderson (2000) over the last 15 years, as well as work by Myrick (1997) and others, has seen the development of comprehensive guidance programs. Gysbers (2001) further supports the integration of these school counseling programs into the educational framework in ways that assist all students toward academic success and reaching their personal and career goals. He stated, "Our mission then is to use the wisdom of the past to further strengthen the work of school counselors within a comprehensive guidance and counseling program framework for today and tomorrow" (p. 104).

To meet these challenges, contemporary counselors have to broaden their roles. Dealing with crises and doing remedial work will continue to be important, but school counselors must move into an arena that includes the developmental/preventive component, which means they also will be adding a teaching role. Paisley and Borders (1995) wrote:

> Currently, the appropriate focus for school counseling is considered to be on comprehensive and developmental programs. Such programs include individual, small-group and large-group counseling as well as consultation and coordination. . . . They will emphasize primary prevention and the promotion of healthy development for all students. (p. 150).

Six years later, Paisley and McMahon (2001) added to these concepts and stated that the ideal school counselor would be culturally and technologically competent and responsive. They suggested that counselors would,

> intentionally and collaboratively design responsive school counseling programs. They would hold themselves accountable rather than wait for someone else to. They would evaluate their programs and share the results with the school community, and use the results to enhance the programs to more effectively meet student needs and support student learning. (p. 114)

A balanced approach emphasizing remedial and crisis intervention, as well as addressing the developmental needs of students (Baker, 1996), will be critical for meeting the changing needs of students in today's diverse society.

Developmental/Preventive Models

Several models of school counseling advocate a strong developmental/preventive emphasis. Developmental guidance and counseling models (Gysbers & Henderson, 2000; Myrick, 1997; VanZandt & Hayslip, 1994, 2001; Vernon & Strub, 1990–1991) came on the scene in the early 1970s. In 1979, the American School Counselor Association adopted this approach and issued the following definition of developmental guidance:

> Developmental guidance is that component of all guidance efforts which fosters planned interventions within educational and other human services programs at all points in the human life cycle to vigorously stimulate and actively facilitate the total development of individuals in all areas: i.e., personal, social, career, emotional, moral–ethical, cognitive, and aesthetic; and to promote the integration of the several components into an individual's life style. (American School Counselor Association [ASCA], 1979)

In 1997, the ASCA published a work titled *National Standards for School Counseling Programs* (Campbell & Dahir, 1997) to provide a framework for school counselors that focuses on what students need to know and do developmentally. These standards were an attempt to move school counseling from its traditional "ancillary" role to one that is integral within the educational system and total development of students. The standards exemplify many of the basic principles of a developmental counseling and guidance approach.

The developmental guidance and counseling approach integrates a counseling curriculum into the total educational process for all students in the school, rather than seeing it as peripheral or tangential. Incorporated into this approach are the following principles identified by Myrick (1997, p. 35):

1. Developmental guidance is for all students.
2. Developmental guidance has an organized and planned curriculum.
3. Developmental guidance is sequential and flexible.
4. Developmental guidance is an integrated part of the total educational process.
5. Developmental guidance involves all school personnel.
6. Developmental guidance helps students learn more effectively and efficiently.
7. Developmental guidance includes counselors who provide specialized counseling services and interventions.

In addition, we believe the following principles are applicable in developmental models:

1. Developmental guidance and counseling helps students cope with issues and problems that are normal to growing up and becoming adults.
2. Developmental guidance and counseling considers the nature of human development, including the general stages and tasks of normal maturation.
3. Developmental guidance and counseling encompasses three approaches: remedial, crisis, and preventative.

Counseling All Students in the Classroom

The core component of a developmental guidance and counseling program is its preventive aspect. Certainly, prevention can be integrated into individual and small-group counseling, but its primary infusion for children and adolescents comes through the counseling and guidance curriculum offered in the classroom. This type of counseling program is available to all students in the school. Through the classroom curriculum, students at every grade level, throughout the entire academic year, are offered programming that attends to their developmental level and personal needs.

Developmental guidance and counseling models span the K–12 years. They are based on the concept that children pass through various developmental stages as they grow and mature. For children to develop in a healthy manner, they must progress successfully through certain kinds of learning and development. Therefore, within the models, student competencies, based on developmental learning theory and national standards, are identified (Campbell & Dahir, 1997). Using these standards as guides, school counselors can develop specific competencies for each grade level, reflecting the developmental characteristics and needs of students for that grade. For example, a first grade competency might be to learn how to set a goal for getting work done in class during the day. In middle school the student may take a situation and set a short, intermediate, and long-term goal for a class project. High school students may address the competency by establishing goals for post-secondary education or employment. These student competencies become the objectives from which the school counselor begins to develop a counseling curriculum.

Student competencies differ among school districts and states. The American School Counselor Association published a guide for school counselors that suggests student competencies for each grade level (ASCA, 1990). States and school districts use these guidelines to write their own list of competencies applicable to their situations and settings. In developing counseling programs, student competencies typically are organized around three domains of development—personal/social, career/vocational, and academic/learning—as is discussed in detail later in this chapter (Gysbers & Henderson, 2000).

Since Gysbers's seminal work on developmental guidance and counseling in the 1970s, developmental models have been adopted in most states throughout the country by state departments of education (e.g., Wisconsin, Oklahoma, Louisiana, Alaska, Indiana) and by school districts (e.g., San Antonio, Texas, and Lincoln, Nebraska). Presentations and workshops are offered on how to design and implement this programming in school settings, and counselor education training programs have begun to teach this type of model to school counselors in training. Some reasons for this national trend are the following:

1. Today's youths are trying to grow up in a complicated and fast-changing society. Their complex needs of personal and social adjustment, academic proficiency, and career and vocational awareness can be met best through a comprehensive, integrative program.
2. Counselors in the schools cannot effectively use a one-to-one counseling approach alone, as it provides services to only a few students. Developmental programming in the classroom enables counselors, teachers, and people in the community to impact all students in their personal, academic, and career development.
3. As the developmental approach is implemented, it becomes cost-effective by providing services to all students in an accountable manner.

The Counselor's New Role as Educator

In the past some teachers went into the field of counseling to escape the classroom. Today's developmental counselors see the classroom as the "front line" of their work. In returning to the mainstream of education, counselors must have the professional skills needed to fulfill all the roles they will be called upon to perform: teacher, therapist, group facilitator, career specialist, crisis manager, mediation trainer, consultant, administrator, researcher, college specialist, test interpreter, and so forth. When administrators hear an explanation of the integrated counseling curriculum, they generally are highly supportive and willing to help make it possible.

Many counselors wonder how they will have the time to implement a counseling curriculum. With good administrative support and program management skills, implementing a fully developed counseling curriculum typically requires only 20–25 percent of the counselor's time. It is a matter of administrative support and program management. The following time utilization plan has been shown to be workable at the high school level:

individual and group counseling	25–30%
developmental programming	20–25%
placement (internal and external)	18%
administrative coordination	15%
information-giving	10%

testing	5%
evaluation/follow-up	2%

Even though large-group counseling is vital to the developmental/preventive focus, counselor time still must be allocated to small-group counseling and individual counseling, as well as other aspects of the counselor's role.

As with any comprehensive program, developmental programming must incorporate a team approach if it is to effectively meet the needs of all students. Thus, teachers must be active participants. Counselors who are trained and prepared in the developmental model take the lead in establishing the curriculum, but they do so by strongly collaborating with teachers, drawing upon their expertise. Furthermore, team teaching is encouraged. Counselors can train teachers in the types of lessons and the process desired for a counseling curriculum. As counselors meet with the large groups, they can model the teaching of personal/social, academic, and career lessons that enhance and promote academic growth.

Ideally, classroom teachers will assume some of the responsibility for teaching the lessons and meeting the objectives identified in the counseling curriculum because counselors cannot do all of the classroom guidance and still have time to do their individual and small-group counseling for which they are uniquely trained. For example, the counselor and teacher would collaborate on an assignment that involves writing an essay on a career option for an English class.

Because time during the school day is at a premium, creative planning is necessary to implement developmental programming. This may be simpler at the grade school level because the suggested 30 minutes a week for counselors to come into the classroom is easier to fit into the teacher's schedule. In the upper grades, when students are attending classes in periods, the counselor may have to negotiate alternatives for leading classroom programs. In some schools, teachers in English, science, social studies, physical education, or other classes allow the counselor to deliver the curriculum in the classroom within agreed-upon timeframes. In other schools, a guidance and counseling period has been established around homerooms or split lunch periods. Myrick (1997) suggested implementing a program in which teachers, serving as student advisors, become involved in developmental guidance and counseling during homeroom or other designated periods.

The use of student advisory periods has become a popular way to implement a developmental program, especially at the middle and high school levels. An advisory period is an identified period of the school day lasting from 15–30 minutes that can be used for delivering a curriculum that addresses student needs. In identifying the teacher as student advisor, Myrick (1997) emphasized the work teachers must do to build a personal relationship with students.

Unfortunately, many teachers are not doing what is needed to build strong relationships with their students. In a survey conducted by the Consortium for School Improvement at the University of Chicago (Sebring et al., 1996), students overwhelmingly indicated that they did not have a personal relationship with their teachers and believed that no one really cared about their development in high school. The Chicago Public Schools have addressed this need with the establishment of student advisories in all high schools with two primary purposes: (a) to establish a personal relationship between students and at least one adult in the school, and (b) to help students develop life skills that will enable them to achieve in school and experience success (Chicago Public Schools, 1997–1998). In the many schools that have student advisory periods, teachers, administrators, and school counselors collaboratively use this time to address students' competencies and needs.

In other schools the developmental curriculum is presented predominantly by the counselor, who develops units and goes into general classes to present the material. In these cases, cooperation is vital to planning and delivering an effective program. The counselor is under heavy scrutiny to use classroom time effectively and efficiently, because students, faculty, and administrators are critics of how the program is evolving. To establish accountability, the counselor must put in place an evaluation procedure that measures outcomes of the student competencies and objectives of the established curriculum. Reporting outcomes to the faculty and administration is a positive step in gaining support. In addition, the evaluation procedure can help counselors improve the effectiveness in future student programming.

Reforming school counseling, changing it from an ancillary role to an integral role in the total educational process, is no easy task. Sink (2002) stated that what appears to be the emphasis for the school counselor of the 21st century is a fusion between counseling and guidance and education. This can be accomplished by encouraging counselors to focus on the following:

> Developing and updating the skills needed to serve all students; exploring innovations in educational and counseling theory and practice; advocating for themselves and their programs; implementing well-designed comprehensive programs; collaborating with one another, other school personnel, and with community agencies and programs; measuring student and program accomplishments and needs; creating a sense of community in their schools; and demonstrating a high degree of professionalism. (p. 161)

Working as an educator in the classroom may require major shifts in the counselor's role and behaviors. Infusing objectives from a counseling curriculum into other areas of teaching requires creativity by classroom teachers. With careful planning, however, this change can be highly productive and is well worth the effort. Students will benefit from a counseling curriculum that assists in their positive development throughout their school years and helps them to refine their skills for living by increasing their decision-making, self-awareness, and coping abilities. Schools will benefit from a curriculum that addresses the complex personal developmental needs of its students in addition to their academic subject-matter needs. The curriculum will give students the tools to approach life's challenges and therefore will help to minimize the number and severity of student difficulties.

For school counselors, the new role of educator means becoming more active and taking an integral role in the total school curriculum. It means moving into the classroom, becoming curriculum specialists, and holding themselves and their programs accountable. The profession no longer can hide behind closed doors or have unclear goals. To move into the developmental program is to put one's expertise on display and to be accountable for one's work. It is a worthy challenge.

Major Principles in a Counseling Curriculum

A counseling curriculum is based on the premise that all students need assistance throughout their school years in accomplishing developmental tasks. Acquiring the necessary skills can lead each student to a sense of personal fulfillment and enhance the student's quality of life as a productive person in society.

A counseling curriculum provides a systematic approach for exposing students to age-appropriate lessons that will help them learn, understand, and eventually master aspects of personal/social development, vocational/career development, and academic/educational development. The primary goal is to help students develop healthy ways to cope and deal with situations that arise during their life journeys. Students can work through developmental and situational crises if they are able to call upon the skills they learned to confront difficulties when they arise.

As an example, students might role-play appropriate ways of handling their feelings when they are angry at school. Having the students explore alternative ways of reacting and consider the consequences of their behaviors in situations that are not emotionally charged will help them gain a better understanding without the emotional component. When the students are faced with a real situation in their personal lives, they will be able to make more appropriate, positive decisions.

Like any other curriculum in the educational schema, a counseling curriculum must be comprehensive, ongoing, and sensitive to the students' readiness to learn. Lessons emphasizing prevention should begin at the elementary level and progress to more difficult or abstract levels as the students develop cognitive and emotional capabilities. All students can benefit from lessons that promote positive self-esteem, for example, but the way the counselor approaches this topic will be quite different depending upon the grade level. For example, first graders may learn to identify their physical characteristics, middle school students may learn to deal with self-consciousness, and high school students may learn how to identify individual strengths that relate to career interests. The main ideas and themes (self-esteem, for example) must be repeated at each grade level through different activities that reflect developmental tasks and challenges and enhance the students' learning.

Some counselors establish monthly themes for the entire student body. The unit taught during a given month reflects that month's theme in developmentally appropriate lessons. One school district that has adopted this approach has established the following schedule (Winneconne School Counselors, 1990):

August:	Getting Acquainted/Orientation/Transition
September:	Academic Fitness/Self-Evaluation/Goal Setting
October:	Choices and Consequences/Decision Making
November:	Liking Me/Self-Esteem
December:	Family
January:	Wellness/Lifestyles/Stress Management
February:	Friendship/Interpersonal Relationship Skills
March:	Citizenship/Civic and Social Responsibility
April:	Feelings/Communication/Coping
May:	Careers/Exploration/Planning

Monthly themes also may be developed around topics based on age-appropriate developmental issues. For example, elementary school students may benefit from themes of sibling rivalry, tattling, and good touch/bad touch. Middle school students may benefit from units on cliques, peer relationships, study skills, or managing emotional ups and downs. High school students might benefit from units on college planning, applying for jobs, dating, and developing a sexual identity.

Counselors also may identify situational topics, which usually are presented to students following a specific event or catastrophe. After the September 11th attacks on America, for example, counselors presented units to students addressing fear, death, and safety. As another example, a unit on loss and grief may be appropriate following the death of a student or staff member in a school.

The counseling curriculum must be well organized. Goals and competencies for each grade level must be identified, followed by units and lesson plans that contain sequential, developmentally appropriate activities that follow a lesson plan format. Students, faculty, staff, and parents all must see the counseling curriculum as an integral component within the total instructional program, and this can be accomplished only if the curriculum is organized and accountable.

Developing the curriculum to fit the needs of a school system is a major task. Counselors must be willing to scrutinize the plethora of materials available from publishers and glean from them the activities or ideas they believe will be the most appropriate. Curriculum resources can be organized into three-ring binders so they can be readily shared with other counselors in the school district or neighboring districts. The materials that can be used in classroom guidance and counseling programming should be reviewed and customized according to the unique characteristics of the setting. (Designing a lesson plan for a developmental program and suggestions for teaching the lesson in the classroom are discussed in detail later in this chapter.)

A counseling curriculum also must be flexible. As new areas of need arise in a program, the curriculum should be revised and embellished. The toughest time will be at the start, when guidance and counseling units have to be created. After a unit has been taught, additional lessons can be added and changes made. When appropriate, outside experts can serve as resources. For example, local police officers might come into the classroom to teach a unit on drug awareness or personal safety. Some school districts hire a representative from a local professional substance abuse center to teach a prevention program to students. Flexibility enables the counseling curriculum to fit the ever-changing needs and circumstances of the setting and the students.

Finally, a counseling curriculum must be accountable, which requires good planning from the beginning. Goals and objectives for the curriculum should be written in behavioral and measurable terms. An evaluation should be done at the end of each unit to determine whether the students understood and grasped the topic or issue presented. The evaluation activity might be a game or an informal test that would not be graded.

In addition, classroom teachers could be questioned about any new behaviors they observe in the students. Year-end evaluations should be done to measure the effectiveness of the curriculum. By planning ahead and implementing evaluative materials from the beginning, the counseling curriculum has a much better chance to be successful and find favor with parents, faculty, and administrators.

All of the components in a counseling curriculum must work together in a holistic and meaningful way. Such a comprehensive approach can greatly contribute to students' healthy development.

A Student Development Program Model

A thorough counseling curriculum carefully considers three components within each of the general (personal/social, career/vocational, and academic/learning) areas of living. These components are life themes, life transitions, and life skills that affect human beings as they grow and develop (Drum & Knott, 1977). The student development program model described here is a step-by-step illustration of how components can be effectively incorporated into a counseling curriculum.

The student development program is a structured, sequenced, large-group activity directed to the needs and interests of all students in a school, and sensitive to the developmental competencies and interests of students at different grade levels. It is a helping process in which the counselor or teacher presents a series of lessons representing a curriculum of counseling. Figure 12.1 depicts the student development program model and the interrelatedness of each aspect with the

Steps:	Definitions:		
1. Identify school level (i.e., elementary, middle, or,high school).	Life Themes:	Major recurring situations and issues throughout the lifespan that need to be addressed developmentally so that people can adequately respond to these situations and cope with these issues.	
2. Identify developmental tasks and needed competencies.	Life Transitions:	Major changes and/or passages throughout the lifespan that impact on a person in such a way as to necessitate adaption and restructuring of current behaviors and realities.	
3. Utilize professional assessment and/or needs assessment.	Life Skills:	Learned behaviors that enable a person to perform the essential tasks of normal developmental growth throughout the lifespan (e.g., problem solving).	
4. Identify developmental program based on the model.			

	Life-Themes	**Life Transitions**	**Life Skills**
Academic			
Personal/ Social			
Career			

FIGURE 12.1   *Structural Framework Form for a Developmental Counseling Program*

three developmental domains discussed below. The developmental approach targets the accomplishment of student competencies in three domains of living: personal/social, career/vocational, and academic/learning domains, as shown in the following list:

   1. *Personal/social:* The curriculum identifies competencies that will assist students in understanding and expressing self and in looking at how they relate to others as individuals and in groups. It helps students see how their thoughts,

feelings, and behaviors shape their personality, their being, and their inter-personal relationships.

2. *Career/vocational:* The curriculum targets competencies that will assist students in exploring career possibilities and opportunities, helps students with career decision making, and enables them to make a successful transition from school to the world of work.

3. *Academic/learning:* The curriculum provides activities and experiences that develop competencies leading to a student's educational success and promotes optimum development of each student's learning potential.

When students are taught a curriculum emphasizing these three domains at every grade level, the preventive aspect is clear. The goal is to teach the students how to deal with normal developmental issues in a way that will increase their self-awareness, self-esteem, and positive relationships with others and will improve their goal-setting, decision-making, career exploration, and study skills. These competencies then can be translated into skills or tools that will lead to healthy choices and responses when students face difficulties or decisions.

Student development program planners also identify specific goals, issues, and situations to be addressed in the classroom in the areas of:

1. *Life themes:* major recurring situations and issues throughout the lifespan that can be addressed developmentally so people can adequately respond to and deal with them. Certain situations occur again and again throughout life. Each time they appear, they may have to be addressed differently, perhaps at a more intensive level, requiring modifications or different skills. Life themes are best approached by teaching life skills that relate to specific recurring situations. As people grow and mature, the best method to handle or cope with these situations may change. Examples of life themes are friendship and love, stress, personal safety, and responsibility.

2. *Life transitions:* major changes and passages throughout the lifespan that impact on a person and necessitate adapting and restructuring current behaviors and realities. Life transitions are specific points in a person's life at which significant changes transpire. Some of these transitions occur at common times for most people, such as starting school and obtaining a driver's license. Other transitions occur at varying times, such as first job, first love, moving, or the death of a significant grandparent or parent. Some students go through painful life transitions before most people do, experiencing a serious illness or injury that alters their life, or having parents divorce, for example. Including life transitions in the curriculum is critical so students can begin to prepare for anxious times and crises by identifying life skills that may help them cope effectively when situations do present themselves.

3. *Life skills*: learned behaviors that enable a person to perform the essential tasks of normal developmental growth throughout the lifespan. These are taught continually in the counseling curriculum. Most relate heavily to the

personal/social area. They include self-acceptance, listening, communication, problem solving, values clarification, identifying and expressing feelings, and so forth.

Life themes and life transitions necessitate that individuals learn life skills that can help them handle recurring situations, issues, changes, and life passages. As counselors identify the themes and transitions in the lives of preschool–grade 12 students, they should design and implement programs that will:

1. Create an awareness of the dynamics involved in each life theme and transition.
2. Help individuals understand how the themes and transitions affect them.
3. Teach students how to change or modify their behaviors to adjust to or resolve specific life themes or transitions.

For example, lessons on stress management should help students realize that sometimes unpleasant circumstances result in an upset stomach or other physical manifestation. They should allow for discussion about how students feel about unpleasant situations and the effects of these situations, and they should teach students how to develop coping skills to deal with unpleasant situations.

Working Within the Structural Framework

As a counseling curriculum is developed, the counselor has to plan for the inclusion of certain essential topics. Counselors are encouraged to prioritize the essential topics and develop units and lessons one topic at a time across the K–12 curriculum. Some planners set up their curriculum to focus on decision making in fifth grade and friendships in sixth grade, for example. This type of haphazard or unsequential planning should be avoided, as students at all grade levels need to learn developmentally appropriate information about each topic at each grade level to assure more comprehensive learning. Suggested essential topics are listed in Table 12.1.

Another set of topics, termed "special needs," may be instituted in a school or community because of the unique needs or characteristics of the local community. For example, a unit on death or loss may be needed if a school has had a series of suicides or catastrophic deaths, or a unit on eating disorders or self-mutilation may be needed if the district has a high prevalence of these disorders.

Figure 12.1 contains a structural framework form that can assist counselors in designing classroom guidance and counseling programs. Often the hardest step in a developmental guidance and counseling program is getting started. This format can be used to begin a new program or to reassess an ongoing program. Prior to using the form, the counselor should:

1. Select a grade level.

TABLE 12.1 *Essential Topics to be Covered in a Counseling Curriculum*

Life Themes	Life Transitions	Life Skills
Personal/Social Domain		
Self-Concept Development	Family Changes (new	Self-Awareness
Friendship and Love	siblings, death, divorce)	Self-Acceptance
Change	New School Orientation	Listening Skills
Conflicts	Significant Life Events	Communications Skills
Stress	(puberty, driver's	Values Clarification
Values	license, first job)	Problem-Solving
Personal Safety	Loss of Friends and	Relationship Skills
Responsibility	Loved Ones	Coping Skills
Grief and Loss		Behavior Management
Death		
Career/Vocational Domain		
Career Exploration	Career Fantasy to	Planning
Use of Leisure Time	Career Exploration	Goal-Setting
Attitude Toward Work	Exploration to Tentative	Career Decision Making
Dual-Career Couples	Career Choice	Employment-Seeking
Career Decisions		Skills
Academic/Learning Area		
Motivations	Preschool to Elementary	Study Skills
Learning Styles	Elementary to Middle	Time Management
Learning Deficiencies	School	Speech and Test Anxiety
Discipline vs. Procrastination	Middle School to High	Reduction
Lifelong Learning	School	Critical Thinking
	High School to College	Analysis and Synthesis
	High School to Work	

2. Identify student needs based on students' developmental level (review of ASCA student competencies, national standards, or another source that addresses student needs is helpful).

3. Consider other pertinent information gathered from needs assessments of students, teachers, parents, and administrators.

Then, in the appropriate column on the form, the counselor should list important life themes, life transitions, and life skills to be addressed at that grade level.

The suggested essential K–12 topics for a student development counseling curriculum, as listed in Table 12.1, cover the personal/social, career/vocational, and academic/learning domains. Within each domain, the three components of life skills, life themes, and life transitions add meaningful organization to the specific units. This structural framework enables counselors to identify the core areas of the counseling curriculum, topics essential for all programs, and topics unique to the individual school setting.

Identifying topics is only the first step, though. Objectives or competencies should be developed for each topic from kindergarten through the senior year in high school. These objectives will serve as the basis for creating lessons and units on each of these topics and for developing a sequential, grade-level curriculum. As an illustration, we present the objectives that Vernon (1998a,b,c) identified for the topic of self-acceptance.

Self–Acceptance (Grades 1–12)

Grade 1

- *To learn that everyone has strengths as well as weaknesses*
- *To learn that everyone is worthwhile regardless of weaknesses*
- *To identify what children like about being who they are*
- *To develop an attitude of self-acceptance*
- *To identify ways in which children are physically growing and changing*
- *To identify competencies associated with physical changes*

Grade 2

- *To develop awareness of abilities and attributes*
- *To learn to accept oneself with these abilities and attributes*
- *To recognize that strengths and limitations are part of one's self-definition*
- *To learn not to put oneself down because of limitations*
- *To identify individual strengths*
- *To learn a strategy to help remember good things about oneself*

Grade 3

- *To learn that how one acts determines self-worth*
- *To learn that nobody is perfect*
- *To learn to accept oneself as less than perfect*
- *To identify characteristics of self, including strengths and weaknesses*
- *To learn to accept compliments*
- *To identify personal strengths*

Grade 4

- *To learn that mistakes are natural*

▪ *To learn that making mistakes does not make one a bad person*
▪ *To identify strengths and weaknesses in the areas of physical, social, and intellectual development*
▪ *To recognize ways to get approval from others and ways to approve of oneself*
▪ *To learn that others' approval is not required to be worthwhile*
▪ *To learn more about individual preferences, characteristics, and abilities*

Grade 5

▪ *To identify one's positive attributes*
▪ *To differentiate between making mistakes and being a total failure*
▪ *To identify specific characteristics that are like or unlike oneself*
▪ *To identify feelings associated with varying rates of development*

Grade 6

▪ *To identify self-characteristics*
▪ *To learn that self-characteristics may change over time*
▪ *To normalize the self-conscious feelings that begin to occur during this period of development and to learn more about the physical changes occurring during this period of rapid growth*
▪ *To learn that all individuals have strengths and weaknesses and not to rate oneself globally as good or bad*
▪ *To learn to take multiple perspectives into account when forming opinions about oneself*
▪ *To learn to separate others' negative perceptions from one's sense of self-worth*

Grade 7

▪ *To learn not to equate self-worth with performance*
▪ *To normalize feelings of self-consciousness during early adolescence*
▪ *To explore ways to deal with self-conscious feelings*
▪ *To develop a better understanding of the self-definition process and how this applies to oneself*
▪ *To identify ways one is like and unlike one's peers*
▪ *To develop awareness of social, emotional, and physical problems associated with eating disorders*

Grade 8

▪ *To develop an understanding of the frequent changes in the way one thinks, feels, and behaves*
▪ *To identify feelings associated with changes during early adolescence*
▪ *To develop an understanding of adolescent egocentricity*
▪ *To learn how adolescent egocentricity affects oneself as well as others*

■■ *To normalize feelings of self-consciousness and develop effective strategies for dealing with those feelings*
■■ *To develop a clearer picture of who one is*

Grade 9

■■ *To learn more about personal values*
■■ *To learn more about one's identity*
■■ *To clarify values and beliefs*
■■ *To learn that one is not invincible*
■■ *To identify consequences of believing that one is invincible*
■■ *To learn that performance in one area is not a reflection of one's total worth as a person*

Grade 10

■■ *To distinguish between all-or-nothing self-rating and rating one's individual traits*
■■ *To clarify aspects of self-identity*
■■ *To learn facts about anorexia and bulimia*
■■ *To identify the social, emotional, cognitive, and physical problems associated with eating disorders*
■■ *To compare self-image with one's perceptions of how others see one*
■■ *To learn not to equate self-worth with others' perceptions of one*

Grade 11

■■ *To learn more about who one is becoming in one's identity quest*
■■ *To learn how to accept oneself and to identify one's positive qualities*
■■ *To identify ways one puts oneself down*
■■ *To differentiate between self-respect and disrespect*
■■ *To identify ways to change things one doesn't respect in oneself but to accept oneself as worthwhile regardless of these things*
■■ *To identify what it means to be independent, ways one is independent, and feelings associated with independence*

Grade 12

■■ *To assess personal strengths*
■■ *To identify present and future roles*
■■ *To distinguish between abuse and self-abuse*
■■ *To identify strategies to deal with self-abusive behaviors or abusive behaviors inflicted by others*
■■ *To clarify how one sees oneself in the future*
■■ *To identify what it means to be dependent, ways one is dependent, and feelings associated with dependence*

How to Design a Lesson

Once objectives have been established, the counselor is ready to design the lessons and units to address the objectives or competencies.

Format for Developing Counseling Lessons and Units

The most common approach for developing a counseling curriculum is to organize units around a theme, central idea, or developmentally age-appropriate topic that may arise out of the life-themes, life-transitions, or life-skills components discussed earlier. The unit may evolve as the result of a needs assessment or an outcome desired by the students, or it may reflect grade-level developmental competencies based on developmental needs and tasks. Myrick (1997) suggested that many units be presented yearly, adjusted to target the appropriate readiness skills for each grade level, and that other units be created in response to specific needs or events. For example, if the school is beginning to see gang activity, the counselor might elect to introduce a unit on gang awareness, taking care to provide lessons that match the students' developmental level.

Units usually have an overall theme and are composed of several lessons or sessions. Although the number of sessions varies with the topic, time allocation, and age level, anywhere from 4 to 10 sessions is appropriate. When designing a unit or series of lessons, the counselor should specify the general objectives and goals he or she intends to meet throughout the sessions. The unit format should include the following:

Grade level
Unit name or topic
Appropriate grade-level competencies
Rationale for the unit
Unit purpose
Unit objectives
Number of sessions
Detailed procedures of all activities
Evaluation criteria and method

In addition to being included in the unit format, a brief rationale for the unit, explaining why it is important, should be included in the curriculum sometimes. This rationale can be presented to the administration, staff, and faculty to summarize the "what and why" of the curriculum. This is especially important if the counselor develops units on sensitive issues such as AIDS or death and loss.

The classroom lesson is the heart of the developmental counseling program. Building upon a model developed by Vernon (1998a,b,c; 1989a,b), each lesson should contain the following components:

1. Purpose and objectives

When developing a lesson, the counselor should begin by writing down the purpose and objective he or she intends to accomplish in that lesson. The objective should be written in the specific terms of a performance/measurable outcome. For example: "The student will respond to another by using an 'I message' appropriately." Broad objectives such as, "The student will develop an understanding of better communication skills" should be avoided.

2. *Stimulus activity/procedure*

   Next, the counselor should design a well-planned activity that will assist him or her in fulfilling that objective. This stimulus activity may be a story, film, role-play, speaker, simulation, reading assignment, or other activity. The counselor should make sure the activity will not take up all of the time allotted for the session. The activity is not the most important part of the lesson; it should only "set the stage" for what the counselor wants to accomplish with the students. A list of the materials and/or supplies needed for the activity should be included here.

3. *Content-level discussion*

   The next part of the lesson should be discussion of the stimulus activity at a content level. For example, the counselor might ask the students to tell a partner what was going on in the story or might have the students discuss in small groups the main problem in the video. This section of the lesson should be relatively short and simple. The focus should be on what the students did in the activity or what they learned about the content of the activity.

4. *Personal-level discussion*

   The stimulus activity then should be discussed at a personal level. For example, the counselor may ask the students to think of when they had a similar experience, or if it has happened to them, or how they felt. The counselor may have the students brainstorm ideas about what they think should be done, or what they would do, to handle the situation. In this component the students apply the main concepts of the lesson to their personal situations. The counselor should allow ample time for this component, as it is the key to the lesson. Counselors will find that most of the published materials applicable to counseling units do not contain questions that focus on the personal level; thus, counselors need to pay special attention to personal-level discussion and spend time developing appropriate questions.

5. *Closure*

   During this part of the lesson, the counselor processes the session and brings some closure to the group. With this step the counselor can utilize the group-process skills in asking the students what they learned in the session. The discussion may reveal insights the students have had about themselves or about others.

The final step in developing a counseling unit is planning evaluation. Evaluation is essential for reporting the value and benefit outcomes to administrative and school board personnel. It also benefits the classroom teacher and the students by calling attention to the work the students are doing and the impact that work is having on the students' thinking, feeling, and behavior.

Evaluations can be done at the end of each session or at the end of a unit. The evaluations should be kept simple and appropriate to the grade level, and they can be creative. Art or creative writing projects can be used. The students might form small groups and role-play for the rest of the class what they have learned. They might be asked to complete checklists or surveys that pinpoint the objectives identified at the start of the unit. The most important purpose of the evaluations is for the counselor to gain insight into the effectiveness of the unit so he or she can decide if or how it should be changed when the unit is taught again. In an effective developmental counseling program, evaluation and accountability go hand in hand.

Unit development and lesson design are challenging and require creativity. Ideas can be created, found in affective education materials, or borrowed from other counseling programs, When using ready-made materials, the counselor should adapt them, as necessary, to the unique needs and objectives of his or her situation. A resource list of suggested affective education materials is provided at the end of this chapter.

The lesson plan format discussed here and outlined in Figure 12.2, was used to develop the following sample lessons, one for elementary students and one for middle school. Both lessons are related to emotional development and illustrate how to design lessons around the same theme but relate the concepts to developmental tasks at each level: Elementary students are just developing feeling vocabularies and becoming aware of their emotions; young adolescents need to learn how to deal effectively with painful emotions.

Sample Lesson Emotions, Grade 2

This lesson is reprinted from *The Passport Program: A Journey through Emotional, Social, Cognitive, and Self-Development,* by A. Vernon (Champaign, IL: Research Press, 1998a, 91–92).

Title:	*A Lot or a Little?*
Lesson Objective:	To learn to differentiate the intensity of emotions and to learn that everyone doesn't feel the same way about the same situation.
Materials:	Chalkboard, a ruler, sheet of paper, and pencil for each student.

Stimulus Activity/Procedure:

1. Introduce the activity by having the students use their rulers to draw a line across their papers (horizontal).

Lesson # _____ Topic_____

(1) Lesson Objectives _____

_____

Materials _____

(2) Stimulus Activity _____

(procedure)_____

_____

(3) Content-Level Discussion Questions

    a) _____

    b) _____

    c) _____

(4) Personal-Level Discussion Questions

    a) _____

    b) _____

    c) _____

(5) Closure_____

Evaluation (may be optional) _____

Notes:

FIGURE 12.2   *Lesson Plan Format*

2. On the model line, write the words *very happy* at one end and the words *very unhappy* on the other end. Write the other words (on) the line as illustrated:

very happy   pretty happy   pretty unhappy   very unhappy

3. Ask the children to listen carefully as you read the following situations, one at a time. After each, they are to put an X on the line to illustrate how they might feel if they were in this situation: very happy, pretty happy, pretty unhappy, very unhappy.

    ■ Your teacher tells you that you did very well on your spelling test.

    ■ Your sister gets to stay up later than you do.

■■ Your best friend didn't walk to school with you today.
■■ Your father yelled at you because you hadn't picked up your room.
■■ Your neighbor's dog chewed your new tennis shoes.
■■ Your big brother took you for a ride on his bike.
■■ Your cousin let you use her new rollerblades.
■■ You can't go out for recess because it is raining.
■■ Your class is going on a field trip to the zoo.
■■ You missed two problems on your math paper.

When you have finished reading the first situation, ask children to raise a hand if they marked this situation *very happy, pretty happy,* and so on. Count each response and put the total on the chalkboard beside each feeling on the continuum. Then proceed to the next situation and follow the same procedure of identifying and tallying the responses.

4. After all the situations have been read and recorded, process the activity by asking the Content and Personalization Questions.

Content Questions

1. Looking back at the responses, did this group have all of the marks on the *very happy* end of the line? Did this group have all of the marks on the *very unhappy* end of the line? Why do you think this group had marks at several different places on the line?

2. Was it hard for you to decide how you felt about some of these situations? If so, why do you think it was hard?

3. Do you think everyone always feels the same way about the same things? Why or why not?

Personalization Questions

1. Think about your day today. Have you felt only very happy or very unhappy, or have you also felt pretty happy or pretty unhappy?

2. Have you ever had a disagreement with someone because that person felt differently about something than you did? Invite sharing of examples.

3. Based on this lesson, what do you need to remember about feelings?

Closure (to the leader)

At this age children are very concrete thinkers. Consequently, they have difficulty understanding the concept of a continuum of feelings. As a result, they frequently assume that someone is either very mad or very unhappy about something without recognizing the range of intensity of emotions. Without this understanding, misinterpretation is common. It is possible to teach children how to develop a broader perspective as part of their emotional development.

Sample Lesson on Emotions, Grade 8

This lesson is reprinted from *The Passport Program: A Journey through Emotional, Social, Cognitive, and Self-Development,* by A. Vernon (Champaign, IL: Research Press, 1998b, 203–204).

Title:	*Pain Relievers*
Lesson Objective:	To distinguish healthy and unhealthy ways to relieve emotional pain.
Materials:	A chalkboard, magazines, scissors, glue, a large sheet of tagboard, and markers for every group of 4 students.

Stimulus Activity/Procedure:

1. Introduce the activity by having students quickly brainstorm examples of painful emotions. As they identify examples, write them on the board. Next discuss the difference between healthy and unhealthy ways of dealing with painful emotions. For example, anger can be a painful emotion. An unhealthy way to deal with anger would be to get drunk. A healthy way to deal with it would be to talk it out.

2. Divide students into groups of four and distribute the materials. Instruct them to make two columns on the bottom half of the tagboard poster and to label one side "Healthy ways to deal with painful emotions" and the other side "Unhealthy ways to deal with painful emotions." Ask each group to list several painful emotions at the top of the poster. Then have them look through the magazines for pictures representing healthy or unhealthy ways to deal with these emotions. If they can't find appropriate pictures, have them draw symbols or use words to represent their suggestions.

3. After the posters have been completed, have the small groups share them with the total group.

4. Discuss the Content and Personalization questions.

Content-Level Discussion Questions:

1. Which was harder to identify: healthy or unhealthy ways to deal with painful emotions?

2. In general, were the small groups in agreement with each other? Were there some ideas that one group labeled unhealthy that you might have considered healthy, and vice versa? Share examples.

3. What makes the unhealthy methods unhealthy? Do you really think they help relieve pain in the long-term? Why or why not?

Personal-Level Discussion Questions:

1. Are your "pain relievers" generally healthy or unhealthy? How do you feel about that?

2. If you have tried unhealthy methods in the past, how has this affected your life? If you had it to do over, what might you do differently, if anything?

3. Did you learn anything from this lesson that will be helpful to you in dealing with painful emotions? Invite sharing.

Closure (To the Leader):

To young adolescents, feelings such as discouragement, ambivalence, depression, shame, and confusion often seem unbearable. Too often they numb their feelings in unhealthy ways. This activity can help them learn more effective means of dealing with painful emotions. As a follow-up you could make available novels that portray healthy ways of dealing with painful emotions.

How To Conduct Classroom Guidance and Counseling Lessons

School counselors who have been trained in a teacher-preparation program have a distinct advantage in developing classroom developmental counseling lessons because they know how to write lesson plans. They also have had training in motivation and classroom management. Counselors who have not had formal training should at least familiarize themselves with the following:

A Knowledge Base of Teaching Skills

Good (1979), Hunter (1976), and Stallings (1984) have developed instructional programs that provide classroom teachers with a format and process for teaching that has been shown to be effective. These programs and others that offer innovative techniques for use in the classroom can increase the knowledge and confidence of school counselors who work in the large-group setting. One of these approaches is called *cooperative learning* (Johnson & Johnson 1994). According to Jones and Jones (1997), a cooperative learning approach "not only enhances learning and positive attitudes toward both subject matter and school in general, but it also creates positive peer relationships and enhances students' self-esteem" (p. 233). Because self-esteem is always a byproduct, and sometimes even the prime objective, in a classroom guidance unit, methods that enhance its potential are imperative.

Another method with a strong impact was introduced by Purkey and Schmidt (1996) and Purkey and Novak (1996). Called "invitational learning," this approach attempts to elevate the importance of school and learning in an environment that heavily emphasizes the unique worth, respect, and dignity of each student. It moves beyond the premise that self-esteem is something that should be the theme of an occasional classroom activity and, instead, holds that the entire educational experience should validate individual worth.

School counselors and teachers must act in a way that makes school inviting to children (Purkey and Schmidt, 1996). By modeling and demonstrating concrete humanistic behavior, the counselor and teacher can help the student relate to the environment, become assertive by developing a sense of control within the classroom, be willing to try new things and make mistakes, and be able to cope with the world. Models such as Johnson and Johnson's and Purkey and Schmidt's provide a base of knowledge for the counselor who will be active in the school setting as the large-group leader. Using these models, the counselor will be able to create a learning environment that encourages the transfer of knowledge and experiences from the classroom to the entire school, the family, and the community.

Some skills important to successfully teaching a counseling curriculum are:

- Classroom management
- Operation of technological equipment
- Time management
- Delivery of a presenting stimulus or lecturette
- Directing smallgroup to whole-class structured activities
- Active listening
- Open-ended questioning
- Facilitating the group process
- Nonjudgmental responses
- Pacing
- Balancing flexibility and staying on task
- Involving all students
- Noting cues for follow-up work with individual students

Developing a Counseling Curriculum

For counselors, conducting guidance and counseling lessons in a classroom is much different from counseling in an office. Counselors with prior teaching experience may find the rewards of classroom teaching to be an enjoyable part of their total counseling work. In conducting classroom guidance units, there are several options, as has been highlighted in the examples throughout this chapter. For example, the counselor could be totally responsible for the design and implementation of the entire classroom unit, or the counselor could be responsible for design and the teacher for implementation.

Another option would involve a collaborative effort in which the counselor and teacher work together to deliver the unit. The counselor would teach some of the lessons, and other lessons would be led by the classroom teacher or qualified community people. For example, the counselor might teach the first three sessions and the teacher the last three sessions. Ultimately, the school counselor is the person who is responsible for implementing the counseling curriculum and for assisting and coordinating the teachers who are also involved. This assistance may include inservice training, team teaching, or modeling by the counselor.

In contrast to normal classroom teaching, which centers on subject matter, teaching a counseling curriculum, or developmental programming, centers on content that is much more personalized. The content of the counseling curriculum (life themes, life transitions, and life skills) necessarily means that the counselor or teacher has to personalize the content to each student. Teachers have to differentiate teaching academic content from teaching a curriculum that is more process-focused and phenomenological. The goal is for students to integrate what they learn in the counseling curriculum into their own individual, family, and social environments. Thus, the counselor and teacher alike strive to have the students internalize the content as it relates to their academic, vocational, and personal/social life and then make behavioral changes.

In this process of personalizing, the counselor or the teacher has to be facilitating and empowering in the classroom. Excellence in education in the classroom demands that teachers become more facilitative in the classroom. Teachers who do this create learning situations that are personally meaningful, positive and nonthreatening, self-initiated, self-evaluated, feeling focused (Wittmer & Myrick, 1989, p. 6).

A counseling curriculum also involves teaching aspects that are more factual and objective. A unit on self-awareness, for example, may include information on nutrition, stress reduction, or using positive self- statements. Those objectives can be infused intentionally into the total school curriculum and become part of a health, English, or reading lesson. As another example, career exploration may be incorporated into a social studies class. In these ways, the counseling curriculum can be integrated within the total curriculum and help to meet the needs of the whole student. The key to this approach is for classroom teachers to be consistent in how they address the objectives within the counseling curriculum so that students are exposed to developmental, sequential programming. The counselor should administer this curriculum and be responsible for seeing that age-level competencies and objectives are clearly and appropriately met.

Teaching a counseling curriculum is one of the most effective and efficient ways of developing students' potential, as the content is developmental and preventive and the counselor or teacher is working with 15 to 30 or more students at the same time. Teaching a developmental counseling curriculum can further the potential of many individuals.

Steps in Classroom Lessons

Counselors and teachers may find the following suggestions useful in conducting classroom lessons:

1. Prepare materials and handouts in advance.

2. Place all materials for a given lesson in a file folder that can be pulled later to update and reuse. (Portfolios work well here.)
3. Arrange ahead of time for any audiovisual equipment, know how to operate it, or arrange for someone else to do it.
4. Be generally knowledgeable and familiar with the entire unit and totally familiar with the lesson that is to be taught that day.
5. Arrive early, and start on time.
6. Keep the classroom atmosphere relaxed, but maintain proper decorum using appropriate classroom-management skills.
7. Follow the structure of the lesson plan, and teach the lesson using group-process skills.
8. Strive to personalize the content with a balance of task orientation and flexibility while keeping an eye on the time.
9. Utilize various-sized groups (dyads, triads, groups of six, or total group) for maximum effectiveness in given activities.
10. Vary the traditional classroom style by having students sit in a circle or on the floor.
11. Make use of student demonstrations, role-plays, or homework with non-threatening assignments.
12. Conclude by generalizing the content to applicable situations in the students' world.

Leading classroom lessons has some pitfalls that can be avoided just by being aware of what could happen. Detailed storytelling by the facilitator and students could bore students or get the lesson off track and should be avoided. If the counselor is overly flexible, students can ramble in their discussions. If the content contains sensitive material for students and their families (e.g., sexual responsibility), the counselor can avoid resistance by letting the parents know in advance about the material. Tactfully presenting the issue to parents might defuse any negative reactions.

The Future of Developmental Programming

The benefits to be gained by developmental programming far outweigh the pitfalls. Developmental programming through classroom lessons is done to avert students' problems or "nip them in the bud." Because the content of developmental programming is preventive in nature, students should be enabled to reach their potential sooner than they would without this intervention.

Practical research is needed to determine the extent to which developmental programming is helpful in problem solving, fosters achievement, reduces dropout rates, alleviates social/emotional problems, promotes readiness for major transitions, and so on. Research by Lapan, Gysbers, and Sun (1997) with high school students indicated that when intentional, developmental guidance programs are in place, students rate the school climate as more positive, feel safer and have a greater sense of belonging, report less disruption and better behavior from peers, and believe more career and college information was presented.

Similar results were reported by Lapan, Gysbers and Petroski (2001) with middle school students. But more must be done to demonstrate effectiveness. Issues of accountability and program evaluation have to be intentionally addressed. This must include outcome data, as well as the impact of school counseling programs on student achievement and positive behavior in schools (Paisley & McMahon, 2001). The counselor's role in creating and implementing a comprehensive school counseling program holds much promise in developing students' potential and achievement in the learning/academic, career/vocational, and personal/social domains.

Summary

A developmental counseling curriculum reaches all students and is delivered by counselors in collaboration with other student services staff, teachers, and community resource persons. Properly trained teachers have an integral role in the delivery of this curriculum when the content of their class activities relates directly to the topics in the counseling curriculum. The curriculum is based on identification of students' age appropriate developmental needs.

A model curriculum has three domains: (a) learning/academic, (b) career/vocational, and (c) personal/social. In each of the domains the curriculum addresses age-appropriate life themes, life transitions, and life skills. A developmental counseling curriculum is an effective and productive means for students to succeed academically, interpersonally, and vocationally. In addition, counselors are viewed as providing an essential part of the total school curriculum designed to facilitate learning and develop the potential of all students.

References

American School Counselor Association. (1979). *Standards for guidance and counseling programs*. Falls Church, VA: American Personnel and Guidance Association.

American School Counselor Association. (1990). *Counseling paints a bright future: Student competencies and guide for school counselors*. Alexandria, VA: Author.

Baker, S. B. (1996). *School counseling for the twenty-first century* (2d ed.). Englewood Cliffs, NJ: Merrill.

Campbell, C. A., & Dahir, C. A. (1997). *The national standards for school counseling programs*. Alexandria, VA: American School Counselor Association.

Chicago Public Schools. (1997–1998). *The students advisory handbook* (working draft). Chicago: Author.

Drum, D. J., & Knott, J. E. (1977). *Structured groups for facilitating development: Acquiring life skills, resolving life themes, and making lift transitions*. New York: Human Sciences Press.

Ellis, T. (1991). Guidance—The heart of education: Three exemplary approaches. In G. R. Walz (compiler), *Counselor quest* (p. 70). Ann Arbor: University of Michigan. (ERIC Counseling and Personnel Services Clearinghouse)

Good, T. (1979). Teacher effectiveness in the elementary school. *Journal of Teacher Education, 30,* 52–64.

Gysbers, N. C. (2001). School guidance and counseling in the 21st century: Remember the past into the future. *Professional School Counseling, 5,* 96–105.

Gysbers, N. C., & Henderson, P. (2000). *Developing and managing your school guidance program.* (3d ed.). Alexandria, VA: American Counseling Association.

Hunter, M. (1976). *Improved instruction.* El Segundo, CA: TIP.

Johnson, D., & Johnson, R. (1994). *Learning together and alone: Cooperative, competitive, and individualistic learnings* (4th ed.). Englewood Cliffs, NJ: Prentice–Hall.

Jones V. E., & Jones, L. S. (1997). *Comprehensive classroom management: Motivating and managing students* (5th ed.). Boston: Allyn & Bacon.

Lapan, R. T., Gysbers, N. C., & Petroski, G. F. (2001). Helping seventh graders be safe and successful: A statewide study of the impact of comprehensive guidance and counseling programs. *Journal of Counseling & Development, 79,* 320–330.

Lapan, R. T., Gysbers, N. C, & Sun, Y. (1997). The impact of more fully implemented guidance programs on the school experiences of high school students: A statewide evaluation study. *Journal of Counseling & Development, 75,* 292–302.

Myrick, R. D. (1997). *Developmental guidance and counseling. A practical approach.* (3d ed.). Minneapolis: Educational Media Corporation.

Paisley, P. O., & Borders, L. D. (1995). School counseling: An evolving specialty. *Journal of Counseling & Development, 74*(2), 150–153.

Paisley, P. O., & McMahon, G. (2001). School counseling for the 21st century: Challenges and opportunities. *Professional School Counseling, 5,* 106–115.

Purkey, W. W., & Novak, J. M. (1996). *Inviting school success. A self-concept approach to teaching and learning* (3d ed.). Belmont, CA: Wadsworth.

Purkey, W W, & Schmidt, J. J. (1996). *Invitational counseling: A self-concept approach to professional practice.* Pacific Grove, CA: Brooks/Cole.

Sebring, P, Sebring, P., Bryk, A. S., Roderick, M., Camburn, E., Luppescu, S., Thum, Y. M., Smith, B., & Kahne, J. (1996). *Charting reform in Chicago: The students speak.* Chicago: Consortium on Chicago School Research.

Sink, C. A. (2002). In search of the profession's finest hour: A critique of four views of 21st century school counseling. *Professional School Counseling, 5,* 156–163.

Stallings, J. (1984). *An accountability model for teacher education.* Nashville, TN: Vanderbilt University, George Peabody College for Teachers, Stallings Teaching and Learning Institute.

VanZandt, C. E., & Hayslip, J. B. (1994). *Your comprehensive school guidance and counseling program.* New York: Longman.

VanZandt, Z., & Hayslip, J. (2001). *Developing your school counseling program: A handbook for systemic planning.* Pacific Grove, CA: Brooks/Cole.

Vernon, A. (1989a). *Thinking, feeling, behaving: An emotional education curriculum for children.* Champaign, IL: Research Press.

Vernon, A. (1989b). *Thinking, feeling, behaving: An emotional education curriculum for adolescents.* Champaign, IL: Research Press.

Vernon, A. (1998a). *The Passport Program: A journey through emotional, social, cognitive, and self-development, grades 1–5.* Champaign, IL: Research Press.

Vernon, A. (1998b). *The Passport Program: A journey through emotional, social, cognitive, and self-development, grades 6–8.* Champaign, IL: Research Press.

Vernon, A. (1998c). *The Passport Program: A journey through emotional, social, cognitive, and self-development (grades 9–12).* Champaign, IL: Research Press.

Vernon, A., & Strub, R. (1990–1991). *Developmental guidance program implementation.* (Counseling and Human Development Foundation Grant Project). Cedar Falls, IA: University of Northern Iowa, Department of Educational Administration and Counseling, University of Northern Iowa, Cedar Falls.

Winneconne School Counselors. 1990. *Winneconne developmental guidance model.* (rev.). Madison, WI: Department of Public Instruction.

Wittmer, J., & Myrick, R. D. (1989). *The teacher as facilitator.* Minneapolis: Educational Media Corporation.

Selected Resources for Developing a Counseling Curriculum

Elementary Level

Anderson, J. (1992). *Thinking, Changing, Rearranging: Improving Self-esteem in Young People.* Portland, OR: Metamorphous Press.

Lessons and activities covering areas including self-esteem, where hurt comes from, beliefs that cause problems, changing language, and changing destructive thoughts. Includes teacher's guide with spirit-duplicating masters and student paperback book. Ages 10+.

Berne, P., & Savary, L. (1999). *Building Self-esteem in Children* (new expanded ed.). New York: Crossroads/Herder & Herder.

68 effective, practical techniques to help parents, educators, and other concerned adults develop healthy relationships with children and foster attitudes and atmosphere in which self-esteem can flourish.

Blum, D. J. (1998). *The School Counselor's Book of Lists.* West Nyack, NY: Center for Applied Research in Education.

Borba, C., & Borba, M. (1993). *Self-Esteem Builders.* San Francisco: Harper.

More than 100 ways to build self-esteem in children. Activities teach students to communicate better, use their talents, and be responsible.

Bowman, R. R., & Myrick, R. D. (1991). *Children Helping Children: Teaching Students to Become Friendly Helpers.* Minneapolis: Educational Media Corp.

Written for elementary and middle school counselors, teachers, and principals who want to improve the learning climate in their schools. Designed to help young students take a more active role in the learning and helping process.

Canfield, J., & Wells, H. (1994). 100 *Ways to Enhance Self-Concept in the Classroom* (2d ed.). Englewood Cliffs, NJ: Prentice–Hall.

A good source of quotations, cartoons, and activities that can be used in developing self-awareness and enhancing positive self-concept. K–12.

Chapman, D. B. (1997). *My Body Is Where I Live.* Circle Pines, MN: American Guidance Service.

Picture book and cassette tape help children develop an appreciation of their bodies and an understanding of the dangers of drugs.

Commissiong, W. (1991). *The Best Face of All.* Chicago: African-American Images.

Takes young readers through a litany of facial features and choices, asking each time, "Which eyes are best?" or "Which are the best noses?" The answers are sometimes practical, sometimes heartwarming, always insightful.

Devencenzi, J., & Pendergast, S. (1999). *Belonging: Self and Social Discovery for Children and Adolescents* (Rev.). San Luis Obispo, CA: Sovereignty Press.

Grollman, E., & Grollman, S. (1985). *Talking About the Handicapped (Mainstreaming).* Boston: Beacon Press.

> A workbook about mainstreaming students with disabilities into a classroom and the resulting feelings and problems.

Guinan, K. (2002). *Peace Quest: Journey with Purpose.* Blair, NE: Kind Regards.

Hendricks, B., & Leben, N. (1994). *Anger Work with Children: How To Focus, Control, and Resolve Anger.* Berkeley: University of California Extension, Center for Media and Independent Learning.

Jolin, J., & Randolph, D. (1997). *How to . . . Career Activities for Every Classroom: Grades K–3* (D. Caulum & R. Lambert, Project Directors). Madison: University of Wisconsin/Wisconsin Alumni Research Foundation.

Jolin, J., & Randolph, D. (1997). *How to . . . Career Activities for Every Classroom: Grades 4–6* (D. Caulum & R. Lambert, Project Directors). Madison: University of Wisconsin/ Wisconsin Alumni Research Foundation.

Kreidler, W. J. (1997). *Conflict Resolution in the Middle School: A Curriculum and Teacher's Guide.* Cambridge, MA: Educators for Social Responsibility.

> Methods for improving pupils' communication skills, cooperation, tolerance, and positive emotional expression. Helps students deal with anger, fear, prejudice, and aggression in the K–6 classroom.

Loomans, D. (1996). *Today I am Lovable: 365 Positive Activities for Kids.* Tiburon, CA: Kramer.

Mannix, D. (1991). *Life Skills Activities for Special Children (workbook).* West Nyack, NJ: Center for Applied Research in Education.

McDaniel, S., & Bielen, P. (1990). *Project Self-Esteem: A Parent Involvement Program for Elementary-Age Children.* Rolling Hills Estates, CA: Jalmar Press.

> A classroom program designed to raise self-concept. Thoroughly tested, inexpensive, effective.

Shapiro, L. E. (1993). *Building Blocks of Self-Esteem.* Secaucus, NJ: Center for Applied Psychology.

Smead, M. (1994). *Skills for Living: Group Counseling Activities for Elementary Students.* Champaign, IL: Research Press.

> Details the skills and steps needed to design, organize, conduct, and evaluate a multi-session group-counseling experience. Includes eight developmentally appropriate topics for groups, including self-esteem, peacemaking, responsibility, and divorce.

Teolis, B. (1996). *Self-Esteem and Conflict-Solving Activities for Grades 4–8.* West Nyack, NY: Center for Applied Research in Education.

VanZandt, Z., & Buchan, B. A. (1997). *Lessons for Life: Career Development Activities Library* (Vol. 1: Elementary grades). West Nyack, NY: Center for Applied Research in Education.

Vernon, A. (1980). *Help Yourself to a Healthier You.* Minneapolis: Burgess.

> Preventive mental health program for grades 1–6. Content includes principles of rational–emotive therapy (self-acceptance, feelings, beliefs, challenging beliefs).

Vernon, A. (1989). *Thinking, Feeling, Behaving: An Emotional Education Curriculum for Children (Grades 1–6).* Champaign, IL: Research Press.

> A comprehensive, developmental curriculum including chapters on feelings, behavior management, self-acceptance, problem solving, and interpersonal relationships.

Vernon, A. (1998). *The Passport Program: A Journey Through Emotional, Social, Cognitive, and Self-Development: Grades 1–5.* Champaign, IL: Research Press.

> A comprehensive, developmental curriculum based on typical developmental issues children need to master. Interactive, creative lessons focus on self acceptance, emotional development, decision making, and interpersonal relationships.

Weltman, B. (1996). *Social Skills Lessons and Activities for Grades 1–3.* West Nyack, NY: Center for Applied Research in Education.

    Separate books also are available for grades 4–6 and grades 7–12.

Youngs, B. (1992). *Enhancing Self-Esteem: A Guide for Professional Educators.* Rolling Hills Estates, CA: Jalmar Press.

    A comprehensive resource delineating ways in which educators' self-esteem is positively or negatively charged in the workplace. Provides tools for rebuilding and nourishing the educator's self-esteem.

Secondary Level

Bodine, J., & Crawford, D. K. (1998). *The Handbook of Conflict Resolution: A Guide to Building Quality Programs in the Schools.* San Francisco: Jossey–Bass.

Capacchione, L. (1992). *The Creative Journal for Teens.* North Hollywood, CA: Newcastle Publishing.

Carlock, J. C. (Ed.). (1998). *Enhancing Self-Esteem.* New York: Taylor & Francis.

    Techniques for enhancing self-esteem presented in a specific sequence and progression. For children, adolescents, and adults.

Cohen, L. M. (1996). *Coping for Capable Kids: Strategies for Parents, Teachers, and Students.* Waco, TX: Prufrock Press

Jackson, T. (1995). *More Activities That Teach.* Cedar City, UT: Red Rock Publishing.

JIST Works. (Eds.). (1998). *Creating Your High School Portfolio: An Interactive School, Career, and Life Planning Workbook.* Indianapolis: Author.

Johnson, D. W. (1997). *Reaching Out* (6th ed.). Boston: Allyn & Bacon.

    A comprehensive source for exercises in interpersonal relations, goal-setting, self-awareness, and communication.

Jolin, J., & Randolph, D. (1997). *How to...Career Activities for Every Classroom: Grades 7–9* (Caulum, D. & Lambert, R. Project Directors). Madison, WI: University of Wisconsin/ Wisconsin Alumni Research Foundation.

Kehayan, A. (1990). *SAGE—Self-Awareness Growth Experience: Grades 7–12.* Rolling Hills Estates, CA: Jalmar Press.

    More than 150 activities emphasizing creativity, problem solving, social intervention, and other developmental areas essential to the behavioral growth of adolescents.

Khalsa, S. N. (1996). *Group Exercises for Enhancing Social Skills and Self-Esteem.* Sarasota, FL: Professional Resource Exchange.

Lindsay, N. (1994). *Pathfinder: Exploring Career & Educational Paths.* Indianapolis: JIST Works.

Silliman, B. (1995). *Resilient Kids and Adults: Coping and Using Life Challenges Creatively.* Laramie: University of Wyoming Cooperative Extension Services, Dept. of Home Economics.

Smead, R. (1990). *Skills for Living: Group Counseling Activities for Young Adolescents.* Champaign, IL: Research Press.

    Details the skills and steps needed to design, organize, conduct, and evaluate a multi-session group counseling experience. Includes eight developmentally appropriate topics for groups, including anger management, grief and loss, and divorce.

Strauss, S., & Espeland, R (1992). *Sexual Harassment and Teens.* Minneapolis: Free Spirit.

    Provides background information for teaching sexual harassment prevention to young people. Includes reproducible pages for handouts and overheads, activities, questions, and a survey.

Tindall, J. (1994). *Peer Power: Book 1: Becoming an Effective Peer Helper* (3d ed.). Muncie, IN: Accelerated Development.

> Peer counseling training featuring four new modules for advanced students: conflict resolution drug and alcohol abuse, intervention and prevention, moving toward wellness through stress management, and developing human potential.

VanZandt, Z., & Buchan, B. A. (1997). *Lessons for Life: Career Development Activities Library* (Vol. 2: Secondary Grades). West Nyack, NY: Center for Applied Research in Education.

VanZandt, Z., & Hayslip, J. (2001). *Developing Your School Counseling Program: A Handbook for Systematic Planning.* Belmont, CA: Wadsworth/Thompson Learning.

Vedral, J. L. (1994). *How To Get Your Kids To Talk: The Question Game for Young Adults.* New York: Ballantine Books.

Vernon, A. (1989). *Thinking, Feeling, Behaving: An Emotional Education Curriculum for Children. (Grades 7–12).* Champaign, IL: Research Press.

> A comprehensive curriculum that includes lessons on self-acceptance, feelings, rational thinking and problem solving, and interpersonal relationships.

Vernon, A. (1998). *The Passport Program: A Journey Through Emotional, Social, Cognitive, and Self-Development: Grades 6–8.* Champaign, IL: Research Press.

> A comprehensive curriculum that includes creative, interactive lessons on self-acceptance, emotions, problem solving/decision making, feelings, and interpersonal relationships. Lessons are based on typical developmental issues that young adolescents face during this period of development.

Vernon, A. (1998). *A Journey Through Emotional, Social, Cognitive, and Self-Development: Grades 9–12.* Champaign, IL: Research Press.

> A comprehensive developmental curriculum that includes creative, interactive lessons on self-acceptance, feelings, behavior management, problem solving, and interpersonal relationships. Lessons are baased on typical developmental issues that adolescents face during this period of development.

Youngs, B. B. (1992). *Six Vital Ingredients of Self-Esteem: How To Develop Them in Your Students.* Normal, IL: Preferred Learning Enterprises.

> Practical ways to help kids manage school, make decisions, accept consequences, manage time, and discipline themselves to set worthwhile goals. Covers developmental stages from age 2 to 18 with implications for self-esteem at each age.

Working With Parents

Ann Vernon

With increasing frequency, helping professionals are interacting with parents in a variety of ways about issues related to their children. Although parenting has never been easy, the stressors on families in today's society make parenting even more difficult, and this is complicated in that families now are more diverse in both membership and functioning (Lauer & Lauer, 1997). In addition to the traditional two-parent family whose children are their biological offspring, single-parent, blended, and never-married families are prevalent. A negative and alarming trend, according to Karpowitz (2000), is that many families are breaking down and are not coping with life effectively. These families are characterized by more violence and tension, less parental supervision, and lack of emotional stability. Children in these families have more psychopathology (Lindahl,

1998). Clearly this trend has significant implications for school and mental health counselors.

According to Gordon (2000), mental health professionals, teachers, administrators, and law-enforcement officials, among others, blame parents for the troubles of youth and for the problems that young people cause. Yet, Gordon asks, who is helping parents? "How much effort is being made to assist parents to become more effective in rearing children? Where can parents learn what they are doing wrong and what they might do differently?" (Gordon, 2000, p. 1). Gordon's points are well taken. Certainly in the present day, parents need various forms of assistance, not blame, as the problems they face make parenting more stressful and challenging than ever (Stephenson, 1996; Vernon, 2002).

More and more parents are expressing feelings of inadequacy about family relationships, and some parents simply don't know what to do with their children (Clark, 1996; Levy & O'Hanlon, 2001). Traditional patterns of parental authority are no longer effective (Stone and Bradley, 1994), but at the same time parents often feel uncomfortable and uncertain about changing what has become familiar (Nelson & Lott, 2000). And, though good parenting always has been a fulltime effort and continues to be one of the most important and challenging tasks a person will ever undertake, it is both surprising and disheartening to acknowledge that parenting doesn't require training or specific qualifications. It is a sad commentary that we receive more instruction about balancing a checkbook and changing a tire than we do about how to parent.

Although the concept of parent education has been around since the 1920's (Fine, Voydanoff, & Donnelly, 1993), the development and marketing of parenting programs is only a few decades old (Ayers, 2000). Stone and Bradley (1994) noted that parents now seem to be more interested in education and training for their role. Without a doubt, parents need help in managing the contemporary challenges of parenting. They also need to develop skills to help themselves and their children deal successfully with developmental stressors and opportunities. In addition to practical skills, they need to understand how their irrational beliefs about themselves as parents or about their children contribute to negative emotional and behavioral reactions that can prevent them from implementing effective parenting skills (Vernon, 2002).

Counselors can assist parents in two ways: through parent education and through consultation. Parent education is valuable for all parents and is preventive and psychoeducational in nature, whereas consultation is recommended for parents who have specific problems after receiving parent training or whose children are experiencing difficulties for which more intensive help is indicated. This chapter addresses the importance of parent education and consultation and the role of counselors in providing these services to parents. It presents information about effective parenting practices, how to develop and implement parent education groups, and how employ a consultation model.

Definitions

Fine (1989) defined parent education as "being concerned mainly with the imparting of information and skills which are supportive of good parenting" (p. 13). Parent education is based on the belief that the influential role of parents produces considerable responsibility for them to provide appropriate guidance for their children. Parent education increases parents' knowledge and helps them develop skills. The focus is preventive: As parents learn to parent more effectively, they will reduce the potential for problems arising from ineffective parenting practices.

Parent consultation is recommended for parents who have specific problems with their child. Parents may contact a counselor to discuss their concerns about a variety of matters—for example, their child's behavior, school performance, or emotional and social adjustment; specific issues related to developmental or learning disabilities (Knowlton & Mulanax, 2000; Lancaster, 2000); or problems associated with more severe problems such as childhood depression or eating disorders. Although education may be part of the consultation process, consultation deals more specifically with an existing problem and therefore is not as preventive in nature.

Outcomes of Parent Education and Consultation

Parent education and consultation are essential components of a counselor's role. Many parents are anxious to learn new techniques or alleviate their anxiety about problems they are having with their children. Parent education and consultation can best be understood by considering some of the expected outcomes of these processes. Stone and Bradley (1994) identified a number of outcomes and benefits of parent education and consultation. This list underscores the value of working with parents.

1. *Improved parent–child relationships.* The primary goal of parent education is to improve relationships between parents and children. As parents become more understanding and accepting, children are less likely to misbehave, and the relationship between parents and children improves.
2. *Improved behavior at home and school.* Parental participation in education groups can result in positive changes in parents' attitude toward children, positive changes in children's behavior, and improvement in the family atmosphere. A study conducted by Kottman and Wilborn (1992) discovered that parents who participated in study groups initiated by counselors had significantly more positive attitudes toward their children than parents who were not exposed to study groups.
3. *Improved acceptance of responsibility.* In their work with parents, both in parent study groups and when conducting consultations, Stone and Bradley

(1994) found that as the relationship between children and their parents improved, children were willing to accept more responsibility.

4. *Parent involvement in the school.* Parents who have positive relationships with their children and whose children are more likely to accept responsibility are more likely to become involved with the school. Parents' involvement with the school often begins with parent education. As parents' attitude toward their children and the school improves, the parents will likely become more involved with the school.

5. *Improvement in school achievement.* Parent education and consultation seem to initiate a chain reaction. When the child's behavior starts to improve, he or she begins to accept more responsibility, the relationship with the parents improves, the parents are more inclined to become involved with the school, and the child's schoolwork improves correspondingly. Because this process tends to be linear, children's feelings about the relationship with their parents is extremely important to children's motivation and school achievement.

For the counselor, the need for parent education and consultation becomes obvious. It is not a matter of whether to offer parent education and consultation but, rather, where, when, and in what format it should be provided. Edwards (2000) suggested that it should be offered to all who function in a parental role, including grandparents raising grandchildren. Single and low-income parents, teenage parents, and never-married parents also should be targeted (Bogenschneider & Stone, 1997).

Generally speaking, research has shown that as a consequence of attending a parent program, parents became less angry and felt less guilty and simultaneously became more effective in helping their children solve problems (Fine et al., 1993). Even though the child may be experiencing a problem, the parents themselves have problems dealing with the child or with their own issues about the child' problem (Vernon, 2002). Therefore, if practitioners work only with the child, they are neglecting an important part of the problem.

Cultural Considerations

Given the fact that our population is increasingly becoming more ethnically diverse and that White Americans will be in the minority in many areas of the United States within the next decade (U.S. Bureau of the Census, 1996), McDermott (2000) stressed the importance of addressing cultural and ethnic diversity if we intend to provide successful parenting services to a variety of populations. Even if parent education and consultation are tailored to the values and cultures of the specific groups, however, accessing the individuals and groups who need assistance is a challenge because many ethnic minorities fear or distrust the services or feel ashamed about admitting that they need help.

It is important not to make generalizations about groups, as many factors determine the actual lifestyle of the individual (Atkinson, Morten, & Sue, 1993). Gender must be taken into consideration, because both sexes have commonalities within their own group that are irrespective of ethnicity (Hays, 1996). Age is another important variable; older members of the ethnic group may have very different values than younger members (Baruth & Manning, 1991).

Professionals working with parents must be aware that the European-American dominant culture values independence and autonomy, competition, and hard work as the keys to success. This culture places a premium on time and an action-orientation characterized by structure and problem resolution (McDermott, 2000). We cannot assume that all other groups share these values; we must become familiar with the characteristics of each group and how their values and characteristics affect parenting practices. For example, the extended family, as contrasted with the nuclear family, is extremely important to African Americans. In the African American family, children belong to the entire group; friends, neighbors, and relatives help discipline and care for the children (Blum & Deussen, 1996). The Asian American family also values the extended family, as well as the work ethic and a group orientation (Atkinson et al., 1996). The extended family also is central to Latino Americans; loyalty to the family and obedience to the father are expected (Atkinson et al., 1993). Because of the tribal system in the Native American culture, children may live in a nuclear family with many family members or even in different homes (Red Horse, 1982, as cited in McDermott, 2000).

Because parenting is perceived and defined differently by different cultural and ethnic groups, knowledge about and sensitivity to these variables will help assure the success of parent education and consultation. As professionals, we need to know our limitations and seek advice and consultation when in doubt.

Parent Education Programs

Parent education frequently is done through groups. The group format provides an opportunity to reach many parents in a relatively short time. The group structure enables counselors to expand their contact with parents and at the same time make use of the group to provide direction and support for each parent. Parents who struggle with their parenting role typically feel rather alone in this situation ("Other parents don't have trouble with their children"). By bringing parents together, they can quickly gain a sense of commonality in that they all face similar concerns as parents.

Identification of parents' needs and concerns is essential in developing good programs. In selecting a parent education approach, Stone and Bradley (1994) suggested taking time to ensure that the approach will provide appropriate information to meet parents' needs, as well as to provide a philosophical foundation that addresses those needs. A program's flexibility in meeting the changing needs of the family as well as the cultural context is a prerequisite for effectiveness. In selecting the appropriate approach, level of education and income also should be considered. Other factors, such as cost, special training of the leaders, and availability and appropriateness of the materials, should be taken into account as well. In addition, the developmental needs of children must be considered in the formulation of any program, as studies have revealed that parents have different concerns about their children at different stages (Fine et al., 1993; Vernon & Al–Mabuk, 1995).

Hundreds of books about parenting are available, as well as many parent education models (Gordon, 2000). If counselors are aware of historical and current trends in parent education, programs can be modified to better meet parents' specific needs. Because there is no magic approach to parent education, counselors often develop the most effective programs by selecting materials from various sources and compiling a program that best addresses the needs of a given group of parents through materials and approaches that are relevant and culturally appropriate.

Stone and Bradley (1994) stressed that parents are not a homogeneous body; they have different needs at different times. These authors noted that parent groups do not have to be large, that timing is crucial, and lack of attendance does not necessarily reflect a lack of concern.

Format and Topics

Parent education can take several approaches, including support groups, parent study groups, and parent education. Support groups typically are not as structured as education groups. The primary goal of support groups is to create an environment in which parents can come together to share concerns about their children and receive some assistance. Support groups may be organized around specific topics, such as a support group for parents of hyperactive or of gifted children, or support groups for single parents, teenage parents, or parents in blended families.

Support groups also can be convened by a leader who facilitates interaction among parents about any issue they want to discuss. This type of support group has no identified topic; members bring their current concerns, and other members respond with suggestions and encouragement. Although support groups may have some educative aspect, the basic purpose of these groups is to encourage discussion and interaction among parents relative to specific concerns they have about their children. They gain knowledge primarily through other parents who share their ideas and experiences, although the leader may introduce content as appropriate.

In contrast, parent education and parent study groups are more highly structured. Although discussion and interaction are encouraged, the primary goal is to develop parenting skills and impart information through a variety of methods such as small-group activities, videos, role-play, and specific skill-building activities. In this type of group, the leader is more active and directive in presenting information, facilitating skill-development opportunities and discussion, and encouraging parents to apply the content to their own situations.

Topics for support, education, and study groups often are the same; only the format and basic goals differ. Topics may address general parenting practices, selected topics, or topics applicable to children at a specific developmental level.

Examples of topics for *general parenting practices* groups are:

- communication techniques ("I versus you" messages, assertive communication, active listening)
- understanding stages of child and adolescent development
- methods of discipline (behavior modification, time-out, logical consequences)
- parenting styles (authoritarian, authoritative, ignoring, permissive)

Groups organized around *selected topics* include:

- parenting gifted children
- parenting children with learning disabilities or ADHD
- parenting children with eating disorders or depression
- parenting oppositional children

Examples of groups organized around issues pertinent to *specific developmental levels* are:

- dealing with preschoolers' separation anxiety
- helping elementary-aged children develop positive peer relationships
- understanding and dealing with adolescent mood swings
- dealing with the transition out of high school

Many more topics could be included in each category. The distinction between general parenting practices, topics pertaining to specific development levels, and selected topics should provide counselors with a variety of ways to approach parenting programs.

In addition to topics, parenting programs can assume a variety of formats. For example, support groups may be *time-limited* (6 to 8 weeks or biweekly sessions lasting from 1 hour to 2 hours each session), or they may meet monthly for 6 months, or they could be ongoing. Parent study and education groups may meet weekly or biweekly for 1 to 2 hours for 6 to 8 weeks, or they may be single-session meetings on selected topics. These single-session meetings may be offered sporadically throughout the year. For example, a counselor may offer four sessions on general parenting practices topics. Parents could choose to attend all sessions or select the ones they find most applicable to their needs.

Another format is a type of *mini-conference* in which parents attend a variety of short, single-session topics during a day or an evening. For example, the conference may last 3 hours, and during this time parents could opt to go to three hour-long sessions on topics such as establishing family rules, conducting family meetings, or helping children develop responsible behaviors. The conference topics could target issues pertinent to specific developmental levels or address selected topics or general parenting matters.

An additional format especially applicable to a parent study group is to organize the group around a book that all parents could read and discuss, such as: *SOS! Help for Parents* (Clark, 1996), *P.E.T.—Parent Effectiveness Training* (Gordon, 2000), *Try and Make Me!* (Levy & O''Hanlon, 2001), *Positive Discipline A-Z* (Nelson, Lott, & Glenn, 1999), or W*hat Growing Up Is All About* (Vernon & Al–Mabuk, 1995). While there are many good parenting resources available, the leader should select a book that is relatively short and easy to read so it is appropriate for various levels of reading ability. Also keep in mind the cost factor if participants have to purchase the book themselves, and be sure to select books that are appropriate for the population you are serving.

Each type and format has advantages and disadvantages, and counselors are encouraged to do a brief needs assessment to see which format would be most relevant to their specific population. Although ongoing groups provide more opportunities to build support, gain knowledge, and develop skills, many parents cannot afford to hire sitters or give up valuable time with their children. For this reason, the mini-conference or the series of single-session programs is often more practical and reaches a larger number of parents. Edwards (2000) suggested offering child care, as well as door prizes and refreshments to help with attendance.

Skills for the Leader

Jacobs, Masson, and Harvill (1998, pp. 113–120) identified a number of leadership skills that counselors, by virtue of their training, possess. The following are applicable for parent education:

1. Communication skills, which usually include active listening, reflection, clarification, questioning, and summarizing
2. Mini-lecturing and information-giving for the purpose of providing interesting, relevant, and stimulating material in a short time
3. Setting a climate in the group that is encouraging and supportive of parents and also appropriate in tone to underscore the material being discussed
4. Leader modeling and self-disclosure to provide parents with an example of effective behavior in interacting with others and a sense of comfort in being able to share their thoughts
5. The leader's voice intonation and eye contact to stimulate the group and set the tone for each session by reinforcing members' participation and energizing the group to participate. The leader assumes an important role in creating an atmosphere of inclusion for all members
6. The leader as a group manager who has to know how to direct the *flow of* conversation by bringing members into the conversation and tempering the participation of overly active members.

Group leaders also have to be able to accept participants as individuals, recognizing that they will vary considerably in the extent to which they can expect participants to change behaviors and integrate the information. Leaders also have to be able to alter the pacing in terms of content in an educational group, as well as demonstrate sensitivity to members' needs (Fine & Wardle, 2000).

Approaches to Parent Education

A number of approaches for parenting education have emerged. These share the same general objective: to help parents learn ways of relating to their children that will promote healthy development. These programs differ in content and also in the use of cognitive, behavioral, and affective modalities to achieve their goals. Each approach emphasizes reeducating parents. Examples of a number of commercially developed programs are:

- *Parenting without Hassles* (Stone & Bradley, 1992)
- *Systematic Training for Training Parenting* (STEP) (Dinkmeyer & McKay, 1993)
- *How to Talk So Kids Will Listen and Listen So Kids Will Talk* (Faber & Mazlish, 1991, 1999)
- *P.E.T.: Parent Effectiveness Training* (Gordon, 1970, 2000)
- *Active Parenting Today* (Popkin, 1995)
- *Tough Love* (York & Wachtel, 1983)

Numerous programs also are available over the Internet. Among them is *The Interaction Network for Children and Families* (http://www.positiveparenting. com/commong.html), which provides courses that parents and teens take together. Another example is *Whole Persons Associates* (http://www.wholeperson.com/wpa/ghb/fi/fi.htm), a video program for parenting adolescents, which covers practical parenting tips with discussion guides and worksheets. As with any parenting program, the counselor should select a program that best addresses the needs of the population with whom they are working.

Organizing a Parent Education Program

Parent education programs can be organized in many different ways, and more and more materials are available to use in developing the program. Some counselors prefer to use commercially developed programs such as those listed above. Other counselors believe that designing their own program is a more effective way to address the specific needs, cultural values, and interests of the target groups.

Stone and Bradley (1994) suggested that the first step in organizing a parent education program is to appoint a committee of professionals and parents. The committee's primary goal is to decide what parent education approach best fits the parents' need. After this committee has been established, members can develop a short needs assessment, which could take the form of a checklist of potential topics and formats for the program.

Based on the results of the needs assessment, the committee can determine the nature of the program—a support group, single or ongoing sessions, a mini-conference, or a multi-session topical education group. Topics also can be identified. Next, the time and place of the meetings can be decided, and the implementation process begins. The following steps are suggested for implementation:

1. Promote the program through flyers, newsletters, personal contact with parents, commercial media, and parent–teacher organizations through the school.
2. Prepare for the parenting sessions. This will include a thorough review of the materials and consideration about how to create a good learning environment, including building a "sense of community" by involving parents in some icebreaker activities. The physical arrangement of the meeting place should enhance good communication through visual contact between all participants and the leader. Good preparation and planning will help to establish credibility as a leader and provide the parents with positive feelings about the program.
3. Establish a means of getting parents to participate through planned activities and assignments that will enable them to identify with the material presented.
4. Order materials that may be used as a supplement to the parenting sessions.
5. Establish an evaluation procedure, the primary purpose of which is to ensure that the parents' needs have been met, to solicit feedback on the quality of the program, and to provide the leader with input for self-improvement. Evaluations can be given orally or in writing.

A Sample Parent Education Program

Counselors are in an ideal position to help parents and children interact well with one another. The parent/child relationship can be enhanced by helping parents communicate more effectively, employ positive behavior management strategies, adopt more effective parenting styles, and tailor their parenting strategies to the developmental needs of their children. The intent is to bring together parents and children in a way that might stimulate ongoing interaction rather than distancing from each other as the children grow older.

A six-session program on general parenting practices focusing on communication is presented below. This model parent–child communication program will help the reader identify the content-and-program sequence. The program could be delivered either through a parent education group or modified for use in parent consultation. Careful selection of material and the use of examples will enable parents to identify with the concepts and more readily incorporate the material into their own parenting styles. The material here has been adapted from a variety of sources including *Parent Effectiveness Training* (Gordon, 2000) and *Positive Discipline for Teenagers* (Nelson & Lott, 2000).

Session 1: Parent Awareness Activity

Objectives: • To sensitize parents to their interactions with their children
              • To help parents differentiate effective and ineffective communication
              • To help parents appreciate the value of effective communication

Procedure: The opening session can sensitize parents to the nature of their communication by first helping them to consider their typical interactions with their children. Although counselors can provide awareness through didactic presentations, experiential activities may be more effective in helping parents review their own behaviors. The latter can be addressed through the introspective consideration of parent and child interchanges.

              Ask parents to divide a sheet of paper into four squares. Then invite them to think about the last positive interchange they had with one of their children, and write in the first square a few words describing what they think made this exchange positive. Next, ask them how they felt about this interchange and write their feeling in the second square. Then ask them to think about the last time they had an unsatisfactory discussion or exchange with one of their children. Instruct them to think about what made that exchange so negative and write that in the third square. Finally, ask how they felt about the negative discussion and write that in the last square.

              To facilitate sharing, play some music and invite the parents to circulate throughout the room, selecting a partner when the music stops. Then invite them to share the information on their first two squares. After 10 minutes, start the music and instruct them to find another partner and share their last two squares when the music stops.

              Ask the parents to tell what it was like to identify the positive and negative exchanges, and the characteristics that described these interchanges. Write this information on newsprint, along with a list of the feelings they had about each of the types of interactions. This information will set the stage for a discussion with parents in which they identify for themselves how their communication is effective and what should be improved.

              Next, ask for a volunteer to play the role of a child, and you as leader will assume the role of a parent. Use a typical example such as checking to see if the child has done his or her homework. In the role play, use as many of the following communication roadblocks as possible (Gordon, 2000): ordering, commanding, and directing; warning and threatening; moralizing and preaching; advising, offering solutions or suggestions; teaching, lecturing, or giving logical arguments; judging, criticizing, disagreeing, or blaming; praising, agreeing; name-calling, ridiculing, or shaming; interpreting, analyzing, and diagnosing; reassuring, sympathizing, consoling, and supporting; questioning, probing, interrogating; and withdrawing, distracting, humoring, or diverting (pp. 49–52).

After presenting the role-play, ask the parents to say what they thought was effective or ineffective about the exchange. Provide more explanation of the roadblocks (Gordon, 2000), and then divide the parents into small groups and have them discuss roadblocks they may use. Emphasize that all parents use these roadblocks from time to time and that the purpose of this session is to help them realize that communication with children isn't easy but that in this group they will have an opportunity to learn new skills and unlearn ineffective behaviors.

As a homework assignment, ask the parents to pay attention to their communication and eliminate as many roadblocks as possible.

Session 2: Undoing the Roadblocks: Effective Listening Skills

Objectives: • To help parents learn and practice effective listening skills

Procedure: Begin this session by reviewing the information from the last session and checking on the homework assignment. Then discuss how listening is the primary skill necessary for good communication. Being a good listener requires verbal and nonverbal skills, eye contact, and a posture that indicates "I'm listening." Listening requires paying close attention to what the child is saying and concentrating on the meaning. By paying close attention to the child, parents can communicate understanding and acceptance (Gordon, 2000).

Introduce the concept of *active listening* (Gordon, 2000). Active listening is just that—it means that that the receiver of a message listens empathically to what the sender is saying and refrains from using the communication roadblocks. Active listening promotes a relationship of warmth between parent and child. Vernon and Al–Mabuk (1995) suggested that active listeners recognize—in addition to spoken words—body language and tone of voice. Active listening requires close attention, sensitivity to feeling, and the ability to express what the child is feeling.

At this point the leader should ask for a volunteer to role-play a teenager who is upset about receiving a bad grade on a test. Invite the other group members to be observers. As the leader, you play the role of the parent and demonstrate active listening. For example, the teenager says, "I'm no good at math. I got a terrible grade on the test." The parent could reflect, "You're discouraged about your ability to perform well in math." In this example the parent attempts to understand what the child feels and means and then states this meaning to the child so he or she feels understood and accepted. The parent is nonjudgmental and encourages the child to feel heard and to continue talking.

After discussing the role-play, invite the parents to work in triads as parent, child, and observer, to practice active listening. After they have each had a turn to play the role of the active listener, discuss their reactions and encourage them to practice this skill throughout the week.

Session 3: The Language of Acceptance

Objectives: • To help parents develop techniques for communicating acceptance of their children

               • To sensitize parents to their own thoughts and actions regarding their children

Procedure: Communicating acceptance extends beyond understanding what the child is saying; it conveys acceptance of the child. Through the language of acceptance, children can believe they are part of the environment and the world of their important adults (Dinkmeyer, McKay, & Dinkmeyer, 1997). The language of acceptance frees children to talk about their feelings and problems and lets them know that they are accepted for who they are, not as they should or could be (Gordon, 2000).

Inform parents that they can show acceptance by listening passively—doing nothing but offering encouragers such as "Oh?" "I see," "Mm–hmm" (Gordon, 2000, p. 44–45). Verbal acceptance can be offered in the form of "door openers" (p. 57), which convey acceptance of the child and respect for him or her as a person. Examples of door openers are: "Your thoughts and feelings are important," "I'm interested in hearing about your experiences," and "I really want to hear your ideas."

As an activity to demonstrate the language of acceptance, lead a discussion with the parents regarding each of the following concepts: acceptance, confidence, appreciation, and recognition of effort. Using newsprint to record their responses, ask parents to provide examples of each form of acceptance. Post the examples on the wall, and divide parents into triads. Instruct them to take turns role-playing parent–child interactions that would give them opportunities to practice the language of acceptance. Invite them to "contract" with members of their triad to practice a certain number of acceptance statements during the following week.

Session 4: "I" Messages

Objectives: • To help parents use "I" messages instead of "you" messages

Procedure: Open this session with a general discussion about "I messages" and "you messages," a concept fundamentally attributed to Gordon (1970). "I messages" are nonjudgmental responses about how we feel. Vernon and Al–Mabuk (1995) referred to "I messages" as a clear way of communicating to the child how you as a parent are feeling without the child becoming defensive. These authors noted that "I messages" are more effective than shaming and blaming. "I messages" give children an opportunity to change their behavior without losing face and helps them learn to be more responsible.

To deliver a good "I message," parents must state clearly how they are feeling and why, and then give the message using the following formula: "When you . . . (describe the unacceptable behavior in a nonjudgmental way), I feel . . . (describe your feelings), because . . . (share what effect the behavior has on you)" (Gordon, 2000, p. 130). By contrast, "you messages" tend to put children on the defensive and accuse them of inappropriate behavior, attitude, or motive. When children feel they are being accused of something, they resist. "You messages" are more likely to evoke argumentive behaviors. An example of a "you message" is: "You never pick up your clothes. Why can't you ever do anything right?" An overgeneralization often accompanies this statement as well.

To further differentiate "I messages" and "you messages," use a typical example of a child not coming home on time. "You message": "You never obey the rules. You were supposed to be home an hour ago. Why can't you follow the rules?" Note that this message is often a put-down and contains many of the communication roadblocks described in a previous session. In contrast, an "I message" is: "When you don't come home on time, I feel worried and angry because I don't know where you are, and you're not obeying the rule."

Following this demonstration, group the parents in triads and have them practice "I messages," taking turns playing the role of the parent, the child, and an observer. After each triad has worked through all three roles, lead a discussion about their reactions to the use of "I messages."

Session 5: Encouragement

Objectives: • To help parents better understand the concept of encouragement
                    • To help parents demonstrate competence in using encouragement

Procedure: As with the previous session, begin with a presentation of the following information about encouragement: The process of encouragement is based on communication skills and is designed to improve a child's sense of self (Dreikurs & Soltz, 1964). All people want to succeed at the activities they undertake. This is a natural human desire. Unfortunately, many people are discouraged, and our society is good at pointing out mistakes. The watchword has been, "We learn from our mistakes," but what is often overlooked with this strategy is that only the strongest can withstand constant bombardment of their errors and persevere.

Inform parents that a more useful strategy is to accentuate the positive and eliminate the negative. If parents want to help children develop a positive self-concept, the key lies in emphasizing what young people can do rather than what they can't do. Parents need to learn how to encourage because it helps children feel good about themselves and enhances their sense of self-control (Vernon & Al–Mabuk, 1995). Encouragement is not a single act on a single occasion. It is ongoing as children attempt to succeed and gain mastery in their world. By expressing faith in children as they are, and not as they could or should be, children feel more self-confident.

Encouragement, the language of acceptance, is based on respect for the child as a human being. It differs from reinforcement in that reinforcement is a reward given after the child has successfully completed a task, whereas encouragement is given before a task has begun or after the child has failed. In these instances, when children may feel insecure, discouraged or self-doubting, support and positive words help. Dinkmeyer and Losoncy (1980) described an encourager as someone who listens effectively, focuses on the positive, is accepting, inspires hope, and recognizes effort and improvement.

Parents can show acceptance by saying things such as, "I like the way you picked up your room," with the emphasis on the task rather than on an evaluation of the child. In accordance with the philosophy, you would not say, "You're a good kid because you picked up your room" because it equates self-worth with performance.

Various authors (Stone & Bradley, 1992; Vernon & Al–Mabuk, 1995) identified the following ways to encourage children:

1. Emphasize strengths.
2. Minimize weaknesses and failure.
3. Show you care.
4. Spend time together.
5. Develop patterns of learning, to build success.

6. Value silence as a means to reduce discouragement.
7. Support effort, not just success.
8. Try to understand the child's point of view.
9. Be positive for both of you.
10. Remember that both adults and children have the right to a bad day.

After the input on encouragement, ask parents to take each of these 10 methods of encouraging and individually develop a list of examples of when they have used or could use each one. Then have them share their examples with others in a small group. Suggest that they make a plan to incorporate at least three methods at home during the following week.

Session 6: Family Meetings

Objectives: • To teach parents how to conduct family meetings to foster open communication

Procedure: Family meetings provide an opportunity for family members to feel a sense of belonging and work together to improve communication and problem-solving skills (Nelson & Lott, 2000). During family meetings, issues such as family rules, routines, decisions, chores, and family outings can be discussed. Reminding family members that all of their thoughts and feelings are considered important conveys acceptance and reinforces the notion that everyone in the family unit is valued, which in turn enhances communication because individuals feel safe to express their point of view.

After this explanation of the purpose of the family meeting, distribute the following guidelines for effective family meetings and invite discussion about them (Nelson & Lott, 2000, p. 173).

1. Start with compliments and appreciations.
2. Prioritize items on the agenda. Ask if any items can be eliminated because they have been handled already. Ask if any should be top priority.
3. Set a timeline for the meeting. Use a timer and a designated timekeeper.
4. Discuss each item and let everyone voice his or her opinion without comments or criticism from others.
5. If the problem calls for more than a discussion, which is more often than not, brainstorm for solutions.
6. Choose one solution that everyone can live with (consensus), and try it for a week.

7. Table difficult issues to discuss at the next regularly scheduled family meeting.

To further clarify the process, ask for four volunteers to assume roles as family members (with at least one as the parent) and conduct a short family meeting according to the guidelines. They are to assume that this is a first meeting with no prior agenda; everything brought up will be a new agenda item. Give them 15 minutes to conduct this mock meeting and indicate that you will serve as a coach to facilitate the process as needed. During the demonstration, other participants should keep notes on questions they have so these can be addressed at the end of the role-play.

Following the demonstration, ask family members to tell how they felt about the process, and encourage discussion from other participants, including any personal experiences with family meetings within their own family units.

As this is the last session, the following activity could be used for closure:

Ask parents to reflect on three things and write them on an index card: (1) what they learned by participating in the group, (2) something they have done differently as a result of what they learned, and (3) what they would like to continue to work on in their parenting role. To encourage sharing, give one of the participants a ball of yarn and ask him or her to share one of his or her responses. Then, while holding the end of the yarn, he or she is to toss the ball of yarn to another parent, who shares, and so forth. Continue in this manner until everyone has had an opportunity to share at least once. When everyone has been "connected" through this activity, invite discussion and closing comments.

Myths About Parenting

When consulting with parents or delivering some form of parent education, counselors should keep in mind that some parents think parenting is instinctive and, therefore, should be easy. This is an unrealistic view that is hard to let go of because most parents wish it were this way (Vernon & Al–Mabuk, 1995). Other myths about parenting identified by Vernon and Al–Mabuk are that children should be perfect, that what works with one child will work with another, and that whatever parenting methods their parents used with them will automatically be best for your children. When parents cling to these myths, they often feel guilty, anxious, frustrated, angry, or uncomfortable. Along with these myths, irrational beliefs contribute to negative feelings and inappropriate parenting behaviors.

Irrational Beliefs About Parenting

Vernon and Al–Mabuk (1995), Vernon (2002), and Wenning (1996) identified the following irrational beliefs that have a significantly negative impact on parents' behavior and emotions:

1. *Demands*—requiring children to behave perfectly. Demands result in anger, which in turn can result in aggressive punishment instead of effective discipline. *Demanding* that children behave is useless, as all children will misbehave to some extent some of the time. Rather than making rigid demands, parents should establish developmentally appropriate behavioral standards but not upset themselves by always demanding perfect behavior.
2. *Self-downing*—equating self-worth as a parent with their child's performance. Parents who engage in self-downing think they are a failure if their children misbehave or don't live up to parental expectations. Parents need to remember that they do the best they can but they can't control every aspect of their children's lives. If their children mess up, the parents aren't worthless.
3. *Awfulizing or catastrophizing*—blowing things out of proportion and overgeneralizing about the effects of a specific action. For example, many parents think it is the end of the world if their children don't always keep their rooms clean or if their teenager has blue hair and wears baggy clothes. While parents might not prefer this, they should look at situations realistically and put them in perspective: Things could be worse.
4. *Low tolerance of frustration or discomfort anxiety*—demanding that parenting should be easy; that they shouldn't have to go through inconvenience or discomfort in parenting. Parents have to expect that parenting will be a challenge with hassles and hurdles, although that certainly will vary from child to child. Parents who have discomfort anxiety are afraid to enforce rules, for example, because they are afraid they can't stand their child's being upset if he or she doesn't like the rules.

When parents hold one or more of these irrational beliefs, it interferes with their ability to be effective. Helping them understand that they are not to blame if something goes wrong with their child, that it is better to prefer than demand, and that they can tolerate the discomfort that is naturally associated with parenting will increase their competence.

Parenting Style

Parenting style is another critical factor. Coercive parenting styles, inconsistency, and lack of parental involvement are clearly associated with greater pathology in children (Lindahl, 1998). Vernon (2002) and Vernon and Al–Mabuk (1995) discussed the parenting styles of authoritarian, authoritative, permissive, and ignoring. They distinguished between *authoritarian* and *authoritative* by suggesting that authoritarian parents are demanding and rigid, using harsh punishment to try to change behavior. In contrast, authoritative parents maintain a reasonable amount of control but do it in a collaborative fashion based on mutual respect. Authoritative parents have reasonable rules and consequences, and they are supportive of their children.

Permissive parents think they can't stand conflict, so they give in because it is easier. These parents generally have very few rules, and they are underinvolved in their children's lives. *Ignoring* parents put their own needs first and provide children with little parental guidance. A parenting style that includes clear explanations, moderate and realistic limit-setting, consequences instead of physical punishment, reasonable consistency and involvement, and communication of warmth results in children who have higher self-esteem, better school achievement, more positive social skills, and more personal happiness (Karpowitz, 2000).

Nelson and Lott (2000) identified three discouraging (short-term) parenting styles and one encouraging (long-term) parenting style. Short-term styles are: (a) controlling/punitive/rewarding, (b) permissive/overprotective/rescuing, and (c) neglectful/giving up on being a parent. These styles take away power from children and do not help them learn to be responsible or to become self-reliant. By contrast, kind and firm parenting, which is similar to the authoritative parenting style, provides opportunities for children to learn and grow.

Counselors also may want to share with parents information on myths, irrational beliefs, and parenting styles, as well as the following information on discipline—another topic with which parents generally need help.

Discipline

Discipline and punishment are not the same thing. Discipline, on the one hand, is about caring. It is not intended to belittle but, rather, to help children learn appropriate behavior and to teach self-discipline, responsibility, and cooperation (Vernon & Al–Mabuk, 1995). Punishment, on the other hand, is delivered in anger (Levy & O'Hanlon, 2001) and is characterized by endless scolding, blaming, shaming, ridicule, and harsh physical measures to thwart unwelcome behavior. When parents try to teach children responsibility by demanding, they often punish harshly when children don't comply. The problem with this approach is that, when children are punished, they punish the parent in return. Needless to say, how parents discipline their child affects the quality of the parent–child relationship.

Although children need limits and controls, these must be reasonable to enable children to become more self-reliant and responsible. Rudolph Dreikurs, a prominent psychiatrist, suggested that parents become knowledgeable leaders of their children instead of authority figures (Dreikurs & Soltz, 1964). Parents should influence their children rather than overpowering them. An effective discipline strategy that helps children develop responsibility and puts parents in the role of leaders rather than authoritarians is to use *consequences*.

Consequences are of two types: natural and logical (Levy & O'Hanlon, 2001). *Natural consequences* follow the natural order of the universe: If you go outside in below-zero temperatures with no coat, you'll probably catch cold. *Logical consequences,* on the other hand, are arranged by parents. For example, a logical consequence of coming home an hour late is that the child will have to come home an hour earlier the next day, or if he or she breaks another child's toy, he or she should have to figure out how to replace it. Logical consequences should relate directly to the specific problem.

In applying consequences, parents should be both kind and firm. Giving children a choice is a good idea: "You can either eat your dinner without playing with your food, or you have to leave the table now and not plan on a snack later. Which do you choose?" The tone of voice can indicate a desire to be kind, and the follow-through can demonstrate firmness. There is a thin line between punishment and consequences. In applying consequences, tone of voice, attitude, and willingness to accept the child's choice are essential. If the voice is harsh and the tone is angry, the child might view the consequence as punishment. Parents need to delay the consequence long enough so they can deliver it effectively and calmly (Levy & O'Hanlon, 2001).

In certain situations the use of consequences is not helpful. These include the following.

1. Don't use consequences when they can't be carried out. An example is when the consequence would result in breaking the law or violate rules or regulations.
2. Don't use consequences that are hard to accept. For example, some parents think that making a child go without lunch if the child doesn't use manners or interact appropriately at the table is detrimental.
3. Don't use consequences when the child may be placed in a dangerous situation, such as if the child is playing with matches. In this situation, simply remove the matches; don't give the child a choice. If a logical consequence is not appropriate, take action and try to use as few words as possible.
4. Don't use consequences if anger gets in the way. This is when a consequence turns into punishment through tone of voice and actions.

Consequences can be effective in managing children's behavior because the consequence links them with the reality of their behavior. Through the use of consequences, parents are able to form a relationship with their children based on mutual rights and mutual respect.

Another discipline strategy that can be effective, especially with younger children, is *time-out*. Although time-out does not teach children how you want them to behave, they do learn what the results will be when they continue to misbehave (Levy & O'Hanlon, 2001). Time-out gives children time to cool down and regroup. The area designated for time-out should be a boring place, and the adult in charge will determine the length of the time-out. The goal of time-out is to help children think about what put them there and how they have to act differently. It can be an effective way to modify behavior.

Problem Solving

It is natural for parents and children to have differences of opinion and, therefore, to have conflicts. To resolve the conflict satisfactorily, parents must move beyond listening to working through the issue at hand. The following problem-solving model is useful for parents (Friend & Cook, 1992), particularly for older children and adolescents.

1. *Understand the problem.* Parents and children need to arrive at a common understanding of the problem and the responsibility each person might have in this situation. All too often parents assume they know what the basis of the problem is and act from that perception. This step is designed to arrive at a common understanding.

2. *Consider the alternatives.* This step is extremely important when the problem affects both parent and child, because each will bring his or her own expectations to the situation. For this step to work, each must actively participate in generating possible alternatives. Although this is hard for most adults, it works best when both parties suggest possible solutions without being judgmental. What is important is to create a number of ideas. If the parent and the child can cooperate in this way, each will feel free to bring thoughts and expectations forward.

3. *Select the best mutual alternative.* Critically consider each suggestion. This is when the hard work and effective communication come into play. Both parent and child must be willing to listen to the other, and each must be willing to express his or her ideas and evaluate the pros and cons of each alternative. This is a most important step, and quite possibly the most time-consuming, because it involves negotiation and compromise. Here, the parent and the child will work out a mutually satisfactory solution. If the decision is not satisfying to both, the solution probably will not work. Therefore, both must be willing to compromise to reach a satisfactory solution.

4. *Discuss the probable results of the chosen solution.* This is an opportunity to examine how to implement the alternatives selected. Two questions must be addressed: What will make the solution work? What will make it fail? By considering each of these questions, both parties begin to gain a perspective on their investment to ensure success.

5. *Establish a commitment.* Once the probable results have been examined, each party knows what he or she must do to be successful. In this step both parent and child are asked to make a commitment to try to carry out the solution.

6. *Plan an evaluation.* This last step is a safety net for the whole process. Before embarking on new actions, the parent and child should set a specific

time to review their solution to the problem. By setting a specific timeframe for review, they have provided a means of checking out their solution and making the necessary adjustments. Possibly they will have to return to the second step, reexamine the alternatives, and consider another choice.

Problem solving is a rather simple model, which parents too often "short-circuit" by not following the entire process. It is a tremendously useful technique for working through conflicts especially with older children and adolescents.

Consultation

One of the best ways to foster child/adolescent development is through the counselor's consultation with parents. Even though consultation is one of the counselor's roles, many counselors hesitate to consult with parents, in part because they are uncertain about the exact nature of consulting and because they believe parents will not be receptive to consultation. Contrary to this belief, most parents who are aware of the availability of consultation will request or accept assistance when needed.

Consulting is distinguished from counseling by the nature of the relationship between the consultant and the consultee (parent). Unlike counseling, in which the counselor works directly with the client, consultation is an indirect process, in which the counselor (consultant) works with the consultee (parent) to bring about change in the client (child). Dougherty (2000) defined consultation as "a process in which a human service professional assists a consultee with a work-related (or caregiving-related) problem with a client system, with the goal of helping both the consultee and the client system in some specified way" (pp. 10–11). Stone and Bradley (1994) described consultation as a process that "involves the service of an outside professional—in this case, you as the counselor; an indirect service to the client—the child; and a problem-solving process implemented by the consultee—generally a teacher or parent" (p. 199).

A goal of consultation is to create positive change. It is collaborative in nature in that the consultant and consultee work together to solve the problem. Consultation is intended to improve consultees' functioning with their child and also to develop consultees' skills so they can handle similar problems independently in the future. Consultees are perceived as parents or anyone else who works with young people and can benefit from consultation. The consultee is a partner with the consultant in a shared problem-solving process in which the concern is to improve parents' functioning with their children.

Various consultation models have been developed, with specific counseling techniques for each. Brown, Pryzwansky, and Schulte (1995) presented a representative model consisting of the following five stages, which are discussed in relation to the following vignette.

Sonja is a 14-year-old eighth grader who has been in a continual battle with her single-parent mother over family rules. In particular, Sonja leaves home for long periods without letting her mother know where she is going and when she will return, often coming home well after midnight. Her mother is concerned that Sonja may be involved with a 21-year-old man. The mother wonders if Sonja is sexually active and experimenting with alcohol or drugs. The mother has contacted you for assistance with Sonja.

Stage One: Phasing-In

The first stage primarily involves relationship building. The counselor as consultant has to develop and be able to exhibit specific relationship skills including listening, understanding, empathy, and self-disclosure, if appropriate. In the case of Sonja, the consultant would spend the first meeting gathering information regarding the mother's (consultee's) concerns about Sonja, the frequency and intensity of the problem, some background information about the family, and the nature of the relationship between mother and daughter. The counselor should work to gain the mother's trust and be supportive.

Stage Two: Problem Identification

The consultant's priority is to clarify the main problem. The appropriate skill during this stage is to provide focus. Additional skills include paraphrasing, restating, goal setting (establishing priorities), and obtaining commitment. In this stage the consultant and the consultee attend to the various concerns the consultee has expressed, and prioritize these concerns. In the scenario here, time is spent on actions the mother has taken regarding her concerns with Sonja. Quite possibly, the consultant will want to determine how the mother reacts when Sonja comes home late and what discussions or arguments have arisen about the family rules and the mother's expectations.

Stage Three: Implementation

The counselor/consultant helps the consultee explore strategies to solve the identified problem. A major skill is the ability to give feedback. Additional skills include dealing with resistance and demonstrating patience and flexibility. The consultant also can provide recommendations for action. In this stage the consultant helps the consultee examine the actions the latter has taken in terms of the success or the extent to which they have worsened the situation. Also, the consultee, the mother in this case, quite possibly has tried to remedy the situation by imposing stricter rules, which have been to no avail.

The goals at this stage in the above case are to establish something the mother can do differently or reinforce strategies that have been successful in the past. The consultant might look at ways for the consultee to spend more time with Sonja doing things they mutually enjoy and helping the mother develop reasonable rules and establish consequences. They should identify specific strategies the mother can accept and implement. Often, when the problem is complex and involves several concerns, a sequence for addressing the various issues should be established. The consultant should provide support and encouragement in helping the consultee implement the plan of action.

Stage Four: Evaluation

In this stage the counselor/consultant and consultee evaluate progress. The evaluation stage ends when the consultee is satisfied with the outcome. This stage involves monitoring the implementation and evaluation strategies. Within a reasonable timeframe to allow the consultee to implement the strategies discussed, the counselor and the consultee identify and review what has transpired. Often, this session includes a detailed review of how things have been going between the mother and Sonja. The intent is to reinforce the things that are working and consider precisely what has happened with the things that have not worked. Usually adjustments are made in the plan of action, and the consultee's commitment to trying different strategies is reaffirmed.

This session may be repeated several times over the next few weeks to months until the consultee believes the relationship has improved. Another possible outcome is that the consultant may refer the consultee—in this case, Sonja's mother—for counseling for her own issues.

Stage Five: Termination

The consultant signifies an ending to the consultation by bringing closure to a consultation agreement. Together the consultant and the consultee review both the positive and the negative outcomes derived from the change in strategy. Although similar to the preceding stage, the purpose at this stage is to provide closure by emphasizing the progress the mother has made and reinforcing her for the behaviors she has adopted in her relationship with Sonja. Although some provision can be made to allow the mother to reinitiate the consultation at later date, the purpose of this last stage is to terminate the relationship.

Summary

Counselors engage in parent education and consultation on behalf of children at all school levels, as well as in mental health settings. Given the struggles that parents face today, coupled with the difficulties young people face as they grow up, both parent education and consultation are vital services.

Parent education imparts information and skills that support good parenting. Three approaches include (a) parent study groups, (b) support groups, and (c) parent education. In support groups, which generally are not as structured as education groups, the primary goal is to create an environment in which parents can come together to share common concerns about their children. Parent education

and parent study groups are more structured and have the primary objective of developing parenting skills and disseminating information. The leader of such a group needs good communication skills, including active listening, reflection, clarification, questioning, and summarizing. He or she also sets an encouraging and supportive group climate and models effective behavior.

Parent consultation is suited to parents who have specific problems with a child. It is different from parent education in that it is indirect; the consultant works with the consultee, the parent, to bring about change in the child. A typical model has five stages: phasing-in, problem identification, implementation, evaluation, and termination.

References

Atkinson, D.R., Morten, G., & Sue, D.W. (1993). *Counseling American minorities: A cross-cultural perspective.* Dubuque, IA: Wm. C. Brown.

Ayers, L. (2000). Gender issues in parenting: parenting teenage girls. In M.J. Fine & S.W. Lee (Eds.), *Handbook of diversity in parent education: The changing faces of parenting and parent education* (pp. 15–35). San Diego: Academic Press.

Baruth, L.G., & Manning, M.L. (1991). *Multicultural counseling: A lifespan perspective* (2d ed). Upper Saddle River, NJ: Macmillan.

Blum, L.M., & Deussen, T. (1996). Negotiating independent motherhood: Working class African Americans talk about marriage and motherhood. *Gender and Society, 10,* 199–211.

Bogenschneider, K., & Stone, M. (1997). Delivering parent education to low and high risk parents of adolescents via age-paced newsletters. *Family Relations, 46*(2), 123–134.

Brown, D., Pryzwansky, W B., & Schulte, A. C. (1995). *Psychological consultation: Introduction to theory and practice* (3d ed.). Boston: Allyn & Bacon.

Clark, L. (1996). *SOS! Help for parents*: *A practical guide for handling common everyday behavior problems.* Bowling Green, KY: Parents Press.

Dinkmeyer, D., & Losoncy, L.E. (1980). *The encouragement book.* Englewood Cliffs, NJ: Prentice–Hall.

Dinkmeyer, D., & McKay, G. (1993). *Systematic training for effective parenting.* Circle Pines, MN: American Guidance Service.

Dinkmeyer, D., McKay, G., & Dinkmeyer, D. (1997). *Systematic training for effective parenting.* Circle Pines, MN: American Guidance Service.

Dougherty, A. M. (2000). *Psychological consultation and collaboration in school and community settings.* Belmont, CA: Brooks/Cole.

Dreikurs, R., & Soltz, V. (1964). *Children the challenge.* New York: Hawthorn.

Edwards, O.W. (2000). Grandparents raising grandchildren. In M.J. Fine & S.W. Lee (Eds.), *Handbook of diversity in parent education: The changing faces of parenting and parent education* (pp. 199–210). San Diego: Academic Press.

Faber, A., and Mazlish, E. (1991). *How to talk so kids will listen and listen so kids will talk.* New York: Avon.

Faber, A., & Mazlish, E. (1996). *How to talk so kids will listen and listen so kids will talk* (2d ed.). New York: Avon.

Fine, M. (Ed.). (1989). *The second handbook on parent education.* New York: Academic Press.

Fine, M. A., Voydanoff, P., & Donnelly, B. W. (1993). Relation between parental control and warmth in child well-being in stepfamilies. *Journal of Family Psychology, 7,* 222–232.

Fine, M.J. & Wardle, K.F. (2000). A psychoeducational program for parents of dysfunctional backgrounds. In M.J. Fine & S.W. Lee (Eds.), *Handbook of diversity in parent education:*

The changing faces of parenting and parent education (pp. 134–152). San Diego: Academic Press.

Friend, M., & Cook, L. (1992). *Interactions: Collaboration skills for school professionals.* White Plains, NY: Longman.

Gordon, T. (1970). *Parent effectiveness training: The proven program for raising responsible children.* New York: Wyden.

Gordon, T. (2000). *Parent effectiveness training: The proven program for raising responsible children.* New York: Three Rivers Press.

Hays, P.A. (1996). Addressing the complexities of culture and gender in counseling. *Journal of Counseling and Development.74*, 332–338.

Jacobs, E., Masson, R., & Harvill, R. (1998). *Group counseling: Strategies and skills* (3d ed.). Pacific Grove, CA: Brooks/Cole.

Karpowitz, D.H. (2000). American families in the 1990's and beyond. In M.J. Fine & S.W. Lee (Eds.), *Handbook of diversity in parent education: The changing faces of parenting and parent education* (pp. 3–12). San Diego: Academic Press.

Knowlton, E., & Mulanax, D. (2000). Education programs for parents and families of children and youth with developmental disabilities. *Handbook of diversity in parent education: The changing faces of parenting and parent education* (pp. 299–312). San Diego: Academic Press.

Kottman, T., & Wilborn, B. L. (1992). Parents helping parents: Multiplying the counselor's effectiveness. *School Counselor 40*, 10–14.

Lancaster, P. E. (2000). Parenting children with learning disabilities. In M.J. Fine & S.W. Lee (Eds.), *Handbook of diversity in parent education: The changing faces of parenting and parent education* (pp. 233–250). San Diego: Academic Press.

Lauer, R.H. & Lauer, J.S. (1997). *Marriage & family: The quest for intimacy* (3d ed.). Madison, WI: Brown & Benchmark.

Levy, R. & O'Hanlon, B. (2001). *Try and make me! Simple strategies that turn off the tantrums and create cooperation.* St. Martin's Press.

Lindahl, K.M. (1998). Family process variables and children's disruptive behavior problems. *Journal of Family Psychology, 12*(3), 420–436.

McDermott, D. (2000). Parenting and ethnicity. In M.J. Fine & S.W. Lee, (Eds.), *Handbook of diversity in parent education: The changing faces of parenting and parent education* (pp. 73–94). San Diego, CA: Academic Press.

Nelson, J., & Lott, L. (2000). *Positive discipline for teenagers: Empowering your teen and yourself through kind and firm parenting* (2d ed.). Roseville, CA: Prima Publishing.

Nelson, J., Lott, L, & H. S. Glenn (1999). *Positive discipline A-Z* (2d ed.). Rocklin, CA: Prima Publishing.

Popkin, M. H. (1995). *Active parenting today.* Atlanta: Active Parenting.

Stephenson, J. B. (1996). Changing families, changing systems: Counseling implications for the twenty-first century. *School Counselor, 44*(2), 85–92.

Stone, L. A. & Bradley, F. O. (1992). *Parenting Without Hassles: Parents and children as partners.* Salem, WI: Sheffield.

Stone, L. A., & Bradley, F. O. (1994). *Foundations of elementary and middle school counseling.* White Plains, NY: Longman.

U.S. Bureau of the Census. (1996). *Statistical Abstracts of the United States* (116th ed.), Washington, DC: U.S. Government Printing Office.

Vernon, A. (2002). *What works when with children and adolescents: A handbook of individual counseling techniques.*

Vernon, A., & Al–Mabuk, R. H. (1995). *What growing up is all about: A parent's guide to child and adolescent development.* Champaign, IL: Research Press.

Wenning, K. (1996). *Winning cooperation from your child! A comprehensive method to stop defiant and aggressive behavior in children.* Northvale, NJ: Jason Aronson.

York, P., & Wachtel, L. (1983). *Toughlove.* New York: Bantam Books.

Chapter 14

Working With Families

Larry Golden

When a child is referred for counseling why work with families? Logistically, counseling with the individual child is easier than bringing in the family. Families are confusing, hard to schedule, and potentially offer powerful resistance to therapeutic change. Nevertheless, the point of view in this chapter is that professionals who seek to help children *must* work with families. The family is in a position to support or sabotage therapeutic goals. Building a healing counselor-child relationship is not enough. To best understand the child's problems, the counselor must see the child in the family context.

The traditional nuclear family idealized in yesteryear television sitcoms such as "Leave It to Beaver," "Father Knows Best," and "Ozzie and Harriet" is becoming a minority, if not a vanishing species. Today's children come from a variety of home situations including blended, single-parent, dual-career, grandparent-headed, and gay and lesbian families. In some respects, the basic dynamics between parents and children are the same now as they have always been. Parents are still responsible for protecting children and preparing them for autonomy. As they get older, children still feel compelled to push against the restraints on their freedom.

Today's children conceivably may reap unexpected benefits from their disordered family lives. Children exposed to the stress of living in blended families, for instance, may develop extraordinary interpersonal skills. These complex families require children to become flexible and alert in relationships. They will have much to offer a world that exposes human beings to rapid change. Regardless of the long-term possibilities, today's families will continue to need support and guidance from mental health professionals during this transitional social and economic era.

This chapter highlights several specific approaches to helping children by working with their families. *Brief family consultation* is a time-limited behavioral approach intended for school settings in which the counselor works with the parents, teacher, and child to bring about rapid behavioral change. *Solution-focused family counseling* builds quickly on a family's prior successes. *Strategic family therapy* offers powerful techniques for changing aspects of the family system that maintain the child's problem behavior. There are also various legal, social service, long-term outpatient, and inpatient (psychiatric hospitalization) treatment approaches that are not addressed by this chapter. The Quick Assessment of Family Functioning appraisal tool can help the practitioner decide which level of intervention to use.

Working With Families in Cultural and Gender Context

If there was ever a client population that confronts counselors with intense cultural dynamics, it is families. When working with families, I draw on everything I've learned about multiculturalism, including knowledge of my personal history. I am a middle-class Jewish American heterosexual married white man. How does this "cultural filter" impact my response to a particular family seeking counseling from me?

I want to be aware of how ethnicity, race, social class and gender color the experience of every individual within every family that I see in counseling. I don't want to make the mistake of treating everyone as if they had equal access to resources. Nor do I want to presume that all members of a minority group share the same familial characteristics. I know that I must be alert to that which is unique.

I've found it helpful to read the chapter in this book by Clemente that describes cultural influences on children in African American, Latino, Native American, and Asian American families. The chapter by McFarland and Tollerud looks at counseling with children in nontraditional families including single-parent families and stepfamilies.

Assessment

Not everyone wants or needs long-term counseling. In physical medicine, treatment of health problems corresponds to their severity. The doctor prescribes an aspirin for a headache but employs surgery or radiation to treat a brain tumor. Likewise, functional families may benefit from short-term behavioral intervention and dysfunctional families may require long-term counseling that goes to the root of individual or systemic pathology.

The difference between a functional family and a dysfunctional family is a values-laden issue. Who is to say which behaviors are functional and which are not? Some of the ambiguity can be eliminated by defining a functional family as one that can benefit from a short-term and relatively nonintrusive approach. Conversely, a dysfunctional family is likely to require a longer period of more intensive therapy. To evaluate the level of functioning of a family, and thereby provide assistance in determining an appropriate level of intervention, the Quick Assessment of Family Functioning (Figure 14. 1) assesses five variables: parental resources, time frame of the problem behavior, communication, hierarchy of authority, and rapport between helping adults (Golden & Sherwood-Hawes, 1997).

To understand how The Quick Assessment of Family Functioning works, consider the following two case studies.

Respond to questions on a scale of "1" to "5": [5] definitely yes; [4] yes; (3) moderately, [2] no; [1] definitely no; [NA] data not available. An average score of "3" or higher indicates that behavior change can be achieved by a brief approach.

_____*Parental Resources.* Can parents provide for the child's basic needs?

_____*Time Frame of the Problem Behavior.* Is the child's misbehavior of short versus chronic duration?

_____*Communication.* Is communication between family members clear and open?

_____*Hierarchy of Authority.* Are parents effective in asserting authority?

_____*Rapport Between Helping Adults.* Does a working relationship exist between counselor, teacher, and parents?

FIGURE 14.1   *The Quick Assessment of Family Functioning*

The Case of Sam: School Phobia

Sam, a 7-year-old second grader, was referred to me, his school counselor, because he was afraid to go to school. Sam lived with his mother and older sister. His parents were divorced when he was only 2. He visited his father regularly on alternate weekends. Sam's mother told me that his "school phobia" started about a month before, when an older child stole his lunch money and threatened to beat him up. In fact, school phobia, school avoidance, and school refusal are various names for a problem that counselors can expect to frequently encounter (Murray, 1997). Although the bully was disciplined and the incident had not recurred, Sam continued to try various strategies (headaches, stomachaches, earaches, elbow aches) to avoid going to school. His mother reported that she'd taken Sam to the doctor and that the doctor found no medical basis for Sam's complaints. She admitted to being "wishy-washy," permitting Sam to stay home rather than force the issue.

To evaluate the family's level of functioning and determine the level of therapy indicated, I used the Quick Assessment of Family Functioning, as described next.

Parental Resources

I had to make a relatively simple decision: Could Sam's parents provide for Sam's basic needs and still have time and energy left to follow through on a behavioral plan? A strong marriage, supportive extended family, gainful employment, and financial security are conditions that predict that a family can hold up its end in a team approach. At the other extreme, very young, immature single parents probably will not have the resources at their disposal to do so. Multigenerational poverty, criminality, alcoholism, suicide threats, and child abuse also indicate that the family might not yield to counseling interventions. Under such emergency conditions, a child is best helped when counselors connect families to community resources and public authorities.

In the case of young Sam, while his parents were divorced, the father continued to be involved. There were no other indicators of extreme family distress. On the scale of "1" to "5" (see Figure 14. 1), I assigned a score of "3."

Time Frame of the Problem Behavior

Is the child's misbehavior of short or chronic duration? If the child's problem behavior is an *adjustment disorder* that results from a recent and identifiable stressor (American Psychiatric Association, 2000), a less intrusive treatment approach, such as brief family consultation or solution-focused therapy, may be effective. The symptoms caused by a stressor can be resolved simply by removing the stressor or teaching the child to better cope with stress. By contrast, if the child's misbehavior is chronic, a more tenacious and powerful intervention, such as strategic family therapy would be required to change these habitual behavior patterns. An example of such a chronic behavior problem is a *conduct disorder* that entails persistent violations of the basic rights of others and society's norms (American Psychiatric Association, 2000).

Sam's problems with school refusal were of short duration, having begun only a month before in response to an identifiable stressor: Score = "5."

Communication

Can family members communicate well enough to solve problems? According to Satir (1972), people close down communication during periods of stress. The counselor should have no trouble straightening out a stress-triggered parent/child misunderstanding in a functional family. In dysfunctional families, however, closed communication is the rule, not the exception. This closed system is maintained by yelling, blaming, sarcasm, or, more ominously, silence. Persistently disturbed communication patterns indicate a need for family therapy.

Take a look at the following interaction between Sam and his mother:

Counselor (to Sam):	Tell your mom what happened this morning when you got to school.
Sam:	Jeffrey called me a carrottop. Then he got William to call me a carrottop.
Mother:	I wish you could just let their stupid teasing roll off your back.
Sam:	I can't. I hate school,
Mother:	Well, I can see that you had a very bad time this morning. I'm angry at those boys for what they said.
Sam:	Me, too!

In this and other conversations, Sam and his mother had done a nice job in communicating empathically. I gave them a score of "5" for communication.

Hierarchy of Authority

Are the parents effective in asserting authority? Imagine an organizational chart that illustrates the decision-making structure. Parents in functional families hold an "executive" position in the family organization. Children are granted freedom commensurate with their demonstrated responsibility. In dysfunctional families, parents surrender authority in the hope that they can avoid conflict with a child. Children in these families often are out of control. Strategic family therapy would be a suitable approach for families that score "low" in this category.

With regard to the case of Sam, asserting authority may have been his mother's Achilles' heal. She had described herself as wishy-washy and admitted that she caved in to Sam's excuses for not going to school. I made a note to see if her efforts at discipline were supported or undermined by Sam's father. At the risk of being harsh, I assigned a score of "2" for hierarchy of authority.

Rapport Between the Helping Adults

Can the parents and helping professionals work together as a team to resolve a child's behavior problem? Dependability is a factor. Do the parents return phone calls? Are they punctual for conferences? Also central to the issue is follow-through. The functional family does its homework. For example, a functional parent probably will follow through on an agreement to telephone the teacher to make sure their child turned in an assignment. A dysfunctional one will not. Without this kind of follow-through, a behavioral plan will fail.

A breakdown can occur at the professional level as well. For example, a burned-out teacher may be more invested in documenting a difficult child's "ticket" to special education than in assisting in a plan to improve the child's classroom behavior.

At the risk of overgeneralizing, counselors tend to establish rapport most easily with parents who are verbally skilled and psychologically sophisticated. However, parents who seem to be unresponsive may be acting in this way because they feel intimidated by professionals or may lack fluency in English. These parents can be effective team members if counselors will reach out.

In Sam's case, there didn't seem to be a problem in this area. His mother was reaching out for help. Score = "5."

My research indicates that an average score of "3" or higher on the Quick Assessment of Family Functioning predicts success in using a time-limited, less extensive behavioral approach such as brief family consultation, which is described later in this chapter (Golden, 1994). Of the five criteria, "hierarchy of authority" seems to be the best predictor of success (Golden, 1994). In the case of Sam, the mean score of "4" predicted that behavior change could be achieved through a brief approach.

The Case of Katrina: A Blended Family

Thirteen-year-old Katrina was referred to my private practice by her mother, Alicia. Alicia was worried about her declining grades and the constant fighting between Katrina and her stepfather, Cliff. For the first interview, I asked to see the entire family, including 2-year-old Brian.

Cliff, age 48, was a successful, hard-driving insurance executive. His own father, now deceased, was an alcoholic. Cliff had two adult children by a previous marriage. Alicia, age 35, was a housewife. Brian was the offspring of Alicia and Cliff's 3-year marriage.

Katrina, the offspring of Alicia's previous marriage, rarely saw her father, who lived in another state. Although her declining grades were a recent phenomenon, she always had been a "below average" student and had been "moody," at least since her parents' divorce when Katrina was 4 years old. On one occasion she told her teacher about "being better off dead."

Alicia and Cliff seemed committed to each other, but Katrina's misbehavior had been the trigger for escalating stress. Cliff blamed Alicia for being overly permissive in her approach to discipline. Alicia acknowledged truth in his statement but saw Cliff as being needlessly harsh. Their polarized strategies effectively neutralized their attempts to discipline Katrina.

The following is my evaluation of Katrina's family using the Quick Assessment of Family Functioning criteria:

Parental resources: My score of "3" reflected the family's healthy financial status weighed against the inherent vulnerability of any blended family (e.g., the possibility of another divorce, legal challenges to child custody).

Time Frame of the Problem Behavior: My score of "2" reflected the knowledge that at least some aspects of Katrina's presenting problems had been observed since she was 4 years old. A long-term problem predicts a lengthy intervention.

Communication: For this criterion, I gave the family a score of "2," reflecting the rift between Cliff and Katrina, as well as the strain of Katrina's behavior on their communication.

Hierarchy of Authority: Based on the information that Cliff and Alicia antagonized each other when disciplining Katrina, eroding their ability to control her behavior, I gave a score of "1" for hierarchy of authority.

Rapport Between Helping Adults: Weighing Alicia's willingness to seek professional help and her rapport with school authorities against Cliff's distrust of any potential dependency on a counseling relationship, I gave a score of "4" for this criterion.

This was a complex and difficult case. From a strategic point of view, Katrina's declining grades and moodiness could have had any of several ulterior motives: (a) to bring marital problems to the forefront, (b) to force Alicia to take Katrina's side against Cliff, or (c) to propel Katrina out of a household in which she did not feel wanted.

Because the average score on the QAFF was under "3" a brief approach did not seem sufficient. Instead, I used an approach that included family counseling, individual counseling, and parent education/marital counseling. Each session had the feel of a three-ring circus, with the 50 minutes usually divided into a segment for each type of counseling. I also arranged a conference at the school to include Alicia, Katrina's teachers, and the school counselor. At the conference, everyone agreed that Katrina would bring home a daily report indicating whether or not she had turned in her assignments. Further, Alicia and Cliff decided on chores they wanted Katrina to do at home—washing dishes, cleaning her room, and so on. Katrina's $10 per week allowance was eliminated, but she could earn as much as $15 a week by turning in assignments and doing her chores, and she could earn additional bonuses by acting on her own initiative instead of requiring parental nagging. Katrina's behavior improved a little, but her mood remained sullen.

In a typical episode involving Cliff and Katrina, which Cliff reported in one of the earlier sessions, Cliff saw dishes in the sink and Katrina lounging on the couch watching TV. Cliff said, "What about the dishes? Or do you think you're some kind of royal princess?" Katrina stormed into her room and slammed the door. Cliff charged in after her: "I want you out of this house! Do us all a favor and run away!" Later, when Cliff and Katrina told Alicia about the incident, she was sympathetic to Cliff's feelings but infuriated by his outburst inviting Katrina to run away. Cliff responded, "As usual, you don't back me up." Alicia snapped back with, "As usual, I've got two children on my hands."

I asked Cliff how he explained to himself Katrina's storming into her room and slamming the door. He identified two possibilities: (a) her mother had raised her to be irresponsible, and (b) she's trying to break up our marriage. I pointed out that thoughts such as these could lead to violent emotions. I asked him to mentally substitute another statement before confronting Katrina again: "She doesn't like being in the same room with me when I call attention to her failings." This relatively moderate statement resulted in Cliff's tempering his emotions and showing more rational behavior.

Like many adolescents, Katrina was a poor candidate for counseling. She assumed that I, as a counselor, was in the business of helping her parents and teachers exercise control over her behavior, which was not far off the mark! I acknowledged that I wanted her to improve her grades and get along better with Cliff and her mother. I also wanted her to know I was interested in her as an individual, separate from her family. I asked her if I understood her goals: (a) to convince her mother and stepfather that she was nobody's puppet, and (b) to plan on leaving home on her own two feet. She concurred. We talked about the different ways a girl her age could rebel strongly against parental authority only to become even more dependent. With a little prompting, Katrina identified pregnancy, drugs, and school failure as being "bogus" paths to freedom. I wondered aloud if a teenager could secretly pursue a goal of leaving home on her own two feet. Jay Haley's book *Leaving Home* (1980) provides a classic conceptualization of the universal phenomenon of teenagers leaving home.

Although Katrina started making small gains, Cliff and Alicia's marriage was slipping downhill. Marriages in blended families can be easily destabilized by misbehaving stepchildren. Cliff concluded that Katrina was purposely misbehaving to wreck the marriage, paving the way for a reconciliation between her mother and father. Although this is a commonly held myth about step-children, my experience is that step-children are ambivalent about the new marriage. They rebel against a step-parent out of loyalty to the noncustodial parent, and they may entertain fantasies of reconciliation, but the last thing on earth they want is to go through another divorce. I shared this point of view with the entire family.

I also told the family that Katrina was now more able to manage her life, and advised Alicia and Cliff to attend to their marriage. Thus, the stage was set for marital counseling.

The procedures of marital counseling are not germane to this chapter. Suffice it to say that eventually the marital format gave way to individual counseling for Cliff. His disturbed childhood with an alcoholic father and his first divorce had left him fearful of dependency, unable to commit, and chronically depressed. I used Rogerian counseling to help Cliff gain insight into the etiology of his condition and cognitive therapy to assist him in achieving mastery over impulsive behaviors.

In summary, this case study illustrates the ways in which a child's problems are woven into the fabric of the family. It also demonstrates several techniques (e.g., behavioral, cognitive, marital) that can be used in counseling with children and their families.

Brief Strategies With Families

There are numerous strategies for helping children and families, including legal, social service, long-term outpatient and inpatient, and brief interventions. The focus here is on *brief* strategies that are especially useful for today's counselors. Counselors who hesitate, across the board, to adopt a brief approach need to examine their own therapeutic bias. Because counseling and psychotherapy originated in psychoanalysis (Corey, 2001), much of what counselors-in-training learn in graduate school is a variation on this Freudian theme. I would imagine that Freud, Jung, Adler, and even Carl Rogers would regard the humble onion as a metaphor for understanding psychotherapy. In this view, the presenting symptom is seen as merely the outer representation of unconscious motivation. The counselor peels away these successive layers of defense to expose the root cause (e.g., negative self-concept, inferiority complex, Oedipal fixation). *This takes a lot of time.*

Few people would argue that the onion is an apt metaphor for personality development, but there is good reason to challenge the assumption that counselors must peel it! Most clients cannot pay for in-depth counseling, and third-party payers such as insurance companies will not. In fact, mental health professionals today see clients an average of only five or six sessions (Budman & Gutman, 1988). Such time constraints are not new to school and agency counselors who carry enormous caseloads. Further, little or no evidence exists that long-term or depth approaches are more effective with children and families than time-efficient strategies.

Brief Family Consultation

Brief family consultation is a time-limited behavioral strategy that can be used in a school or agency setting. This intervention is especially suitable for the school counselor because it requires no special training in family therapy and is highly time-efficient. Further, it is congruent with the school counselor's consultative role. I developed the Brief Family Consultation model at the Parent Consultation Center, a collaborative project of the University of Texas at San Antonio and local school districts. The research that was generated by this ten-year project indicates that school counselors can expect success when they use this approach with reasonably well-functioning families (Golden, 1994). Features of the Brief Family Consultation model are as follows:

1. *The intervention is limited to a maximum of five conferences.* The time limit conserves resources, permitting a large number of families to be served. The time limit also encourages an intensive "do-or-die" effort. Families should be made aware that they will not receive "therapy." To make this distinction explicit, client contacts are termed "conferences," not "sessions," and practitioners call themselves "consultants," not "counselors."

2. *Only functional families are referred.* Referrals for brief family consultation should be made by professionals, such as school counselors, who understand that a dysfunctional family is unlikely to benefit from such a limited approach. If dysfunctional families are referred mistakenly, the behavioral objectives can be narrowed to increase the chance that they will be achieved. When expectations for behavior change are unrealistic, everyone is the loser. Alternatively, a family therapy approach may be deemed most beneficial, in which case the family may need to be referred to another counselor.

3. *The goal is behavior change.* The parents, child, and consultant sign a contract specifying behavioral targets and consequences. Progress is reviewed at each conference so the targets and consequences can be fine-tuned. The best-laid plans are defeated by ambivalence. The motto is, "Go for it!" The consultant often uses a form such as the Target Behavior Form presented in Figure 14.2, which was developed at the Parent Consultation Center.

4. *The consultant coordinates a team effort that includes parents, teachers, and the child.* A brief strategy works best when all of the key players are involved. Counselors who believe they are doing a good job of helping children without contacting other significant adults are laboring under an illusion. Counselors need all the help they can get! As a general rule, parents and teachers should be included in any attempt to solve a child's behavior problem.

5. *The consultant supports parental authority.* The distressed child likely is making a plea, albeit indirect, for parental control. Out of feelings of guilt and confusion, even competent parents may permit the child more freedom than is appropriate. Parents should be encouraged to take charge of resources

Conference # _____

Child _____ Parents _____

Date _____ Consultant(s) _____

1. _____

This target behavior is being achieved now. Circle the number that best describes your opinion:

definitely not   1   2   3   4   5   definitely

2. _____

This target behavior is being achieved now. Circle the number that best describes your opinion:

definitely not   1   2   3   4   5   definitely

What will happen during this coming week? _____

What will parent do? _____

What will child do? _____

What will consultant do? _____

Next conference date _____ Time _____

FIGURE 14.2   *Target Behavior Form for Brief Family Consultation*

that could serve as reinforcers. For example, a child who is "independently wealthy," sporting a big allowance and a roomful of electronic games, is in a position to disregard his or her parents' demands for behavior change. These parents would be well advised to terminate the allowance and remove the games. The child *earns* these rewards by achieving behavioral goals.

Family group consultation is a variation of brief family consultation (Golden & McWhirter, 1975). Several families are seen together, with the advantage of mutual support and social reinforcement. Counselors function as group facilitators and behavioral consultants. Generally, conferences last one and one-half hours with each conference divided into three half-hour segments. During the first portion, families report on progress during the past week. During the second segment, the large group breaks into separate subgroups for parents and children. Two counselors are needed, one to facilitate each group. The subgroups analyze the reasons for the success or failure of the prior week's plans. During the third segment, the large group reassembles and each family commits to specific goals for the coming week. This type of family support group meets for about 5 weeks, because establishing a new behavior takes at least that long. If the group meets for longer than 5 weeks, families start dropping out.

Brief family consultation has limitations. The behavioral approach that is used works well with elementary-age children. Typically, young children trust that the adults in their lives know what's best for them and respond eagerly to rewards and praise. Adolescents, however, may regard adults as agents of oppression and resent the manipulation inherent in "carrot-and-stick" tactics (Golden & Sherwood-Hawes, 1997). Teenagers respond more readily to a cognitive approach that endorses their compelling drive for independent decision making and action.

The Case of Alejandro: Hyperactive Behavior

This case illustrates both the efficacy and limits of brief family consultation. Alejandro R.'s fourth-grade teacher referred him to the school counselor. Alejandro and his mother, a single parent, attended the first conference. The presenting problem was that Alejandro was "hyper." His teacher complained that he would not remain seated in class; he poked, tripped, and teased the other children, and failed to complete assigned work. Mrs. R. also reported behavior problems at home. For example, Alejandro had to be constantly "nagged" to finish the morning routine of getting dressed, brushing his teeth, eating breakfast, and so on. If his mother pushed him too hard, Alejandro "threw a fit." Alejandro spent every third weekend with his father, and Mrs. R. said that Alejandro's behavioral problems were more extreme after these visitations. She also reported that Alejandro wet the bed following his weekends with his father. Prior to the divorce, which was finalized the summer before Alejandro started third grade, there had only been occasional teacher complaints about behavior problems.

The counselor asked if any activities held Alejandro's attention for longer than 30 minutes. Mrs. R. said that Alejandro could stay riveted on computer games for hours, he was an alert soccer player, and he could concentrate for extended periods when he drew pictures of dinosaurs. Apparently, Alejandro's hyperactivity was selective.

In consultation with the teacher, it was agreed to target on-task, in-seat behavior during reading. By the second conference, Mrs. R. had asked for and was getting daily written reports from Alejandro's teacher. For each 5-minute period that Alejandro stayed in his seat and remained on-task during reading group, the teacher affixed a star to a chart that Alejandro kept at his desk. At home, the stars were redeemed for a variety of prizes chosen by Alejandro—a trip to the zoo, pizza, video game playing time.

By the third conference, there had been a dramatic improvement. The fourth conference followed a weekend visitation with Mr. K., and the "hyper" behavior returned full force. Within a day, however, Alejandro was back on track. At the fifth and final conference, Mrs. R. and Alejandro proudly displayed a string of star-laden charts from the classroom teacher.

The bed-wetting, however, was getting worse. Mrs. R. was convinced that the tension caused by Alejandro's visitations with Mr. K. was to blame. She said that Alejandro's father wanted to punish her, and that he used Alejandro as a tool for his revenge. She felt that Alejandro might be better off if he didn't see his father at all. In an individual interview, Alejandro reported that both parents said "mean" things about the other, and he felt "torn in two pieces." The school counselor explained to Mrs. R. that her son was paying a high price for this ongoing conflict, and made a referral for family counseling.

The family therapist saw the parents, both separately and together, for a total of 20 sessions. Occasionally, Alejandro was included. The goals of family therapy were to (a) convince both parents that Alejandro would suffer if they were unable to manage their mutual animosity; (b) create a path for direct communication, thereby preventing messages being sent through Alejandro; and (c) encouraging the premise that Alejandro could love both his parents without being disloyal to either. As the parents were able to mediate their hostile impulses toward each other, Alejandro's bed-wetting became less frequent.

The success of the brief consultation demonstrates the efficiency of behavioral techniques and a team approach. Parental sniping, however, threatened to sabotage the behavioral gains. The family therapist brought rationality to an otherwise chaotic family system, and the parents responded with alacrity to brief consultation and family therapy. Alejandro was the direct beneficiary of this intervention because children require order and predictability in their lives.

With the benefit of hindsight, I used the Quick Assessment of Family Functioning to evaluate the R. family on a scale of "1" (very weak) to "5" (very strong). The scores that I gave the R. family predict only limited success using brief family consultation.

1. *Parental Resources:* Although the parents were divorced, Mrs. R., the custodial parent, was financially secure. Mr. R. made regular child-support payments. But the power of this family to resolve problems was diminished by the recent divorce and continuing antagonism. Score = "2."
2. *Time Frame of the Problem Behavior:* "Hyper" behavior and bed-wetting were reported as only occasional problems prior to the fourth grade. Score = "5."

3. *Communication:* These parents used communication as a weapon in their ongoing conflict. Score = "1."
4. *Hierarchy of Authority:* Mrs. R. was a decisive disciplinarian. Her fear that Alejandro would someday choose his father over her, however, served to undermine her authority. Score = "2."
5. *Rapport Between Helping Adults:* Mrs. R. was conscientious in follow-through on reports from Alejandro's teacher. Both parents were willing to participate in family therapy. Score = "4."

Solution-Focused Family Counseling

Steve de Shazer and Imsoo Berg developed solution-focused therapy at the Brief Family Therapy Center in Milwaukee, Wisconsin. It is a quick intervention and easily adapts to the school setting (Hayes, 1997). For the solution-focused counselor some problems can be solved by deciding they aren't problems (Berg, 1991). For example, parents might attribute an adolescent's disrespectful behavior to deep-seated psychopathology or decide, instead, that their teen is going through a normal, albeit unpleasant, developmental stage. In other instances, the counselor helps the family look at their past and current successes to find easy and natural solutions to the current problem.

De Shazer (1984) declared the "death of resistance" to therapy, suggesting that when clients don't follow the counselor's directives, it is their way of teaching the counselor the best way to help them. Solution-focused family counseling rejects the notion that the child's problem serves an ulterior purpose (e.g., a child fails to learn to read in order to get revenge on his or her domineering mother). The presenting problem is taken at face value, not as a symptom of underlying pathology.

Parents become discouraged when they believe they are unable to help their troubled child. This pessimism generates rigid, "more-of-the-same" attempts at problem solving. The solution-focused counselor emphasizes the family's past and current success as a starting point toward a solution.

De Shazer (1985) and his colleagues use universal formulas that seem to help clients work toward solutions regardless of the presenting problem. The following are some of these "skeleton keys," presented here in an abbreviated form.

1. *The Exception Question.* "When did you *not* have the problem when by all rights you should have?" Family members come to counseling prepared to document their complaints against one another. The result is blaming. The exception question flips this negativism onto its positive side. For example, a parent who wishes to control her temper is directed to observe what she does when she is successful in overcoming the urge to "lose it" with her child. If this successful strategy worked once, why not again?
2. *The Miracle Question.* "Suppose one night while you are asleep, there is a miracle and this problem is solved. How would you know? What would be different?" This technique focuses on problem solving.

3. *The Good News.* The counselor takes time at every session to compliment the family's strengths. Too often, counselors attend to weaknesses and failures.

4. *The First Step.* "How will you know that your child is on the right track?" The family is helped to see that a long journey begins with a single step and that small changes snowball into bigger ones. This intervention removes the burdensome (for the counselor as well as the client!) expectation that the child must be "cured."

5. *The Task.* "Between now and the next session, notice what you or your child or both of you are doing that you want to see continue." Again, the orientation changes from negative to positive. Solution-focused therapy is a relentless pursuit of the positive.

By way of limitations, solution-focused therapy tends to minimize a client's problems (Wylie, 1992). If there is no complaint, there is no problem. But the "power of positive thinking" has its limits (Wylie, 1992). Focusing on successes rather than failures may help the overanxious parent of an underachieving child, but what does this approach offer a child who is being sexually abused? Some families consciously or unconsciously conspire to deny serious problems such as child abuse or alcoholism. These dangerous conditions demand alarm bells, not positive reframing. At the least, solution-focused therapy is a good beginning, a way to start therapy on a positive note. Counselors, however, must recognize when stronger interventions are needed to break through denial.

Strategic Family Therapy

The field of family therapy splinters into various schools or camps, among them Bowenian, experiential, humanistic, psychodynamic, strategic, structural, and systemic. I regard strategic family therapy as very near the vital center of the field and include it in this chapter because it is both powerful and time-efficient. Strategic family therapy is associated with the Mental Research Institute in Palo Alto, California, and with certain individuals, most notably Gregory Bateson, Don Jackson, Paul Watzlawick, and Jay Haley (Corey, 2001).

Strategic family therapy holds that children misbehave and display symptoms to keep the family system, albeit dysfunctional, afloat. For example, a child may feel that her bed-wetting is distracting or detouring her parents' conflicted marriage and thereby is preventing a divorce. Strategic family counselors attempt to change only those aspects of the family system that maintain the child's symptomatic behavior. In the situation just mentioned, the best strategy is to resolve the marital conflict as opposed to treating the bed-wetting. Then the bed-wetting will no longer serve a systemic function.

Some of the major features of strategic family therapy are as follows:

1. *The goal is to eliminate the presenting problem.* Frequently, the child and family have an unspoken investment in maintaining the child's symptom. In

these instances, the presenting problem often can be solved with a straight-forward behavioral contract. The counselor designs and implements a strategy (hence, "strategic" family therapy) to change the family system so the symptom no longer serves a purpose. The counselor does this by directing family members to perform therapeutic tasks that will change the way they communicate or work together (Goldenberg & Goldenberg, 2000). Insight is "frosting on the cake" and not necessary to resolve the presenting problem.

2. *The strategic counselor is active and directive.* Families bring a contradiction to therapy: Help us change, but don't upset the applecart. Homeostasis—the tendency of a system to maintain the status quo, works against change. Haley (1984) openly acknowledged that change can be painful and that counselors are justified in using their power to bring it about.

3. *Paradoxical injunctions are used to defeat resistance.* Some children (as well as parents) are so oppositional that they defy the counselor. The strategic counselor makes use of this tendency by telling the client *not* to change. For example, the counselor could tell an oppositional child to continue to be rebellious against his or her parents. If the paradox works, the child will obey the parents to defy the counselor.

4. *Reframing is used to bring about a cognitive shift.* Perception is relative. Because the counselor can't be sure of a child's motive, why not choose a motive that supports health and control rather than pathology and despair? For example, a father accounts for his teen's running away from home as follows: "He's incorrigible, irresponsible, and downright stupid!" These words describe an individual who probably is incapable of change and would not choose to change even if he could. A more therapeutically useful explanation would be: "He's chosen a 'gutsy' but dangerous way to strike out on his own." This reframe, though not necessarily more true than the first, invites possibilities. An effective reframe forces a cognitive shift that reduces resistance to behavioral change. Even though strategic family therapy finds few adherents among school counselors, the strategy of reframing is relevant to their work.

Opponents of the strategic approach have charged it with a "blame the family" bias (Wylie, 1992). In some cases a youngster's symptom has an intrapsychic basis that strategic counselors could too easily ignore. Counselor Richard Schwartz described such a case with a bulimic client:

> A young woman had been "detriangulated" from her family. She had given up her role as family protector, had moved into her own apartment, and was enjoying her job. Her parents had accepted the change and, according to the standard theory that her symptom served the function of keeping her stuck, she should have been, by then, no longer bingeing and purging. Alas, she remained bulimic, apparently "unaware *of* her cure" (Wylie, 1992, p. 23).

The paradoxical injunction, a favored method of strategic counselors, should be used sparingly. A paradox is a way to trick someone into behaving the way the counselor thinks best. This reverse psychology is somewhat disrespectful. On occasion it backfires in an unpleasant way, such as with a double reverse. For example, the counselor could direct an oppositional student *not* to study for an exam in order to test the theory that studying is a waste of time. The student could confound the strategy by not studying and failing the exam and then telling the counselor that he had tried his best.

Summary

This chapter discussed a number of ways for counselors to help children by working with their families and described an assessment tool that practitioners can use to decide what type of approach—brief or more intensive—would be most appropriate. This tool, the Quick Assessment of Family Functioning, differentiates between functional and dysfunctional families based on five variables: parent resources, time frame of the problem behavior, communication, hierarchy of authority, and rapport between helping adults.

The overwhelming need for mental health services and the sharp limitations on economic resources in today's society lend support to the use of brief approaches for working with children and families. The simple decision to include the family is in itself a brief strategy. Family approaches, however, are more than a "quick fix." Family strategies recognize the role parents play in maintaining and solving childhood behavior problems and affirm the parents' capacity to assist their children with the next, inevitable developmental crisis. It is important to recognize that brief approaches are best suited to functional families that face situational difficulties. Dysfunctional families with a long history of disordered behavior may require a long-term intervention that gets to the root cause of the presenting symptom.

The simplest approach is *brief family consultation,* which is limited to a maximum of five "conferences" (the preferred term). The consultant coordinates a team, consisting of parents, teacher, and the child, to achieve the goal of rapid behavior change. A variation of brief family consultation, *family group consultation,* incorporates several families into one group, with the advantage of mutual support and social reinforcement.

Solution-focused therapy rejects a "problem" focus. Instead, the counselor builds quickly on a family's prior successes. Certain reliable "formula" tasks, discussed briefly in this chapter, are used with all clients regardless of the presenting problem. The goal is to achieve small steps in the right direction rather than a complete "cure."

Strategic family therapy is more powerfull than the other approaches discussed. The goal is to eliminate the presenting problem. When the family system serves to maintain this problem, the counselor may try to change destructive patterns of communication or to redistribute power among family members. To this end, the strategic counselor is active and directive. Paradoxical injunctions are used to defeat resistance, and refraining is used to bring about a cognitive shift.

No matter what approach is used, whether brief or more intensive, counselors are encouraged to include families in their efforts to help children. Why ignore the potential of a family to assist or hinder the development of any of its members?

References

American Psychiatric Association (2000). *Diagnostic and statistical manual of mental disorders: DSM–IV-TR.* (4th edition, text revision). Washington, DC: Author.

Berg, I. K. (1991). *Family preservation: A brief therapy workbook.* London: Brief Therapy Press.

Budman, S. H., & Gutman, A. S. (1988). *Theory and practice of brief therapy.* New York: Guilford.

Corey, G. (2001). *Theory and practice of counseling and psychotherapy* (6th ed.). Pacific Grove, CA: Brooks/Cole.

De Shazer, S. (1984). The death of resistance. *Family Process, 23,* 11–17.

De Shazer, S. (1985). *Keys to solution in brief therapy.* New York: Norton.

Golden, L. (1994). Brief strategies in counseling with families. *Family Counseling and Therapy, 4,* 1–10.

Golden, L., & McWhirter, J. (1975). Practicum experiences in family group consultation. *Arizona Personnel and Guidance Association Journal, 1,* 44–46.

Golden, L., & Sherwood–Hawes, A. (1997). Counseling children and adolescents. In D. Capuzzi & D. Gross (Eds.), *Introduction to the counseling profession* (2nd ed., pp. 329–347). Boston: Allyn & Bacon.

Goldenberg, I., & Goldenberg, H. (2000). *Family therapy: An overview* (5th ed.). Pacific Grove, CA: Brooks/Cole.

Haley, J. (1980). *Leaving home: The therapy of disturbed young people.* New York: McGraw-Hill.

Haley, J. (1984). *Ordeal therapy.* San Francisco: Jossey-Bass.

Hayes, L. L. (1997, September). Solution-focused counseling in schools. *Counseling Today,* 14–16.

Murray, B. (1997, September). School phobias hold many children back. APA *Monitor* pp. 38–39.

Satir, V (1972). *Peoplemaking.* Palo Alto, CA: Science and Behavior Books.

Wylie, M. S. (1992, January/February). The evolution of a revolution. *Family Therapy Networker* 17–29, 98–99.

Name Index

Subject Index